lonely planet

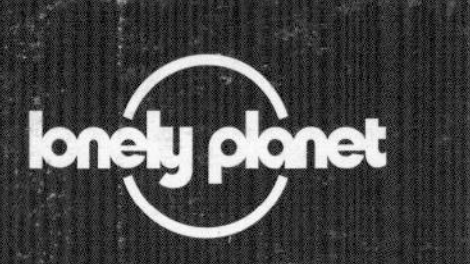

Tunisia

Abigail Hole
Michael Grosberg, Daniel Robinson

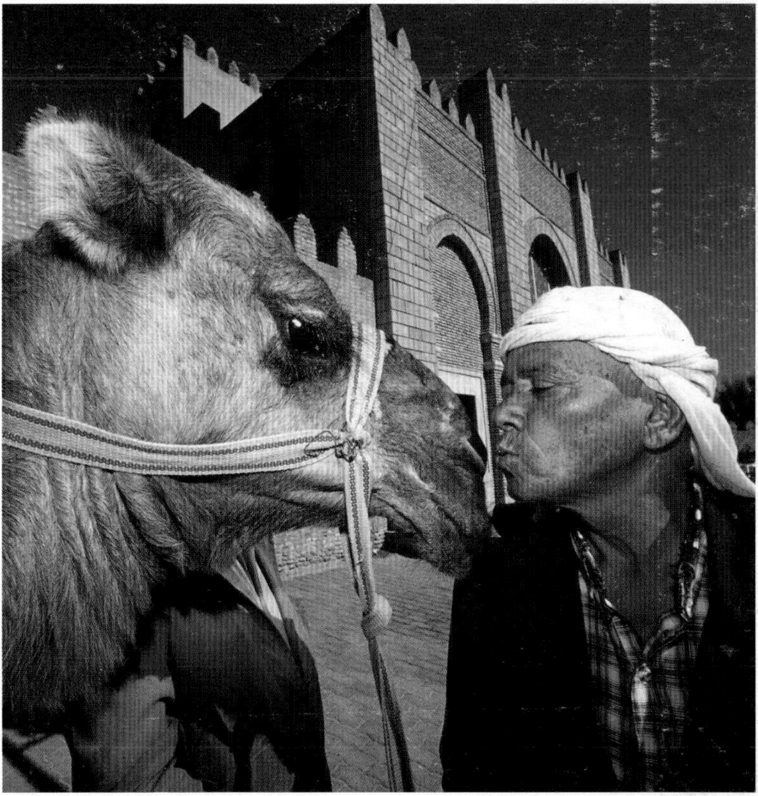

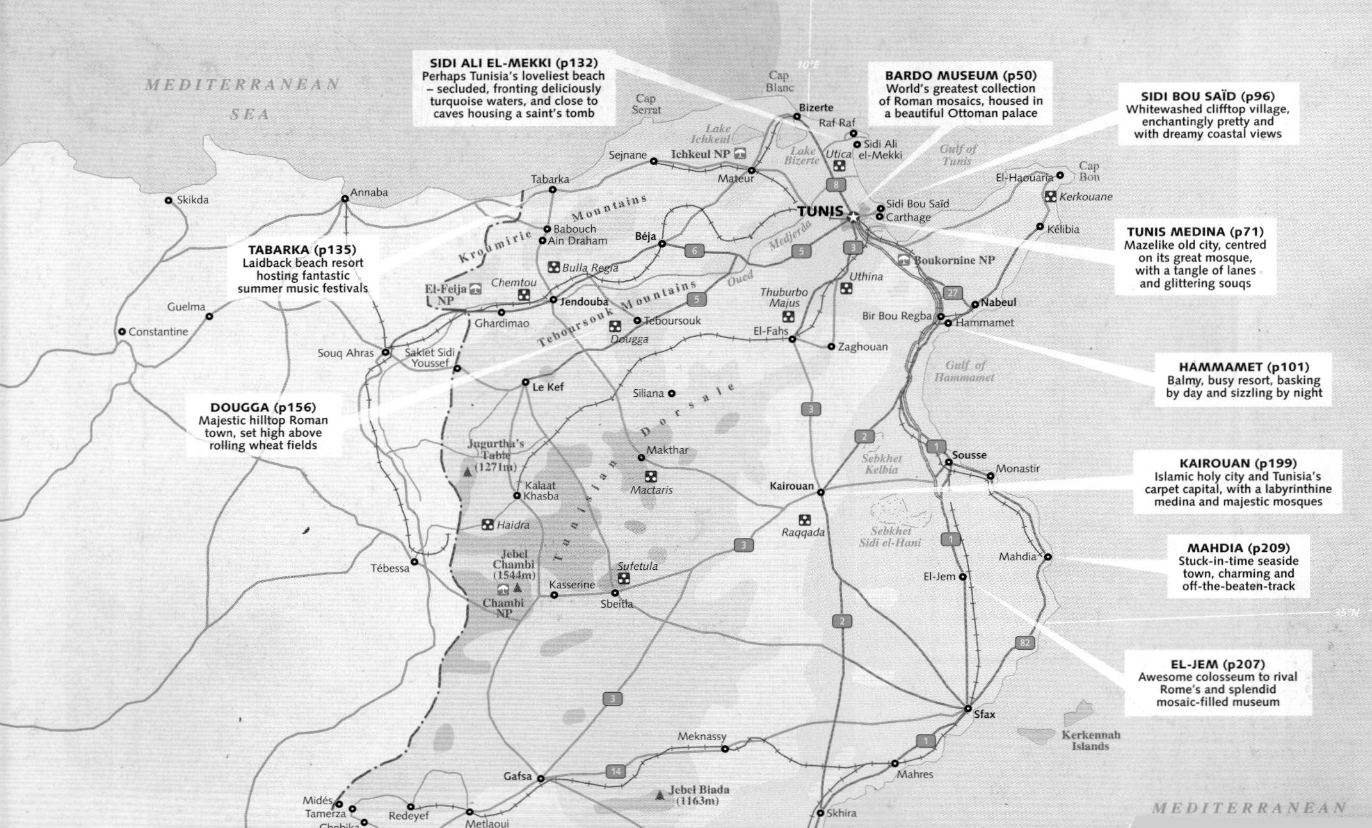
SIDI ALI EL-MEKKI (p132)
Perhaps Tunisia's loveliest beach – secluded, fronting deliciously turquoise waters, and close to caves housing a saint's tomb
BARDO MUSEUM (p50)
World's greatest collection of Roman mosaics, housed in a beautiful Ottoman palace
SIDI BOU SAÏD (p96)
Whitewashed clifftop village, enchantingly pretty and with dreamy coastal views
TUNIS MEDINA (p71)
Mazelike old city, centred on its great mosque, with a tangle of lanes and glittering souqs
TABARKA (p135)
Laidback beach resort hosting fantastic summer music festivals
HAMMAMET (p101)
Balmy, busy resort, basking by day and sizzling by night
DOUGGA (p156)
Majestic hilltop Roman town, set high above rolling wheat fields
KAIROUAN (p199)
Islamic holy city and Tunisia's carpet capital, with a labyrinthine medina and majestic mosques
MAHDIA (p209)
Stuck-in-time seaside town, charming and off-the-beaten-track
EL-JEM (p207)
Awesome colosseum to rival Rome's and splendid mosaic-filled museum
MEDITERRANEAN SEA
MEDITERRANEAN
10°E
35°N
Cap Blanc
Cap Serrat
Cap Bon
Bizerte
Raf Raf
Sidi Ali el-Mekki
Lake Ichkeul
Lake Bizerte
Utica
Gulf of Tunis
Sejnane
Ichkeul NP
Mateur
El-Haouaria
Kerkouane
Skikda
Annaba
Tabarka
TUNIS
Sidi Bou Saïd
Carthage
Kélibia
Kroumirie Mountains
Babouch
Ain Draham
Béja
Medjerda
Boukornine NP
Bulla Regia
Uthina
El-Feija NP
Chemtou
Jendouba
Oued
Thuburbo Majus
Nabeul
Teboursouk Mountains
Guelma
Constantine
Ghardimao
Teboursouk
Dougga
El-Fahs
Bir Bou Regba
Hammamet
Zaghouan
Souq Ahras
Sakiet Sidi Youssef
Le Kef
Siliana
Gulf of Hammamet
Tunisian Dorsale
Jugurtha's Table (1271m)
Makthar
Sebkhet Kelbia
Sousse
Monastir
Mactaris
Kairouan
Kalaat Khasba
Raqqada
Sebkhet Sidi el-Hani
Haidra
Mahdia
Tébessa
Jebel Chambi (1544m)
Chambi NP
Sufetula
Kasserine
Sbeitla
El-Jem
Sfax
Kerkennah Islands
Meknassy
Gafsa
Mahres
Jebel Biada (1163m)
Midés
Tamerza
Chebika
Redeyef
Metlaoui
Skhira

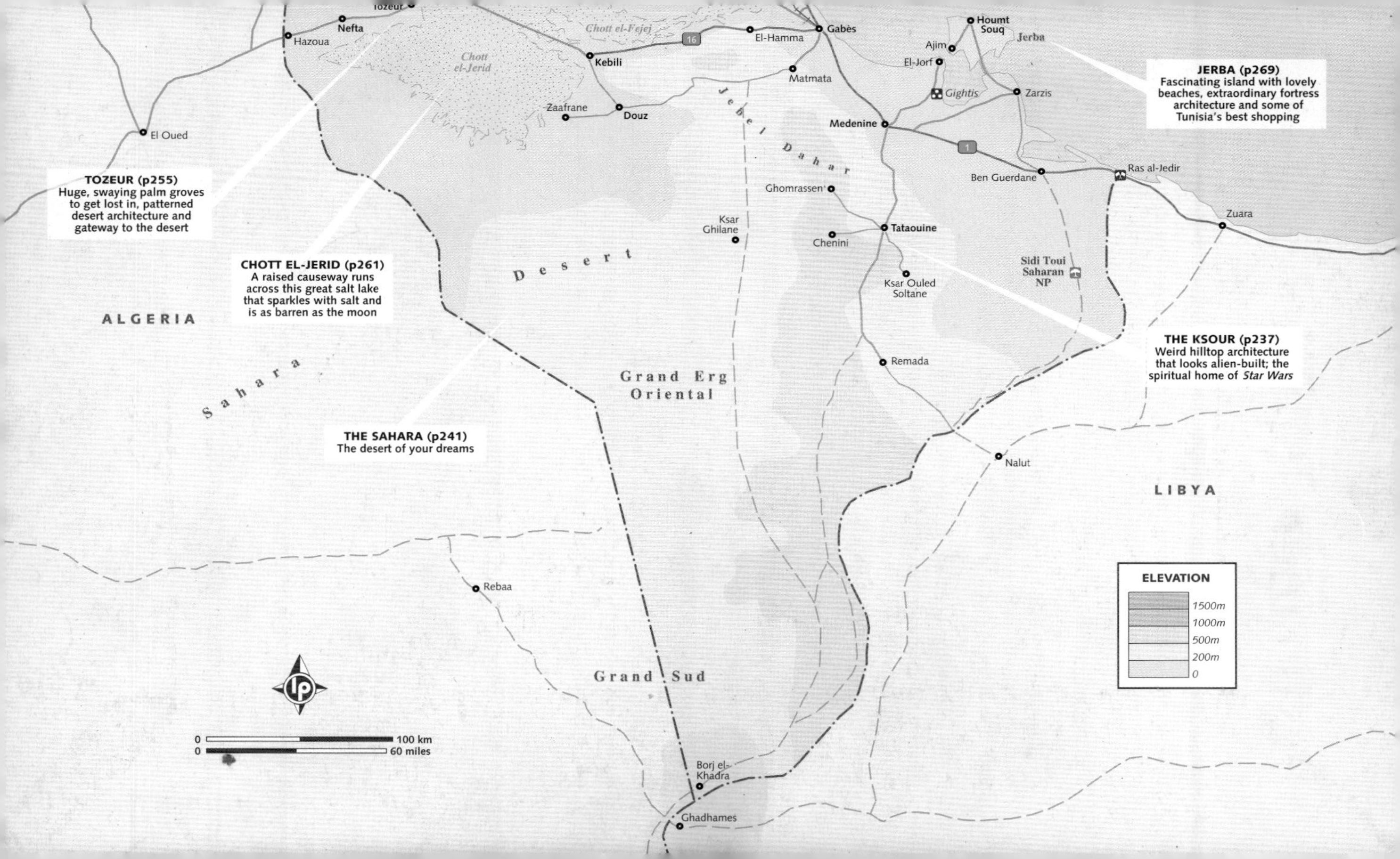

JERBA (p269)
Fascinating island with lovely beaches, extraordinary fortress architecture and some of Tunisia's best shopping
TOZEUR (p255)
Huge, swaying palm groves to get lost in, patterned desert architecture and gateway to the desert
CHOTT EL-JERID (p261)
A raised causeway runs across this great salt lake that sparkles with salt and is as barren as the moon
THE SAHARA (p241)
The desert of your dreams
THE KSOUR (p237)
Weird hilltop architecture that looks alien-built; the spiritual home of *Star Wars*
ALGERIA
LIBYA
Sahara
Desert
Grand Erg Oriental
Grand Sud
Jebel Dahar
Chott el-Fejej
Chott el-Jerid
Jerba
Tozeur
Nefta
Hazoua
El Oued
Kebili
Douz
Zaafrane
El-Hamma
Gabès
Matmata
Houmt Souq
Ajim
El-Jorf
Gightis
Zarzis
Medenine
Ben Guerdane
Ras al-Jedir
Zuara
Ghomrassen
Ksar Ghilane
Tataouine
Chenini
Ksar Ouled Soltane
Sidi Toui Saharan NP
Remada
Nalut
Rebaa
Borj el-Khadra
Ghadhames
16
1
ELEVATION
1500m
1000m
500m
200m
0
0
100 km
0
60 miles

Destination Tunisia

This is Africa at its most Mediterranean, brimming with olives, dates and oranges. Less hassle than Morocco, more exotic than Italy, and with enough history, diversity and beaches to pack a continent, Tunisia is a thrilling, underrated destination. The Islamic call to prayer divides the day, but it's a laid-back place, where women choose whether or not to wear the veil and people can drink alcohol if they please.

Tunisia is prime territory for a straightforward sun, sand and sea holiday, where you can bliss out along the balmy Mediterranean coast. It has the extra advantage that the resorts avoid the excesses that scar some southern European coasts.

The south is the heartland of the indigenous Berber culture. Its desertscapes and alien-seeming architecture were considered weird enough to stand in for 'a galaxy far, far away' in the *Star Wars* films – the latest contributor to this small country's imperial baggage, a lineage that includes the Phoenicians, Romans, Ottomans, and French.

In the south lie undulating Lawrence-of-Arabia desertscapes, and yet, less than a day's journey to the north, you can trek in moss-green mountains covered in alpine forest, see the incredible remnants of Roman occupation and discover off-the-beaten track beaches. And sandwiched between the desert and the northern peaks are huge, eerie salt lakes, the palm-fringed desert islands of Jerba and Kerkennah, the holy city of Kairouan, the great El-Jem colosseum, and the cosmopolitan capital Tunis.

Tunisia is a rarity: it's small enough so that travel is a breeze, yet you can experience different cultures and geographical extremes over the course of an afternoon. Don't miss out on this gentle, fun country and the Tunisians themselves: warm, hospitable, and gracious hosts.

CRAIG PERSHOU

Architecture & Monuments

BETHUNE CARMICHAEL

Wander through the magnificent remains of the Roman city of Dougga (p156)

CRAIG PERSHOUSE

View the impressive colosseum (p208) at El-Jem, the third largest in the Roman Empire

Gaze at the otherwordly structure of a *ksar*, at Ksar Ouled Soltane (p237) near Tataouine

BETHUNE CARMICHAEL

Natural Beauty

BETHUNE CARMICHAEL

Take a trek with the locals to Jugurtha's Table (p177), Le-Kef for a spectacular view

Indulge in a day at the beach at Monastir (p198) with the *ribat* in the distance

JANE SWEENEY

Bathe in hot springs by the beach at Korbous (p121), Cap Bon Peninsula

CHRISTOPHER GROENHOU

CHRISTOPHER GROENHOUT

Drink a last coffee on the edge of the dunes before joining an expedition (p248) into the Sahara

BETHUNE CARMICHAEL

Take a winding desert trip on the way to Tataouine (p230)

Experience the rare sight of Chott el-Jerid lake (p261) complete with water

CHRISTOPHER GROENHOUT

Amazing Experiences

PHILIP GAME

Spend a night underground in one of Matmata's troglodyte hotels (p228)

CHRISTOPHER GROENHO

Join a camel trek into the desert (p248)

Succumb to temptation in Kairouan and purchase a carpet (p206)

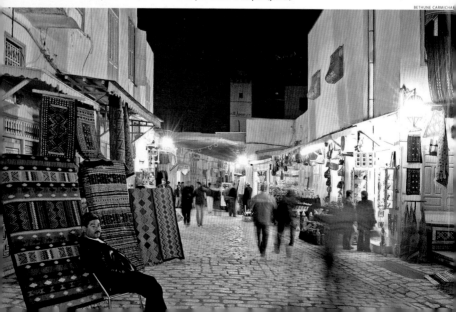

BETHUNE CARMICHA

Contents

The Authors	**11**
Getting Started	**13**
Itineraries	**17**
Snapshot	**23**
History	**24**
The Culture	**36**
Arts & Architecture	**44**
Environment	**54**
Food & Drink	**58**
Tunis	**66**
History	67
Orientation	67
Information	68
Dangers & Annoyances	70
Sights & Activities	71
Walking Tour	77
Courses	79
Tunis for Children	79
Tours	80
Festivals & Events	80
Sleeping	80
Eating	81
Drinking	84
Entertainment	84
Shopping	85
Getting There & Away	86
Getting Around	87
AROUND TUNIS	**89**
La Goulette	89
Carthage	90
Sidi Bou Saïd	96
La Marsa	98
Gammarth	99
Hammam Lif	99
Cap Bon	**100**
Hammamet	101
Nabeul	109
Around Nabeul	114
Kélibia	114
Kerkouane	117
El-Haouaria	119
Soliman	120
Korbous	121
Northern Tunisia	**122**
Bizerte	123
East Of Bizerte	130
From Bizerte to Tabarka	132
Tabarka	135
Ain Draham	139
Around Ain Draham	142
Béja	143
Jendouba	143
Bulla Regia	145
Chemtou	147
Ghardimao	149
Central West & the Tell	**150**
South Of Tunis	151
Dougga	156
Teboursouk	159
Le Kef	160
Around Le Kef	164
Makthar (Mactaris)	165
Haidra (Ammædara)	167
Jugurtha's Table	177
Kasserine	177
Sbeitla (Sufetula)	180
The Central Coast & Kairouan	**184**
Sousse	185
Around Sousse	195
Monastir	196
Kairouan	199
Around Kairouan	207
El-jem	207
Mahdia	209
Sfax	213
Kerkennah Islands	220

Gabès, Matmata & the Ksour 222
Gabès 223
Matmata 227
Around Matmata 229
Tataouine 230
Around Tataouine 234
Medenine 238
Around Medenine 239

The Sahara 241
Douz 243
Around Douz 249
South into the Sahara 250
Ksar Ghilane 251
Around Ksar Ghilane 252
Grand Sud 253

Tozeur & the Jerid 254
Tozeur 255
Around Tozeur 261
Nefta 263
Gafsa 265
Around Gafsa 267

Jerba 269
Houmt Souq 272
Erriadh (Hara Seghira) 277
Guellala 278
Guellala to Zone Touristique 279
Zone Touristique 280
Southeastern Coast 282

Directory 283
Accommodation 283
Activities 285
Business Hours 287
Children 287
Climate Charts 288
Courses 288
Customs 288
Dangers & Annoyances 289
Discount Cards 290
Embassies & Consulates 290
Festivals & Events 291
Food & Drink 292
Gay & Lesbian Travellers 292
Holidays 292
Insurance 293
Internet Access 293
Legal Matters 293
Maps 294
Men Travellers 294
Money 294
Photography 295
Post 296
Shopping 296
Solo Travellers 298
Telephone & Fax 298
Time 299
Toilets 299
Tourist Information 299
Travellers with Disabilities 300
Visas 300
Women Travellers 300

Transport 302

Health 314

Language 319

Glossary 331

Behind the Scenes 334

Index 337

World Time Zones 342

Map Legend 344

Regional Map Contents

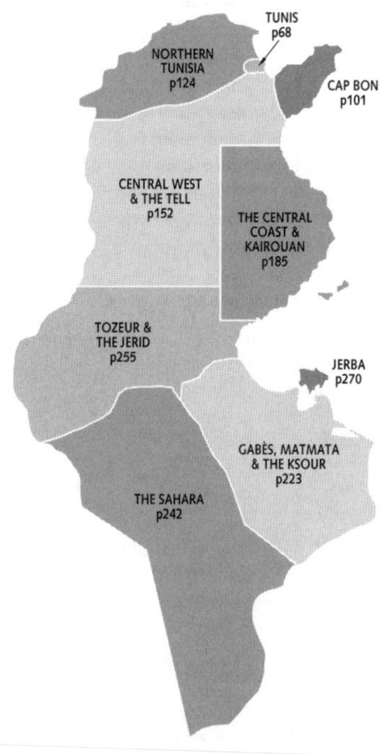

The Authors

ABIGAIL HOLE

Coordinating Author, Tunis, Cap Bon

From London, Abigail first wrote on Tunisia for Lonely Planet's *Africa on a Shoestring,* spending months in Africa and also researching Mali, Mauritania and Egypt. Shortly afterwards, she returned to Tunisia to co-write the 3rd edition of Lonely Planet's *Tunisia*. She came back to coordinate this book and revisit Tunis and Cap Bon, but this time did the research with the help of her one-year-old son. She lives in Rome with her Italian partner.

My Favourite Trip

I'd start off in **Sidi Bou Saïd** (p96), commuting into Tunis to get lost in its **medina** (p71) and visit the incredible **Bardo Museum** (p50). Next I'd take a road trip around little-known spots along the Cap Bon and the North Coast – stopping at **Kélibia** (p114), **El-Haouaria** (p119) and balmy **Sidi Ali el-Mekki beach** (p132) near Bizerte, before camping out at **Cap Serrat** (p134). I'd make sure I got to climb **Jugurtha's Table** (p177), the ancient natural fortress with views over Algeria, before going further south. I'd explore the whitewashed fortresses of **Jerba** (p269), the underground houses of **Matmata** (p228), and the alien architecture around **Tataouine** (p230). From here I would head further south, deep into the desert from **Ksar Ghilane** (p251), before returning to cross the eerie causeway across **Chott el-Jerid** (p261).

Cap Serrat
Sidi Ali el-Mekki Beach
El-Haouaria
Tunis
Kélibia
Jugurtha's Table
Sidi Bou Saïd
Matmata
Jerba
Chott el-Jerid
Ksar Ghilane
Tataouine

MICHAEL GROSBERG

The Central Coast & Kairouan, Gabès, Matmata & the Ksour, The Sahara, Tozeur & the Jerid, Jerba

After a childhood spent stateside in the Washington, DC area and with a valuable philosophy degree in hand, Michael took a job doing something with developing a resort on an island in the Pacific after which he left for a long overland trip through Asia. He later made his way to South Africa where he did journalism and NGO work and found time to travel all over Africa. He returned to New York City for graduate school in comparative literature and, in an attempt to land a coveted fellowship – which he did not receive – to study in an exotic desert locale, he immersed himself in the literature of North Africa. He has taught literature and writing in several NYC colleges in addition to Lonely Planet assignments that have taken him around the world.

DANIEL ROBINSON **History, Northern Tunisia, Central West & the Tell**

Daniel's interest in the cultures and history of North Africa began in high school, when he spent two semesters living with Moroccan émigré families. It deepened when he did a Near Eastern Studies degree at Princeton and during the three years he lived in France, dining on couscous and *briq* at every opportunity. Over the years, his travel writing – including Lonely Planet guides to France and Paris – has been published in nine languages. Daniel's favourite out-of-the-way bits of Tunisia include the Roman baths at Hammam Mellegue and the beach of Sidi Ali el-Mekki, but the high point of his research for this volume – conducted almost entirely by louage, bus and train – was Tabarka's spirited *Raï* festival.

CONTRIBUTING AUTHORS

Rafik Tlatli wrote the Food & Drink chapter, with Abigail Hole. Rafik is the hotelier of Hôtel Les Jasmins and also the head chef at Restaurant Slovénia in Nabeul. He has written *Saveurs de Tunisie, Delice de Tunisie* and many books of recipes, and has made regular radio and TV broadcasts on cooking in France, Italy and Russia as well as Tunisia. He is the founder and president of the National Association of Chefs in Cap Bon. Rafik has organised a master chef competition in Tunis for the past 14 years and an annual gastronomic conference in Tunis since 1998, and has also run seminars on Tunisian cuisine in countries ranging from Japan to Sweden.

LONELY PLANET AUTHORS

Why is our travel information the best in the world? It's simple: our authors are independent, dedicated travellers. They don't research using just the internet or phone, and they don't take freebies in exchange for positive coverage. They travel widely, to all the popular spots and off the beaten track. They personally visit thousands of hotels, restaurants, cafés, bars, galleries, palaces, museums and more – and they take pride in getting all the details right, and telling it how it is. For more, see the authors section on www.lonelyplanet.com.

Getting Started

Tunisia is an easily accessible country to visit – bureaucratic obstacles are few – so your preparations will mostly involve deciding where to go and what to pack. This book's itineraries (p17) give some pointers about routes, and the top 10 lists in this chapter suggest some highlights. Reading – online or in old-fashioned book format – before your visit or while you're there always adds to a trip, so give the travel literature and websites suggested in this chapter a try, and look out for the other book and online recommendations in the History, Culture, Food & Drink and Arts & Architecture chapters.

WHEN TO GO

The best times to travel in northern and central Tunisia are from April to June, and from September to October. At these times, you're almost guaranteed sunny, but not too hot, days, the sea is warm enough to swim (though perhaps not in April and October), and high season prices and crowds have not yet arrived. The countryside is at its prettiest after the winter rains in early spring.

See Climate Charts (p288) for more information.

However, if your holidays are in July and August, you are assured brilliantly sunny days, and coastal towns are at their liveliest. The Tunisian tourist authorities also run a number of superb festivals at old Roman sites; see p291 for more details. The downside is that you'll be sharing the beaches with about two million northern European holidaymakers, prices will be higher and accommodation chock-a-block.

For desert trips, temperature is an essential consideration. The best times to travel are from late September to November and March to early May. November is just after the date harvest; prices are cheaper. Douz and Tozeur have desert festivals (see p292). In July and August, the soaring temperatures mean that exploring the Sahara is really only possible overnight. Not only is it baking hot, but you'll have to cope with the sandy sirocco – desert wind. The search for air-con and iced-lollies will be all-consuming.

DON'T LEAVE HOME WITHOUT...

Try to leave some room in your luggage for souvenirs, but there are some essential (and not-so-essential) items that you could consider:

- a Swiss Army knife with a bottle opener and corkscrew in case you buy alcohol from a supermarket
- a hat, sunglasses and sun lotion – essential on the beach and in the Sahara; extra-force sunscreen if travelling with kids (it's expensive here!)
- a small sewing kit – useful for emergency repairs
- a small cool pack – good for carrying drinks, essential if you're travelling with a baby and need to keep milk and/or food chilled
- for women travelling outside the main resorts, an extra beach cover-up, such as shorts and a T-shirt to wear in the water
- a small football – a great way to meet local kids (and their families)

Tampons are usually only found in resort supermarkets, but most other toiletries are widely available. Condoms are cheap and readily available at pharmacies.

In winter, Tunisia is surprisingly cold, and you should pack lots of warm clothes – many places don't have good heating. If you're looking for winter sun in February, it's not guaranteed; it might rain and it'll definitely be too cold for lying on the beach. However, there'll be few other travellers around and prices will be rock bottom.

For a detailed summary of the low, mid and high season periods in Tunisia, see p283.

COSTS & MONEY

Tunisia is an inexpensive country for Western visitors, particularly compared with Europe.

Scrimpers could get by on TD20 to TD25 a day, staying in hostels, eating at cheap local restaurants and travelling only every few days.

For a more comfortable stay, midrange travellers will need to spend a minimum of TD50 to TD60 daily, enough to get a comfortable room, travel around and eat and drink well. Allow some more cash on top so you can buy souvenirs.

At the upper end of the scale, if you're staying in top-end hotels, eating at the best restaurants, buying crafts, and taking safaris or having some spa treatments, TD200 to TD300 per day will keep you in comfort.

If you've already paid for a package at a resort, you'll only have to pay for things like meals outside the resort, excursions, souvenirs and the occasional taxi.

HOW MUCH?

Hammam from TD1.5 (basic scrub)

International newspapers TD2-6

Bottle of Tunisian wine from TD4 (supermarkets); from TD9 (restaurants)

Entry ticket to ancient sites TD3-6

TRAVEL LITERATURE

There's little travel writing on Tunisia in English, but what there is often captures a particular epoch, provides fascinating cultural insights, and is hugely entertaining.

Ibn Khaldun was a prolific 15th-century traveller, whose North African travels – and long Tunisian visit – informed his remarkably accessible *The Muqaddimah,* peppered with sharp and sympathetic observations.

Daniel Bruun lived with the Berber people in Matmata during 1898, and his *The Cave Dwellers of Southern Tunisia: Recollections of a Sojourn with the Khalifa of Matmata* is a window on a forgotten world with its idiosyncratic portrait of Berber Tunisia before the tourists arrived.

Norman Douglas' *Fountains in the Sand* is a stiff-upper-lip, colonial account of a 1912 journey through southwestern Tunisia, entertaining enough despite his intolerance of all things Tunisian.

OK, so it's set in Morocco, but *The Sheltering Sky,* a gothic fiction about travels in the North African desert, is an evocative book to take on your travels. It describes North Africa pre-WWII, when its protagonists lose themselves in a sinister, alien, terrifyingly foreign world – it will certainly help to put any holiday blues you have into perspective.

Jolly-hockey-sticks, easy reading is *Among the Faithful,* by Dahris Martin, offering a unique portrait of Kairouan by a young American woman who lived there in the 1920s.

Barnaby Rogerson's *A Traveller's History of North Africa* includes some good essays on Tunisian history, placed within the wider North African context.

Paul Theroux's *The Pillars of Hercules* contains a frustratingly brief chapter on Tunisia; he amusingly describes an encounter with a carpet tout, as well as visits to Sfax and the Kerkennah Islands.

Less grumpy than Theroux, Michael Palin's more entertaining than in-depth *Sahara* covers Jerba, Matmata, El-Jem, Sousse and Sidi Bou Saïd, and revisits some *Monty Python's Life of Brian* movie sets.

TOP TENS

Architectural Treasures

- **Punic city of Kerkouane** (p117) – the best-preserved Punic site in the world
- **Roman Colosseum at El-Jem** (p208) – an astonishing monument to pleasure, rising from the plains
- **Roman city of Dougga** (p156) – perched on a hilltop, fascinating like no other Roman city
- **Ribat at Monastir** (p197) – film-directors' favourite and the best of Tunisia's fortresses
- **Great Mosque of Kairouan** (p202) – austere Aghlabid exterior and extravagant prayer hall
- **Village of Chenini** (p236) – crumbling hilltop Berber village built into the mountain
- **Ksar Ouled Soltane** (p237) – fantastical fortified Berber granary stores
- **Troglodyte houses, Matmata** (p228) – underground Berber houses in real-life *Star Wars* set
- **Medina at Sfax** (p215) – the medina least touched by tourism
- **Tunis' Ville Nouvelle** (p77) – elegant French-Tunisian fusion with neoclassical façades

Amazing Experiences

- **Saharan adventure** (p252) – trekking over a great sand sea
- **Beach Babylon** (p285) – catching some rays and splashing about in the Mediterranean
- **Scrub a dub dub** (p286) – getting squeaky clean in an ancient, atmospheric *hammam* (public bathhouse)
- **The call to prayer from Byrsa** (p90) – timing your visit so you can hear the plaintive wail of the muezzin while exploring the ruins at Carthage
- **Tunis' medina** (p71) – from the rich central souqs to the narrow whitewashed outskirts, it's another world
- **Sunset at Dougga** (p156) – watching the sunset from Tunisia's most spectacular Roman city
- **Jugurtha's Table** (p177) – walking up the hacked stone steps to this remote, plateau fortress
- **Midès Gorge** (p262) – trekking the amazing gorge between Midès and Tamerza
- **Chott el-Jerid** (p261) – taking the causeway across this sparkling, pancake-flat salt lake
- **Dancing in Tabarka** (p138) – making it to a music festival in this laid-back seaside town

Kids' Stuff

- **Tamerza's waterfalls** (p262) – swimming in the pools at this desert oasis
- **Camel rides!** (p286) – riding across desert dunes on camel-back
- **Star Wars sets** (p22) – finding the *Star Wars* locations and sets in the desert
- **Underground adventure** (p228) – exploring •troglodyte houses and staying at one of Matmata's underground hotels in *Star Wars* country
- **Hot springs** (p251) – unforgettable paddling in Ksar Ghilane's desert springs
- **Beach bonanza** (p285) – some of the Mediterranean's best beaches
- **Seaside fun** (p286) – every kind of watery sport, from bouncy banana-boating to parasailing
- **El-Jem Colosseum** (p208) – the gory history and splendour of this mighty Roman stadium will fire young imaginations
- **Crocodiles!** (p281) – they pack the pond at Parc Djerba Explore
- **Chak Wak Park** (p256) – Tozeur's open-air museum, with crazy outdoor dioramas of dinosaurs and Noah's Ark

Desert Divers, by Sven Linqvist, is a recent book describing the author's Saharan travels and examining the stereotypes and prejudices of past literary tourists such as André Gide and Antoine de St-Exupery.

Robert D Kaplan's *Mediterranean Winter* is the tale of an off-season Mediterranean journey beginning in Tunisia, bringing alive historical characters and revisiting Kaplan's youth.

INTERNET RESOURCES

The internet is a great place to discover more about Tunisia, though information is closely monitored by the Tunisian government.

Access Tunisia (www.access-Tunisia.com) Handy portal with excellent links.

Adventures of Tunisia (www.lexicorient.com/tunisia/) Comprehensive site with chatty information and photos for 140 Tunisian destinations.

Film Scouts (www.filmscouts.com/scripts/matinee.cfm?Film=eng-pat&File=locatns) Good summary of sites used in filming *The English Patient,* including those in Tunisia.

Lonely Planet (www.lonelyplanet.com) Succinct summaries, postcards from other travellers and the Thorn Tree forum.

Travel & Tourism Guide to Tunisia (www.tourismtunisia.com) Helpful Tunisian National Tourist Office website; includes festival dates, hotel details and destination summaries.

Tunis Post (www.tunispost.com) Portal to international news sites with uncensored Tunisia stories.

Tunisia Guide (www.tunisiaguide.com) US Tunisia Tourist Office website; includes cultural and travel information, and a list of tour operators.

Tunisia Online (www.tunisiaonline.com) Government-run site with good sections on the environment, women, history and tourism, and Tunisian news in English, French and Arabic.

Tunisia.com (www.tunisia.com) Useful guide with information on flights, tours, hotels, business, culture, shopping and property rental, and an online community.

Itineraries

CLASSIC ROUTES

MOSQUES, MEDINAS & THE COLOSSEUM **12 Days / Tunis to Sfax**

Start your stay in **Tunis** (p66), Tunisia's laid-back, cosmopolitan capital, with the exceptional **Bardo Museum** (p50) and Unesco World Heritage–listed **medina** (p71). It's also a good base for day trips to ancient **Carthage** (p90) and the enchanting whitewashed village of **Sidi Bou Saïd** (p96), which also has some charming places to stay. Allow three to four days for Tunis and its surrounds, then head south to **Sousse** (p185), where a buzzing Ville Nouvelle stretches along the popular beach, and the sandcastle medina contains some of Tunisia's finest architecture. From here you can visit **Monastir** (p196) with its superb *ribat* (fortified monastery; scene of much silliness in the *Life of Brian*) and mausoleum to Habib Bourguiba; the mystical holy city of **Kairouan** (p199); and the amazingly well preserved Roman colosseum towering over **El-Jem** (p208). It's worth staying at least overnight in atmospheric, seaside **Mahdia** (p209), the perfect antidote to busy resorts and towns. Further down the coast, **Sfax** (p213) has Tunisia's best-preserved medina, and provides an insight into what the other coastal towns must have been like pre-tourism.

This 300km route wends its way from Tunisia's largest city to its second largest, past an astounding array of architectural forms and fascinating ruins. It takes between 12 days and two weeks.

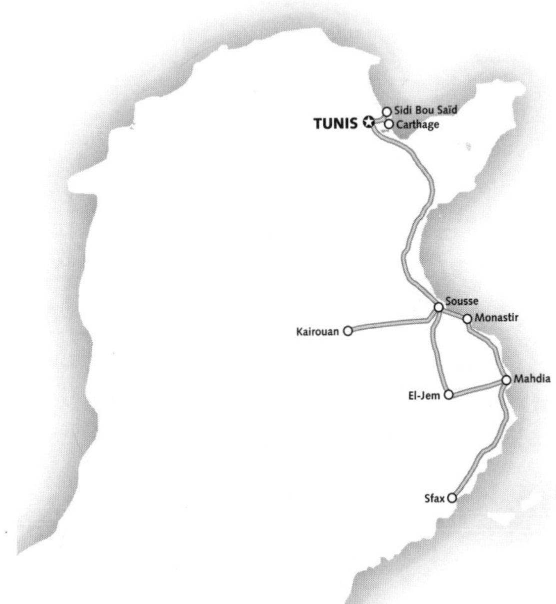

JERBA, BERBERS, SALT & THE SAHARA **10 Days / Jerba to Ong Jemal**

Jerba (p269) is a desert island, but a very much inhabited one, with white-washed, defensive architecture – even the houses look like mini-forts (see the boxed text, p274) – and some good beaches, including **Sidi Mahres** (p280) on the east coast. The island's main town, **Houmt Souq** (p272) is a fascinating mix of covered souqs, good restaurants and vine-covered squares, and you can sleep here in enchanting restored *funduqs* (inns; p276).

From here you can launch off into the south. Amazing stops are the extraordinary underground Berber houses at **Matmata** (p227) and the picturesque Arab-Berber **ksour district** (p237) around Tataouine, with their unique architecture, alien enough to attract the makers of the *Star Wars* films to use them as locations. You could spend at least three or four days exploring these areas, which include the stunning abandoned Berber villages of **Chenini** and **Douiret** (p236) that seem to dissolve into the hilltops, and the alien-looking **Ksar Ouled Soltane** (p237), used to store Berber grain. Via 4WD, you can push south to **Ksar Ghilane** (p251) on the edge of the **Grand Erg Oriental** (p252): an endless sea of sand. Equally you could launch a Saharan expedition from the laid-back town of **Douz** (p243) or **Tozeur** (p255), with its distinctive brick-pattern architecture, both of which are set amid enormous palm groves. If travelling between them, you'll travel over a 2m-high causeway across the strange flat landscape of the **Chott el-Jerid** (p261) – an experience not to be missed. From Tozeur you can also take a trip to the *Star Wars* Mos Espa set at **Ong Jemal** (p263) or the oasis villages of **Tamerza**, **Midès** and **Chebika** (p261) close to the Algerian border.

It takes a week or two to travel the 540km from the sunny coast to the desert interior via Berber villages, oasis towns, salt lakes, and seas of sand dunes.

ROADS LESS TRAVELLED

CAP BON SECRETS & NORTHERN SURPRISES 10 Days / Kélibia to Haidra

Travelling off the beaten track in Tunisia is surprisingly easy. Relatively few foreign tourists travel outside the main resorts, and beyond these you can find rugged coastline, deserted beaches and lush mountains. You can even feel away from it all on Cap Bon, Tunisia's most touristed area: start your journey in **Kélibia** (p114), exploring the beaches at **El-Mansourah** (p115), before going to end-of-the-world **El-Haouaria** (p119) and taking some cobweb-clearing cliff walks. Next, go north to **Bizerte** (p123), a bustling port with an old-world feel, from where you can visit (preferably not at weekends) the largely empty beautiful beach at **Sidi Ali el-Mekki** (p132). Another great coastal stop is hidden-away **Cap Serrat** (p134), then travel up winding mountain roads to reach red-roofed **Ain Draham** (p139), deep in the forests of the Kroumirie Mountains, from where you can go trekking in the green, green hills or even indulge in a spa on the border with Algeria. Hilltop **Le Kef** (p160) is your next stop, a remote walled town with a defensive atmosphere. South into Tunisia's central plains, there are the spectacular natural fortress of **Jugurtha's Table** (p177), with stairs hacked up the side and views into Algeria, and the remote Roman site of **Haidra** (p167). Covering all these sites could stretch from one to two weeks depending how long you choose to laze on the beach or lose yourself in the hills.

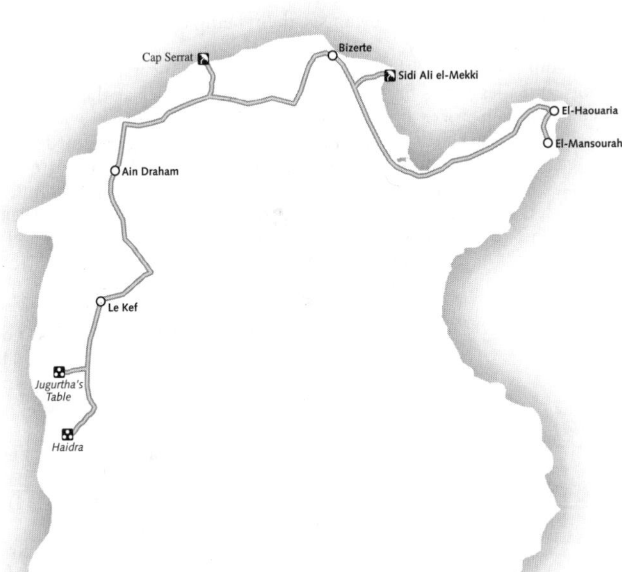

This route takes you away from the crowds to quiet beaches, forested mountains and remote archaeological sites. It will take a week or two and covers around 370km.

TAILORED TRIPS

ADVENTUROUS AGENDA

At first glance it seems like Tunisia's a place for relaxation, not exhilaration, but there's plenty of adventure potential here. Around **Ain Draham** (p139), in the north, you can trek into the Kroumirie Mountains among tall cork forests, for incredible views. Further south you can explore **Jugurtha's Table** (p177), a great flat-topped mountain, and climb the rough-hewn steps to the top. Your reward will be views over the surrounding plains and into Algeria. Further south still, take a dazzling hike along the spectacular gorge between **Midès** (p262) and **Tamerza** (p262), stopping for swims in the springs and feeling smug about what those in the 4WDs are missing. Next stop, the Sahara. At **El-Faouar** (p249), 30km south of Douz, you can go dune-skiing, then travel southeast another 100km or so to **Ksar Ghilane** (p251), to see a sea of endless dunes. From here you can venture to remote **Ksar Tarcine** (p252), a desolate outpost of the Roman Empire. Stop off in **Hammamet** (p101) for some high-velocity water sports (you can even dive WWII wrecks). Also recommended is the tip of Cap Bon for wild, windy cliff walks around end-of-the-world **El-Haouaria** (p119).

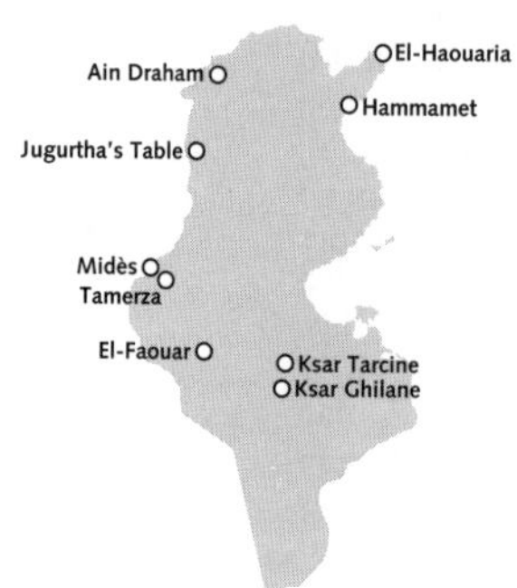

CRAFTY BUSINESS

Tunisian crafts are bright and beautiful – specialities include rugs, ceramics, basketware and brass. You can see them being created and buy them on this colourful itinerary.

Start your journey in **Nabeul** (p109), Tunisia's main ceramics centre to see pots and tiles being fired and painted, and wonder at the amazing choice at bargain prices in its coloured pottery shops. Visit a weaving cooperative at **Beni Khiar** (p114) and see huge looms being operated with practised skill. A few kilometres away is **Dar Chaabane** (p114), a centre for stone-carving, where you can watch this fascinating craft and commission yourself a couple of columns. In central Tunisia, don't miss **Kairouan** (p199), with Tunisia's finest selection of carpets and leatherware. The idyllic island of **Jerba** (p269) is another good place to buy a carpet if you're not already loaded up, and also to visit **Guellala** (p278) village, another great pottery centre, lined with workshops and galleries. If you still haven't tracked down that perfect rug, try **Tozeur** (p255), one of the main gateways to the desert, where brilliant designs brighten the sand-coloured architecture.

A reason to stop in **Ain Draham** (p139), besides the Alpine scenery, is to visit the local carpet cooperative. Further north is **Sejnane** (p134), with its distinctive naïve ceramic figures.

Any craft you wanted to buy on your journey but missed or didn't want to carry, you can find in **Tunis** (p85).

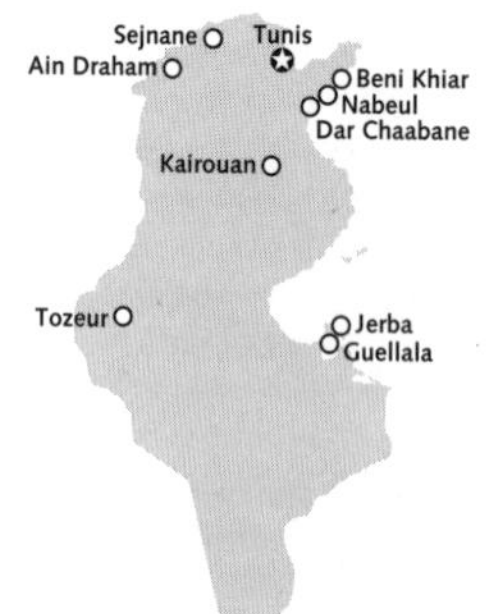

NATURAL SPLENDOUR

South is the **Sahara** (p241) of your dreams, undulating southwest into Algeria: silent, shifting gold. Best is to get as far as **Ksar Ghilane** (p251), with the huge, strangely blank dunes beyond. North of the desert lies **Chott el-Jerid** (p261) a great, sparkling salt lake, weirdly flat and projecting mirages, with an amazing 2m-high causeway across the centre. North of the *chott* (salt lake), don't miss the trek across the extraordinary **Midès** (p262) gorge.

Around the coast, take your pick of beaches – **Sidi Ali el-Mekki** (p132) is a perfect white-sand curve lapped by azure sea, **Kélibia** (p114) in Cap Bon wins the prize for softest sand and clearest blue water and **Hammamet** (p101) is justly famed for its long, golden, greenery-fringed curve.

Jugurtha's Table (p177) is a flat-topped mountain that rears up from the plains like an island, with hacked stone steps leading to views over Algerian peaks. Further north, the Kroumirie range rises and falls on an Alpine scale, blanketed in tall cork-oak forest in the area around **Ain Draham** (p139).

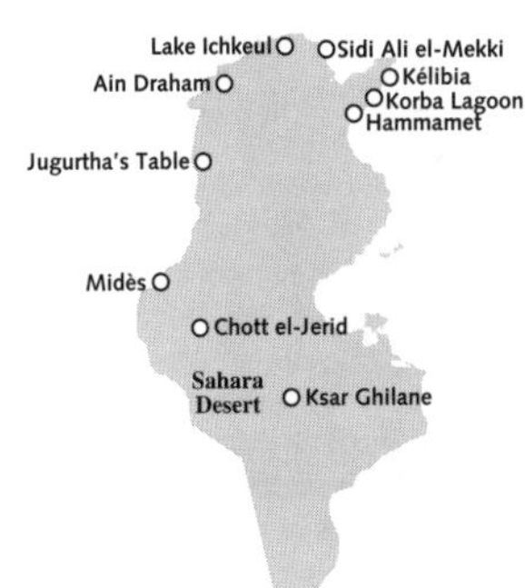

Near Bizerte is huge **Lake Ichkeul** (p132) with its buffalo and birdlife. Another wonderful place for birdlife is the **Korba Lagoon** (p114) in Cap Bon, which stretches 15km along a pearly-white stretch of sandy coast, and can turn pink with flamingos.

FOLLOWING THE FESTIVALS

Summer is the best time in Tunisia for music lovers, although you'd need to stick around for a couple of months to catch everything. Laid-back seaside Tabarka, in the north, is the hub of the music festival calendar – hosting most events in its charming little amphitheatre – with the world-renowned **Tabarka International Jazz Festival** (p138) in July.

By mid-July, the **El-Jem International Symphonic Music Festival** (p209) is under way, with classical music set in the glinting-gold sandstone Roman colosseum at El-Jem. Around the same time, there's no better place to watch classical drama than the Roman theatres of Carthage and Dougga during the **Carthage International Festival** (p95). It's followed soon after by the **Hammamet International Festival** (p101) with a mix of international film, music and theatre groups. Tabarka again takes centre stage in August and early September, with a **World Music Festival**, **Latin Music Festival** and **Raï Festival** (p138) showcasing the best of *raï* from Algeria, just across the border.

If you've missed all of this, Ramadan in October or November signals the **Medina Festival** (p80) in Tunis, with evening concerts in the evocative medina, which comes alive at this time of year. November is also the best time to visit the south when Douz hosts the **Sahara Festival** (p245), a local shindig that predates tourism, followed almost immediately by the **Oasis Festival** (p258) in Tozeur.

Precise dates change from year to year so check out the ONTT's website (www.tourismtunisia.com/culture/festlist.html). For a fuller listing of festivals, see p291.

STAR WARS – A SPACESPOTTER'S GUIDE

Not only are many of the settings for *Star Wars* in the south instantly recognisable, but also plenty of sets are still in place. You could conceivably see all these sites in a week to 10 days.

Tozeur is a good starting point, and tour operators here can help you track down sights. Nearby **Ong Jemal** (p263) was Darth Maul's lookout in *The Phantom Menace,* where he tussled with Qui-Gon. Nearby **Mos Espa** (p263) is a remote desert set used for the prequel films. Also accessible from Tozeur, **Sidi Bouhlel** is known as Star Wars Canyon. It's where jawas parked their sandcrawlers, R2D2 trundled plaintively along, Luke was attacked by Tusken raiders, and Ben and Luke overlooked Mos Eisley. West of Nefta, **Chott el-Jerid** (p261) saw Luke soulfully contemplating two suns from the edge of a crater. Around the fringes of the Chott, the desolate flats doubled as Junland Wastes populated by Krayt dragons and sand people. Ask at the Nefta tourist office (p264) for directions.

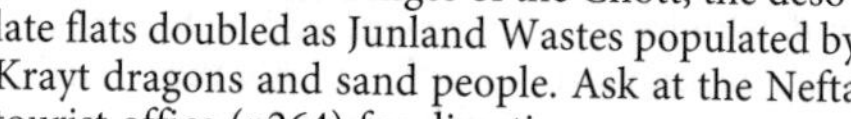

East, in Matmata, is the famous **Sidi Driss Hotel** (p229), which was used in four movies, including *Star Wars* – Luke tucked into blue milkshakes and tussled over the harvest with his Uncle Owen in the dining room. Anakin Skywalker's *Phantom Menace* slave quarters are in **Medenine** (p238), while the Mos Espa slave quarters were represented by the fabulous **Ksar Haddada** (p235). Here Qui-Gon discovered Anakin's parentage in *The Phantom Menace*. South of Tataouine, the extraordinary **Ksar Ouled Soltane** (p237) also provided (even more evocative) slave quarters.

A great *Star Wars* locations website is Star Wars Traveller (www.toysrgus.com/travel/tunisia.html). The book *Tataouine Tours: On Location* by Jeremy Beckett goes into all these sites in detail.

Snapshot

Tunisia's position at the tip of Africa and the edge of the Mediterranean made it a coveted prize of the Carthaginians, Romans, Arabs, Turkish, and French. Its importance has not entirely dimmed; it's a highly significant spot – a moderate Islamic country at the hub of North Africa. The government since independence in 1956 has determinedly pursued a secular political agenda, while retaining its Islamic credentials to keep on side with its neighbours, as well as to maintain harmony within the country.

On the surface Tunisia feels Westernised, particularly in the towns, and especially when compared with its neighbours – Algeria, Libya and Morocco. But the influence is skin deep. The family is very strong here, and social mores enduringly traditional. People cast their eyes towards the West as a land of opportunity but at the same time recoil from it. You will find people eager to talk about the 'War on Terror' and its many ramifications, and it can be extremely worthwhile to discuss the assumptions people here have about the West, as well as the West's misconceptions about Islam. The Tunisian-on-the-street is horrified at the idea that Islam has been typecast as the enemy of Western democracy, and as saddened and disheartened by terrorism as people are in the West. However, not without some justification, people here see some policies in the West, particularly hostility against the Palestinians, Iraq and Afghanistan and support for Israel (especially in view of the latest events in Lebanon) as an attack on Islam.

This desire to talk about politics does not extend to local issues. Local people have learned not to be candid about their feelings regarding the government. Free speech may be enshrined in the constitution but it's not actually allowed, with a controlled press encouraged to practise self-censorship, and anyone who disagrees openly with the government liable to end up in prison. President Ben Ali won his fourth five-year term in power in 2004 with over 95% of the vote. The main opposition, the Democratic Progressive Party, withdrew before the election, stating that participation would have given the proceedings the semblance of democracy.

Some may say that freedom of speech is a small price to pay for the benefits this stable government brings. Ben Ali has continued along the tack of the great architect of independence, Habib Bourguiba, who ruled for an imperious but radical 30 years and set the country on its secular course, paying particular attention to establishing the status of women, enshrining their rights and ensuring equal treatment of men and women, which is unique in the Arab world. Islamic fundamentalism is kept at bay, there's free access to education up to university level, a free health service, and the economy is relatively strong. However, all is not rosy in the jasmine-scented Tunisian garden: unemployment is a problem, the gap between rich and poor notable, many people look abroad for their salvation, and the price being paid for tranquillity is freedom.

Nonetheless, Tunisians are justly proud of their country and its achievements, its peacefulness and relative prosperity – quality of life here for most people is streets ahead of the rest of North Africa – and its strong links with both Europe and America, and the rest of the Arab world.

FAST FACTS

Population: 10.175 million

Unemployment: 14.2%

Inflation: 2.1%

GDP per capita: US$8300

Life expectancy: 77 years for women (up from 51 years in 1966); 73 years for men (around 10 years less than French women and men)

Main crops: olives, olive oil, grain, tomatoes, citrus fruit, dates and almonds

Wine production: 24,000 metric tonnes per year

Petrol and petroleum products: 25% of Tunisian exports

Birth rate: 15.52 births per 1000, almost twice that in Italy

The Punic Wars officially ended in 1985, when the mayors of Rome and Carthage signed a treaty, over 2000 years after hostilities ceased.

History

All the great empires of the Mediterranean basin have ruled Tunisia, leaving fascinating – and in many cases stunningly beautiful – vestiges that continue to captivate and astound visitors to this day.

Carthage: a History, by Serge Lancel, is a detailed but accessible history of the Punic state from its foundation to its ultimate destruction by Rome in 146 BC.

Tunisia was home to the mighty city-state of Carthage, which flourished for six centuries but was eventually brought to its knees by its arch-enemy, Rome. Eight centuries later, the country lay in the path of Islam's conquering armies, who overwhelmed Tunisia's Byzantine and Berber rulers and drew the country into the Arab sphere of influence. Over a thousand years later, after three centuries of at least nominal Ottoman rule, the French made Tunisia a protectorate. After gaining its independence in 1956, Tunisia was ruled for three decades by one of the Arab world's great modernisers, Habib Bourguiba.

FIRST PEOPLES

About 200,000 years ago, Stone Age people eked out an existence using primitive stone tools near the southern oasis town of Kélibia. Back then, the Sahara was covered in forest, scrub and savannah grasses, a fact that anyone who's ever been in Douz in mid-August will find almost impossible to imagine.

Some 8000 years ago, at the end of the last Ice Age, precipitation decreased and the Sahara began to dry out, effectively cutting Tunisia off from the rest of Africa. People began arriving from the east, the most significant of whom were the Capsians. Named after the city of Gafsa (ancient Capsa), near which finely sculpted stone and bone implements from this era have been found, they lived in southern Tunisia until about 4500 BC. Some mosaics from ancient Capsa can be seen in the museum in Gafsa (see p265).

The area covered by modern Tunisia is, apart from the Sahara, remarkably similar to that ruled by Carthage 2500 years ago.

Waves of migration from southern Europe continued until around 2500 BC. It is from these varied Neolithic peoples that the Berbers (see the boxed text, p233) are thought to have descended.

THE RISE & FALL OF CARTHAGE

The name that looms largest in Tunisian history is Carthage (in Phoenician, Kart-Hadasht; in Latin, Carthago). Now a well-heeled northern suburb of Tunis (see p90), this great trading city emerged to dominate the western Mediterranean in the 6th century BC.

The Phoenicians were first drawn to the Tunisian coast in their search for trading posts along the maritime route between their mother city of Tyre (now in southern Lebanon) and the silver mines of southern Spain. Their first settlement in Tunisia, founded in 1101 BC, was Utica (Utique; see p130), about 35km northwest of Tunis. Other early Phoenician ports along the North African coast included Hadrumetum (Sousse), Hippo Diarrhytus (Bizerte) and Thrabaka (Tabarka).

Carthage was founded in 814 BC by the Phoenician queen Elissa (Dido), whose story is told in the city's elaborate foundation myth (see the boxed text, p91), a version of which appears in Virgil's epic poem

TIMELINE

1101 BC	814 BC
Phoenicians found first settlement in Tunisia at Utica	City of Carthage founded by Phoenicians

The Aeneid. A response to the growing Greek presence in the region, Carthage was intended as the start of a more permanent Phoenician presence in Tunisia.

While Tyre suffered at the hands of the Assyrians in the 7th and 6th centuries BC, Carthage went from strength to strength. It soon grew into the great metropolis of the Phoenician world, its wealth and trading craft protected by a powerful navy. By the end of the 6th century BC, Carthage had become the main power in the western Mediterranean, controlling the North African coast from Tripolitania (western Libya) to the Atlantic, with colonies in the Balearic Islands, Corsica, Malta, Sardinia and Sicily.

The cultivation of olives was introduced to Tunisia by the Phoenicians. Today, Tunisia's 56 million olive trees cover 16,000 sq km – by area, that's 19% of the world's olive groves.

During the 5th and 4th centuries BC, Carthage turned its attentions to expanding its land empire in Africa, carving out territory – similar in extent to modern-day Tunisia – that stretched from Tabarka in the northwest to Sfax in the southeast. This Carthaginian entity included the fertile lands of the Cap Bon Peninsula and the Medjerda Valley, which supplied Carthage with a large and exportable agricultural surplus.

It was inevitable that this regional primacy would lead to conflict with the other great powers of the Mediterranean: first Greece, and then Rome. Carthage fought numerous wars with the Greeks over Sicily, which is just 150km northeast of Carthage, most notably in 310 BC. By the time the Carthaginians finally took control of the island in the middle of the 3rd century BC, they found themselves squaring off against an even more formidable rival, the mighty Roman Empire.

The scene was thus set for the first of the three Punic Wars that would preoccupy the two powers for the next 100 years. (Phoenician civilisation in North Africa and its language, which was quite similar to Hebrew, came to be called 'Punic' because the Romans referred to the people of Carthage as 'Poeni', a version of Phoenician.) Rome launched the first war in 263 BC with a campaign to win control of Sicily. Roman successes on land and the supremacy of Carthage's navy ensured a stalemate that dragged on for 20 years.

Rome finally achieved a breakthrough when its fledgling navy destroyed the Carthaginian fleet off Trapani (eastern Sicily) in 242 BC. Navyless and close to bankrupt, Carthage was forced to accept Roman terms and abandon Sicily; in 238 BC it was forced to give up Sardinia and Corsica, too. Trouble on the Carthaginian home front grew as unpaid mercenaries revolted, sparking a bitter conflict, the savagery of which inspired Gustave Flaubert's over-the-top novel *Salammbô* (1862).

The award-winning Franco-Tunisian film *A Summer in La Goulette* (1996), set in 1967, is an entertaining portrayal of three friends – a Muslim, a Jew and a Catholic – and the generation gap facing their families.

Carthage's defeat in the Battle of Zama in 202 BC meant that it again had to relinquish overseas territories. Nevertheless, over the next 50 years it re-established itself as a commercial centre – despite losing much of its African territory to the Numidian king Massinissa, whose cavalry fought for the Romans alongside Scipio at Zama (see p26).

Carthage's resurgence caused increasing unease in Rome. Whipped up by men such as Cato the Elder, the eminent statesman and writer, Rome launched the Third Punic War with the intention of settling the issue once and for all. In 149 BC, the Roman army again landed at Utica and laid siege to Carthage for three years. When the city finally fell in 146 BC, the Romans showed no mercy. Carthage was utterly destroyed

263–242 BC

First Punic War between the Romans and the Carthaginians

218–202 BC

Second Punic War; the glory years and decline of the Carthaginian general Hannibal

HANNIBAL BARCA

Acclaimed by some as the finest military leader in history, the great Carthaginian general Hannibal Barca came within a whisker of erasing the emerging Roman Empire from the history books in the course of the Second Punic War (218–202 BC).

Hannibal, born in 247 BC, was the son of Hamilcar Barca, Carthage's leading general during the First Punic War. That conflict ended with Carthage's loss of Sicily, Sardinia and Corsica, leaving Hamilcar thirsting for revenge.

Frustrated by Carthage's powerful merchant lobby, which preferred trade to war, Hamilcar established an alternative power-base in Spain and made the nine-year-old Hannibal swear an oath of eternal enmity to Rome at the altar of Carthage's great Temple of Baal. This fabled structure was dedicated to Baal Hammon, the main Carthaginian deity, to whom the Carthaginians were notorious for sacrificing children.

Having taken control of Spain in 221 BC, Hannibal set off three years later at the head of an army said to have numbered 90,000 infantrymen backed by 12,000 cavalry and 37 elephants. Hannibal's journey took him across hostile Gaul (modern-day southern France) before an epic crossing of the Alps that saw him descend into the plains of northern Italy in the spring of 217 BC. Only 17 elephants survived the crossing, and his army had shrunk to just 23,000.

Hannibal's finest hour came the following year at the Battle of Cannae (216 BC), where Hannibal virtually annihilated a Roman army of 80,000 despite being vastly outnumbered. His tactic of employing a 'soft centre' to his line, which lured the Romans forward into a trap, makes this one of the most studied battles in history.

Despite his success on the battlefield, Hannibal was unable to break Rome. More than a decade of hide-and-seek followed as Rome sought to contain Hannibal without engaging him in battle. Finally Rome sent Scipio to retake Spain and attack Carthage in 204 BC, forcing the recall of Hannibal from Italy. The two generals faced off at the Battle of Zama (near Siliana) in 202 BC, resulting in Hannibal's only defeat and in Scipio earning the moniker Scipio Africanus.

After the war Hannibal moved briefly into Carthaginian politics before being forced by a plot to flee. He spent the last years of his life touting his skills as a military adviser around the eastern fringes of the Roman Empire before committing suicide in 183 BC when he was betrayed to the Romans.

and then ceremonially cursed, its agricultural lands symbolically sown with salt – so the story goes – to ensure that they would remain forever barren. The survivors were sold into slavery (p90).

The Carthaginians may have been great traders and merchants but they were also ruthless rulers who had oppressed and heavily taxed the indigenous Berber peoples around them. It is often claimed that the Berbers learnt advanced agricultural methods from the Carthaginians but, in fact, many were forced to flee into the desert and mountain hinterland. It is unlikely that many mourned Carthage's brutal demise.

ROME – FROM NEGLECT TO FULL CONTROL

With Carthage in ruins and Roman expansionary priorities lying elsewhere, Rome seemed at a loss as to what to do with its new acquisition. It was happy to leave most of the country to the Numidians (a Berber kingdom) and doubtless they, in turn, were happy to be left alone after centuries of Carthaginian oppression. Under Massinissa, the Numidians had established a kingdom that stretched from western Algeria to Libya.

146 BC

Carthage wiped off the map, sown with salt and cursed by the Romans

44 BC

Julius Caesar resettles Carthage as a Roman city

THE ORIGINS OF 'AFRICA'

Once the Romans had completed their destruction of Carthage, they looked around for a name for their newly acquired territory.

The search ended about 50km to the west of Carthage, in the band of low hills running north from the Medjerda River between the towns of Membressa (modern Mejez el-Bab) and Matar (Mateur). This was the homeland of the Afri, a tribe – apparently Berber – whose loyalty the Romans were keen to cultivate as part of their efforts to create a buffer against the Numidian kingdom further to the west.

The new province of Africa Terra (land of the Afri) occupied the northeastern third of modern Tunisia. As the boundaries of Roman rule were extended east and west along the continent's north coast, 'Africa' came to refer to an ever larger area. Eventually the name became synonymous with the entire 30-million-sq-km continent – only a small part of which was known to the Romans – spreading first among Europeans and later among the native peoples.

Its major towns included Sicca Veneria (Le Kef; p160), Thugga (Dougga; p156) and Vaga (Béja; p143). On Massinissa's death in 148 BC, Rome attempted to cut the kingdom down to size by dividing it up between his three sons.

This policy worked until the kingdom was reunited by Massinissa's grandson Jugurtha, an absolutely ruthless master of the arts of internecine warfare, whose massacre of some Roman traders sparked a war that lasted from 112 to 105 BC. According to some researchers, his mountain base was an impregnable mesa (flat-topped mountain) in far western Tunisia, known to this day as Jugurtha's Table (see p177). Jugurtha was eventually betrayed by his father-in-law, King Bocchus I of Mauretania, captured, paraded through the streets of Rome and then executed.

Rome decided to give the Numidians another chance, splitting their kingdom into a western half centred on Cirta Regia (in modern Algeria) and an eastern half based at Zama, near Siliana. The last of the Zama kings, Juba I, backed the wrong side in the Roman civil war – centred on the power struggle between Julius Caesar and Pompey – and was trounced by Julius Caesar at the Battle of Thapsus in 46 BC.

The 1959 constitution of the Republic of Tunisia states that the president must be a Muslim.

Rome was now firmly in control of its African outpost and Roman settlement began in earnest. Julius Caesar re-established Carthage as a Roman city in 44 BC and it became the capital of the expanded colony of Africa Proconsularis.

By the 1st century AD, the wheat-growing plains of the Medjerda Valley and the Tell Plateau were supplying more than 60% of the Roman Empire's grain requirements. Wealthy citizens donated the monumental public buildings – including baths, theatres and temples – that were a hallmark of the Roman cities of the region. The Berbers – and a number of Jewish communities – prospered and some Berbers were granted Roman citizenship, though it is not clear to what degree Roman civilisation supplanted the local Berber and Punic languages and cultures among the common people. After all, whereas Spain and France ended up speaking Latin-based languages, North Africa did not.

During this time, Roman Africa supplied the wild animals used in colosseum shows, as well as slaves, gold, ivory, olive oil, ostrich plumes

AD 439–533

Decline of Rome and occupation of North Africa by the Vandals

533–647

Tunisia comes under renascent Byzantine Empire

and *garum* (a fishpaste delicacy). The great Roman cities based on this prosperity – including Bulla Regia (p145), Dougga (p156), El-Jem (Thysdrus; p207), Haidra (p167), Sbeitla (Sufetula; p180) and Thuburbo Majus (p153) – are now among Tunisia's principal tourist attractions.

THE VANDALS & THE BYZANTINES

By the beginning of the 5th century AD, Roman power was in terminal decline and the Vandal king Gaiseric (or Genseric), who had been busy marauding in southern Spain, decided that Rome's North African colonies looked like easy pickings. He set off across the Straits of Gibraltar in AD 429, bringing about 80,000 men, women and children with him in one of history's most astonishing invasions. Within 10 years, the Vandals – who were avid Arian Christians – had fought their way across to Carthage, which they made the capital of a short-lived empire. The Vandals built no great monuments and left few cultural or archaeological traces (except for some churches) of their rule, which hastened North Africa's economic decline. Gaiseric, infamously, went on to plunder Rome in AD 455.

Habib Bourguiba of Tunisia: The Tragedy of Longevity, by Derek Hopwood, is probably the best account of the Bourguiba years, with a thoughtful mix of analysis and criticism.

In the meantime, the Byzantine emperor Justinian, based in Constantinople (Istanbul), had revived the eastern half of the now-Christianised Roman Empire and had similar plans for its western territories. In two battles near Carthage, his general Flavius Belisarius defeated the Vandals in AD 533, ushering in 150 years of Byzantine rule. Like most occupiers before them, the Byzantines lived in a state of instability and constant siege, with Berber chieftains in control of the bulk of the country. They built with their customary zeal, however, and many of Tunisia's Roman sites feature 6th-century Byzantine churches and fortifications.

THE ARRIVAL OF ISLAM & THE ARABS

In the mid-7th century AD, the armies of the new religion of Islam (see p39) swept out of Arabia to permanently change the face of North Africa. Islam's green banner was flying over Egypt by AD 640 – just eight years after Mohammed's death – and soon after, Tripoli was in Muslim hands. The Arabs soon inflicted defeat on the Byzantines' Tunisian armies (see p180) but quickly withdrew with their spoils, allowing the Byzantines to hold on to their possessions.

It was not until nearly 30 years later that Islamic rule was secured. For three years, beginning in AD 669, Okba ibn Nafaa al-Fihri swept across North Africa, stopping on the way to establish Qayrawan (Kairouan; see p201), considered by many Sunni Muslims to be Islam's fourth holiest city (after Mecca, Medina and Jerusalem).

Most of the Berbers – up to this point mainly Christian but some also Jewish or pagan – adopted the religion of the invaders readily enough. However, they did not accept Arab rule, and in AD 683 the Arabs were forced to abandon North Africa after Okba was defeated and killed by a combined Berber-Byzantine army. The victors were led by the Berber chieftain Qusayla, who then established his own Islamic kingdom based at Kairouan.

The Arabs soon regrouped, retaking Kairouan in AD 689 and dislodging the Byzantines from Carthage in AD 698. However, they continued

647
First Islamic conquests in Tunisia

669–672
Islamic conquest of North Africa by armies of Okba ibn Nafaa al-Fihri

to encounter spirited resistance from the Berbers, who had rallied behind the legendary princess Al-Kahina (see the boxed text, p233). She defeated the Arabs at Tébessa (Algeria) in AD 696, but was eventually cornered and killed after a legendary last stand at El-Jem in AD 701 (see p208). North Africa, with Kairouan as its capital, became a province of the rapidly expanding Islamic empire controlled by the Umayyad caliphs, based in Damascus.

Meanwhile, the tyrannical behaviour of Arab militia stationed in North Africa had pushed the Berbers to the brink of yet another rebellion. Further inflaming matters was the Berbers' affinity for the teachings of the Kharijites, a puritanical Islamic sect – divided into a variety of feuding factions – whose egalitarian beliefs contrasted sharply with the arrogant and worldly ways of the Umayyad elite, whom they continued to resist.

ISLAMIC DYNASTIES

Tunisia, like much of North Africa, was always too geographically distant from the great centres of Islamic power – such as Baghdad, Damascus, Cairo and Istanbul – to be ruled directly, a circumstance that resulted in a great deal of fighting between rival Muslim groups, both Berber and Arab, and gave rise to a succession of local Islamic dynasties.

A History of the Arab Peoples, by Albert Hourani, is a sweeping and nuanced history of the Arab world and Islam.

In AD 797 Ibrahim ibn al-Aghlab was appointed by the Baghdad-based Abbasid dynasty – which overthrew the Umayyads in AD 750 – as governor of the province of Ifriqiyya (the Arabic name for Africa). With Kairouan as his capital, he soon established effective control of Tunisia, eastern Algeria and the Libyan province of Tripolitania. He was rewarded for these efforts by Harun al-Rashid – whose magnificent Baghdad court may have inspired *The Thousand and One Nights* – with an appointment as hereditary emir, thus establishing the successful Aghlabid dynasty, which ruled Tunisia – nominally as vassals of the Abbasids – for over a century. Arguably, the Aghlabids left the country with its most enduring Islamic architectural legacies. The Great Mosque in Kairouan (p202) and the *ribats* (forts) at Sousse (p189) and Monastir (p197) were all built during the Aghlabid period.

Next came the Fatimids (named after Fatima, Mohammed's daughter), a group of Berber Shiites from the Kabylie region of central Algeria on a mission from God, as they saw it, to depose the religiously illegitimate Abbasid caliphate and declare their leader, Obeid Allah, as caliph. Through alliances with disaffected Berber tribes, the Fatimids quickly conquered North Africa, defeating the Aghlabids in AD 909; a year later Obeid Allah was declared the 'true caliph' at Raqqada, south of Kairouan.

Anticipating reprisals, the Fatimids built a new capital, Mahdia (see p209), on a small, easily defended coastal headland and set about plotting the conquest of Egypt. In AD 969 they took control of the Nile Valley and founded another new capital, Cairo.

A new dynasty, the Zirids, arose in Ifriqiyya but pressure began to mount for a return to religious orthodoxy. In 1045 the Zirids caved in and officially returned to the Sunni mainstream, in open defiance of the Cairo-based Fatimids. The Fatimid reaction was devastating: the Bani Hilal and Bani Sulaim nomadic tribes of upper Egypt invaded the Maghreb en masse, and over the following century North Africa was slowly reduced to ruins. For a

797–909
Tunisia ruled by Aghlabid dynasty

909
Fatimids arrive in Tunisia and establish rule

time in the mid-1100s even the Normans – yes, those Vikings who invaded England in 1066 – held parts of the Tunisian coast.

The power vacuum was eventually filled by the puritanical Almohads, who came to power in Morocco at the beginning of the 12th century. They completed their conquest of North Africa with the capture of Mahdia in 1160 but their empire almost immediately began to crumble. The Maghreb split into three parts: Ifriqiyya (Tunisia) came under the Hafsids; Algeria came under the Banu Abd al-Wad; and Morocco came under the Merenids. Although borders have changed and rulers have come and gone, this division remains more or less intact today.

In 1270 the French King Louis IX, better known as Saint Louis, died at Tunis of the plague while leading the ill-fated Eighth Crusade – the crusaders chose Tunis as their first target with the hope of using it as a staging ground for an invasion of Egypt, to be followed by an assault on the Holy Land. His funeral was a solemn affair held at Notre Dame in Paris. Among the things named after Louis IX: L'Acropolium, Carthage's one-time cathedral (p93) and the US city of St Louis, Missouri.

THE OTTOMAN TURKS

While the Ottoman Turks and the Spanish fought for control of the Mediterranean – yet another regional conflict not of Tunisian making – local resistance came from Muslim corsairs, or pirates. The most famous were the Barbarossa brothers, Aruj and Khair ed-Din, who had established themselves on the island of Jerba. Aruj captured Algiers from the Spanish but was killed when they retook the city in 1518. Khair ed-Din turned for help to the Turks, who jumped at the chance to get involved. He was given the Turkish title of *beylerbey* (governor) and supplied with troops.

Tunisia has some of the world's most draconian internet censorship. Sites with political, human rights and erotic content are blocked and, in internet cafés, bandwidth is limited.

Tunis was to change hands four more times before Sinan Pasha finally claimed it for the Turks in 1574, forcing the last of the Hafsids into exile. Tunis then became a *sanjak* (province) of the Ottoman Empire. In 1598 Othman Dey seized power, downgrading the Ottoman pasha to a mere figurehead. Internecine warfare and endless power struggles persisted until the early 18th century, when Hussein ben Ali founded the Husseinite line of beys, who ruled Tunisia – at least in title – until the country became a republic in 1957.

The Arab world's first constitution *(destour)* was promulgated in Tunisia in 1861.

THE FRENCH PROTECTORATE

In the mid-1810s, Great Britain, the Netherlands, France and the far-off United States, tired of predations by pirates based in the Barbary States (Tripoli, Tunis and Algiers), dispatched naval vessels to North Africa, forcing Tunisia to ban piracy in 1816. In 1846 the Bey of Tunis abolished slavery, a Westernising reform that, like the end of highly profitable raids by Tunisian corsairs, exacted a heavy toll on his country's treasury, necessitating heavy borrowing – in the form of high-interest loans – from European banks. By 1869 the country was broke and control of its finances was handed over to an international commission, an ignominious state of affairs for this once-prosperous trading nation.

12th–16th centuries

Hafsids rule Tunisia after demise of Moroccan Almohads

1574

Sinan Pasha claims Tunisia for the Turkish Ottoman Empire

In 1881 the French sent 30,000 troops into Tunisia on the pretext of countering border raids by Tunisian tribesmen into French-occupied Algeria. They stayed. The bey remained as Tunisia's titular head but was forced to sign the Treaty of Kassar Saïd, which put real power in the hands of a French resident-general. The British, France's great colonial rivals, accepted French domination of Tunisia in exchange for French acquiescence in the British occupation of Cyprus.

The 1883 Convention of La Marsa established parallel justice systems, under which Europeans were judged under French law and local Tunisians under a modified form of Islamic law.

The French went about the business of land acquisition more discreetly than they did in neighbouring Algeria. In Tunisia, they managed to get their hands on the best fertile land without confiscating property from individuals. Rather, they took over large tracts of the Cap Bon Peninsula and the Medjerda Valley that had previously been controlled by the bey or used by nomads for grazing. The citrus groves of Cap Bon are a legacy of this time, as are the vineyards that provide the bulk of the country's wine grapes.

The south was too arid for agriculture and was largely ignored until the beginning of the 20th century, when phosphate was discovered in the hills west of Gafsa. The massive mining operation begun by the French remains an important export-earner for the Tunisian economy.

The Sultan's Admiral, by Ernie Bradford, is a lively biography of the famous 16th-century pirate Khair ed-Din, who terrorised Christian shipping in the western Mediterranean and paved the way for the Ottoman conquest.

WORLD WAR II

After France's capitulation to Nazi Germany in June 1940, Tunisia's colonial government remained loyal to the collaborationist Vichy regime led by Marshall Philippe Pétain and, among other things, enacted anti-Jewish laws.

In November 1942, after British forces defeated Rommel at El Alamein (Egypt) and American forces landed in Morocco and Algeria, the Germans sent troops from Sicily to northern Tunisia in an attempt to turn back the Allied armies now advancing on the country from both the east and the west. Conditions for the Allies were difficult – their supply lines were long and the weather was cold and rainy – and they found themselves in a stalemate until February 1943 (see The Battle of Kasserine Pass boxed text on p178).

The Allies – mainly Americans and British – lost more than 15,000 men (see WWII Military Cemeteries boxed text on p144) before capturing Tunis and Bizerte – and more than 250,000 Axis POWs – in May 1943. The Allied victory put an end to Nazi plans to round up the country's entire Jewish community.

The Pillar of Salt, by Albert Memmi, is an autobiographical coming-of-age novel about a Tunisian-Jewish youth, powerfully drawn to French culture, growing up in Tunis before and during WWII.

THE ROAD TO INDEPENDENCE

The first Tunisian nationalist political party, the Destour (Constitution) Party, was formed in 1920. Its demands for democratic government were supported by the bey but the French responded with troops and arrests and, for a while, managed to derail nationalist initiatives.

In 1934 a young, charismatic, Sorbonne-educated lawyer, Habib Bourguiba (1903–2000), broke away from the Destour Party, founding the Néo-Destour Party. Support for the new grouping quickly spread, but

1881–83
French military action and treaties hand effective control of Tunisia to the French resident-general

1920
Tunisia's first political party, the Destour, demands equal rights for Europeans and Tunisians

after the French turned their guns on demonstrators in Tunis on 9 April 1938, killing dozens of people, the party was banned and Bourguiba arrested and deported to France. French suppression merely increased the Néo-Destour's popular support.

Charles De Gaulle's Free French forces took control of Tunisia after the German defeat in 1943 and quickly implemented uncompromising antinationalist policies. The bey was deposed and Bourguiba, who had returned to Tunisia in 1943, fled to Cairo, from where he organised a successful propaganda campaign aimed at bringing the Néo-Destour's proindependence demands to international attention. By 1951 – the year neighbouring Libya received its independence – the French were ready to make concessions. A nationalist government was set up and Bourguiba was allowed to return but the French soon changed their minds – and exiled Bourguiba for a third time. Nationalist guerrilla violence followed and the country was soon in a state of disarray.

Modern Tunisia, by Andrew Borowiec, is one of the more readable modern histories of Tunisia, with a particular focus on its battle against Islamic fundamentalism.

In July 1954, just two months after the defeat of French forces by Ho Chi Minh at Dien Bien Phu in Vietnam, French premier Pierre Mendès-France announced France's readiness for negotiations about Tunisian autonomy. In June 1955 an agreement was reached and Bourguiba – who had spent half of the previous two decades in detention – returned to Tunis to a hero's welcome.

Tunisia was formally granted full independence on 20 March 1956, with Bourguiba as prime minister. (Eighteen days earlier Morocco had also been granted independence.) Within a year, the last bey had been deposed, the country had been declared a republic and Bourguiba became Tunisia's first president.

TUNISIA UNDER BOURGUIBA

During his early years in power, Habib Bourguiba supported proindependence forces in Algeria. In 1958 French aircraft – in pursuit of Algerian rebels – bombed the Tunisian border village of Sakhiet Sidi Youssef (40km west of Le Kef), killing 62 civilians and creating international outrage.

In their attempts to silence Habib Bourguiba, the French both exiled him from Tunisia and sent him into internal exile in Tabarka, Remada and, for two years, the tiny Mediterranean island of Galite.

In 1961 Bourguiba demanded that France evacuate its military enclave at Bizerte, the last bit of Tunisia still under French control. When Tunisian troops invaded the French base, French paratroops – flown in from Algeria – and aircraft launched a bloody retaliatory operation in which more than 1000 Tunisians died during 90 hours of fierce fighting. The French finally withdrew from Bizerte in 1963.

Bourguiba, whose principles were socialist and secular, was quick to introduce sweeping legal and social changes, adopting a policy of Westernisation in order to modernise Tunisia's economy and society. The results of his bold efforts to emancipate women (see p43), including the abolition of polygamy, are a prominent feature of Tunisian life to this day, and Tunisia became a showcase for successful postcolonial development.

Bourguiba regarded Islam as a force that was holding the country back and therefore sought to deprive religious leaders of their grass-roots role in shaping society, in part by closing religious schools and abolishing Sharia (Islamic law) courts. In addition, more than 60,000 hectares of

1934
Habib Bourguiba forms Néo-Destour Party and begins struggle for independence

May 1943
American and British forces end the Nazi occupation of Tunisia

land that had financed mosques and religious institutions were confiscated. Not surprisingly, clerics vehemently opposed the changes and for a time resistance flared, particularly in Kairouan.

In 1975 the National Assembly made Bourguiba president-for-life.

The 1970s saw the gradual emergence of an Islamic opposition whose support increased dramatically following the use of the military to crush a general strike in January 1978, killing dozens of people. Under increasing pressure at home and abroad, Bourguiba called the first multiparty elections in 1981, though the Islamic opposition was not allowed to run and there were cries of foul play.

President Ben Ali, who came to power in 1987, would have to rule until 2018 to match Habib Bourguiba's 31 years in office.

Anxious to preserve its power and desperate to avoid the upheaval and violence caused by Islamic militants in Algeria and Egypt, Bourguiba's government spent much of the '80s conducting a harsh and effective clampdown against the Islamist opposition. In very early 1984 the withdrawal of a bread subsidy sparked six days of rioting notable for slogans such as 'God is great' and 'down with America'; more than 70 people died. To ease tensions, the bread subsidies were reinstated and a number of jailed Islamist politicians freed.

While this epic struggle for the heart and soul of Tunisia was being slowly played out, Bourguiba's decades-long reign was stagnating and he was seen as being increasingly out of touch with the concerns and needs of the common people.

On 7 November 1987, Prime Minister Zine el-Abidine ben Ali, afraid that executing several Islamists convicted of plotting to overthrow the government – as demanded by Bourguiba – would spark a popular uprising, seized power in a bloodless palace coup. A team of doctors declared the 83-year-old president physically and mentally incapable of carrying out his duties.

Bourguiba died in 2000 at the age of 96, having lived out his last years in Monastir.

TUNISIA UNDER BEN ALI

Ben Ali has continued with most of his predecessor's policies, both domestic (secularist and politically repressive) and foreign (moderate and pro-Western).

In the early 1990s an alleged Islamist coup plot was uncovered and thousands of suspected fundamentalists were imprisoned; many others fled into exile. Human rights groups and, for a time, the French government led the way in calling for greater respect for human rights, and

BOURGUIBA LEGACY

No person did more than Habib Bourguiba to shape modern Tunisia. He will be remembered not only for having led his country to independence from France but also for creating a strong secular Tunisian identity, advancing women's rights, instituting bold reforms that in some cases ran counter to Sharia law, vastly increasing literacy and bringing Tunisians a standard of living that puts Tunisia near the top of the pile in the developing world.

The bronze door of Bourguiba's mausoleum in Monastir (see p198) is marked with the words: 'The Supreme Combatant, the Liberator of Women, the Builder of Modern Tunisia'.

20 March 1956
Tunisia granted independence from France

1957
Tunisia declared a republic, rule of the beys ended, Habib Bourguiba becomes president

The film *Indigènes* (2006) exposes France's ingratitude towards the 130,000 Tunisians, Algerians and Moroccans who fought to liberate France from Nazi rule during WWII.

at one point Tunisia seemed on the way to becoming something of a pariah state.

Since several bombings by Algerian Islamists in France in the mid-1990s and, even more so, since 9/11, the international pressure on Ben Ali has eased significantly, although his government has continued to restrict political parties, censor the press and the internet, limit religious freedoms and engage in the surveillance and harassment of intellectuals, opposition activists and journalists. Indeed, in some policy-wonk circles, Tunisia is now seen as something of a model of how a moderate, secular and relatively open Arab state can resist fundamentalism, if not democratically then at least effectively. In 2006 Ben Ali issued a statement critical of the wearing of headscarves by Tunisian women.

After eviscerating the Islamist opposition in the early 1990s, Ben Ali cleverly tried to appease the wider population. He headed off on a heavily publicised pilgrimage to Mecca to establish his own credentials as a good Muslim, and ordered that the Ramadan fast be observed in public. He also promised a multiparty political system, released political prisoners, abolished the State Security Court and limited police powers of detention. Political exiles were invited to return and many decided that it was safe to do so.

Ben Ali confirmed his hold on power in elections in 1989, 1994, 1999 and 2004. The 2004 poll left Ben Ali's Rassemblement Constitutionnel Démocratique (RCD) with 152 seats in the 189-seat Chamber of Deputies while the official opposition, the Mouvement des Démocrates Socialistes (MDS), won 14 seats. Four other parties shared the remaining 23 seats. Ben Ali retained the presidency with 94.5% of the vote, his lowest vote total ever.

Despite high unemployment, Tunisia's economy continues to be among the most successful in the developing world. Significant infrastructure investments have eased rural poverty and brought running water and electricity to even the remotest villages. In 1995 Tunisia became the first Arab state to be integrated into the European Economic Area, and agreements with Italy allow Tunisians to work in its agricultural sector. Overall, the economy is growing steadily, helping to cement Tunisia's reputation as relatively prosperous, stable and modern nation.

Tunisia's foreign policy has long been characterised by moderation and efforts to facilitate dialogue and reconciliation. For a decade starting in 1979, Tunisia served as the headquarters of the Arab League after the organisation quit Cairo to protest the 1978 peace treaty between Egypt and Israel. And in 1982 Tunisia welcomed Yasser Arafat and the Palestine Liberation Organisation (PLO) after they were forced out of Beirut by the Israelis; the organisation was based at Hammam Plage, just south of Tunis, until mid-1994, when most of the PLO moved to the West Bank and Gaza under the terms of the Oslo Accords. Around the same time, Tunisia and Israel established low-level diplomatic relations, maintaining interest offices in Tel Aviv and Tunis until the outbreak of Palestinian-Israeli violence in October 2000. Even today, Israelis have no problem getting visas to visit Tunisia.

In April 2002 a suicide bombing at a historic synagogue in Jerba (see the boxed text, p278), blamed on Al-Qaeda, killed 21 people, causing

1981

Tunisia's first multiparty election

7 November 1987

Ben Ali ousts Habib Bourguiba in bloodless coup to become Tunisia's second president

FROM TUNIS TO VIRGINIA TO WASHINGTON – & BACK TO VIRGINIA

Former United States Senator George Allen (Republican of Virginia), an unswerving Bush loyalist, was known for chewing tobacco, wearing cowboy boots, listening to country music and promoting a very conservative Christian social agenda. His amiable, down-home manner endeared him to conservative white voters, some of whom were, if not attracted, then certainly not deterred by his image as something of a redneck (his college nickname was 'Neck'), based in part on his affinity for the Confederate flag and his having opposed Virginia's Martin Luther King Day. Conservative Republicans were touting him as a presidential candidate for 2008.

Imagine his shock, then, when the senator, at age 53, after a full and rewarding life as a good ol' boy, discovered that he is, in fact, an African-American of sorts. More precisely, it turns out that he is half Tunisian and, more specifically, half Tunisian-Jewish. *Time* dubbed him 'the unlikeliest Semite in Christendom'.

Allen had known that his mother, Henriette (Etty), née Lumbroso, had been born in Tunisia but had been told that the family's background was European colonial, with roots in France, Italy and Spain. In fact, the Lumbrosos were prominent members of Tunis' ancient Jewish community and had lived in Tunisia for hundreds of years, tracing their roots back to Moorish Spain. Back in the early 1700s, one Lumbroso had even been the Chief Rabbi of Tunis.

During the Nazi occupation of Tunisia, Etty had seen her father, Felix, dragged from their home in the middle of the night and sent to a forced labour camp. This event so traumatised her that after the war, she and Allen's father – a famous American football coach – decided that the safest thing to do was to hide the family's Jewish background from absolutely everyone, including their children. Only at age 83 did Etty reveal the truth, a disclosure that might have had zero impact on Allen's political career had he handled it with tact and sensitivity, rather than losing his cool at a televised press conference and bragging about his mother's pork chops.

Combined with his on-camera use of a racial epithet a few weeks earlier, the way Allen responded to his outing as an African did significant damage to his reputation and saved the seemingly hopeless campaign of his Democratic rival in the November 2006 Congressional elections, Jim Webb. Webb's cliff-hanger victory – by just 7200 votes – secured the Democrats control of the Senate by 51 seats to 49.

widespread outrage in a country that is proud of its legacy of religious tolerance.

Tunisia expressed opposition to the US-led alliance in the 1991 Gulf War and was even less enthusiastic about the US-led overthrow of Saddam Hussein in 2003. The Tunisian 'street' is vehemently opposed to the occupation of Iraq and anti-American (or at least anti-Bush) positions figure prominently in the statements of Tunisian opposition groups.

Today there is no suggestion that the Tunisian government is anything other than in complete control. Politics is not a popular (or advisable) topic of conversation, but many Tunisians express what could be genuine admiration for Ben Ali's leadership. Not only are Tunisians proud of their country's reputation for stability and economic success in a volatile and largely impoverished region, but a glance west towards Algeria – still struggling with Islamist violence after 15 years of civil strife in which at least 150,000 people have died – or east to Libya – led for almost four decades by the erratic Muammar Gaddafi – provides ample evidence that things could be an awful lot worse.

Football-mad Tunisians were delighted when their country – hosts of the tournament – beat Morocco to win the African Cup of Nations title in 2004.

2000

Death of Habib Bourguiba in Monastir

2004

Ben Ali re-elected president with 94.5% of the vote

The Culture

THE NATIONAL PSYCHE

Tunisians are proud of the achievements of their government and of their tolerant, hospitable society, but, then again, they're not really allowed to say what they think. Despite their pride, many people would leave if they could. In Europe they can maybe moonlight as a security guard or pick up work as a hospital porter before moving onto something better.

Tunisia banned the *hejab* (women's headscarf) in schools and public administration in 1981, over 20 years before France did the same.

The exodus to Europe is mostly economic and to fulfil ambitions – like anyone choosing to work abroad. Tunisia offers its people an excellent education, but then jobs for graduates are scarce. European society, free from family strictures and tantalisingly close, tempts many graduates and those less-qualified away from treading water.

Tunisia is much freer than other Arabic Muslim societies. People have choices; this is obvious when you see a family walking along the street with two daughters dressed entirely differently – one in jeans and a T-shirt, the other in a long robe and veil. However, traditions are constraints below the surface. Women may dress in Western fashions, but they will still be expected to be virgins when they marry. People may have flooded to the cities but there is a village mentality here that resists the change.

Only 150km from Europe, here there's widespread admiration for the achievements of the West as well as condemnation for the perceived injustices done in the West's name elsewhere in the region. Tunisia shares with the Arab world a history of invasion and colonial meddling. Despite this, the country has a tradition of gracious hospitality that has its roots in the nomadic Bedouin traditions of refuge and hospitality, as well as in the verses of the Quran.

While 90.2% of Tunisian households possess a TV, only 35.6% have a telephone, 21% own a car and 16.5% are without running water.

LIFESTYLE

Since independence in 1956, Tunisia's population has more than doubled and people have flooded to the cities. Over 60% of the population is urban. Society today divides between the cosmopolitan mores of big cities and rural, small-town traditions.

In some ways Tunisia resembles Italy, its near neighbour. The family is all important, and the individual is always subordinate to its interest. An inner sanctum is protected and supported by a morass of relatives. In Tunisia's recent past this was taken to the extent that an extended family would all live together in one house. Hence the size of upper-class family

RESPONSIBLE TRAVEL

- Most importantly – dress appropriately to show consideration for local culture. Women should keep their arms and legs covered and avoid exposing too much flesh.
- Couples should avoid demonstrations of affection in public – it's offensive to many local people to see people kiss or even hold hands in public.
- If you're staying in a resort, venture outside it to discover the real Tunisia – eat in a local restaurant, visit some sights, try a beach outside the tourist resorts, tussle over goods in the medina or take a louage (shared taxi) trip.
- Talk to local people about Islamic and Arabic culture and find out how people view the West – you might be able to dispel some preconceptions.

INSIDE A TUNISIAN WEDDING

'It's ludicrous how much it costs to hire a room for a wedding,' said Khaled dolefully, 'thousands of dinars for just a few hours. People invite everyone they know and everyone they don't. Families are broken by the expense. And then the marriage breaks up a few months later!' He laughed cynically. Not everyone has Khaled's pessimistic attitude to marriage, but everyone agrees it is expensive, convoluted and all inclusive. Marriages are the biggest excuse Tunisians have to party. If you visit in summer – wedding season – expect your sleep to be disturbed by processions of cars through the streets, horns blaring, and loud music continuing until the early hours. What you're hearing is the riotous joy of a Tunisian wedding.

Nowadays, in Tunisian towns and cities, people usually find their own partner. But in traditional families, parents search for prospective sons- and daughters-in-law when their children reach marriageable age. It is rumoured that mothers often go to the *hammam* (public bathhouse) on scouting expeditions for their sons, to find the most beautiful women, after which they conduct discreet research into the woman's family background, her job prospects and other aspects of eligibility. When the parents have made their choice (after having consulted their daughter in all but the most traditional rural families), the girl is asked for her agreement. Under Tunisian law, she has a right to refuse, which is respected by most families.

If the girl agrees, a meeting between the two families is arranged – as you might imagine, a somewhat formal and awkward occasion. If all goes well, contracts are exchanged and the legal formalities completed. Between then and the wedding, the couple is allowed a series of meetings. Again, they're not exactly intimate occasions as they're usually accompanied by family members; anything (from gossip to illicit acts) could be fatal to a woman's honour and hence her marriage prospects.

Weddings traditionally last three to seven days, for the duration of which the woman is secluded from public view with the women of her family.

On the first day of the wedding, the groom does the rounds with his male friends, buying gifts (clothes, jewellery, perfumes) for his wife. These are displayed in the satin quilted baskets you can see on sale in Tunisia's souqs. He then, with great ceremony, delivers these gifts to the eagerly awaiting women of the wife's family.

On day two the husband and wife remain with their families and enjoy an evening of feasting in the company of an all-male or all-female cast of family members. It is also on the second day that the man shaves off his beard (which he has been growing for a month) and the woman goes to the *hammam* and has all the hair from her body removed. Her hands and feet are decorated with henna.

On the last day, in the early evening, cars gather to begin the noisy procession of friends and family through the streets, announcing the joyful news. In the south, revellers traditionally passed through town on foot, alongside the bride astride a camel but concealed by a canopy.

And there is a party to end all parties in the expensively rented room. The couple are seated on glitzy thrones, the woman heavily made up (usually in fashionable 'Lebanese style'), sweating nervously under the lights and scrutiny of the crowds.

At the end of the night, the husband and wife retire to the man's house (nowadays usually a hotel), alone together for the first time, for one week's seclusion and consummation of the marriage. Thankfully, the older women no longer wait outside for the blood-stained sheet as proof of the woman's virginity.

As for Khaled, he is middle-aged and divorced. Would he do it again? 'Yes! But I would marry for love and have the party in my garden.'

homes, such as Dar Ben Abdullah in Tunis (p76) and Dar el-Annabi in Sidi Bou Saïd (p96). Today, with increased migration and emigration, this is less likely, but the pull of home is strong and those who have left will return for frequent visits.

The absence of government unemployment benefits also contributes to the enduring strength of family ties: the unemployed survive thanks to familial support and often one working adult has to provide for four or five other adults. Social security does, however, provide old-age and disability pensions, free health care and education.

Female literacy rose from 24% in 1966 to 77% in 2004.

Tunisia is a deeply religious society – religion is part of daily life and pervades all significant ceremonies. When a baby is born to a Muslim family, the first words uttered to it are the call to prayer. A week later this is followed by a ceremony in which the baby's head is shaved and an animal sacrificed. The major event of a boy's childhood is circumcision, which normally takes place sometime between the ages of seven and 12. When a person dies, a burial service is held at the mosque and the body is then buried with the feet facing Mecca. Yet Tunisian life is balanced between the observance of Islam and secular values, and religion is a private affair.

POPULATION

After 14 centuries of intermarriage, the indigenous Berbers and later-on-the-scene Arabs are thoroughly entwined. You are most likely to find stronger evidences of Berber traditions in the south, along the northern fringe of the Sahara.

The Tunisian divorce rate is 0.82 per 1000 people, less than a third of the UK rate (3.08 per 1000), but nearly four times that in Italy (0.27 per 1000).

Muslims make up 98% of the population, the other 2% being Jews and Christians.

Government family-planning programmes have slowed the population growth rate to 1.6%, but Tunisia has a very young population, which places a great strain on social services, particularly with the pressure on jobs.

SPORT

Football is the sport closest to Tunisian hearts. The Tunisian national team, nicknamed 'the Carthage Eagles', is one of the strongest teams in Africa having qualified for the World Cup finals in 1978, 1998, 2002 and 2006 (though they haven't so far made it out of the first round). Tunisia hosted the 2004 African Cup of Nations and the country erupted in delight when they won the tournament (2–1 against old enemies Morocco). In 2006, they made it only to the quarterfinals.

They've never had it so good: life expectancy has risen from 51 years at the time of independence (1956) to 77 years today. Poverty now stands at 4%, compared with 22% of the population in 1975.

Tunisian club teams are also among the best on the continent with Espérance Sportive de Tunisie (Tunis) and Etoile Sportif du Sahel (Sousse) regularly reaching the final of the continent-wide club competitions. These two clubs routinely dominate the domestic competition. The competition runs from early October until the end of March, with matches played on Saturday and Sunday afternoon starting at 3pm. You'll find fixtures and results in the local papers. For information on games in Tunis, see p84.

Tunisians are also proud of the Tunisian players plying their trade with clubs in the major European competitions. Their pride even encompasses any player of North African origins, such as Zinedine Zidane (whose background is Berber-Algerian).

MEDIA

If much of what you see, read or hear sounds like a presidential press release, that's because it is. Tunisian TV, radio and newspapers are all under government auspices.

For TV, there are only two (Arabic-language) channels, both controlled by a government intent on protecting itself from criticism and its citizens from anything vaguely corrupting. Most Tunisians get around the stultifying local programming by buying satellite dishes (often smuggled from Algeria).

NO NEWS IS GOOD NEWS

There was a flurry of protest when Tunisia was chosen by the UN to host a World Summit on the Information Society (WIIS) in 2005.

It was an ironic choice considering Tunisia's treatment of journalists who challenge the government. Zouhair Yahyaoui was imprisoned for 18 months in 2002 for 'spreading false news' (publishing articles criticising the government's actions, or suggesting that there is corruption at the top) – he had published articles satirising the government on his website, TunisZine. Released in November 2003, the dissident journalist died in 2005 at the premature age of 36.

Mohammed Abbou, a human rights lawyer, has been imprisoned since March 2005, sentenced to three and a half years in prison for his open criticism of the government online. When two journalists, Slim Boukhdir and Taoufik Al-Ayachi, went to try to interview his wife at her home, they were beaten by police.

The government has enshrined freedom of information in the constitution, and introduced press liberalisation measures in 2005. However, this is an area where actions speak louder than words. Reporters sans Frontiers (www.rsf.org) states 'Journalists and media are actively discouraged from being more independent by means of bureaucratic harassment, advertising boycotts and police violence.'

There's more variety to be found in newspapers (French and Arabic), but they're still heavily censored. The music radio stations are less potentially subversive (at least in the government's eyes) and therefore far more entertaining.

As for new media, numerous internet sites are blocked by the government, including some political sites and most pornography. See the boxed text, above for more on censorship.

And one tip: if you're watching Tunisian TV in Sousse and you see pictures of the president waving to crowds in Sousse, don't expect a handshake; chances are that it's file footage being shown to disguise his real location.

RELIGION

Tunisia is 98% Muslim, and Islam is the State religion, but the government has spent much of the last five decades cracking down hard on those who wish to mix religion with politics.

In addition to the more than 95% of Tunisians who are Sunni Muslim (the orthodox majority in Islam), there are small communities of Kharijites (a minority Muslim sect). Jews (see the boxed text, p278) and Christians make up the other 2%.

Tunisian Jews (www.harissa.com) Homepage of Tunisian Jewish community and diaspora – easy to negotiate and informative.

Islam

THE RISE OF ISLAM

'Islam' means submission. The call to submit to God's will was the essence of Allah's message conveyed through the Prophet Mohammed. The religion shares its roots with the other great monotheistic faiths that sprang from the harsh land of the Middle East – Judaism and Christianity – but it's considerably younger.

Mohammed was born into a trading family in the Arabian city of Mecca (in present-day Saudi Arabia) in AD 570. He began to receive revelations in AD 610 and later started imparting the content of Allah's message to the Meccans. He gathered quite a following against the idolaters of Mecca, and his movement especially appealed to the poor. The powerful families became increasingly outraged and, by AD 622, had made life sufficiently unpleasant for Mohammed and his followers; they fled to Medina (after which all Arabic walled cities are named), an oasis town some 300km to the north and now Islam's second holiest city. (This migration – the Hejira – marks the beginning of the Islamic calendar, year 1 AH or AD 622.) In Medina, Mohammed continued to preach.

Islam: A Short History, by Karen Armstrong, provides a contemporary and sympathetic study of Islam from its birth to its modern struggle against misrepresentation.

By AD 632, Mohammed had revisited Mecca and many of the tribes in the surrounding area had sworn allegiance to him and the new faith. Mecca became the symbolic centre of the faith, containing as it did the Kaaba, which housed the black stone supposedly given to Ibrahim (Abraham) by the angel Jibril (Gabriel). Mohammed determined that Muslims should face Mecca when praying outside the city.

On Mohammed's death in AD 632, his followers quickly conquered the areas that make up modern Syria, Iraq, Lebanon, Israel and the Palestinian Territories. This was accomplished under Mohammed's four successors, the caliphs (or Companions of Mohammed).

Islam spread west, fanning out across North Africa. By the end of the 7th century, the Muslims had reached the Atlantic and thought themselves sufficiently in control of the Gezirat al-Maghreb (Island of the West, or North Africa beyond Egypt) to march on Spain in AD 710.

After Mohammed's death came the most serious split in the faith. Some followers felt that a relative of Mohammed's should be the new Caliph and chose Ali, a cousin, married to Mohammed's daughter Fatima. These broke away to become the Shiite branch, while the mainstream were called the Sunni, though divisions appeared within this group too, with varying ways of interpreting the Quran. Most Tunisians are Sunnis. There are also small other radical sects, such as the Ibadis based on Jerba (see the boxed text, p280). Another variation is Sufism (see the boxed text, p42), reaching the mystic parts that mainstream Islam does not reach.

THE QURAN

The holy book of Islam is the Quran – the word of Allah, revelations communicated to Mohammed in verse via the angel Jibril. Not only is it a fascinating and holy text, but also a masterpiece of Arabic literature – essential reading for anyone who wants to understand Islam from its source. It contains many references to the earlier prophets of Judaism and Christianity: Adam, Abraham, Noah, Moses and Jesus, a line that ends definitively with the greatest, the Prophet Mohammed.

Banipal (www.banipal.co.uk) is a literary magazine in English publishing work by and articles about Arabic writers.

In the past, young boys whose families could afford it were sent to Quranic schools where they would learn all 6200 verses by rote.

Tunisians are mostly Sunnis belonging to the Malekite school of Quranic interpretation, which is somewhat less rigid in its application and interpretation of the Quran than the other schools.

THE FIVE PILLARS OF ISLAM

To live a devout life, Muslims are expected to observe the Five Pillars of Islam:

Shahada This is the profession of faith, Islam's basic tenet: 'There is no God but Allah, and Mohammed is the Prophet of Allah' *(Allahu akbar, Ashhadu an la Ilah ila Allah, Ashhadu an Mohammed rasul Allah)*. You will hear this during the call to prayer and it is repeated at many other events, such as births and deaths. The first part has virtually become an exclamation, good for any time of life or situation.

Sala Sometimes written 'salat', this is the obligation of prayer, ideally five times a day – at sunset, after dark, at dawn, midday and in the afternoon – when muezzins (mosque officials) call the faithful to pray. Although Muslims can pray anywhere, it is considered best to do so together in a mosque.

Zakat Giving of alms to the poor is an essential part of the social teaching of Islam and you will often see Tunisians giving alms to beggars.

Sawm Ramadan, the ninth month of the Muslim calendar, commemorates the revelation of the Quran to Mohammed. In a demonstration of Muslims' renewal of faith, they are asked not to let anything pass their lips, and are expected to refrain from sex, from dawn to dusk for a month. For specific dates, see p291.
Haj The pinnacle of a devout Muslim's life is the pilgrimage to Mecca. Ideally, the pilgrim should go to Mecca in the last month of the year, Zuul Hijja, to join Muslims from all over the world.

THE CALL TO PRAYER

Allahu akbar, Allahu akbar
Ashhadu an la Ilah ila Allah
Ashhadu an Mohammed rasul Allah
Haya ala as-sala
Haya ala as-sala

God is most great, God is most great
I testify that there is no God but God
I testify that Mohammed is God's Prophet
Come to prayer
Come to prayer

The first slivers of dawn are flickering on the horizon, and the deep quiet of a city asleep is pierced by the cries of the muezzin exhorting the faithful to the first of the day's prayers. Like church bells, the sound summons Muslims to enter a mosque to pray, or pray where they are if they cannot. The midday prayers on Friday, when the sheikh of the mosque delivers his weekly *khutba* (sermon) are considered the most important. The mosque also serves as a kind of community centre, and often groups of children or adults receive Quranic lessons here, while others pray quietly or simply shelter in the tranquil peace. For more about the mosque and its architecture, see p52.

ISLAMIC CUSTOMS

Muslims carry out certain rituals attached to prayer. First they must wash their hands, arms, feet, head and neck in running water; all mosques have an area set aside for this purpose. If they are not in a mosque and there is no water available, clean sand suffices; and where there is no sand, they must go through the motions of washing. Then they must face Mecca (all mosques are oriented so that the *mihrab*, or prayer niche, faces Mecca) and follow a set pattern of gestures.

In everyday life, Muslims are prohibited from drinking alcohol and eating pork (considered unclean).

Islam Online (www.islamonline.net/English/index.shtml) offers world news from an Islamic perspective as well as interesting information about Islamic rituals and even an 'Ask a scholar' inquiry line.

ISLAMIC HOLIDAYS

The main Muslim religious holidays are tied to the lunar Hejira calendar, which is about 11 days shorter than the Gregorian (Western) calendar. This means that in Western terms the holidays fall at different times each year; see p291 for the dates of Islamic holidays.
Ras as-Sana New Year's day, celebrated on the first day of the Hejira calendar year, 1 Moharram.
Moulid an-Nabi A lesser feast celebrating the birth of the Prophet Mohammed on 12 Rabi' al-Awal. In the Maghreb this is generally known as *mouloud*.
Ramadan and Eid al-Fitr Most Muslims, though not all with equal rigour, take part in the fasting that characterises the month of Ramadan, a time when the faithful are called upon as a community to renew their relationship with God. Ramadan is the month in which the Quran was first revealed. From dawn to dusk, a Muslim is expected to refrain from eating, drinking, smoking and having sex. This can be a difficult discipline, and only people in good health are asked to participate. Pregnant women,

SUFISM

Famed for whirling dervishes and extreme selfmutilation (pushing skewers into their cheeks, eating glass or walking on coals), Sufis have unusual ways of getting closer to God.

Ascetics wishing to achieve a mystical communion with God through spiritual development rather than through study of the Quran formed the Islamic order of Sufism. This offshoot fulfilled a need many people felt for a more mystical side to the Islamic religion. The name comes from *suf,* meaning 'wool', referring to the simple cord worn by the ascetics as a belt.

There are many hundreds of orders, and they tend to gather at the mosque or tomb of their holy man (or *wali,* a term loosely translated as holy man or saint) and follow a particular *tariq* (path), or way of worshipping. A particular aspect of Berber Sufism in North Africa is maraboutism – the worship of a holy man endowed with magical powers.

For orthodox Muslims, this kind of veneration is akin to idol worship, but Sufis don't see it that way. The *wali* is a friend of God and so an intermediary. The great *moussems* (pilgrimages) to saints' tombs are more a celebration of the triumph of the spirit than an act of worship. Despite the conflict with religious orthodoxy, the Sufi emergence was tolerated because they provided a link to local rites and superstitions, and were thus able to attract large numbers of people who had not otherwise embraced Islam.

children, and people engaged in exacting physical work, in *jihad,* or travelling are also considered exempt. Every evening during Ramadan is a celebration. *Iftar,* the breaking of the day's fast, is a time of animated activity, when the people of the local community gather not only to eat and drink but also to pray. Non-Muslims are not expected to participate, even if more pious Muslims suggest you do. Restaurants and cafés open during the day may be harder to find, and at any rate you should try to avoid openly flouting the fast. The end of Ramadan, or more accurately the first days of the following month of Shawwal, marks the Eid al-Fitr, the Festival of Breaking of the Fast (also known as the Eid as-Sagheer, the Small Feast), which generally lasts for four or five days, during which time everything grinds to a halt. It's not a good time to travel, but can be a great experience if you are invited to share in some of the festivities with a family. Ramadan is widely observed in Tunisia.

Haj and Eid al-Adha The fifth pillar of Islam, a sacred duty of all who can afford it, is to make the pilgrimage to Mecca – the haj. It can be done at any time, but at least one should be accomplished in Zuul Hijja, the 12th month of the Muslim year. The high point is the visit to the Kaaba, the stone of Ibrahim in the centre of the *haram,* the sacred area into which non-Muslims are forbidden to enter. The faithful, dressed in a white robe, circle the Kaaba seven times and kiss the black stone. The haj culminates in the ritual slaughter of a lamb (commemorating Ibrahim's sacrifice) at Mina. This marks the end of the pilgrimage and the beginning of the Eid al-Adha, or Feast of the Sacrifice (aka the Grand Feast, or Eid al-Kebir). Throughout the Muslim world the act of sacrifice is repeated, and the streets of towns and cities run with the blood of slaughtered sheep and goats.

Ramadan was forbidden during the government of Habib Bourguiba.

CONTEMPORARY ISLAM

Tunisia is a liberal, tolerant society, and most Tunisians are quite relaxed about their faith.

Scientifically and philosophically, Arabic culture left that of the West far behind for many centuries: the reason Classical texts are available to us today is that they were translated into Arabic; the word Algebra comes from the Arabic; and famous Islamic universities, such as that at Zaytouna (see p71) in Tunis, were great centres of learning. However, the Enlightenment in the West had a far-reaching impact, and leaps in Western military and shipping technology led to a change in the balance of world power at the end of the 18th century.

North African colonialism meant that Islam occupied a historic position as the counterbalance to Western occupation, and is enduringly seen as the alternative to a society resting on Western values. Tunisia has successfully embraced some aspects of Westernisation – including its progressive treatment of women. But capitalism and urbanisation accentuate the familiar divisions seen here between the poor and dispossessed and the upwardly mobile middle classes. This may account for why Islam has seen some resurgence in recent years, particularly among poorer young people with few opportunities. The view of Islam as a counterculture is accentuated by the bigger global picture, in which international disputes based on economics and power are simplified as a clash of civilisations and religion gives people a reason to live in an environment with few choices.

The Tunisian government maintains a balancing act between promoting Islam (important for its regional status) and the adoption of occidental values (for economic and social reasons) and has been so far remarkably successful in negotiating this tightrope – in part assisted by a suppression of free speech and omnipresent police force, but perhaps also due to the nature of Tunisians themselves: magnanimous and moderate.

The Arabs, by Peter Mansfield, explores history and society in the Middle East, discussing the centuries-long struggle for dominance between Christendom and the Islamic world, with a chapter on each state.

WOMEN IN TUNISIA

Conditions for women in Tunisia are better than just about anywhere in the Islamic world – to Western eyes, at least. One of the many titles that Habib Bourguiba, Tunisia's first president, awarded to himself during his reign was 'The Liberator of Women'. Many Tunisian women agree. Bourguiba, whose first wife was French, was a staunch supporter of women's rights. His 1956 Personal Status Code banned polygamy and ended divorce by renunciation. It also placed restrictions on the tradition of arranged marriages, setting a minimum marriage age of 17 for girls and giving them the right to refuse a proposed marriage. The code is regularly updated, most recently in 2005, when the President announced that the marrying age would be unified (to 18) and women's custodial right on divorce would be safeguarded.

Behind Closed Doors: Women's Oral Narratives in Tunisia, by Monia Hajaiej, fascinatingly lays bare the lives of Tunisian women from a local female perspective.

Bourguiba regarded the *hejab* (the veil worn by Muslim women) as demeaning and called it an 'odious rag'. He banned it from schools as part of a campaign to phase it out. Many Tunisian women consider not wearing the *hejab* to be an expression of their liberty and you will see many women without. However, a resurgence of conservative elements has led to it being more prevalent, notably among young women.

Since 1956 there have been dramatic improvements in conditions for women across the country, not only in the standards of literacy, but also in terms of health – infant mortality is only 26 per thousand births, compared with 139 in 1966.

André Gide's *The Immoralist* starts off in Tunisia, where a man on his honeymoon discovers his preference for Arab boys.

Yet Tunisia is also filled with men grumbling about how women are favoured and how dangerous it is – for the women, you understand – to give them such freedom. It is this attitude that indicates the real situation that many Tunisian women face. They live dual lives – encouraged to participate by relatively favourable legal and socioeconomic conditions, yet restricted by traditional family values. Away from cosmopolitan city centres or the beachside resort towns, the public social domain remains that of the man, while women largely remain in the home.

Arts & Architecture

You may be pushed to name a Tunisian writer or poet and might never have seen a Tunisian film, but this is your chance to fill this gap – some fascinating books, poems and films have been produced by local artists, providing a striking insight into the country, so read on for recommendations. During your visit, you'll quickly become aware how much art pervades the everyday – decorative arts turn markets and buildings into a whirl of colour and traditional music provides a soundtrack to every taxi or louage trip. Tunisia also has a particularly magnificent architectural heritage, with the extraordinary Berber buildings in the south, and the remains of great civilisations from Roman to Islamic dotted right across the country.

ARTS

LITERATURE

The *Tremor of Forgery,* by Patricia Highsmith, has been acclaimed by some as her best novel, a mysterious, gripping thriller, set against an edgy Tunisian backdrop.

Tunisia's national poet is Abu el-Kacem el-Chabbi (also spelled Abdulkacem Chebbi; 1909–34), whose rousing poem *Will to Live* is taught to every schoolchild. From Tozeur, he was educated at Tunis' Zaytouna Mosque. He died aged only 25, but his poetry had a huge impact. Combining the classical Arabic tradition with a landscape-inspired Romanticism, it expresses the stultifying sense of living under a colonial power. To read more, get his collected works *Songs of Life.*

His contemporary Ali Duaji (1909–49) wrote fascinating, urbane sketches of early 20th-century Tunisia, influenced by Twain, Camus and Flaubert. Good reads include *Bar-Hopping along the Mediterranean* – an amused, ironic view of colonial culture – and *Sleepless Nights.*

Most modern Tunisian writers live in Europe, where the financial rewards are greater and the dangers arising from offending the government fewer. Mustapha Tlili (1937–), based in New York, is most famous for *Lion Mountain* (1988), a character-packed examination of postcolonial mores and the impact of modernity on a remote, imaginary mountain village. You won't find this controversial text on sale in Tunisia. The internationally acclaimed Albert Memmi lives in Paris and writes in French about the identity crisis faced by North African Jews like himself. His books include *The Colonizer and the Colonized,* about the political, social and sexual impact of the French occupation of Tunisia. From a Bedouin family, Hassouna Mosbahi (shortlisted for the 2001 Caine Prize for African writing) lives in Germany, and his works include *Adieu Rosalie* and *Return to Tarshish,* both dealing with the tragedy of an exile lost between two worlds.

Sabiha Khemir's *Waiting in the Future for the Past to Come* is a series of connected stories about a small coastal town postindependence.

You should be able to track down most of the above in English translation. If you read French, you'll have access to still more works.

CINEMA

Tunisia is a familiar setting for international films, but also has a small, renowned local film industry. It's easier to see its art-house offerings abroad than when you visit the country – most cinemas show a mix of Hollywood blockbusters, Bollywood bonanzas and Egyptian slapstick.

Acclaimed directors include Ferid Boughedir, whose *Halfaouine* – a coming-of-age piece about sexuality and tradition in the 1960s in one of Tunis' most charismatic districts – featured at the Cannes Film Festival in 1990. His *A Summer in La Goulette* (1996) is a comedy set in 1967 Tunis where three daughters seek Muslim, Christian and Jewish boyfriends at the time of the Arab-Israeli war.

Female director Moufida Tlatli won a special prize at Cannes in 1994 for her film *Silence of the Palace*, about a 1950s upper-class home from the servants' point of view. Her 2001 *Season of Men* is about a Jerban woman bringing up an autistic son.

Nouri Bouzid is a controversial, interesting director: *L'Homme de Cendres* (Man of Ashes; 1986) deals with prostitution, child abuse and the relationship between Muslims and Jews; *Les Sabots en Or* (Gold Shoes) is about imprisonment and torture and was banned in Tunisia; the pertinent *Bezness* looked at sexual tourism (*bezness* is local slang for the beach-gigolo 'business') from the perspective of a young man desperate for a way out of Sousse; and *Une Fille de Bonne Famille* (A Girl of Good Family) examined marital breakdown.

Radio Tunis (www.radiotunis.com/music.htl) is a great place for listening to Tunisian music and songs.

Another film worth seeking out is *Keswa: Le Fil Perdu* (1999), directed by Kalthoum Bornaz, a renowned female director, whose satirical portrayal of a young Tunisian woman defying her family's wishes for an arranged marriage is both funny and thought-provoking.

The biennial Carthage International Film Festival (see p95) offers a good opportunity to view the latest work from regional directors. There's also a biennial short film festival in Kélibia (Cap Bon), which is a good chance to check out local talent.

MUSIC

Western music is based on the octave, which has 12 tones, and its instruments only allow for half tones. The structure of the Arabic scale differs. The octave can contain up to 17 tones, with traditional stringed instruments allowing quarter tones. Arabic music also tends to remain within a narrow range of notes, without jumping between octaves.

In Tunisia, traditional music takes the form of *malouf* (meaning 'normal'), a national institution introduced in the 15th century by Andalusian refugees. It combines instrumental pieces (which serve as preludes and breaks) and vocal works performed in a *nouba* – a nine-part sequence.

Tunisie: Anthologie du Malouf is a great all-round selection, available as five (for devotees) or one (for tourists) CD sets.

Traditionally, *malouf* was performed by small ensembles using a *rbab* (a kind of two-stringed violin), *oud* (lute) and *darbuka* (drum, usually made of terracotta and goatskin), with a solo vocalist. Today, ensembles are more likely to be composed of large instrumental and choral groups, playing both Western and traditional Arabic instruments.

Malouf was superseded by a new, lighter style of music introduced from Egypt in the mid-1920s, but underwent a revival in the 1930s when Baron d'Erlanger, a musicologist living in the Tunis suburb of Sidi Bou Saïd, founded the Rachidia Ensemble, which became the official centre for *malouf*. This is where most of Tunisia's leading musicians have trained and is still Tunisia's best place to hear classical music. At the baron's mansion you can also see his amazing collection of musical instruments (see p96).

After independence, *malouf* was adopted as a symbol of national identity. Since then, it has become institutionalised, with the government offering courses in *malouf* at the National Conservatory of Music in Tunis and an annual cycle of festivals and competitions culminating in the International Festival of Malouf held in July in Testour.

Stars of the scene include the all-female orchestra the El-Azifet Ensemble, Sonia M'Barek, and Lotfi Bouchnak (listen to *Live in Berlin* to hear some old-school *malouf*). *Oud* players who combine traditional *malouf* with jazz and other influences include Anouar Brahem (try his *Astrakan Café* or *Le Pas du Chat* CDs) and Dhafer Youssef (try *Electric Sufi*).

The main opportunity to hear traditional music in Tunisia is at festivals, which mostly take place in summer. Restaurants in Tunis featuring traditional music, though not necessarily *malouf*, are Dar el-Jeld (p82), Le Malouf (p83) and Lucullus (in La Goulette; p90).

For a taste of Tunisian music try *Mawkatash: Love Songs*, by Latifa, Tunisia's foremost diva; Ghalia Benali and Timnaa's seductive *Wild Harissa* showcasing an extraordinary voice, and Sonia M'Barek's *Takht*, a classic of modern *malouf*.

During the summer, there are sometimes weekend free concerts on Ave Habib Bourguiba, as well as occasional classical music concerts at the Centre of Arabic and Mediterranean Music (it's better known as the Dar Ennejma Ezzahra; p96) in Sidi Bou Saïd and at L'Acropolium (p93) in Carthage. Tabarka also hosts some outstanding music festivals (see p135 and p291 for details). During the summer, festivals at Hammamet (p106) and Nabeul also star traditional musicians and singers.

Most of the music that forms Tunisia's soundtrack is classical Arabic or Arabic pop. You'll hear the omnipresent Umm Kulthoum – *the* rags-to-riches Egyptian diva whose passionate classicism forms a soundtrack for North Africa; love songs performed by some raven-haired songstress from Cairo; or Algerian dance music – *raï* – which is a special favourite of louage (shared-taxi) drivers – a good barometer of popular (male) taste.

Modern Tunisian pop favourites include Sabar Rbaï and Salma Echarfi, churning out catchy romantic hits. Traditional Arabic music is not that fashionable among young people, though if you get a group of them having a singsong and you wouldn't know it. Contemporary live music venues are few and far between. However, Western-style reggae, heavy metal and jazz groups – big hits with Tunisian youth – play regularly at Tunis' Théâtre l'Etoile du Nord (p84) – check the website for details. You'll also catch good live acts at Le Boeuf sur le Toit (p84), including Sunday jazz.

You can buy tapes (around TD1) at newspaper stands and supermarkets, which are a great way to get a flavour of Tunisian sounds.

DANCE

When Tunisian men dance to Arabic music, they hold their arms out stiffly at their sides, wiggle their hips, and never think shimmying around with other men makes them look sissy. Women move in a sensual, belly-dancing style that takes much skill to perfect. You're most likely to see dancing at a bar or restaurant where a band's playing, at a wedding or at a festival.

Music from Tunisia (www.focusmm.com/tunisia/tn_musmn.htm) contains a short summary of the main themes of Tunisian music and links to songs from musicians little known outside Tunisia.

Traditional Berber dances date back to pre-Islamic times and can sometimes be seen at resort hotels. They include the dramatic Dance of the Vases, performed by dancers with – yes – vases balanced on their heads. This is a highlight of the Festival of the Ksour, held around Tataouine in November.

CALLIGRAPHY & PAINTING

Calligraphy is a historic and holy art form: it's believed that Arabic was revealed by Allah to the Prophet Mohammed in the form of the Quran.

Early calligraphers used an angular script called Kufic that was perfect for stone carving; the eastern wall and minaret of the Great Mosque in Sfax (p216), and above the entrance to the Mosque of the Three Doors in Kairouan (p203) are among the finest examples. Nja Mahdaoui is renowned among modern calligraphists for his free-flowing style.

Rachid Koreíchi is an Algerian, partly based in Tunis, who produces works featuring symbols and characters in various materials. You can see his huge embroidered works in cloth at luxury hotel Villa Didon (p96) in Carthage.

Painting as a figurative rather than decorative art form came to Tunisia with the French. Murals and ceiling paintings were particularly popular in the 15th and 19th centuries.

Calligraphy is a primary art form in Islamic cultures because representations of the human form are considered to be heresy.

Contemporary painting ranges from the highly geometric forms of Hédi Turki to Western styles that aim to encapsulate daily life, including scenes of cafés, *hammams* (public bathhouses) and music and dance performances – figurative works that are unusual within the framework of an Islamic society. Works by Yahia Turki (widely considered to be the father of Tunisian painting) and Ammar Farhat fall into this last category. Art patron Baron Erlanger, who lived in Sidi Bou Saïd, was a keen amateur painter, and his impressive renditions of the everyday are on view at his mansion studio (p96).

In the 1940s, artists established the nationalist École de Tunis in order to counter French dominance, and this was responsible for popularising Tunisian life as artistic subject matter.

Under the French, the ambient lifestyle of Tunisia attracted European artists who were entranced by the North African light and architecture. Most famously, Tunisia inspired the Swiss and German expressionists Paul Klee and Auguste Macke, who visited the country together in 1914. It was a turning point for Klee, whose encounter with North African colour led to his move towards abstraction, with paintings such as *Hammamet with its Mosque*. Wonderful works by Macke – who tragically died in action during WW1 the following year – include *St Germain near Tunis, Tunisian Landscape* and *Turkish Café*.

Modern art galleries are mainly confined to Tunis and its suburbs, especially the artist's haven of Sidi Bou Saïd. The English-language weekly *Tunisia News* lists exhibitions. **Espace Diwan 9** (Map pp72-3; 9 rue Sidi ben Arous; 9am-8pm Mon-Sat, to 7pm Oct-Mar) in the Tunis medina, and **Librairie Claire Fontaine** (Map pp72-3; 14 rue d'Alger) have some excellent art books.

AMAZING MOSAICS

Tunisia has the world's best collection of mosaics, at Tunis' Bardo Museum (p50). Its masterpieces form an extraordinary document of Roman interests, lifestyle and beliefs.

The ancient Greeks created the first mosaics, and the technique caught on in places influenced by Greek culture, becoming increasingly sophisticated. At Punic Kerkouane (p117) in Cap Bon, you can see mosaic used to create a simple white-on-red scatter pattern. But it was the Romans who took the art to dizzy heights, using it to decorate their private and public spaces, with elaborate pictures designed to show their wealth. Most mosaics are the type known as *opus tessellatum,* in which patterns are formed out of little squares called *tesserae* (from the Latin, meaning cubes or dice). The technique involved laying out a bed of mortar in which the *tesserae* were placed.

Tunisian Roman mosaics date mainly from the 2nd to 6th centuries AD. Those from the 3rd century onwards show a distinctive African style, as local artists assimilated and improved upon the art. African mosaics are characterised by large, dramatic, colourful compositions – in Italy the style tended towards black and white. As elsewhere in the empire, the mosaics depict realistic subjects, in this case amphitheatre games, hunting and everyday life on the African estates. The most elaborate mosaics were always in reception rooms, to impress visitors and clients.

Byzantines continued the art, but their mosaics were much more simple, naïve works.

Apart from the Bardo, there are beautiful mosaics on display at the museum in Sousse, at the El-Jem museum (p209), and in situ in Bulla Regia (p145).

Other places in Tunis worth investigating include **Galerie Yahia** (☎ 71 330 235; Palmarium, 4 rue de Gréce) and **Galerie Gorgi** (☎ 71 892 129; 23 Rue Jugurtha, Le Belvédère). The Palais Khereddine (p76) also often has impressive art exhibitions. In Hammamet you can see and buy the etchings of Baker Ben Fredj (p109).

CRAFTS

Wandering through Tunisian souqs, you will be dazzled by colour, busy patterns, rustic beauty and a share of tourist tat. Like Morocco (but resembling a less-virtuoso cousin) Tunisia has an impressive decorative tradition, with vibrant rugs, bright ceramics, finely worked brassware and heavy folk silver jewellery.

A holy man named Sidi Kacem Ezzilizi is credited with importing tile-making from Andalusia in the 15th century, and his tomb now forms a small Tunis museum (see p76) to the craft. In the 16th century, tilemakers and potters worked around the area close to Bab Souika in the Tunis medina. The Ottomans injected Turkish style, and you can see fine examples at Dar Othman (p76) and Ottoman-era mosques in the Tunis medina (p74). In the 19th century, Italianate was all the rage, as evident in grand mansions such as Tunis' Dar Ben Abdullah (p76).

Designs and Patterns from North African Carpets and Textiles, by Jacques Revault, is the essential companion for those thinking of buying a carpet in Tunisia and a handy weapon against the touts.

Ceramics used to be a functional craft supplying local needs, but as times have changed, the pottery trade nowadays caters mainly for tourists. Nabeul is the largest centre, selling Andalusian-influenced, tourist-friendly designs, while Sejnane in the north turns out a distinct Berber style, specialising in rustic figurines. For more information on contemporary ceramics and where to buy them, see Shopping in the Directory (p297).

Carpet-making is a centuries-old craft and one of the most beautiful. Knotted carpets are divided into *alloucha* or *zarbia* variations. *Alloucha* use natural colours – beige, black and white – with simple motifs. *Zarbia* are richly multicoloured. Woven carpets are known as *mergoum,* are brighter coloured and stem from the nomadic Berber tradition. Kairouan is the biggest carpet centre in the country; again, see Shopping (p297) for good places to buy.

ARCHITECTURE

With waves of invaders and immigrants stamping their styles and erecting monuments over the last 2500 years, Tunisia has an incredible array of architectural heritage.

Here are the world's most complete vestiges of the great ancient Punic civilisation. That said, not much is left, but the few remains are remarkable for their neat town planning and fastidious private bathrooms. There are also a few remnants of the Numidians, contemporary to the Carthaginians, most in Chemtou (p147), with a 21m-high Libyo-Punic mausoleum at Dougga (p156).

In contrast, Roman vestiges are typically prolific. The Romans were great engineers and many of their buildings remain remarkably intact, such as the city of Dougga (p156) in the north, and the great stadium of El-Jem (p208).

But most pervasive and formidable is the architecture of Islam, which ranges from the austere functionality of the early Aghlabids to the exuberant work of the later Andalusians and Ottomans. One of the pleasures of travelling in Tunisia is getting lost in its seemingly unplanned medinas (walled cities), each harbouring a great mosque at its centre.

In the south, the Berbers were responsible for some of the most astonishing forms of indigenous architecture anywhere. Weird enough to stand in for an alien world, they have become a favourite of the makers of the *Star Wars* movies. Also worth seeking out is the traditional relief brickwork found in Tozeur and Nefta, which uses protruding sand-coloured bricks to create intricate monochrome patterns.

Jerba's highly distinctive architecture reflects the island's long history as a stronghold of the fiercely autonomous Kharijite sect. The buildings, painted dazzling white, were all designed with defence in mind, and resemble fortresses regardless of their function. For more information on Jerban architecture, see the boxed text in the Jerba chapter (p274).

PUNIC – TOWN PLANNING & BATHTUBS

Before the discovery of Kerkouane (Cap Bon) in 1952, little was known about Punic architecture. Its cities were razed to the ground, then built upon, by their conquerors, so what little knowledge we had was gleaned from foundations like those at Carthage.

At Kerkouane you can see the Punic building technique *opus Africanum* – rubble walls strengthened at intervals with stone slabs. This Punic technique was adapted by Roman and Byzantine builders – for example, at the Capitole in Dougga. The town's most remarkable feature is its unique, neat bathtubs. Almost every house has one, armchair-shaped and lined with red cement. Each has a well within easy reach and a drain for dirty water. These were people who obviously valued cleanliness (and privacy) highly.

Virgil's epic *The Aeneid* is a beautiful work of literature, based around legends of Carthage and telling the love story of Queen Dido and Aeneas.

All the houses have a similar layout – small-scale and arranged around a courtyard (the earliest surviving Tunisian courtyard homes), with a staircase leading to a roof terrace. Simple red-and-white mosaics decorate the floors – in one case adorned by a symbol of Tanit, a Punic god, seemingly to ward off the Evil Eye. Town planning was obviously highly developed, and it seems that Kerkouane would have been an idyllic place to live, with an amazing (but unfortunately vulnerable) setting beside the azure sea.

ROMAN – UNDERGROUND, OVERGROUND

Wherever they went, the Romans left great buildings and feats of engineering rearing up from the landscape. Here remain ruins of the Zaghouan to Tunis aqueduct, the El-Jem colosseum and impressive cities: Dougga, Thurburbo Majus, Carthage, Bulla Regia, Sbeitla, Haidra and Oudhna. Also fascinating are the mines where the famous Chemtou (p147) marble was extracted, prized all over the empire.

All Roman cities had a capitole, grand public baths and a forum – a focal square that was the centre of public life, surrounded by temples and civil buildings. Streets usually followed an orderly, oh-so-Roman grid.

Roman temples weren't usually converted into churches with the coming of Christianity – they could not fit congregations, being only built to accommodate important people and priests.

Particularly remarkable are the lavish mosaics that decorated these buildings. The towns here were prosperous, and the agricultural magnates who inhabited them wanted to show their wealth. For more on mosaics, see the boxed text (p47).

Bulla Regia is a unique site. Always creative in using architecture to shape their environment, here the Romans built underground rooms to escape the summer heat and winter cold. They used hollow tubes to create overhead vaults that were sufficiently light (a similar technique can be seen in Rome, where amphorae were often embedded into upper walls to lighten the load). The site gives the rare opportunity to walk inside a complete Roman room.

BARDO MUSEUM

The **Bardo Museum** (☎ 71 513 650; admission TD6, camera TD1; 9.30am-4.30pm Tue-Sun mid-Sep–Mar, 9am-5pm Tue-Sun Apr & Jun–mid-Sep, closes early during Ramadan) is dominated by the superb mosaics that adorned Roman Africa's sumptuous villas. If you visit any of Tunisia's ancient sites, the Bardo will complete the picture – here is the art they once contained.

Not only is the collection extraordinary, but it's housed in one of Tunisia's finest palaces – the former official residence of the Husseinite beys, commissioned by the Hafsid sultan Al-Mustansir (1249–77). It was rebuilt in the late 17th century, steadily enlarged by a succession of Husseinites, and became a museum in 1888. There are plans afoot to revamp the Bardo, with a proposed extension of 8000 sq metres that will vastly increase its exhibition space and capacity for visitors and a complete overhaul of its presentation that will result in spectacular state-of-the-art displays, but at the time of going to press the possible timescale for these changes was still undecided.

Currently on the ground floor, highlights include the re-creation of the 40,000-year-old Hermaion d'El Guettar, a religious monument with a striking resemblance to a heap of rubble, probably the world's oldest spiritual monument. The next room houses the infamous 3rd-century BC stele from Carthage (see p95), showing a priest carrying a child, possibly to be sacrificed. Look out for the unusual 6th-century cruciform baptismal font from El-Kantara. Nearby are statues from Bulla Regia (p145), starring Apollo: huge, languorous and sensual, with how-does-it-stay-on drapery.

Moving up a floor, don't miss the Islamic Museum housed in an older section of the palace, with formal reception rooms furnished in the 19th-century Husseinite style.

Centrepiece of the 1st floor is a grand, colonnaded reception room with an icing-sugar ceiling and triumphant statuary from Roman Carthage (see p90), arranged around large floor mosaics from Oudhna (Uthina; see p151), including an industrious portrait of 3rd-century farm life.

Some of the finest mosaics are on this floor. Don't miss that from the Sousse villa of a wealthy horse breeder, covering nearly 140 sq metres, featuring a triumphant Neptune (the sea god was a popular theme in coastal towns). The nearby Lord Julius mosaic is famous for its depiction of life on a wealthy lord's estate. En route to the Dougga room you'll see a gigantic foot and head – belonging to a 7.5m-high statue of Jupiter from Thuburbo Majus (see p153).

In the Dougga room, there's a celebrated work depicting huge dark-skinned cyclops working Vulcan's forge, from the site baths. However, the highlight comes from seaside La Chebba: an exquisite piece depicting the Triumph of Neptune. It's so well preserved, it appears years rather than millennia old. Another hugely virtuoso piece depicts Ulysses. The wandering hero – with a real look of wonder on his face – is strapped to his shipmast so he might listen to the Sirens without being lured towards them. The dangerous creatures line up stage right, while the other sailors are looking away, their ears stopped with wax.

Also on the 1st floor is the palace concert room – room 13 – which feels as if you are inside a music box. Nearby is the bey's private apartment, elaborately tiled and stuccoed and now containing the only contemporary portrait of the poet Virgil, holding a copy of his *Aeneid,* and flanked by Muses – a nervous-looking Clio (history) and more-composed Melpomene (tragedy). Other 1st-floor highlights are the incredible Greek bronzes from a 1st-century BC shipwreck.

Moving up to the top floor, look out for an ancient bronze of a drunken Hercules looking decidedly unheroic, and an interesting mosaic, verging on the absurd, showing ostriches being used for hunting. But finest of the 2nd-floor exhibits are from the minor, yet wealthy Roman port of Acholla, 40km north of Sfax. These are some of Africa's oldest mosaics. Many of the pieces come from the Trajan Baths, and provide an idea of the overall scale of decoration.

The Bardo is 4km west of central Tunis. You can get here by taxi – about TD4 from the centre, or by *métro léger* (Tunis' tram network) to Le Bardo station on line 4 (TD0.5). The entrance is on the northern side (rue Mongi Slim), while the station is on the museum's southern side (blvd du 20 Mars 1956).

To avoid the tour groups, it's best to arrive early, late or at lunchtime. In summer, start on the 2nd floor, as it gets hot in the afternoon. It'll take at least half a day to visit, and it's even worthwhile making two trips to avoid museum overkill. It's well worth looking at the collection in detail and the museum shop sells an excellent illustrated guide (€8) in various languages.

BARDO MUSEUM

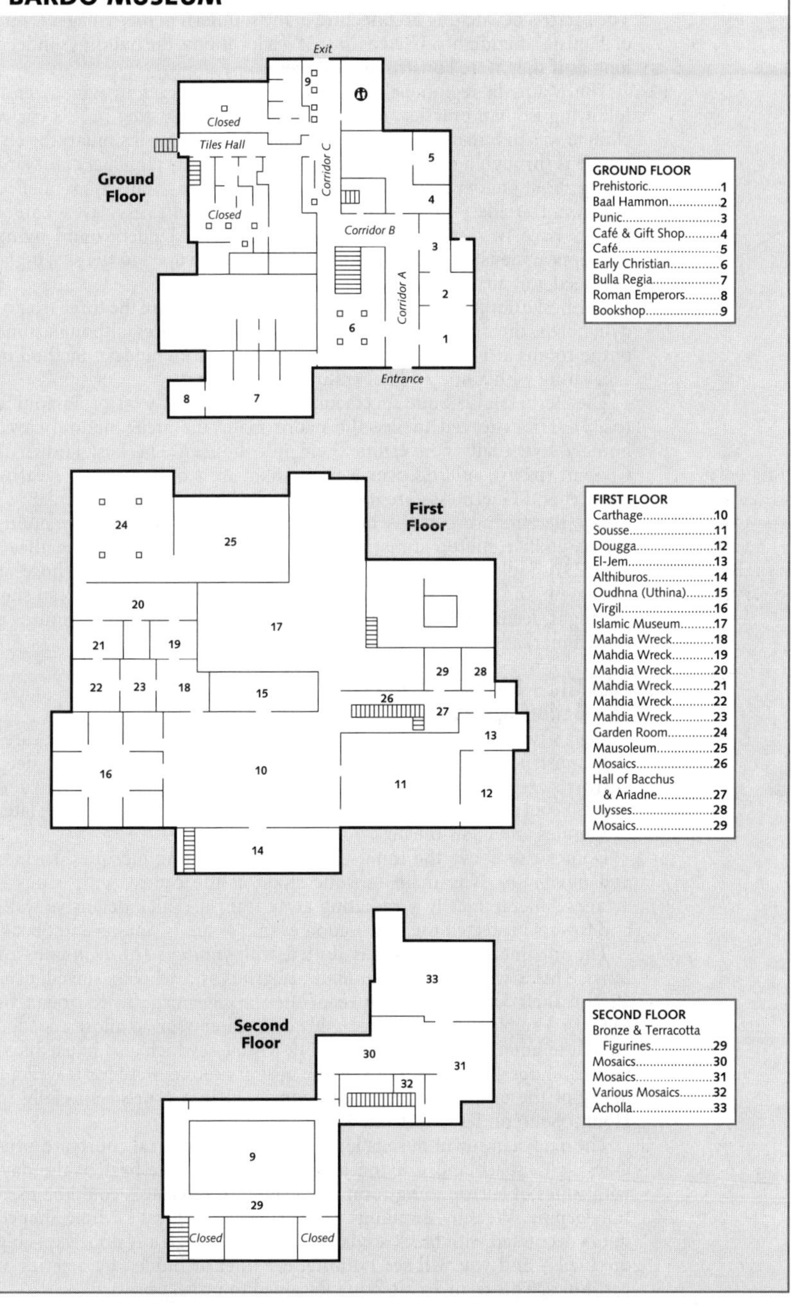
Exit
Closed
Tiles Hall
Corridor C
Ground Floor
Closed
Corridor B
Corridor A
Entrance
First Floor
Second Floor
Closed
Closed
GROUND FLOOR
Prehistoric....................1
Baal Hammon..............2
Punic..........................3
Café & Gift Shop..........4
Café............................5
Early Christian..............6
Bulla Regia...................7
Roman Emperors..........8
Bookshop.....................9
FIRST FLOOR
Carthage.....................10
Sousse........................11
Dougga.......................12
El-Jem........................13
Althiburos...................14
Oudhna (Uthina)........15
Virgil..........................16
Islamic Museum.........17
Mahdia Wreck............18
Mahdia Wreck............19
Mahdia Wreck............20
Mahdia Wreck............21
Mahdia Wreck............22
Mahdia Wreck............23
Garden Room.............24
Mausoleum................25
Mosaics......................26
Hall of Bacchus & Ariadne................27
Ulysses.......................28
Mosaics......................29
SECOND FLOOR
Bronze & Terracotta Figurines.................29
Mosaics......................30
Mosaics......................31
Various Mosaics.........32
Acholla.......................33

BERBER – TROGLODYTE & TOP OF THE WORLD

The bizarre, bewitching architecture of the southern Berber villages is one of Tunisia's highlights. Used as *Star Wars* locations, the buildings indeed look as if they were constructed by aliens.

The Matmata region bakes in summer and freezes in winter, and, following Roman practice, the Berber solution to existing in this tricky climate was to burrow underground. Their houses are all similar: the entrance is through a narrow tunnel, a central (usually circular) courtyard is dug about 6m deep into the irregular terrain, and rooms are tunnelled out from the sides – like living in a crater, lined with cosy caves. Larger houses have two or three connected courtyards. Underground living may appear claustrophobic, but the courtyards are open to the sky, high-ceilinged and airy.

The best examples to check out in Matmata (p228) are the three troglodyte hotels, the Marhala, the Sidi Driss and Les Berbères, although some of the rooms at Les Berbères were built by the more modern method of excavating with a hoe and backfilling over the roof.

The Berbers also built spectacular hilltop villages west of Tataouine (p235). Tribes forced to flee the plains made the area's natural caves homely, eventually converting them into houses. The best known is Chenini (p236), spilling over a peak 18km west of Tataouine. Nearby Douiret and Guermessa are much less visited but just as spectacular.

Fish and Hand of Fatima symbols, often seen on doorways, are to ward off the bad luck brought by envious looks, otherwise known as the Evil Eye.

The Berbers are perhaps best known for their extraordinary multistorey, podlike, hilltop granaries *(ksour)*. For more information on these, see p237. Sadly, many *ksour* are falling into ruin. However, those at Metameur and Ksar Hallouf contain budget hotels – where you can stay the night, feeling like a Hobbit – while the *ksar* at Medenine houses a tourist market.

ISLAMIC – PRIVACY & DEFENCE

The Medina & Traditional Houses

Tunisia's twisting, ancient medinas may seem chaotic, but they're carefully constructed according to Islamic architectural principles. The deep narrow streets keep the sun's rays from the centre during the day and draw in cool air at night. Earth, stone and wood absorb water, which later evaporates and cools the air.

Domes rise above the inner-city tangle, indicating mosques, shrines and *hammams*. The main mosque stood at the centre, with souqs – arranged hierarchically – radiating away from it. Thick defensive walls and towers protected the city – good examples are in Sousse and Sfax.

The medina in Tunisia was dotted with *funduqs* (*caravanserais* or inns). This is where traders, nomads, pilgrims and scholars stayed, usually on their way somewhere else (often a pilgrimage to Kairouan or Mecca). The plain doorway was wide and tall enough to allow a loaded animal to enter. Livestock were kept downstairs, which also housed teahouses, shops and warehouses, while upstairs rooms were for travellers. Many of these *funduqs* have been converted into hotels, especially in Houmt Souq on Jerba (see p276).

The Tunisian townhouse is known as a *dar*. A central courtyard provides light, space and a living area that's cool in the heat of the day, with suites of surrounding rooms. At night, roof terraces could be used for sleeping. Wealthy dwellings were signalled by great keyhole-shaped doors decorated with black studs. But glance through any doorway – big or small – and you will see nothing, the interior hidden by a series of vestibules. This is an architecture designed to protect privacy.

The Mosque

All mosques *(masjid)* follow the layout of the Prophet's house in Medina, which had an enclosed, oblong courtyard with huts (housing Mohammed's wives) along one side and a rough portico, or *zulla,* providing shade at one end for the poorer worshippers.

The courtyard has become the *sahn,* the portico the arcaded *riwaqs* and the houses the *haram* or prayer hall. The prayer hall is usually divided by aisles in order to segregate the sexes. A broad central aisle leads to the *mihrab,* a vaulted niche in the *qibla* wall. The *mihrab* is built to face Mecca, and so indicating the direction of prayer. It's also the site of the *minbar,* a pulpit from where the *khutba* (weekly sermon) is delivered.

All medina buildings, domestic or religious, were based around courtyards, inspired by the Prophet Mohammed's house in Medina.

The courtyards of many Tunisian mosques are open to all, but nowhere will non-Muslims be allowed into the prayer hall.

Almost every mosque (Sousse's Great Mosque is an unusual exception; see p189) has a minaret (from the word *menara,* meaning lighthouse) – the tower from where Muslims are called to prayer. Alongside many are elaborately decorated *medersas* (Quranic schools), residential colleges teaching theology and Muslim law. They comprise an open-air courtyard, with an ablutions fountain in the centre and a main prayer hall at the far end, surrounded by an upper gallery of student cells. The Medersa Bachia and Medersa Slimania in the Tunis medina (see p75) can both be visited by non-Muslims.

The many small whitewashed domes that you'll see all over Tunisia are *marabout* (Muslim holy men) tombs. A *zaouia* is a tomb complex, typically containing a prayer hall and accommodation for visitors. Some of the best are in Kairouan.

Military Architecture

Thick defensive walls guarded ancient Tunisian towns, also serving as barracks, granaries and arsenals. Towers dotted the perimeter, crenellated walls sheltered defenders, and there were few gates, all clanged shut at night. The best examples, in Sfax and Sousse, were both built by the Aghlabids in the 9th century.

The Islamic *bab* (gate) was flanked by two stone-block towers. Usually horseshoe arches, the gates were often beautifully decorated with geometric, flower-and-foliage or shell-inspired friezes. Favourites include those of Sfax, Kairouan and Monastir. Another form is the *skifa,* like Mahdia's Skifa el-Kahla (p211), which features a long, vaulted passageway protected by a series of gates.

In Tunisia, a kasbah refers to the main fortress guarding a medina, usually built astride the city's walls, or positioned in a commanding corner. None is as imposing as that towering over the remote town of Le Kef (p162).

A *borj* was a mini fort added to bolster a medina's defences at key points, such as the Borj Ennar in Sfax (p217), or a free-standing fort like Jerba's Borj Ghazi Mustapha (p274), while a *ribat* was a cross between a fort and a monastery, occupied by Islamic warriors, who divided their time between the somewhat disparate occupations of fighting and quiet contemplation of the Quran. Most have now disappeared, save the *ribats* of Sousse (p189) and Monastir (p197).

Environment

Tunisia was once lush and green, home to lions and elephants. As Europe shivered under an Ice Age snow blanket, the Sahel and the Sahara encompassed savannah, lakes, rivers and forests. Today's arid plains and sands are the result of desertification and deforestation, but Tunisia is nonetheless remarkably diverse, ranging from inky-green forested mountains to golden, shifting desert.

Sahara, by Marq de Villiers and Sheila Hirtle, markets itself as the biography of the world's greatest desert and doesn't do a bad job; little specifically on Tunisia but essential for desert heads.

THE LAND

Tunisia looks small (164,150 sq km or 63,360 sq miles) hemmed in by Algeria and Libya, but is larger than England and Wales combined. It's only 150km from Europe – Sicily lies to the northeast. Tunisia measures 750km from north to south but only 150km from east to west.

It has an astonishing 1400km of Mediterranean coastline, alternating between jagged rocks and balmy beaches, which forms Tunisia's eastern and northern boundaries.

The Tunisian Dorsale is the main mountain range – the continuation of Morocco and Algeria's Atlas mountains. It runs from Tébessa in Algeria (northwest) to Zaghouan, south of Tunis, tapering off to form Cap Bon. Its – and Tunisia's – highest peak is Jebel Chambi (1544m). The Tell – rolling high plains – and the Oued Medjerda's lush valley lie to the north.

The Medjerda, rising in eastern Algeria, is the only permanent river, north of which lie the oak-forested Kroumirie Mountains.

South of the Dorsale range is a bald plain dropping down to *chotts* (salt lakes), eerie expanses shimmering with the ice-glow of salt. Beyond these, the land gives way to desert.

Some critics think *Desert Wind* (Francis Kohler) – a documentary about 13 men discovering stuff about masculinity alongside their Swiss therapist in the Tunisian desert – is a load of hot air, but the setting is sublime.

WILDLIFE

Animals

Hannibal's elephants hailed from here: North African forest elephants that once roamed the land. Great cats, including lions and cheetahs, were also common – the Romans captured them to appear in their amphitheatres. Populations began to diminish when the Romans began clearing the forests to grow wheat.

These days, wild boar is the only plentiful large mammal left, but you're as likely to spot this shy creature as clock President Ben Ali at a Hammamet disco. Sightings of mongoose, porcupines and genets (an arboreal, catlike carnivore) are even rarer. All live in the northern forests. Jackals are more common and striped hyena are occasionally found in the south. Red squirrels nimble around woodland areas.

You'll see plenty of camels in the south. With their big flat feet and ability to store enough body fat to survive without nourishment for six months, camels are ideally suited to the desert. The desert harbours other well-adapted animals, such as gazelles – who gain all their fluids from plants – gerbils, hares, the cute squirrel-like suslik, and addax (impressively spiral-horned antelopes).

Revel in Philippe Boursellier's exquisite Sahara shots in the hardback *Call of the Desert the Sahara,* a beautiful photographic extravaganza.

There's more chance of spotting snakes, including horned vipers, which rest beneath the sand's surface, awaiting their prey, and the desert varanid (lizard) – a distant, small cousin of Indonesia's Komodo dragon. Scorpions are also common. These measure around 6cm, huddle in the shade and wiggle their legs to keep cool. They only sting in self-defence, but some are fatally poisonous – if you do get stung, seek medical attention.

COOL FOR CATS

They scatter across medina lanes, explore rubbish heaps, and beg under restaurant tables. From battered and forlorn to well-kept domestic animals, cats have a special status here, evident from their sheer numbers.

The Prophet Mohammed had a special affection for felines as shown by several stories in the Hadith (a collection of his reported sayings). A touching tale describes how once, when Mohammed was summoned to prayer, a cat was asleep on his robe, and he cut off his sleeve rather than disturb it. Another cat warned him of danger so he escaped a snake bite, and a woman who starved a cat was said to be later tortured in hell.

Despite their preferential treatment, many Tunisian cats nevertheless suffer a great deal and it can be distressing to see. In Tunis if you see a cat (or other animal) needing help, call the **Societé pour la Protection des Animaux** (☎ 71 390 167; www.protection-des-animaux.org; ave du 3 Août, 1009 El-Ouardia, Tunis) and you can take it to be treated (for a fee of TD5).

ENDANGERED SPECIES

It's (mostly European) hunters storming through the undergrowth as well as environmental degradation that have endangered Tunisian species. The animals that survived the bombast are now under government protection, including the addax, maned mouflon, oryx, ostrich, serval and fennec (a pretty, nocturnal desert fox with radarlike ears and fur-soled feet to protect against scorching sands). Some of these had disappeared but have been reintroduced in special programmes. Sadly the monk seal has probably disappeared from the Cap Bon coast.

Scorpions may outlive us all: they can live in the desert heat, resist for a year without food or water, survive being frozen and have a strong resistance to nuclear radiation.

BIRDS

The number of resident bird species is comparatively small, but in spring and autumn, skies, cliffs, lakes and lagoons become thick with birds stopping off en route between Europe and sub-Saharan Africa. Having survived the Sahara, and the hunters' guns in Sicily and Malta, Tunisia provides a welcome respite.

Over two hundred species have been recorded here, including storks, hawks, eagles, colourful bee-eaters and rollers, and many wading birds and waterfowl. Flamingos turn Korba Lagoon pink during the nesting season over the winter.

In the desert oases you can see larks, as well as the aptly named trumpeter finch, while birds of prey gather around mountainous, forested areas and Cap Bon's sea cliffs.

See p286 for information about bird-watching sites.

The fastest bird in the world is the peregrine falcon, which lives in Tunisia's rocky northern cliffs. It can fly at up to 300km/hr when swooping for its prey.

Plants

Bougainvillea, introduced from Brazil in 1829, is everywhere, its brilliant papery colour (the flowers lie within the bright outer leaves) pouring over whitewashed walls. Jasmine fills the air with its delicious, almost edible scent; its blooms – the pinker ones have the stronger perfume – are used to create the posies – *mashmoum* – and garlands sold everywhere.

The Kroumirie Mountains are thick with evergreen holm and cork oak. Striking red fruit load the strawberry tree in November and December, hence its name, while in autumn it's covered in fragrant white flowers.

All-consuming eucalyptus, the fast-growing tree from Australia, spreads across the north.

Pockets of the Tell's ancient Aleppo pine forests remain, while further south, the *Acacia raddiana* forest of Bou Hedma National Park is what's left of Tunisia's savannah.

Tunisia Online (www.tunisiaonline.com/environment) is a government site with quite a detailed section on environmental programmes and links to organisations.

Olive trees fill the semi-arid Sahel region, cultivated since pre-Roman times. You'll also see knobbly cactuses loaded with spine-covered *Opuntia tomentose* (prickly pear or Barbary fig).

The Jericho rose scuds around the desert, carried by the wind, its branches curled up in a tight ball enclosing its seeds. It opens only on contact with moisture. In the oases, towering date palms shelter a surprising variety of fruit trees.

NATIONAL PARKS

There are eight national parks and 18 natural reserves, covering around 6% of Tunisia's land area.

The only park with visitor facilities is Unesco-listed Ichkeul National Park (see p132), near Bizerte. The others are difficult to reach, and some double as military areas. A government and World Bank project since 2002 seeks to revamp park management, but it remains to be seen whether this will improve access.

Other national parks include the following:

Bou Hedma 85km east of Gafsa, last 16,000 hectares of acacia forest. Reintroduced addax, maned mouflon, oryx and ostrich.

Boukornine 18km south of Tunis at Hammam Lif, Boukornine (1900 hectares) surrounds Jebel Boukornine (576m). Persian cyclamens, wild boars, jackals, porcupines and the military.

Chambi (p179) 15km west of Kasserine, 6700 hectares of forest surround Jebel Chambi (1544m). Aleppo pine, cork oak and juniper; mountain gazelles, striped hyenas and 16 reptilian species.

El-Feija 20km northwest of Ghardimao, 2600 hectares of cork oak forest; 500 orchid species, Barbary deer, wild boar, jackal and (reintroduced) serval.

Orbata West of Gafsa, 3000 hectares include desert mountain habitat for mouflon sheep.

Sidi Toui Saharan 50km south of Ben Guerdane, 6300 hectares of arid plains and dunes; gazelle, jackal and successfully reintroduced fennec fox. Also reintroduced rare antelopes.

Zaghouan 60km south of Tunis, 2000 hectares; rare Saharan golden eagle.

Ever since the Romans started clearing woodland for their fields, the environment has suffered degradation, with forests shrinking from 30% then to 2% today.

ENVIRONMENTAL ISSUES

Tunisia has been heavily farmed since Roman times, and forestry degradation has meant an attendant loss of biodiversity. The ecology of the high plains has been destroyed, and Tunisia loses around 23,000 arable hectares to erosion annually. Massive erosion gullies scar the Tell's wheat-growing regions, and much former agricultural land is suitable only for grazing. Rapid urbanisation has led to traffic, rubbish, water and sewage problems. However, to combat these problems, the government does have a national sustainable development strategy that includes environmental education and is much more developed in this area than most African countries. Practical effects are slow but it's a step in the right direction and 3% of GDP is devoted to environmental protection.

The website of the Sahara and Sahel Observatory, an organisation combating desertification in Africa is www.unesco.org/oss.

Water scarcity is a major issue, but your conservation can help combat this problem. The tourist industry's requirements have depleted artesian water levels and dried up springs. Dam construction ensures that most places in the north receive adequate supply, but in Jerba, supply pressures have damaged agriculture and made the water undrinkable.

There's a depressing amount of litter in the countryside. One author witnessed a train guard carefully sweep up the rubbish in all the train carriages and then just as carefully push it out of the gap between carriages onto the track. It's distressing for visitors to see the scale of the problem and the lack of concern or comprehension on the part of many residents. This is another area where the government is making big efforts to promote education and cleaning programmes, but progress is slow.

RESPONSIBLE TRAVEL

Tunisia has problems with water shortages in some areas and it is important to conserve water where you can. To avoid adding to plastic disposal, use purified, boiled or tap (many hotels have a drinkable water supply, but check first) water to refill mineral water bottles. Obviously, avoid adding to Tunisia's rubbish problem and burn litter or take it away with you if camping out in the desert. Also when camping, avoid the use of firewood (carry a small gas stove for cooking).

Check www.tunisiaonline.com/environment for information on ongoing environmental programmes and links to organisations. Becasse (www.becasse-ecologie.com) is an organisation offering green courses and nature trips.

Industrial pollution, with toxic waste pumped into the sea, has damaged the marine environment of the shallow Gulf of Gabès, where local fishing stocks (and fishermen's livelihoods) are under threat – a five-year World Bank–funded project, from 2005, aims to reverse the trend of degradation.

Food & Drink

Rafik Tlatli & Abigail Hole

Tunisians like it hot. Couscous packs a punch, *harissa* (chilli paste) is an appetiser and salads can be conversation stoppers.

This Mediterranean cuisine is packed with sun-focused flavours, and based around grains, vegetables, fruits, seafood, liquid-gold olive oil and garlic – local foodstuffs that you'll see celebrated in many Roman mosaics.

Rafik Tlatli is the hotelier of Hôtel Les Jasmins and the head chef at the Restaurant Slovénia in Nabeul. He has written a number of books, and made regular radio and TV broadcasts on cooking in Europe and Tunisia.

Centuries of immigrants colonised cooking as well as the country, bringing Roman, Arabic, Jewish, Turkish, Andalusian, French and Italian tastebuds into the equation. The Berbers introduced couscous, the Maghreb staple. Combinations of meat, fruit and cinnamon derive from Persian cuisine, a Turkish import. However, the most obvious influence is French.

Tunisia's key position during the early spice trade brought cumin, caraway, saffron, mustard, cayenne, ginger, cinnamon, dried rosebuds, black pepper and sugar to the table.

STAPLES & SPECIALITIES

Breakfast *(ftoor is-sbah)* traditionally consists of milk, coffee, eggs, *assida* (a belly-filling pudding made with flour or semolina, oil and dates), fritters, *sohlob* (sorghum, sugar, cinnamon and ginger), or, in winter, *hsou* (spicy semolina and caper-based soup). The French influence, however, means that you'll more likely find people tucking into coffee and a deliciously authentic croissant or *pain au chocolat*.

Once the breadbasket of the Roman Empire, Tunisia's biggest import is now wheat.

For lunch *(ftour)* and dinner *(ashaa)*, starters include soups, salads, vegetables, *tajine* (unlike its Moroccan namesake, an omelette with white beans or potatoes, breadcrumbs, chopped meat, cheese and egg) or fish, followed by a plain dish of couscous or pasta.

Harissa

Tunisian cooking revolves around *harissa,* a fire-red concoction made from crushed dried chilli, garlic, salt and caraway seeds. Served neat with a pool of olive oil – you dip your bread into the mix as an appetiser – it gives the mouth a tantalising jolt.

It was the Spanish who introduced hot peppers to Tunisia. The word *harissa* comes from the Arabic, meaning 'break into pieces', as the paste is traditionally made by pounding red chillies in a mortar. An old tale says that a man can judge his wife's affections by the spice in his food – if it's bland then love is dead.

The www.harissa.com website is dedicated to Tunisian Jews. It has weird syntax, but some good stuff on dishes and background on Judaism in Tunisia.

Bread

Bread is eaten with every meal – ideally still warm from the local *boulangerie.* It's frequently a baguette (long crusty French loaf), but often, particularly in the countryside, it's *tabouna*. This traditional Berber bread is flat, round and heavy, subtly flavoured with *hab hlaoua* (aniseed), and named after the traditional clay-domed ovens in which it's baked. You can see such ovens among the 4th-century BC Punic ruins at Kerkouane (p117). The price of bread is subsidised and controlled – price rises in 1984 led to riots.

Starters

Kemia are small tasty dishes, usually served as appetisers. Besides such nibbles as nuts, olives, *poutargue* (mullet roe), dried fish, and spiced

TRAVEL YOUR TASTEBUDS

People often have a milk drink – *Iben* – when eating couscous: an acquired taste that's worth a try.

Barbary figs (aka prickly pears) are the green cactus fruits you'll see piled high from October to December. Introduced by the Spanish in the 16th century, these are covered in fine spines that'll leave your hand like a cactus if you try to pick one up. Tip: get the vendor to peel it for you.

octopus, particular delights are the crushed vegetable dishes that tingle on the tongue, such as carrots, pumpkin or courgette, mixed with spices and *imalah* (pickled carrots and cauliflower).

Perhaps Tunisia's most prolific starter is the smoky-tasting *salade mechouia,* a delicious blend of roasted peppers, garlic and *harissa.* It's a coolly refreshing way to start a meal, mopped up with crusty white bread. *Salade Tunisienne* is another hit: comprising finely chopped tomatoes, onion and peppers, seasoned with lemon juice, olive oil and mint. *Omni houria* – cooked carrots mashed with garlic and olive oil – is also a quenching, lightly spiced taste, served cold. A winter favourite is *chorba:* a punchy, oily, tomato-based soup.

Mediterranean Cooking Revised Edition, by the expert Mediterranean cookery writer Paula Wolfert, pays particular attention to Tunisian specialities and traditions, laying emphasis on healthy but robust eating.

The *briq* is a Tunisian curiosity that's of Middle Eastern origin, a delicate deep-fried envelope of pastry that's usually filled with a satisfying slurp of egg (skilfully rendered so that the white is cooked and the yolk is runny). It might be stuffed with onions, parsley, potato, capers, tuna, egg, seafood, chicken or meat, though *briqs* can be stickily sweet too, filled with almond or sesame paste and drenched in honey.

Seafood

With 1400km of coastline, Tunisia has excellent fresh seafood, including sole, red mullet, mackerel, grouper, perch, octopus and squid. Favoured seasonings are garlic, saffron, cumin, paprika, turmeric or dried rosebuds (providing an aromatic, rose-tinged flavour), though often fish is simply grilled with lemon and olive oil, or baked or fried in olive oil. The traditional accompaniment for fried fish is *tastira,* a delicate mixture of chopped fried tomatoes and eggs, seasoned with caraway seeds, salt and olive oil.

Tunisia is unusual in North Africa in that it often serves couscous with fish.

Look out for *kabkabou,* an aromatic, tangy baked dish with saffron, preserved lemons, tomatoes and capers, and simple, tasty fish *brochettes* (kebabs), alternating between chunky fish and fresh vegetables.

Mussels, clams, calamari, prawns and oysters also feature widely, as well as crayfish and lobster (particularly around Tabarka), which are boiled and often served with a roux (white sauce made from butter and flour) and mayonnaise. Succulent large prawns are grilled, sautéed with garlic and parsley, or simmered in a *gargoulette* (clay cooking pot).

Meat

Merguez (spicy lamb or goat sausages) are hard to beat, but some cheap joints sell delicious roast chicken – best when piping hot, with a pile of chips. Around Ain Draham you can sometimes eat *marcassin* (wild boar piglet), though it's off-limits to Muslims and has been illegal in recent years. Camel meat is a southern novelty.

Particularly interesting are dishes combining meat, fruit and spices. Tunisians like *maraqa,* a slow-cooked stew, normally lamb, in versions such as *koucha,* with chilli, tomatoes and potatoes, *klaya,* with paprika, or *kamounia,* cooked in cumin. You can find a similar cooking style in Provence, where dishes were brought back by French settlers in North Africa.

THE DEPENDABLE DATE

Until recently, life in the Sahara was almost entirely dependent on one remarkable plant: the date palm *(Phoenix dactylifera)*.

So important was it to desert life that the traditional way of assessing the size of an oasis was in terms of the number of palms it could support, rather than the number of people.

A date palm can live to be over 100 years old, growing up to 24m high. The trees start producing fruit at around 20-30 years. The fruit supplies begin to decline at about 70 years, so they are normally cut down around then (at around 20m, before they reach their full potential height).

Nowadays palms are mainly used for their fruit, but in the past the trunk was used for building, or hollowed out to channel water. The branches are used for roofs and fences, while leaf fibres can be woven into mats and ropes and the woody fruiting stems make good brooms. Nothing went to waste. Even the date pits are used: in the old days they were roasted and ground to make an ersatz coffee; today they are ground up as animal fodder.

The date palm's very presence is an indicator of the desert's most precious resource, water. The tree is specific in its climatic requirements. There is an old Arab saying that it likes 'its feet in heaven and its head in hell', a reference to its need for sizzling summer temperatures and lots of water – about 500L a day in summer.

There are more than 100 varieties of date, finest of which is the *deglat ennour* (finger of light), so called because the flesh is almost translucent. It constitutes 50% of all plantings in Tunisia.

If you can, try to make it to Douz in October for the date harvest, when the abundant dates are at their succulent best.

Couscous

The national dish, couscous (semolina granules) is the pride of the Maghreb, eaten by rich and poor alike. There are more than 300 ways of serving up this grainy, soft cereal. It's *the* dish to eat at celebrations, usually communally, with people delving into a large single deep bowl, and this is when it's at its best.

Recette de Couscous, by Magali Morsy, includes couscous recipes from all over North Africa.

Couscous is prepared by steaming wet grains in a *couscoussière*, a two-piece pot. The sieve-lined upper part holds the couscous, while the sauce (vegetables, chickpeas, beef, chicken, lamb or fish) cooks slowly underneath. The scented steam rises to cook the grains, which expand up to three times their original size.

Fruit, Nuts & Sweets

Tunisia has wonderful, sun-ripened fruit. The intense, subtle flavours are an extraordinary surprise to those accustomed to imported foodstuffs.

In May try juicy *bousa'a* – medlar-fruit – orange in colour and plum-like in taste. At the end of June look out for *boutabguia (pêche de vigne)*. All peaches are mouth-wateringly good but this warm-yellow variety has an unusual compact texture. Grapes are finest at the end of August – try fragrant white muscats from around Kélibia, or *razzegoui,* a large white grape, shaded pink. Summer sees roadsides stacked with succulent *della* (melon).

Romans didn't eat oranges. Citrus fruit trees were probably only introduced here from China in the early medieval period.

Mishmish are extraordinarily delicate apricots; you might want to couple them with some crunchy, sweet *inzas bouguidma* (meaning 'bite-sized'; miniature pears). From September, blush-red pomegranates join the dessert menu; specify if you want them *sans sucre* (unsugared). Fresh almonds *(almandes)* appear in July and August (their pods are green and suedelike) – crack them open to find a gleaming pale kernel.

Tunisian cakes are sweet, nutty and delectable, including baklava – sticky filo pastry filled with nuts and honey, *samsa* – filo pastry and ground roast almonds, baked in lemon and rosewater syrup, and *bouza* – hazelnut cream with grilled sesame seeds. *Makhroud* – small date-stuffed, honey-soaked wheat cakes are a speciality of sugar-loving Kairouan.

DRINKS

Cafés deck every corner, crammed with men passing the time and shooting the breeze.

Drinks of choice include coffee: the best is thick and gritty *ahwa arbi* (Turkish coffee) fragrant with orange blossom or rosewater. Other versions, all benefiting from sugar to make them palatable, are *express* (espresso coffee), *café direct* (coffee with milk) or *capucin* (espresso with a dash of milk).

Délice de Tunisie, edited by Rafik Tlatli, is a French book that brings together specialities of 10 different regions, chosen by Tunisian chefs.

Thé à la menthe (mint tea) is the classic North African tipple, but here you'll also be offered *thé au pignon* – with pine nuts, or *thé à l'almande* – with almonds, which react with the hot tea to create a delectable buttery taste.

Most cafés sell refreshing *citronade* – lemon juice, water and sugar – and many offer delicious freshly squeezed orange juice. Look out for seasonal juices or milkshakes with fresh fruit – always specify if you want just a little sugar otherwise it'll be assumed that you want a lot. If *lait de poule* is offered, it's not 'chicken's milk' but a fruit milkshake with egg white.

Alcohol

Although Tunisia is a Muslim country, alcohol is remarkably easily available, with locals frequenting bars (mostly all-male preserves), though the annual tourist influx raises the number of consumers by an impressive 50%. Beer is popular. Celtia, the local brand, is a drinkable lager (particularly ice cold) – and also the cheapest. German Löwenbräu is also brewed locally. For information on wine, see the boxed text, below.

A popular aperitif is *boukha* – a gloopily sweet, aromatic spirit made from distilled figs, served at room temperature or chilled, and often mixed with Coke. Also popular are aniseed drinks such as Pastis – a French relic – and whisky, which has a snobbish appeal. Herb-based *Thibarine* is made from an ancient recipe in the Thibar region near Dougga. *Sarabi,* from Soukra (near Tunis), is as sweet as you'd expect a liqueur distilled from dates.

Laghmi, fermented palm sap, is found in the southern oases, and can be powerful – check the quality before surrendering your stomach.

WINE: THE ESSENTIALS

Tunisia has had some practice in wine-producing: Dionysus, god of wine, staggers all over Roman mosaics, and Magon, contemporary to the Phoenicians, wrote about techniques of production still used today. The French and the Italians planted the first industrial vineyards in the 19th century.

Tunisia's wines come from its northern vineyards – important regions are Nabeul, Cap Bon, Bizerte, Ben Arous and Zaghouan. The main grapes are Carignan, Grenache, Beldi and Cinsault. Wines are strong, mostly full-bodied reds – Magon Supérior is recommended – and light, fruity rosés – Château Mornag is good. Among the whites, Blanc de Blanc is a safe bet. Kélibia (Cap Bon) produces a very drinkable musky, dry muscat.

You can buy wine in some supermarkets and many restaurants (though not the cheapest ones).

CELEBRATIONS

Like most cultures, Tunisians celebrate with food, and you can measure the event's importance by the amount of scoff.

Saveur de Tunisie, by Rafik Tlatli, in French, supplies innovations in Tunisian cooking.

There are many special celebratory dishes, such as *zrir* (nut paste served in small glasses), which is served after childbirth to help revitalise the mother.

Marriage

Marriage is the ultimate feast. Hospitality is all important and families feel it their obligation to celebrate in style. Sometimes festivities last as long as seven days, with the culinary part kicking off on the fourth day, known as Outia Sghira, when a bull is slaughtered to provide meat for the following feasts. On Outia Kbira, the fifth day, guests eat meat and chickpea couscous followed by baklava. The sixth day sees a *really* big meal featuring *tajine, market ommalah* (meatball stew), *salade mechouia* and *klaya* (meat and paprika stew).

On the big day, lunch is pasta with meat sauce, and *mloukhia,* a dark-green, pungent stew with powdered corète (aka *mloukhia;* a herb) that has a unique, some might say slimy, taste, and is traditionally eaten for new starts. In the evening everyone eats couscous, followed by fruit, leaving room for baklava and other sweets.

The website www.globalgourmet.com/destinations/tunisia features gastronomic morsels – both recipes and cultural.

Ramadan

The flipside of the Muslim holy month, with its daylight-hours fasting, is night-time no-holds-barred feasting.

Each night, people break their fast by drinking water and eating a date. Afterwards they tuck into some hearty *chorba* (oily spicy soup, made from meat or chicken and celeriac with pasta), an egg *briq,* and then couscous or pasta.

Once the day's hunger has been sated, it's time to socialise until late, topping up on fruits, sweets and cakes, tea or coffee.

Before sunrise, people wake to eat *shour,* a light meal, and energise for the day by snaffling some *mesfouf,* a comforting milky couscous dessert, with dates, raisins, chopped almonds, sugar and cinnamon.

Eid al-Fitr

Eid al-Fitr – the lesser *eid* – marks the end of Ramadan. This small festival is big on cakes, such as baklava, *ghraïba* made from fine semolina, or *makhroud.*

For three days families visit each other bearing sweets. Children not only get to enjoy this sugar fest, but are dressed in brand-new clothes.

The Great Book of Couscous: Classic Cuisines of Morocco, Algeria and Tunisia, by Copeland Marks, includes recipes, visits to markets and chefs' homes and comparisons of the North African cuisines.

Eid al-Adha

Eid al-Adha is the greater *eid,* taking place 70 days after Eid al-Fitr. It's a bad time for sheep as each family slaughters an animal and serves it up for at least a week in dishes such as *m'rouzia,* a stew with raisins and chestnuts, or *daouara,* sausage made of sheep liver and lungs, parsley and mint.

Ras as-Sana

Ras as-Sana is the first day of the lunar or Hejira year, when people eat the verdant dish of *mloukhia* – because the year is green.

People in the Nabeul region prepare a special couscous dish, *kadid* (salted dried meat conserved since Eid al-Adha), decorated by a hard-boiled egg, chickpeas, sweets, dried fruit and a doll made from coloured sugar.

Moulid an-Nabi

Moulid an-Nabi commemorates the Prophet's birthday, and in the morning everyone tucks into *assida:* either the simple version made from fine semolina or flour, oil and honey, or the more refined, Ottoman-influenced sort, of pinenuts, cream, hazelnuts, pistachios and almonds. Again, it's sweet-toothed Kairouan that makes it the best.

La Cuisine Tunisienne d'Ommok Sannafa, by Mohamed Kouki, is a French and Arabic classic on Tunisian cooking.

WHERE TO EAT & DRINK

Eateries are firmly divided. Fast-food places serve hamburgers, chips and sandwiches. Up a level, basic local haunts don't usually serve alcohol and are either *gargottes* – offering sandwiches, chicken, fish, and couscous, or *rotîsseries,* selling fried and roasted meats. *Meshoui* are popular roadside joints selling barbecued meat.

Restaurants touristiques are more formal, and not just for tourists, despite the name. They're assessed by the ONTT (national tourist office), marked with one to three forks, serve Tunisian and international specialities, and serve alcohol.

Cafés in Tunisia range from stand-up pâtisseries fit for a swallow of caffeine and a pastry to leisurely male-dominated gossip havens, where clientele play chess and dominoes and smoke *sheeshas* – tobacco water pipes. These contraptions cool the fragrant smoke, making for a gentle puff with attendant musical gurgle; you can have *mwassi* (honey-soaked) or *tufa* (apple-flavoured) tobacco. Some cafés have a mixed clientele, particularly in Tunis, and there are also a few all-women places tucked away.

If you were writing a book called *101 Uses for Tinned Tuna,* this would be the place to research. Tuna loads sandwiches, pizzas and salads, is sprinkled on pasta and decks *harissa* as an hors d'oeuvre.

Most bars are raucous, smoky all-male dives. For a more salubrious drink, in a place where women will feel comfortable, head for a reputable hotel bar, or a restaurant. Liquor stores and supermarkets sell alcohol, but put your bottles in bags when carrying them around in public.

Quick Eats

Tunisians have developed snacking into a fine art, with countless solutions for a hungry rumble.

Popular on winter mornings, particularly with labourers, is *lablabi,* a set-you-up-for-the-week chickpea, *harissa* and cumin soup. It's served in brown-glazed terracotta bowls (you'll see them stacked up where it's sold) filled with broken bread with the soup poured over the top. Sometimes egg and tuna are stirred in too.

Tunisian sandwiches are great. A favourite is the casse-croûte, a jaw-challenging half-baguette – usually you choose from a selection of *harissa, salade mechouia,* cucumber, tomato, egg, tuna and olives. The *chapatti* is a folded disc of bread, lightly fried to make it hot and crispy, filled with finely chopped, lightly spiced potatoes, tuna and egg.

TUNISIA'S TOP FIVE EATING SPOTS

- **Dar el-Jeld** (see p82) Exquisite traditional cuisine in a beautiful mansion.
- **Dar Bel Hadj** (see p82) Less well known than El-Jeld, this has delicious food in a similarly sublime setting.
- **Restaurant Slovénia** (see p113) Innovative Tunisian dishes and international influences.
- **Le Restô** (see p96) Blue-as-can-be Tunis Gulf views and international food with a Tunisian slant.
- **Le Petit Mousse** (see p129) Bizerte's finest, with French cuisine on a seaside terrace.

Another important part of life is the doughnut (*yoyo* or *beignet*), made of soft yielding dough dipped in oil and sugar or enveloped in honey. *Babalouni* or *shishi* are large doughnuts eaten in the afternoon – so don't try getting a big doughnut in the morning.

250 Recettes Classique de Cuisine Tunisienne, by Edmond Zeitoun, has mouthwatering Jewish-Tunisian recipes.

VEGETARIANS & VEGANS

Tunisians eat meat if they can afford it, and they find it strange that people might not through choice, while veganism is an unheard-of curiosity. But fruit, vegetables, grains and nuts are staples here, so you'll have no cause to go hungry. Your best bet will be starters: *salades Tunisienne* or *mechouia* are delicious and ubiquitous, though you'll have to ask that they hold the tuna and egg. The *briq* is often meat-free, and *Ojai* (fresh tomatoes and chillies blended into a spicy sauce; often prawns, *merguez* or brains are added with eggs stirred in at the last minute), *shashouka, lablabi* and *tajine* are other options if you check what's going into them – often a meat stock will be used. Vegans will find eating out difficult, and will have to self-cater most of the time.

EATING WITH KIDS

Tunisians adore children and you'll be fêted guests at any restaurant, though you might not feel comfortable at very upmarket ones. The climate means that you'll often be eating outside, which is ideal. There's rarely a children's menu, but kids can share dishes or choose from the starters. In the resorts you'll have tons of child-friendly choices as many restaurants serve chicken, crepes, pasta, pizzas, sandwiches and so on. Baby food and formula milk are available from pharmacies.

The Momo Cookbook: A Gastronomic Journey Through North Africa, produced by the London restaurant Momo, has recipes, covers background to cookery culture and has delectable photography.

If you're spending the day sightseeing, it's a good idea to take a picnic, in case you can't find any suitable food along the way.

Travelling with young children, it's handy to stay somewhere with some kitchen facilities, so you can prepare some meals rather than constantly eating out. For additional information on travelling with children, see p287.

HABITS & CUSTOMS

Families often eat sitting around a *mida,* a round, low table, where food is served in a big communal dish. Men and women eat together here, unlike in some Arabic countries, but in some traditional families, women leave the table at the end of the meal and the men stay (Western women are regarded as honorary men). If the family is religious, meals start and end invoking Allah: first *bis millah,* and last *ilhamdulillah.*

When invited to a Tunisian home, you should bring a gift: something from your own country is ideal, but otherwise sweets from an upmarket Tunisian pâtisserie, fruit, nuts or flowers are also good.

DOS & DON'TS

- Do dress well when invited to someone's home.
- Don't pass things and eat with your left hand – it's reserved for less salubrious tasks like wiping your bottom.
- Do eat everything up, and don't refuse if someone offers you more.
- Do ask God's pardon if you burp: *Astakhfirou Allah.*
- Don't start eating before the father of the family.

EAT YOUR WORDS

Useful Phrases

What do you recommend?	*shnuwwa tansahnee?*
Not too spicy, please.	*mush haar*
Could you please bring me some/more?	*bi-rabbee zeednee shwayya?*
Thanks, that was delicious.	*barkallah oo feek, bneen barsha*
I don't eat meat, chicken or fish. (I'm a vegetarian.)	*ana ma naakulsh lham wala djaaj wala hoot*
I don't eat meat or dairy products. (I'm a vegan.)	*ana végétarien ma naakulsh lham wala haleeb oo moushtakaatoo*
I have a wheat/nut allergy.	*ana andee hassaaseeya lil qamah/il boofroowa*
little sugar	*shwayya sukur*
without sugar	*bilaash sukur*

Food Glossary

SPECIALITIES

kammounia	meat stew with cumin
keftaji	spicy ratatouille usually served with meatballs
koucha	lamb, potatoes and tomatoes, seasoned with rosemary, mint, turmeric and capsicum, baked in a clay pot
loup à la sfaxienne	perch baked with tomatoes, onions, peppers, garlic and capers
mérou au citron	grouper poached in a sauce of lemon, *harissa* and cumin
ragoût de gnaouia	meat and vegetable stew, rich red in colour and eaten with bread
shakshouka (also spelt *chakchouka*)	peppers, onions and tomatoes combined with scrambled eggs

EATING OUT

ashaa	dinner
farsheeta	fork
ftoor	lunch
ftoor is-sbah	breakfast
il-fatoora	bill/check
migharfa	spoon
muqlee	fried
skeena	knife

BASICS

adham	eggs
batata maqliyya	chips
beera	beer
ghalla	fruit
khubz	bread
maa ma'danee	mineral water
rooz	rice
shrab	wine
sukur	sugar
zeet	oil
zeetoon	olives
zibda	butter

MEAT & SEAFOOD

'alloosh	lamb
brochette	kebab
crevettes	prawns
djaaj	chicken
espadon	swordfish
hoot	fish
langouste	crayfish
lham	meat
loup de mer	perch
mérou	grouper
mullet	mullet
pulpe	octopus
rouget	red mullet
ton	tuna

Tunis تونس

Arabian, African and Mediterranean, Middle Eastern and European, yet curiously provincial – the laid back capital of Tunis has two distinct hearts.

The new city, created by French colonials in the 19th century, is an orderly European grid, with wrought-iron balconies, cafés and pâtisseries bordering the boulevards. The city's main drag, palm-lined ave Habib Bourguiba, is prime territory for promenading, coffee-drinking, gossiping and idly watching the passing human traffic.

Founded by the Arabs in the 8th century, the medina, the old city, is the city's historic and symbolic heart. Here you enter a tangled maze of narrow streets, winding and arched, with giant keyhole-shaped doors, scattering cats, alley communities, workshops and glittering souqs selling everything but your mother. Here all the lanes, however twisted, will eventually lead to the great mosque. People watch people go by from within kaleidoscopic-tiled coffeehouses, suckling on hubbly-bubbly pipes and indulging in chat, chequers and chess.

Outside the two-part centre lie some even bigger attractions: the ruins of once-magnificent Carthage, set among the great white mansions of Tunis' contemporary upper classes; the astounding, enormous collection of Roman mosaics housed in the Bardo's Ottoman palace; and the flower-laden cliff-top village of Sidi Bou Saïd that inspired Paul Klee and August Macke to experiment with colour.

However urban Tunis (home to 90% of Tunisia's population) might feel compared with the rest of the country, you are never far from the beach. The suburbs stretch endlessly out along deep-blue seafronts, where in summer everyone walks in search of a breeze.

HIGHLIGHTS

- Get lost and shop till you drop in the **medina** (p71)
- See Baron Erlanger's fantastical mansion and sip tea at sunset in **Sidi Bou Saïd** (p96)
- Be amazed by the incredible Roman mosaics at the palatial **Bardo Museum** (p50)
- Imagine the glories of ancient **Carthage** (p90)
- Scrub, sweat and socialise at a stuck-in-time **Hammam Sahib** (p71) in Halfaouine

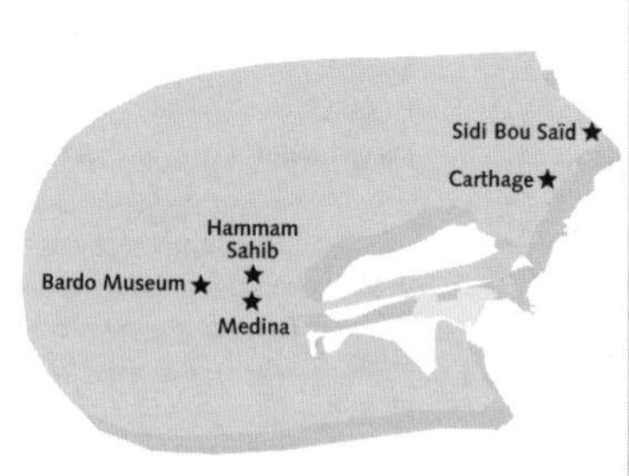

HISTORY

Once insignificant,Tunis (ancient Tynes) features on 5th-century BC maps, and the Roman general Regulus camped here in 255 BC during the First Punic War.

The Carthaginians and the Romans ruled from Byrsa Hill, on the coast to the east, but after ousting the Byzantines in AD 695, the victorious Arab Hassan bin Nooman decided to build at Tunis, which he felt was in a better defensive position. The medina was sited on a narrow band of high ground flanked by the Sebkhet Sejoumi (a salt lake) to the southwest and Lake Tunis to the east. A deep-water channel was dug across the lake to access the sea.

The city was born with the building of the Zaytouna (Great) Mosque (p71) in AD 732, but it was in the 9th century, when Aghlabid ruler Ibrahim ibn Ahmed II moved his court here, that it became the seat of power.

Tunis declined under the Fatimids, who chose Mahdia as their capital in the 10th century, and escaped the ravages of the 11th-century Hilalian invasion, emerging again as capital following the Almohad North African conquest in 1160.

The city flourished and trade boomed under the Hafsids, who ruled from 1229 to 1574. The population more than tripled (to about 60,000). Souqs (markets), mosques, *medersas* (Quranic schools) and the Zaytouna Mosque University were established.

Tunis suffered badly during Turkish-Spanish tussles, leading to the fall of the Hafsids. Much of the city was destroyed and the population fled. Sinan Pasha finally secured the city for the Ottomans in 1574, and people began to return, including refugees fleeing religious persecution: Moorish Andalusians from Spain and Jews from Livorno in Italy. Many were fine artisans who played an important role in the city's reconstruction.

In the 19th century, the colonising French built their elegant Ville Nouvelle (new town) on land reclaimed from Lake Tunis, moving the city's focus and causing the medina to decline.

ORIENTATION

Almost everything of practical importance to travellers is within the Ville Nouvelle.

The main east–west road is ave Habib Bourguiba, running from Lake Tunis to place de l'Indépendance, with the medina at its western end. A causeway at the eastern end carries road and light-rail traffic east across Lake Tunis to La Goulette, and then north along the coast to the suburbs of Carthage, Sidi Bou Saïd, La Marsa and Gammarth.

The main north–south thoroughfare is the street known as ave de Carthage to the south of ave Habib Bourguiba and as ave de Paris to the north. Just west of ave de Carthage is place Barcelone, hub of the city's excellent *métro léger* (tram network). The train station is on the square's southern side.

Maps

The tourist office hands out a good, free map of Tunis, as well as one of the medina that's fairly accurate. The best maps are produced by the **Office de la Topographie et de la Cartographie** (☎ 71 832 933; www.otc.nat.tn; 13 rue de Jordanie), including *Tunis – Ariana/Bardo*, covering the city centre, and *La Marsa, Sidi Bou Saïd, Carthage & La Goulette*, showing

TUNIS IN...

Two Days

Head to the **Bardo** (p50) in the morning, returning to the centre for lunch and to explore the **medina** (p71), before a promenade and reviving drink on **avenue Habib Bourguiba**. Finish up at the extraordinary 18th-century medina restaurant **Dar el-Jeld** (p82). The next day, explore the ancient sites of **Carthage** (p90) and then visit the whitewashed village of **Sidi Bou Saïd** (p96), drinking in the views and having dinner at one of the village's restaurants.

Four Days

Spend a day wandering the **medina** (p71) and have dinner at **Dar el-Jeld** (p82). The next day go to **Carthage** (p90) and finish up in romantic blue-and-white **Sidi Bou Saïd** (p96). Head to the **Bardo** (p50) the third day. On your last day, return to the medina to stock up on souvenirs and atmosphere.

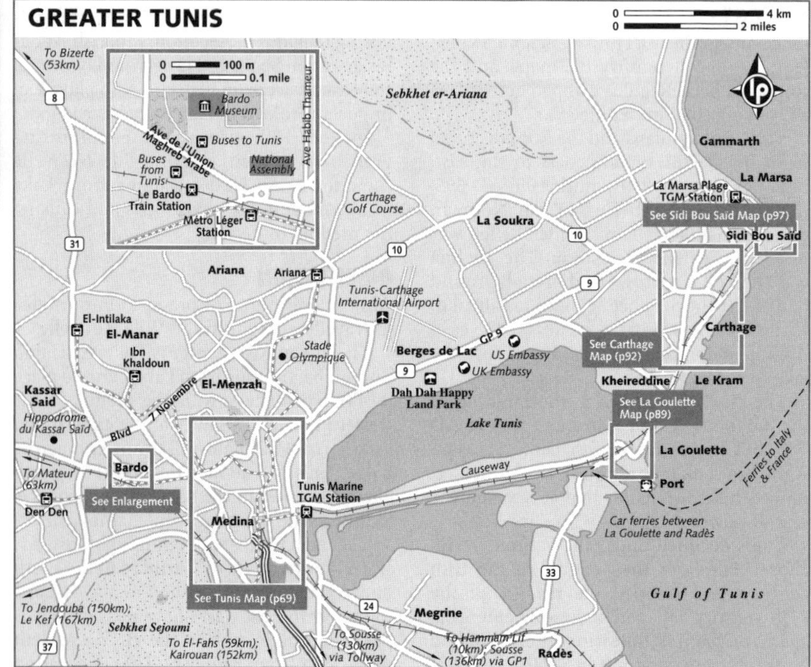

the coastal suburbs. Both are on a scale of 1:10,000 and cost TD9.

These maps are on sale at the office or at Espace Diwan 9 (see below).

INFORMATION

Bookshops

Al-Kitab (Map pp72–3; 43 ave Habib Bourguiba; 8am-9pm Mon-Fri, 8am-11pm Sat) Maps, travel guides and cookery books, and a few English titles.

Espace Diwan 9 (Map pp72-3; 9 rue Sidi ben Arous; 9am-8pm Mon-Sat Apr-Sep, to 7pm Oct-Mar) A good selection of books about Tunisia; also sells CDs, old books and photographs.

Librairie Claire Fontaine (Map pp72-3; 14 rue d'Alger) Excellent selection of French books, and some lovely coffee-table books on Tunisia in French and English.

Second-hand bookshop (Map pp72-3; rue d'Angleterre) Some English titles; owner will buy and exchange books.

Cultural Centres

British Council (Map p69; ☎ 71 848 588; www.britishcouncil.org/tunisia.htm; 87 ave Mohamed V)

Centre Culturel Français (Map p69; ☎ 71 105 262; 87 ave de la Liberté)

Centre d'Information Americain (☎ 71 107 000; route de l'Aouina)

Centre Russe (Map p69; ☎ 71 780 953; 34 ave de la Liberté)

Goethe Institut (Map p69; ☎ 71 844 973; 6 rue du Sénegal)

Institut Cervantes (Map p69; ☎ 71 788 847; 120 ave de la Liberté)

Emergency

Ambulance (☎ 190)

Police (Map pp72-3; ☎ 197) The most central police station is on rue Jamel Abdelnasser; some English spoken.

Internet Access

You can access free wi-fi at El-Hana International (see Brasserie Les 2 Avenues, p84) on ave Habib Bourguiba.

Publinet (per hr TD1.5-2) ave Habib Bourguiba (Map pp72-3; 28 ave Habib Bourguiba); rue de Grèce (Map pp72-3; rue de Grèce); rue Mokhtar (Map pp72-3; rue Mokhtar)

Laundry

Lavarie Tahar (Map pp72-3; 15 rue d'Allemagne; 7am-6.30pm Mon-Sat) Charges TD6 to wash and dry 5kg.

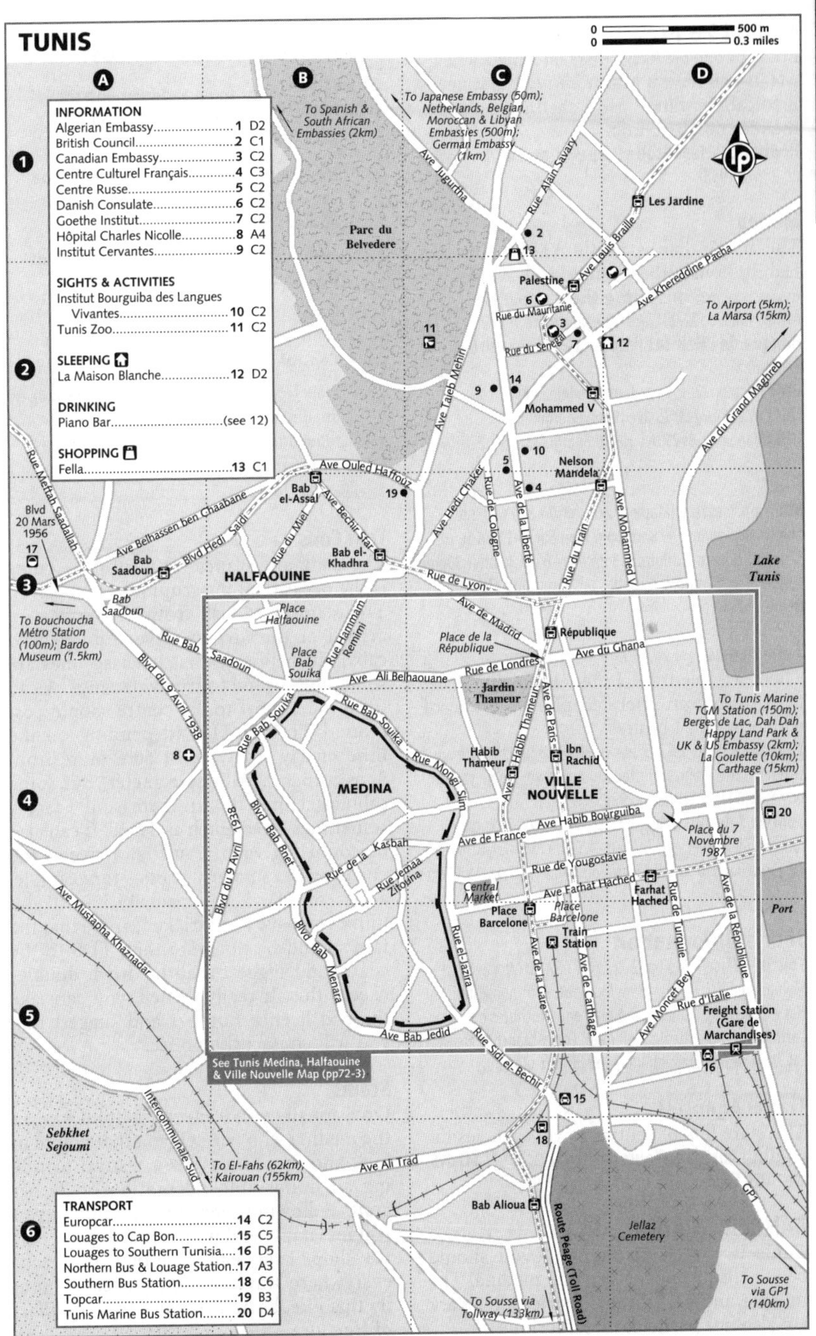
TUNIS
0 500 m
0 0.3 miles
A
B
C
D
1
2
3
4
5
6
INFORMATION
Algerian Embassy......1 D2
British Council......2 C1
Canadian Embassy......3 C2
Centre Culturel Français......4 C3
Centre Russe......5 C2
Danish Consulate......6 C2
Goethe Institut......7 C2
Hôpital Charles Nicolle......8 A4
Institut Cervantes......9 C2
SIGHTS & ACTIVITIES
Institut Bourguiba des Langues Vivantes......10 C2
Tunis Zoo......11 C2
SLEEPING
La Maison Blanche......12 D2
DRINKING
Piano Bar......(see 12)
SHOPPING
Fella......13 C1
TRANSPORT
Europcar......14 C2
Louages to Cap Bon......15 C5
Louages to Southern Tunisia......16 D5
Northern Bus & Louage Station......17 A3
Southern Bus Station......18 C6
Topcar......19 B3
Tunis Marine Bus Station......20 D4
To Spanish & South African Embassies (2km)
To Japanese Embassy (50m); Netherlands, Belgian, Moroccan & Libyan Embassies (500m); German Embassy (1km)
Parc du Belvedere
Ave Jugurtha
Rue Alain Savary
Les Jardine
Ave Louis Braille
Palestine
Ave Khereddine Pacha
Rue du Mauritanie
Rue du Senegal
To Airport (5km); La Marsa (15km)
Ave Taïeb Mehiri
Mohammed V
Ave du Grand Maghreb
Nelson Mandela
Ave Ouled Haffouz
Bab el-Assal
Ave Bechir Sfar
Ave Hedi Chaker
Rue de Cologne
Ave de la Liberté
Rue du Train
Ave Mohammed V
Blvd 20 Mars 1956
Rue Meftah Saadallah
Ave Belhassen ben Chaabane
Blvd Hedi Saidi
Rue du Miel
Bab el-Khadhra
Bab Saadoun
HALFAOUINE
Rue de Lyon
Lake Tunis
To Bouchoucha Métro Station (100m); Bardo Museum (1.5km)
Place Halfaouine
Place Bab Souika
Rue Hammam Remimi
Ave de Madrid
Place de la République
République
Ave du Ghana
Rue de Londres
Rue Bab Saadoun
Ave Ali Belhaouane
Jardin Thameur
Blvd du 9 Avril 1938
Rue Bab Souika
Rue Monji Slim
Habib Thameur
Ave Habib Thameur
Ave de Paris
Ibn Rachid
To Tunis Marine TGM Station (150m); Berges de Lac, Dah Dah Happy Land Park & UK & US Embassy (2km); La Goulette (10km); Carthage (15km)
MEDINA
VILLE NOUVELLE
Ave Habib Bourguiba
Place du 7 Novembre 1987
Ave de France
Rue de la Kasbah
Rue Jemaa Zitouna
Blvd Bab Bnet
Rue de Yougoslavie
Ave Farhat Hached
Farhat Hached
Central Market
Place Barcelone
Train Station
Rue de Turquie
Ave de la République
Port
Ave Mustapha Khaznadar
Blvd Bab Menara
Rue el-Jazira
Ave de la Gare
Ave de Carthage
Ave Moncef Bey
Rue d'Italie
Freight Station (Gare de Marchandises)
Ave Bab Jedid
Rue Sidi el-Bechir
See Tunis Medina, Halfaouine & Ville Nouvelle Map (pp72-3)
Sebkhet Sejoumi
Intercommunale Sud
To El-Fahs (62km); Kairouan (155km)
Ave Ali Trad
Bab Alioua
Route Péage (Toll Road)
Jellaz Cemetery
GP1
To Sousse via GP1 (140km)
To Sousse via Tollway (133km)

Medical Services

Local paper *La Presse* lists late-night chemists. If you have a minor ailment that needs medical assistance, ask a chemist to recommend a nearby clinic.

Hôpital Charles Nicolle (Map p69; ☎ 71 578 346; blvd du 9 Avril 1938)

Money

The major banks (with ATMs) line ave Habib Bourguiba; banks and ATMs are everywhere, including the airport.

Amen (Map pp72-3; Place du 7 Novembre 1987)
Banque de l'Habitat (Map pp72-3; 44 ave Habib Bourguiba)
BIAT (Map pp72-3; 1 rue Jamel Abdelnasser)
UBCI (Map pp72-3; 23 ave Habib Bourguiba)
UIB (Map pp72-3; 29 ave Habib Bourguiba)

Post

Main post office (Map pp72-3; ☎ 71 320 610; rue Charles de Gaulle; 8am-6pm Mon-Sat, 9-11am Sun Sep-Jun, 7.30am-1.30pm, 6-8pm Mon-Fri, 7.30am-1.30pm Sat, 9-11am Sun Jul & Aug) Has poste restante (TD0.4 per item).

Telephone

There are plentiful Publitel telephone offices, with coin-operated phones, some of which open 24 hours.

Tunisiana (Map pp72-3; ave Habib Bourguiba) There are several of these offices dotted around town, where you can buy a local SIM card (see p299).

Tunisie Telecom (Map pp72-3; ☎ 71 801 717; rue Jamel Abdelnasser; 8.15am-4.30pm Mon-Fri, 8.15am-12.15pm Sat Sep-Jun, 7.15am-1pm Mon-Fri, 7.15-11.15am Sat Jul & Aug)

Tourist Information

Tourist office (Map pp72-3; ☎ 71 341 077; 1 ave Mohammed V; 8am-6pm Mon-Sat, 9am-noon Sun) Has a Tunis map, Tunisia road map and brochures on Carthage and the medina (all free). Other branches are at the train station (same hours) and airport (24 hours).

Travel Agencies

There are lots of central travel agencies including **Carthage Tours** (Map pp72-3; ☎ 71 347 015; ave Habib Bourguiba)

DANGERS & ANNOYANCES

Tunis is a safe city, though you should beware of pickpockets in the medina. The medina and Halfaouine district after dark are also not particularly salubrious.

TOP FIVE PLACES TO GET LOST

- Bin the map and wander around the warren surrounding the **Zaytouna Mosque** (opposite).
- Meander around the northwest medina close to **Mosque of Sidi Mehres** (p75) and out to Place Halfaouine.
- Take some wrong turns around the **Sidi Bou Saïd backstreets** (p96).
- Dive into olive-and-*harissa* (chilli paste) central – the buzzing area around Tunis' **Central Market** (p83).
- Walk from site to site in **Carthage** (p90), imagining away the glitzy suburb and following the footsteps of Dido, Aeneas and Hannibal.

Taxi Cons

The main annoyance for visitors to Tunis is the occasional unscrupulous taxi driver. You're most at risk from con-artists on arrival at the airport. Avoid unlicensed cabs, but be aware that licensed ones are sometimes prone to tricky dealings. A cab from the airport to the centre should cost around TD4 to TD7 (depending on the time of day – fares cost 50% more from 9pm to 5am). All use a meter, but some cabbies change this to increase the fare – sometimes by as much as TD20. It can also be confusing when you first arrive as the currency has so many digits – for example, a fare of TD3.5 will read 03,500. If you think you have been tricked, argue that the fare should be no more than TD8 to the centre and suggest that the driver double-checks this. If really rattled, you can take the taxi licence number and suggest that you will contact the police.

Scams

Occasionally you'll meet a helpful soul in the medina who will tell you that you're in luck and must hurry to a festival featuring an unmissable celebration of Berber craft. Following them to the festival, you will inevitably end up in an artisan or carpet shop. Even Paul Theroux, the been-everywhere travel writer, got caught out by this one, as he describes in *The Pillars of Hercules*.

SIGHTS & ACTIVITIES

The medina's tangled streets contain many major sights, but there's also the fantastic Bardo Museum in a northwest suburb (p50), and the ancient remains of Carthage (p90) and charming Sidi Bou Saïd (p96) outside the city to the north.

Medina

Once the medina *was* Tunis. It was founded by the Arabs in the 7th century. Nowadays, to go from the new town into its closely knit streets, packed with generations of palaces and monuments, is to enter a different world. The medina at Tunis is a listed Unesco World Heritage site.

A maze of tunnels and alleys dotted with hidden mansions, the medina's architecture is ideal for the climate, as the narrow streets are cool in summer and warm in winter. As space ran out, residents built upwards, constructing vaults and rooms above the streets. This gives the central lanes a subterranean feel, with shafts of sunlight filtering through. Apparently the vaults had to be built high enough to accommodate a loaded camel.

In the 19th century, the French developed the Ville Nouvelle, depriving the medina of its role. The city's great families began to leave their ancestral homes for suburban seaside pads, and the medina declined, housing rural people settling in the capital. *Zaouias* (the complexes surrounding a tomb of a saint) and palaces were converted to cope with the new arrivals. Today, less than 15,000 people live here, and the main trade is in souvenirs.

Large parts of the northern section were demolished in the 1930s and 1940s to clear the slums and improve vehicle access. Fortunately, the demolition days are long finished, and several organisations are devoted to conservation. The medina's most spruced-up area lies near Place du Gouvernement.

The arteries around the Zaytouna Mosque are packed with souvenir shops (with lots of lovely things to buy as well as trash). Away from these you will find arched winding streets, backstreet workshops, local markets and children playing football.

ZAYTOUNA (GREAT) MOSQUE

Everything in the medina leads to or from the **Zaytouna Mosque** (Map pp72-3; admission TD2; 🕙 non-Muslims 8am-2.30pm Thu-Tue). Zaytouna means 'olive tree' – it's said the founder, Hassan Ibn Nooman, conqueror of Byzantine Carthage, held lessons under a tree here.

Entering, it's impossible not to be awed by the calm of the open space after the busy souqs.

STEAM & SOCIABILITY

Three things, the older they are, the better they are: the well, the *hammam* and the friend.

Arab proverb

You haven't fully experienced Tunisia until you've been scrubbed down with an oven scourer by an enthusiastic elderly masseur. The oldest and most atmospheric *hammams* (public bathhouses) are in the medina, keeping residents steamed and cleaned. Often recognisable by their candy-striped red-and-green doorways and undecorated domes, they feel as if they haven't changed (or been cleaned) for hundreds of years. It's an amazingly exotic, sensual and relaxing experience. You'll need a towel, and you might want a scrubbing mitt, shampoo and soap. To avoid undue attention, be aware that people don't bathe naked, but wear their underwear (men wear shorts). It usually costs TD1, while a massage costs another TD1. There are bucketloads to choose from, but the following are all favourites:

El-Kachachine (Map pp72-3; 30 Souq des Libraires) One of the medina's finest; men only.
El-Methihra (Map pp72-3; 11 rue el-Methira) Friendly, ancient, small scale and tiled, with lots of places to lie down and recuperate. Women bathe in the afternoons, men in the evenings.
Sahib (Map pp72-3; place Halfaouine) This *hammam*, with echoing domed rooms, glorious and dilapidated, was immortalised in the film *Halfaouine*. Women bathe in the afternoons, men in the evenings.
Zitouni (Map pp72-3; rue des Juges) Women-only, clean, with a good hot room; it's newer and fresher than the others.

TUNIS MEDINA, HALFAOUINE & VILLE NOUVELLE

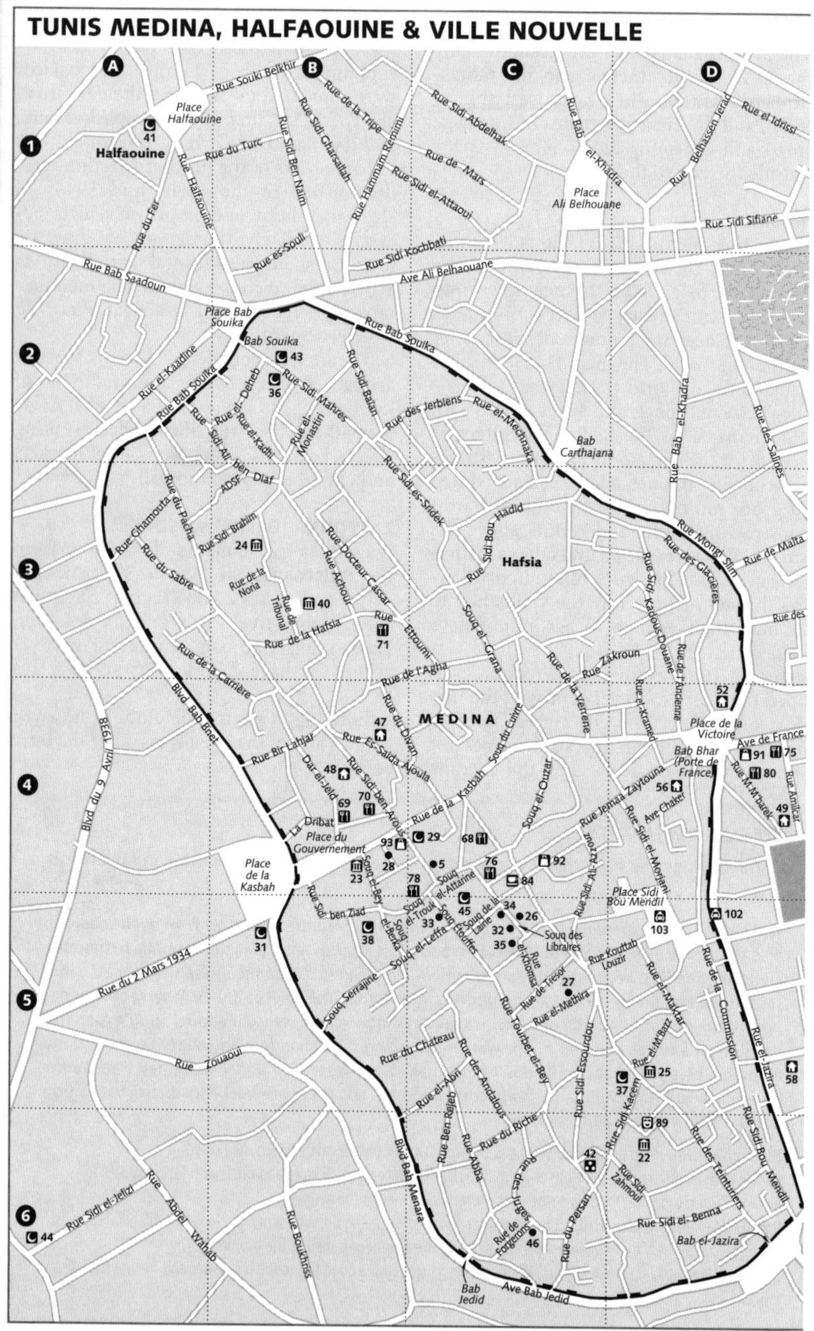

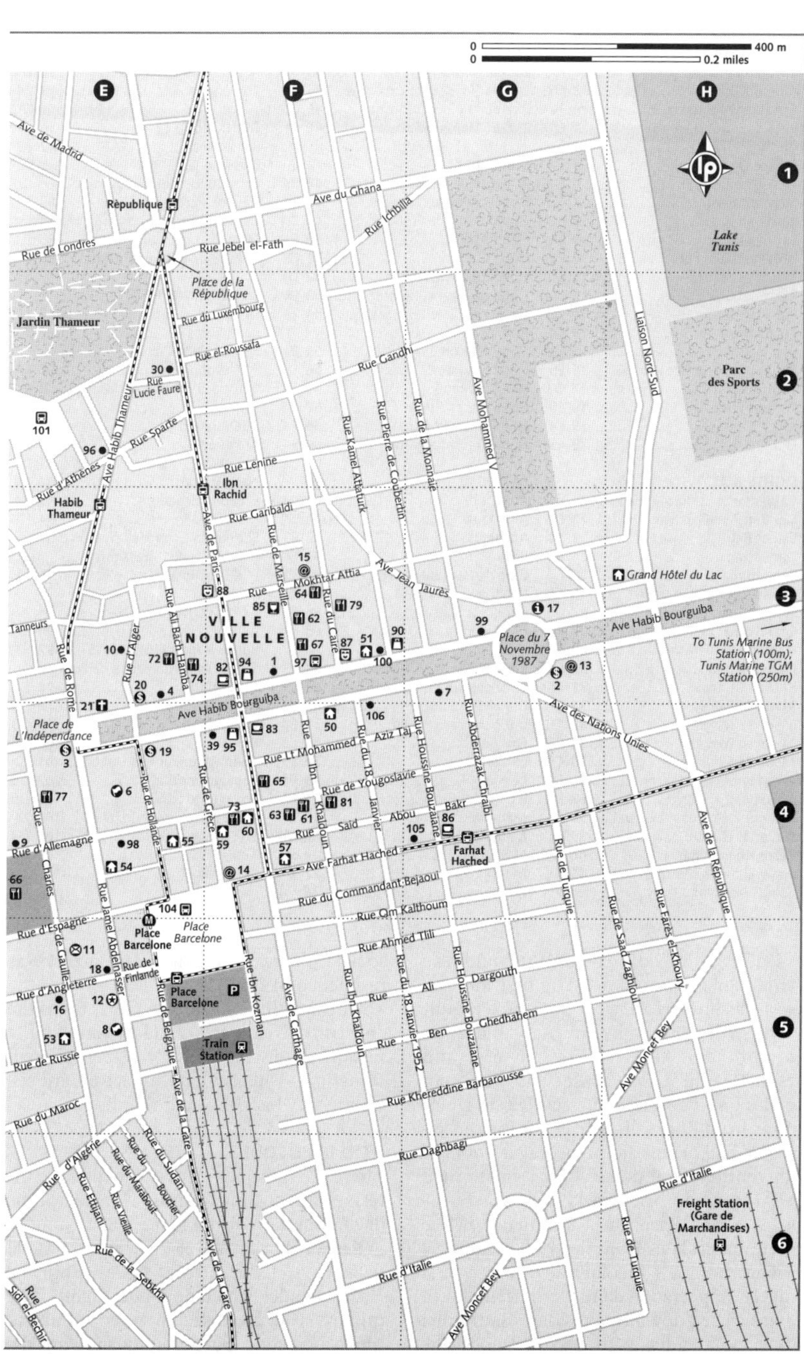
0 400 m
0 0.2 miles
E
F
G
H
1
2
3
4
5
6
Ave de Madrid
Rèpublique
Ave du Ghana
Rue Ichbilia
Lake Tunis
Rue de Londres
Rue Jebel el-Fath
Place de la République
Rue du Luxembourg
Jardin Thameur
Rue el-Roussafa
Rue Gandhi
Liaison Nord-Sud
Parc des Sports
Rue Lucie Faure
Ave Habib Thameur
Rue Sparte
Rue Lenine
Rue d'Athènes
Habib Thameur
Ibn Rachid
Rue Garibaldi
Rue Kamel Attaturk
Rue Pierre de Coubertin
Rue de la Monnaie
Ave Mohammed V
Ave de Paris
Rue de Marseille
Rue Mokhtar Attia
Ave Jean Jaurès
Grand Hôtel du Lac
VILLE NOUVELLE
Rue Ali Bach Hamba
Rue du Caire
Tanneurs
Rue de Rome
Rue d'Alger
Place du 7 Novembre 1987
Ave Habib Bourguiba
To Tunis Marine Bus Station (100m); Tunis Marine TGM Station (250m)
Ave des Nations Unies
Place de L'Indépendance
Rue Lt Mohammed Aziz Taj
Rue Ibn Khaldoun
Rue du 18 Janvier
Rue Houssine Bouzaiane
Rue Abderazak Chraibi
Rue de Hollande
Rue de Grèce
Rue de Yougoslavie
Rue Said Abou Bakr
Rue Charles de Gaulle
Rue d'Allemagne
Ave Farhat Hached
Farhat Hached
Rue de Turquie
Rue de Saad Zaghloul
Rue Farès el-Khoury
Ave de la République
Rue du Commandant Bejaoui
Rue Om Kalthoum
Rue Jamel Abdelnasser
Place Barcelone
Rue d'Espagne
Rue Ahmed Tlili
Rue de Finlande
Rue Ibn Kozman
Ave de Carthage
Rue Ibn Khaldoun
Rue du 18 Janvier 1952
Rue Houssine Bouzaiane
Rue d'Angleterre
Rue Ali Dargouth
Rue de Belgique
Rue Ben Ghedhahem
Ave Moncef Bey
Train Station
Rue de Russie
Ave de la Gare
Rue Khereddine Barbarousse
Rue du Maroc
Rue du Sudan
Rue Daghbagi
Rue d'Algérie
Rue du Boucher
Rue du Marabout
Rue Ettijani
Rue Vieille
Rue d'Italie
Freight Station (Gare de Marchandises)
Rue de la Sebkha
Rue Sidi el-Bechir
1
2
3
4
6
7
8
9
10
11
12
13
14
15
16
17
18
19
20
21
30
39
50
51
53
54
55
57
59
60
61
62
63
64
65
66
67
72
73
74
77
79
81
82
83
85
86
87
88
90
94
95
96
97
98
99
100
101
104
105
106

INFORMATION
Al-Kitab **1** F3
Amen **2** G3
Banque de l'Habitat (see 94)
BIAT **3** E4
Carthage Tours **4** E3
Espace Diwan 9 **5** C4
French Embassy **6** E4
Interior Ministry **7** G3
Italian Embassy **8** E5
Lavarie Tahar **9** E4
Librairie Claire Fontaine **10** E3
Main Post Office **11** E5
Police **12** E5
Publinet **13** G3
Publinet **14** F4
Publinet **15** F3
Second-hand Bookshop **16** E5
Tourist Office **17** G3
Tunisie Telecom **18** E5
UBCI **19** E4
UIB **20** E3

SIGHTS & ACTIVITIES
Cathedral of St Vincent de Paul **21** E4
Dar Ben Abdallah Museum **22** D6
Dar el-Bey **23** B4
Dar Lasram **24** B3
Dar Othman **25** D5
El-Kachachine Hammam **26** C5
El-Methihra Hammam **27** C5
Grand Souq des Chechias **28** B4
Hamuda Pasha Mosque **29** C4
Hôtel Majestic **30** E2
Kasbah Mosque **31** B5
Medersa Bachia **32** C5
Medersa Mouradia **33** C5
Medersa Palmier **34** C5
Medersa Slimania **35** C5
Mosque of Sidi Mahres **36** B2
Mosque of the Dyers **37** D5
Mosque of Youssef Dey **38** B5
National Theatre **39** F4
Palais Khereddine **40** B3
Sahib El-Tabía Mosque **41** A1
Sahib Hammam (see 41)
Tourbet el-Bey **42** C6
Zaouia of Sidi Mahres **43** B2
Zaouia Sidi Kacem Ezzilizi **44** A6
Zaytouna (Great) Mosque **45** C5
Zitouni Hammam **46** C6

SLEEPING
Auberge de Jeunesse **47** B4
Dar El-Medina **48** B4
Grand Hôtel de France **49** D4
Hôtel Africa **50** F4
Hôtel Carlton **51** F3
Hôtel de la Medina **52** D4
Hôtel de l'Agriculture **53** E5
Hôtel de Suisse **54** E4
Hôtel Excel (see 51)
Hôtel Maison Dorée **55** E4
Hôtel Marhaba **56** D4
Hôtel Omrane **57** F4
Hôtel rue de Russie **58** D5
Hôtel Salammbô **59** F4
Hôtel Transatlantique **60** F4

EATING
Abid **61** F4
Al-Mazar (see 67)
Andalous **62** F3
Bolero **63** F4
Café de Paris Brasserie (see 83)
Capitole (see 83)
Capri **64** F3
Carcassonne **65** F4
Central Market **66** E4
Chez Nous **67** F3
Dar Bel Hadj **68** C4
Dar el-Jeld **69** B4
Dar Hamouda Pacha **70** B4
Fast Food **71** B3
Le Carthage **72** E3
Le Malouf **73** F4
L'Orient **74** E3
Magasin Général **75** D4
Mahdaoui **76** C4
Margaritas (see 55)
Monoprix **77** E4
M'Rabet **78** C4
Neptune **79** F3
Restaurante Les 3 Étoiles **80** D4
Tontonville **81** F4

DRINKING
Bar Jamaica **82** F3
Brasserie Les 2 Avenues (see 82)
Café Chaoechin (see 28)
Café de Paris **83** F4
Café Ez-Zitouna **84** C4
Oscars **85** F3
Théatre de l'Etoile du Nord **86** G4

ENTERTAINMENT
La Pamasse **87** F3
Le Colisée (see 94)
Maison de la Culture Ibn Khaldoun **88** F3
Théatre d'Art Ben Abdallah **89** D6

SHOPPING
Antique Shop **90** F3
Delma **91** D4
Hanout Arab **92** C4
Labedi Apiculture **93** B4
Mains des Femmes **94** F3
Société de Commercialisation des Produits de l'Artisanats (SOCOPA) **95** F4

TRANSPORT
Air France **96** E2
Bus to Airport (35) **97** F3
Compagnie Tunisienne de Navigation (CTN) **98** E4
EgyptAir (see 82)
Europcar **99** G3
Hertz **100** F3
Jardin Thameur Bus Station **101** E2
Louages for Algeria **102** D5
Louages to Libya **103** D5
Place Barcelone Bus Station **104** E4
SNCM **105** G4
Tunisair **106** F4
Tunisiana (see 106)

Dating from various eras, the building's remarkably harmonious. The first mosque here was built in AD 734, but it was rebuilt in the 9th century by the Aghlabid ruler Ibrahim ibn Ahmed (AD 856–63), and resembles the Great Mosque in Kairouan in design. The builders recycled 184 columns from Roman Carthage for the central prayer hall. The adjoining prayer room is 9th century. The dome, with its patterned red-and-white brickwork, shows a European – even Byzantine – influence, while the minaret dates from the 19th century.

The mosque's theological faculty was a hugely important Islamic university until it was closed down by President Bourguiba after independence to try to reduce the social influence of religion. The faculty was re-opened in 1987.

Non-Muslims are allowed in as far as the courtyard. Nearby shops allow views of the mosque from their roof terraces, though sometimes you also have to face a hard sell on the way back through the shop.

OTHER MOSQUES

There are mosques all over the medina; interiors are off-limits to non-Muslims. Some of the finest are listed here.

Kasbah Mosque (Map pp72-3; place de la Kasbah) dates from 1235 and was once within the Hafsid citadel, which no longer stands. The minaret's lozenge design pays tribute to Moroccan style, purposefully showing the

Hafsids' links with the Almohad strand of Islam. It was hugely influential, serving as a model for the Zaytouna Mosque minaret. The call to prayer is quietly signalled by a white flag.

Mosque of Youssef Dey (Map pp72-3; Souq el-Berka) was Tunis' first Ottoman-style mosque (1616), designed by Andalusian architect Ibn Ghalib in a colourful mishmash of styles. It was surrounded by Turkish souqs – El-Trouk (tailors), El-Berka (slaves) and El-Bechamkia (slippers) and catered to the Turkish traders. Look out for the minaret crowned with a miniature green-tiled pyramid – this was the first, much-copied octagonal minaret in Tunis, serving as propaganda for the new masters. The mosque contains the tombs of Youssef Dey and his family – another innovative Ottoman custom.

Hamuda Pasha Mosque (Map pp72-3; rue Sidi ben Arous) is a 17th-century, harmonious, richly decorated building that reflects the prosperity of the times. Its witch's-hat minaret is octagonal – typical of the Turkish Hanefite strand of Islam.

Mosque of Sidi Mahres (Map pp72-3; rue Sidi Mahres), built in 1692, is named after Tunis' patron saint, who saved the city after it was captured by Abu Yazd during a rebellion against Fatimid rule in AD 944. He also allowed Jews to settle within the walls, and reorganised the souqs. His tomb lies opposite the entrance, in the **Zaouia of Sidi Mahres**. The mosque is ranked as one of the city's finest Ottoman buildings, with a cluster of white domes resembling a heap of eggs. But there's something missing. It's the minaret – never added as the project ran into difficulties following 17th-century political upheaval. Women come here to pray to be endowed with a husband or children. The surrounding busy local souqs are an interesting place for a wander and for picking up cheap pottery.

Mosque of the Dyers (Map pp72-3; rue des Teinturiers) was built in 1716 by Hussein ben Ali, founder of the Husseinite line of beys (provincial governors). It has an adjoining *medersa* (Quranic school), and another Ottoman octagonal minaret. Hussein buried two holy men in the mausoleum, leaving a space between them for his own tomb, but his nephew Ali Pasha drove him from power and buried his own father in Hussein's spot.

Sahib El-Tabía Mosque (Map pp72-3; place Halfaouine) dates from the 19th century, when Halfaouine was an emerging fashionable quarter. It forms part of Tunis' only *külliye* – a *medersa,* souq, *hammam* and tomb complex. It's almost Venetian looking; the railings and black marble were imported from the continent. The minaret was only added in 1970.

MEDERSAS

Medersas are schools for study of the Quran. They declined in the late 19th century when broader education came into vogue. The following fine examples – mostly still used as schools – are clustered around the Zaytouna Mosque.

With an ornately studded door, the **Medersa Mouradia** (Map pp72-3; 37 Souq Étouffes; admission free; 9am-4.30pm Mon-Sat Sep-Jun) was built in 1673 by Mourad II, son of Husseinite bey Ali Pasha, on the ruins of a Turkish barracks destroyed during a rebellion. It's used to train apprentices in traditional crafts.

Medersa Palmier (Map pp72-3; 11 Souq des Libraires; closed to public), still a Quranic school, was constructed in 1714 on the site of a *funduq* (travellers' inn) and named after a long-gone tree. Identify it by its yellow studded door.

Ali Pasha built **Medersa Slimania** (Map pp72-3; cnr Souq des Libraires & Souq el-Kachachine; 9.30am-4.30pm Mon-Sat) in 1754, a marvel of stucco and tiling, to commemorate his son Suleiman, poisoned by his brother. Once a Quranic school for girls, it now houses an association of former students.

The 1752 **Medersa Bachia** (Map pp72-3; 19 Souq des Libraires) has what was once a small public fountain beside the entrance. Also constructed by Ali Pasha, it now houses an artisans' school.

SOUQS

The medina markets were organised into different commercial areas. Refined trades surrounded the Zaytouna Mosque, while dirtier businesses such as tanners or blacksmiths stayed on the outskirts. The markets are either named after their traditional trade or their founding community, such as **Souq el-Grana** – the Livornese Jews' Souq.

The main markets include the **Souq el-Attarine** – the Perfume Makers' Souq, dating from the 13th century, near the Zaytouna Mosque. Today it's largely souvenirs, but there are plenty of essential oils too. The quilted satin baskets on sale are for wedding gifts. Also leading from the mosque is the 13th-century **Souq des Libraires**, the Booksellers' Souq, lined with *medersas* and a *hammam* (p71).

Souq el-Attarine leads into the **Souq el-Trouk**, the Turkish Souq – traditionally the tailors' souq, and still selling some outfits among the souvenirs.

Souq Étouffes runs alongside the mosque, and was once the elegant cloth market, wide, with green-and-red striped columns; it still sells cloth and clothes.

Also close to the mosque, the narrow **Souq de la Laine**, the Wool Souq, is now packed with silver shops. North of here, barrel-vaulted **Souq el-Berka** dates from Ottoman times: this was the slave souq where prisoners of Muslim corsairs (pirates) were brought, sometimes from the prison at La Goulette, to be sold from a wooden block. When piracy dwindled, the human market was supplied by sub-Saharan Africa. The trade was abolished in 1846 and it's now a goldsmith's market.

One of the biggest souqs is the **Grand Souq des Chechias** (Map pp72–3), northeast of the mosque, where dusty shopfronts are brimful with blood-red hats, and you can see them being shaped and hammered. In the 17th century, this was one of Tunisia's biggest industries. A million red-felt skullcaps, used originally as the basis for building a turban, were made annually by 15,000 craftsmen, and exported worldwide.

MUSEUMS, MAUSOLEUMS, MONUMENTS & PALACES

Bab Bhar, also called the Porte de France or French Gate, is a huge freestanding arch that was the medina's eastern gateway until the surrounding walls were demolished by the French to create place de la Victoire.

The **Tourbet el-Bey** (Map pp72-3; admission TD2, plus camera TD1; 🕒 9.30am-4.30pm) has the green fish-scale domes typical of mausoleums. Inside is a mishmash of tiles and intricate stucco, built during Ali Pasha II's reign (1758–82). Many subsequent Husseinite beys, princesses, ministers and trusted advisers ended up here. The male tombs are topped with strange, anonymous marble renditions of their preferred headgear, be it turban or *chechia* (small, red, felt hat), with the number of tassels showing their importance. The enthusiastic, French-speaking guardian is knowledgeable.

Built in 1796, one of the medina's finest former palaces houses the **Dar Ben Abdallah Museum** (Centre for Popular Arts & Traditions; Map pp72-3; Impasse Ben Abdallah; admission TD2, plus camera TD1; 🕒 9.30am-4.30pm Mon-Sat), a chance to imagine how the wealthy lived within the medina. It belonged to a high-ranking officer, and had a 19th-century makeover in fashionable Italianate style. Four of the rooms have been used to create scenes of 19th-century bourgeois life, including tea drinking and wedding preparations. There's a café opposite, see p84.

Dar Lasram (Map pp72-3; 24 rue de Tribunal; admission free; 🕒 8.30am-1pm & 3-5.30pm Mon-Sat) is another magnificent mansion. From the 18th century, the Lasram family provided the beys with scribes. Today it's home to the Association de Sauvegarde de la Medina, which oversees medina conservation. The interior has magnificent intensely tiled rooms and courtyards, and medina maps, plans and photographs.

Palais Khereddine (Map pp72-3; ☎ 564 110; place du Tribunal; admission free; 🕒 10am-7pm Mon-Sat) is on a pretty, palm-shaded square. This 19th-century palace, later split to house two schools – one for Jews, one for Muslims – is grandly named the Museum of Tunis, and hosts some excellent free, art exhibitions.

Dar Othman (Map pp72-3; rue el-M'Bazz) was built by Othman Dey in the early 17th century. His business – piracy – was obviously lucrative, and he also happened to be Governor of Tunis. The palace is a wonderful example of period architecture, distinguished by its exuberantly busy façade. Some rooms are now offices (some to the Conservation de la Medina organisation), but you are welcome to visit the courtyards. The unusual interior garden was planted in 1936.

Dar el-Bey (Map pp72-3; Place du Gouvernement; 🕒 closed to public) was the Husseinite rulers' city pad, but the beys preferred the Bardo, so it was used as an official guesthouse until 1881, when the French arrived.

Zaouia Sidi Kacem Ezzilizi (Map pp72-3; rue Sidi el Jelizi; 🕒 8am-6pm Tue-Sun) is the tomb of an Andalusian craftsman who's credited with bringing tile-making to Tunis. The restored building has some beautiful Tunisian ceramics, ranging from medieval to modern.

Ville Nouvelle

The Ville Nouvelle is an entirely different city, with tall shuttered windows, wrought-iron balconies, cafés and pâtisseries. There are some fine examples of colonial architecture, ranging from the exuberant to the bizarre.

Cathedral of St Vincent de Paul (Map pp72-3; place de l'Indépendance) sits comfortably in the bizarre camp. This custard-coloured 1883 cathedral melds Gothic, Byzantine and Moorish elements. There are regular masses in French and Italian and it's open variable hours.

The **statue** opposite the cathedral is of Ibn Khaldun, the great Tunis-born Islamic teacher and philosopher – many of his ideas, such as the cyclical nature of history, were way ahead of his time.

Fabulously ornate façades dot the city. Supreme examples include the Art Nouveau **National Theatre** (Map pp72-3; ave Habib Bourguiba), built by the French in 1902, which has a meringue-sculpted frontage that looks as if you could crack it off and eat it. The **Hôtel Majestic** (Map pp72-3; 36 ave de Paris) is another splendid almost-edible confection – currently closed for renovation, though not a lot seems to be happening.

Other grand structures, such as the neoclassical **main post office** (Map pp72-3; rue Charles de Gaulle), built in 1893, and **French embassy** (Map pp72-3; place de l'Indépendance, ave Habib Bourguiba), built in 1856, were designed for the colonial power to assert its authority.

Resembling a much younger cousin of London's Big Ben, a burnished metal **clock tower** forms a glimmering landmark to wards the western end of ave Habib Bourguiba. It was erected to commemorate Independence Day (7 November).

Beaches

Access the Tunis beaches via TGM from Tunis Marine station (Map p68). La Marsa is the best, and less crowded than those at La Goulette, Sidi Bou Saïd and Carthage (but note the patch nearest the president's palace at Carthage is quite pristine).

Thalassotherapy

Thalassotherapy is Greek for sea treatment, and describes a range of therapies that use seawater to detoxify and relieve joint pain. Near Tunis you can indulge in myriad treatments at reasonable prices at the La Residence's luxurious spa (see p99).

WALKING TOUR

This tour takes in the medina's main sights, and the area's best cafés are marked on the map so you can stop for breaks on the way.

Start at the **Bab Bhar** (**1**; opposite). Note rue des Glaciéres, leading off right – this is where huge blocks of Alpine ice for sale were stored in the 18th and 19th centuries. To the left of the road, on the square, is the **former British Embassy (2)**, used for filming scenes from the *English Patient*. The embassy moved to a more secure setting in 2004. From here head along rue Jemaa Zaytouna, the main tourist drag, where nestled between the stuffed camels are jewellery, ceramics, glassware and eager shopkeepers. Near the top, at number 73, you'll pass the fine **National Library (3)**, once a barracks, built in 1814 by Hamouda Bey to house Berber soldiers who'd been recruited after an Ottoman mutiny. Next, head to the **Zaytouna Mosque** (**4**; p71). Amble southwards along **Souq des Libraires** (**5**; opposite). The western side is lined with **medersas** (**6**; p75) formerly linked to the Zaytouna Mosque theological faculty. Carry on along rue el-Khomsa, packed with carpentry workshops, then turn right at rue de Tresor and go south along rue des Teinturiers – street of the dyers. On the corner is the extravagant **Mosque of the Dyers** (**7**; p75).

Opposite, an archway leads to rue el-M'Bazz and **Dar Othman** (**8**; opposite).

Bear right along rue Sidi Kacem and you'll hit the **Dar Ben Abdallah Museum** (**9**; opposite). Further on are the green fish-scale domes of the **Tourbet el-Bey** (**10**; opposite). From here head north along rue Tourbet el-Bey. If you like, make a detour, turning left down rue des Juges, then right along **rue des Forgerons (11)** – the blacksmiths' street – full of noisy dark forges and smoke-blackened workers. A right at the end will take you to **Bab Jedid (12)**, one of three gates built by the Hafsids, and the only one still standing.

Retrace your steps back to the main route, following rue Tourbet el-Bey; at No 41 is the **Mosque of M'sed el-Kobba (13)**, aka Kuttab Ibn Khaldoun (a *kuttab* is a Quranic primary school). The famous historian Ibn Khaldun (1332–1406) was born at No 33 and

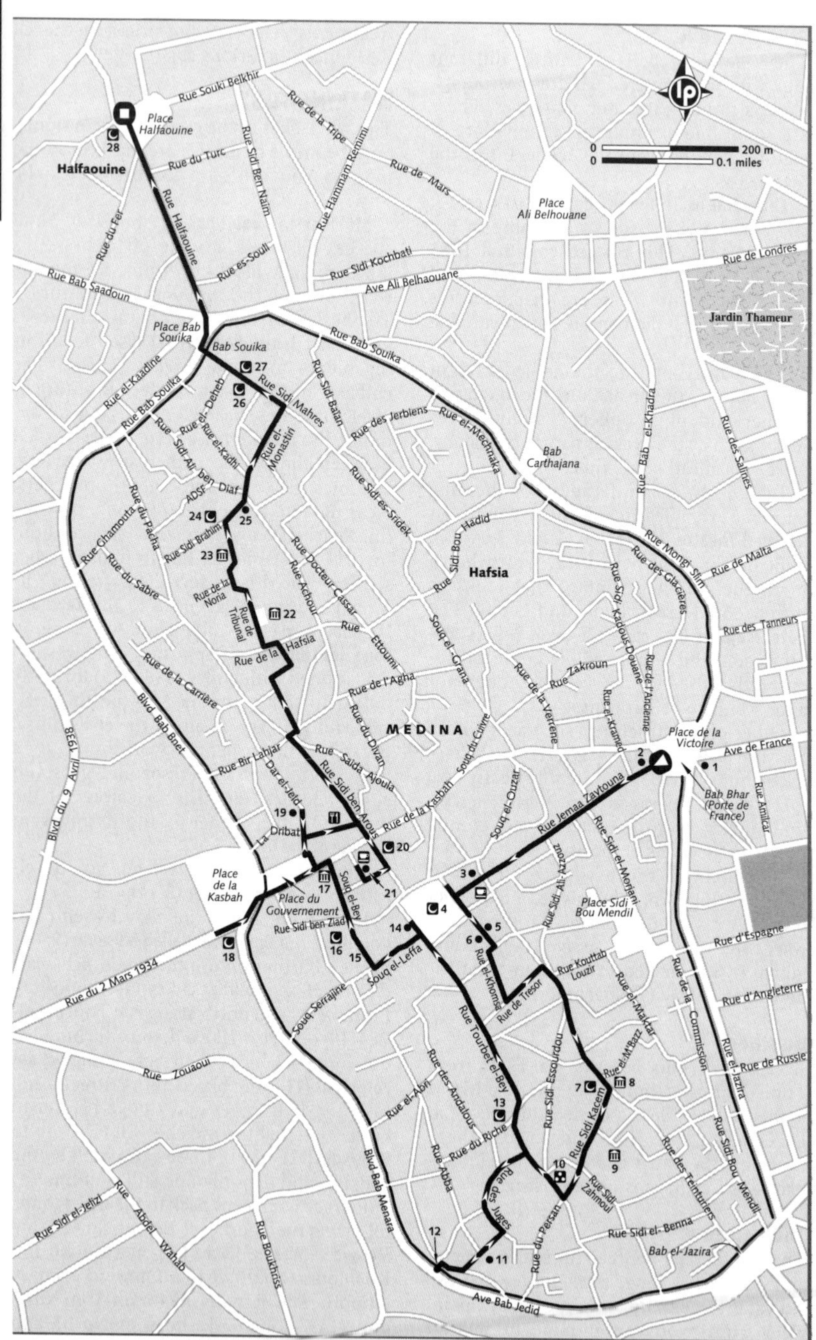
200 m
0.1 miles
Place Halfaouine
Halfaouine
Rue Souki Belkhir
Rue du Turc
Rue Sidi Ben Naim
Rue de la Tripe
Rue Hammam Remimi
Rue de Mars
Place Ali Belhouane
Rue Halfaouine
Rue du Fer
Rue es-Soull
Rue Sidi Kochbati
Ave Ali Belhaouane
Rue de Londres
Rue Bab Saadoun
Jardin Thameur
Place Bab Souika
Bab Souika
Rue Bab Souika
Rue Sidi Mahres
Rue el-Kaadine
Rue el-Deheb
Rue el-Kadhi
Rue el-Monastiri
Rue Sidi Baian
Rue des Jerbiens
Rue el-Mechnaka
Bab Carthajana
Rue Bab el-Khadra
Rue des Salines
Rue Sidi Ali ben Diaf
ADSF
Rue Gharnouta
Rue du Pacha
Rue Sidi Brahim
Rue Sidi es-Sridek
Rue Sidi Bou Hadid
Hafsia
Rue Mongi Slim
Rue des Glacières
Rue de Malta
Rue Sidi Kadous
Rue du Sabre
Rue de la Noria
Rue de Tribunal
Rue Docteur Cassar
Rue Achour
Rue Ettoumi
Souq el-Grana
Rue des Tanneurs
Rue de la Hafsia
Rue de la Carrière
Rue de l'Agha
Rue Zakroun
Rue de la Verrerie
Rue Douane
Rue de l'Ancienne
Rue el-Kramed
Blvd Bab Bnet
Rue du Divan
MEDINA
Souq du Cuivre
Place de la Victoire
Ave de France
Blvd du 9 Avril 1938
Rue Bir Lahjar
Dar el-Jeld
Rue Saida Ajoula
Rue Sidi ben Arous
Rue de la Kasbah
Souq el-Ouzar
Rue Jemaa Zaytouna
Bab Bhar (Porte de France)
Rue Amilcar
La Dribat
Rue Sidi el-Morjani
Rue Sidi Ali Azzouz
Place de la Kasbah
Place du Gouvernement
Souq el-Bey
Rue Sidi ben Ziad
Place Sidi Bou Mendil
Rue d'Espagne
Rue du 2 Mars 1934
Souq el-Leffa
Rue el-Khomsa
Rue de Tresor
Rue Kouttab Louzir
Rue el-Maktar
Rue de la Commission
Rue d'Angleterre
Souq Serrajine
Rue Tourbet el-Bey
Rue Sidi Essourdou
Rue el-M'Bazz
Rue Sidi Kacem
Rue de Russie
Rue el-Jazira
Rue Zouaoui
Rue el-Abri
Rue des Andalous
Rue du Riche
Rue Abba
Rue des Juges
Rue Sidi Zahmoul
Rue des Teinturiers
Rue Sidi Bou Mendil
Blvd Bab Menara
Rue Sidi el-Jelizi
Rue Abdel Wahab
Rue Boukhriss
Rue du Persan
Rue Sidi el-Benna
Bab el-Jazira
Ave Bab Jedid
1
2
3
4
5
6
7
8
9
10
11
12
13
14
15
16
17
18
19
20
21
22
23
24
25
26
27
28

WALK FACTS

Start place de la Victoire
Finish place Halfaouine
Distance 2.5km
Duration two to three hours

taught briefly at the mosque before leaving for Cairo. When you reach the Zaytouna Mosque again, you'll see **Medersa Mouradia** (**14**; see p75), then turn southwest along Souq el-Leffa. Along this street several shops allow access to their rooftops for great views.

Next, turn north along **Souq el-Berka** (**15**; p76). You'll see the **Mosque of Youssef Dey** (**16**; p75). Nose out along Souq el-Bey, with more jewellery shops, and you'll come out at the peaceful Place du Gouvernement, surrounded by government buildings. The **Dar el-Bey** (**17**; p76), is on the south side, and to the west is place de la Kasbah – the kasbah itself was destroyed by the French in 1883 and all that remains is the **Kasbah Mosque** (**18**; p74).

Take Dar el-Jeld northwards and you can visit immaculately restored **Le Diwan (19)**, an 18th-century mansion that's now an upmarket craft shop and banqueting hall. This corner of the medina is particularly kempt, with whitewashed façades, trailing flowers and big studded doors indicating wealthy houses. Nip back up Dar el-Jeld and take a left after its eponymous huge-doored restaurant. Head down the pretty little alley, to reach rue Sidi ben Arous. Turn right. You'll see the **Hamuda Pasha Mosque** (**20**; p75).

Now, it's time you bought one of those traditional red-felt hats favoured by comedians and elderly men. Turn right into the **Grand Souq des Chechias** (**21**; p76). After some age-old sales pitch, carry back along rue Sidi ben Arous. When you reach a junction turn right and then almost immediately left, continuing north, following the lanes till you pass **Palais Khereddine** (**22**; p76), then continue straight, passing **Dar Lasram** (**23**; p76) on your left. When you reach rue Sidi Brahim, turn right. You will pass the **Zaouia of Sidi Ibrahim Riahi (24)**, a Sufi teacher from Testour, on your left. Follow the road straight, passing the 17th-century **Medersa el-Achouria (25)** on your right, until you reach rue Sidi Mahres. Turning left, you will plunge into a street packed with busy local souqs, surrounding the **Mosque of Sidi Mahres** (**26**; p75) and **Zaouia of Sidi Mahres** (**27**; p75). Coming out of the medina onto place Bab Souika, take rue Halfaouine as far as **Sahib El-Tabía Mosque** (**28**; p75). You are well away from the tourist hordes now, in one of Tunis' most colourful local districts – take the chance to do some aimless wandering.

COURSES

Language

Institut Bourguiba des Langues Vivantes (Map p69; ☎ 71 832 418; www.iblv.rnu.tn; 47 ave de la Liberté) Beginners' and advanced courses in Modern and Tunisian Arabic. A one-month course in July or August costs TD480.

Langue Arabe pour Étrangers (Arabic for Foreigners; ☎ 71 845 892; www.arabic-tunisia.freeservers.com; 6 rue de Rhodes Mutuelleville) Offers intensive (four hours daily for 12 days; €350) beginners', intermediate and advanced Modern Arabic courses all year.

Université Libre de Tunis (ULT; ☎ 71 890 391; www.ult-eil.org; Faculté des Arts, des Lettres et des Sciences Humaines, 30 ave Kheireddine Pacha) Private university offers 80-/240-hour Modern Arabic courses costing €600/1800.

Dance

During winter, the École Serguei Diaghilev de Ballet et Danse Classique at the **Centre Russe** (Map p69; ☎ 71 780 953; ave de la Liberté) gives lessons in classical and Tunisian dance.

TUNIS FOR CHILDREN

If there's one thing Tunisians like more than *harissa* it's children, and having little ones along with you will ensure you lots of smiles and local contact. And as Tunis is so laid-back and small, it's an easy place to be with kids. There's quick access to beaches if sightseeing seems too much like hard work.

The entertaining **Dah Dah Happy Land Park** (Map p68; ☎ 71 860 888; ave Principal, Berges de Lac; 1 ticket TD0.5, 12 tickets TD5; 🕒 6pm-1am) is an amusement park with lots of rides. It's part of the developing, trendy district of Berges de Lac, and there's a lively corniche (coastal road) to wander up and down. A taxi from the centre costs about TD3.5.

Tunis Zoo (Map p69; ☎ 71 841 540; Parc du Belvedere; adult/child TD0.5/0.3; 🕒 9am-4.30pm Tue-Sun Oct-Mar, to 7.30pm Apr-Sep) is another child-friendly hit, in a shady, peaceful park with some interesting animals including monkeys and colourful parrots, though cages look cramped.

Children will enjoy the colourful medina souqs, and can be bribed with stuffed camels, though be aware that the main drags can get very crowded and pushchairs are difficult to manoeuvre (your shoulders are a better option). Some will enjoy a short dose of the **Bardo Museum** (see p50) with its Roman mosaics – the pictures tell stories and feature lots of animals, and the **Dar Ben Abdallah Museum** (p76) with its waxwork figures. A great place is **Sidi Bou Saïd** (p96), with its relaxing pace, marina, beach and elaborate mansions. In Carthage there's a small beach and the **Oceanographic Museum** (p95) with an aquarium. If you stay in either of these tranquil suburbs, you'll have an easy walk to the beach. For more on beaches see p77.

If all else fails, the upmarket hotels usually provide babysitting services.

TOURS

Tours of Tunis can easily be arranged at the coastal resorts, but are difficult to set up within the city. However, if you want to go on a tour encompassing the medina, Bardo Museum, Carthage and Sidi Bou Saïd (a daunting amount for one day so you be better of by choosing just two of these), contact **Carthage Tours** (Map pp72-3; ☎ 71 344 066; 1st fl, 2 rue Ali Bach Hamba; 🕑 8am-6pm Mon-Sat), which can arrange a private car for around TD200 with guide for four people. They also arrange a three-day tour to the Sahara (TD230 per person) but be warned that this tour will entail a long drive there and back.

FESTIVALS & EVENTS

There's a **medina festival**, featuring live traditional music, during Ramadan (see p292).

Other festivals take place in Carthage (see p95) and Sidi Bou Saïd (see p97). You'll find information about these festivals in the local press or at the tourist office.

SLEEPING

Tunis offers wide-ranging accommodation for all budgets. Most of the top-end places are out of the centre or in the northern suburbs – see under Carthage (p96), Sidi Bou Saïd (p97), La Marsa (p98) and Gammarth (p99) for more details. For apartment rental, see p285.

Medina & Halfaouine

The medina is an exciting place to stay, with an excellent youth hostel and one beautiful four-star. Otherwise it mainly contains budget hotels, many of which include six-legged friends and a soundtrack of bodily functions in the price.

BUDGET

Auberge de Jeunesse (Map pp72-3; ☎ 71 567 850; 25 rue Es-Saida Ajoula; dm incl breakfast TD8) In the thick of the medina, this occupies the 18th-century Dar Saida Ajoula palace and has single-sex dorms. It has plenty of regulations (closed 10am to 2pm, a 10pm curfew, no showers between 7.30pm and 9am). However, it's still a bargain: clean, and the large dorm has fine murals.

Hôtel Marhaba (Map pp72-3; ☎ 71 327 605; 5 rue de la Commission; s/d with shared bathroom TD12/15, tr/q with bathroom TD30/40) With a great medina-side location, this place is central and clean. It has narrow, iron-framed lumpy beds, is always busy (favoured by Tunisian families) and is fine for lone women. Avoid a room close to a bathroom as the acoustics can be unpleasant. Hot showers cost TD1.

Hôtel de la Medina (Map pp72-3; ☎ 71 327 497; 1 rue des Glaciéres; r with shared bathroom TD15) Many of the spartan, whitewashed, blue-shuttered rooms here have great views over the square. This has a hostel-like feel, is OK for lone women, and has cleanish showers (TD1).

TOP END

our pick Dar El-Medina (Map pp72-3; ☎ 71 563 022; www.darelmedina.com; 64 rue Sidi ben Arous; r TD170, larger r TD220; ❄) There's nowhere like this in Tunis, a converted 19th-century medina mansion. Run by the family who have lived here for generations, it has been beautifully converted, in a simple mix of traditional and contemporary style. All rooms are different. Downstairs includes an elaborately stuccoed and painted salon and the converted kitchen, also now a sitting room. From the multilevel roof terrace you can hear the evening call to prayer echo across the city.

Ville Nouvelle

The Ville Nouvelle contains most of the midrange, faded-colonial French hotels, characterised by tall ceilings, balconies and good value, and there are numerous lusher, newer places.

BUDGET

Hôtel de Suisse (Map pp72-3; ☎ 71 323 821; 5 rue de Suisse; s/d with shower TD10/20) The rooms here are spartan but reasonably clean, with showers in a corner alcove. The 1st-floor rooms have balconies so low that you are almost on street level. Don't leave valuables in your room here.

Grand Hôtel de France (Map pp72-3; ☎ 71 326 244; hotelfrancetunis@yahoo.fr; 8 rue Mustapha Mbarek; s/d with shared bathroom TD17/23, with bathroom TD19/27, with air-con TD24/32; ❄) Airy and light, with lashings of colonial faded elegance, this has tiling details and lots of wrought iron. Ask for a room with balcony – those at the back overlook a leafy inner courtyard.

MIDRANGE

Hôtel Transatlantique (Map pp72-3; ☎ 71 240 680; 106 rue de Yougoslavie; s/d with shared bathroom TD20/28, with private bathroom TD29/35) This hotel is distinguished by elaborate tiling in the reception. The assorted, slightly ramshackle rooms are plain and clean, with high ceilings, shutters and lots of light. Beds are hardish and doubles small.

Hôtel de l'Agriculture (Map pp72-3; ☎ 71 326 394; 25 rue Charles de Gaulle; s/d TD25/35) Rooms here are pokey, but clean and bright, decorated in blue and white, with neat little bathrooms. Management is friendly and there's a *salon de thé* (teahouse) attached.

Hôtel Salammbô (Map pp72-3; ☎ 71 350 732; hotel.salammbo@gnet.tn; 6 rue de Grèce; s with shared shower/private bathroom TD18/30, d with shared/private bathroom TD27/36; ❄) Salammbô has spic-and-span, basic rooms. The cheaper they are, the more stairs you have to climb; pricier rooms have air-conditioning (cheaper ones have a fan). Some have balconies, and staff are friendly and efficient. The double beds are small.

Hôtel Maison Dorée (Map pp72-3; ☎ 71 240 632; 3 rue el-Koufa; s/d with shower TD27.50/35, with private bathroom TD33/43, with air-con TD38/46; ❄) Maison Dorée is charming: simple and spotless with an old-fashioned, French-feeling formality. Most of its rooms (varied in shape and atmosphere; ask to see a couple) have shuttered balconies and comforting, polished-wood, 1950s furnishings; the restaurant is also good.

Hôtel rue de Russie (Map pp72-3; ☎ 71 328 883; 18 rue de Russie; s/d TD35/50; ❄) Despite the unbothered reception, this is good value with smartish rooms that have busily pattern-tiled bathrooms. Ask for one overlooking the street or the interior courtyard.

Hôtel Carlton (Map pp72-3; ☎ 71 330 644; www.hotelcarltontunis.com; 31 ave Habib Bourguiba; s/d/tr TD57/83/98; ❄) This small, well-maintained three-star hotel has plain rooms with satellite TV. Spa treatments are available. Rooms at the front have balconies with views over Tunis' main drag.

Hôtel Excel (Map pp72-3; ☎ 71 355 161; 35 ave Habib Bourguiba; s/d with private bathroom TD50/70; ❄) Next door to the Carlton, and similar. Rooms here may not be big but have a nice, fresh feel. Those with views over the busy avenue are best.

Hôtel Omrane (Map pp72-3; ☎ 71 345 277; www.hotel-omrane.com.tn; 65 ave Farhat Hached; s/d TD55/78) Central, a bit characterless, but comfortable, rooms here are smartish if a bit dull, with TV. A cheap favourite for the business crowd .

TOP-END

Hôtel Africa (Map pp72-3; ☎ 71 347 477; 50 ave Habib Bourguiba; d from TD200) The ashtray architecture of the chandelier sets the scene at this glitzy, refurbished business-oriented place, with good views and spacious rooms.

La Maison Blanche (Map p69; ☎ 71 844 718; 45 ave Mohamed V; s/d TD195/220; ❄) A bit out of the way, the White House has a rare amount of character: elaborate furnishings in light, bright rooms with curvaceous windows. The piano bar is darkly Art Deco.

EATING

You can eat well here, and meals out are very good value. Apart from the wide range of central eateries, even more choice can be found in the city's delightful seafront suburbs – Sidi Bou Saïd and Gammarth have some upmarket joints with wonderful sea views.

Medina

The medina contains Tunis' grandest restaurants (and daytime hole-in-the-wall places for the hard up), housed in exquisite 18th-century mansions.

BUDGET

Fast Food (Map pp72-3; rue Ettoumi) This popular pocket-sized place does great sandwiches for around TD1.5.

Mahdaoui (Map pp72-3; 2 rue Jema Zaytouna; mains TD3.7-7; 🕑 noon-3.30pm Mon-Sat) Central and

THE MEDINA'S BEST CAFÉS

Café Ez-Zitouna (Map pp72-3; rue Jemaa Zaytouna) Beautifully tiled arched rooms, full of fragrant smoke, open to the street.
M'Rabet (Map pp72-3; Souk el-Trouk) Traditional Turkish café, with pillars painted in stick-of-rock stripes, rush-mat seating on raised platforms and an airy courtyard.
Dar Hamouda Pacha (Map pp72-3; rue Sidi ben Arous) Whitewashed alcoves around small, calm courtyards, and mute-coloured sofas, this is the chichi way to smoke your *sheesha* (waterpipe used to smoke tobacco); has good Turkish coffee.
Café Chaoechin (Map pp72-3; Grand Souq des Chechias) The oldest, where *sheeshas* gurgle among the ornate cubby-holes of the hat-makers' souq, with rickety painted tables under tiled arches.
Dar El-Medina (Map pp72-3; 64 rue Sidi ben Arous) Tunis' loveliest hotel (p80) has several salons and a roof terrace where you can take a tea, coffee, fruit juice or *sheesha*.

cheap, here the tables fill a narrow alley by the Zaytouna Mosque. The simple daily menu offers couscous, fish, chicken, lamb (sometimes half a head – yikes) and so on – greasy but pretty good. If you get here late, there won't be much choice left.

MIDRANGE

M'Rabet (Map pp72-3; Souk el-Trouk; mains TD7-12; ⌚ noon-3.30pm & 7.30-10pm Mon-Sat) Above the busy traditional café, this is a formal small restaurant with nice views of the Zaytouna Mosque, specialising in Tunisian dishes and mainly catering to groups.

TOP END

Dar Hamouda Pacha (Map pp72-3; ☎ 71 561 746; 56 rue Sidi ben Arous; mains TD13-18; ⌚ café 8am-8.30pm, restaurant 8-10.30pm Mon-Sat) This is an intimate, elegant café and restaurant with chairs scattered among white arches and small courtyards hung with old black-and-white photographs. It's popular with well-to-do courting Tunisian couples. Cuisine is Tunisian-French.

Dar Bel Hadj (Map pp72-3; ☎ 71 200 894; 17 rue des Tamis; mains TD18-26; ⌚ noon-3pm & 8-10.30pm Mon-Sat) North of the Zaytouna Mosque, this is another grand traditional restaurant in a sumptuous 17th-century mansion, an extraordinary surprise after the medina's narrow streets. The food is delicious and recommended. Try the Tunisian mixed hors d'oeuvres and the *brochettes de mérou* (grouper kebabs). The restaurant's golf buggy will pick you up and drop you off from Place de Gouvernement in the evening.

our pick **Dar el-Jeld** (☎ 71 560 916; 5-10 rue Dar el-Jeld; meals around TD35) This is special from the moment you knock on the grand bee-yellow arched doorway, which opens into an elaborate 18th-century mansion – it's like stepping into a lavishly decorated jewellery box. The magnificent dining room is in a covered central courtyard, with secluded alcove tables around the edge. Start with the mixed hors d'oeuvres, then try delicious traditional Tunisian dishes such as *kabkabou* (fish with tomatoes, capers and olives), all accompanied by the twanging tones of the resident elderly musician.

Ville Nouvelle

BUDGET

Carcassonne (Map pp72-3; 8 ave de Carthage; mains TD1.8-2, 4-course set menu TD4.5; ⌚ noon-10pm) Remarkable value is the name of the game at this small, popular, friendly place, with quality traditional food in pleasant, relaxed surroundings. Service is fast.

Restaurante Les 3 Étoiles (Map pp72-3; rue Mustafa M'barek; mains TD2.5-4; ⌚ 11.30am-11.30pm) Just by the medina, near Bab Bhar, this is a great basic little place with cheap-as-chips food – fill-you-up couscous or blow-your-top *salade mechouia* (grilled peppers and tomatoes with olive oil and garlic, served garnished with olives or tuna) – whirring fans, plastic tablecloths and satisfied customers.

Neptune (Map pp72-3; ☎ 71 254 820; 3 rue de Caire; dishes TD3.2-7.8; ⌚ noon-10pm) With its curly wrought-iron chairs, Formica tabletops and wicker-framed mirrors that could have been plucked from 1970s suburbia, this chirpy place has simple Tunisian favourites, including fresh fish.

Abid (Map pp72-3; ☎ 71 257 052; 98 rue de Yougoslavie; mains TD3.8-8.5; ⌚ 11am-midnight) With busily tiled interior, TV, flickering neon and simple Tunisian staples (specialising in spicy Sfaxian dishes), this is a good-value neighbourhood favourite.

Margaritas (Map pp72-3; ☎ 71 240 632; Hôtel Maison Dorée, 3 rue el-Koufa; 3-course menu TD7.5, mains TD4.5-11.5; ⌚ noon-3pm & 7.30-9.30pm Mon-Sat; ⊠) You get great service, cooking and value at this business and tourist favourite: a small hotel restaurant decorated in dusky mauve and dark wood.

Café de Paris Brasserie (Map pp72-3; ☎ 71 240 583; ave Habib Bourguiba; mains TD4-12; 11.30am-10pm;) A very handy little place (great for kids), with a nice, clean interior and a few outside tables, pizzas, couscous and a varied range of salads, such as Roquefort and walnut. Also serves alcohol.

Capitole (Map pp72-3; ☎ 71 256 601; ave Habib Bourguiba; mains TD5.5-13) This long-standing place has tasty traditional food, served in a slightly flouncy function room, with views over the busy main drag below.

MIDRANGE

Al-Mazar (Map pp72-3; ☎ 71 340 423; 11 rue de Marseille; mains TD4-13.9; 10am-2am;) As befits a bar cunningly disguised as a restaurant, this is buzzing and convivial; lone women might find it intimidating. With paintings on the walls and big globe lampshades, you might think yourself in Paris. The food is excellent, with special mention going to the *harissa* and to the chocolate mousse.

Capri (Map pp72-3; ☎ 71 257 695; 34 rue Mokhtar Attia; mains TD6-11.8, pizzas TD5.5-7; noon-11pm;) A bit cramped, with lots of pinewood on two levels, this is a lively place popular with heavily smoking businessmen. It serves alcohol alongside good simple seafood.

Tontonville (Map pp72-3; ☎ 71 253 918; 96 rue de Yougoslavie; mains TD7-12, set menu TD7; noon-3.30pm & 7-9.30pm Mon-Sat) This buzzing place has plain, no-nonsense décor, heavily curtained from the street, so punters can tuck into the alcohol on offer with impunity. It also has lots of great fish. The *salade mechouia* served with the dishes comes with a kick.

L'Orient (Map pp72-3; ☎ 71 252 061; rue Ali Bach Hamba; dishes TD5-18; noon-3.30pm & 7-11pm) Clutter, a busy vibe, tall ceilings, brick arches, swords, shells and yellow-and-green swirling tiling all supply a strong Andalusian flavour, matched by the seafood slant of the menu.

Bolero (Map pp72-3; ☎ 71 245 928; 6 Passage el-Guattar; mains TD6.5-14; noon-3pm & 7.30-9.30pm) Tucked down a seedy alley, this cosy corner with red tablecloths and low lighting is favoured by Tunis businessmen, who retreat here for long lunches to peruse the long wine list. It specialises in grilled meats and seafood and prides itself on its paella.

Le Malouf (Map pp72-3; ☎ 71 254 246; rue de Yougoslavie; mains TD11-26; 11.30am-3pm & 7pm-midnight Mon-Sat;) If you fancy some pasta, this Italian-owned place is where to head. It's smart, with big artworks decorating the interior and courtyard tables out the front – a charming find in central Tunis. A guitar duo cranks up the atmosphere on Thursday, Friday and Saturday nights.

Le Carthage (Map pp72-3; ☎ 71 255 614; 10 rue Ali Bach Hamba; mains TD12-19; noon-3pm & 7-11pm Mon-Sat;) Heavy on the camp and kitsch statuary, but with prize-winning couscous and specialising in seafood, this is an intimate, popular choice.

Andalous (Map pp72-3; ☎ 71 241 756; 13 rue de Marseille; mains TD13-16.5; noon-3pm & 5-11pm Mon-Sat;) Dimly lit by ornate lanterns and decorated with carved wooden screens, this has a Moroccan feel, affable waiters and tasty seafood and meat dishes.

Chez Nous (Map pp72-3; ☎ 71 243 043; 5 rue de Marseille; mains TD14-25; noon-2.30pm & 7.30-10.30pm Mon-Sat;) This feels like an Italian-American mobsters' haunt. Nothing fancy, in a snug back room, but the food is good and there are faded black-and-white photos of faded stars on the walls.

SELF-CATERING

Central market (Map pp72-3; rue Charles de Gaulle; 6am-3pm) This market dates from the 19th century and is a hugely colourful place to wander and stock up on food, with a mouth-watering selection of cheeses, fresh bread, *harissa,* olives and pickles (surrounding shops sell tempting piles of the same) as well as fruit and veg.

Central supermarkets include **Monoprix** (Map pp72-3; rue Charles de Gaulle; 8.30am-9pm Mon-Sat, 8.30am-3pm Sun) and the **Magasin Général** (Map pp72-3; ave de France; 8.30am-9pm Mon-Sat, 8.30am-1pm Sun). Both stock a range of local wines.

Berges du Lac

The burgeoning lakeside Berges de Lac development is a popular evening hangout, with some flashy cafés and restaurants.

La Croisette (☎ 71 963 287; Corniche du Lac, Les Berges du Lac; noon-midnight) The Berges du Lac development is trendy and prices reflect this, but this popular *salon de thé*-restaurant has a lovely waterside setting, sells anything from ice cream and cakes to pizzas, and is surrounded by fairy lights.

DRINKING

Most city-centre bars are raucous all-male preserves. For more refined nightlife, head out to the northern suburbs (p89). For medina cafés, see the boxed text (p82).

Bar Jamaica (Map pp72-3; Hotel el-Hana International, ave Habib Bourguiba; 4pm-midnight) Zip up to El-Hana's 10th floor for fabulous views. This small bar is lit with funky blue neon, plays a mix of lounge and pop music, has tables outside, and attracts a mixed crowd of men and women, both Tunisian and foreign.

Brasserie les 2 Avenues (Map pp72-3; Hotel el-Hana International, ave Habib Bourguiba; 7am-midnight) This has a pavement location for a prime view of the avenue's people parade.

Café de Paris (Map pp72-3; ave Habib Bourguiba; 6am-midnight) One of the avenue's main people-watching hubs, this has a good mix of men and women and lots of outside tables.

Oscars (Map pp72-3; rue de Marseille) The vaguely cine-themed (perhaps the name refers to the awards ceremony) bar-restaurant upstairs is fun, though not for single women. There's live music and dancers at the weekend.

Piano Bar (Map p69; La Maison Blanche, 45 ave Mohamed V) A good place for a refined, subdued drink, this five-star hotel bar is Art Deco and dark-wood heaven.

Théâtre de l'Etoile du Nord (Map pp72-3; 71 254 066; www.etoiledunord.org; 41 ave Farhat Hached; around 8pm) As boho as Tunis gets, this vibrant theatre has a unique artsy café (no alcohol) catering to a mixed crowd of men and women. Lone women will feel comfortable here.

Le Boeuf sur le Toit (71 764 807; 3 ave Fatouma Bourguiba) Out in the up-and-coming suburb of La Soukra, 'the beef on the roof' is named after a surrealist ballet; it's a restaurant with a dance floor and terrace, and regular DJs, live gigs and Sunday jazz evenings, attracting Tunisia's most cosmopolitan crowd.

ENTERTAINMENT

Théâtre de l'Etoile du Nord (Map pp72-3; 71 254 066; www.etoiledunord.org; 41 ave Farhat Hached; admission around TD3; 8pm) This is a fringe theatre housed in an ex-garage. There are regular plays (in French and Arabic) and concerts (from reggae to heavy metal) – check the website for forthcoming events.

Théâtre d'Art Ben Abdallah (Map pp72-3; 20 443 540; Space 06 Impasse Ben Abdallah; 9am-8pm) This venue, in the converted stables of the Dar Ben Abdallah Museum, has theatre and cinema performances in French and Tunisian and a small café.

There are plenty of cinemas, mainly showing Egyptian films, Bollywood-style action movies or soft porn, but you'll also find recent Hollywood offerings, dubbed into French. The local press has listings. Admission costs around TD3 at plush places such as **La Parnasse** (Map pp72-3; 71 353 513; 63 ave Habib Bourguiba) and **Le Colisée** (Map pp72-3; 71 252 057; 45 ave Habib Bourguiba), though older films are often cheaper. The only arthouse cinema is **Maison de la Culture Ibn Khaldoun** (Map pp72-3; 71 241 901; 16 rue Ibn Khaldoun).

There's traditional live music on offer at restaurants such as Le Malouf (p83) and Lucullus (p90). The upstairs bar at Oscars (left) has lively weekend entertainment. Look out for classical music concerts at the Dar Ennejma Ezzahra (Centre of Arabic & Mediterranean Music; p96) in Sidi Bou Saïd and at L'Acropolium (p93) in Carthage. Big stars dazzle at Carthage's amphitheatre during the International Festival (see p95).

Wealthy Tunisians and tourists are most likely to be getting down at any of Tunis' clubs. The best are out in the northern suburb of La Marsa: try the club at the Hôtel Plaza Corniche (p99).

Villa Didon (p96), in Carthage, has a great bar with superb views. It cranks it up on Friday night, with DJs till 1am, when you'll need to reserve a table and be prepared to spend pots of cash.

Sport

Five of the 14 soccer teams in the Tunisian first division are from Tunis, including rivals Club Africain and Espérance Sportive de Tunisie. Both use **Stade Olympique** (Map p68; El-Menzah) as a home ground. Admission starts at TD7 and matches are usually at 2pm on Sunday. To get there, take *métro léger* line 2 from République to Cité Sportive.

Fixture details are in the Saturday press. Teams are referred to by their initials – CA for Club Africain, and EST for Espérance Sportive de Tunisie. Other Tunis clubs include Stade Tunisien (ST) and Club Olympique de Transports (COT) from the west; Avenir Sportif de La Marsa (ASM) from La Marsa; and Club Sportif de Hammam Lif (CSHL), from the south.

THE PLO IN TUNISIA

Yasser Arafat set up his Tunisian headquarters in 1982, after the Palestinian Liberation Organisation (PLO) were expelled from Lebanon by the Israeli army.

Arafat & co – including Mahmoud Abbas, current PLO chief – were warmly greeted by President Habib Bourguiba despite Tunisia's moderate policy on Israel and misgivings regarding the PLO's activities, and they set up headquarters at Borj Cedria near Tunis.

The Tunisian government promised that they would not interfere in Palestinian affairs, and this policy held, even when, following terrorist attacks, Israel retaliated by bombing the Tunisian base. The PLO had agreed not to launch attacks from Tunisia, but then blatantly broke their promise when they seized the Italian *Achille Lauro* cruise ship, killing a wheelchair-bound passenger. Relations between guests and hosts were rocky after this, but recovered and, in 1988, the PLO renounced terrorism and recognised Israel. After this change in policy 70 countries recognised the PLO as the leaders of the Palestinian Arabs and Arafat's prospects began to look up.

Arafat returned to Gaza in 1994, following the Oslo peace accords. Others who opposed the peace settlement, such as hardliner Farouk Kaddoumi (a founder of the PLO) stayed in Tunisia, where he still lives – he became head of Fatah, Arafat's political organisation, after Arafat's death.

Leila Ben Ali, the Tunisian president's wife, is a close personal friend of Suha Arafat, the PLO leader's wealthy widow. The couple had married secretly in Tunis when she was aged 28 (he was 61). Following the many accusations of corruption among the PLO's high ranks, the pair became embroiled in controversy about alleged multimillion-dollar transfers into Mrs Arafat's bank account, who was – some said – paid $100,000 a month to maintain herself and her daughter. Today, Suha Arafat divides her time between Tunis and Paris, owns shares in Tunisiana, the Tunisia mobile communications company, and recently adamantly denied rumours that she had remarried (Leila Ben Ali's brother).

SHOPPING

The medina is the best place to shop – for information about the souqs see p75. Prices can start ludicrously high, so put on your haggle hat.

Delma (Map pp72-3; 24 ave de France) Impress your date with dates. This upmarket shop sells Tamerza dates stuffed with pistachio paste or dried apricots, or covered in sesame seeds. They're pricier than you'll find in the supermarket but the boxes make good gifts (0.5kg for TD15).

Société de Commercialisation des Produits de l'Artisanats (SOCOPA; Map pp72-3; La Palmarium, ave Habib Bourguiba; 9am-7.30pm Mon-Sat, 9am-1pm Sun, 8am-11pm, 4.30-8.30pm Sep-Jun; daily Jul & Aug) The government emporium sells good-quality, fixed-price crafts, including ceramics, rugs and silver jewellery. Get an idea of costs here before heading into the medina.

Mains des Femmes (Map pp72-3; 1st fl, 47 ave Habib Bourguiba; 8.30am-2.30pm Mon-Sat Jul & Aug, 9am-6.30pm Mon-Fri, 8.30am-noon & 3-6pm Sat Sep-Jun) This shop is the fixed-price outlet for handicrafts produced by rural women's cooperatives, with rugs, including kilims and *mergoums* (woven carpets with geometric designs) and embroidered blankets.

Hanout Arab (Map pp72-3; 52 rue Jemaa Zaytouna; 9am-7pm Mon-Sat) On the main tourist drag, this is an unusual, fixed-price shop with distinctive Tunisian crafts, including textiles, jewellery and ochre-and-black Sejnane pottery.

Fella (Map p69; ☎ 785 924; 9 place Pasteur; 9am-noon & 3.30-6pm Mon-Sat) This small fixed-price chichi boutique has kept stars from Umm Kolthum to Grace Kelly in handmade floaty robes and household ornaments.

Central Market (Map pp72-3; rue Charles de Gaulle; 6am-3pm) In and around the busy food market, you can buy excellent olives, olive oil, *harissa* and pickles, as well as a wide range of basketware.

Antique Shop (Map pp72-3; 27 ave Habib Bourguiba) This not-signed antiques shop may seem singularly uninterested in selling anything, but they do have classy antiques at prices to match.

Labedi Apiculture (Map pp72-3; 38 rue Sidi ben Arous) A fascinating shop, this sells local bee products, including eucalyptus honey, royal jelly hand cream and aromatic hair oils.

TUNIS

GETTING THERE & AWAY

Air

Tuninter (☎ 71 942 323, 754 000; www.tuninter.com.tn) flies direct to Jerba (TD85) and Tozeur (TD66). Getting a booking in the middle of summer can be hard. Buy tickets from **Tunisair** (Map pp72-3; ☎ 71 330 100; 48 ave Habib Bourguiba), at the airport, from travel agents, or direct from Tuninter.

For details of international flights to/from Tunis, see p302.

Airline offices in Tunis include the following:

Air France (Map pp72-3; ☎ 71 105 324; www.airfrance.com; 1 rue d'Athènes)
Alitalia (☎ 71 767 722; www.alitalia.com; Tunis-Carthage Airport)
British Airways (☎ 71 963 120; www.british-airways.com; rue du Lac Michigan, 1053 Berges du Lac)
EgyptAir (Map pp72-3; ☎ 71 341 182; 1st fl, Complexe el-Hana International, 49 ave Habib Bourguiba)
Lufthansa Airlines (☎ 71 751 096; www.lufthansa.com; Tunis-Carthage Airport)
Royal Air Maroc (☎ 71 845 700; www.royalairmaroc.com; 6 ave Kheireddine Pacha, 1073 Montplaisir)
Tunisair (Map pp72-3; ☎ 71 330 100; 48 ave Habib Bourguiba)

Boat

Ferries from Europe arrive at La Goulette, at the eastern end of the causeway across Lake Tunis. A taxi to the city centre costs about TD4. This is a good investment as it's quite a long walk from here to La Goulette Vieille station.

In summer, reserve tickets from Europe as early as possible, especially if you want to take a vehicle.

The **Compagnie Tunisienne de Navigation** (CTN; Map pp72-3; ☎ 71 322 802; 122 rue de Yougoslavie) handles tickets for ferries operated by CTN and its French partner SNCM to Genoa and Marseilles. **Carthage Tours** (Map pp72-3; ☎ 71 344 066; 59 ave Habib Bourguiba) sells tickets for Tirrenia Navigazione to Trapani, Naples and La Spezia.

See p306 for more details.

Bus

Tunis has two intercity bus stations – one for buses south and the other for buses north.

French-language *La Presse* carries details of SNTRI departures from both stations daily, but these schedules list only final destinations and not the stops en route.

SOUTHERN BUS STATION

All the buses that head to destinations in southern Tunisia leave from the **southern bus station** (Map p69; ☎ 71 399 391, 399 440; Gare Routière Sud de Bab el-Fellah), which is situated south of the city centre opposite the huge Jellaz Cemetery. You can walk, or you could catch *métro léger* line 1 to Bab Alioua, 200m from the bus station.

Destination	Fare (TD)	Duration	Frequency (per day)
Ben Guerdane	24.4	8hr	3
Douz	24.1	8hr	3
El-Haouaria	4.5	2hr	7
El-Jem	10	3hr	6
Gabès	16.3	6½hr	10
Gafsa	16.6	5hr	8
Hammamet	3.45	50 mins-1¼hr	half-hourly
Jerba	21.3	8hr	3
Kairouan	7.5	3hr	hourly
Korba	3.1	3½hr	3
Makthar	7.2	3hr	7
Matmata	18.6	8 hr	1
Medenine	20	7hr	5
Nabeul	2.9/3.4	1½hr	half-hourly
Nefta	21.5	7hrs	2
Sbeitla	10.5	4hr	7
Sfax	12.5	5hr	8
Sousse	7.7	2½hr	8
Tamerza	21.1	7hrs	3
Tataouine	21.25	8hr	3
Tozeur	20.75	7hr	5
Zaghouan	2.4	1¼hr	14

NORTHERN BUS STATION

Buses north leave from the **northern bus station** (Map p69; ☎ 71 562 299, 563 653; Gare Routière Nord de Bab Saadoun), about 2km northwest of the city centre.

The easiest way to get there is by *métro léger* line 4 to Bouchoucha station, which is about 150m west of the bus station on blvd 20 Mars 1956.

Destination	Fare (TD)	Duration	Frequency (per day)
Ain Draham	10	4hr	4
Bizerte	3.4	1hr	half-hourly
Jendouba	7	3hr	6
Le Kef	9	3hr	hourly
Tabarka	8.5	3½hr	6
Teboursouk	6	2½hr	hourly

Car

All the major car-hire companies have offices at the airport and in town. For details of rates, see p310.

Avis (rue 8612, Impasse 4, Charguia; ☎ 71 205 347; avis@planet.tn)
Europcar (☎ 71 340 303; 🕑 8am-12.45pm & 2-7pm, to 1pm Jul & Aug) ave Habib Bourguiba (Map pp72-3; 17 ave Habib Bourguiba); ave de la Liberté (Map p69; 99 ave de la Liberté)
Hertz (Map pp72-3; ☎ 71 256 451; 29 ave Habib Bourguiba; 🕑 8am-1pm & 2-7pm Mon-Sat)
Topcar (Map p69; ☎ 71 800 875; www.topcartunisie.com; 7 rue de Mahdia)

Louage

Tunis has three main louage (shared taxi) stations. Cap Bon louages leave from opposite the southern bus station, and services to other southern destinations leave from the station at the eastern end of rue El-Aid el-Jebbari, off ave Moncef Bey. Louages to the north leave near the northern bus station.

The **louage station** (place Sidi Bou Mendil) in the medina serves Libya (Tripoli, TD40, 20 hours); services to Algeria leave from nearby. Prices are usually equivalent to bus fares.

Train

Trains leave from **Tunis Ville train station** (Map pp72-3; ☎ 71 345 511; www.sncft.com.tn; place Barcelone). Trains get crowded in summer, especially going south, and to nab a seat, it's a good idea to reserve the day before. There's a discount of 15% on return tickets.

Destination	Fare (2nd/1st/confort)	Duration	Frequency (per day)
Bizerte	3.4	1¾hr	3-4
El Jem	8.9/11.8/12.5	3hr	6
Gabès	15.4/20.7/22.1	6hr	4
Gafsa	14.4/19.3/20.5	7½hr	2
Ghardimao	8.4/10.5/11.2	3hr	4
Hammamet	3.8/5/5.3	1-1½hr	9*
Jendouba	6.8/8.5/9.1	2¾hr	5
Kalaat Kasba	7.9/12.9	5hr	2
Mahdia	8.9/11.8/12.5	4hr	1
Metlaoui	15.4/20.7/22.1	8½hr	2
Monastir	7.9/10.4/11	3hr	1
Nabeul	3.8/5/5.3	1¼ -1½hr	9*
Sfax	10.5/14.1/15	3-4hr	7
Sousse	6.5/8.6/9.2	2hr	9
Tozeur	17/21/22	8½hr	2

*only one is direct, the rest require a change at Bir Bou Regba

GETTING AROUND

To/From the Airport

Tunis-Carthage International Airport is 8km northeast: a taxi to the centre costs around TD4 to TD7 from 9pm to 5am, or bus 35 heads to/from ave Habib Bourguiba (TD0.6, half-hourly 6.30am to 5.30pm). Note that the TGM L'Aeroport station is not near the airport.

Transtu

The bus, métro and TGM networks come under the umbrella organisation **Transtu** (www.snt-smlt.com.tn). For service information check the website.

BUS

Yellow city buses run citywide, but you'll mainly need them to get to the airport. The destination, point of origin and route number are displayed in Arabic by the back door, but routes of interest to tourists have the destination marked in Latin script too. The basic fare is TD0.5 on most routes, and you buy your ticket on board.

There are three main bus terminuses in Tunis: Tunis Marine (Map p68), near the TGM station at the causeway end of ave Habib Bourguiba; place Barcelone (Map pp72–3); and Jardin Thameur (Map pp72–3), off ave Habib Thameur. Tunis Marine is the starting point for bus 35 to the airport, which also has stops on ave Habib Bourguiba.

MÉTRO LÉGER

The *métro léger* is much easier to use than the buses. It's not a metro system as we know it, but a tram network. There are five main routes – see the map, p88. There are route maps in Arabic and French inside the trams.

Tickets are sold at the small kiosks at each station entrance. They must be bought before you travel. The basic fare costs TD0.45.

Services using lines 3, 4 and 5 between République and place Barcelone travel south along ave de Paris and ave de Carthage and north on rue de Hollande and ave Habib Thameur.

TGM

The TGM is a suburban train line connecting central Tunis with the beachside

MÉTRO LÉGER & TGM ROUTES

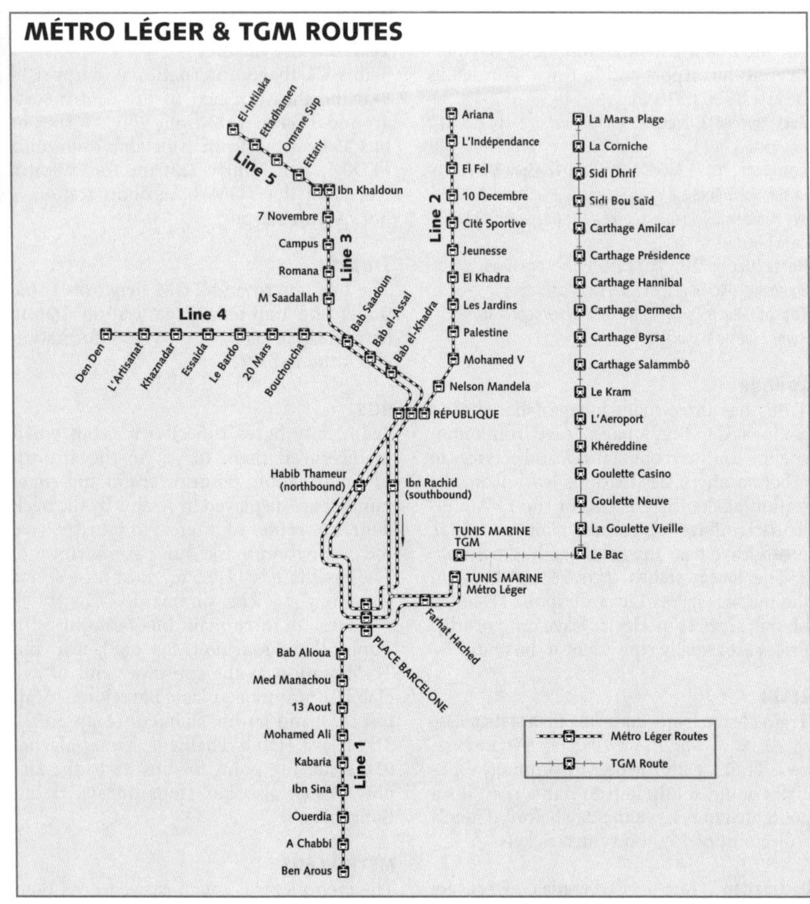

suburbs of La Goulette, Carthage, Sidi Bou Saïd and La Marsa. It's fast, cheap and convenient, though sometimes crowded; avoid the rush hours (7.30am to 8.30am and 5pm to 6.30pm). The first train leaves Tunis Marine at 5am, and the last train at midnight. Departures range from every 12 minutes during peak hours to every 40 minutes. First class is worth the extra cost at busy times, costing TD0.65 to La Goulette (20 minutes) and TD1.1 to Carthage (30 minutes), Sidi Bou Saïd (35 minutes) and La Marsa Plage (45 minutes).

Taxi

Taxis are cheap by European standards and are all fitted with meters. On the day rate, a short hop costs around TD1; a longer trip such as to the Bardo costs TD4, to Sidi Bou Saïd around TD12. The evening rate is 50% more (9pm to 5am) and there's a TD0.37 surcharge for each piece of luggage. Other than at the airport, where some drivers are intent on negotiating a set fare, drivers usually use the meter. Be warned that the occasional driver fiddles the meter to charge a higher fare (see p70 for more information). Taxis are also sometimes frustratingly all busy, and during peak hours you just have to be patient and lucky. They can be booked by phone – ask at your hotel reception – but the meter begins ticking when the taxi sets out to collect you. For more information call ☎ 1853.

AROUND TUNIS

La Goulette, Carthage, Sidi Bou Saïd, La Marsa and Hammam Lif were once distinct villages and towns, remote from the capital. This changed when the French built the causeway across Lake Tunis in the 19th century, and today they are Tunis suburbs, each retaining a distinct atmosphere.

La Goulette is a clattering seaside escape, where locals flock to its fish restaurants. Carthage is home to rich, important Tunisians, as it has been for millennia – dotted among the luxurious villas are the fascinating remains of the ancient city. Sidi Bou Saïd, further along the coast, is a chic, clifftop village. More wealthy villas stretch out along the balmy blue-edged beaches at La Marsa and Gammarth, and Hammam Lif revels in seedy charm, overlooked by a dramatic split-summit mountain.

LA GOULETTE حلق الواد

The historic port of La Goulette, 10km from the centre, is a local favourite, with hordes flocking to eat at its fish restaurants, cram the beach and revel in the summer breezes. The down-to-earth name means 'the gullet' in French, referring to its position on the narrow channel connecting Lake Tunis to the open sea. It has a rough-and-ready feel, and the beach is grubby, but the restaurants are good and there's a night-time buzz – it's still packed around midnight.

This gullet remains a major port, handling cargo and European passenger ferries. The principal monument is the massive fort – the Ottoman **Borj el-Karrak** (ave Farhet Hached; admission free; 7.30am-2pm), built over a Spanish ruin. It was used as a prison from the 16th century and slaves were taken from here to be sold in the medina's slave market: Souq el-Berka. They were used to row the corsair galleys.

Today, it's a rambling ruin with not much to see inside. A family inhabit the most imposing parts – arched caverns surrounding an inner courtyard – and they don't appreciate visitors wandering through, though you're welcome to visit the castle's upper storey.

History

The Arabs developed the port here after their 7th-century conquest, and it became a strategic defensive outpost – the dimensions of the Ottoman fort show its importance.

In Ottoman times, La Goulette housed one of the state-approved corsair fleets that preyed on Christian shipping in the Mediterranean. West of the kasbah, a small, walled town grew from the profits, housing a substantial Jewish community. In colonial times, many Italians moved in, developing the area known as Little Sicily to the north. Today, both communities have moved on.

Sleeping, Eating & Drinking

If you fancy a room with a sea view, close to central Tunis, there are a few pleasant beachfront hotels here. This is also a great place to eat fish. Most eateries are clustered

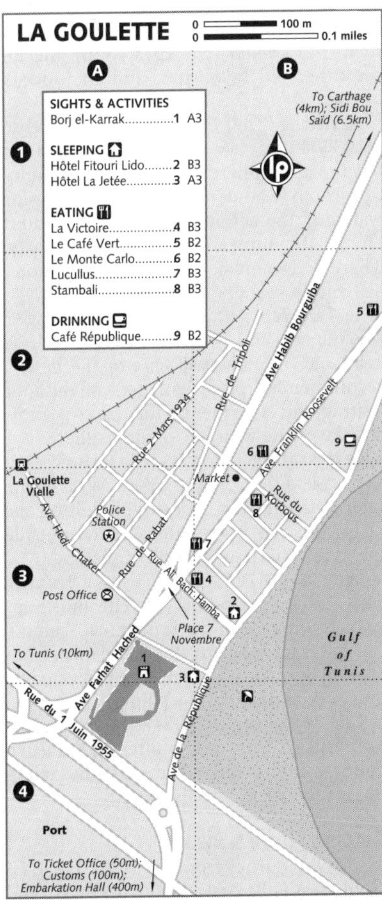

around place 7 Novembre and ave Franklin Roosevelt, from cheap-and-cheerful to swish-and-swanky.

Hôtel La Jetée (☎ 71 736 000; ave del la République; s/d TD55/100; ❄) This smart, pretty seaside hotel has large, comfortable rooms with balconies. Ask for a room with a sea view.

Hôtel Fitouri Lido (☎ 71 738 333; rue Ali Bach Hamba; s/d TD45/70; ❄) Also worthwhile, this hotel has spacious rooms with marble floors and the wrought-iron curly furnishings so beloved of Tunisian midrange hotels. Balconies mostly overlook the busy beach (again, it's worth the few extra dinars for a sea view).

Stambali (☎ 71 738 506; ave Franklin Roosevelt; dishes TD0.5-6) This is a cheap, simple tiles-and-Formica local haunt, where you can tuck into *lablabi* (chickpea soup) and all the other old favourites, and sit indoors or out.

La Victoire (☎ 71 735 398; 1 ave Franklin Roosevelt; mains TD10-16; noon-midnight; ❄) Upstairs has the atmosphere of a Rotary Club function room – however, it's a good place for watching the action on the street without any traffic fumes, and the fish is tasty. There's also outside seating and a non-air-con downstairs room.

Le Café Vert (☎ 71 736 156; 68 ave Franklin Roosevelt; mains TD5.5-16, 3-course lunch TD12; 12.30-3pm & 7.30-11.30pm Tue-Sun) One of the best, a recommended place with lots of outdoor seating, this is further up the road – a Tunisian favourite with lots of atmosphere.

Le Monte Carlo (☎ 71 766 729; 4 ave Franklin Roosevelt; mains TD9-16; noon-1.30am) With white tablecloths and big pictures of fruit on the walls, this has a nice atmosphere, outside tables and the usual excellent seafood.

Lucullus (☎ 71 737 100; 1 ave Habib Bourguiba; mains TD7-20; noon-1am; ❄) The most upmarket joint around, serving great seafood, this has traditional music and a dancer from around 8pm, on a large terrace protected by greenery and shaded by palms.

Café République (ave de la République; 9am-4am) This seafront café – offering the usual coffee, mint tea and cold drinks – has tables out on the rocks and the beach.

Getting There & Away

The TGM journey from Tunis Marine to La Goulette Vieille costs TD0.7/0.5 in 1st/2nd and takes 15 minutes. A taxi to the city centre costs TD4 to TD6.

CARTHAGE قرطاج

Carthage was a great ancient city, inspiring legends, poetry and envy. Hannibal lived here, the military genius who the Romans were only able to beat by ensuring they never fought him. Virgil wrote his *Aeneid* about the tragic romance between Carthaginian Dido (who founded the city) and Roman Aeneas, and symbolised the battle to the death between the two civilisations.

It was an awesome place. The city walls were 34km long, and houses ran from the top of Byrsa Hill right down to the waterfront. It was famous for its navy: protected within interconnecting harbours, the source of its wealth and dominance. The city's founders, the Phoenicians (from present-day Lebanon), were exceptional businesspeople – the historian Pliny credits them with inventing trade – and a huge Mediterranean power. However, they maintained a distance from their empire. They used mercenaries to fight their battles, and never fought for the hearts of people, unlike the Romans, who absorbed whole communities where they conquered.

The Romans trashed the Carthaginian city, and the Vandals destroyed the Roman replacement – not much of either is left today. However, with a dose of imagination, the fragments that remain evoke Carthage's epic history. On the World Heritage list, the site preserves its natural splendour, with lush vegetation and awesome views.

The highlights are the Punic Quarter on Byrsa Hill, the Punic Ports, the haunting Sanctuary of Tophet and several subsequent Roman structures, including the impressive Antonine Baths, the amphitheatre and Roman villas.

History

According to legend, the Phoenicians founded Carthage in 814 BC. Ruling from Tyre in modern Lebanon, their power was at its peak, and Qart Hadasht (Phoenician for 'new city') was founded to consolidate their North African gains.

It was ideally placed: a narrow, hilly promontory flanked by the sea on three sides – Sebkhet er-Ariana, the salt lake to

DIDO GOES TRAVELLING

The legend surrounding Carthage's foundation in 814 BC evolved from the efforts of Greek and Roman writers to come up with a suitably aristocratic background for one of the great cities of the ancient Mediterranean world. They based the story on the few facts known to them about Carthage's Phoenician origins, and emphasised the blue-blooded nature of the link. The best-known version features in Virgil's *Aeneid*.

The story begins in the Phoenician capital of Tyre in the time of King Pygmalion. According to Virgil, Pygmalion coveted the wealth of the high priest Sichaeus, who was married to his sister, Princess Elissa. Pygmalion arranged for Sichaeus to be murdered and, concealing his involvement from Elissa, attempted to lay his hands on the loot. The ghost of Sichaeus, however, told Elissa what had happened and advised her to flee – as well as revealing the location of his treasure. Elissa decided to take his advice, and tricked Pygmalion into providing her with ships on the pretext of moving to a new palace down the coast, away from the memory of her husband. Thus she was able to load up all her belongings without raising Pygmalion's suspicions. At the last moment, she was joined by 80 noblemen, including her brother Barca.

They fled first to Cyprus, where they were joined by 80 suitable wives and the island's high priest, before setting sail for North Africa. By now Elissa had become Elissa Didon (aka Queen Dido), meaning 'the wanderer' in Phoenician. On arriving in North Africa, Elissa set about the job of acquiring land on which to found a city. She struck a deal with the locals whereby she could have as much land as could be covered with an ox hide. The wily Elissa cut the hide into thin strips, which she used to surround the hill that became the Byrsa (the name comes from the Greek for 'ox hide'). This part of the legend is possibly a snide Roman dig at the Carthaginians' reputation for sharp business practices. Virgil also added a subsequent doomed romance between Queen Dido and Aeneas of Rome, which drove her to suicide.

the north of Tunis, was connected to the sea at this time. At the centre of a shipping network, it dominated the Mediterranean and trade from the continent.

Tyre came under increasing threat from the Assyrians during the 7th century BC, and Carthage took over as the seat of Phoenician power.

After two ferocious wars with rival Rome, Carthage fell during the third conflict. After a furious fight, 50,000 Carthaginians were taken away to slavery and 1000 remained defiantly besieged. Their commander, Hasdrubal, surrendered, his wife and children committed suicide by immolation, and the site was levelled and symbolically sprinkled with salt.

It was not until over a century later, in 44 BC, that Augustus re-established the city, and it became a provincial capital in 29 BC. Within 200 years, it was the third-largest imperial city behind Rome and Alexandria, with 300,000 residents, three forums, a circus holding 70,000, mammoth baths and an amphitheatre.

After the Roman Empire fell, the Vandals and Byzantines both ruled from Carthage but, following the Arab conquest, Hassan Ibn Nooman ruled from Tunis. Carthage returned to agriculture as its chief activity, and in the 16th century Leo the African reported its production of peaches, pomegranates, olives and figs. In the 19th century the French plundered the ruins for inscriptions to display in the Louvre – the ship carrying them sunk near Toulon.

Today Tunis' most exclusive suburb, filled with sleek villas, Carthage retains its significance – the president's palace is here, in a location chosen for its symbolic as well as its natural advantages.

Sights & Activities

A **multiple-entry ticket** (ticket TD6, plus camera TD1; 8.30am-5pm mid-Sep–Mar, 8am-7pm Apr–mid-Sep) valid for one day allows entry to all the widely spread sights listed below – from the Sanctuary of Tophet in the south to the Antonine Baths in the north it's 2km. You can use the TGM to cover larger distances. If you only have a few hours, visit the museum and the surrounding Punic ruins, then walk downhill to the Antonine Baths.

Otherwise an all-inclusive route is to start at the Sanctuary of Tophet, walk to the Punic Ports, then take the TGM one

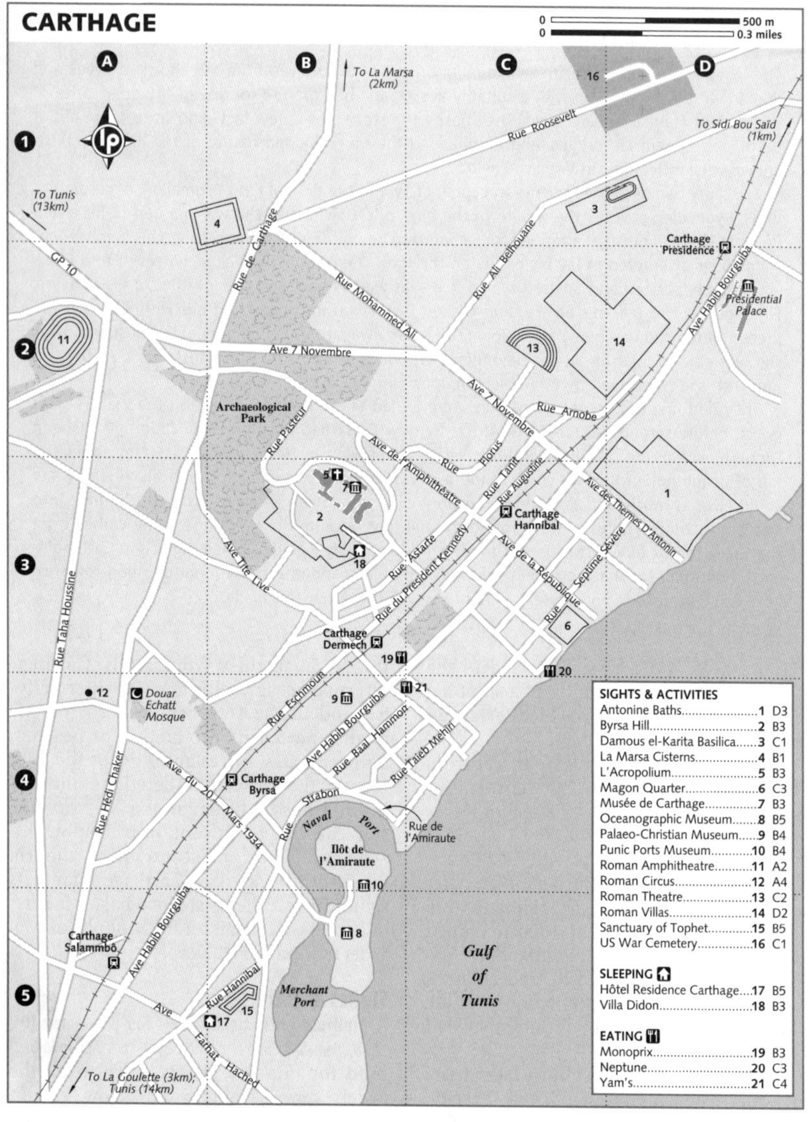

stop from Carthage Byrsa to Dermech to get to the Palaeo-Christian museum. Next, walk up Byrsa Hill for the museum and Punic quarter. Then take a taxi to the further-flung sights: the Roman circus and amphitheatre, the Malga Cistern and Damous el-Karita basilica, getting the driver to drop you at the Roman Theatre, from where you can walk to the Roman villas, Magon quarter and Antonine Baths. To cover all this you will need near superhuman stamina; you're advised to be selective or make several visits.

Also located at Carthage are L'Acropolium (Cathedral of St Louis), the Oceanographic Museum and the US War Cemetery.

BYRSA HILL

Getting off the TGM at Carthage Hannibal or Carthage Dermech, it's a short, steep walk to the top of Byrsa Hill. The entire site is visible from the summit, with amazing views through cypress trees to the ancient Punic ports and the intense blue of the Tunis Gulf.

The hill was the ancient city's spiritual heart. In Punic times, it was occupied by a temple to the Carthaginian god Eschmoun. The Romans destroyed most of the Punic structures and levelled off the top, to create a massive space – 336m by 323m – to hold their capitol and forum. Here stood temples, a library, a 30m-high judicial basilica and several piazzas. All this was in turn destroyed as the fall of Rome unleashed a free-for-all for building materials, but the foundations were left, which have allowed archaeologists to work out the layout and scale of the buildings, delineated on small podiums outside the museum.

Most exciting, just below the summit, is a small, well-preserved section of a Punic residential quarter that was buried and filled with earth – and thus preserved – during Roman levelling operations. This dates from the time of Hannibal (around the 3rd century BC) and is a marvellously evocative place to wander. The neat remains show a street grid with small, careful, domestic structures, some of which were once five storeys high, complete with subterranean cisterns and ground-floor shops.

Musée de Carthage

Housed in the former French cathedral seminary, here the ground floor features some fine 5th-century AD mosaics with lots of peachy bottoms; a Roman sculpture of a boozy Silenus and Maenad continues the sensual theme. There are lamps dating from the 4th century BC to the 7th century AD, some still blackened by smoke. Particularly striking among the Punic remains are the domestic objects – masks painted on fragile ostrich shells, some beautiful engraved 3rd-century razors with duck-shaped handles, and a 4th-century BC terracotta baby bottle in the shape of a bird. There's also a fragment of a Punic town-planning inscription. But the highlight are two magnificent 4th-century BC stone-carved sarcophagi, showing a reclining man and woman – naturalistic representations that seem less ancient than they are, and echo Egyptian and Etruscan influences.

Upstairs, the displays are divided into different themes, one of which describes the final siege of Punic Carthage (149–146 BC) and shows the Punic terracotta bullets and the Roman lead ones. With a few centuries' worth of hindsight, the Roman versions look more lethal. There is some beautifully worked jewellery from a Punic tomb, and many more fragments from daily life and work more than 2000 years ago, such as amphorae and fishing bits and bobs.

L'Acropolium

The 1884 French-built **L'Acropolium** (Cathedral of St Louis; admission TD2.5; 9am-6pm) is a Gothic extravaganza, an assertion of colonial power symbolically plonked in this historic location. It was dedicated to the 13th-century French saint-king Louis who died on the beach at Carthage in 1270 during the ill-fated Eighth Crusade (he was hoping to convert the Hafsid ruler; instead his troops wilted in the heat). The deconsecrated cathedral's ice-cream interior has been restored and houses frequent, interesting exhibitions and concerts (hence the name change).

ROMAN AMPHITHEATRE, LA MARSA CISTERNS & ROMAN CIRCUS

These minor sights are on the hill's western side. The Roman amphitheatre is about a 15-minute walk down from the museum. Once one of the largest in the Roman Empire, with a capacity for 36,000, today only the neat overgrown oval of the stage remains. It's an evocative place, with a sinister exposed subterranean passage where once the theatre's victims cowered. Contrary to legend, St Perpetua and St Felicity were not martyred here, but probably at a military camp outside Carthage.

Across the road is a huge 2nd-century pipe network – remains of the voluminous cisterns that housed Roman Carthage's water supply. The reservoir was nearly 1km long, fed by a huge aqueduct carrying mountain spring water from Zaghouan.

The circus, used for chariot racing, is around 1km south, and once seated 70,000, but only the barest outline can be discerned today. It was later a cemetery.

US WAR CEMETERY

Around 750m along the road from the cisterns, a neat forest of white crosses bears testament to the Americans killed here during WWII. There are 2840 graves at the **cemetery** (rue Roosevelt), and a Wall of Remembrance to 3724 others never found. Like all war cemeteries, its dignified simplicity quietly underlines the horror of so many lives lost.

DAMOUS EL-KARITA BASILICA

This once monumental church is around 1km from the cemetery though it's along a not-very-scenic stretch of road. The basilica was 65m by 45m, with nine aisles, and the remaining lines of broken grey columns clearly stake out this huge scale, if not much else. Steps lead into a well-preserved underground rotunda, 9.5m in diameter, the basement of a building that was possibly a baptistery or a saint's tomb.

ROMAN THEATRE & VILLAS

The Roman theatre has been largely reconstructed, forming an impressive, if not Roman, venue for the annual Carthage International Festival (see opposite). The tiered seating is original; it's thought it could accommodate 5000 spectators. Excavations show that it was lavishly decorated, with lots of marble flourishes. Churchill once gave a speech to the British Army here.

Just east are the **Roman villas** (rue Arnobe), a chance to see a Roman quarter of the city, with Villa of the Aviary as its centrepiece. You get a real sense of refined Roman life from the much-reconstructed houses – with sumptuous marble, mosaics and views.

ANTONINE BATHS

The Romans chose a sublime seaside setting for this fabulous bath complex, a short walk across the road from the Roman villas. Begun under Hadrian and finished in the 2nd century, it was the largest outside Rome, supplied with water by the great Zaghouan aqueduct. Just the foundations remain, but their size is awesome. A plan and model of the baths above the main complex help you read the buildings.

A circular *caldarium* (hot room) was flanked by smaller saunas, and led onto a small *tepidarium* (warm room), which allowed access to the huge 22m by 42m *frigidarium* (cold room) at the centre, which had eight colossal pillars. Beyond this was a wonderful, 17.5m by 13.5m, seaside swimming pool, no trace of which remains. Either side of the *frigidarium* were *palestras* and gymnasiums, where people could indulge in naked wrestling and other such frisky sports.

A sole 15m-high *frigidarium* column gives a sense of the sometime height, its capital alone weighing 8 tons, and huge fragments of marble inscription supply a taste of the décor. To the southwest a huge semicircular construction was discovered, with around 80 seats, which archaeologists at first thought a theatre. It turned out to be a large group of communal latrines.

The baths were destroyed by the Vandals doing what they did best in AD 439, and the stone reused by the Arabs during the construction of Tunis.

The shady palm-filled garden contains other remains too, including a tiny early Christian funerary chapel, a cool underground refuge, with some beautiful naïve terracotta tiles showing Biblical scenes. It was moved here from the northern part of Carthage and rebuilt.

MAGON QUARTER

The **Magon Quarter** (rue Septime Sévère) is a few blocks south of the Antonine Baths. Excavations have uncovered a small area of Roman workshops superimposed on a 5th-century BC Punic residential artisans' quarter. It's now surrounded by a garden. Like the Byrsa quarter, the layout is ordered, and the small houses are endowed with cisterns. There's little to see, but it's a pretty seafront promenade.

PALAEO-CHRISTIAN MUSEUM

Near Carthage Dermech TGM station, this small **museum** (8.30am-5pm mid-Sep–Mar, 8am-7pm Apr–mid-Sep) has good displays on the Punic ports and excavation methods. First-century AD buckles, forceps and needles are among its relics. There's a fine 5th-century marble of Ganymede and the Eagle.

The museum grounds include ruins of the city's most important Byzantine church, the 6th-century Basilica of Carthagenna. It was huge: 36.35m by 25.5m, with a 14-sq-metre basilica, three naves and western and eastern apses.

PUNIC PORTS

Close to Carthage Byrsa TGM station, it's easy to discern the shape of these two ancient ports, the legendary, coveted basis of Carthage's power and prosperity. The southern, oblong commercial port linked to the northern circular military port by a narrow channel. This arrangement made the naval base secure as only the commercial port had sea access. It was arranged so that the military port was hidden from outside, but the Carthaginian navy could see out to sea. The military base had moorings for an incredible 220 vessels in dry docks and around the quay-lined edge. The 7-hectare commercial port was bordered by quays and warehouses.

The ports were filled in by Scipio after the destruction of Carthage in 146 BC, but in the 2nd century the Romans reinvented the islet as a circular forum, with two temples, and used the port to house their fleet for shipping wheat to Rome. Rises in sea level meant the quay walls had to be raised several times. By the end of the 6th century, the harbour had fallen into disuse.

Today the Îlot de l'Amiraute, at the centre of the naval basin, has a miniscule museum, the **Punic Ports Museum** (🕑 8.30am-5pm mid-Sep–Mar, 8am-7pm Apr–mid-Sep), housing interesting reconstructions of the Punic dockyards and the equally impressive Roman port complex.

Nearby, the **Oceanographic Museum** (Dar el-Hout; ☎ 71 730 420; 28 rue 2 Mars; admission TD1; 🕑 10am-1pm & 3-6pm Tue-Sat, 10am-6pm Sun) contains enthusiastic displays of model boats, conservation methods and stuffed, pickled and live wildlife, from giant whale skeletons to preserved vultures. Downstairs is an aquarium with some disconsolate fish.

SANCTUARY OF TOPHET

The chilling **Sanctuary of Tophet** (rue Hannibal), just east of Carthage Salammbô TGM station, was first excavated in 1921. French archaeologists uncovered a sacrificial site and burial ground, where it's believed Carthaginian children were sacrificed to the deities Baal Hammon and Tanit – a stele now in the Bardo Museum shows a priest carrying a child, perhaps to sacrifice. It's an extraordinary, haunting place, with a mass of stubby stelae engraved with simple geometric shapes and symbols under shady trees. Some later Roman foundations shelter more stelae, a particularly spooky spot. The name Tophet is Hebrew for 'place of burning' and comes from Bible references to child sacrifice, such as in Jeremiah: '[people of Judah] have built the altar called Tophet…and there they burn to death their little sons and daughters'.

More than 20,000 urns have been discovered here, each containing the ashes of a child (mostly newborn, but also older children up to the age of four) and marked with a stelae. Many also contained the burned bones of lambs or goat kids. The majority have been dated to the period between the 4th and 2nd centuries BC when Carthage was embroiled in numerous wars and rebellions, and the need to appease the gods was at its greatest. However, there is some controversy about interpretations of the site – see below.

The Romans later built workshops, warehouses and a temple over the site.

GOLF

Carthage Golf Course (☎ 71 863 619; www.golfcarthage.com) Created in 1927, this is the oldest in the country, with 18 challenging holes set among eucalyptus, cypress and pine trees and running alongside citrus orchards.

Festivals & Events

Carthage International Festival (www.festival-carthage.com.tn) takes place in July and August, with internationally renowned music, dance and theatre in the spectacular open-air setting of the Roman theatre.

SACRIFICING THE TRUTH?

Ancient Greek and Roman spin doctors had a hand in propagating stories of Carthaginian child sacrifice. Plutarch and Diodorus claimed this was common at Carthage and the remains at the Sanctuary of Tophet seem to support this view. However, some claim that the children offered to the gods were stillborn or had died of natural causes. Punic people were continually painted as tainted – it was claimed that they also traded and stole children. If a Roman said that you had *fides punica,* he meant you were mighty unreliable. Carthaginian child sacrifice certainly formed a telling contrast with the more noble classical Western civilisations (some of whom merely threw people to wild beasts).

The biennial **Carthage International Film Festival**, held in Tunis' major cinemas, concentrates on Middle Eastern and African cinema. The two-week festival is next due in Autumn 2008 – it's in Burkina Faso on alternate (odd-numbered) years.

Sleeping & Eating

Hôtel Residence Carthage (☎ 71 730 786; 16 rue Hannibal; s/d with breakfast TD57/114; ❄) About 100m from the Tophet, this is a classic small hotel, with sunny rooms decked in old-fashioned furnishings, overlooking gardens. Its three-fork Moroccan restaurant, Le Punique, is pretty smart, with an inviting conservatory.

Villa Didon (www.villadidon.com; Byrsa Hill; ste TD350) A 10-room designer hotel, with furnishings by Starck and Arad and some wonderful North African contemporary art, this is superbly sited on top of Byrsa Hill. Rooms are huge and modernist, with open-plan bathrooms (the Jacuzzi stands on a platform opposite the bed). Large windows and private balconies have stunning views. There's a spa, chic bar (well worth a stop) and Le Restô restaurant, with adventurous international cuisine and the same amazing panoramas.

Monoprix (ave Habib Bourguiba; 🕑 8.30am-10pm) There's a branch next to Carthage Dermech TGM station, if you're self-catering.

Neptune (☎ 71 731 456; mains TD6-14) Seating at this restaurant is on a smashing small seaside terrace, a calm and breezy spot to sit on a hot day or evening. It serves upmarket fish and seafood dishes.

Yam's (☎ 71 720 047; 52 ave Habib Bourguiba; snacks around TD3; 🕑 7am-midnight; ❄) Just below Carthage Dermech TGM station, Yam's is a spic-and-span *salon de thé* with shady wicker roadside seating. It offers milkshakes, fruit juices and palatable pancakes – a good pitstop between sights.

Getting There & Away

The journey from Tunis Marine to any of the six Carthage TGM stations costs TD1.1/0.65 in 1st/2nd class, and takes about 30 minutes.

SIDI BOU SAÏD سيدي بو سعيد

With cascading bougainvillea and flaming-red geraniums against gleaming whitewash, bright-blue window grills, narrow, steep cobbled streets, and jaw-dropping glimpses of azure coast, the cliff-top village of Sidi Bou Saïd has to be one of the prettiest spots in Tunisia. It's also everyone's favourite tourist trap, but wears this remarkably well, remaining untacky and genuinely chic without being exclusive.

It clusters around the Mosque and Zaouia of Sidi Bou Saïd, a 13th-century Sufi saint. The distinctive architecture is Andalusian-inspired, a result of the influx of Spanish Muslims in the 16th century. Longstanding local families and expats have ensured that the buildings retained their character; the village was given protected status in 1915. Previous visitors include Paul Klee, Auguste Macke, André Gide, Michel Foucault, and Osbert and Edith Sitwell.

The centre of activity is small, cobbled place Sidi Bou Saïd, lined with cafés, sweet stalls and souvenir shops. At the bottom of the cliff lies a busy beach and a yacht-bobbing marina.

Sights & Activities

The **lighthouse** above the village stands on the site of an ancient *ribat* (fort), built in the early 9th century as part of a coastal early-warning system that included the *ribats* of Sousse (p189) and Monastir (p197).

Dar el-Annabi (rue Habib Thameur; admission TD3; 🕑 9am-6.30pm) is an 18th-century family home. It's vibrantly tiled and centred around several courtyards filled with jasmine, henna and bougainvillea. Rooms on display include a prayer room, reception rooms and a lovely little library, all carefully presented, with grand wax figures and black-and-white family photos adding a sense of authenticity. The superb panorama from the top terrace sweeps across the village, bay and Carthage.

Dar Ennejma Ezzahra (Centre of Arabic & Mediterranean Music; ☎ 71 740 102; admission adult/child TD3/1.5 🕑 9am-1pm & 2-5pm Tue-Sun) was built between 1912 and 1922 by the extraordinary patron of the arts, French-American Baron Rodolphe d'Erlanger and his Italian-American wife. It's a wonderful extravaganza of Arabian–Art Deco, a pocket of time filled with virtuoso carving, his impressive amateur paintings and amazing collection of gramophones and musical instruments. The Baron was largely responsible for the revival of Tunisian traditional music and wrote a treatise on its history. He tragically

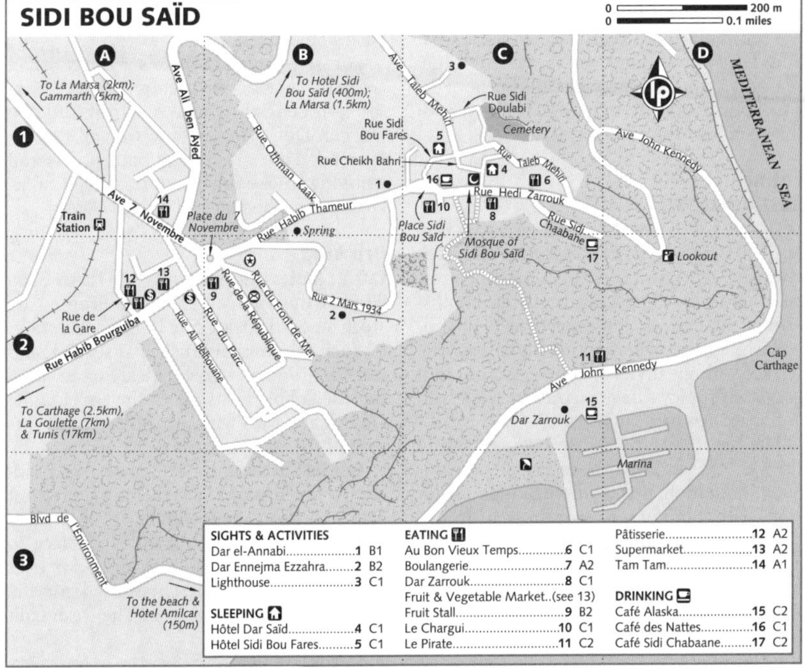

lost his son in WWII and died of TB when in his 60s. The mansion occasionally hosts much-recommended performances of rare classical music (ring for details).

The street heading off to the right at the top end of the main square takes you to the top of a steep stepped path leading down through pine forest to the marina and a small beach. The walk from Sidi Bou Saïd takes about 40 minutes.

Hôtel Dar Saïd (right), has a sleek sea-going yacht, **Dar Zarrouk** (☎ 71 729 666; rue Larbi Zarrouk; 4½hrs/day/weekend/week TD400/700/1200/3000 May-Oct, TD300/500/800/2000 Nov-Apr) with a two-person crew for rent. It takes up to eight people, including the crew.

Festivals & Events

Sidi Bou Saïd has a festival called **Kharja**, held in July or August in honour of the Muslim saint who lived here, when Sufi brotherhoods have a procession up to his shrine.

Sleeping

Despite lacking a certain imagination when it comes to names, there are some exceedingly lovely hotels here and it makes a tranquil base.

Hôtel Amilcar (☎ 71 740 788; www.hotel-amilcar.com; s/d low season TD22/44, high season TD34/68; ⊠ 🏊 P) A 1970s monster lurks at the foot of Sidi Bou Saïd's picturesque cliff. This has big plain rooms with sea views and a good location, and is something of a bargain if you overlook the ugly architecture and occasional blaring music by the pool.

Hôtel Sidi Bou Fares (☎ 71 740 091; 15 rue Sidi Bou Fares; s/d TD28/68) Simple, barrel-vaulted rooms with prettily tiled walls surround a courtyard full of blooming shrubs, vines, a shady fig tree and scattered chairs and tables. The friendly staff speak excellent English.

Hôtel Sidi Bou Saïd (☎ 71 740 411; s/d TD90/120) About 1km north of Sidi Bou Saïd off the road to La Marsa, this modern place is set high up and has sweeping views across the bay and luxurious rooms.

Hôtel Dar Saïd (☎ 71 729 666; www.darsaid.com.tn; rue Toumi; r from TD245, with view TD315; ⊠ 🏊) This boutique hotel is one of the country's most charming. It feels secluded but is in the centre of old Sidi Bou Saïd, housed in a converted, grand (but not imposing) villa. It's centred around pretty, tiled courtyards and has views filled with piercing-blue sea and pink bougainvilleas. The pool is small but pretty and overlooks the bay, and there's a lovely garden terrace.

Eating

RESTAURANTS

Le Chargui (☎ 71 740 987; rue Hedi Zarrouk; mains TD5-12; noon-midnight Apr-Oct, noon-8pm Nov-Mar) The cheapest central option, in a big open-air courtyard with whitewashed concrete booths around low tables. It's draped in blue and has white rugs, neon lighting and a rooftop terrace with great views. Food is simple and good, with spicy *salade mechouia,* fresh fish and tasty *merguez* sausages.

Tam Tam (☎ 71 728 535; ave 7 Novembre; mains TD5.5-18; noon-midnight Tue-Sun Sep-Jun;) Near the station, this is where Sidi Bou Saïd is at, with a buzzing mix of dressed-up locals, TV screens and modern-diner design. There are a few outside tables. Food is a well-executed mix of Italian, Eastern and American dishes. Try the scrummy *petites brochettes de poulet* (chicken kebabs) and fruit cocktails.

Au Bon Vieux Temps (☎ 71 744 733; 56 rue Hedi Zarrouk; mains TD17-24; noon-midnight;) This small, gorgeous choice has a ridiculously romantic terrace centred on a trickling fountain. Drink in the amazing sea views while tucking into excellent French and Tunisian food. This place has filled many illustrious bellies, from Madame Chirac's to the princess of Thailand's.

Dar Zarrouk (☎ 71 740 591; rue Toumi; mains TD18-28; 12.30-2.30pm & 7.30-10.30pm Tue-Sun;) Linked to Hôtel Dar Saïd (see p97), this restaurant scores masses on atmosphere, its long wide terrace with white sun-shaded tables overlooking the deep-blue bay. However, food is good but not brilliant and, despite many waiters, service can get a bit muddled.

Le Pirate (☎ 71 748 266; ave John Kennedy; mains TD19.5-28; noon-3pm & 8-11pm;) By the marina, this is another upmarket, creamily decorated place, with candlelit garden seating under palm trees and white canopies, serving seafood with a French slant.

QUICK EATS

A popular stall around the corner from Café des Nattes sells *bombalouni* (doughnuts) and almond *briqs* (deep-fried flaky pastry envelopes).

For self-caterers, there's a **supermarket** (ave Habib Bourguiba; 8.30am-8pm Mon-Sat, 8.30am-1pm Sun), beneath which is a fruit and veg market. Down some stairs west of the supermarket are an excellent boulangerie and **pâtisserie** (rue de la Gare). Try a fresh fruit milkshake from the **fruit stall** (place du 7 Novembre).

Drinking

Café de Nattes (place Sidi Bou Saïd; 7am-midnight) This is the village epicentre. Fronted by steep steps, the trad-café interior has stick-of-rock columns and rush-mat seating, and outside are small terraces ideal for checking out the cobbled catwalk of the street while sipping mint tea with pinenuts. At the bottom of the steps is a cheaper popular café.

Café Sidi Chabaane (rue Sidi Chabaane; 7am-midnight Apr-Sep, to 8pm Oct-Mar) One of the prettiest café settings around, with layers of terraces cut into the cliff. This is an ideal place to watch the sunset, with high-up views over the blue-green sea, yacht-stuffed marina and sandy swathe of beach. The fresh fruit juices are very good.

Café Alaska (Marina; 8am-1am Apr-Sep, to 7pm Oct-Mar) This large marina-edged tree-shaded café is a busy local option in the evening, with great sandwiches.

Getting There & Away

Sidi Bou Saïd is about 17km northeast of Tunis. The easiest way to travel is by TGM train from Tunis Marine (1st/2nd class TD1.1/0.7, 35 minutes). It's a 15-minute, steepish walk from the station to the top of the hill and the centre of the old part of the village. A daytime taxi costs around TD12.

LA MARSA المرسى

La Marsa, once the Ottoman beys' summer base, is an exclusive beachside suburb at the end of the TGM line, with grand, dazzling-white villas. The palm-lined beach stretches north around a bay that finishes beneath the cliffs of the five-star resort village of Gammarth. It's relatively uncrowded on weekdays, but everyone in Tunis seems to descend at weekends. There's a restored 16th-century palace, **Al-Abdallya**, signposted from beside Tunisie Telecom on ave Habib Bourguiba, which the caretaker will be delighted to show you, though if there's no temporary exhibition, there's little to see other than newly whitewashed arched interiors.

There's a **Publinet Le Net Club** (rue Cheïkh Zarrouk 4; per hr TD2; 9am-midnight Mon-Sat, 10am-midnight Sun), a block away from Pension Predl.

Off ave Habib Bourguiba, **Pension Predl** (71 950 378; 26 rue Mohamed Salah Malki; s/d with shared bathroom TD20/40) is unusual in that it's a pension in a Tunisian home. It's basic but has clean, high-ceilinged rooms. A timeless living room filled with homey clutter is centred around a linoleum-covered table and several sofas.

A few minutes walk from the TGM station, American-owned and highly kitsch **Hôtel Plaza Corniche** (71 743 489; rue du Maroc; s/d TD80/110;), with plastic palms and bright flower-sprigged rooms with balconies, is a popular place for a poolside evening drink. There's also a lively disco – reputedly one of Tunis' best.

The refined French **Au Bon Vieux Temps** (71 774 733; rue Hedi Zarrouk; mains TD14-20; noon-3pm & 6pm-midnight Mon-Sat;), just by the TGM station, is intimate inside and has a small tree-shaded terrace.

Café Le Saf Saf (place Saf Saf; snacks TD1-6; 7am-midnight) is a lovely traditional café, with good snacks as well as tea and coffee. It has a tiled courtyard with shady trees centred around a wooden wheel that was once turned by a camel.

GAMMARTH قمّرت

Beneath the cliffs of Cap Gammarth, 2km north of La Marsa and really just an extension of it, is this rich, leafy suburb with lots of sleek seaside villas, a curve of coast, some excellent restaurants and a gamut of five-star hotels.

The hugely glamorous, if a bit soulless, five-star **La Residence** (71 910 101; www.theresidence-tunis.com; Les Côtes de Carthage; s/d from €298/312) is famous for its fabulous spa – all domes, arches and columns in marble, with around 30 treatment rooms where you can do everything from lymphatic drainage to seaweed wraps. If you can't afford to stay, you can use the facilities if you book a treatment.

With a great seafront location, **Les Ombrelles** (71 742 964; ave Taieb M'hiri; mains TD10-20;) has tasty, straightforward seafood. The interior dining room is a warm yellow and the whole place is candlelit at night, with lovely outdoor seating. It's slightly arrogant, though, and service can be unfriendly.

A graceful white-painted villa, **Les Dunes** (23 401 000; 130 ave Taieb M'hiri; mains TD12-24; noon-3pm Tue-Sun, 8pm-midnight daily;) has a terrace overlooking the sea (though it's across a road) and serves Italian food, specialising – of course – in seafood. The piped music is a bit cheesy.

There are truly big-blue views from **Le Grand Bleu** (71 913 700; ave Taieb M'hiri; mains TD17-22; 12.30-3pm & 8-11.30pm, bar 11am-2am;), perched high above the bay, a gilded, expense-account haunt with excellent seafood. It's a place to impress, with a large terrace, white-tableclothed tables set wide apart and shoals of waiters. There's also a popular piano bar.

You can walk around the bay from La Marsa, which takes about 45 minutes. A cab from La Marsa will cost around TD1.

HAMMAM LIF

This dilapidated southern suburb has been a spa resort for thousands of years. In colloquial Arabic, Lif means 'nose', as the baths here were reputedly good for clearing the sinuses. Bou Kornine – with its twin peaks (the name means two humps) – looms above the district. This is the shadowy mountain you can see from across the bay in Carthage and Sidi Bou Saïd.

Hammam Lif is a popular place to promenade along the seafront, survey your fellow citizens and search out a breeze (or even leap in the sea) on summer evenings, with interesting buildings and loads of food stalls. The corniche is busy until at least 1am. You can reach here by frequent trains from Tunis Ville (20 to 30 minutes) or by taxi (TD4).

Cap Bon الوطى القبا

Cap Bon is Tunisia's tourism hot spot, pointing its crooked thumb towards Sicily, only 150km away. It has long had close links with Europe – geologists speculate that the land masses were once joined – split by the rising Mediterranean 30,000 years ago. Crowded with citrus trees and vineyards, the region is famous for its wine, particularly Kélibia's fragrant muscat.

The action centres on the resort of Hammamet, stretching along an amber-sanded beach that has attracted tourists since the 1920s. Then a jet-set playground, it's now a popular package destination. Clever planning restrictions have kept it an attractive place to visit. Hotels have large capacities but don't tower over the bay, and are surrounded by greenery.

Venture away from Hammamet and the busy craft centre of Nabeul and you'll find Cap Bon a surprising adventure. Its other towns have a charming nothing-much-to-do feel, and if you have your own transport and want to find a deserted beach, you're in luck.

Kélibia, a northern backwater, has a small, busy port, a mighty fortress and a dazzling beach, with only one hotel plonked on it so far. Nearby are the ruins of Punic Kerkouane – the most complete remains of the Carthaginian civilisation. Small town El-Haouaria, at the peninsula's northern tip, feels even more remote, lying near coastal quarries that date back more than 2500 years and supplied stone for Rome's Colosseum.

The west is more rugged and difficult to get around. A dramatic road clinging to the rocky coast leads to faded small spa Korbous, where a scalding hot spring spills directly into the sea, as if performing a magic trick.

HIGHLIGHTS

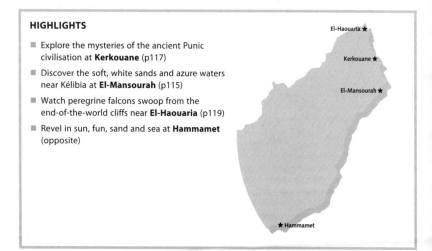

- Explore the mysteries of the ancient Punic civilisation at **Kerkouane** (p117)
- Discover the soft, white sands and azure waters near Kélibia at **El-Mansourah** (p115)
- Watch peregrine falcons swoop from the end-of-the-world cliffs near **El-Haouaria** (p119)
- Revel in sun, fun, sand and sea at **Hammamet** (opposite)

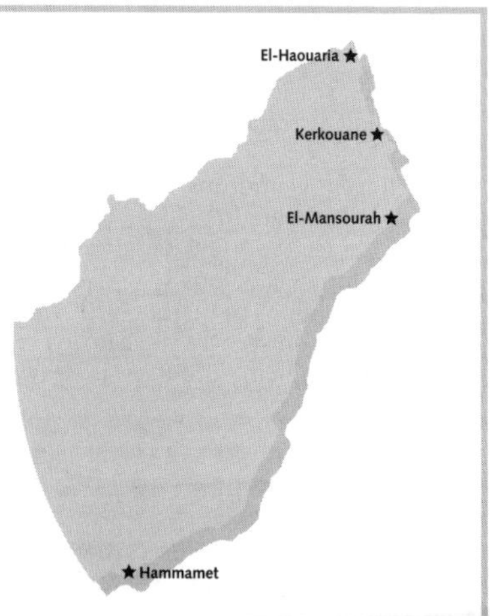

History

Cap Bon was under Carthaginian control by the early 5th century BC, a lush agricultural region that kept the Punic capital in fruit and veg, and formed a key – if not very successful – part of its defence system, centred on fortified Aspis (Kélibia). The problem was that it was geographically vulnerable. Both Agathocles of Syracuse (in 310 BC) and the Roman general Regulus (in 256 BC) invaded through here during their respective assaults on Carthage, sacking Aspis en route. Kerkouane survived Agathocles, but was trashed by Regulus and abandoned forever.

The Romans called the region the 'beautiful peninsula' – Pulchri Promontorium – and settled in. They took over Aspis, renaming it Clypea, and built the large town of Neapolis (Nabeul). The countryside is dotted with relics of other settlements. Prosperity continued until the Arabic conquest. Clypea became a Byzantine stronghold that held out against the Arabs until the late 7th century AD, long after the rest of Tunisia had fallen.

But then piracy and unrest led to decline from the 14th to 16th centuries. Cap Bon was constantly threatened from the sea, forcing many coastal communities to shift inland – you'll notice that Nabeul and Kélibia are a few kilometres from the coast.

A wave of Andalusian immigrants arrived from the 15th century (feeling persecution by Christians in Spain), revitalising the area, and it was favoured by European settlers during the 19th-century French era: the countryside is dotted with the ruins of old, red-tiled farmhouses and great agricultural buildings. The French developed the vast citrus groves around Beni Khalled and Menzel Bou Zelfa and the vineyards around Grombalia.

An exclusive kind of tourism took off in the 1920s, triggered largely by Romanian millionaire George Sebastian building his luxurious villa outside Hammamet. Less-welcome visitors took over the villa in 1943 when Axis forces retreated to Cap Bon and ran their campaign from there, until the surrender that ended the North African phase of WWII. Today it's Tunisia's biggest resort, a holiday playground. Even President Ben Ali has a holiday home here.

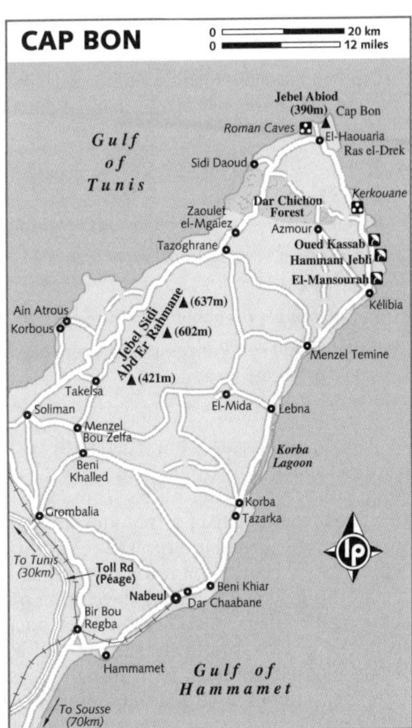

Climate

Cap Bon has a blessedly balmy climate – as a coastal region it is cooler during the summer and warmer in winter than other parts of Tunisia.

Getting There & Away

The nearest airport is Tunis-Carthage. There are many buses and louages (shared-taxis) serving the region, with Hammamet and Korbous around an hour from the capital. Nabeul and Hammamet are also connected to Tunis by train.

Getting Around

Louages and buses connect the coastal towns. It's more difficult to cross the Cap Bon peninsula – Soliman and Korbous are better reached from Tunis.

HAMMAMET حمّامات

pop 52,000

With a soft curve of sandy beach, densely blue Mediterranean, little Noddy trains, all-facility hotels, with everything you need to make life easier, Hammamet ('the baths'

TOP FIVE OFF-THE-BEATEN-TRACK BEACHES

Cap Bon has more than enough beaches for everyone and there are some lovely undiscovered spots. Let us know what you think of these and if you discover any more at lonelyplanet.com/feedback.

- Across the causeway over Korba Lagoon is a remarkable white-sanded beach (p114), a local secret.
- A few kilometres beyond lovely El-Mansourah near Kélibia try Hammam Jebli (p115).
- Near the Centre National de la Jeunes, 7km north of Kélibia, lies pearly white Oued Kassab (p115).
- The locals know about Ras el-Drek (p120) but you'll rarely meet other foreign tourists here.
- At Barrage Port Princes (p121), overlooked by a golden-stone castle, is a charming small bay in a protected area.

in Arabic) is Tunisia's biggest resort, with a hotel capacity of 57,000. But early planning constraints said hotels should not overreach the height of a tree and, though there are some broad interpretations of this, buildings in Hammamet are restrained – it's nothing like the brutal developments scarring Spanish coasts. Hotels, set back from the beach, are mostly surrounded by lushly planted gardens, with lots of trees. However, there's a strange equation here between the traditional elements of a Tunisian town (mosques, the call to prayer, women in headscarves and men in cafés) and a European-favoured resort, with skimpily dressed tourists wandering down to the beach.

The town feels small-scale, attractive and cheery. The small, picturesque centre is packed with restaurants and shops, overlooked by its Disney-perfect medina (walled city), and the sea is surreally dotted by galleon-style tourist boats. Evenings usher in a carnival atmosphere.

The metamorphosis from quiet fishing village began in the 1920s with the arrival of millionaire George Sebastian (his villa now houses Hammamet's International Cultural Centre) and the European jet set. Today, hotels stretch all the way to the fantasy tourist zone of Yasmine Hammamet, 5km to the south. Where the hotels stop, abruptly, the beach is once again wild and untouched.

Orientation

Hammamet's medina is central, overlooking the sea on a small spit of land jutting out into the Gulf of Hammamet. There are two main streets in the town. Ave Habib Bourguiba runs north from the medina and links up with the road to Hammamet Sud (around 2km) and the newest development of Yasmine Hammamet. Ave de la République meanwhile heads northeast from the medina to Hammamet Nord and on to Nabeul.

Information

EMERGENCY

Infirmary (☎ 72 282 333; 29 ave Habib Bourguiba)
Police (Map p103; ☎ 72 280 079; ave Habib Bourguiba)

INTERNET ACCESS

Access costs TD1.5 to TD2 per hour.
Publinet (117 ave de la Libération; 🕑 8.30am-11pm)
Publinet (Map p103; ave Taieb Azzabi; 🕑 9am-11pm)
Publinet La Gare (163 ave Habib Bourguiba; 🕑 7am-midnight)

MONEY

Banks and plenty of ATMs are concentrated around the junction of aves Habib Bourguiba and de la République.

Many hotels and shops can also change cash and travellers cheques.

POST

Main post office (Map p103; ave de la République; 🕑 8am-6pm Mon-Sat, 8am-12.30pm Sun Sep-Jun, 7.30am-1pm & 5-11pm Mon-Sat Jul, 9-11am Sun Jul & Aug)

TOURIST INFORMATION

ONTT (Map p103; ☎ 72 280 423; ave de la République & ave Ali Belhouane; 🕑 9am-1pm & 3-8pm Mon-Sat, 9am-1pm Sun Sep-Jun, 9am-midnight Jul & Aug) Provides free maps of Hammamet and Nabeul.

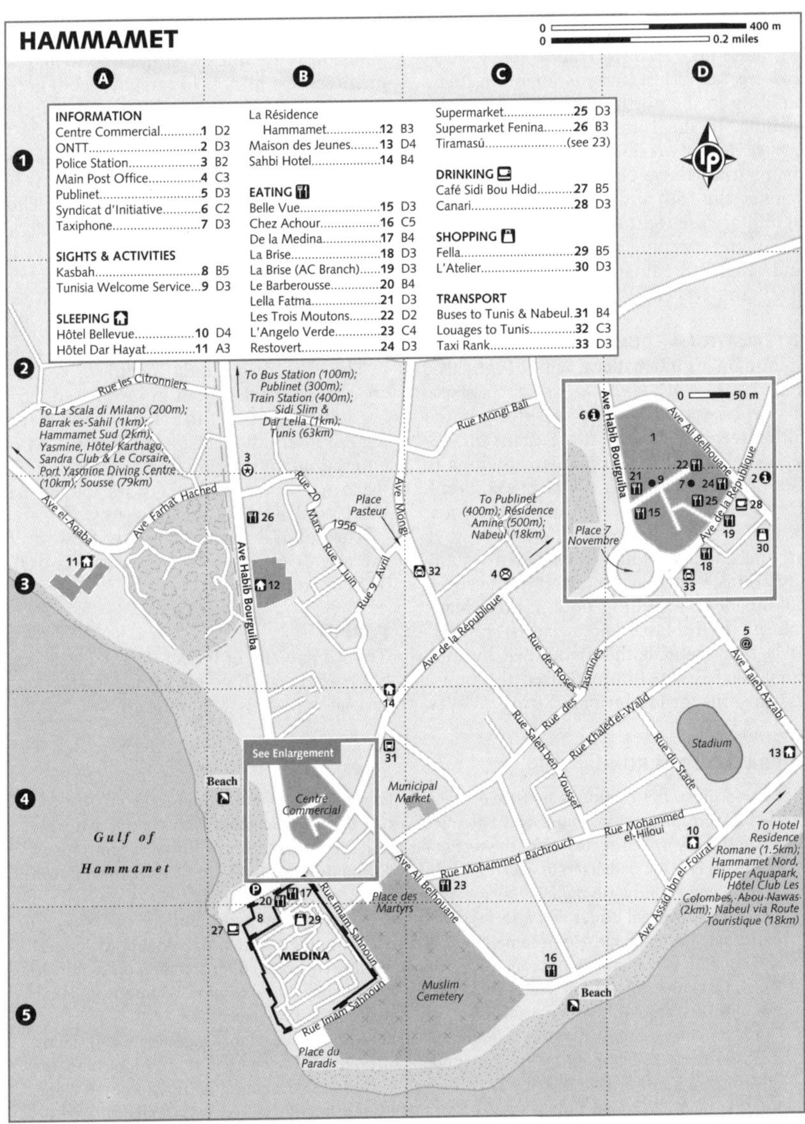

Syndicat d'Initiative (Map p103; ☎ 72 262 891; ave Habib Bourguiba; 🕑 8am-8pm Mon-Sat) This small office carries similar items to the ONTT, but charges for its city map.

Sights

MEDINA

The Hafsid Ottomans built this sandcastle medina (1463–74), with 2m-thick walls, on the site of a 9th-century Aghlabid structure. Up to 1881 the medina *was* Hammamet – a fortified village of 300 inhabitants. The three gates were closed at night and for Friday prayer. Souvenir shops envelope the weblike old souqs, but the southern residential district is particularly well preserved.

The **Kasbah** (Map p103; ☎ 72 782 264; admission TD3, camera TD1; 🕑 8am-5pm Oct-Mar, 8am-6pm Apr-Jun & Sep, 8am-8pm Jul & Aug) is an immaculate building in the northwestern corner of the medina. In the 15th century this was the city governor's residence (a sole tower remains from those days). Adapted for firearms in the 16th and 17th centuries, it was in military use right up to the 19th century. There are sweeping views across the coast and tangled medina from a small (expensive) ramparts café.

INTERNATIONAL CULTURAL CENTRE

Hammamet's **International Culture Centre** (Map p105; ☎ 72 280 410; ave des Nations Unies; admission TD3; 🕑 8am-6pm Feb-Sep, 8am-5pm Oct-Jan) is the ultimate party house. It's a mansion designed and built by Romanian millionaire George Sebastian from 1920 to 1932. Frank Lloyd Wright said it was one of the most beautiful places he knew: the appreciative architect was just one of Sebastian's many illustrious, bohemian guests. It has a central colonnaded swimming pool, a huge black marble dining table and a baptistery font-style four-seater bath surrounded by mirrors. Nazi Erwin Rommel used the house as an Axis headquarters during WWII, and after the war British Prime Minister Winston Churchill stayed here to write his memoirs. It's bizarre to imagine them here in these decadent surroundings – hopefully they enjoyed the four-person bathtub.

The house feels unloved, but its faded feel evokes a sense of good times past. It now hosts interesting displays of art. The terrace faces a rich view of flowers, greenery and sea-flooded horizon, and you can walk down to the beach, where there is a small café serving drinks. It's a particularly lovely stretch of beach frontage and it's usually empty, so bring your beach kit with you.

The 14-acre grounds include a Greek-style amphitheatre, built in 1962, used during July and August to stage Hammamet's annual International Cultural Festival, with entertainment ranging from classical theatre to Arabic music. Tickets are sold at the tourist office and at the door.

The cultural centre is 3km northwest of the town centre – a taxi will set you back TD1 or so.

PUPPUT بوپات

The Roman site of **Pupput** (Map p105; route Touristique; admission TD2; 🕑 9am-5pm mid-Sep–Mar, 8am-7pm Apr–mid-Sep) is 6.5km southwest of the

CRAXI ON THE RUN

Bettino Craxi, the notorious mid-1980s Italian prime minister, fled to Hammamet in 1994 following corruption charges. He had been accused of bribery connected with contracts for the Milan subway system. Craxi spent the rest of his life in seaside exile, under the wing of his friend President Ben Ali. Convicted in absentia on multiple counts, Craxi faced up to 10 years in prison in his home country. He died at the age of 66 in 2000.

The controversial leader was a socialist who had modernised his party, crushing the left wing and changing its image. He became Italy's first socialist prime minister in 1983 and its longest serving (four years) until Berlusconi. He is internationally remembered for standing up to Ronald Reagan over the *Achille Lauro* cruise ship PLO hijack, when he refused to allow US troops to detain the hijackers, arguing that, on Sicilian soil, the Americans had no jurisdiction.

His star fell when investigators from the Italian corruption crack-team 'Operation Clean Hands' exposed huge bribes paid by businesspeople to politicians – charges that demolished the government. Craxi argued that it was common knowledge that political parties accepted illegal funding. A disillusioned public were unimpressed and he was pelted with coins outside his residence in Rome. Fleeing to Tunisia, he stayed here rather than return to Italy for required medical treatment for complications relating to his diabetes, which contributed to his eventual ill-health. He spent his time making pottery, campaigning to free his name and visiting his favourite restaurant, La Scala di Milano (see p108). His tombstone – in Hammamet's Catholic Cemetery – reads 'My freedom is my life'.

One of Craxi's good political friends was one Silvio Berlusconi, media magnate and ex-Italian prime minister, who apparently has also bought a villa in Sidi Bou Saïd – who knows when it might come in handy.

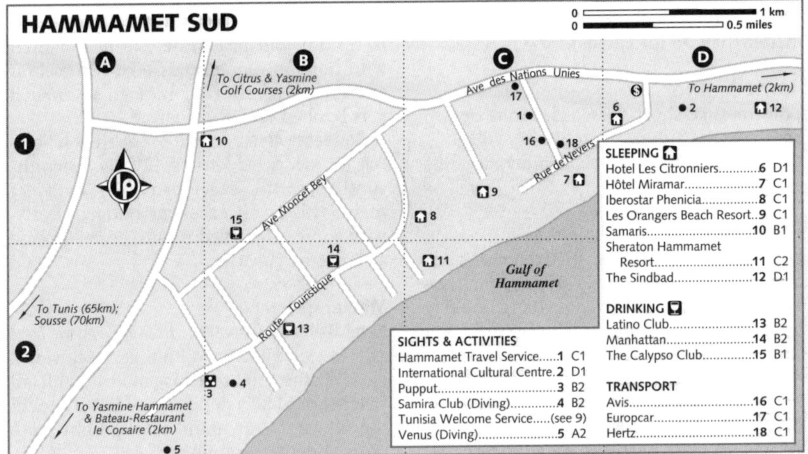

Hammamet town centre. Wedged between Hammamet's hotels and nightclubs, this was once a staging post on the Roman road from Carthage to Hadrumetum (Sousse). The name suggests that it occupies the site of an earlier Punic settlement. The Byzantine and Roman remains are scant, but of interest if you're a history buff. The 5th-century House of Figured Peristyle retains a couple of columns and some mosaic flooring, but most memorable are the bleached-out Byzantine tomb mosaics displayed on a wall.

Activities

BEACHES

Hammamet is all about beaches. The best stretches northwest from the medina. Dotted by private hotel areas, it has plenty of public bits, and water-sports facilities at regular intervals (see below). There's a lovely stretch outside the International Cultural Centre (see opposite). If you have your own transport, you can drive out beyond Yasmine – after the buildings stop, the beach is empty and wild, and seems to go on forever.

The beach running towards Nabeul is also well worth spreading your towel on.

WATER-SPORTS

Places offering paragliding (TD25), water skiing (TD10 to TD15), jet skis (TD35 for 10 minutes), windsurfing (TD25 per hour) and other such delights punctuate the beaches at Hammamet Nord and Sud from April to September.

A couple of hotels have open-water diving centres offering certification courses (around TD380) and sets of five dives (TD180). There are some WWII wrecks and sea life to explore, and readers have had fun learning to dive here – Odysea has received good reports.

Samira Club (Map p105; ☎ 72 226 484)
Venus (Map p105; ☎ 72 227 211)
Port Yasmine Diving Centre (☎ 72 319 741; charrad.jalel@planet.tm)
Odysea Diving School (Hotel Le Sultan; ☎ 72 280 588; www.odyseadiving.com)

FLIPPER AQUAPARK

A water park in Hammamet Nord, **Flipper Aquapark** (Map p103; ☎ 72 261 800; www.aquaflipper.com; Route Touristique; adult/child TD15/10; 🕑 10am-7pm) has winding slides and splashy features for small and big kids. It gets pretty busy.

GOLF

Golf is big business, with two clubs west of town.

Citrus (Map p105; ☎ 72 226 500; www.citrusgolf.com), beside the main Tunis–Sousse road, is a huge, lush complex laid out among citrus and olive trees. Built in the 1990s, it includes two demanding 18-hole courses and a nine-hole short course. Green fees cost TD45/86 for nine/18 holes. **Yasmine** (Map p105; ☎ 72 227 665; www.golfyasmine.com), about 2km to the north, has an 18-hole course and a beginners' nine-hole. Green fees are TD48/69.

Both clubs demand proof of handicap (better than 36 for Citrus).

HORSE RIDING

You can take short horse rides (one or two hours) in the hills or out to Berber villages – most of the bigger hotels can arrange this for you.

Tours

Lots of tour companies run excursions, including a half-day tour to Berber villages – Takrouna, Zriba and Jeradou – and one-day tours whizzing round Carthage, Sidi Bou Saïd and the Bardo Museum. Try:

Hammamet Travel Service (Map p105; ☎ 72 280 193; www.hts-tunisia.com; ave Dag Hammarskjöld)

Tunisia Welcome Service (☎ 72 280 544; www.tunisia-orangers.com) Hammamet (Map p103; Centre Commercial, ave Habib Bourguiba); Hammamet Sud (Map p105; rue de Nevers)

Festivals & Events

In July and August, the International Festival features international stars from everywhere from Ireland to Mali, as well as closer-to-home Tunisian and Algerian musicians. Concerts take place in the International Cultural Centre's seaside amphitheatre, and films show at various venues. Get a programme from the tourist office.

Sleeping

Three-star-plus places usually offer air-con, a pool and sizable rooms. Such is Hammamet's capacity that you can usually walk up and get a room, and discounts apply (always worth a try) if business is slack. Prices plummet in winter. Rates here include breakfast unless otherwise stated, and children under 12 usually cost 30% to 100% less. There's often a supplement of TD4 to TD20 for a sea view, which is worth paying if you can afford it. If you book via a package deal before you arrive, you'll get big discounts on these rack rates.

CENTRE

If you want to be near the best restaurants and a stuffed-camel's throw from the medina, this is where to stay.

Budget

Maison des Jeunes (Map p103; ☎ 72 280 440; ave Assad ibn el-Fourat; d with shared bathroom TD6, dm TD3) A cut above most Maisons des Jeunes, this is central *and* beachside, clean and nice, with hot showers. Rooms take two to four and have seafront balconies. In summer it gets booked up, so call ahead.

Résidence Amine (☎ 72 765 500; ave de la Libération; s/d with private bathroom TD15/30) Friendly, spotless, with eager-to-please management, this is an excellent budget choice, with some huge, tiled rooms, all set around an internal courtyard.

Midrange

Hôtel Bellevue (Map p103; ☎ 72 281 121; ave Assad ibn el-Fourat; s/d TD30/60) With breezy sea views, close to the medina, this small beachfront hotel should be a good choice but it's looking very run-down and a bit grubby, with crumbling bathrooms.

La Résidence Hammamet (Map p103; ☎ 72 280 733; www.hammamet-residence.com; 54 ave Habib Bourguiba; s/d/tr/q with private bathroom & kitchenette TD46.5/77/96/112; ❄ 🏊) Central, and a bargain if you can get a discount, this is a cheaper package place with sizable wrought-iron furnished studios around a leafy courtyard. It also has a rooftop pool, private beach and a shop where you can buy alcohol. Prices listed don't include breakfast, as it's not up to much.

Top End

Hotel Residence Romane (☎ 72 263 103; rommene.sami@gnet.tn; rue Assad Ben Fourat; s/d TD57/78, 2-/4-person apt TD110; ❄ 🏊) With attractive, spacious, unfussy rooms with balconies, this is a great choice. The hotel is well kept and nicely decorated and the pool is surrounded by greenery.

Sahbi Hôtel (Map p103; ☎ 72 266 130; ave de la République; s/d TD56/88; ❄) This is central and above a lavish carpet shop and overhung with greenery. Large, prettily decorated rooms are a bit musty, but discounts are readily available.

Hôtel Dar Hayat (Map p103; ☎ 72 283 399; ave el-Aqaba; s/d TD150/250; ❄ 🏊) Smaller than most upmarket Hammamet hotels, this has bright, elegant rooms with fantastic sea views and an unusual amount of charm, but it feels a bit tired considering the price.

NORD

The beach here is lovely and quieter than the south, but the hotels tend to be older and less flashy.

Top-End

Abou Nawas (☎ 72 281 344; Route Touristique el-Merezka; s/d TD78/95; ❄ 🏊) This is up to the usual luxurious standard of the Abou Nawas chain, beachside, with green grounds, attractive, comfortable rooms and friendly service.

Hôtel Club Les Colombes (☎ 72 280 899; Route Touristique el-Merezka; s/d full board TD90/150; ❄ 🏊) Right on the beach, this is a well-established if rather staid hotel with a quiet atmosphere. The rooms have terrific sea views.

SUD

The south not only has the balmiest curve of beach but also the bulk of the nightlife.

Budget

Samaris (Map p105; ☎ 72 226 353; ave des Nations Unies; camping per adult/child/tent/car/van/hot shower TD2.8/2/2/2/2.8/2.3, s/d with private bathroom TD26/52) It's surprising to go from the busy road into this leafy, courtyard-centred place, a few kilometres from the beach. Rooms are old-fashioned but pleasing enough and it's worth staying here for the lush gardens. The camp site is shady and pretty.

Midrange

Hôtel Les Citronniers (Map p105; ☎ 72 281 650; rue de Nevers; www.hotellescitronniers.com; s/d TD40/60; 🏊) A small, cheery, lower-end package hotel, this has a good location near the beach, a terrace out the front serving beer, a pool and simple clean rooms with balconies.

Top End

Hôtel Miramar (Map p105; ☎ 72 280 344; rue de Nevers; s/d TD127/194; ❄ 🏊) Rooms at this large hotel are big and nicely decorated. There are also George Sebastian–inspired (see p101) suites with two terraces.

Les Orangers Beach Resort (Map p105; ☎ 72 280 144; www.orangers.com.tn; rue de Nevers; s/d full board TD147/252; ❄ 🏊) This is something like a much more luxurious, more international version of Butlins. Here you have everything you need for a holiday, with pools, bars, private beach and lots of entertainment. It's huge (391 rooms) and great for families.

The Sindbad (Map p105; ☎ 72 280 122; www.hotel-sindbad.com; ave des Nations Unies; s/d TD166/210; ❄ 🏊) The flashy Sindbad gets good reviews. It has an exclusive feel, excellent service and spacious rooms set in lush grounds with shady terraces. There's also a good pool and private beach.

Iberostar Phenicia (Map p105; ☎ 72 226 533; www.iberostar.com; s/d full board TD175/290; ❄ 🏊) Built in the '70s by the presidential architect, this massive place (capacity 720) has been revamped to become a designer hotel, with sharply designed modern rooms that make a refreshing change. There's a practice golf course and putting green.

Sheraton Hammamet Resort (Map p105; ☎ 72 226 555; www.sheraton.com; s/d TD195/300; ❄ 🏊) The tasteful Sheraton has an excellent reputation, with helpful staff and good disabled access. With a mere 201 rooms (plus two suites), it feels appealingly smaller scale, with simple and luxurious whitewashed, bungalows set in gardens around an attractive pool. Ask for a sea view.

YASMINE

This is Hammamet's newest development. It's on a different scale, with stark palm-lined boulevards featuring huge mall-style hotels (mostly four- and five-stars) and a marina. If you're on a package, you'll doubtless revel in all-inclusive luxury (the beach is nice too), but if not you've no reason to come here. It did have Carthageland, a theme park enclosed in a spanking-new medina, which added a touch of Vegas-style weirdness, but this was closed long-term at the time of research due to an accident. Special mention should go to five-star neo-castle Lella Baya for out-and-out architectural eccentricity.

Top-End

Flora Park (☎ 72 227 727; www.solmelia.com; s/d TD120/190; ❄ 🏊) Unusual in this area, this is a boutique hotel, a bit away from the beach (you have to cross a few roads to reach it), but with an intimate feel, nice spa and tasteful rooms.

Hôtel Karthago (☎ 72 240 666; www.karthagohotels.com; Station Touristique; d TD210; ❄ 🏊) This mammoth marina and beachside five-star is very swish, with a cream-coloured, gold-studded central atrium reminiscent of a huge '70s cruise liner crossed with an airport. The rooms echo the ship design, and there's a classy spa and huge pool. There's an ice rink next door.

Hasdrubal Thalassa (☎ 72 248 800; www.hasdrubal-hotels.com; ave Medina; junior/ambassador/prestige ste TD450/720/1000;) One of the Leading Hotels in the World group, this place is hugely swish, if a bit far-flung, with lots of marble, ostentatious pool and super spa. Most people stay here to indulge in its tremendous treatments.

Eating

RESTAURANTS

There are hoards of good restaurants and many open very late (to around 2am) in July and August.

La Brise (Map p103; ave de la République; mains TD4-8.5; 10.30am-12.30am, to 9pm Oct-Mar;) The best of the cheapies. A friendly place with some outside tables near the medina and nice food in hearty portions. The air-con branch is very spiffy and clean, with blue and yellow tiling.

Restovert (Map p103; ☎ 72 278 200; ave de la République; dishes TD5.8-8.5; 9am-1am) Plastered with film posters, this little 1st-floor place is a popular hang-out for young Hammamet, with a balcony for street-surveillance and lots of tasty snacks, such as crepes and panini.

L'Angolo Verde (Map p103; ☎ 72 262 641; rue Ali Belhaouane; mains TD5.8-12.5; 11am-11pm;) A happening, tucked-away spot, this place is popular and great for children. There's some tree-shaded pavement seating and a long, trendy menu that includes good pizzas, pasta, crepes and panini (no alcohol). Next door is Tiramasú (open noon to 1am) with yummy Italian ice cream.

Chez Achour (Map p103; ☎ 72 280 140; rue Ali Belhouane; mains TD7.5-21;) This attractive place is great for a special night out, with seating in a garden courtyard decorated by white lanterns and sunshades. It serves up excellent seafood.

Dar Lella (☎ 72 279 128; off ave du Koweit; mains TD8.5-18.5; 10am-3pm & 6.30pm-midnight;) Sumptuously decorated (as if ready for a wedding) in a mix of Berber and European styles, this place serves upmarket tradi tional food and has outside lawn seating.

La Scala di Milano (Map p103; ☎ 98 618 713; La Corniche; mains TD10-16;) Well worth the short walk from the centre, this restaurant has some of Hammamet's best cooking, with excellent pasta, bruschetta, fish and meat dishes and a charming small garden. It was disgraced Italian former prime minister Bettino Craxi's favourite haunt, and his chair is enshrined here to prove it. Run by and attracts characters.

Sidi Slim (☎ 72 279 124; 156 ave du Koweit; mains TD10-18.5; noon-11.30pm;) With fussy décor involving some crazy-paving arches, upmarket local favourite Sidi Slim is welcoming, has good seafood and meat dishes and comes recommended.

Les Trois Moutons (Map p103; ☎ 72 280 981; Centre Commercial; mains TD11-20;) This is one of Hammamet's classier restaurants, with an interior like a pretty conservatory stage-set and it serves lots of seafood.

Le Corsaire (☎ 72 240 323; Port Yasmine Hammamet; mains TD13-23; noon-midnight) At this upmarket boat restaurant floating in the marina. you can sit on the top deck and tuck into top seafood, with great views over the slick, flag-fluttering yachts.

Other recommendations:

Belle Vue (Map p103; ☎ 72 280 825; ave Habib Bourguiba; mains TD6-12.5; 8-2am) Next door to and cheaper than Lella Fatma, Belle Vue has received favourable reports from travellers.

De la Medina (Map p103; ☎ 72 281 728; mains TD7-15; noon-midnight) Seating on medina ramparts, but the view is the main draw rather than the food or service.

Lella Fatma (Map p103; ☎ 72 280 756; ave Habib Bourguiba; mains TD8.9-17.9; 11am-11pm) Opposite the medina, this place is good for people-watching and has reliably palatable food.

Le Barberousse (Map p103; ☎ 72 280 037; mains TD12-24; 12.30pm-midnight) Also on the medina walls, this is more upmarket than De la Medina, but the lovely beachside views are again the main attraction.

SELF-CATERING

Self-caterers can stock up at the Municipal Market between ave de la République and rue des Jasmines. You can buy beer and a fine selection of local wines at the town's small main **supermarket** (ave de la République; 8.30am-8pm). Smaller **Supermarket Fenina** (82 ave Habib Bourguiba; 8.30am-10pm Mon-Sat, 10am-1.30pm Sun) is well stocked and has fewer queues.

Drinking

Hammamet has some of Tunisia's best nightlife, though this says more about the dearth elsewhere: discos have a cattle-market vibe and clientele is a lively mix of Tunisians and foreign tourists. The best are in Hammamet Sud, bumping and grinding on two parallel streets, so if you get hacked off with one you can head elsewhere. They peak on Friday and Saturday, charge around TD10, which includes one drink, and open from about 10pm till 4am or 5am.

Manhattan (Map p105; ☎ 72 226 226) A long-standing classic cheesy club, with big flashing lights and pop house tunes.

The Calypso Club (Map p105; ☎ 72 227 530; www.calypsotunisia.com; ave Moncef Bey) Advertising itself as the best club in Tunisia, this is the haunt of Tunisia's loaded youth and has pricey drinks, go-go dancers and the most see-and-be-seen atmosphere.

Latino Club (Map p105; Route Touristique) This is perhaps Hammamet's best club, with a lively mix from salsa to Arabic pop. Hip Spanish tourists arrive at the airport and head straight here, such is its fame.

Café Sidi Bou Hdid (Map p103; snacks around TD2; 5.30am-2am) Between the medina walls and the sea, with a mix of locals and tourists, this is a lovely place for an orange juice or a *sheesha,* with tables and chairs or rug-draped low seats and tables.

Canari (Map p103; ave de la République; snacks TD2-4; 9am-1am, to 10pm Oct-Mar) A popular café with a large, watch-the-world-go-by terrace, this is good for fresh juices and milkshakes. In the back is a bakery and pâtisserie selling wonderful Tunisian sweets and French pastries.

Shopping

Jewellery, leather, clothes, ceramics and carpets are sold in and around the medina. There's lots of choice, though you'll have to sift through some tack and there are better deals elsewhere.

Fella (Map p103; ☎ 72 280 426; Medina; 9am-1pm & 4-9pm Tue-Sun) Sophia Loren, Umm Kolthum, Grace Kelly and Greta Garbo have all floated around in Fella at some point. The boutique has immaculate handmade Tunisian dresses, jewellery and bits and pieces. A nice *fouta* (cotton beach sheet) costs TD12.

L'Atelier (Map p103; ☎ 72 261 918; rue Ali Belhouane; 9am-1pm & 4-9.30pm) This small gallery has original, metal-framed etchings by Baker Ben Fredj, starting at TD66.

Getting There & Away

BUS

There are buses to/from Nabeul (TD0.8, 30 minutes, half-hourly) and Tunis (TD3.5, 50 minutes to 1¼ hours, half-hourly) departing and arriving from near the tourist office. Buy tickets on board. There are buses to Sousse (TD5.5, SRTG TD3.8, 1½ hours, five daily), but it's easier to get there via louage (see below).

CAR

Car rental agencies include the following:

Avis (Map p105; ☎ 72 280 164; rue de Nevers)
Europcar (Map p105; ☎ 72 280 146; rue des Hôtels)
Hertz (Map p105; ☎ 72 266 466; rue de Nevers)

LOUAGE

Louages to Tunis (TD4, one hour) leave from Place Pasteur, about 800m northeast of the medina. Other louages, to Sousse (TD4.4, one hour) and Kairouan (TD4.7, 1½ hours), leave from Barrak es-Sahil, 2km northwest of town.

TRAIN

There are trains to/from Nabeul (TD0.6, 20 minutes, 12 to 13 daily) and Tunis (TD3.8, one to 1½ hours, nine daily) – only one Tunis train is direct, the others involve a change at Bir Bou Regba. From Bir Bou Regba you can make connections to Sousse, Sfax and beyond. Hammamet station is about 1.5km from the centre, at the northern end of ave Habib Bourguiba.

Getting Around

The main taxi rank is by the medina. It costs TD3.5 to Hammamet Sud. There are several Noddy trains, run by different companies, chugging around all the major hotels (leaving from outside the medina), and buses run from here to Yasmine Hammamet (TD0.5, half-hourly).

NABEUL نابل

pop 57,400

Nabeul, 18km north of Hammamet, is a working town: the administrative centre of Cap Bon and Tunisia's biggest ceramics centre. It also has an attractive white-sand beach, though lacking shade – it's cleanest in front of the resort hotels, and there are a few beach cafés open in high season. There is a Friday souvenir market that has become hugely famous for no particular reason. Quieter than Hammamet and with fewer hotels, Nabeul has some unusually good pensions. It also has a unique line in kitsch roundabout architecture. An arts festival featuring traditional music is held in late July and early August.

Orientation

Nabeul is spread out. The centre is about 1.5km inland – a legacy of the 16th century when pirates terrorised the coast. Now that pirates are no longer a pest, the town has slowly spread back seawards.

The two areas are linked by ave Habib Bourguiba, which runs through the middle from the northwest (the road from Tunis), and finishes by the beach. The town centres around the intersections of ave Habib Bourguiba, ave Habib Thameur and rue Farhat Hached (Souq de l'Artisanat).

Information

EMERGENCY

Hospital (Map p112; ☎ 72 285 633; ave Habib Thameur)
Police (Map p112; ☎ 72 285 474; ave Habib Bourguiba)

INTERNET ACCESS

Publinet (Map p112; ave Hedi Chaker; per hr TD2; 🕑 9am-11pm Mon-Sat, 10am-11pm Sun)
Publinet (Map p112; ave Habib Thameur; per hr TD2; 🕑 8am-11pm)

MONEY

There are plenty of banks with ATMs, mostly along aves Habib Thameur and Habib Bourguiba.

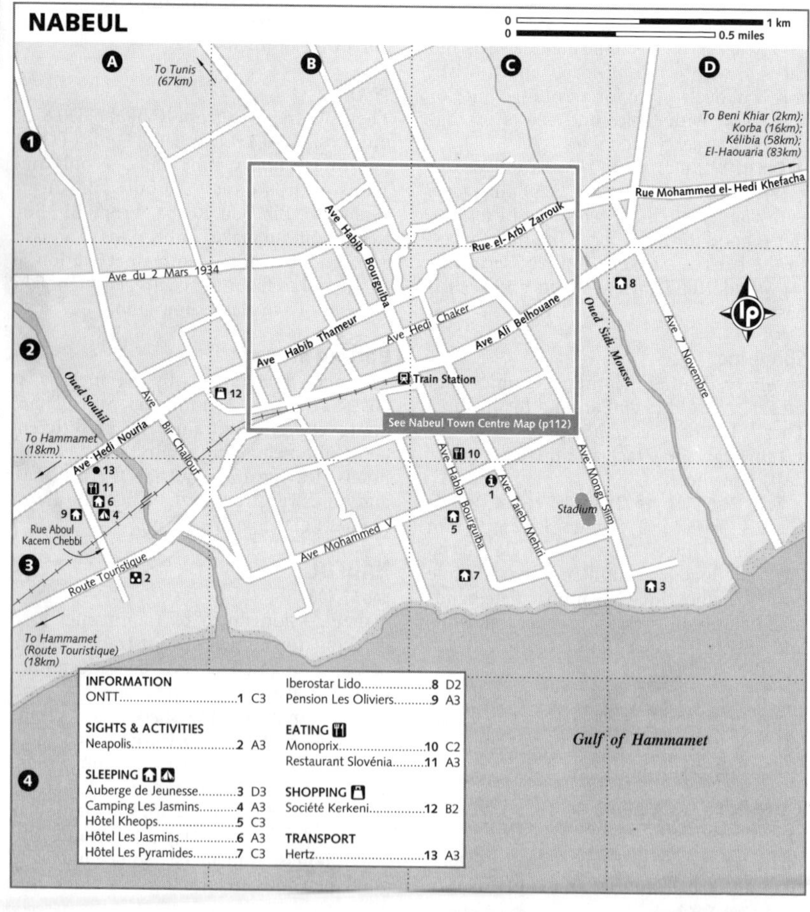

POST

Main post office (Map p112; ave Habib Bourguiba)

TOURIST INFORMATION

ONTT (Map p110; ☎ 72 286 800; ave Taieb Mehiri; 🕑 8.30am-1pm & 4-8pm Mon-Sat) Has maps of Nabeul and Hammamet.

Syndicat d'Initiative (Map p112; ave Habib Bourguiba; 🕑 9am-1pm Tue-Sun) Small but convenient, supplies similar stuff to the ONTT.

Sights & Activities

MARKET

Nabeul's bustling, buzzing Friday market is a major tourist event. Thousands of day-trippers turn up to tussle over jewellery, leather, glass, brass and particularly ceramics – the standard things you can buy everywhere in Tunisia but all bunched together in one place. Unsurprisingly, prices are high; stallholders are used to people with more money than time.

Rues Farhat Hached (Souq de l'Artisanat) and el-Arbi Zarrouk get packed. They're busiest between 9am and noon. By 2pm, life is slowly returning to normal.

MUSEUMS

Nabeul's small but impressive **museum** (Map p112; ave Habib Bourguiba; admission TD3, plus camera TD1; 🕑 9am-1pm & 3-7pm Tue-Sun Apr–mid-Sep, 9.30am-4.30pm Tue-Sun mid-Sep–Mar) covers Cap Bon's history and displays Punic jewellery and some amazing statues from Thinissut in an open-air Carthaginian sanctuary. These include a life-size terracotta lion-headed goddess, sphinxes and the nurturing goddess – an ancestor of the Madonna and child. There's also information on the local Roman site Neapolis, with well-restored mosaics and displays on Tunisia's fish-salting factories, which produced the yummy-sounding *garum* sauce (made from fermented fish guts).

This small private museum, **Dar Zmen** (Map p112; ☎ 72 281 461; Imp. No 5; admission TD4), has some lovely antiques, especially jewellery, engravings and furniture, all housed in a beautifully tiled 19th-century house (once home to a Nabeul governor). Some of the rooms are laid out with a bridal trousseau. There's also a bey's (provincial governor in the Ottoman Empire) bedroom and a Berber tent. The pricey admission includes a cup of mint tea.

TOP OF THE POTS

Traditionally known for their fine Punic- and Roman-influenced pots and vases, and for the ornate decoration introduced by 17th-century Andalusian immigrants, Nabeul potters turn out astounding (some in the worst sense) ceramics. There are some beautiful examples of traditional work, particularly bowls and tiling pictures. You can get a good idea of reasonable prices at the well-stocked **ONAT emporium** (Map p112; ave Habib Thameur) – there are artisans' workshops at the back too.

You'll find massive choice at the Friday market, or try the following shops, where you can see artists and potters at work.

Société Kerkeni (Map p110; ☎ 72 221 808; 121 ave Habib Thameur; 🕑 8am-9pm) Some gloriously exuberant designs and a huge fixed-price range.

Hassen Kharraz (Map p112; ave Habib Thameur; 🕑 9am-1pm & 2.30-8.30pm) The most upmarket, this is where to go if you've got a gilt craving. There's also some appealingly cute stuff with animal decorations.

NEAPOLIS نيابوليس

Ancient **Neapolis** (Map p110; route Touristique; admission TD2, camera TD1; 🕑 9am-1pm & 4-7pm Tue-Sun), meaning 'New City' in Greek, is a seaside site, about 1.5km southwest of the centre. The Punic settlement, established in the 5th century BC, was invaded by Agathocles in 310 BC, and destroyed during the Third Punic War. It was later re-established as a Roman town, and a major producer of fermented-fish-guts *garum* sauce, which must have made for fragrant streets. Several full amphorae were unearthed in the 1960s, and after extensive excavations the site is open, though there's not a lot to see. Nabeul museum displays information about the site and some beautiful mosaics found here in 'House of the Nymphs'. There's a clean, attractive stretch of beach in front of the site, with a few small seasonal restaurants.

Tours

Delta Travel (Map p112; ☎ 72 271 077; 3rd fl, 113 ave Habib Bourguiba) runs excursions to Dougga and so on, and longer trips down south. You can also arrange tours at **Nova Rent Car** (☎ 72 222 072; 54 ave Habib Bourguiba; 🕑 8am-1pm & 4-8pm).

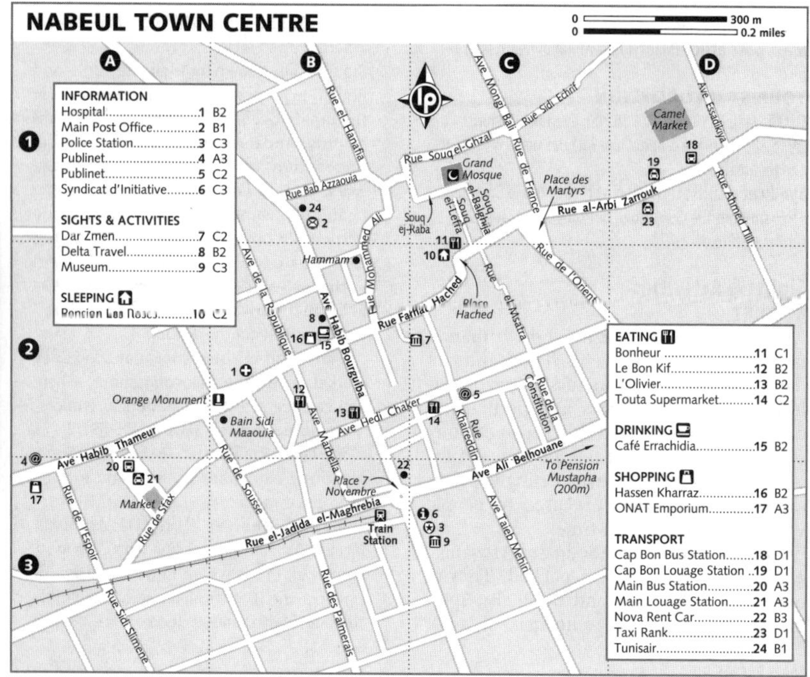

Sleeping

Nabeul has lots of character-filled, family-run pensions and several midrange hotels.

BUDGET

Camping Les Jasmins (Map p110; ☎ 72 285 343; rue Aboul Kacem Chebbi; adult/child/tent/caravan/vehicle/hot shower TD2.8/2/2/2.5/2/2.3;) Les Jasmins, next to Hôtel Les Jasmins, occupies a shady olive grove and is a five-minute walk from an uncrowded stretch of beach.

Auberge de Jeunesse (Map p110; ☎ 72 285 547; ave Mongi Slim; camping per person/tent/caravan TD1/5/5, dm TD5) On the beach, this has a great location, and separate spic-and-span single-sex dorms in barrel-ceilinged *ghorfas* (rooms), each with their own bathroom. There's a camping area too.

Pension Les Roses (Map p112; ☎ 72 285 570; Place Hached; s/d with shared bathroom TD8.5/17, plus hot showers TD1) In souq central, Les Roses is friendly and good for the price. It feels like a step back in time – with shuttered windows onto balconies and basic, cleanish, fanless rooms.

Pension Mustapha (☎ 72 222 262; rue Habib el-Karma & ave Ali Belhouane; s/d TD17/30) Sited on a busy junction, this is nevertheless a good choice: friendly and clean; prices include breakfast and rooms have fans and some have balconies.

MIDRANGE & TOP END

our pick **Pension Les Oliviers** (Map p110; ☎ 72 286 865; rue Aboul Kacem Chebbi; s/d TD41/51) This is a Nabeul gem; it has simple rooms with balconies and is surrounded by olive and citrus groves. It's near a clean, unbusy stretch of beach. You can have breakfast on the lawn. The charming owners (ex-high-school teachers) speak excellent English, and can direct you to worthy places to see and buy ceramics.

Iberostar Lido (Map p110; ☎ central reservations Spain 34 922 070300 ; www.iberostar.com; ave 7 Novembre; 3-night minimum stay, s/d TD50/70;) This has been recommended by a reader and is an appealing place, with helpful staff, some bungalows, bright rooms, sea views and lush grounds. The food is apparently good too.

Hôtel Les Jasmins (Map p110; ☎ 72 285 343; off ave Hedi Nouria; www.hotellesjasmins.com; s/d TD50/78;) Relaxed, tree-shaded and attractive, the rooms here are in two-storey whitewashed buildings and have balconies. There are tables set amid the woodland for breakfast and other meals, or there's Restaurant Slovénia (see below) next door. It's 300m from the beach.

Hôtel Les Pyramides (Map p110; ☎ 72 285 775; ave Habib Bourguiba; s/d TD86/108;) Packed with Eastern European tours, this big package place has nothing-special rooms with small balconies, but it's near the beach. Facilities include tennis courts and a disco.

Hôtel Kheops (Map p110; ☎ 72 285 444; ave Habib Bourguiba; s/d TD110/144;) Nabeul's snazziest hotel, with good facilities, this place is nonetheless down-at-heel. It looks like a great artificial pudding and is usually packed with Eastern European package tourists. Rooms are large but business-hotel sombre (trouser press anyone?). There's a mammoth pool.

Eating & Drinking

Self-caterers should head for **Touta supermarket** (Map p112; ave Hedi Chaker; 8.30am-8pm) or **Monoprix** (Map p110; ave Habib Bourguiba; 8.30am-8pm). There are also a few good restaurants around town.

Bonheur (Map p112; ☎ 72 220 563; rue Farhat Hached; mains TD3-8; 10am-5pm year-round, 7-11pm Aug-Sep) The best of the cheapies, tucked off the main pedestrianised shopping street, this place has the requisite tiled walls and TV, fast service and simple dishes such as couscous and *brochettes* (kebabs) – it also serves beer.

Le Bon Kif (Map p112; ☎ 72 222 783; 25 ave Marbella; mains TD5-18;) This is a relaxed and pleasant choice, with the regular menu of reasonably good couscous, seafood and meat dishes. There's a small tiled courtyard.

Restaurant Slovénia (Map p112; ☎ 72 285 343; Hôtel Les Jasmins; mains TD10-16; noon-3pm & 6pm-midnight;) Nabeul's finest restaurant, run by one of Tunisia's most innovative chefs, Rafik Tlatli. The cooking has Tunisian, Indonesian, Andalusian and Slovenian influences. Try delicious dishes such as lamb with rosemary or crispy-coated prawns. Seating is in a low-lit leafy garden or cosy interior.

L'Olivier (Map p112; ☎ 72 286 613; ave Hedi Chaker; mains TD11-20; noon-3pm & 6-11pm;) This snug place, on two levels, is one of Nabeul's best, with an excellent reputation for cooking with a French slant. There's lots of seafood.

Café Errachidia (Map p112; ave Habib Thameur; 9am-midnight) This lovely café is perfect for people-watching on the porch with a *sheesha* (water pipe) and a mint tea or excellent Turkish coffee, accompanied by the café's own delicious biscuits.

Getting There & Away

AIR

Tunisair (Map p112; ☎ 72 286 092; 178 ave Habib Bourguiba) faces the post office. The nearest airport is Tunis-Carthage.

BUS

The bus station is on ave Habib Thameur. Buses go to Hammamet (TD0.7, 30 minutes, half-hourly 5.30am to 9pm, to 11pm July and August) and Tunis (normal/confort TD3.4/2.9, 1½ hours, half-hourly 6am to 8pm). Buy tickets on board. Other services include Kairouan (TD5.4, 2¼ hours, three daily) and buses to Zaghouan and Sousse (TD6, SRTG TD4.4, two hours, five daily).

Buses for elsewhere in Cap Bon leave from rue el-Arbi Zarrouk, including those to Kélibia (TD2.6, 1¼ hours, 13 daily). For El-Haouaria take a Kélibia bus and then take a louage or a taxi. For information, head to the main bus station.

CAR

There are lots of rental agencies:

Hertz (Map p110; ☎ 72 285 327; ave Habib Thameur)
Nova Rent (Map p112; ☎ 72 222 072; 54 ave Habib Bourguiba; 8am-1pm & 4-8pm)

LOUAGE

Cap Bon services, including Kélibia (TD3.2, one hour) and Korba (TD1), leave from next to the bus station on rue el-Arbi Zarrouk. For El-Haouaria take a louage to Kélibia then a taxi or another louage. Other services leave from behind the main bus station on ave Habib Thameur; destinations include Tunis (TD3.5), Kairouan (TD6), Sousse (TD5.2) and Zaghouan (TD3.5).

TAXI

A shared taxi to Hammamet charges TD1 to TD2, while one all to yourself costs TD6 to TD8.

TRAIN

The station is central, on ave Habib Bourguiba. There are trains to Hammamet

(TD0.6, 20 minutes, 12 to 13 daily) and Tunis (TD3.8, one to 1½ hours, nine daily). Only one Tunis train is direct, otherwise you must change at Bir Bou Regba, from where there are also connections to Sousse, Sfax and beyond.

Getting Around

Nabeul is reasonably spread out, and in summer it's an effort to walk from the centre to the beach. A taxi costs about TD1 (TD0.5 shared); you can take a *calèche* (horse-drawn carriage), but bargain hard and agree on a price before setting off (around TD10 per hour).

AROUND NABEUL

Dar Chaabane دار شعبان

This small village, 4km northeast of Nabeul on the road to Kélibia, is Tunisia's stonework capital. Most people here are masons, and the main street is lined with workshops, carving everything from ashtrays to antelopes. It's an interesting skill to watch, and if you need a couple of monumental lions, you're in luck. Workshops can arrange international delivery.

Any bus heading north can drop you here, or you can take a local bus from the beach (TD0.3, hourly 9.30am to 6.30pm July and August). A taxi costs about TD3 from Nabeul.

Beni Khiar بني‌خيار

This village, about 2km east of Nabeul, is a weaving centre, where you can visit **Cooperative des Tisserands el-Faouz** (☎ 72 229 387; ⏲ 8am-noon & 3-6pm). It's a fascinating place, the all-male workers skilfully operating the ferociously complex looms and spinning wool. Some have worked here for more than 30 years. There's a small shop selling their products at low fixed prices.

There are buses (TD0.3, hourly 10am to 6pm, to 8pm Sunday July and August) from the beach, or a taxi costs about TD3.

Korba Lagoon قربة

A long, narrow lagoon that follows the coast for 15km, this beautiful dark-blue stretch, edged by a streak of white sand, is one of the finest bird-watching areas in Tunisia – the wetlands attract a spectacular wealth of birdlife. In winter, the lagoon becomes dappled in pink as flamingos amass; juveniles can be seen year-round.

It begins at the little town of Korba – whose main business is producing tomatoes – 16km northeast of Nabeul, and gets more tranquil and scenic the further north you head. Around 3km after Korba on the Korba–Kélibia road, a causeway runs across the lagoon – cross it to reach a white-sand beach that lacks shade but is beautifully clean. It's popular with local farm workers who come here in trucks, by tractor and with their donkeys.

The main road to Menzel Temine and Kélibia runs parallel to the lagoon, so any bus or louage travelling north can drop you where you choose. Buses to Korba leave about hourly (TD1, 15 minutes).

KÉLIBIA قليبية

pop 36,000

Kélibia, 58km north of Nabeul, appeals partly because it's a resolutely ordinary town with few tourists. But it's also blessed with nearby El-Mansourah beach: a silver-sanded strand edged by translucent sea, overseen by a towering fort.

The town centre, a mix of functional shops and men-packed cafés, is 2km inland. It survives on fishing and agriculture, with tourism as a sideline – foreign voices you hear in the restaurants are as likely to be here on business as on holiday. The attractions are all on the coast to the east, where you'll find a small beach, the picturesque port and a few low-key resort hotels. The town's also famous for Muscat Sec de Kélibia, a fragrant dry white wine.

Every other year, in July, Kélibia hosts an international film shorts festival, which is worth a look.

History

Once there was a Berber settlement here, taken over by the Carthaginians in the 5th century BC. They called it Aspis, meaning 'shield', either for its defensive status or the shape of the land. Whatever the reason, the fort they built was key to Carthage's defence. It proved ineffective against both Agathocles and Regulus, but the town made it through to be reborn as Roman Clypea, traces of which are scattered around town in excavated fragments. It remained one of Tunisia's major cities until the 11th

PIRATES!

The north African coast, known as the Barbary (a medieval term for the Maghreb) Coast, was once overrun with pirates. Piracy had been a popular career option since the decline of the Roman Empire, but it was in the 14th century that it became really rife, right up to the early 19th century.

Previously raids were carried out for political gain, but piracy reached its height in the 17th century when it was all about slaves and cash. The Tunis rulers lined their pockets with plunder. Colonial expansion led to an explosion of shipping and the pickings were rich. Muslim pirates preyed on Christian shipping on the Mediterranean, and Christian swashbucklers from across the water gave as good as they got. The Barbary pirates captured thousands of Christian slaves, using them to power their galley ships.

From the 17th century the introduction of sailing ships increased the pirates' scope, but didn't reduce the appetite for the lucrative slave business – important people were held to ransom and less-illustrious ones sold in the markets.

European countries didn't try to discourage this lawless trade, as each nation was keen to suppress others by forming alliances and negotiating immunities. It was only in the early 19th century that Europeans began to clamp down in earnest, particularly after a cheeky raid by a Tunisian crew who carried off 158 people from Sardinia. However, piracy wasn't fully suppressed till 1830 and the arrival of the French.

century, but was later damaged by Sicilian pirate attacks, and even moved inland to escape raids.

Orientation & Information

Most travellers will arrive at the bus and louage station on ave Ali Belhouane. The centre is just east, around the junction of rue Ibn Khaldoun and ave Habib Bourguiba. To get there, head north along ave Ali Belhouane (towards El-Haouaria) from the bus and louage station, and then turn right into rue Ibn Khaldoun. There's no tourist office. There are a couple of banks (ATMs often don't work at weekends), a supermarket on rue Ibn Khaldoun, and the post office is on ave Habib Bourguiba. The fort and port are 2km east of here along ave des Martyrs.

There's a central **publinet** (59 rue des Martyrs; per hr TD1.5; 8.30am-midnight).

Sights & Activities

BEACHES & THE PORT

At **El-Mansourah beach**, 2km north, soft white sand tapers gently into blissfully clear-as-glass sea. It's exposed (a sunshade is handy) but otherwise brilliant. There are a few buildings, with just one monster mustard-coloured hotel, Club Kélibia (packages only) marring the background, but if you walk beyond this, empty beach stretches on as far as the eye can see.

There are beaches from here nearly all the way to Kerkouane, with a particularly fine stretch at **Hammam Jebli**, about 4km from Kélibia. Beyond this **Oued Kassab** is another lovely section.

The beach at Kélibia itself is small and not that flash, but nearby, close to the fort, is the interesting **fishing port**, packed with boats decked in fluttering flags, overlooked by a few restaurants and cafés.

FORT & ROMAN EXCAVATIONS

The fabulous polygonal **fort** (admission TD3; 9am-5pm mid-Sep–Mar, 9am-8pm Apr–mid-Sep) dominates the harbour, on a hilltop shrouded by eucalyptus. Views from the ramparts are so broad that the horizon curves like the rim of a vase.

Built by the Carthaginians for use by their maritime police, the fort was dismantled in the 3rd century BC, during the First Punic War, but reconstructed after the war ended. It successfully repelled the Romans during the Second Punic War, but the Romans razed it in the 2nd century BC, and political unity in the Mediterranean meant there was no need for fortifications here. In AD 580, the Byzantines set up their usual small fort within the old walls, still visible, and it was their last refuge when driven out of Carthage in AD 698. It became important following the Arabic conquest, and was rebuilt to defend against the Normans.

From the 13th to 16th centuries it became a Sufi religious centre, seeing action again in the 16th century during Turkish-Spanish spats. The Ottomans rebuilt the fort in the 17th century, and it next withstood bombardment by the French. The most recent additions are gun emplacements, built by Italian–German forces during WWII.

A road leads up to the fort from opposite the Maison des Jeunes on the Mansourah road.

From the battlements you get a good view of some excavated villas at the base of the hill – the remains of Roman Clypea.

Sleeping

Kélibia doesn't have many hotels; most are at the beach by the harbour.

Centre National de la Jeunes (☎ 72 721 601, 72 22 767 613; camping per person TD3) Set on the coast under fluttering eucalyptus trees, 7km north of Kélibia, this pretty 200-person site is mainly used by youth groups, but the friendly staff welcome independent travellers. It's 10m from the beautiful beach of Oued Kassab and a small excavated Punic-Roman site.

Maison des Jeunes (☎ 72 296 105; dm TD5) This institutional blue-and-white building supplies the basic place to lay your head. It's often full in summer so call ahead. Single female travellers may not feel comfortable here.

Hôtel Florida (☎ 72 296 248; Kélibia Plage; s/d with private bathroom TD21/33) Built in 1946, this is a shabby option that's not recommended for single women; it has a nice shaded terrace by the water's edge that's beloved by boozing locals. Small, run-down, fairly clean rooms open onto a little garden.

Hôtel Palmarina (☎ 72 274 062; Kélibia Plage; s/d TD46/72; ❄ 🏊) This is one of the town's better choices. It has a pool and pleasant rooms with shady, sea-facing balconies, but is fraying at the edges and lacks much care.

Pension Anis (☎ 72 295 777; ave Erriadh; s/d/tr with shared bathroom TD30/40/47, d with private bathroom TD60; ❄) Next to the municipal market, this pleasant place is notably friendly and relaxed, with nice staff and a mostly Tunisian clientele. It has pristine rooms, some of which are huge, if a bit stuffy and lacking views. There's an excellent restaurant (see Eating, right).

Hôtel Mamounia (☎ 72 296 088; s/d with private bathroom TD63/86; 🏊) This faded place is pleasantly small-scale, and features simple rooms with balconies, a seaside setting and a small pool. It's ludicrously overpriced, but rates may drop to TD50 or less a double.

Eating

Kélibia has a small but good array of restaurants.

Petit Paris (rue Petit Paris; mains TD2.5-12; 🕑 9am-2am) If you're on the beach but don't feel like a full-on meal, this cheery place has great views over the sea and offers lots of snack food.

Pension Anis (☎ 72 295 777; ave Erriadh; mains TD8-12; 🕑 10am-3pm & 6.30-11.30pm; ❄) Kélibia's best restaurant. Its unusually wide range of dishes – specialising in rich seafood – attracts a wide range of customers. The intimate, stuck-in-time interior is divided by wooden lattices, and there's a respectable wine list and good service.

Le Goéland (☎ 72 273 074; Port de Kélibia; mains TD8-16; ❄) At the port, this has fantastic sea views from its two breezy levels, and reliable food – the traditional Tunisian options, lots of seafood and pizzas.

Les Arcades (☎ 72 274 062; Hôtel Palmarina, Kélibia Plage; TD6-18; ❄) A hotel restaurant with tasty salads and hearty fish and meat dishes. It's airy, quiet and decorated with some kitsch stained-glass.

El-Mansourah (☎ 72 295 169; El-Mansourah Plage; mains TD13-17; ☎ noon-midnight; ❄) On a small headland at the south of Mansourah beach, this place has tables set into rocks in the sea, overlooking crystal-clear rockpools. Perfect for a long lunch of fresh fish, washed down with chilled Kélibia muscat.

Drinking

Café Sidi el-Bahri (☎ 72 296 675; 🕑 7am-3am) In the port, this is a place to while away time over tea and a *sheesha,* though it also has OK snacks. It has a great setting with seating right down to a rocky beach and is particularly popular at night.

Café el-Borj (🕑 9am-2am) This is a little domed place just below the fort with colourful rugs spread over stepped seating overlooking woodland, and there's a roof terrace. The splendid views make this a memorable place for a mint tea or Turkish coffee (though a bit overpriced at TD2 a pop) and a *sheesha.*

Getting There & Away

Buses and louages all leave from ave Ali Belhouane. There are buses to Tunis (TD5, 2¼ hours, hourly), Nabeul (TD2.5, 1¼ hours, hourly) and El-Haouaria (TD1, 40 minutes, hourly). There are also regular louages to these destinations – louage is the best way to get to El-Haouaria (TD1.5). There is a single daily bus to Kairouan (TD7.5, 3½ hours), Sousse (TD6.8, three hours) and Monastir (TD7.6, 3½ hours).

Getting Around

The bus station is 2.5km from the harbour and beach. A taxi to the bus station costs about TD1.5 (shared TD0.5). Buses go to/from Mansourah beach hourly from 10.30am to 6.30pm (TD0.3).

KERKOUANE كركوان

Set on a dazzling curve of turquoise coast, the remote Punic settlement of **Kerkouane** (admission TD3, camera TD1; 9am-4pm mid-Sep–Mar, 9am-6pm Apr–mid-Sep, museum open Tue-Sun only), 12km north of Kélibia, is the world's best-preserved example of a Carthaginian city. Abandoned in its prime in the middle of the 3rd century BC and never reoccupied, it offers a unique insight into all things Punic. There's a useful guidebook (TD15) available at the site shop.

The site is clearly signposted off the road between Kélibia and El-Haouaria. Buses and

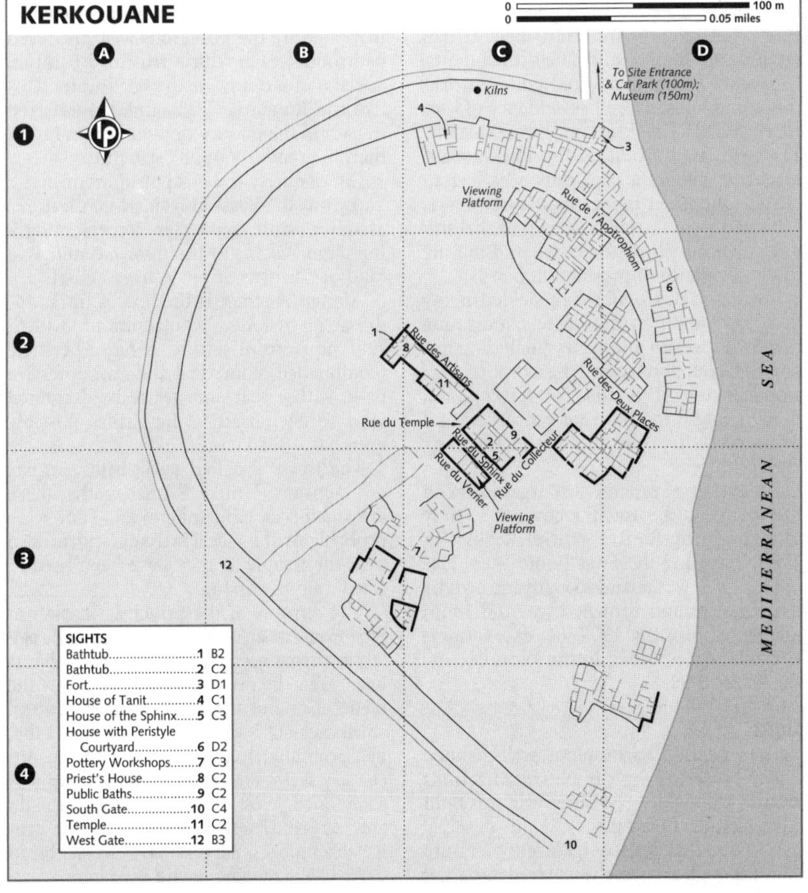

louages can drop you at the turn-off, leaving a pleasant walk of 1.5km to the site.

History

Little is known of the town's history, not even its name. Kerkouane was coined by French archaeologists, who stumbled on the site in 1952.

Finds suggest it was an established Berber town when the Phoenicians arrived in the 8th century BC, but Berber and Phoenician cultures blended and it evolved into a Punic town. The oldest remains date to the early 6th century BC, but the ruins today are mainly 4th- to 3rd-century BC.

Although ancient writers waxed about the fertility of the peninsula, no evidence of agricultural activity has been found here. Kerkouane, it seems, was home to an urban elite of merchants and craftsmen. It had around 300 houses and 2000 inhabitants. Excavations have uncovered pottery workshops and kilns, as well as evidence of jewellery and glass making, and stone carving. The town also produced the Phoenicians' favourite colour: a dye known as Tyrian purple (after their first capital, Tyre). It was extracted from murex, a species of shellfish once plentiful along the coast, and the site retains evidence of production here.

The large necropolis has yielded many decorative and precious objects, indicating the town's wealth and tastes (including imported Greek pottery and the extraordinary woodcarving *Woman of Kerkouane*), though many tombs were ransacked and damaged by treasure hunters in the early 20th century.

An earlier plunderer was Agathocles in 310 BC, but the town recovered – only to be burnt by Roman general Regulus in 256 BC, during the First Punic War. This time the site was abandoned, overgrown by dwarf palms and drowned by sands until uncovered during 1957–61 excavations. Kerkouane was added to the World Heritage list in 1982.

Sights

Kerkouane was a harmonious, well-planned town, protected by double fortifications around 15m wide. The outer wall was built after Agathocles' attack.

Cap Bon was exalted in ancient literature and, although exaggeration played its part, it was doubtless a region of plenty– historian Diodorus wrote of Agathocles' invasion: 'all the lands that he had to cross were set with gardens and orchards watered by numerous springs. There were well-constructed country houses, built with lime…' To protect this good life, forts and towers were added, such as the small coastal **fort** on the northern side and the fortifications around the south gate. None of which did any good when Regulus went on the rampage.

The main entrance was through the distinctive **west gate**, also known as the Port du Couchant (Sunset Gate), built into an overlap between the walls. The houses are the main attraction, particularly those of the wealthy northeastern quarter, with some wonderful examples of *opus signinum* flooring (scatter-pattern mosaic). Most remarkable are the numerous well-preserved bathrooms, each with a red-lined bathtub, a well and a drain for the used water. Unlike the Romans, Carthaginians preferred to bath in the privacy of their homes rather than in grandiose public structures.

Check out 3 rue de l'Apotrophiom, better known as the **House of Tanit**, which features a simple white Tanit sign (representing a Punic god) set into the floor, seemingly a kind of talisman or protective symbol.

Along the street is the town's finest address: 35 rue de l'Apotrophiom, with a sublime seafront setting. It has a peristyle (colonnaded) courtyard and an impressive bath, with a seat and armrests, decorated with white mosaic – the bather possibly even had a sea view.

The town also had **public baths**, on rue des Artisans. Unlike Roman baths, these are small-scale and functional. They were probably used by local artisans, and are also near the temple so may have been used to wash up pre-worship.

The remains of the principal **temple** run west from rue du Temple. Along one side **pottery workshops** used to produce votive objects have been discovered. The temple was the scene of one of the site's strangest finds: a small cache of Roman lamps and bowls that had been hidden away, dating from the 3rd century AD – 500 years after the town was abandoned. West of the temple, at 2 rue du Sphinx, is the **Priest's House**. In its centre, protected within a small room, is a circular bread oven, like the *tabounas* still used here.

Rue du Sphinx is named after a sphinx on a solid gold ring (which you can see in the museum) found at No 1 (**House of the Sphinx**), which has a fine bathroom with a double bath.

MUSEUM

The museum holds startling finds from the site necropolis, most notably the 3rd- to 4th-century BC *Woman of Kerkouane*, a full-size cypress-wood sarcophagus, thought to represent the goddess Astarte. There are also some beautiful pieces of gold jewellery, everyday objects such as razors, kohl pots, tweezers and baby bottles, and funerary statues. Imported Greek, southern Italian and Egyptian artefacts demonstrate the sophistication of the residents' taste and their wealth. Labels and explanations are in French and Arabic.

Sleeping

Résidence Dar Zenaïdi (☎ 22 774 705; darzenaidi@planet.tn; s/d with private bathroom TD75/100;) Off the road to Kerkouane is this large white house, with five big airy, nicely decorated rooms with countryside views, and a pool. Reception is filled with traditional hand-painted furniture.

EL-HAOUARIA الهوارية

pop 10,300

Under the mountainous tip of Cap Bon, the middle-of-nowhere town of El-Haouaria feels appealingly out of the way. It has the enticing unspoilt beach of Ras el-Drek on the southern side of the point, and some impressive cliff walks up to nearby desolate headland Jebel Abiod, jutting out to sea and just 150km from Sicily. The town is famous for its coastal caves, 3km northwest of town, cut into the cliffs by the Phoenicians, who used the stone in building many settlements, including Kerkouane and Carthage. They are often referred to as Grottes Romaines (Roman caves), as the Romans were partial to El-Haouaria's stone too, and continued the practice. El-Haouaria is also famous for falconry, and has a festival devoted to hawking in July.

From this part of the coast you can spot the shadowy rocky islands of Zembra and Zembretta, off-limits as nature reserves and favoured nesting spots for grey pelicans.

Apparently the cliffs south of the Roman caves are good for cliff jumping – we were unable to verify this so, if you do, let us know how you get on at www.lonelyplanet.com/feedback.

The town has a choice of hotels and restaurants and there are a couple of banks on the main street.

Sights & Activities

JEBEL ABIOD

This 390m peak, north of town, is the northeastern tip of the Tunisian Dorsale and feels like the edge of the world. You can either walk up or drive along the road to the top, from where there are magnificent views over sheer cliffs, dropping down to incredible blue sea. It's a fantastic bird-watching spot, a prime migration route for thousands of raptors travelling between Africa and Europe. In May and June, the skies can be thick with birds waiting for the thermals to carry them across the Straits of Sicily. You can find information on local species at **Les Amis des Oiseaux** (☎ 72 269 200), which also runs bird-watching outings, signposted off the northern end of the main street.

According to readers, you can hike up the peak from the town:

> A 40-minute hike following the path north of Pension Dar Toubib leads to an absolutely spectacular view (including an old wrecked ship). We managed to find two decent camping spots and were not bothered by anyone as we slept under the stars.
>
> *James B & Daniel K*

Otherwise access to the mountain is by a road that leads north of rue Ali Belhouane in the town centre. The road finishes at a telecommunications tower at the summit – an eerie, desolate place humming with radio waves. For beautiful views, there is a path on the left, a few hundred metres before you reach the summit, marked by a sign headed 'Zone de el-Haouria'. The rocky but gentle path leads to a dip in the cliffs and a small shack, a stunningly peaceful place.

ROMAN CAVES

This remarkable complex of **Roman caves** (admission TD3, camera TD1; 9am-5pm mid-Sep–Mar, 8am-7pm Apr–mid-Sep) is on the dramatic stretch of rocky coast to the west of El-Haouaria. The cliffs here are formed of an

CAP BON

easily worked, highly prized yellow sandstone, and the Carthaginians began exploiting this in the 6th century BC, later followed by the Romans, who prised stone out here to build the Colosseum in Rome and the stadium at El-Jem (see p208). Small pyramid-shaped shafts remain, lit by hacked-out oblong skylights; you can still make out the marks of quarrying tools on the walls.

The quarriers discovered that the quality of the stone was much better at the base of the cliff than on the surface, and opted to tunnel into the cliffs rather than to cut down. The end result, after almost 1000 years of quarrying, was caves stretching almost 1km along the coast. It was a highly sophisticated operation. The cut stone was dragged out through the caves and loaded onto ships for transportation.

The caves are signposted 3km west of town. It takes about 45 minutes to walk here, but there's plenty of passing traffic for hitchers (for information on the risks associated with hitching see p311).

RAS EL-DREK

Also known as El-Haouaria *plage*, this lovely white-sand beach is a local favourite, backed by clusters of villas (many are for rent) and a couple of cafés. To reach here, follow indications for Le Port (there is a small fishing port nearby) and/or 'Restaurante les Pecheurs, Pointe de Cap Bon' from town. It's about 3km from the centre and louages run here in season, or a taxi costs around TD2.5.

BOAT TRIPS

Excursions by boat run from Le Daurade. They are for a minimum of 12 people and cost TD50 per person for a full day.

Festivals & Events

El-Haouaria has a tradition of falconry, and stages an annual **Festival d'Epervier** for four days in July, with daily demonstrations of the birds near the caves, sailing shows, live music and market stalls. Sparrowhawks are captured during their spring migration, trained for the festival and then released afterwards.

Sleeping

Besides the town's few hotels, there are numerous notices of places to rent around town and by the beach.

Pension Dar Toubib (☎ 72 297 163; s/d with private bathroom TD24/48) This is El-Haouaria's nicest place to stay. It's welcoming and has a relaxed, traveller-friendly feel. Rooms are bright, cheery and spacious, if basic, and set around a garden courtyard. To get here, follow the 'Hotel' signs from the main square out towards the mountain. It's a 10-minute walk. If the owner's not here, ask around and someone will track him down.

Hôtel L'Epervier (☎ 72 297 017; 3 ave Habib Bourguiba; s/d TD30/50) In the middle of town, this friendly place has a variety of comfortable, old-fashioned rooms with small terraces, set around a small courtyard. There's a good restaurant.

Pension Les Grottes (☎ 72 269 072; www.centregrotte.com.tn; Route les Grottes; s/d TD35/70;) Although this has a good hilltop position and small pool, there's a somewhat desolate atmosphere, though the restaurant is busy with local men. Rooms are small and bright but the bungalow architecture is not that attractive and makes little of the views.

Eating

La Daurade (☎ 72 269 080; mains TD5-15; noon-midnight) Out by the caves, this friendly place has an incredible seaside setting and excellent seafood. There are lovely open terraces and seating down to the water's edge. No alcohol is served. Management can arrange boat trips (see left).

Hôtel L'Epervier (3 ave Habib Bourguiba; mains TD8-15) has tree-shaded courtyard seating, and **Pension Les Grottes** (Route les Grottes; mains TD6-15) has a reasonable restaurant with good views, popular with local drinkers. Both serve alcohol.

Getting There & Away

El-Haouaria is well served by public transport. There are buses travelling along the north coast to Tunis (TD4.5, two hours, seven daily), via Soliman, and to Kélibia (TD1, 40 minutes, eight daily). There are regular louages to Kélibia (TD1.5), and less frequent ones to Tunis (TD4.5).

SOLIMAN سليمان

Soliman, 10km southwest of Korbous, is a popular local beach getaway – packed at weekends – that's quick to access from Tunis. The white-sand beach has lots of cafés and a couple of package hotels, and is framed by shadowy mountains, but it has a desultory feel. If you are hankering after a beach stay, it's worth striking out further into Cap Bon.

Buses and louages run to/from Soliman (TD1.4, one hour) from Tunis. You can then catch a shared taxi to the beach (TD0.5).

KORBOUS قربص

Korbous is just one street, with two hotels, a spa and a *hammam*, all set in a narrow ravine and surrounded by cliffs. It's an old-fashioned beauty spot, with the faded feel that permeates forgotten British seaside resorts and spa towns. It's famous for its hot springs and the few stalls in the main street specialise in scrubbing mitts and big knickers.

The approach to Korbous from Soliman is spectacular, especially the final 6km when the road hugs the coastal cliff-face. The road south along the coast has been closed for the last six or so years, but may have reopened by the time you read this, and should be fantastically dramatic. At Aïn Atrous, about 1.5km north of Korbous, a hot spring empties directly into the sea, providing a small patch of heated ocean that's always jostling with people. It's a unique place: the spring has been channelled through several small pools before it reaches the sea, so you can dangle your feet above the steaming, sulphurous water. Next to the spring there are a few small hole-in-the-wall restaurants specialising in grilled fish priced from around TD4.

Readers have camped near Korbous:

> Due east of the main road in town – a 10-minute climb up the valley – is a nice spot that we were told is used by scouts for campouts. It seems the villagers are used to people coming into town and camping there. We too found a nice spot there!
>
> *James B & Daniel K*

But if you prefer a hotel, welcoming **Hôtel Residence des Thermes** (☎ 72 284 520; ave 7 Novembre; s/d with private bathroom TD35/50; ❄) has simple white-walled rooms, with balconies, some bigger and better than others and there's a pleasant restaurant.

Hôtel Les Sources (☎ 72 284 540; ave 7 Novembre; s/d TD46/72; P ❄ 🏊) has more facilities, unintentionally funky '70s textiles in the rooms, good balcony views and a pool (TD4), but is somehow less appealing than Residence des Thermes. It's a bit run-down and was something of a building site when we visited – apparently it will reopen as a five-star hotel, which will have to be seen to be believed.

Restaurant Dhib (☎ 72 284 523; ave 7 Novembre; mains TD2.5-6; 🕑 11.30am-9pm) is Korbous' sole restaurant outside the hotels. It's simple with the usual Tunisian favourites on the menu and outdoor seating on a small street-side terrace.

In the centre are the run-down **Stations Thermales et Touristiques** (☎ 72 284 585; 🕑 8am-8pm), offering some daunting-sounding water treatments and more-relaxing massages that are something of a bargain: a general massage costs TD8 for 20 minutes, while an anti-cellulite 30-minute massage costs TD15.

Nearby is the ancient and suitably decrepit **hammam** (Turkish bath; admission TD1.5; 🕑 8am-8pm). It's a popular, atmospheric place, with separate sections for men and women, and the subterranean pool is remarkably hot.

If you have your own transport, there is an appealing golden curve of beach at **Barrage Port Princes**, a protected area. Coming from Korbous, take the Doula road, pass through Doula and carry straight on towards Bir Meroua for 3km, then turn left at the road signposted Barrage Port Princes. The road is paved for around 3km to 4km, then becomes a dirt track that is passable in dry weather. Follow this for around 4km (when the road forks, take the left fork). On the headland is a golden-stone castle (private property), otherwise the remote beach has a small rickety pier, a small shop and some sunshades.

Getting There & Away

It's easier to get to Korbous from Tunis than from the southern side of Cap Bon. From Tunis' southern bus station, there are buses to Soliman (TD1.4, one hour) from where you can take a shared or private taxi or direct louages (TD2.5).

Northern Tunisia

Beloved by Tunisians but often overlooked by visitors from abroad, Northern Tunisia may just be the country's most underappreciated region. Not only does it have some of Tunisia's finest and most secluded beaches, but it's also home to extensive forests, rugged hills that drop precipitously into the glinting blue Mediterranean, and rolling farmland that's magnificently lush in winter and golden in summer.

Bizerte, the region's main city, is endowed with a picturesque ancient port and a bustling – and largely untouristed – commercial centre. It's an excellent base for exploring Ichkeul National Park – one look at the lake and you'll understand why it's a Unesco World Heritage site – and some of the handful of Tunisian beaches that can give southern Thailand a run for its money, including Sidi Ali el-Mekki and Cap Serrat.

Tabarka, out near Algeria, is a slow-moving seaside town with a passable beach, tree-shaded cafés, an excellent golf course, Tunisia's finest scuba diving and, in summer, four of Tunisia's hottest music festivals.

Heading south from Tabarka along narrow, winding roads takes you into the Kroumirie Mountains, thick with cork oak and ideal for hiking (with a guide). The main town is Ain Draham, a friendly, one-time colonial hill station that's high enough to get snow in winter.

Further south, Jendouba is the best base for exploring the subterranean Roman villas of Bulla Regia and the ancient Chemtou quarries, renowned for their unique yellow marble. Béja has an interesting old medina and an evocative Commonwealth military cemetery, while Ghardimao is truly the end of the line.

HIGHLIGHTS

- Frolic in the calm, shallow waters of **Sidi Ali el-Mekki** (p132), perhaps Tunisia's finest beach
- Sip something cold or hot at the enchanting old port in **Bizerte** (p125)
- Enjoy top-flight international talent at one of the four summer music festivals in **Tabarka** (p138)
- Explore the exquisite underground Roman villas of **Bulla Regia** (p145)
- Ramble through the cork forests around **Ain Draham** (p140)
- Marvel at the living creatures and wild landscapes of **Ichkeul National Park** (p132)

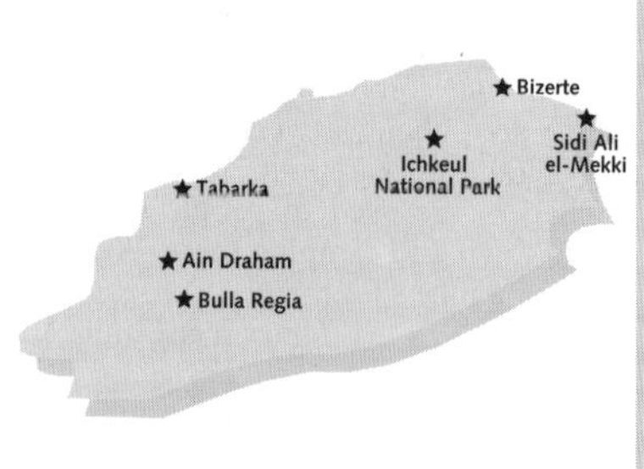

History

Northern Tunisia has been fought over for millennia not only because of its strategic ports but also because it's one of the country's richest agricultural regions.

It was first settled by European migrants between 6000 BC and 2500 BC, then the Phoenicians gained a foothold here when they established Utica in 1100 BC. During the Second Punic War (204 BC) the Roman general Scipio landed at Utica. The Romans gained power a century later but were content to let the Numidians rule. Over time, the Romans – with a main base at Vega (Béja) – rebuilt the earlier Punic settlements and made the most of the region's prodigious wheat-growing capacity – hence the glorious wealth of settlements such as Bulla Regia.

With the coming of the Arabs and Islam, the seat of power moved southwards to Kairouan. The Spanish and the Ottoman Turks played pass-the-parcel with the region's strategic centres in the 16th century, when piracy was rife.

In the 19th century, Tunisia's northern riches proved very attractive to the French. During WWII, in the spring of 1943, the area became a battleground, as a number of military cemeteries testify.

Climate

Summers are hot and dry along the coast but up in the Kroumirie Mountains it's a few degrees cooler – that's why Ain Draham was such a popular hill station during the colonial period. In winter the mountains along the Algerian border can get surprisingly cold – in December and January there's often snow. During the winter of 2005 Ain Draham got a record 1.7m of the white fluffy stuff!

National Parks

Ichkeul National Park (p133) supports a remarkable variety of plants, insects, mammals and, especially, birdlife. Near the border with Algeria, forested El-Feija National Park (p149) is known for its wild gazelles and rare Barbary deer.

Getting There & Around

Tunis-Carthage International Airport is linked to Bizerte by bus (see p129). Tabarka's international airport is served by the occasional European charter.

Buses and louages (shared-taxis) to every city and large town in the region leave from Tunis' northern (Bab Saadoun) bus station (see p86). Trains link Tunis with Bizerte, Béja, Jendouba and Ghardimao.

With a bit of patience, you can use public transport to get to and between virtually all the places mentioned in this chapter.

BIZERTE بنزرت

pop 113,400

Many visitors to Bizerte tend to hang out mainly in the Zone Touristique, with its row of beachside hotels, but the city centre – endowed with a picturesque old port, a sprawling outdoor market, colonial architecture and a marina – is great for aimless ambling, people-watching in cafés and dining.

Bizerte makes a good base for excursions to Ichkeul National Park and the beaches of Raf Raf and Sidi Ali el-Mekki.

History

The Phoenicians founded the port in the 8th century BC as Hippo Zarytus and later built the first canal connecting Lake Bizerte (Lac de Bizerte) to the sea, opening up one of the finest harbours in the western Mediterranean. The Romans destroyed the city in 146 BC to avenge its part in the Punic Wars but rebuilt it 100 years later as Hippo Diarrhytus. The city was later occupied by the Vandals and the Byzantines.

In AD 678 the Arabs captured the town and renamed it Bizerte. The Spanish occupied the town from 1535 to 1570, then the Ottomans took over and it became an important base for the Muslim corsairs (pirates) preying on Christian shipping in the Mediterranean.

The 1800s saw Bizerte in decline until the opening of the Suez Canal in 1869 gave the port renewed significance. The French transformed the town, digging a new canal (completed in 1895) to handle modern steamships. They filled in the old shipping canal dug by the Carthaginians, building in its place the Ville Nouvelle (new town).

France held onto Bizerte and its strategic naval base after Tunisia became independent in 1956. More than 1000 Tunisians died in 1961 in fierce clashes that broke out after Habib Bourguiba demanded that the French leave, something they finally did in 1963 (see p32).

NORTHERN TUNISIA

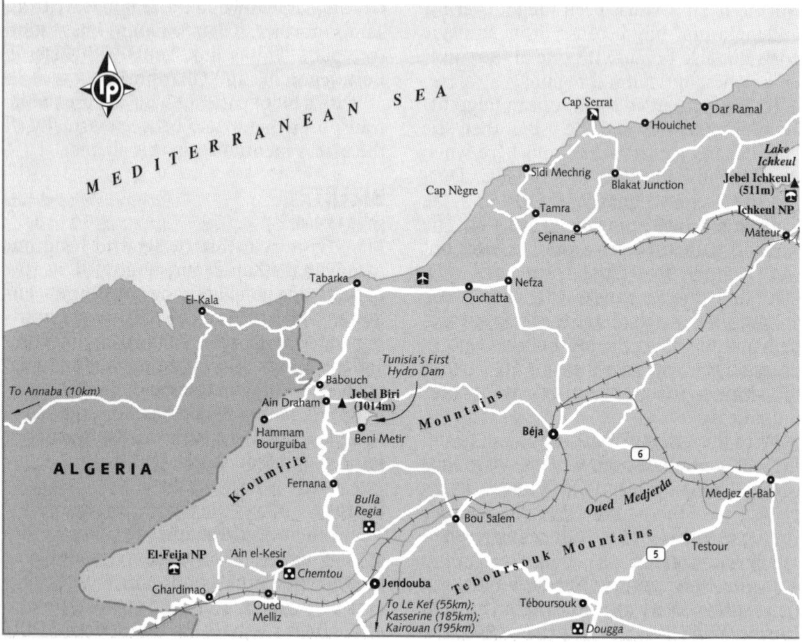

Orientation

The Ville Nouvelle, now the city's commercial centre, stretches from the shipping canal north to east-west–oriented ave Habib Bourguiba. North of there, around the café-lined old port (Vieux Port in French), you'll find the huge outdoor market, the medina and the kasbah.

North-south–oriented blvd Habib Bourguiba (not to be confused with the avenue of the same name) leads from the marina *(port de plaisance)* northward to the Zone Touristique, with its beaches and hotels, eventually – 3km north of the kasbah – becoming ave de la Corniche.

The shipping canal is spanned by a modern drawbridge leading southeast to Tunis.

Information

There are lots of currency exchange and ATM options around place du 7 Novembre 1987, especially between the town hall and the Main Bus Station.

Banque du Sud (rue Habib Thameur) Situated 50m west of the town hall.

BIAT Bank (rue Moncef Bey cnr rue Habib Thameur)

BNA Bank (rue Habib Thameur cnr rue 1 Juin 1955)

Centre Public d'Internet (rue Salah bin Ali; internet per hr TD2; 8am-10pm)

Cyber House (rue Habib Thameur cnr rue d'Alger; internet per hr TD2; 9am-10pm) Quiet and modern.

La Muse Internet Café (rue du 1 Mai cnr rue de Grèce; internet per hr TD1.2; 8am-midnight) Popular with young locals, this place also serves hot and cold drinks (see p129).

Maison des Jeunes (blvd Hassen en-Nouri; internet per hr TD1; 9am-8pm Jun-Aug, 9am-noon & 4-8pm Sep-May) This hostel has an internet room.

Main post office (ave d'Algérie)

Office de la Topographie et de la Cartographie (rue 2 Mars 1934 cnr ave d'Algérie; 8am-noon & 2-6pm Mon-Fri Sep-Jun, 7am-noon Jul & Aug) Sells good maps of Tunisia, Bizerte, Tabarka and Ain Draham (about TD5 each). Take the payment voucher to the BIAT bank and then come back to pick up your map.

SOS Infirmerie Chida (☎ 72 434 640 or 21 074 433; 5 rue du Théâtre; 24 hr) Can administer first aid and summon a doctor if necessary. Phone to arrange a house call. The staff speak French and a bit of English. Situated one block west of Rue Thaalbi, just north of ave Habib Bourguiba.

Tourist office (ONTT; ☎ 72 432 897; crtb.ontt@email.ati.tn; Bizerta Resort; 8.30am-1pm & 3-5.30pm Mon-Thu,

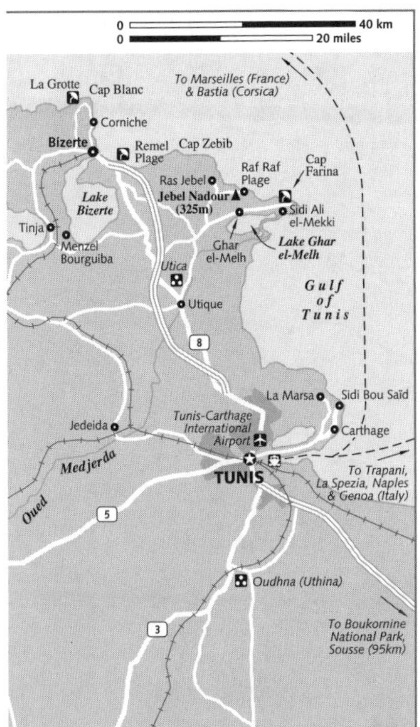

8am-1pm Fri & Sat Sep-Jun, 8am-2pm Mon-Sat Jul & Aug) Can supply you with a town map and brochures. The anonymous entrance is on the south side of the Bizerta Resort.

Sights & Activities

OLD PORT & MEDINA

The old port, lined with cafés, its multicoloured fishing boats making squiggly reflections in the water, is an enchanting place for a stroll. Two blocks west of the port's southern end is **place Bouchacha**, now the centre of a vast **outdoor and indoor market** where locals come to find both edibles and durables.

Northwest and north of the port is the medina, known as the Ville Arabe (Arab Town) during the French period. The richly decorated, lavishly tiled **Zaouia of Sidi Mokhtar** (5 rue de la Grande Mosquée; 8.30am-1pm & 3.30-5.30pm Mon-Thu, Fri morning & Sat morning Sep-Jun, 8.30am-1pm Mon-Sat Jul & Aug), well worth a look in, is home to the **Association de Sauvegarde de la Medina de Bizerte** (☎ 72 430 424; www.asm.bizerte1.com), the group responsible for medina conservation. Displays include a fascinating map of Bizerte in 1881 – before the old canal was filled in – and old photos of the city. If you leave ID you can borrow books on Tunisian history and architecture in French. On sale is *Bizerte – Identité et Mémoire* (TD40), an excellent illustrated book about the city (in French).

Next door, the **Great Mosque** (Grande Mosquée; rue des Armuriers), built in 1652, has an octagonal, stone-built minaret decorated with blue and white tiling. The women's section, in back, affords views of the old port. At prayer times it might be possible to get a peek of the courtyard, with its slender marble columns and delicate stone arches.

West of here is the heart of the medina. The area was damaged during WWII by Allied bombing but its alleys, with blue grills and keyhole-shaped doors, are worth a wander. The tiny **rue de Forgerons**, still true to its name, is lined with cluttered blacksmiths' workshops.

On the north side of the entrance to the old port stand the 10m-high fortified walls of the **kasbah**. Along with its kid brother, the **ksibah** (small fort) on the southern side, it was originally built by the Byzantines in the 6th century AD. Today's kasbah, constructed in the Ottoman period (17th century), encloses a warren of tranquil residential streets. Inside the **Kasbah Mosque**, straight ahead as you walk through the kasbah's only gate (situated on its western side), 30 stone columns – topped with an assortment of recycled ancient marble capitals – hold up 20 elegant stone cupolas. It was being renovated as we went to press.

From outside the eastern buttress, steps lead up to the **ramparts** (adult/child TD0.5/0.25; 9am-12.30pm & 3-8pm). On top, with a view of the port, is a café, an evening favourite with local couples.

SPANISH FORT

Built from 1570 to 1573 by Ulj Ali, the military ruler of Algiers, *after* he had booted out the Spanish (thus the confusing name), this **fortress** (ave du 15 Octobre 1963; admission free; 8am-5pm) overlooks the medina from the north. All that remains are two long wall sections and one citadel. The views across the town, over the modern cement amphitheatre, are stupendous.

KSIBAH

This squat little fort, facing the kasbah, was modified by the Aghlabids, who added the

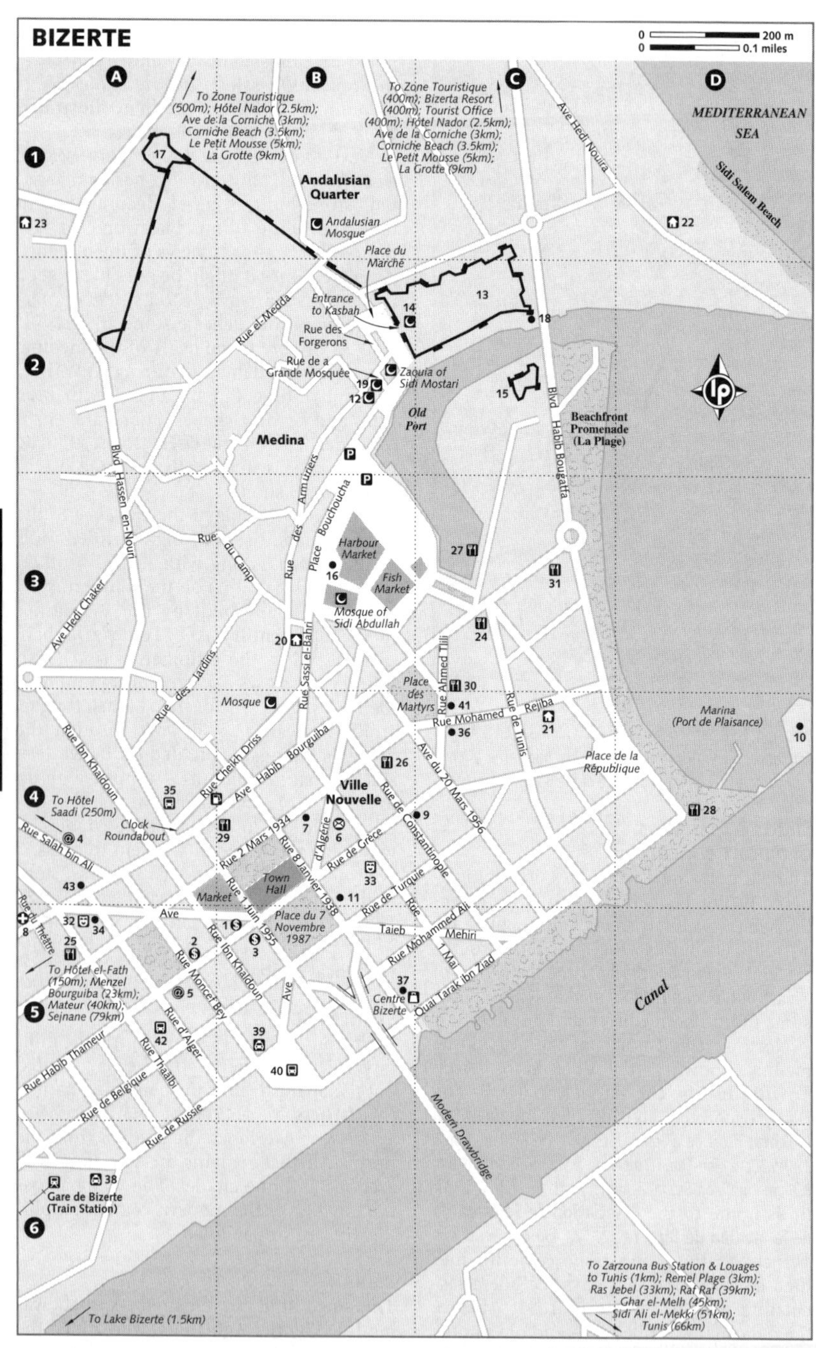
BIZERTE
0 200 m
0 0.1 miles
To Zone Touristique (500m); Hótel Nador (2.5km); Ave de la Corniche (3km); Corniche Beach (3.5km); Le Petit Mousse (5km); La Grotte (9km)
To Zone Touristique (400m); Bizerta Resort (400m); Tourist Office (400m); Hotel Nador (2.5km); Ave de la Corniche (3km); Corniche Beach (3.5km); Le Petit Mousse (5km); La Grotte (9km)
MEDITERRANEAN SEA
Sidi Salem Beach
Ave Hedi Nouira
Andalusian Quarter
Andalusian Mosque
Place du Marché
Entrance to Kasbah
Rue des Forgerons
Rue de a Grande Mosquée
Zaouia of Sidi Mostari
Old Port
Rue el-Medda
Medina
Blvd Habib Bougatfa
Beachfront Promenade (La Plage)
Blvd Hassen en-Nouri
Rue des Armuriers
Place Bouchoucha
Harbour Market
Fish Market
Mosque of Sidi Abdullah
Rue du Camp
Ave Hedi Chaker
Rue Sassi el-Bahri
Rue des Jardins
Mosque
Place des Martyrs
Rue Ahmed Tlili
Rue Mohamed Rejiba
Rue de Tunis
Marina (Port de Plaisance)
Place de la République
Rue Ibn Khaldoun
Rue Cheikh Driss
Ave Habib Bourguiba
Ville Nouvelle
Rue de Constantinople
Ave du 20 Mars 1956
To Hôtel Saadi (250m)
Clock Roundabout
Rue Salah bin Ali
Rue 2 Mars 1934
Rue 8 Janvier 1938
Rue d'Algérie
Rue de Grèce
Rue de Turquie
Town Hall
Market
Rue 1 Juin 1955
Place du 7 Novembre 1987
Ave Taieb Mehiri
Rue Mohammed Ali
Rue 1 Mai
Rue du Théâtre
To Hôtel el-Fath (150m); Menzel Bourguiba (23km); Mateur (40km); Sejnane (79km)
Rue Moncef Bey
Rue Ibn Khaldoun
Centre Bizerte
Quai Tarak ibn Ziad
Canal
Rue d'Alger
Rue Thaâlbi
Rue Habib Thameur
Rue de Belgique
Rue de Russie
Modern Drawbridge
Gare de Bizerte (Train Station)
To Lake Bizerte (1.5km)
To Zarzouna Bus Station & Louages to Tunis (1km); Remel Plage (3km); Ras Jebel (33km); Raf Raf (39km); Ghar el-Melh (45km); Sidi Ali el-Mekki (51km); Tunis (66km)
NORTHERN TUNISIA

INFORMATION
Banque du Sud....1 B5
BIAT Bank....2 A5
BNA Bank....3 B5
Centre Public d'Internet....4 A4
Cyber House....5 A5
La Muse Internet Café....(see 33)
Main Post Office....6 B4
Maison des Jeunes Internet....(see 23)
Office de la Topographie et de la Cartographie....7 B4
SOS Infirmerie Chida....8 A5

SIGHTS & ACTIVITIES
Abri Public Sign....9 C4
Association de Sauvegarde de la Medina de Bizerte....(see 19)
Bizerte Plongée....10 D4
Deconsecrated Cathedral....11 B4
Great Mosque....12 B2
Kasbah....13 C2
Kasbah Mosque....14 B2
Ksibah....15 C2
Oceanographic Museum....(see 15)
Outdoor & Indoor Market Area....16 B3
Pedal Boat Rental....(see 27)
Spanish Fort....17 A1
Steps to Ramparts....18 C2
Zaouia of Sidi Mokhtar....19 B2

SLEEPING
Hôtel Africain....20 B3
Hôtel de la Plage....21 C4
Hôtel Sidi Salem....22 D1
Maison des Jeunes....23 A1

EATING
Café-Pâtisserie Bellahouel....24 C3
Du Bonheur....25 A5
La Cuisine Tunisienne....26 B4
Le Phénicien....27 C3
Le Sport Nautique....28 D4
Monoprix Supermarket....29 B4
Pizzeria Le Grand Bleu....30 C3
Popular Eateries....31 C3

ENTERTAINMENT
Cinéma Le Paris....32 A5
Espace Culturel La Muse....33 B4

TRANSPORT
ADA Car Rental....34 A5
Buses to Corniche & Cap Blanc....35 A4
Europcar....36 C4
Hertz....37 B5
Louages to Menzel Bourguiba, Mateur & Sejnane....38 A6
Louages to Ras Jebel & Raf Raf....39 B5
Main Bus Station....40 B5
Opera Car Car Rental....41 C4
SNTRI Bus Station....42 A5
Tunisair....43 A4

attractive arched *skifa* (gate) and a courtyard with a set of cells – not for prisoners but for silent Quran study.

Also known as Fort Sidi Henni, it now houses a small, dull **Oceanographic Museum** (adult/child TD0.5/0.25; 9am-12.30pm & 3pm or 4-8pm) and has a rooftop café with good views over the old port.

FRENCH ARCHITECTURE

There's some attractive French architecture from the 1920s and 1930s along **rue de Grèce**. On one building at the corner of rue d'Istamboul, you can see a faint painted sign pointing the way to an *abri-public* (bomb shelter) that dates from the Nazi occupation (see p31) – the collaborationist local authorities painted it so French civilians could find shelter from Allied bombers.

The deconsecrated **cathedral** (place du 7 Novembre 1987), a concrete modernist structure with vertical stripes of stained glass, is now a cultural centre.

BEACHES & PROMENADES

In the evenings young love flourishes – to the degree that cultural norms allow – along the romantic **beachfront promenade** (known to locals as La Plage) along the east side of blvd Habib Bourguiba between the lively **marina**, where people fish off the jetty and sip coffee in cafés, and the ksibah.

The **beaches** north of the kasbah, situated a few hundred metres east of the main road, are sweeping and balmy but are fronted by a string of rather isolated hotels. Further north, up past the Y-junction (about 3km from the kasbah), **ave de la Corniche**, another favourite venue for an evening promenade, runs along a narrow strip of **beach** with dried kelp piled up on the sand.

Following ave de la Corniche northward all the way to the radar station, looping around the headland and then heading west will take you to **La Grotte**, a dramatic – if narrow – beach that's popular with Tunisian families. It's protected to the west by the white cliffs of Cap Blanc, one of the northernmost points on the African continent. From June to September, there are several **basic eateries**, one of which has a very rudimentary bathroom. From the centre, a one-way taxi fare to La Grotte, which is 9km from the kasbah, costs about TD3.5. Local bus 2 goes to the roundabout just below the radar station (tell the driver you're going to La Grotte); from there you'll have to walk the last 3km or so.

Perhaps the best local beach is **Remel Plage**, a long stretch of sand with a backdrop of pine groves that begins about 3km southeast of the centre of town, across the drawbridge over the canal. Any bus heading east, or local bus 8, can drop you at the turn-off, from where it's a 15-minute walk. From the centre a cab costs about TD3 one-way.

Activities

Bizerte Plongée (72 420 411; www.tunisieplongee.com in French), based at the marina, runs scuba-diving excursions (including wreck dives) and rents equipment.

Pedal boats (per hr TD6; Jun-Aug) can be hired at the old port, next to the fake Phoenician warship.

Courses

Courses on offer at **Espace Culturel La Muse** (☎ 72 424 514; krsenda@yahoo.fr; rue du 1 Mai cnr rue de Grèce) include Tunisian and classical written Arabic (available one-on-one by the hour), painting and guitar.

The **Maison des Jeunes** (☎ 72 431 608; dmj.bizerte@jeunesse.tn; blvd Hassen en-Nouri) sponsors all sorts of courses for young people, including karate, aerobics, chess, spelunking and theatre.

Sleeping

Bizerte's budget options are all in the centre, while its midrange and top-end places are spread out along the coast north of the city, mostly in the Zone Touristique.

BUDGET

Hôtel Saadi (☎ 23 737 545; rue Salah Ben Ali; s/d/tr with shared bathroom TD7.5/15/22.5) The best of the super-cheapies, this clean, welcoming place has 14 smallish rooms (without sinks), some with balconies overlooking a small football stadium. Situated about 400m northwest of the centre in a tranquil but nondescript part of town. There's a *hammam* (public bathhouse) half a block away.

Maison des Jeunes (☎ 72 431 608; dmj.bizerte@jeunesse.tn; blvd Hassen en-Nouri; dm TD8) Open to travellers of all ages, this welcoming youth centre, about 1km north of the centre, has a bright, airy campus. The 80 beds are pretty tightly packed in but the rooms – including four-bed family rooms – while basic, are clean. Unlike the *foyer garçons* (men's building), the *foyer filles* (women's building) has toilets in the rooms. In July and August it's a good idea to reserve ahead.

Hôtel Africain (☎ 72 434 412; 59 rue Sassi el-Bahri; s/d with shared bathroom TD10/20) In the middle of the happening market area, the 13 rooms of this hotel (some with windows that open onto the hallway) have high ceilings but are very basic, lacking even a sink. The bathroom is clean but on the ground floor – bit of a hike if you're up on the 2nd floor.

Hôtel el-Fath (☎ 72 430 596; 136 ave Habib Bourguiba; s/d with shower in Jul & Aug TD15/30, Sep-Jun TD10/20) This modest establishment (also known as Hôtel el-Fateh), very near the main mosque, has lots of North African–style tilework but, alas, cannot be described as spotless. Some rooms have balconies. Situated about 350m west of the centre.

MIDRANGE

Hôtel de la Plage (☎ 72 436 510; 34 rue Mohamed Rejiba; s/d TD17/35, with shared bathroom TD15/30) Clean, simple and friendly, this place has an excellent central location and 25 smallish but cheerful rooms. A pretty good deal, though the showers may not always be hot and the rooms at the front can be noisy at night

Hôtel Nador (☎ 72 443 022; fax 72 433 817; Zone Touristique; s/d Jul & Aug TD30/50, Sep-Jun TD25/40; ❄ 🏊) By the beach 2.5km north of the kasbah and 250m east of the road to the corniche, this sprawling hotel, built in 1967, has huge gardens, an old-fashioned outdoor pool and a slight jet-set era vibe. The 106 rooms have barrel-vaulted ceilings, spotless bathrooms and balconies with garden views. A taxi to the centre costs TD1.5. After renovations, planned for 2007, room prices may rise by TD5 or TD10. Offers good value.

Le Petit Mousse (☎ 72 432 185; fax 72 438 871; ave de la Corniche; d May-Aug TD80, Sep-Apr TD60) Dating from 1946, this intimate 12-room hotel, 5km north of the centre, occupies a blue and white building across the road from the narrow corniche beach. Has an excellent restaurant (see opposite).

Hôtel Sidi Salem (☎ 72 420 365; www.hotel-sidisalem.com; ave Hedi Nouria; s/d Jul & Aug TD65/90, Apr-Jun & Sep-Oct TD50/70, Nov-Mar TD40/60; ❄ 🏊) The bougainvillea-draped garden is scraggly and half the grass is dead but this establishment, just 300m east of the kasbah, has large rooms facing a wide sandy beach, lots of sports facilities and a disco on Friday and Saturday nights (from 10pm).

TOP END

Bizerta Resort (☎ 72 436 966; fax 72 422 955; hbizerta@gnet.tn; ave Hedi Nouira; s/d TD69/130 mid-Jul–mid-Sep, TD60/110 Apr–mid-Jul & mid-Sep–Oct; TD47/85 Nov-Mar; ❄ 🏊) This four-star place – whose amenities include indoor and outdoor pools, a Jacuzzi, a fitness room, a sauna and a *hammam* – is the best place in town to lounge languorously in the luscious lap of luxury. Opened in 1998, it has 104 stylish rooms and a sleek bar with generously stuffed wing chairs. Situated on the beach 700m north of the kasbah.

Eating & Drinking

Self-caterers should check out the sprawling, indoor and outdoor **food market** (around place Bouchoucha; 🕑 7am or 8am-about 8pm), just west of the old port, or the **Monoprix supermarket** (ave Habib Bourguiba; ⏰ 8am-almost midnight), just east of rue 1 Juin 1955.

There's a cluster of popular eateries open till late at night along the easternmost bit of ave Habib Bourguiba and around the corner (to the south) on blvd Habib Bourguiba. The old port is lined with cafés.

Up along ave de la Corniche there are a number of ice cream and crepe places as well as several proper restaurants specialising in rather pricey fish and seafood.

Café-Patisserie Bellahouel (ave Habib Bourguiba cnr rue de Tunis; ⏰ 5.30am-almost midnight) Facing the old port, this place has super-fresh pastries (about TD0.4) and excellent coffee you can sip while seated at little, round sidewalk tables. A perfect place to start the day!

La Cuisine Tunisienne (7 rue 2 Mars 1934; mains TD2.5-4; ⏰ noon-11pm Mon-Sat, noon-3pm Sun) A cheap-and-cheerful eatery with a good choice of traditional Tunisian standards. Not gourmet but offers reliable good value.

Pizzeria Le Grand Bleu (☎ 20 241 129; rue Ahmad Tlili; pizza TD4-5; ⏰ noon-10 or 11pm) A spotless, brightly lit ground-floor pizzeria with pretty good pies, lasagne, shwarma and sandwiches.

Restaurant Le Grand Bleu (☎ 97 464 750; rue Ahmed Tlili; pasta TD6-10, meat mains TD10-12; ⏰ noon-3pm & 7.30pm or 8pm-midnight or later; ❄) A genuine Italian restaurant – the chef is from Italy – with tacky Italianate décor and 12 kinds of spaghetti. Upstairs from the pizzeria.

Du Bonheur (☎ 72 431 047; 31 rue Thaâlbi; meat mains TD8.5-14, fish per 100g TD4.5; ⏰ 11am-1am or later; ❄) Decked out in the traditional North African style, this restaurant serves tasty Tunisian specialities, including couscous (TD7 to TD8.9), at tables separated by *mushrabiya* (traditional wooden screens that allow people – especially women – to see out without being seen). The prettiest seats are way in back. Not to be confused with the all-male bar of the same name a few doors down.

Le Phénicien (☎ 72 424 480; old port; couscous TD11-14, meat mains TD14-24, fish per 100g TD6-10; ⏰ noon-2am or 3am; ❄) So now you know what that wooden monstrosity 'moored' at the old port is – opened in 2005, it's an upscale fish and seafood restaurant that's supposed to look like a Phoenician warship. Surprisingly, the food is good and, though tacky, this place is very popular with well-off Tunisians. The bar (alcohol served) on the upper deck affords superb harbour views.

Le Sport Nautique (☎ 72 432 262; quai Tarak ibn Ziad; fish per 100g TD6.5-7.5, meat mains TD14-24, couscous TD18-22; ⏰ noon-2.30pm & 8-10pm; ❄) Established for the French colonial elite back in 1928, this highly regarded restaurant offers delightful views of the marina from its breezy terrace. You select the fish you'd like from a trolley wheeled elegantly to your table.

Le Petit Mousse (☎ 72 432 185; ave de la Corniche; fish per 100g TD7-9.5; ⏰ 12.30-3.30pm & 8-11pm early May-Sep, noon-3pm & 7-10pm Oct-early May) The corniche's most upmarket fish and seafood place, this elegant establishment also serves French dishes such as *coq au vin* (TD16.5). Has a balmy, candlelit veranda with sea views and, downstairs, garden seating. Attached to a hotel of the same name (see opposite)

Entertainment

Espace Culturel La Muse (☎ 72 424 514; krsenda@yahoo.fr; rue du 1 Mai cnr rue de Grèce) Opened in late 2005, this privately funded cultural centre, behind the former cathedral, organises film screenings and concerts (eg guitar). It's a good place to meet young locals, perhaps to converse in English. You can also grab a bite, sip coffee, check your email, play chess and view paintings by Tunisian artists.

Cinéma Le Paris (end of ave Taieb Mehiri; admission TD2) screens first-run films in Arabic.

Getting There & Away

Bizerte's intercity public transport is decentralised, which is a nice way of saying that there are three bus stations and three louage stations, each serving different destinations.

AIR

The nearest airport is Tunis-Carthage. **Tunisair** (☎ 72 432 201; 76 ave Habib Bourguiba) has a local office.

BUS

From the **Zarzouna Bus Station** (☎ 72 593 161; rue de Tunis), 1.5km south of the centre (across the drawbridge over the canal), express buses go to Tunis' northern (Bab Saadoun) bus station (TD3.5, one hour, at least hourly till 7pm). Nonexpress buses to Tunis (TD3, 1¼ hours, every half-hour till 7pm), via Utica, take Route Nationale 8.

The buses to Tunis-Carthage International Airport (TD3.5, one hour, 11 daily) are yellow and have destination signs in Arabic. At the airport, the stop is way over to the left as you exit the terminal building. There are departures every one to 2½ hours – until 7pm from the airport, till 5.30pm from Bizerte.

Destinations served by STRB buses departing from the Main Bus Station, at the southern end of rue Ibn Khaldoun, include Ain Draham via Tabarka; Mateur (TD1.8, every two hours); Menzel Bourguiba (TD1, every half-hour); Ras Jebel (TD1.7, seven daily), where there is onward transport to Raf Raf and Ghar el-Melh; Sejnane (TD4, twice daily), which has links to Cap Serrat and Sidi Mechrig; and Tabarka (TD7.4, 3¼ hours, at 6am, with an SRT Jendouba bus at about noon).

Long-haul buses depart from the **SNTRI bus station** (☎ 72 431 222; rue d'Alger) Destinations include Jerba (TD23.9, 11 hours, at 6am and 6.30pm), Kairouan (TD12.3, four hours, at 6am), Sfax and Sousse.

CAR

Bizerte's multitude of small car-hire agencies include the following:

ADA (☎ 72 431 508; 27 rue d'Alger) Affiliated with France's largest discount car rental chain.

Europcar (☎ 72 439 018 or 20 44 796; 19 rue Rejiba, cnr rue Mohamed Rejiba)

Hertz (☎ 72 438 388; rue 8 Janvier 1938) On the side of Centre Bizerte.

Opera Car (☎ 72 421 427; rue Ahmed Tlili) Can arrange a car with a driver.

LOUAGE

Red-stripe louages to Tunis leave from next to the Zarzouna Bus Station.

Across rue de Russie from the Main Bus Station, blue-stripe louages depart frequently for Ras Jebel (TD1.9), where you can catch onward louages to Raf Raf and Ghar el-Melh.

From the parking lot just outside the train station, blue- and yellow-stripe louages go Sejnane (TD3.9) and blue ones go to Mateur (TD2.2), Menzel Bourguiba (TD1.2), Nefza and Tabarka (one daily).

TRAIN

The **Gare de Bizerte** (train station; rue de Russie) is linked to Tunis (TD3.2, with air-con TD4, 1¾ hours, four daily) via Tinja and Mateur.

Getting Around

The white local buses are decorated with colourful abstract doves, apparently the work of some Picasso wannabe. Buses 2 and 21 (half-hourly) link the corner of blvd Hassen en-Nouri and ave Habib Bourguiba with ave de la Corniche.

Buses heading east, such as local bus 8, can drop you at the Remel Plage turn-off (TD0.3, every 15 minutes).

EAST OF BIZERTE

Utique (Utica) أوتيك (أوتيقا)

Utica, the first Phoenician city in North Africa, was founded in about 1100 BC, 300 years before Carthage. Situated at the mouth of Oued Medjerda, it soon became a thriving port and remained important – and a rival of Carthage – for more than 1000 years.

Having defected to the Roman camp before the Third Punic War, Utica became the capital of the Roman province of Africa after the destruction of Carthage in 146 BC. Caught up in the Roman civil war in the 1st century BC, Utica supported Pompey. When the local commander, the Roman statesman Cato the Younger (Cato of Utica), realised that all was lost, he committed suicide rather than be captured – becoming a symbol of probity in public life the hard way – and Julius Caesar entered the city.

Under Hadrian Utica continued to flourish. A new aqueduct was built, along with a forum, baths and some elaborate residences. The city's days were numbered, though, by the fickle waters of Oued Medjerda, which silted up because of the increase in wheat cultivation under the Romans. By the beginning of the 2nd century AD, the river was no longer navigable and the port had been rendered useless.

These days, the **Site Archéologique d'Utique** (Utica ruins; admission TD3, plus camera TD1; 🕓 8am-7pm Apr–mid-Sep, 8.30am-5.30pm mid-Sep–Mar, museum closed Mon) – now 15km from the coast – occupies a low hill overlooking rich farmland. The remains are a bit sparse compared with some of Tunisia's other ancient cities but there are some fine mosaics and the tranquil site is cypress-shaded and flower-filled.

The best place to start a visit is the Musée d'Utique (museum), 2km off Route Nationale 8 (the old Bizerte–Tunis road). The Punic room shows everyday objects found at the necropolis, including make-up utensils, razors and some beautiful jewellery. Imported Greek pottery indicates the sophistication of the Punic settlement, while in the Roman room you can admire the marble garden statuary that was all the rage 2000 years ago. A new mosaics gallery opened in mid-2006.

At ancient Utica itself, 800m down the road from the museum, three Roman villas are the main attraction. A number of glorious mosaics – protected from the elements by low wooden roofs – have been left *in situ*; if you take a tour, the guide will spray water on them to bring out the rich colours.

The **House of the Cascade** (Maison de la Cascade), with a central patio, is named after a fountain in a northern room decorated with a fishing-scene mosaic. One glorious basin mosaic shows a fishing cupid in a boat, while the **triclinium** (dining room) is floored in green marble (from Greece) and golden marble (from Chemtou) in striking geometric patterns. A mammoth mosaic from Utica with a sea-god theme can be seen at the Bardo Museum (see p50).

Pretty much the only way to see the squat toilet, the glories of Roman water engineering (including the rainwater collection system) and the gruesome 7th- or 8th-century BC *in situ* skeleton of a teenage girl is to hire a guide – for an informative tour in French, Italian or Arabic call **Hedi Selini** (☎ 96 151 317).

Signs at the site are in Arabic, English, French and German. A book on Utique (in French) is on sale at the ticket counter.

GETTING THERE & AWAY

Utica can easily be visited on a day trip from Bizerte or Tunis, perhaps in combination with one of the nearby beaches.

The turn-off to the archaeological site, marked 'Utique Ruines', is just east of the small town of Utique, 33km north of Tunis on Route Nationale 8, the old (ie non-toll) road to Bizerte.

By public transport, take a non-express Tunis–Bizerte bus and ask the driver to drop you on the main road; from there it's a 2km walk to the museum.

Raf Raf Plage رفراف

The unpretentious beach at Raf Raf – often crowded with Tunisian families – consists of a long narrow crescent of sand, much of it lined by whitewashed low-rise buildings, and a slightly ramshackle promenade. Offshore, framed by luscious turquoise waters, loom the cliffs of a dramatic sand-coloured island, **Jazirat Bilou**.

The drive to Raf Raf and its *plage* (beach), 4km beyond the uninteresting *centre-ville* (village centre), takes you through rolling hills whose tans and olivey greens contrast sublimely with the deep blues of the Mediterranean.

SLEEPING & EATING

The only accommodation option is the midrange **Hôtel Dalia** (☎ 72 441 688/630; s/d Sep-Jun TD35/70, Jul & Aug TD55/90; ❄), 150m up the hill from the beach. The 10 small, bright rooms come with little balconies.

LAKE ICHKEUL BIRDLIFE

Providing its seasonal variations in salinity are in balance, Lake Ichkeul is a true haven for our feathered friends. Some hunt along the shoreline or probe the soft mud at the water's edge; others stride into the shallows on long legs in search of their dinner; and yet others, such as the brightly coloured kingfisher, dive in search of underwater prey.

Most spectacular are the greater flamingos – if you're in luck, you'll see one of Tunisia's ornithological highlights, a mass of pink above the shimmering waters. Other large migrants that pass through include squacco herons, cattle egrets and white storks, famed bringers of babies and beloved symbol of France's Alsace region. Warblers, finches and rails dart about the dense vegetation surrounding the lake.

Autumn sees the arrival of birds – especially ducks and geese – fleeing the approaching winter in northern and eastern Europe and Russia. Their usual migration routes are via Corsica and then Sicily or over the Italian boot. On one occasion a Eurasian wigeon banded in Britain was recorded.

Birds of prey you might see gliding over Jebel Ichkeul include Bonelli's eagles, short-toed eagles, Eleonora's falcons and Egyptian vultures.

Restaurants serving sandwiches, pizza and fresh fish – caught by the small local fishing fleet – and a few fruit and veggie vendors line the seafront.

GETTING THERE & AWAY

Ras Jebel, 6km west of Raf Raf, is the nearest public transport hub, with services to Bizerte (TD1.7, seven daily). Raf Raf is linked to Ras Jebel by taxi (TD1.2 per person; the stand faces the Hôtel Dalia) and bus (TD0.65).

Ghar el-Melh غار الملح

The village of Ghar el-Melh, on the other (southern) side of Jebel Nadour (325m) from Raf Raf, snoozes beside a silted-up lagoon. Surprisingly, it's endowed with three imposing, stone-built **Ottoman forts**, each worth a look inside, and a small, somnolent **fishing port** with a relaxing little café. The road through town passes under an arched section near the **old market**.

Ghar el-Melh was founded during the reign of Osta Murad Dey (1637–40) as the pirate base of Porto Farina. Its notoriety was such that in 1654 it was attacked and temporarily knocked out of action by the celebrated English naval heavy Sir Francis Drake. After privateering was abolished at the beginning of the 19th century, the Husseinite beys attempted to turn the port into a major naval base. Ahmed Bey (1837–55) ordered the construction of two new forts, a defensive wall and a port but his efforts were soon foiled by the silt-laden waters of the Oued Medjerda, which clogged the lagoon. Attempts at dredging failed and the port was abandoned in favour of La Goulette, near Tunis.

GETTING THERE & AWAY

Ghar el-Melh is only a few kilometres south of Raf Raf but about 20km by road. The town is linked to Bizerte by louages and by bus (TD1.5, one hour, two daily). There's no public transport out to Sidi Ali el-Mekki.

Sidi Ali el-Mekki سيدي علي المكي

Sidi Ali el-Mekki beach, on the southern side of Cap Farina at the edge of the Ghar el-Melh lagoon, is one of the handful of beaches in Tunisia that's in the same league as southern Thailand. Favoured by well-off Tunisians, it has broad expanses of fine-grain sand and lusciously transparent waters that shade from jade to turquoise to aquamarine.

From mid-June to mid-Sept the beach has life guards, Gilligan's Island–type fibre parasols (TD5, including a table and four chairs), refreshment kiosks and even its own little Garde Nationale post. There are rudimentary toilets and showers.

Thanks to the protection afforded by pine-forested **Cape Sidi Ali el-Mekki**, to the north, the waves are generally tiny, making this an ideal beach for small kids. An ice plant–lined **trail** leads from the beach to the tip of the cape, a distance of about 3km.

The whitewashed structures up on the hillside are caves housing the **tomb of Sidi Ali el-Mekki** and the tombs of other local saints. They attract a mixture of the devout, who light candles in the hope of saintly intercession, and the curious, attracted at least in part by the spectacular view. Come dressed in a bit more than swimwear.

SLEEPING & EATING

It may be possible to rent a straw shack. Camping is OK too.

Restaurant Cap Farina (☎ 98 442 851; fish TD14; daily mid-May–mid-Oct, Sat & Sun mid-Oct–mid-May) serves salads and delicious fresh fish and seafood, barbecued on pine cones.

GETTING THERE & AWAY

Situated 6km east of Ghar el-Melh, Sidi Ali el-Mekki is not served by public transport, though you could walk or try hitching (for the risks of hitching, see p311). Parking costs TD0.6 – pay at the gate.

FROM BIZERTE TO TABARKA

The area west of Bizerte is hilly and rural, with wide expanses of undulating grain fields between secluded villages. The dramatic coastline, largely uninhabited, consists of a series of rugged promontories and sparkling blue bays and is only accessible at a few points.

Louages go virtually everywhere people live but you'll need patience to get to the more remote villages along the coast.

Ichkeul National Park بحيرة اشكل

A Unesco Natural World Heritage site since 1980, the sublimely beautiful, 120-sq-km **Ichkeul National Park** (Parc National d'Ichkeul; TD1;

(8am-5pm, once inside you can stay till dusk) encompasses **Lake Ichkeul**, a shallow, brackish lake – in the most extraordinarily gentle shades of blue and green – surrounded by marshland that floods in winter; and **Jebel Ichkeul** (511m), whose reddish bulk rises from the surrounding flats and low hills like a Mediterranean version of Uluru (Ayers Rock).

Lake Ichkeul covers about 89 sq km in summer, when its average depth is about 1m, expanding in winter to flood 30 sq km of the surrounding marshland. It's a paradise for birds and bird-watchers (see p131), though the entire lake ecosystem is now under threat (see below).

Ichkeul was managed as a hunting reserve at least as far back as the 13th century and today is home to wild boar, crested porcupines, Egyptian mongoose, wild cats and four species of bat. Otters have been hunted almost to extinction. The 60 water buffalos, descendants of a pair given to Ahmed Bey in 1840, can weigh up to 1000kg.

The rather dated exhibits in the small **Écomusée** (visitors centre), opened in 1989, present the lake's unique ecosystem in French and Arabic. One wall chart describes the lake as being like 'a very rich soup' that, like any broth, can be ruined by too much salt. Another chart illustrates various bird species' feeding habits. Nearby, **trails** lead around the hill and up its flanks.

There are **hot springs**, popular with locals, on the northeastern edge of Jebel Ichkeul.

There's no accommodation in the park and camping is not permitted. The best time to spot wildlife is early in the morning or around dusk.

GETTING THERE & AWAY

Entry to the park, about 30km southwest of Bizerte, is on the eastern flank of Jebel Ichkeul, which overlooks the lake from the south. The turn-off is about midway between Tinja and Mateur, near where the train tracks cross the highway – look for a sign reading 'Parc Echkel'.

At the gate to the park you must register and pay an entry fee (TD1) before

AN ECOSYSTEM AT RISK

Lake Ichkeul is one of the four most important wetlands in the western Mediterranean (the other three are the Camargue in France, Doñana in Spain and El Kala in Algeria).

For countless millennia the lake's unique ecosystem thrived thanks to seasonal variations in salinity. During the autumn rainy season, six seasonal rivers brought in fresh water, reducing salinity to about 5g per litre, whereas from July to October evaporation and the inflow of saltwater from nearby Lake Bizerte, a nearby marine lagoon, brought salinity up to above 30g per litre.

In recent years, following the construction of dams on three of the rivers – to provide much-needed water for homes and agriculture – winter and summer salinity levels have increased significantly. The consequences have been fast and devastating. Narrow-leaved pondweed *(Potamogeton pectinatus)* – the major source of food of waterfowl – has been replaced by salt-tolerant plants that the birds cannot eat. The result has been a precipitous drop in the number of migrant and wintering birds: two decades ago some 200,000 waterfowl spent the winter at Lake Ichkeul; today only 50,000 do so. Over this same period, the number of wintering greylag geese has dropped from 20,000 to under 1000.

Rushes and reeds, too, are sensitive to salinity and their disappearance from marshlands is having a severe impact on the birds that used to construct nests in them, such as herons, egrets and the threatened marbled teal. Indeed, none of these species now nest here. Mammals, such as the otter, for whom the rushes and reeds provided shelter, have also been affected, as has the insect population, including some huge dragonflies.

Unless the lake again receives sufficient freshwater, it is in danger of becoming a saltwater lagoon, resulting in a tragic loss of biodiversity – that's why, in 1996, the park was placed on Unesco's List of World Heritage in Danger. In 1986 226 species of bird, including 34 that bred here, were recorded. How many will be left in another five or 10 years?

Each foreign visitor to Ichkeul National Park is a tangible expression of the lake's international ecological importance and of its potential – if the ecosystem is properly protected – as a magnet for ecotourism and thus for local economic development.

continuing for 3km along a mostly gravel road to a complex of bright white buildings; the Écomusée is up the stairs.

Buses (about TD1.5 from Bizerte, every two hours) and louages between Bizerte and Mateur can drop you at the 'Parc Echkel' turn-off but from there you'll either have to walk (about 7km) or hitch. Traffic is light, especially from the park entrance to the Écomusée.

Sejnane سجنان

Sejnane is set amid hilly grain fields and grey-green forests but the sole reason to come to this hardscrabble town, 71km southwest of Bizerte, is to catch a bus or louage to somewhere else. The only thing even half worth seeing is the **storks' nests** – check out the roof of the freight-only train station, 250m up the road from the Mobil petrol station, and the adjacent, long abandoned mining rig.

The main street is a chaotic, dirty jumble of cafés, cheapie eateries, market stalls, shops and flocks of louages. At the far end, at the top of the open-air market, is a basic **hospital**. All this hustle and bustle attracts some rough-edged characters, in no way hostile but hardly models of politesse.

Sejnane has no hotels.

GETTING THERE & AWAY

Buses and louages can be found at or near the main junction, next to the Mobil petrol station. SNTRI buses travelling the northern route (via Mateur) between Tabarka (TD2.5) and Tunis (TD5.5) stop here, as do louages to Bizerte (TD3.9, one hour; until about 6pm), Cap Serrat beach (TD1.3, one or two daily in winter, more in summer), Mateur (TD2.5) and Sidi Mechrig (TD1.2, eight daily). Transport from Sejnane to Tabarka is infrequent – a louage trip may require changing at Nefza and Ouchtata.

SEJNANE WARE

The techniques used by the potters of the Berber villages around Sejnane to make their distinctive wares date back to Neolithic times. Clay is hand-moulded into unusual animal figurines and bowls of different shapes and sizes, then open-fired on mounds of glowing coals before being decorated with rusty reds and deep browns.

You'll find Sejnane ware on sale at tourist shops countrywide (and in Bizerte's open-air market) as well as at roadside stands around (but not in) Sejnane – for instance, a few kilometres out of town along the roads to Bizerte and Mateur.

Cap Serrat Beach رأس سرّاط

Cap Serrat Beach is dazzling, serene and secluded. Situated across the small Zeyatine River – lined with marshes and eucalyptus trees – from the shaded parking area, it's definitely one of Tunisia's mellowest beaches, a quiet, friendly place to chill. The two rocky islands offshore are known as **Les Frères** (the brothers).

To the northwest, the cape is topped by a white **lighthouse**, while to the east are gentle, sandy hills. The whole area, including the inland eucalyptus forests, can be explored on a network of **trails**. You can sometimes spot wild boar.

Alas, the beach – a long, wide expanse of sand that gets hit with some pretty vigorous waves – is not the cleanest. In addition to the usual blight of plastic bottles, the sand is strewn with dark-brown discs – on closer inspection you'll see that they're dried cow pats (pies). The showers (TD0.25) are pretty dilapidated. It's possible to hire a small boat, skipper included.

SLEEPING & EATING

Tunisians and foreigners alike camp on the sand under the trees.

Le Pirate (☎ 23 694 746 or 23 968 939; d TD40, ⏰ Mar-Dec, call ahead in Jan & Feb) serves excellent grilled fish (per 100g including salad and desert starts from TD4) on an outdoor terrace and also has three basic but rather pricey rooms. Everything, including the toilets, is absolutely spotlessly clean.

GETTING THERE & AWAY

The road to Cap Serrat, 27km north of Sejnane, snakes through eucalyptus and pine plantations filled with beehives – in summer you can buy honey at the roadside. A rough road hugs the coast from Cap Serrat to Sidi Mechrig, some 20km to the west – in winter it requires a 4WD as some bits are sandy.

Louages to Cap Serrat from Sejnane (TD1.3), well connected with Bizerte, run a few times a day in July and August but only once or twice a day in winter, in the morning. It's more convenient to take a louage from Bizerte to Blakat junction, midway between Sejnane and Cap Serrat, and then a *camionnette* (small truck) to Cap Serrat.

Sidi Mechrig سيدي مشرق

Sidi Mechrig is a tiny coastal settlement with no mobile phone reception, one guest house, a small but modern fishing port and a stretch of sandy beach overlooked by three **Roman arches** – the remains of an ancient bathhouse. Unfortunately, it's not as laid back as Cap Serrat and the beach is strewn with detritus that's been washed ashore. Beyond the small fishing port (a bit northeast of the beach) you can see the Cap Serrat lighthouse.

Trails lead to a pretty little spring and through the nearby pine forest to the tomb of Sidi Bou Tayeb. The trail along the coast goes to Jebel Chitane and the tomb of Oma Nowala, a woman saint.

SLEEPING & EATING

Auberge-Restaurant Sidi Mechrig (d/q with common bathroom TN30/50; year-round), next to the Garde Nationale post, overlooks the beach. The 10 large rooms have high ceilings, big beds with new mattresses, and patterned tile floors from the late French period. The **restaurant** (fish TD8.50-10) serves grilled fish and various Tunisian dishes, including couscous; everything comes with salad and chips. A cold beer is recommended.

GETTING THERE & AWAY

The signless turn-off to Sidi Mechrig is 10km west of Sejnane on the road to Tabarka, a bit before Tamra. From there it's a further 17km through eucalyptus tree plantations and past scattered houses.

Sidi Mechrig is linked with Sejnane by louage (TD1.2, eight daily) and a few buses a day, timed to get local kids to school.

THE WILD SIDE

The remote, sparsely populated area north of the Bizerte–Sejnane highway (highway 51), between Cap Blanc and Cap Serrat, is well worth exploring if you've got a car, a taste for dramatic landscapes, some time to burn and the patience to get lost. The reward at the end of the serpentine, one-lane roads to nowhere, through undulating fields of grain and along maquis-covered hills: some truly wild Mediterranean coastline. If you reach the dirt-poor hamlets of **Dar Ramal** or **Houichet** you've truly arrived at the end of the line.

There don't seem to be accurate maps of the area. Both Michelin's 1:800,000-scale map of Tunisia and the 1:750,000-scale map produced by Tunisia's Office de la Topographie are pretty useless out here – worse than useless since they show roads that don't exist. Mobile phone coverage is patchy. Bring food and water as there are no shops.

TABARKA طبرقة

pop 13,600

Just 22km from Algeria, the port town of Tabarka sits at the western edge of a beach-fringed bay, south of a rocky peninsula crowned by an imposing Genoese fort. Renowned for affording Tunisia's best scuba diving, its focal point is the marina, which serves both pleasure craft and fishing boats – the latter bring in the fresh fish and seafood served around town. During July and August Tabarka hosts four fabulous music festivals.

Tabarka is a good base for exploring the Kroumirie Mountains, Ain Draham and several Roman sites, including Bulla Regia.

History

Like so many North African coastal towns, Tabarka began life as a Phoenician settlement. Originally called Thabraca (Shaded Place), it remained a minor outpost until Roman times, when it became a major port thanks to the export of Chemtou marble. It also served as the exit point for many African big cats en route to the colosseums of Rome and elsewhere.

In the 16th and 17th centuries, Tabarka was one of the bases for the Barbary Coast corsairs. They included the notorious Khair ed-Din Barbarossa, who was obliged to hand over Tabarka Island to the Genoese in the 1540s as ransom for the release of his cohort, Dragut. The castle the Genoese built enabled them to retain Tabarka against the Ottomans until 1741, when it fell to the bey of Tunis.

The French constructed both the causeway to the island and the modern town. Despite these developments, Tabarka remained enough of a backwater for the

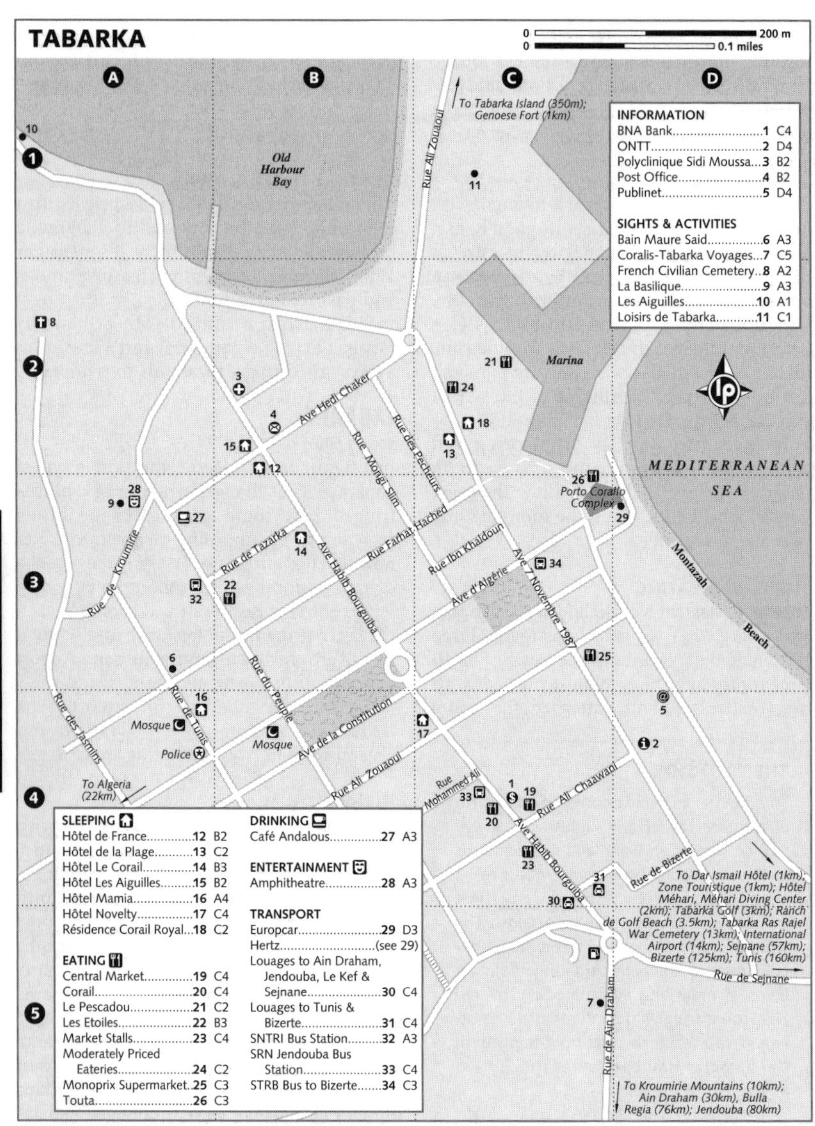

French to consider it a suitable place of exile for Habib Bourguiba in 1952.

Orientation

The marina is just northeast of the town centre. The main drag is northwest-to-southeast–oriented ave Habib Bourguiba, which ends at a roundabout (and a petrol station) from which roads head south to Ain Draham and east to Sejnane and Bizerte. The Zone Touristique begins 1.5km east of the marina.

Information

There are a few banks situated along ave Habib Bourguiba. Useful websites include the western flank of Jebel Biri (1014m), the highest peak of the Kroumirie Mountains, while all around are rounded hills covered in cork forest. The town is a great base for hiking, mountain biking and horse riding (see below).

Ain Draham was popular with colonial hunters – the last of Tunisia's lions and leopards were shot around here early last century. Hunting continues to be an attraction, with wild boars now the primary target, but most visitors come to relax and escape the summer heat and a few come to do serious training at the well-equipped sports centre.

The road linking Tabarka with Ain Draham is one of Tunisia's most beautiful. As it climbs through rich countryside, it passes from the coastal plain into the Kroumirie Mountains' famous cork oak forests, affording views of the deep-blue sea and the verdant valleys leading down to it.

Orientation & Information

The simplest way to navigate around Ain Draham is to measure distances from the fountain roundabout at the northern edge of town, in the middle of the T-junction formed by the intersection of two main roads: ave 7 November 1987, which heads southward down the hill past the bus station and on to Jendouba, and ave Habib Bourguiba, which heads both northwest towards Tabarka and southeast (up the slope) to the centre of town, from where it arches southward a eventually joins ave 7 November 1987 form the main road to Jendouba.

Hospital (☎ 78 655 047; rue Habib Thameur; ⏲ 24h Situated 600m southwest of the fountain roundabout on the other side of the valley from the town centre. Look f a sign reading *urgences*.

Maison des Jeunes Internet Room (☎ 78 655 08 ave Habib Bourguiba; internet per hr TD1.2; ⏲ 9am or 10am-almost midnight) To the left and up the stairs fro the main building.

Post office (ave Habib Bourguiba) About 400m up the from the fountain roundabout.

STB Bank (ave Habib Bourguiba) About 250m up the hi from the fountain roundabout. Ain Draham does not hav any ATMs.

Sights & Activities

Strung out along the main commerci street, ave Habib Bourguiba, are colonia era buildings, cafés, a few restaurants an small food, clothing and crafts shops. Th town is especially animated on Monda which is market day.

One local walking option is to head ou along the road towards Tabarka to th Hôtel Nour el-Ain, in an area known a **Col des Ruines**. From the western edge o the hotel parking lot, up the stairs, a trai heads up the hill to a cement water-tan and then continues south and southwes through the pine and oak forests back t town. The whole circuit takes about tw hours.

ECOTOURISM IN THE KROUMIRIE MOUNTAINS

The hills, forests and plains around Ain Draham have huge ecotourism potential that, so far, is almost entirely untapped, in part because the absence of decent maps pretty much precludes heading out on your own. Fortunately, Ain Draham's **Royal Rihana Hôtel** (see opposite; ☎ 78 655 391; www.royalrihana-hotel.com; ⏲ generally May-Oct) organises a variety of guided outdoors expeditions. Groups usually have to have at least eight participants.

The Rihana's experienced team offers **hikes and treks** through the mountains, along the coast and/or to Roman sites. Full board is provided and accommodation en route is either in hotels or in Berber-style tents. Four/eight nights in a tent cost TD489/832; reserve at least a week ahead.

For **mountain biking**, you can either base yourself in Ain Draham and take guided day trips (the hotel provides hot lunches) or head out on a longer expedition; one/two/seven nights cost TD269/342/489.

If you've got a group of at least 20, one option is a nine-day **back-roads cycling trip** (€999), with about 100km of riding a day, from Ain Draham to Le Kef, Sbeitla, Kairouan, Mahdia, Hammamet, Kélibia and Tunis. In each governorate the group is accompanied by a local police escort. You'll need to bring your own bicycle.

Horse-riding trips cost TD489/589/929 for four/five/nine nights.

www.tabarka.org (in French) and www.tabarka.de (in German).

BNA Bank (ave Habib Bourguiba) Faces the SRN Jendouba bus office.

Polyclinique Sidi Moussa (☎ 78 671 200; 5 ave Habib Bourguiba; ⏲ 24hr) Can deal with medical needs and emergencies.

Post office (rue Hedi Chaker cnr ave Habib Bourguiba)

Publinet (internet per hr TD2; ⏲ 8am-9pm or 10pm) Next to the tourist office.

Tourist Office (ONTT; ☎ 78 673 555; crtt.ontt@email.ati.tn; ave 7 Novembre 1987; ⏲ 8am-10pm daily Jul & Aug, 8.30am-1pm & 3-5.45pm Mon-Sat Sep-Jun) Occupies the old train station.

Sights

The heart of Tabarka is its **marina** (*port de plaisance*), just northeast of the town centre. If you tire of strolling on dry land, you can ask around for a boat offering sea excursions.

About 1km north of the marina on rocky **Tabarka Island** (Île de Tabarka), turned into a peninsula by the French, stands a magnificent **Genoese fort**, now occupied by the Tunisian army. It can be admired only from the outside.

Across the **Old Harbour Bay** (*Ancien Port*) from the peninsula, **Les Aiguilles** (lays ai-*gwee*; The Needles) – a grouping of spiky pinnacles of rock – and the adjacent **jetty** are a popular destination for photo-ops and short evening strolls.

On the hillside above Les Aiguilles is an old **French civilian cemetery** with views of the port – to get there, take rue Farhat Hached west to rue des Jasmins and turn right.

The **Basilique** (La Basilique) is a Roman cistern turned into a church by French missionaries at the end of the 19th century. Delicate and airy it's not – inside you can see some massive square columns holding up some equally massive arches. The 1500-seat **amphitheatre** out front hosts Tabarka's four famous music festivals (see Festivals, p138).

About 14km east of Tabarka, just west of the turnoff to the airport, is the neatly tended **Tabarka Ras Rajel War Cemetery**, in which 500 Commonwealth soldiers who died in WWII – 60 of them unidentified – are buried.

Activities

BEACHES

Montazah Beach begins at the marina and stretches eastward around the bay, past the big hotels of the Zone Touristique. The further from the marina you go the cleaner it gets.

HAMMAM

Bring along shorts, a towel, flip-flops, shampoo and soap to **Bain Maure Said** (rue Farhat Hached cnr rue de Tunis; bath TD1.2, massage TD1.2; ⏲ for women noon-5pm, for men 5-8pm Sat-Thu, for men 5am-noon, for women noon-8pm Fri). Documents can be deposited in little boxes.

DIVING

Based at the marina, **Loisirs de Tabarka** (☎ 78 670 664; www.loisirsdetabarka.com; rue Ali Zouaoui; ⏲ about Mar-Oct) offers CMAS level 1/2 courses with six/eight dives for TD330/430 and packages of 1/6/10 dives for TD27/138/200 (from July to September TD30/144/220), not including equipment (TD20 per dive). Excursion options include an all-day trip to the protected Galite Islands, three hours from Tabarka, which are famed for their fantastic sealife (TD70 per person including a barbecue; minimum 12 people).

Hidden away in the Hôtel Méhari complex 2.5km east of town, the experienced **Méhari Diving Center** (☎ 78 673 136; www.meharidivingcenter.com; Zone Touristique) runs level 1/2/3/4 CMASPADI-SSI courses for TD230/280/350/400; 1/6/10 dives cost TD25/132/200 (a bit more for night dives), not including equipment rental (TD15 per dive).

HORSE & CAMEL RIDING

Ranch de Golf Beach (☎ 98 824 144; Zone Touristique; ⏲ year-round), just to the left of the gate to the Golf Beach Hotel, charges TD25 for a two-hour guided horse-ride along the beach and through the forest; the price for a camel ride is the same.

GOLF

The **Tabarka Golf Club** (☎ 78 671 031; www.tabarkagolf.com; Zone Touristique; 9/18 holes TD35/55; ⏲ year-round) has a fine 18-hole layout. Theoretically you need a handicap of 36 but in practice just having a golf handicap certificate (*carte verte* in French) is sufficient. Renting a half-series of clubs costs TD7. Reservations, necessary for groups in spring and autumn, can be made by email or fax (summer is the low season here). Three- to seven-day beginners' courses and private lessons (30 minutes costs TD22) are available.

Tours

Coralis-Tabarka Voyages (☎ 78 673 740; coralis@gnet.tn; 13 route de Ain Draham; 8.30am-1pm & 3-6pm Mon-Sat & sometimes Sun May–mid-Oct, open mornings only Jul & Aug) runs half-day excursions to Bulla Regia (TN30; every Sunday and perhaps other days) and all-day trips to Dougga and Chemtou (TD50; once or twice a week). Reserve a day or two ahead.

Festivals

Tabarka is famous far and wide for its four first-rate, summertime **music festivals** (www.tabarkajazz.com in French; admission TD10-20). The season kicks off with the outstanding, weeklong **Jazz Festival** (second week of July) and is followed by the **World Music Festival** (mid-August), the **Latinos Festival** (late August) and, to cap off the season, the **Raï Festival** (at the tail end of August), which brings to town *raï* superstars from France and Algeria.

The main events take place in the amphitheatre just outside the Basilique but are supposed to be transferred to a larger amphitheatre northwest of town as soon as it's built.

Sleeping

Budget options are scarce. The most luxurious places are along the beach in the Zone Touristique, 1.5km to 4km west of the marina. Prices rise precipitously in July and August.

Campervans can park near the marina for a fee.

BUDGET

Hôtel Mamia (☎ 78 671 058; fax 78 670 638; 3 rue de Tunis; s/d/tr with toilet Jul-Sep TD22/30/45, Oct-Jun TD15/20/30) The windows of the simple, clean rooms open onto a plant-filled courtyard, where you'll find the showers. The management may make you feel as if you're inconveniencing them. Situated across the street from a mosque.

Hôtel Le Corail (☎ /fax 78 673 082; rue de Tazarka; d with hall bathroom TD35, with bath & toilet TN50-65, about 50% less mid-Sep–Jun) This place has 20 light and airy rooms – the better ones have pretty tile floors and high ceilings, the cheaper ones are spartan and have an old-fashioned feel. Scrubbing till the end of eternity would not make the hall bathrooms feel really clean; the plumbing is a bit iffy.

MIDRANGE

Hôtel La Plage (☎ 78 670 039; 11 ave 7 Novembre 1987; s/d with shared bathroom late Jun–mid-Sep TD25/44, with shower TD30/50, with air-con TD45/70, s/d with shared bathroom mid-Sep–late Jun TD15/20, with shower TD20/35, with air-con TD20/35) Clean, small and central, the nicest rooms here have balconies overlooking the street. The entrance has some crazy fibreglass seashell action but otherwise the reception is dour. Watch out for the hard, lumpy pillows.

Hôtel Les Aiguilles (☎ 78 673 789; fax 78 673 604; hotel.lesaiguilles@wanadoo.tn; 18 ave Habib Bourguiba; s/d late Jun–mid-Sep TD55/80, Apr-late Jun & mid-Sep–Oct TD30/40, Nov-Mar TD20/30) Housed in an old colonial building, this welcoming, 19-room place is nothing fancy but the rooms come with high ceilings and proper bathrooms and, in some cases, sea views. Excellent value except in summer.

Hôtel Novelty (☎ 78 670 176; fax 78 673 008; 68 ave Habib Bourguiba; s/d Jul–mid-Sep TD45/90, Apr-Jun & mid-Sep–Oct TD30/60, Nov-Mar TD25/50) This establishment, very centrally located, has 26 bright and airy rooms, all of them simply furnished but neat and clean. Watch out for the low ceiling over the staircase.

Hôtel de France (☎ 78 670 600; fax 78 671 132; ave Hedi Chaker cnr ave Habib Bourguiba; s/d Jul–mid-Sep TD65/100 , Apr-Jun & mid-Sep–Oct TD50/70, Nov-Mar TD30/40) This lift-equipped three-star, with a popular pavement café, has 16 smart, recently renovated rooms with TV; some also come with tiny balconies and good views over the bay. Bourguiba stayed here during his brief exile.

Résidence Corail Royal (☎ 78 670 370; ave 7 Novembre 1987; 2-/4-/6-/8-person apartments with 1/2/3/4 rooms Jul–mid-Sep TD110/160/205/230, Apr-Jun & mid-Sep–Oct TD56/90/120/150, Nov-Mar TD46/80/110/140) Right next to the marina, these 59 self-catering apartments have spacious kitchenettes and elaborately tiled bathrooms; some come with sea views. Overpriced in summer but a good deal the rest of the time.

TOP END

Hôtel Méhari (☎ 78 670 184; www.goldenyasmin.com; Zone Touristique; s/d Jul-Aug TD107/164, mid-Mar–Jun & Sep-Oct 72/110, Nov & Mar TD54/100) Part of the Golden Yasmin chain, this luxurious complex, 2.5km east of the marina, offers a fine strip of beach, two swimming pools, tennis, a fitness centre, a Jacuzzi, a *hammam*, massage, *thalassothérapie* (saltwater therapy) and an on-site dive club (see p137). Kids have a 'mini-club'. Bungalow studio apartments costs TD125 (TD80 in winter).

Dar Ismail (☎ 78 670 188; www.hoteldarismail.com; Zone Touristique; s/d Jul–mid-Sep TD95/190, mid-Sep–Jun TD63/126) Situated 1.5km east of the marina, this five-star, Moorish-themed place, painted in glitzy shades of tangerine, has peachy, comfortable rooms and all the comforts – plus a fine stretch of beach and lots of grass. A business centre with internet is due to open in 2007

Eating

Not surprisingly, fish and seafood – especially grilled fish – are a Tabarka speciality.

There's a bunch of moderately priced eateries at the northwestern end of ave 7 Novembre 1987 and some cheapies with a local clientele along rue du Peuple near ave Farhat Hached (around Les Etoiles – see below). The fish restaurants around the marina are more upscale.

A number of midrange hotels have restaurants with good-value three-course meals – places to try include the Hôtel Les Aiguilles (TD12) and the Hotel Novelty (TD10).

Les Etoiles (rue du Peuple; grilled fish TD4) Perhaps the best of several similar simple places on this street. Has outside tables and a nice local feel.

Corail (ave Habib Bourguiba; mains TD6.5, 3-course set menu TD8) This cheap-and-cheerful place has a good set menu, some outside tables and jolly management.

Le Pescadou (☎ 98 237 996; marina; fish & meat mains TD8-10; closed Ramadan & weekdays in winter) One of the sea-based specialities here is bouillabaisse.

Touta (☎ 78 671 018; marina; fish per 100g TD6; 11.30am-midnight or 1am, closed for a few months in winter) Specialises in locally caught fish and seafood, including langouste (crayfish; per 100g TD9). Has a great marina setting.

Self-caterers will find fruits and veggies at the **central market** (rue Ali Chaawani). There are more market stalls just across ave Habib Bourguiba and the usual items can be found at the **Monoprix supermarket** (ave 7 Novembre 1987; 8.30am-10pm).

Drinking

Café Andalous (ave Hedi Chaker) This old-time, teetotal café is worth a visit just to see the wall tiles, made long ago in Tunis b
the wood-and-copper figurines o
man Turks strung along the ceilir
the chandeliers, which have to be
be believed. During the jazz festival
one of the venues for live music.

Getting There & Away

AIR

Little happens at Tabarka's inter
airport, 15km east of the city, ex
the occasional European charter fl

BUS

Buses to Tunis (3¼ hours, six d
Mateur or Béja depart from the
station (rue du Peuple).

The **SRN Jendouba bus office** (84 ave
guiba cnr rue Mohammed Ali) handles bus
Draham (TD1.1, 40 minutes, a doz
Bizerte (TD7.4, 3¼ hours, at 6.45
an STRB bus from Restaurant Sid
at 12.30pm), Jendouba (TD2.9, 1
four daily) and Le Kef (TD5.5, 3
twice daily).

CAR

Car-hire companies include the f
Europcar (☎ 98 237 967; Porto Corallo com
Hertz (☎ 78 670 670; Porto Corallo comple

LOUAGE

Louages congregate near the sou
end of ave Habib Bourguiba. L
Tunis (TF8.7, 2½ hours, freque
tures) and Bizerte (one daily) leav
east side of the street, while loua
Draham (TD1.3), Jendouba (TD3
(TD6.5) and Mateur via Sejnane
at about 6am) leave from the w
the street.

Getting Around

A taxi from Tabarka to the air
TD10 (TD15 at night).

A cab ride from the town ce
Zone Touristique costs TD1.5 t
pending on how far out you go.

AIN DRAHAM

pop 15,300

Often snow-covered in Decemb
uary, Ain Draham (altitude 90
30km inland from Tabarka, is T
station. Its steep-roofed houses

LES TAPIS DE KROUMIRIE

Bold, colourful carpets and handbags, many decorated with simple, traditional Berber motifs, are woven in Ain Draham by a small women's cooperative called **Les Tapis de Kroumirie** (☎ 78 655 226; rue Abou el-Kacem Echebbi; 8am-1pm & 2-5pm or 5.30pm, closed Fri afternoon & Sat afternoon). Launched in the 1980s by two French doctors and operated with the help of Ain Draham's Centre d'Action Sociale (Social Action Centre), it aims both to provide employment for poor women and to preserve local carpet-making traditions.

At the friendly, airy workshop, where you can see women working the looms (other women prefer to work at home), two varieties of thick-pile wool carpets are available. A *tapis de Kroumirie* has 40,000 knots per square metre, while a *tapis berbère* (Berber carpet), made with thicker yarn, has 10,000 knots per square metre. Kilims (woven rugs) made of wool or cotton are also on offer. All the wool is spun by hand and coloured using vegetable dyes. Prices are fixed but they're not high – a woven handbag costs TD10 to TD18, while carpets are TD60 to TD80 per square metre.

The most straightforward way to get to Les Tapis de Kroumirie – though it involves a bit of up-and-down – is to walk down the flight of stairs next to the post office on ave Habib Bourguiba and then, at the bottom, turn left for 50m. The workshop is on the 1st floor, above the Ministère des Affaires Sociales office.

Products made by Les Tapis de Kroumirie are available in Tunis at **Mains de Femmes** (☎ 71 330 789; 47 ave Habib Bourguiba), an exhibition of women's crafts run by a nonprofit organisation.

You can also walk to the top of **Jebel Biri** – the path starts near the Hôtel Rihana and takes about three hours return.

Sleeping

Maison des Jeunes (☎ 78 655 087; ave Habib Bourguiba; dm TD6) About 1km up the hill from the fountain roundabout, this hostel has 90 beds in basic rooms.

Hôtel Les Pins (☎ 78 656 200; fax 78 656 182; ave Habib Bourguiba; s/d Nov-Jun TD25/38, Jul-Oct TD34/52) Situated 200m up the hill from the fountain roundabout, this welcoming hotel has a haut-relief pine tree over the entrance, a salmon-pink lobby and 21 spacious rooms with piping hot water year-round. Somehow all this comes together to give the place a vaguely chalet feel. An excellent deal.

Hôtel Beau Séjour (☎ 78 655 363; s/d TD35/50) Painted white with green shutters, this former hunting lodge feels like the setting for an Agatha Christie novel – perhaps it's the fangy, dive-bombing boars mounted on the lobby wall across from the old brick fireplace. The 18 rooms have balconies reached via French windows. The café serves beer.

Royal Rihana Hôtel (☎ 78 655 391; www.royalrihana-hotel.com; s/d Sep-Jun TD54/98, Jul & Aug TD59/98;) With hammered copper hunting scenes behind reception and pictures of dead boars nearby, this unique hotel – the name is also spelled Rayhana – has a masculine feel. The 74 rooms are spotless, practical and unpretentious and have wonderful forest views; amenities include a barside fireplace with roaring fires in winter, a grape-shaded patio and an indoor pool. The idiosyncratic décor grows on you. See the internet site for seasonal deals. Situated 2km south of the fountain roundabout along ave Habib Bourguiba, up the slope from the sky-blue statue of a giant mouse with huge white ears.

Eating

There's a cluster of eateries right just west of the fountain roundabout. These include Restaurant L'Escale (not to be confused with the café of the same name), which serves excellent quarter-chickens with spicy sauce (TD2.2) and, in the evening, super *m'lawi* (TD0.85; rolled chapatis filled with tuna, potato salad and other goodies). About 800m up ave Habib Bourguiba, Restaurant du Grand Maghreb, painted brick-red with green trim, serves pizzas (TD1.5 to TD4).

Shopping

For details on wool items hand-woven by local women, see above.

On ave Habib Bourguiba up near the Maison des Jeunes, shops sell locally made carved wood items and planters made of cork bark that look like the cross-section of a tree trunk but weigh almost nothing.

Getting There & Away

BUS

The **SRT Jendouba bus station** (☎ 78 655 022; ave 7 Novembre 1987), 150m down the hill from the fountain roundabout, sends buses off to Beni Metir (TD0.70, one bus daily at 12.30pm), Bizerte (at 6am via Tabarka), Hammam Bourguiba (TD0.85, two daily), Jendouba (TD1.9, four daily), Le Kef (three daily) and Tabarka (TD1.1, a dozen daily). SNTRI buses go to Tunis (five daily).

LOUAGE & TAXI

On the street outside the bus station there are blue-stripe services to Tabarka (TD1.3, 40 minutes) and Jendouba (TD2.2, 45 minutes) and red-stripes to Tunis. Yellow-stripe louages to Fernana stop 250m down the hill from the bus station.

Taxis occasionally go to Beni Metir (TD5). A taxi to Hammam Bourguiba costs TD4 (TD1.2 per person).

NORTHERN TUNISIA

AROUND AIN DRAHAM

Hammam Bourguiba حمّام بورقيبة

An enchanting winding drive through forested hills takes you to this remote village 17km southwest of Ain Draham. In a small valley just 4km from the Algerian border, it feels on the edge of something and in the middle of nowhere. The hot springs here, a favourite of former president Habib Bourguiba, are renowned for their health benefits.

Hammam Bourguiba makes a fine day trip from Ain Draham and is a good base for walks in the surrounding forest and valleys (eg to the reservoir). Stay away from the frontier.

ACTIVITIES

Hôtel El Mouradi's **Centre de Cure** (🕑 8am-1pm & 3-6pm, closed during Ramadan), frequented mainly by wealthy Tunisians, is able to offer a variety of water cures and beauty treatments thanks to two natural hot springs, known as Source Eucalyptus (38.5°C) and Source Les Pins (50°C to 56°C). Set at the base of a forested hill, this ultramodern place is, in the French spa tradition, somewhat clinical – gotta love the staff in neo-nurse gear.

The 2½- to three-hour **Forfait Bien-Être** (wellness package deal; TD60) includes time in the **pool** (🕑 9am-1pm & 4-6pm, women only 3-4pm), a massage bath and a massage. Other options include *hydrothérapie* (a sort of computer-controlled Jacuzzi), something called 'starlight' (a Jacuzzi with underwater lights that change colour), an *application algue générale* (you get smeared in sea algae in a sort of hot, all-encompassing water bed; TD12), shiatsu (for 45 minutes TD45) and even a *douche nasale* (nasal shower; TD3). Just using the pool costs TD5. The high season here lasts from October to mid-May.

There's a total disconnect between the luxurious, gated spa and the impoverished village of Hammam Bourguiba, which consists of little more than a school and a few shops. Fortunately, the villagers – and visitors on a tight budget – can enjoy the joys of lounging around in hot spring water at the **Hammam Shaabi**, (people's bath; admission TD0.40). It's located in an unmarked building with blue-barred windows next to a giant white water-tank 150m up the hillside through the eucalyptus grove from the Garde Nationale post. The men's section is to the left, the women's to the right. A massage costs about TD1. Bring bathing gear and flip-flops.

SLEEPING

Hôtel El Mouradi (☎ 78 654 055; www.elmouradi.com; s/d TD77/104, incl full board TD101/152; ❄ 🏊) This four-star luxury hotel, attached to the spa (see left), has 152 very comfortable rooms and 30 bungalows. Details on promotional rates are available online or by phone.

GETTING THERE & AWAY

There are two daily buses from Ain Draham (TD0.85), or you can take a taxi (TD1.2 per person). There are also infrequent louages.

Beni Metir بني متير

The quiet village of Beni Metir, 10km southeast of Ain Draham down a winding road, was built by the French starting in 1948 to house the workers who constructed Tunisia's first hydroelectric dam, then – as now – the town's *raison d'être*.

Locals are proud of their distinctive **market square**, surrounded by an ensemble of white arcaded buildings with striking red and black doors and windows – both the architecture and the colour scheme date from the French period. The squat, deconsecrated **church**, with a pointy cement belfry, is now a children's club.

The surrounding cork oak forests are a great venue for relaxing day walks – options include following the lakeshore towards the dam or heading out to **Ein Jemel** (Spring of the Camels), a few kilometres from town.

SLEEPING & EATING

The **Centre de Stages et de Vacances** (☎ 78 649 200 or 98 500 944; market square; dm q TD5/20) This 100-bed, 35-room hostel, in an old French building, has large rooms with soft, comfortable beds. It's well kept and clean.

A few tiny cafés and grocery shops can be found at or near the market square.

GETTING THERE & AWAY

The best public transport connections are with Fernana (TD1 per person by taxi), 15km south of Beni Metir and 19 km south of Ain Draham on the Ain Draham–Jendouba road.

One bus a day links Ain Draham with Beni Metir. Louages on this route are infrequent; hiring a private taxi may cost TD5 to TD10.

BÉJA باجة

pop 56,400

Not many tourists make it to Béja, a solid small city set among curvaceous grain hills, but the medina and war cemetery make it worth a short stop.

From the train station, walking up the hill takes you to **place de l'Indépendance**, the main square – check out the imposing **town hall**, with its columns and balcony. From here, the **medina** is 300m further west, past a **deconsecrated church** that's now used for cultural events. The medina's southeast-to-northwest–oriented main street is lined with shops and fruit-and-veggie vendors.

The **Great Mosque** (rue de la Mosquée) has a square minaret with terracotta tiles on the sides and candy-striped Moorish arches up top. About 150m northwest is the fish-scale dome of the **Zaouia of Sidi Abdel Kader**, with a tile panel over its green door. It isn't really open to the public though you might be able to peek into the tiled courtyard.

A few streets north of the mosque its the white-domed **Zaouia of Marabout Sidi Boutef Faha** but it, too, is pretty derelict inside, though people do come to light candles. Inside you can see henna handprints left prior to circumcision and marriage ceremonies.

From there, walking down the hill will take you to an overgrown and partly looted colonial-era **Christian cemetery** with lots of Italian names, some of them from as late as the 1990s.

Turn right at the train tracks and you'll soon come to the **Commonwealth Military Cemetery** (rue Mohamed ben Kahla; see p144), a neat, serene field of 396 graves, 87 of them unidentified; most perished in the spring of 1943 during the Allied offensive. To get to the cemetery from the train station, walk north along the tracks for 500m.

Sleeping & Eating

Maison des Jeunes (rue 18 Janvier; dm TD4; 💻) A basic hostel across the street from the bus station. Offers internet access to guests and nonguests alike.

Hôtel Phénix (☎ 78 450 188; www.phenix.com.tn; 6-8 ave de la République; s/d/tr/q TD30/40/50/60; ❄) Just east of place de l'Indépendance, this very central hotel has 14 clean, bright, spacious rooms – the front ones, with little balconies over the street, are best. Excellent value.

Favoured by visiting government ministers, the **Phénix restaurant** (meat mains TD7-13; 🕑 noon-midnight; ❄), the best in town, serves Tunisian cuisine as well as fish, pasta and pizza. There are several cheaper restaurants along the same street.

Getting There & Away

The **SRT Béja bus station** (rue 18 Janvier) is across the train tracks from the train station – to get there take the road to Tunis and cross the grassy area. Destinations include Ain Draham (two daily), Bizerte (four daily), Teboursouk (one daily) and Tunis (three daily).

Louages to Bizerte, Sousse, Teboursouk and Tunis leave from the train station.

The **train station** (ave Habib Thameur) is linked five times a day with Tunis (TD4, 1¼ hours) and Jendouba (TD2.6, 1¼ hours).

Béja's taxis don't seem to have meters.

JENDOUBA جندوبة

pop 44,700

Jendouba, a quiet governorate capital 153km west of Tunis and 60km north of Le Kef, is regarded by most as pretty dull but it has a gentle feel and the centre comes alive somewhat in the early evening. Linked

THE PRICE OF VICTORY

The painful progress of the Allies' WWII North African campaign (p31) is marked by a series of **military cemeteries**.

War dead from Great Britain and the countries of the Commonwealth are buried near where they fell in eight cemeteries designed and maintained by the Commonwealth War Graves Commission (www.cwgc.org), which has responsibility for about 2500 WWI and WWII cemeteries worldwide. Sombre and dignified, with neat lawns and uniform rows of white stone markers, each is an immaculately maintained corner of British pastoral. Many of the gravestones bear a personal dedication chosen by next of kin; others are marked simply, 'A Soldier of the Second World War/Known unto God'.

Tunisia's largest Commonwealth cemetery is 3km outside **Mejez el-Bab** (also spelled Medjez-El-Bab), 60km southwest of Tunis on the road to Béja. It contains the graves of 2903 WWII soldiers, 385 of them unidentified; a memorial bears the names of another 2000 soldiers who fell in Tunisia and Algeria but have no known graves. The birdsong in the surrounding trees seems appropriately haunting and chaotic.

There are other Commonwealth cemeteries at **Béja** (see p143), **Bordj El Amri** (Massicault; 30km southwest of Tunis on the road to Béja), **Oued Zarga** (80km southwest of Tunis towards Béja), **Tabarka** (Ras Rajal; p137), **Thibar** (30km southwest of Béja towards Teboursouk), Enfidha (Enfidaville; 95km southeast of Tunis) and **Sfax** (4km south of the city on the road to Gabès).

American war dead are buried at the **North Africa American Cemetery & Memorial** (www.abmc.gov) at Carthage, five minutes on foot from the Carthage Amilcar TGM suburban rail station.

There are French cemeteries at **Enfidha** (95km southeast of Tunis) and **Gammarth** (see p99) and a German military cemetery at **Borj Cédria**, on the Gulf of Tunis about 25km southeast of the capital.

by train to Tunis, it's an important transport hub and makes a good base for visits to Bulla Regia and Chemtou. Wednesday is market day.

Orientation & Information

The train station (with storks' nests on top), police station, post office and two banks (UIB and STB), both with ATMs, are right around place de la République, the filthy but shaded main square in front of the train station.

From there, rue Mohammed Ali, the narrow tree-lined main commercial street, heads south; after about 350m you get to a Mobil petrol station (at the corner) and place 7 Novembre, a giant roundabout with a towering sculpture that looks like a giant Lego rocketship. The bus and louage station is 200m further on (ie south, just past the Hôtel Simitthu).

Publinet (internet per hr TD1.2; ⌚ 8am-11pm or midnight) is diagonally across the street from the Hôtel Atlas.

Sleeping & Eating

Hôtel Atlas (☎ 78 603 217; rue 1 Juin 1955; s/d TD18/25) Just off place de la République behind the police station, this hostelry is bare-bones and a bit out of date but the rooms are clean and – despite the tissue-paper-thin sheets and lumpy pillows – relatively comfortable. It's convenient if you're travelling by train.

Hôtel Simitthu (☎ 78 604 043; blvd 9 Avril 1938; s/d TD30/44) About 100m south of place 7 Novembre and just north of the bus and louage station, this place is dull, musty and overpriced – but convenient if you're travelling by bus. Simitthu was the Numidian name for Chemtou.

For self-caterers there's a **Monoprix supermarket** (place de la République; ⌚ 8am-2pm & 4-9pm) facing the train station and a great bread and pastry **bakery** (rue Youssef) facing the Mobil petrol station.

Getting There & Away

The **bus and louage stations** (blvd 9 Avril 1938) are about 200m south of place 7 Novembre, ie just south of the Hôtel Simitthu. SRT Jendouba buses go to Ain Draham (TD1.9, nine daily), Béja (twice daily in the morning), Bizerte (TD6.7, twice daily), Le Kef (TD2.5, six daily) and Tabarka (three daily). SNTRI buses serve Tunis (TD7.8, six daily).

From the **louage station** next to the bus station, red louages go to Bizerte, Le Kef (TD3.2), Tunis and, via Kairouan, to Sousse (TD12.2).

Louages to Ain Draham and Tabarka stop just across the train tracks from the Total petrol station – the spot is 200m northwest of place 7 Novembre and 250m southwest (along the tracks) from the train station.

Five trains a day link the **train station** (place de la République) with Béja (TD2.6, 1¼ hours), Ghardimao (TD2, 26 minutes) and Tunis (TD6.8, 2½ hours).

BULLA REGIA بلا ريجية

Famed for its extraordinary underground villas, the Roman city of **Bulla Regia** (admission TD3, camera TD1; 8am-7pm Apr–mid-Sep, 8.30am-5.30pm mid-Sep–Mar), 7km northwest of Jendouba, offers a rare opportunity to walk into complete, superbly preserved Roman rooms rather than having to extrapolate how things once looked from waist-high walls.

To escape the summer heat, the ever-inventive Romans retreated below the surface, building elegant homes – complete with colonnaded courtyards – that echo the troglodyte Berber homes at Matmata. The name each villa is known by reflects the theme of the mosaics found inside; some (but not all) of the best are now in the Bardo Museum (p50).

As you tour the site watch your step so you don't plummet into a cistern.

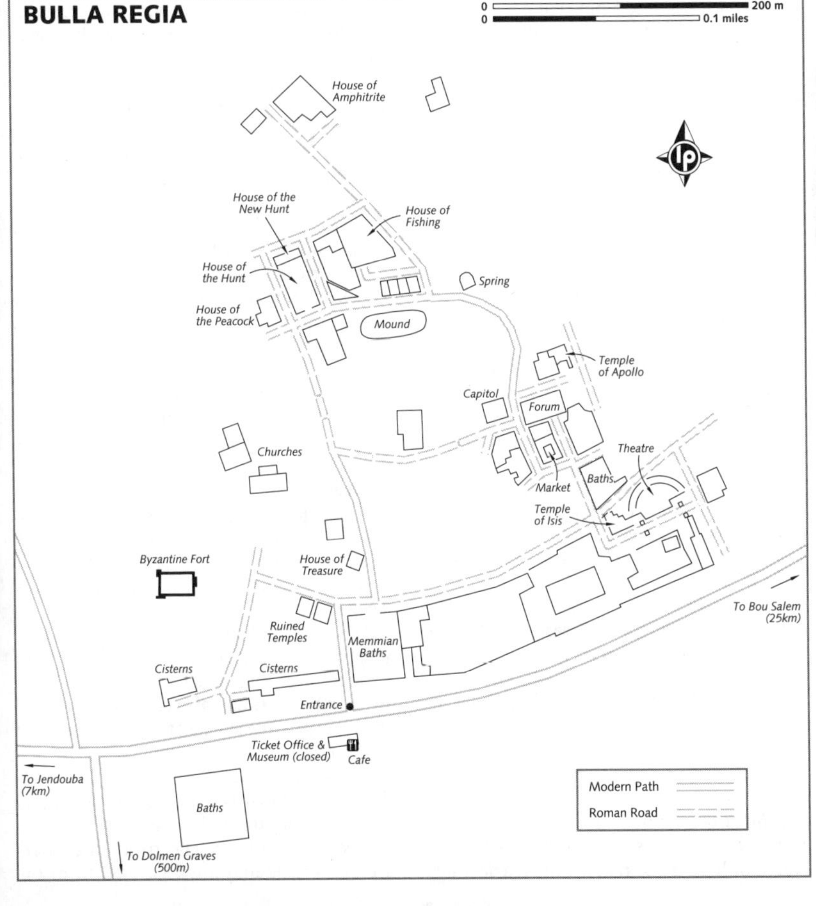

History

The dolmens (Neolithic tombs) that dot the surrounding hills show that the area was inhabited long before the Romans arrived. The town of Bulla emerged in about the 5th century BC as part of Carthage's move to develop the Medjerda Valley as a wheat-growing area. 'Regia' (royal) was added later when it became the capital of one of the short-lived Numidian kingdoms tolerated by Rome following the destruction of Carthage.

Bulla Regia flourished under Roman rule, its citizens growing rich on wheat – and, through grand construction projects, made sure their neighbours knew it. The town reached the peak of its prosperity in the 2nd and 3rd centuries AD; most of the site's buildings date from that era.

Bulla Regia was subsequently occupied by the Byzantines, who as usual added a fort, but was abandoned after the Arab conquest in the 7th century.

Sights

The **Memmian Baths** (Thermes), to the right of the entrance, were named after Julia Memmia, wife of Emperor Septimius Severus. The most extensive of the site's above-ground structures, its rooms are surrounded by arched service areas – a reminder of the slaves who kept the waters hot and Roman backs scrubbed.

Walking northwards, following the signs to the Quartier des Maisons (villas quarter), takes you to the city's wealthiest residential neighbourhood. The villas – seven of which have been excavated – vary in their level of sophistication but are all built to the same basic plan, with a central courtyard open to the sky. As you descend into each, you'll feel a significant drop in temperature – just what the Romans intended.

The first home you come to is the small, subterranean **House of Treasure** (Maison du Trésor), named after a cache of Byzantine coins discovered here. The large dining room is decorated with a geometrically patterned mosaic; next door is a bedroom.

Continuing north, you pass two side-by-side, 6th-century Byzantine **churches** *(basilique chrétienne)*, with some columns and a walk-in, cross-shaped baptismal font. North of here is the rather unloved-feeling, subterranean **House of the Peacock**, named after a mosaic that's now in the Bardo.

Across the road is the truly impressive **House of the Hunt** (Maison de la Chasse), centred on an underground hall with eight ornate pillars; hexagonal holes at the top of each cleverly reduce the structure's weight. Off the courtyard is a spacious mosaic-floored dining room, an indication of the lavish lifestyle once enjoyed here. Upstairs are some neat, side-by-side latrines, next to the building's private *hammam* – this place was really state of the art.

Next door, an above-ground hunting mosaic has been left *in situ* at the **House of the New Hunt** (Maison de la Nouvelle Chasse). Large chunks are missing but there's still plenty left to view, including an action-packed lion hunt. Underground is a five-column hall with a swirling geometric floor.

Take the path east and then north to Bulla Regia's star attraction, the **House of Amphitrite**; the entrance is near the metal grate in the pavement. The underground mosaic is exquisite – a perfectly preserved portrait of a nude Venus flanked by two centaurs, one shocked (having his hair tugged), the other quizzical. At the base are some lively cupids riding dolphins – one of them is checking himself out in a mirror at the same time. Leaping fish add to the vibrancy and balance of this masterpiece.

South of here is the spacious **House of Fishing** (Maison de la Pêche), the earliest of the villas. This place had a fountain in the basement; a small room contains a mosaic with a fishing theme.

Heading southeast, you'll pass on your left the **spring** that once supplied ancient Bulla Regia with water – and still delivers its cool waters to nearby Jendouba. There's a fine panorama from atop the nearby **mound**.

Walking east and then south will take you to the **forum**, surrounded by the ruins of two temples – the **capitol**, to the west; and, to the north, the **Temple of Apollo**, which yielded the truly godlike statue of Apollo displayed at the Bardo.

Just south of here is the **market** and a little further down is a small but beautifully preserved **theatre** with a large mosaic of a not-very-fierce bear. The front three tiers are extra wide and are separated from the rest by the remains of a low wall – VIP seating. Southwest are the remains of the small **Temple of Isis**, which honoured the Egyptian goddess, a fashionable addition to the Roman pantheon.

The hill south of the ticket office is covered with Neolithic **dolmen graves**.

Getting There & Away

The turn-off to Bulla Regia is about 4km north of Jendouba on the road to Ain Draham; from there, the site is 3km east.

SRT Jendouba buses link Jendouba's bus station with Bulla Regia hourly until 7pm (6pm in winter). A taxi from Jendouba costs about TD4 one-way.

Any bus or louage travelling between Jendouba and Ain Draham can drop you off at the Bulla Regia turn-off, from where it's an easy hitch or a pleasant 3km walk (if it's not too hot).

CHEMTOU شمتو

The largest marble quarry in ancient North Africa, **Chemtou** (admission TD3, camera TD1; 8am-7pm May–mid-Sep, 8.30am-5.30pm mid-Sep–Apr) was the source of an unusual pink-veined yellow marble that was prized throughout the Roman world as the exotic stone that most resembled gold. It's daunting even to contemplate the work that went into carving out and transporting the huge blocks of stone. The site is brought to life by an excellent museum.

A café is supposed to open here sometime in 2007 – until then bring along food and drink.

History

The site, on the northern bank of Oued Medjerda, was originally the Numidian settlement of Simitthu. Marble from here was used to construct the celebrated Monument of Micipsa at Cirta (modern Constantine in Algeria) in 130 BC.

The region came under Roman control after the battle of Thapsus in 46 BC, when Caesar defeated the combined forces of Pompey and the last Numidian king, Juba I. Its marble became a symbol of Roman might and wealth – not only was it golden but it expressed the empire's domination over exotic lands. After Julius Caesar's assassination, a 6m-high column of Chemtou marble was erected in his honour in Rome's forum.

The Roman settlement here was founded during the reign of Augustus (27 BC–AD 16) and thanks to the marble craze it quickly developed into an important town. The quarrying operations here were said to have been the most sophisticated in the Roman world – each block of marble carried the stamp of the emperor of the day, that of the proconsul for Africa and the quarry supervisor, and a reference mark. The workers were slaves.

Initially, the blocks were hauled to Oued Medjerda on rollers and floated downstream to the port of Utica (Utique) on barges. By the beginning of the 2nd century, silt had all but closed the river to barge traffic, obliging the Romans to build a special road across the Kroumirie Mountains to link the quarries with the port of Thabraca (Tabarka).

The quarries were worked until Byzantine times but were abandoned following the 7th-century Arab invasion. These days marble is quarried just east of the archaeological site.

Sights

Chemtou sprawls over a wide area between Oued Medjerda and the band of low hills that were the source of the town's 'marbelous' wealth.

Despite the town's proximity to the river, drinking water was brought in by aqueduct from a spring in the hills 30km to the north. If you arrive from the north, the first ruins you see are the remains of this aqueduct advancing across the landscape. It ends at the ruins of the **municipal baths**, to the right of the access road, which continues past a Roman **theatre**.

The first-rate **archaeological museum** is the star attraction here. Labelling is in Arabic, French and German, reflecting the source of the museum's funding ('you pay for it, you get to choose the language'), but the layout is clear enough. An informative 20-minute **film** on the site, available in six languages, is usually shown only to groups but if you ask nicely a private screening can probably be arranged. Highlights include a chart showing how, 200 million years ago, Tunisia used to be located approximately where New York now is; exhibits on the technology used to quarry and transport marble; a fine mosaic floor representing the four seasons; a re-creation of the Monument of Micipsa, which once crowned a nearby hilltop; and an impressive marble plaque designed to glorify the emperor – an early, rather cumbersome version of today's political bumper stickers and campaign buttons.

To the left as you exit the museum is a small section of original **Roman road** used to transport marble down to the river. Excavations of the **forum**, a few hundred metres to the west, have revealed that it was built on the foundations of a Numidian temple.

The **quarries**, three in all, are in the little hills north of the museum. Chemtou marble ranges in colour from dark red to green but the most highly prized hue was golden yellow.

A path leads up to the top of the easternmost hill, where you can see the ruins

THEIR BARK IS BETTER THAN THEIR PLIGHT

Money may not grow on trees but cork does, and if you live in the mountains of northwestern Tunisia it might as well be the same thing.

Cork is something of a miracle material: it's durable, light, almost impermeable to liquids and highly elastic. That's why it's long been used to make stoppers for wine bottles. In the Kroumirie Mountains you often see chunks of the stuff lying around and when you hold it and probe it with your fingers and weigh it in your hand it's hard to believe that it is what it is.

From the point of view of environmental sustainability, cork is an ideal product: not only is it 100% biodegradable but it's also completely renewable. Raw cork is harvested in the late spring and early summer by removing the outer bark of cork oaks, which look a bit reddish and bald for a while but immediately begin regrowing their protective outer layer. After nine to 12 years, a tree's cork sheath is again as thick as a wine stopper is wide and can once more be harvested.

Each harvest cycle, a cork oak – which lives for one to three centuries – produces between 25kg and 60kg of raw cork. Only about one-eighth of this can be turned into bottle stoppers; the rest is used for less lucrative products such as corkboard, floor tiles and coasters.

Cork oak forests are hugely important ecologically. Able to thrive in the often-harsh climate and marginal soils around the western Mediterranean, they are home to an exceptionally high number of plant and animal species. In Tunisia, they provide a habitat for the extremely rare zen oak and – in winter – for countless migratory birds from northern Europe. The almost-extinct Barbary deer *(Cervus elaphus barbarus)*, Africa's only native deer, lives exclusively in the cork oak forests of northwestern Tunisia and adjacent parts of Algeria. As they grow back a new layer of cork, the trees take three to five times more CO_2 out of the atmosphere than non-harvested trees.

Cork harvesting makes forests a valuable source of income for remote rural communities, creating a powerful economic incentive for local people to protect them from degradation. Bottle stoppers are the cork industry's *raison d'être*. In 2005, 1kg of top-quality, one-piece cork stoppers was worth a whopping €46, compared with just €6.60 for 1kg of agglomerated cork stoppers and €3 for 1kg of decorative corkboard.

In a roundabout way, the greatest threat to Tunisia's cork oak forests comes from the Australian wine industry, which has led the switchover from natural cork bottle stoppers to cheaper synthetic ones or even – *quelle horreur* – aluminium screw-tops. About 35% of the stoppers used by Australia's wineries are now noncork, and if current worldwide trends continue – even in France one in 10 bottles of wine now has a noncork cork – the demand for cork stoppers, and thus the price of raw cork, could plummet.

Ecotourism, including trekking in the forests around Ain Draham (see p140), and the purchase of Kroumirie cork souvenirs will be able to make up for only a tiny part of the income loss should the global cork market crash.

The WWF (www.panda.org) fears that cork oak forests that no longer produce income for local communities face poor management, conversion to agriculture, overgrazing, fragmentation and accelerated human encroachment, processes that could result in increased erosion, more frequent forest fires, biodiversity loss and even desertification. That's why they've launched a worldwide campaign to encourage the wine industry to continue to use genuine cork bottle stoppers.

of a Numidian **temple**, later converted into a temple to Saturn by the Romans and then a Byzantine church.

A few kilometres south there's a **Roman bridge** over Oued Medjerda, just downstream from the modern bridge. Situated further along from the bridge are the ruins of a **turbine mill**.

Getting There & Away

Chemtou is in the middle of nowhere. More specifically, it's 16km west of the Bulla Regia turn-off on the Jendouba–Ain Draham road, which is about 4km northwest of Jendouba. You can also take the Jendouba–Ghardimao road to Oued Melliz and turn right.

A taxi from Jendouba or Bulla Regia to Chemtou costs about TD15 to TD20 one-way and TD30 to TD40 return, including a couple of hours at the site. Chemtou is quite spread out so you might want to arrange in advance to be driven from site to site.

Doing a bit of walking is also an option (bring plenty of water). Chemtou is about 3km north of the Jendouba–Ghardimao road – ask your bus or louage driver to leave you at the turn-off. To get back, walk to the highway and then continue on another kilometre or so to the village of Oued Melliz, where there are local louages to Jendouba. Another option is to go via Ain el-Kesir, a village 3km north of Chemtou, which also has occasional louages to Jendouba.

GHARDIMAO غار ألدّماء

pop 19,400

Ghardimao, 36km west of Jendouba, has an almost appealingly dead-end feel, with the sort of brooding, still atmosphere that in a Western movie precedes a shoot out. This really is the end of the line, especially since the suspension of the Al-Maghreb al-Arabi (Trans-Maghreb Express) train service that once linked Tunisia with Morocco via Algeria.

Welcome to Tunisia's wild west, surrounded by countryside whose stark beauty is tempered by the tension of the frontier. The town itself bakes lazily in the relentless west Tunisian sun, exuding a general air of dereliction

Truly off the beaten path is **El-Feija National Park**, about 20km to the northwest near the Algerian frontier, whose mature oak forests are home to the rare Barbary deer. Endemic trees include the African oak and the cork oak, which grow alongside aromatic plants such as lavender and myrtle.

Orientation & Information

The main drag, ave Habib Bourguiba, is on the other side of a partly tree-shaded square from the train station.

There are some shops and a **BNA bank** (no ATM) at the main square on ave Habib Bourguiba, marked by a stone pedestal holding aloft a broken clock whose sole remaining hand twists slowly in the wind – some say it was caught in the crossfire between the sheriff and a notorious Algerian smuggler.

It may be possible to connect to the internet at **Al-Maktaba al-Arabi** (ave Habib Bourguiba; per hr TD1; 24hrs), a writing supplies shop with one computer in the back. With a blue awning out front, it's 100m southwest of the Maison des Jeunes (no accommodation available), housed in a deconsecrated French church.

Sleeping & Eating

If you get stuck here the only accommodation option is the **Hôtel Tebournik** (☎ 78 660 043; s/d with shared bathrooms TD10/20), which has 11 passable rooms, some with balconies. The name is spelled 'rnik' on the sign, probably because the other letters were shot off one day at high noon. Across the sunbaked square from the train station, this place has a restaurant (mains TD3 to TD5) and one of only two beer-serving saloons in town.

At the main square there are several small eateries and an arcaded food market.

Getting There & Away

Trains go to/from Tunis (TD8.4, three hours) via Jendouba (TD2, 26 minutes) and Béja (TD3.8, 1¾ hours) five times a day.

Central West & the Tell

The hills and mountains of the Tunisian Dorsale and the Tell – the high plains north of the Dorsale that were the granary of ancient Rome – offer visitors a variety of enchanting options far from the coastal crowds.

The Romans bequeathed to this region a number of exceptional cities, now in ruins but rich in beguiling hints of their prosperous past. The undoubted highlight is Dougga, spread over an enchanting hillside overlooking grain fields and gentle hills. Also spectacular is Sufetula (Sbeitla), which has the feel of a Roman frontier town and is especially magical in the early morning light.

The Roman cities of Mactaris (Makthar) and Ammædara (Haidra) still evoke the sense of luxury and isolation characteristic of more remote Roman outposts, and serve as poignant symbols of western Tunisia's lonely sense of having been left behind by history.

Less than an hour from Tunis, the Roman cities of Thuburbo Majus and Uthina (Oudhna) also present evocative ruins, though the majority of their most outstanding mosaics are now in Tunis' Bardo Museum. Jugurtha's Table, almost on the Algerian frontier, is a remote, hauntingly beautiful mesa where Berber resistance to Roman rule enjoyed its proudest hour before being swept away.

For fans of urban delights, the friendly city of Le Kef, guarded by a towering kasbah, captures the Tell's irrepressible spirit. With its cobbled streets, cafés that time forgot and panoramic hillside setting, it's one of Tunisia's best-kept secrets. Kasserine may not be Tunisia's most scintillating city but it's a good base for exploring areas out near Algeria.

HIGHLIGHTS

- Exploring glorious, golden **Dougga** (p156), perhaps Tunisia's most enchanting Roman site
- Taking the waters like a Roman in remote **Hammam Mellegue** (p164)
- Wandering among the Roman temples of **Sufetula** (Sbeitla; p182), magical in the early-morning light
- Chilling in **Le Kef** (p160), an atmospheric hilltop town with a proud multicultural history
- Hiking up **Jugurtha's Table** (p177), a spectacular natural fortress in the middle of nowhere

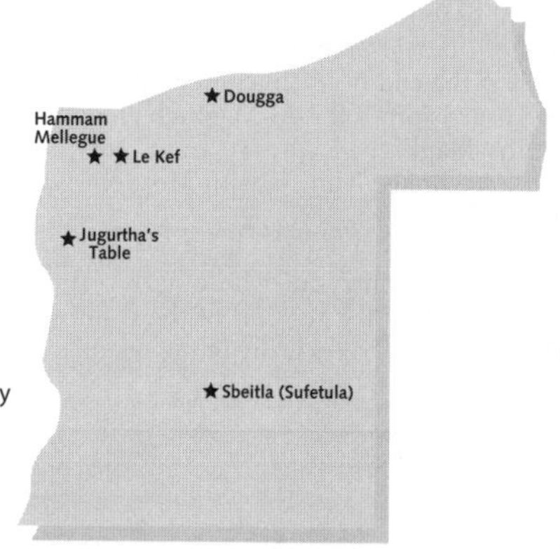

History

After Rome defeated Carthage in the 2nd century BC, the hinterlands of its new African provinces were largely left to the Berber tribes of the interior, most notably the Numidians, who accommodated Roman rule even as they rebelled against it. The final Berber resistance to the Romans came at Jugurtha's Table, the legendary stronghold where the Numidian king Jugurtha made his last stand at the end of the 2nd century BC. In subsequent centuries, the area's Roman towns grew prosperous on the proceeds of agricultural production and served as staging posts along lucrative trade routes. After the departure of the Romans, the area slid into obscurity.

Climate

This region's desolate terrain briefly comes to life in spring with spectacular displays of wildflowers. The summers are very hot, whereas the winters – particularly at higher elevations – can be cold and bleak.

Getting There & Around

Even the smallest towns have at least one daily bus, plus louages (shared taxis), to Tunis; Le Kef and Dougga (Teboursouk) are especially easy to get to. Two trains a day link Tunis with Kalaat Khasba, midway between Le Kef and Kasserine and served by buses to both cities.

Every place in this chapter is accessible both by private car and by public transport of one form or another. Destinations visitable on day trips from Tunis include Oudhna, Thuburbo Majus, Zaghouan and Dougga. Le Kef is a convenient base for excursions to Dougga, Makthar, Hammam Mellegue, Jugurtha's Table and Haidra, while Kasserine makes a good base for trips to Sbeitla, Haidra and Jugurtha's Table. Visiting Haidra and Jugurtha's Table by louage on a day trip from either Le Kef or Kasserine is one of Tunisia's ultimate public transport challenges.

SOUTH OF TUNIS

Oudhna (Uthina) أوذنة (أوتينا)

Fascinating but little-visited, the ruins of ancient **Uthina** (admission TD3; 9am-7pm Apr–mid-Sep, 8am-5pm mid-Sep–Mar), near the village of Oudhna, are about 28km south of Tunis. Still being excavated, the site has some of Tunisia's most impressive *in situ* mosaics. Photography is forbidden.

There's a map of the site with a brief text in Arabic, English, French and Italian between the tiny ticket booth and the amphitheatre.

HISTORY

The Roman historian Pliny mentions the town as a Berber settlement named Adys and as one of the first Roman colonies in Africa. A major battle between Carthage and the Roman general Regulus took place here during the first Punic War (255 BC).

Uthina, the centre of a fertile agricultural region, was founded by the emperor Augustus at the beginning of the 1st century AD and settled with Roman army veterans. Like many of Tunisia's Roman towns, its prosperity peaked in the 2nd and 3rd centuries. Christianity took a powerful hold here and the town was home to many bishops but declined after the Vandal conquest.

SIGHTS

The best place to begin a visit is at Uthina's highest point, the **capitol**, known locally as Al-Kalaa (the fortress). Partly restored stone steps lead up to five newly built, oversized fluted columns. At the top, surprisingly, is an elegant – if run-down – French colonial **farmhouse**. Constructed atop the capitol with supreme colonial arrogance, it unintentionally juxtaposes two disappeared empires – both speaking Latin or a Latin derivative – that once ruled vast swathes of North Africa. There are great views from the farmhouse's back terrace.

Below the colonial homestead are magnificent vaulted chambers from the Roman or Byzantine periods; underneath that there are more Roman chambers.

The former **forum**, to the southeast, is occupied by dilapidated colonial outbuildings now used by the maintenance staff.

South of the forum, at the end of an **aqueduct** that supplied water from springs at nearby Jebel Rassas, are the remains of a **reservoir**. Most of the water was delivered to a network of enormous arched **cisterns** 200m south of the reservoir. Some have collapsed although others remain in remarkably good condition – huge, dank watertight rooms.

The jumble of collapsed masonry chunks east of the capitol mark the site of the main

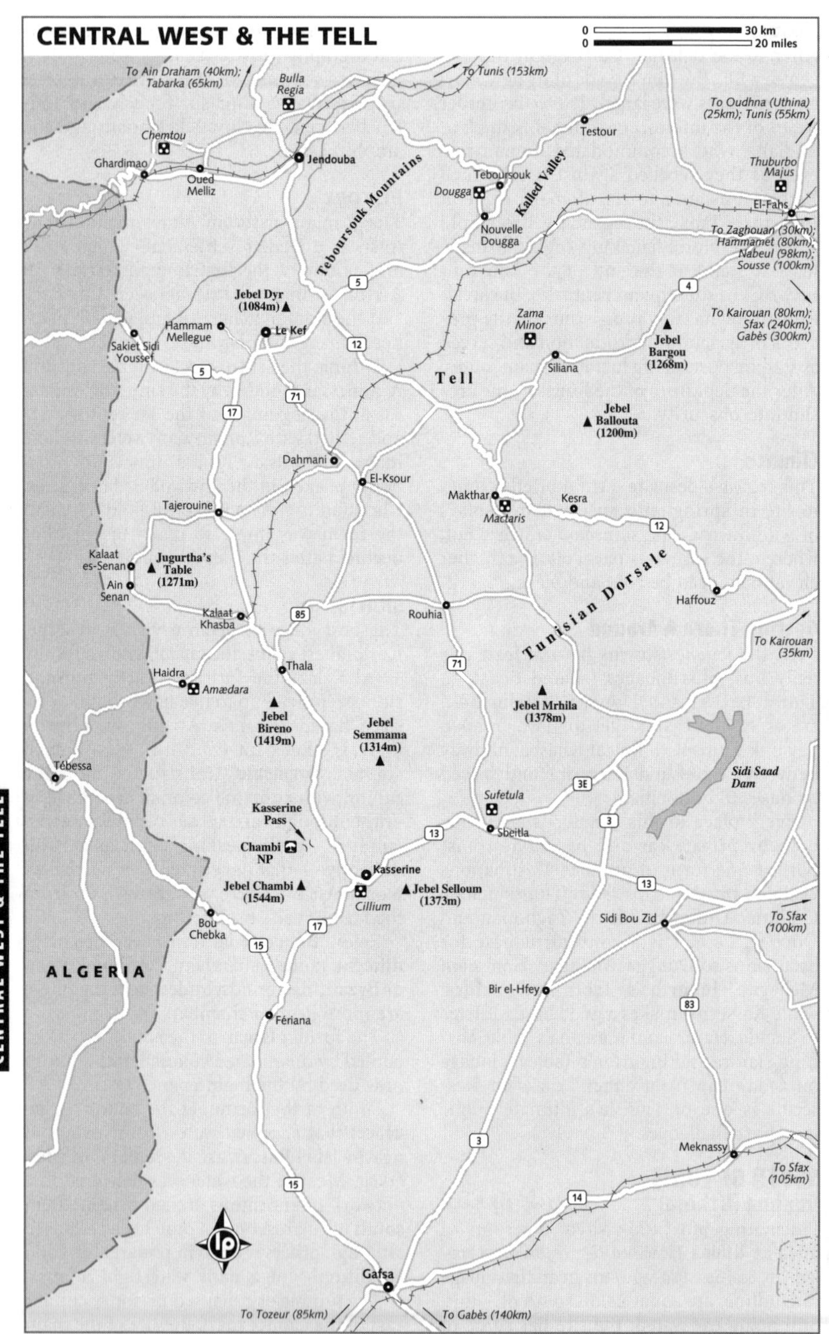
CENTRAL WEST & THE TELL
0 30 km
0 20 miles
To Ain Draham (40km); Tabarka (65km)
Bulla Regia
To Tunis (153km)
To Oudhna (Uthina) (25km); Tunis (55km)
Chemtou
Testour
Ghardimao
Jendouba
Oued Melliz
Teboursouk Mountains
Kalled Valley
Teboursouk
Dougga
Thuburbo Majus
El-Fahs
Nouvelle Dougga
To Zaghouan (30km); Hammamet (80km); Nabeul (98km); Sousse (100km)
Jebel Dyr (1084m)
To Kairouan (80km); Sfax (240km); Gabès (300km)
Zama Minor
Hammam Mellegue
Le Kef
Jebel Bargou (1268m)
Sakiet Sidi Youssef
Siliana
Tell
Jebel Ballouta (1200m)
Dahmani
El-Ksour
Makthar
Mactaris
Kesra
Tajerouine
Kalaat es-Senan
Jugurtha's Table (1271m)
Ain Senan
Tunisian Dorsale
Haffouz
Kalaat Khasba
Rouhia
To Kairouan (35km)
Thala
Haidra
Amædara
Jebel Bireno (1419m)
Jebel Semmama (1314m)
Jebel Mrhila (1378m)
Sidi Saad Dam
Tébessa
Sufetula
Kasserine Pass
Sbeitla
Chambi NP
Kasserine
Jebel Chambi (1544m)
Cillium
Jebel Selloum (1373m)
Bou Chebka
Sidi Bou Zid
To Sfax (100km)
ALGERIA
Bir el-Hfey
Fériana
Meknassy
To Sfax (105km)
Gafsa
To Tozeur (85km)
To Gabès (140km)
5
12
71
17
85
4
3E
3
13
15
83
14

public baths – nicknamed Touir Ellil (the bat tunnel) – which were damaged by explosions while being used as an arms depot during WWII. The subterranean level is in good condition. A beautiful black marble bust with a Libyan hairstyle, now in the Bardo Museum, was discovered here.

To the north, just north of the access road, are the **Baths of the Laberii**, which take their name from the inscription on the lovely mosaic of Orpheus charming the animals, now in the Bardo Museum. There are still some fine mosaics *in situ,* including a delightful one depicting fishers and fish. During the Byzantine period the northeast part of the complex was a pottery workshop and many Christian artefacts were discovered here.

The baths stand beside the remains of the celebrated **House of the Laberii**, also known as the House of Ikarios (named after a beautiful mosaic showing Ikarios giving a vine to the king of Attica), a sumptuous villa of over 30 rooms and probably the best house in town. You can still see the remains of the colonnade that surrounded a garden. All the rooms were paved with mosaics, the most exquisite of which are now on display – where else? – at the Bardo Museum.

The **amphitheatre**, near the entrance, could hold more than 10,000 spectators and is a good indication of the stature of the Roman town. Among its features: cells for the criminals and wild beasts whose 15 minutes of fame, in front of roaring crowds, were often cut short. The amphitheatre was still being excavated when we went to print.

GETTING THERE & AWAY

If you're driving from Tunis, take the highway towards Kairouan for about 20km until you get to the spot where the ancient Zaghouan-Carthage aqueduct begins following a side road. From there the site is a further 7.5km – look for the sign to 'Uthina Site Archaeologique' next to the enormous base of a fake Roman column. If you get lost, your best bet is to scan the horizon for the silhouette of hilltop ruins.

From Tunis, bus 25 goes to the village of Baruta (TD0.8, 45 minutes, about twice an hour), from where it's a few walkable kilometres to the archaeological site. In Tunis the stop is about 500m southeast of place Barcelone, just off rue de Carthage a block north of rue d'Italie.

Other options include taking a taxi from Tunis to El-Fahs and negotiating with a louage or taxi driver to take you to both Thurburbo Majus and Oudhna and then back to Tunis – the whole trip should cost about TD40.

Thuburbo Majus طبربو ماجوس

Surrounded by shimmering wheat fields and olive groves just like those that made its fortune, the Roman city of **Thuburbo Majus** (admission TD31, plus camera TD1; 8.30am-5.30pm mid-Sep–Mar, 8am-7pm Apr–mid-Sep), 60km southwest of Tunis near the utterly skipable town of El-Fahs, has a prosperous air – even in its ruinous state. In the 2nd century it had 10,000 inhabitants, the wealthiest of whom tried to outdo each other by donating public buildings and fine mosaics; many of the latter are on display in the Bardo Museum (see p50).

So far, about 7 hectares of Thuburbo Majus' (pronounced *ma*-yoose or *ma*-juice) 40 hectares have been excavated. You can get a sense of the size of the Roman town by looking for the three extant city gates, situated north, southwest and east of the capital.

Wall panels near the ticket office provide background on the site in Arabic, English and French.

HISTORY

The town was here long before the Romans arrived – this ancient Berber settlement was one of the first to come under Punic control in the 5th century BC as part of Carthage's drive to build an African empire. It remained loyal to Carthage until that city's bitter end at the hands of the Romans.

Forced to pay tribute after the fall of Carthage (146 BC), Thuburbo Majus became something of a backwater until it was declared a municipality following a visit by the emperor Hadrian in AD 128. The town soon developed into an important trading centre for local agricultural produce – oil, wheat and wine. Most of the buildings date from the second half of the 2nd century, although there was a second phase of construction at the end of the 4th century.

SIGHTS

On a platform dominating the surrounding residential ruins is the **capitol**, with four

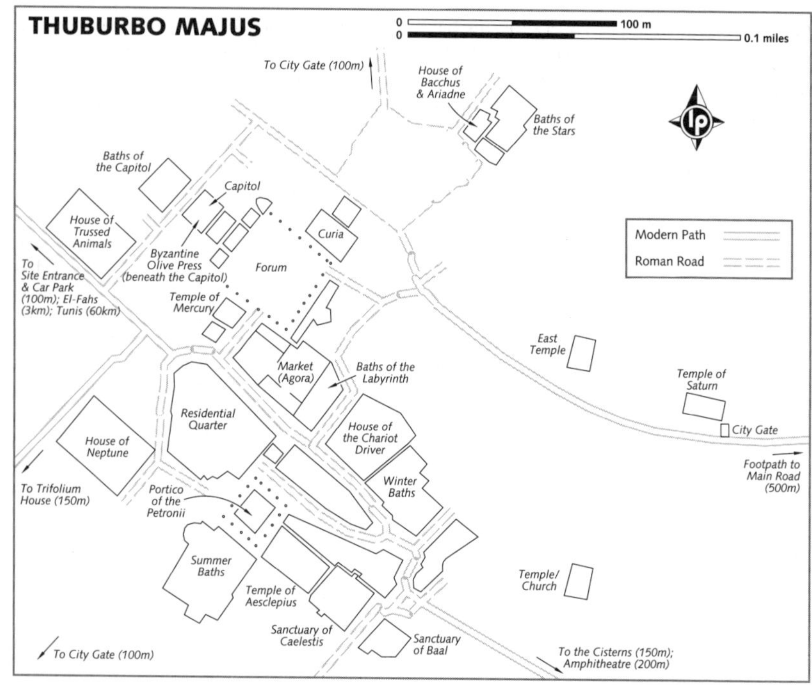

giant pillars of veined pink limestone marking the entrance to the **temple**. Built in AD 168, it is reached by a wide flight of stairs leading up from the **forum** (AD 161–2), which is colonnaded on three sides.

The capitol was dedicated to two emperors, Marcus Aurelius and Commodus, and was under the protection of the ancient trinity of Jupiter, Minerva and Juno. The giant sandalled foot and head of an enormous statue of Jupiter, estimated to have stood 7.5m high, were found here; they now reside in the Bardo Museum.

The ruins of a Byzantine **olive press** occupy the space beneath the capitol. As elsewhere, Byzantine builders showed themselves willing to adapt any available structure, cleverly making use of what was a bathing pool to catch oil.

On the southwestern side of the forum, the **Temple of Mercury**, with an unusual circular design, abuts the **market** – Mercury was the god of trade as well as messenger of the gods. The market stalls can be discerned on three sides of the courtyard below the temple.

Directly behind the market is a very un-Roman tangle of residential streets, obviously laid out before the Romans arrived. Beyond is the spacious **House of Neptune**, with some impressive geometric-patterned mosaics.

The imposing **Portico of the Petronii** is named after the family of Petronius Felix, who paid for the construction of this gymnasium complex in AD 225. It was surrounded by Corinthian columns made of an unusual yellow-veined grey marble; one row remains standing, still holding aloft a Latin inscription. This is where people played sports before heading to the baths. In the southeastern corner some letters are carved – part of a game.

The biggest of Thuburbo Majus' five bath complexes was the **Summer Baths**, adjacent to the Portico of the Petronii, which cover 2800 sq metres. The **Winter Baths**, 150m to the east, feature a grand entrance flanked by four veined marble columns. Both were full of mosaics – the finest are now on display in the Bardo Museum, though some can still be seen *in situ*.

The smaller **Baths of the Labyrinth**, southeast of the *agora* (market), and the **Baths of the Stars**, northeast of the capitol, are named after their mosaics. The **Baths of the Capitol** are just west of the capitol.

About 50m south of the Winter Baths, the **Sanctuary of Baal** is a small square temple that's easily identified by the two yellow-veined grey pillars atop its steps. It was dedicated to Baal Hammon, whose cult survived (in Romanised form) long after the fall of Carthage.

The adjacent **Sanctuary of Caelestis**, reached through a freestanding yellow-stone arch, was for another adapted god – this time the Roman version of Tanit. The temple was later converted into a Byzantine church, traces of which can still be seen.

A rough path leads southeast from the Sanctuary of Baal towards the ruins, set into the hill, of the massive arched **cisterns** that once supplied the town with water. The mound beyond the cisterns marks the site of a small **amphitheatre**. Another rough path leads north from here to a low hill topped by the remains of a **Temple of Saturn**.

GETTING THERE & AWAY

Thuburbo Majus, an easy day trip from Tunis, is just west of the Tunis-Kairouan road, 3km north of El-Fahs. There is no public transport to the site but any bus between Tunis and Kairouan can drop you at the turn-off, leaving a 15-minute walk to the site. The sight of a city gate, marking the northern edge of the city, is an indication that you're getting close.

To get to El-Fahs from Tunis, you can either take a louage from the Cap Bon louage station (TD3.4) or a bus from the southern bus station. A taxi from El-Fahs out to Thuburbo Majus should cost between TD5 and TD7 return, including an hour or so at the site.

Zaghouan زغوان

pop 15,800

This sleepy town snuggles at the foot of rugged, rocky, red-hued Jebel Zaghouan (1295m), whose summit – sometimes snow-dusted in winter – is a vertical 1km higher than Zaghouan itself. The top is accessible by road.

During the reign of the Roman emperor Hadrian, a 132km-long aqueduct to supply water to Carthage was built in just 11 years (AD 120–31). Long stretches, in remarkably good condition (thanks, in part, to repairs by the Byzantines and in medieval times), still stride across the countryside along the Tunis–El-Fahs road. Today, the town's springs supply deliciously refreshing water to a number of **public fountains** elaborately decorated with tiles.

The old town's charming main street, rue Sidi Ali Azouz, stretches from the yellow and green **minaret**, just west of the old **French church** (now a school), southward along the ridge, passing wall fountains spouting mineral water, and houses with dark green doors and old wooden *mushrabiya* (traditional wooden screens that allow people – especially women – inside their homes to see out without being seen) windows. Roman columns, incorporated into the corners of buildings and the sides of archways, protected them from being scraped by passing carts and carriages.

The city's architectural highlight is the **Zaouia of Sidi Ali Azouz** (rue Sidi Ali Azouz; 🕒 daily), 10m down the hill from the arch, which has a green fish-scale dome and, inside, superb tiled walls, colourful stained glass and intricately carved plaster ceilings. The guardian expects a tip of TD2.

About 2km southwest of the old town along the well-signposted continuation of rue Sidi Ali Azouz, on a forested hillside, is the **Temple des Eaux** (Water Temple; admission free; 🕒 24hrs). Also known as the Nymphaeum, it's a semi-circular shrine – built under Hadrian – to the spring that kept Carthage in water. It's surrounded by 24 arches and 12 niches that once held statues depicting the months. The attractive **garden café** has a cage of chattering parakeets. As we go to press, the site is being renovated and a museum is planned.

Zaghouan is known for its *kaak al-warka*, round cakes stuffed with almond paste and flavoured with rosewater. There are markets here on Thursday afternoon and Friday morning.

SLEEPING & EATING

There are no hotels in Zaghouan.

Restaurant La Source (☎ 72 675 661; ave 7 Novembre; meat mains TD6-10) A proper restaurant with tasty food and reasonable prices, this is the only place in town that serves wine and beer.

About 100m up the hillside, on a reed-shaded section of the street just above the Roman arch, you'll find lots of cheap little **chicken and sandwich joints**.

GETTING THERE & AWAY

The bus and louage stations are a little way down the hill and to the left from Restaurant La Source. Buses, whose destinations include Tunis, El-Fahs, Nabeul/Hammamet and Sousse, also stop in town.

Louages from Tunis to Zaghouan (TD3.5, 50 minutes) – the best way to get here from the capital – depart from the Cap Bon station. Louages also link Zaghouan with El-Fahs (TD1.4,), Nabeul (TD3.8) and Sousse (TD4.4).

DOUGGA دقة

A Roman city with a view, **Dougga** (☎ 78 466 636; admission TD3, plus camera TD1; 🕒 8am-7pm Apr–mid-Sep, 8.30am-5.30pm mid-Sep–Mar) is set on an enchanting hillside surrounded by olive groves and overlooking fields of grain, with forested hills beyond. Built of yellowish-tan stone, its mellow tones meld harmoniously with the brown, tan and dark-green landscape of the Kalled Valley and the Teboursouk Mountains.

One of the most magnificent Roman monuments in Africa, Dougga's ancient remains – a Unesco World Heritage site since 1997 – are startlingly complete, giving a beguiling glimpse of how well-heeled Romans lived, flitting between the baths (including the fine Thermes de Caracalla), the imposing Capitole, the 3500-seat theatre and various temples (21 have been identified). The city was built on the site of ancient Thugga, a Numidian settlement, which explains why the streets are so uncharacteristically tangled. The 2nd-century BC Libyo-Punic Mausoleum is the country's finest pre-Roman monument.

The best time to visit is early in the morning or late in the day; allow at least three hours. You won't find much shade so if you're neither a mad dog nor an Englishman you might want to avoid the midday sun. There's a café selling snacks but Dougga is a magical setting for a picnic.

History

This prime real estate – endowed with natural springs – has been occupied since the 2nd millennium BC, judging by the dolmen graves on the ridge above the ruins. It was already a substantial settlement by the time Carthage advanced into the interior in the 4th century BC. The town stayed under Carthaginian control throughout the 3rd century BC but became part of the kingdom of the Numidian king Massinissa at the end of the Second Punic War.

Thugga lay outside the boundaries of the first Roman province of Africa, which was created after the destruction of Carthage in 146 BC, and remained a Numidian town until 46 BC, when the last Numidian king, Juba I, backed the wrong side (Pompey) in the Roman Civil War.

Thugga became Dougga, part of the expanded province of Africa Nova, and the slow process of Romanisation began. Dougga's prosperity peaked between the 2nd and 4th centuries, when it was home to an estimated 5000 people.

The town declined during the Vandal occupation and the population had all but disappeared by the time the Byzantines arrived in AD 533 and set about remodelling Dougga as a fort. The ruins of an **Aghlabid bathhouse**, southwest of the Capitole, show that the site was still inhabited in the 10th century.

People continued to live among the ruins until the early 1950s, when the inhabitants were moved to nearby Nouvelle Dougga (New Dougga).

Orientation

Dougga has two entrances: one faces Teboursouk, 8km to the northeast, at the eastern edge of the site; the other, at the southwestern edge, is 4km up the slope from the Nouvelle Dougga junction on the Le Kef–Teboursouk road.

Sights

The route outlined below begins at the Teboursouk entrance.

THEATRE

Nestled into the hillside, the outstanding theatre, whose 19 tiers could accommodate an audience of 3500, was built in AD 188 by one of the city's wealthier residents, Marcus Quadrutus. Today, it serves as a superb setting for classical drama during the month-long **Dougga Festival** (running from early July

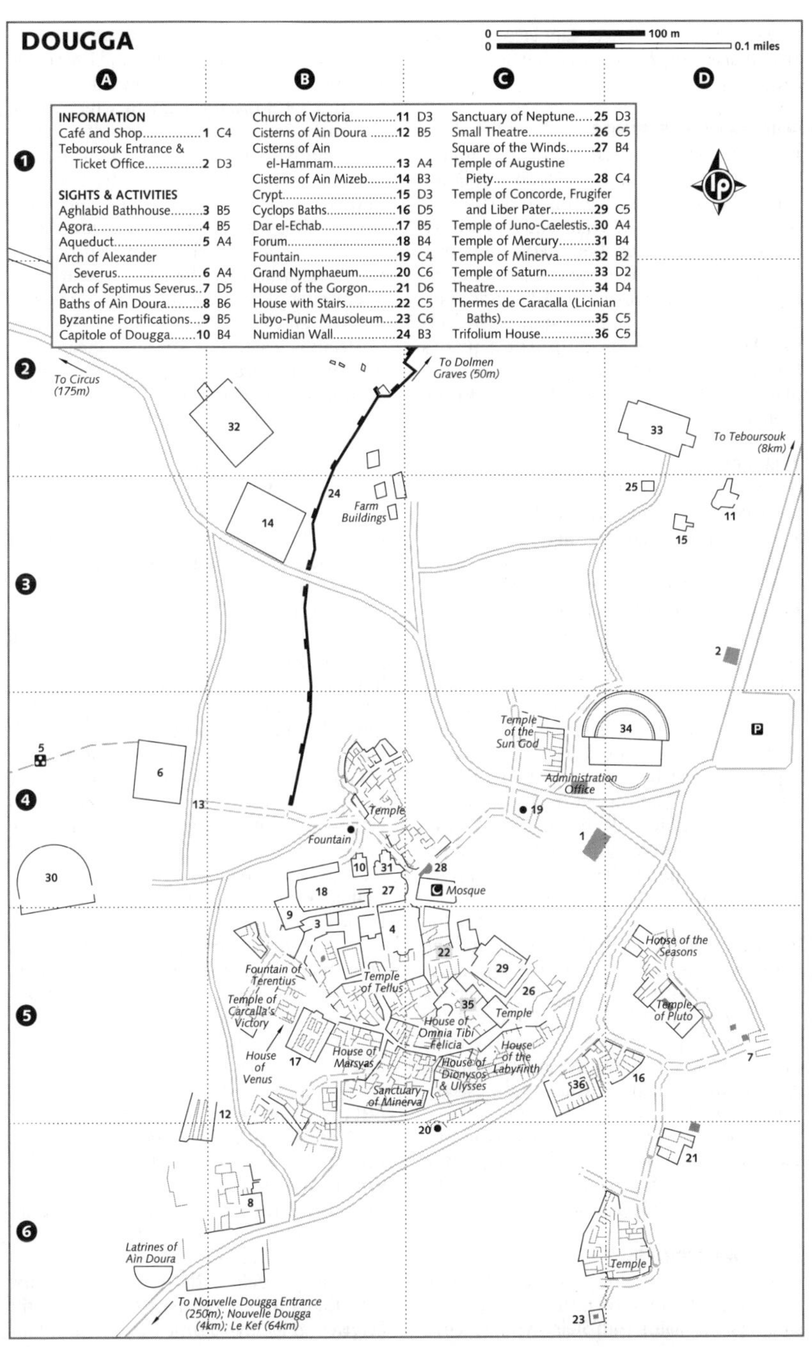
DOUGGA
0 100 m
0 0.1 miles
A
B
C
D
1
2
3
4
5
6
INFORMATION
Café and Shop................1 C4
Teboursouk Entrance & Ticket Office................2 D3
SIGHTS & ACTIVITIES
Aghlabid Bathhouse.........3 B5
Agora.............................4 B5
Aqueduct........................5 A4
Arch of Alexander Severus.......................6 A4
Arch of Septimus Severus..7 D5
Baths of Ain Doura..........8 B6
Byzantine Fortifications....9 B5
Capitole of Dougga.......10 B4
Church of Victoria............11 D3
Cisterns of Ain Doura 12 B5
Cisterns of Ain el-Hammam.................13 A4
Cisterns of Ain Mizeb.........14 B3
Crypt...............................15 D3
Cyclops Baths...................16 D5
Dar el-Echab.....................17 B5
Forum...............................18 B4
Fountain...........................19 C4
Grand Nymphaeum...........20 C6
House of the Gorgon........21 D6
House with Stairs..............22 C5
Libyo-Punic Mausoleum....23 C6
Numidian Wall..................24 B3
Sanctuary of Neptune.....25 D3
Small Theatre..................26 C5
Square of the Winds........27 B4
Temple of Augustine Piety...........................28 C4
Temple of Concorde, Frugifer and Liber Pater............29 C5
Temple of Juno-Caelestis..30 A4
Temple of Mercury..........31 B4
Temple of Minerva..........32 B2
Temple of Saturn............33 D2
Theatre...........................34 D4
Thermes de Caracalla (Licinian Baths)..........................35 C5
Trifolium House...............36 C5
To Circus (175m)
To Dolmen Graves (50m)
To Teboursouk (8km)
Farm Buildings
Temple of the Sun God
Administration Office
Temple
Fountain
Mosque
House of the Seasons
Temple of Pluto
Fountain of Terentius
Temple of Tellus
Temple of Carcalla's Victory
House of Venus
House of Omnia Tibi Felicia
House of Marsyas
House of Dionysos & Ulysses
House of the Labyrinth
Sanctuary of Minerva
Latrines of Ain Doura
To Nouvelle Dougga Entrance (250m); Nouvelle Dougga (4km); Le Kef (64km)

to early August). Travel agencies in Tunis and major resort areas organise festival excursions.

SQUARE OF THE WINDS

From the theatre, head south and follow the Roman road that leads downhill towards the Capitole, passing the ruins of a small **fountain**. The road emerges at the Square of the Winds, bounded by temples and named after the large circular engraving listing the names of the 12 winds. You can make out some of the names, including Africanus (the sirocco). The Square's function is unclear but it was probably a marketplace, used in conjunction with the **agora** to the south.

TEMPLES

The town is dominated by the imposing hilltop **Capitole** (Capitol; AD 166). In remarkable condition, it has 10m-high walls and six mighty, one-piece fluted columns – each 8m high – supporting the portico. The massive walls are the finest known example of a construction technique called *opus africanum*, which uses large stones to strengthen walls built of small stones and rubble.

The walls enclose the temple's inner sanctum. The three large niches in the north wall once housed a giant statue of Jupiter flanked by smaller statues of Juno and Minerva. The carved frieze shows the emperor Antonius Pius being carried off in an eagle's claws, with an inscription dedicating the temple to the gods Jupiter, Juno and Minerva.

The Byzantines were responsible for the **fortifications** that enclose the capitole and the **forum**, built on the orders of General Solomon and constructed using stones filched from surrounding buildings. Look out for stones bearing the dedication from the Temple of Mercury (see next paragraph), which have wound up at knee height on the eastern wall, facing the Square of the Winds.

The meagre remains of the **Temple of Mercury** are to the north of the square. To the east are four square pillars belonging to the tiny 2nd-century **Temple of Augustine Piety**.

BATHS & LATRINES

If you head south along the path running past the building known, for obvious reasons, as the **House with Stairs**, you reach a large but poorly preserved **temple** complex dedicated to **Concorde, Frugifer** and **Liber Pater**. Beyond, facing southeast towards the valley, is a **small theatre**, next to which stand the early 3rd-century **Thermes de Caracalla** (Licinian Baths) – their size is a further indication of the town's prosperity. The walls of this extensive complex – especially those surrounding the grand *frigidarium* (cold room) – remain largely intact. A tunnel for the slaves, who kept the baths operating, is a reminder of how the good-life enjoyed by the Roman elite was maintained.

Heading east, and straight ahead over the staggered crossroads, you come across an unusual solid square doorframe to the south. It marks the entrance to an unidentified temple referred to as **Dar el-Echab**, after the family who once occupied the site. Carry on past Dar el-Echab, and then head south. The route turns into a rough path that winds downhill past the ruined **Cisterns of Ain Doura** to the **Baths of Ain Doura**, the city's main summer baths.

If you head back uphill from here along the dirt road that crosses the site, you'll pass the **grand nymphaeum** on the left. This huge, partly restored fountain is thought to have been supplied with water by an underground conduit from the Cisterns of Ain el-Hammam (see opposite), 300m northwest.

Continue along the road for another 75m, then turn right, descending the steps leading to **Trifolium House**. This is believed to have been the town brothel – the discreet name was inspired by the small clover-leaf-shaped room in the northwest corner of the house.

Next door are the **Cyclops Baths**, named after the remarkable mosaic found here (now in the Bardo Museum). The baths themselves are in disrepair, except for the sociably horseshoe-shaped row of 12 latrines just inside the entrance.

ARCH OF SEPTIMIUS SEVERUS & LIBYO-PUNIC MAUSOLEUM

From here you can head east along the paved Roman road that leads downhill to the ruins of the Arch of Septimius Severus, built in AD 205 to honour Rome's first African-born emperor.

Turn right before the arch and follow the path that winds south past the **House of the Gorgon** to the Libyo-Punic Mausoleum. This triple-tiered, obelisk-shaped monument, an amazing 21m high, is crowned by a small pyramid with a seated lion at the pinnacle. It was built during the reign of Massinissa at the beginning of the 2nd century BC and is dedicated, according to a bilingual (Libyan and Punic) inscription, to 'Ateban, son of Ypmatat, son of Palu'. The inscription, which once occupied the vacant window at the base, was removed by the British consul to Tunis in 1842, who destroyed the whole monument in the process. The stone was taken to England (it's now in the British Museum); the monument itself was rebuilt by French archaeologists in 1910.

The well-preserved **Arch of Alexander Severus**, built between AD 222 and 235, marks the city's western entrance. A path leads southwest from here through olive trees to the roughly contemporary **Temple of Juno-Caelestis**, dedicated to the Roman version of the Carthaginian god Tanit. Funded by a resident made a *flamen* (a Roman priest) in AD 222, it was adapted as a church in the 5th century. The pillar-surrounded sanctuary retains an impressive portico, reached via a flight of steps.

CISTERNS, TEMPLES & A CHURCH

Immediately west of the Arch of Alexander Severus are the cavernous **Cisterns of Ain el-Hammam**, added during the reign of Commodius (AD 180–192) to meet the city's growing demand for water. They were supplied via an **aqueduct**, sections of which are visible among the olive trees west of the cisterns, fed by springs 12km to the southwest.

A rough path leads north through the trees from here, emerging after 150m in front of the nine **Cisterns of Ain Mizeb**. The city's main water supply, they were fed by a spring some 200m to the west and remain in excellent condition.

Follow the dirt road that leads northwest, and then cut across the fields to the **Temple of Minerva**. Looking northwest from here, it's possible to discern the outline of the **circus**, now an elongated wheat field filling a saddle between two hills.

Turn right and aim for the rocky ridge to the northeast, which is dotted with dozens of primitive **dolmen graves**. These are just north of the so-called **Numidian Wall**, which protected the city in pre-Roman days.

Cross the wall and follow the paths that curve across the hill towards the **Temple of Saturn**. This great temple must have been a magnificent sight after its completion in AD 195 but today only six stunted columns remain. Built on a platform facing east over the valley of Oued Kalled, it dominated the ancient city's northern approach. The structure stands on the site of an earlier temple to Baal Hammon, the chief Punic deity, who became Saturn in Roman times and was the favoured god of Roman Africa.

The reconstructed apse south of the temple is all that remains of the **Sanctuary of Neptune**.

The ruins of the Vandal **Church of Victoria**, on the slope east of the sanctuary, are the only evidence of Christianity at Dougga. The church was built in the early 5th century using stone taken from the surrounding temples. The small **crypt** next door is packed with large stone sarcophagi and still has relics from the saint.

From here, you can follow the path south to the theatre.

Getting There & Away

Dougga can easily be visited on a day trip from Tunis or Le Kef – or en route between the two cities. The nearest town, about 8km northeast of Dougga, is Teboursouk – see p160 for details on getting there by public transport.

From Teboursouk's louage station, hiring an entire yellow-striped louage or a yellow taxi to Dougga should cost about TD7 one way or TD10 to TD15 return (the driver will return to pick you up at a pre-set time), though iffy operators may demand a lot more or set an exorbitant per-person rate.

If you're coming from Le Kef, you can get off the bus at the Nouvelle Dougga turn-off on the main road. From here it's a 4km walk – you *might* be able to hitch a ride with locals but don't count on it. See Hitching, p311 for general information about possible dangers.

TEBOURSOUK تبورسوق

pop 12,700

The small town of Teboursouk (*tuh*-burr-suck – swallow all the vowels), 68km northeast of Le Kef, has a fine setting high up in pine-forested hills but there's nothing specific to see here. Market day is Thursday.

Nearby Dougga's popularity with tourists seems to have attracted a few unsavoury types who try to take advantage of visitors.

Readers have written to us to complain that while their backpacks were in the keeping of unnamed local businesses, they were rifled through and items were stolen. However, it *may* be possible to leave your bags safely at Restaurant L'Arrêt Chez Adel, next to the SNTRI office (it's one of several adjacent eateries), if you eat lunch there.

If you've got your heart set on getting out to the ruins early or staying late, the 33-room, two-star **Hôtel Thugga** (☎ 78 466 647; s/d TD30/44; ❄), about 1km down the hill from the centre of Teboursouk and 8km from Dougga, is a decent tourist-class choice. The only hostelry in town, it's clean and comfortable and has a restaurant.

Getting There & Away

All SNTRI services operating between Tunis (TD5.5, 1¾ hours, hourly until 5pm) and Le Kef (TD3.5, one hour, almost hourly until 8.15pm) stop at Teboursouk's SNTRI office, which is in the town centre. Across the street, louages leave for Béja, Tunis and Le Kef.

See p159 for information on details about how to get to Dougga.

LE KEF الكاف

pop 46,000

High in the hills at an elevation of 780m, Le Kef (El Kef or al-Kaf, Arabic for 'rock') is topped by a storybook kasbah offering panoramic views. On the slope below is the medina, a maze of narrow cobbled streets and blue-shuttered low-rise buildings whose highlights include a fine museum that focuses on Berber culture and Muslim, Christian and Jewish places of worship.

Le Kef, 175km southwest of Tunis and only 40km from the Algerian frontier, is one of Tunisia's most underrated tourist destinations. Particularly friendly and with lots of local pride, it's an excellent base for exploring the Roman sites of Dougga and Haidra as well as Jugurtha's Table. The city is cold in winter and oven-hot in the summer.

The area around the bus station looks distinctly unpromising but things get much more interesting as you walk up the hill.

A website (in French) with lots of historical information and old photos of Le Kef is http://lekef-carte.postale.chez-alice.fr.

History

Established around 500 BC by Carthage to protect the western parts of its newly won empire, the first town on this strategic site was called Sicca and was known for the temple prostitutes who hung out at its sanctuary to the goddess Astarte, whose portfolio included love. In Roman times, the sanctuary was dedicated to Venus and so the town became known as Sicca Veneria.

When Carthage couldn't pay its mercenaries, they were sent here and rose in revolt, whereupon more mercenaries were sent to sort things out, triggering a horrific four-year battle (inspiring Flaubert's novel *Salammbô*). After the fall of Carthage, Le Kef became a stronghold of the Numidian king Jugurtha during his rebellion against Rome.

The Vandals came and went, followed by the Byzantines and then the Arabs, who captured the town in AD 688 and took to calling it Shakbanaria (a corruption of Sicca Veneria). Locals rebelled against the central government at pretty much every opportunity before becoming autonomous after the Hilalian invasions of the 11th century. The town fell briefly to the Almohads in 1159 but soon returned to its independent ways. By the time the Ottomans arrived in the 16th century, the region had become the private fiefdom of the Beni Cherif tribe.

Le Kef prospered under the Ottomans, who rebuilt its fortifications, and this upward spiral continued under the beys. Hussein ben Ali, who founded the Husseinite dynasty of beys (1705–1957), was born here.

Orientation & Information

Most things of interest to travellers are either around place de l'Indépendance or in the western half of the medina, which is on the slopes below (south of) the kasbah. The bus and louage stations are about 600m southwest of place de l'Indépendance.

Charged with protecting the city's historic sites, the two offices of the **Association de Sauvegarde de la Medina** (ASM; ☎ 78 200 476, 78 201 367; 🕒 8am-1pm & 3-6pm) also function as makeshift tourist offices. **ASM Bureau** (place de l'Indépendance) is housed in the mausoleum of

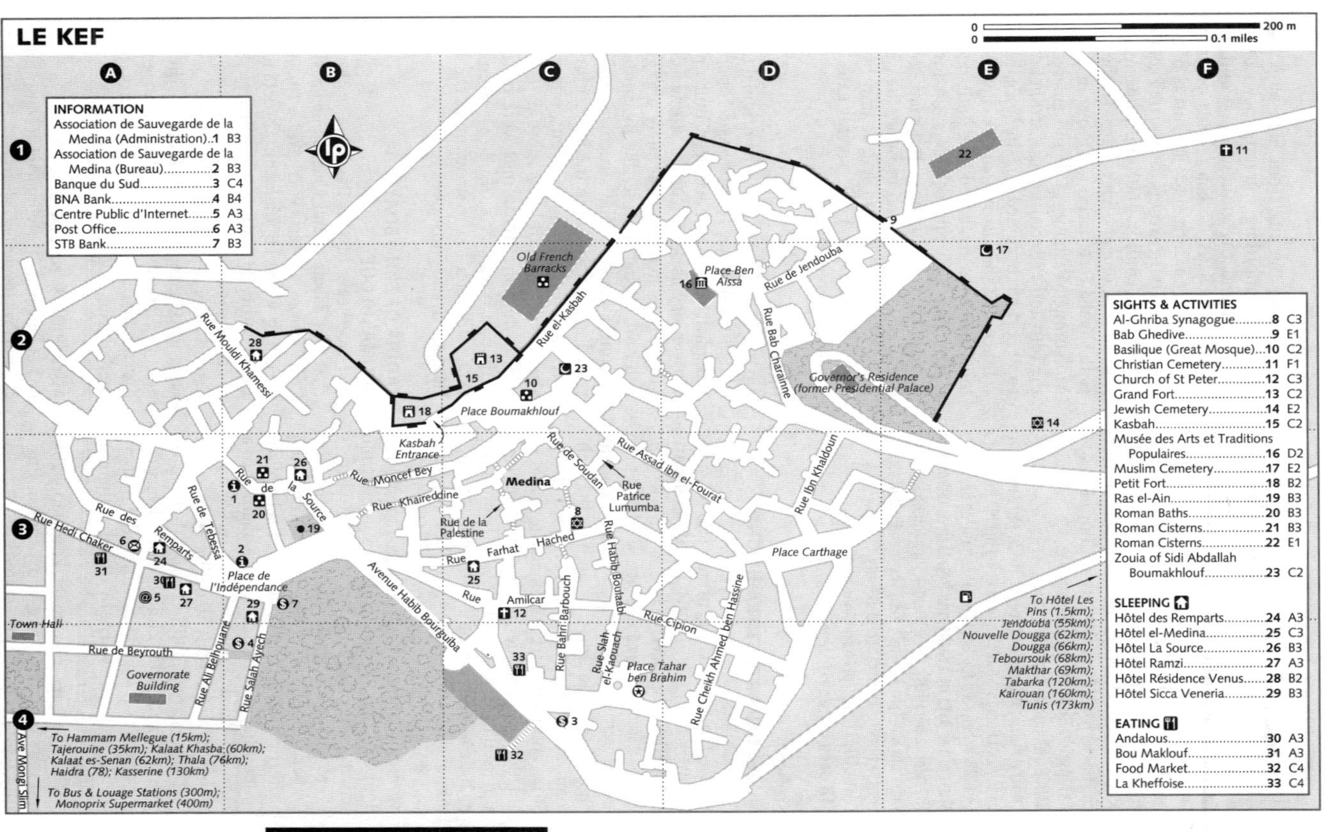
LE KEF
0 200 m
0 0.1 miles
INFORMATION
Association de Sauvegarde de la Medina (Administration)..1 B3
Association de Sauvegarde de la Medina (Bureau)..2 B3
Banque du Sud..3 C4
BNA Bank..4 B4
Centre Public d'Internet..5 A3
Post Office..6 A3
STB Bank..7 B3
SIGHTS & ACTIVITIES
Al-Ghriba Synagogue..8 C3
Bab Ghedive..9 E1
Basilique (Great Mosque)..10 C2
Christian Cemetery..11 F1
Church of St Peter..12 C3
Grand Fort..13 C2
Jewish Cemetery..14 E2
Kasbah..15 C2
Musée des Arts et Traditions Populaires..16 D2
Muslim Cemetery..17 E2
Petit Fort..18 B2
Ras el-Ain..19 B3
Roman Baths..20 B3
Roman Cisterns..21 B3
Roman Cisterns..22 E1
Zouia of Sidi Abdallah Boumakhlouf..23 C2
SLEEPING
Hôtel des Remparts..24 A3
Hôtel el-Medina..25 C3
Hôtel La Source..26 B3
Hôtel Ramzi..27 A3
Hôtel Résidence Venus..28 B2
Hôtel Sicca Veneria..29 B3
EATING
Andalous..30 A3
Bou Maklouf..31 A3
Food Market..32 C4
La Kheffoise..33 C4
To Hôtel Les Pins (1.5km); Jendouba (55km); Nouvelle Dougga (62km); Dougga (66km); Teboursouk (68km); Makthar (69km); Tabarka (120km); Kairouan (160km); Tunis (173km)
To Hammam Mellegue (15km); Tajerouine (35km); Kalaat Khasba (60km); Kalaat es-Senan (62km); Thala (76km); Haidra (78); Kasserine (130km)
To Bus & Louage Stations (300m); Monoprix Supermarket (400m)
Old French Barracks
Governor's Residence (former Presidential Palace)
Medina
Kasbah Entrance
Place Ben Aissa
Place Boumakhlouf
Place Carthage
Place de l'Indépendance
Place Tahar ben Brahim
Town Hall
Governorate Building
Rue el-Kasbah
Rue de Jendouba
Rue Bab Charainne
Rue Ibn Khaldoun
Rue Cheikh Ahmed ben Hassine
Rue Assad ibn el-Fourat
Rue Patrice Lumumba
Rue de Soudan
Rue Habib Boulaabi
Rue Slah el-Kaouach
Rue Cipion
Rue Bahri Barbouch
Rue Farhat Hached
Rue Amilcar
Rue de la Palestine
Rue Khaireddine
Rue Moncef Bey
Rue de la Source
Rue Mouldi Khamessi
Rue de Tebessa
Rue des Remparts
Rue Hedi Chaker
Rue de Beyrouth
Rue Ali Belhouane
Rue Salah Ayech
Avenue Habib Bourguiba
Ave Mongi Slim

a 19th-century saint, Sidi Hacine bou Karma (look for the orange ceramic wall map of Le Kef out front); **ASM Administration** (rue de la Source) is located inside Dar el-Kahia (look for the little marble ASM plaque out front), a large, tile-decorated mansion from the 18th and 19th centuries that's worth seeing. A room off the courtyard has old photos of Le Kef and wall charts (in French) with historical background on the city's monuments.

Banque du Sud (ave Habib Bourguiba)

BNA Bank (rue de Beyrouth)

Centre Public d'Internet (per hr TD1.5; 8am-2am) On the 2nd floor in a building 50m down the hill from the post office, between rue Hedi Chaker and rue de Beyrouth.

Musée des Arts et Traditions Populaires (admission TD2, plus camera TD1; 9.30am-4.30pm mid-Sep–Mar, 9am-1pm & 4-7pm Apr–mid-Sep) The friendly staff can provide tips and information on the city.

Post office (rue Hedi Chaker) Has an ATM.

STB Bank (place de l'Indépendance)

Sights

MUSÉE DES ARTS ET TRADITIONS POPULAIRES

Housed in a sprawling, ornate Sufi religious complex founded in 1784, the **Musée des Arts et Traditions Populaires** (admission TD2, plus camera TD1; 9.30am-4.30pm mid-Sep–Mar, 9am-1pm & 4-7pm Apr–mid-Sep) is worth a stop. There are many highlights, including the tomb of the Rahmaniya Sufi leader Sidi Ali ben Aissa (1901–56), a complete Berber nomads' tent and an old flour mill made in Marseilles in 1860 and used in Le Kef until 1992. Other features include a mock-up of a traditional Quranic school for young boys, Berber bagpipes and a room covering *travaux féminins* – 'women's labours' such as weaving, milling flour and making couscous (a summertime activity). Plus there's heavy silver jewellery – 1½ to 2kg of it – traditionally worn daily by Berber women (silver is believed to provide protection against the Evil Eye). Each child a woman had was indicated by a chain with a *khomsa* (Hand of Fatima) for a girl or a full-moon shape for a boy dangling at the end.

Chances are you didn't know that camels hate cold and, when chilled, can get very aggressive – that's why, in winter, the Berbers kept them toasty warm by dressing them in a huge sombrero.

The staff are extremely knowledgeable and may be able to give you a tour in English (a small tip is appreciated).

KASBAH

Dominating the city from high atop Jebel Eddir and affording stunning views of the old town and the grainfields beyond, the grand, crenellated **kasbah** (8am-7pm, to 8pm or later Mon-Fri, may be closed 1-2pm) consists of two fortresses. To the west is the square **Petit Fort** (small fort), built in 1601 and protected by four towers, one at each corner. To the east is the **Grand Fort** (large fort), begun under Mohammed Pasha in 1679 and enlarged in the 18th and 19th centuries. A stronghold of some sort has occupied this site since the 5th century BC; the last military occupant was the Tunisian army, based here until 1992.

The guardian appreciates a tip for accompanying you around the main points of interest: the Turkish mosque, the prison cells, a bronze cannon left behind by the Dey of Algiers in 1705, several gates and walls of various vintages.

BASILIQUE

No one is quite sure what the original function of the **Basilique** (8am-noon & 3-6pm) was, though it seems to have been built in the 4th century as some sort of storage depot for precious items such as silver and grain. Later on, probably under the Byzantines, it became a church. The structure was converted into a mosque in the 8th century, in the wake of the Arab invasions, but today, after restorations, it looks more-or-less like it did when the Byzantines were in town. Although it was secularised in 1966, many locals still refer to the structure as the **Great Mosque** (Grand Mosquée).

ZAOUIA OF SIDI ABDALLAH BOUMAKHLOUF

Just northeast of the Basilique is the enchanting **Zaouia of Sidi Abdallah Boumakhlouf** (10am-noon & 3-6pm, all day Wed & Fri), with gleaming white cupolas and an octagonal, 19th-century Hanafite-style minaret. Built at the beginning of the 17th century, it's named after the town's Fez-born patron saint who, along with his family, is buried here in elaborate tombs cloaked in green. Just outside is a bewitchingly pretty, tree-shaded square with a café.

AL-GHRIBA SYNAGOGUE

Le Kef long had a thriving Jewish community; **Al-Ghriba Synagogue** (rue Farhat Hached; 7am-7pm), in the heart of the former Jewish quarter, the Hara, pays tribute to that now-vanished part of local culture. Inside the structure, restored in 1994, you can see old wooden memorial plaques; a marriage invitation from 1952; a Torah scroll, hand-written on parchment; a circumcision chair that causes some male visitors, instinctively, to cup their hands over their crotch; a truly spooky chandelier (it's hard to believe that such items where once fashionable!); and fragments of old newspapers whose Arabic text is written in Hebrew characters (this seldom-seen language, Judeo-Arabic, is to Arabic what Yiddish is to German). The caretaker will let you in; there's no entry fee but you should give him a tip of at least TD2.

CHURCH OF ST PETER

The remains of the 4th-century **Église St Pierre** (Dar el-Kous; rue Amilcar; 8am-noon or 1pm & 3-6pm) are two blocks southwest of the synagogue. Remarkably well-preserved, the structure – built on the site of a pagan temple – has a narthex, a large nave, two side aisles and an impressive apse that was added in Byzantine times. It's often locked.

RAS EL-AIN

Le Kef owes its very existence to the **Ras el-Ain spring** (place de l'Indépendance, cnr rue de la Source), whose waters once supplied the **Roman baths** (rue de la Source) just to the west; note the hexagonal hall and the remains of a 5th-century church. Spring waters were also used to fill the **Roman cisterns**, across rue de la Source from the baths.

BAB GHEDIVE

Stepping through this city gate – the only one of the city's five gates still extant – is like a journey through the looking glass, from the city to the countryside. Just outside is a huge underground **Roman cistern** – a spooky, gloomy cavern that's popular with secret boozers after dark. Small red cliffs form a backdrop to the town – villagers walk down from here with their donkeys to collect water from the pump. East of the cisterns, past the **Muslim cemetery**, is an old **Christian cemetery**, with wrought-iron grave decorations. Down the hill, 200m west of the former Governor's Residence (formerly Bourguiba's Presidential Palace), is a large **Jewish cemetery**.

Sleeping

Le Kef has a good selection of clean, comfortable accommodation options.

BUDGET

Hôtel el-Medina (☎ 78 204 183; 18 rue Farhat Hached; s/d with shared bathroom TD6/12) Very basic but pretty clean, this 13-room place has beds reminiscent of a hospital and the hall toilets lack toilet seats. On the brighter side, there are fine views from the rooms at the back and from the rooftop terrace.

Hôtel La Source (☎ 78 204 397; rue de la Source; per person TD6-15) Run by a real character, this nine-room place, arranged around a traditional courtyard, has peeling paint, some iffy plumbing, cracked and off-kilter floor tiles and beds that are, shall we say, a bit rickety – but you can't beat it for atmosphere. To stay in the spectacularly tiled, 18th-century 'family room' – the most extraordinary hotel room in town – with its ornate Andalusian ceiling is to live the life of a bey, albeit one whose fortunes are in genteel decline.

Hôtel des Remparts (☎ 78 202 100; 5 rue des Remparts; s/d TD10/20) On a quiet street, this hostelry – slightly ragged at the edges – has simple, bright rooms, some with big windows.

MIDRANGE

Hôtel Sicca Veneria (☎ 78 202 389; place de l'Indépendance; s/d TD22/38) This 32-room, lift-equipped place is very central but the rooms – some with balconies – are boring. The entrance is around the corner on rue Salah Ayech.

Hôtel Ramzi (☎ 78 203 079; rue Hedi Chaker; s/d TD25/50, without toilet or shower TD20/40) This is a central and very welcoming hotel whose 14 rooms are clean and decorated with lots of colourful wall tiles. It has a restaurant.

Hôtel-Résidence Venus (☎ 78 204 695; www.hotel-lespins.com, in French; rue Mouldi Khamessi; s/d TD28/40) Nestled beneath the outer walls of the old kasbah, this especially friendly pension has twittering canaries in the courtyard, great views from the rooftop and 20 rooms that are simple, clean and pleasant. It's under the same management as Hôtel Les Pins and if you ask nicely they'll let you use the pool there. The manager can arrange transport to Hammam Mellegue (TD29).

Hôtel Les Pins (☎ 78 204 021; www.hotel-lespins.com, in French; s/d TD30/42;) About 1.5km east of town on the road to Tunis, this good-value hotel – surrounding a courtyard pool – is lovely, clean and bright, with lots of colourful tiling. All rooms have nicely tiled bathrooms and some come with views.

Eating

La Kheffoise (☎ 78 203 887; ave Habib Bourguiba; pizzas TD2) This spotless little bakery and pizzeria has seating on a small interior balcony.

Bou Maklouf (☎ 98 285 211; rue Hedi Chaker; mains TD3.5-7; 🕑 to midnight) This good-value cheapie is very popular for lunch, when specialities include couscous, *lablabi* (soup) and the town's best chicken and chips. The selection is more limited in the evening.

Andalous (rue Hedi Chaker; mains TD7) This simple place, run by a motherly woman who's clearly proud of her establishment, serves excellent *salade mechouia* (traditional Tunisian salad of grilled peppers and tomatoes, with olives) and tasty fish and couscous.

Edibles are sold at the **food market**, down from ave Habib Bourguiba. To get to the **Monoprix supermarket** (🕑 8am-1pm & 4-8pm) from the bus station, walk 50m up the hill and then 250m right (east) – just follow the signs.

Getting There & Away

BUS

From the **bus station** (ave Mongi Slim), located about 600m southwest of place de l'Indépendance, the Société Régionale de Transport du Gouvernorat du Kef (SRTG Kef) has bus services to Bizerte (TD8.5, twice daily); Gafsa (twice daily); Jendouba (TD3.2, one hour, twice daily); Kairouan (TD7.5, four daily) via Makthar (TD3, 1¼ hours, last bus back at 3pm or 3.30pm); Kasserine (TD5.6, two hours, five daily) via Tajerouine (linked to Jugurtha's Table by louage), Kalaat Khasba (linked to Tunis by two trains a day) and Thala (linked to Haidra by louage); Nabeul (TD9.4, twice daily) via Hammamet (TD8.5); Sfax (TD12.2, four daily); and Sousse (TD9.4, twice daily).

SNTRI services to Tunis (TD8.3, 3¼ hours, hourly except around noon) can drop you in Nouvelle Dougga (TD3.2, one hour), from where you can walk to Dougga, or in Teboursouk (TD3.5, 1¼ hours), linked to Dougga by taxi.

For details on transport to Hammam Mellegue see right.

LOUAGE

Red-stripe louages to Jendouba (TD3.1, one hour), Béja, Makthar and Kasserine (TD6.5) leave from the bus station parking lot. Louages to Sousse, leaving early in the morning, Teboursouk (TD8.7) and Tunis (TD8.7) stop across the street.

AROUND LE KEF

Hammam Mellegue حمّام ملاّق

For an unbelievably relaxing hot-water soak, head to the tiny, isolated hamlet of Hammam Mellegue, 15km west of Le Kef, where you can have a real Roman bath in a stunningly beautiful natural setting. Overlooking the broad, sandy sweep of the murky green Oued Mellegue, the *hammam* (public bathhouse) is hidden away at the base of a dramatic escarpment surrounded by reddish bluffs dotted with pine trees. The only electricity comes from photovoltaic cells.

Although much of the 2nd-century bath complex is little more than a roofless jumble of walls and arches, the **caldarium** (hot room; admission TD1; 🕑 all day) is an extraordinary place that remains virtually unchanged more than 1800 years after it was built.

A large wooden door opens onto a steam-filled chamber lit by a skylight set into the barrel-vaulted ceiling. Ancient stone steps lead down the pool, worn smooth by the feet of 40 generations and turned dark red by iron elements in the water, which is fed by hot springs whose waters emerge from the ground at 35°C. It is emptied by removing wet rags from the ancient drain pipes, connected by gravity with Oued Mellegue, and refilled from pipes connected to the spring. There are two chambers, one each for men and women.

The water is slightly saline (you can drink it direct from the inflow pipe) and is said by locals to be good for rheumatism and the problems of the digestive tract.

Bring a bathing suit, towel, flip-flops and plenty of drinking water; for security bring your stuff into the caldarium with you.

If you'd like to stay out here you can either camp or rent a very rudimentary room (TD2.5).

GETTING THERE & AWAY

Hammam Mellegue attracts only a handful of Tunisians and virtually no foreigners, in part because it's so hard to get to.

BE A ROMAN!

To experience the luxurious, sensual life once lived by wealthy Romans – indeed, to actually *transform* yourself into a Roman, at least for a little while – you don't have to learn to look nonchalant in a toga or develop a taste for lead-tainted wine. A 45-minute trip from Le Kef along an almost impassable dirt track is all it takes!

Hammam Mellegue (opposite), whose spa facilities have hardly changed in 1800 years, affords the real Roman bath experience, absolutely genuine in every detail. Even the mobile phone reception out here is no better than it would have been back when Scipio Africanus sent his SMS messages with runners.

To achieve maximum authenticity, you might try chatting in Latin while lolling about in the steaming spring water. 'This is *ne plus ultra*, dude – it's a good thing no one here is *in loco parentis*', you might remark to your companion. 'Instead of heading back to *terra firma*, I'd like to stay here *ad infinitum*, though I wouldn't want to drink that salty spring water *ad nauseum*. Paying TD1 *per capita per diem* for a *bona fide* Roman experience isn't bad – I wonder what it costs here *per annum*? If you dare splash me that will be a *casus belli* – not only will you become a *persona non grata* for the rest of the day you'll find me *in absentia* until you say *mea culpa*.'

Of course, if your brain is a *tabula rasa* you can always mutter '*et cetera, et cetera*'.

If you've got a car, follow the signs from Le Kef to Sakiet Sidi Youssef; the turn-off to Hammam Mellegue is about 3km southwest of town at the far end of the military base – look for a sign to the 'Forêts du Kef'. Further on, the signless route passes by some Tunisian army training bases so stay on the road as the area is sensitive security-wise and there may be old ordnance lying around (that's what those skull-and-crossbones markings are about). The first 9km, which pass through rolling wheat country, are in pretty good condition. The final 3km get dodgy as the road descends to Oued Mellegue. In summer the track, steep and washed out in places, is passable (but just barely) to non-4WD vehicles; during the winter rains? Fugeddaboudit, unless you've got a Land Rover.

There is no public transport to Hammam Mellegue but it's possible to hire a vehicle with a driver in Le Kef. One option is to suss things out with a yellow-striped louage driver across the street from the bus station – a round-trip by *camionnette* (small truck) should cost about TD20 (a bonus for the driver: a long, hot soak). It might be simpler, though, to hire an ancient Peugeot pickup with a driver (TD29) through the Hôtel-Résidence Venus (p163).

MAKTHAR (MACTARIS) مكثر

pop 9000

The ruins of ancient Mactaris are in the middle of nowhere on the road between Le Kef (69km northwest) and Kairouan (114km to the east). If you like classic Roman public spaces – Mactaris boasts a fine triumphal arch, a forum and a superb bath complex – it's worth the effort to get out here but don't plan to stay overnight as the modern town is bleak and the only accommodation option unbelievably unappealing.

History

Ancient Mactaris was one of many native towns incorporated into the Carthaginian Empire at the end of the 5th century BC as part of Carthage's push to take control of its hinterlands. Captured by the Numidian king Massinissa before the Third Punic War, it remained in Numidian hands until the beginning of the 1st century AD, when Rome began to take the settlement of Africa seriously.

The Roman town reached the peak of its prosperity in the 2nd century; in subsequent centuries the Vandals and the Byzantines both left their mark. Mactaris continued to be occupied until the 11th century, when it was destroyed during the Hilalian invasions.

Orientation & Information

The archaeological site is on the southeastern edge of town, near the junction of the roads to Kairouan and Le Kef; the entrance is next to a roundabout with a fountain in the middle. About 100m to the west there's a second roundabout with a Roman column in the centre – from there it's 250m north to the Hôtel Maktaris, the bus shelter and the louage station. The dust-blown town centre

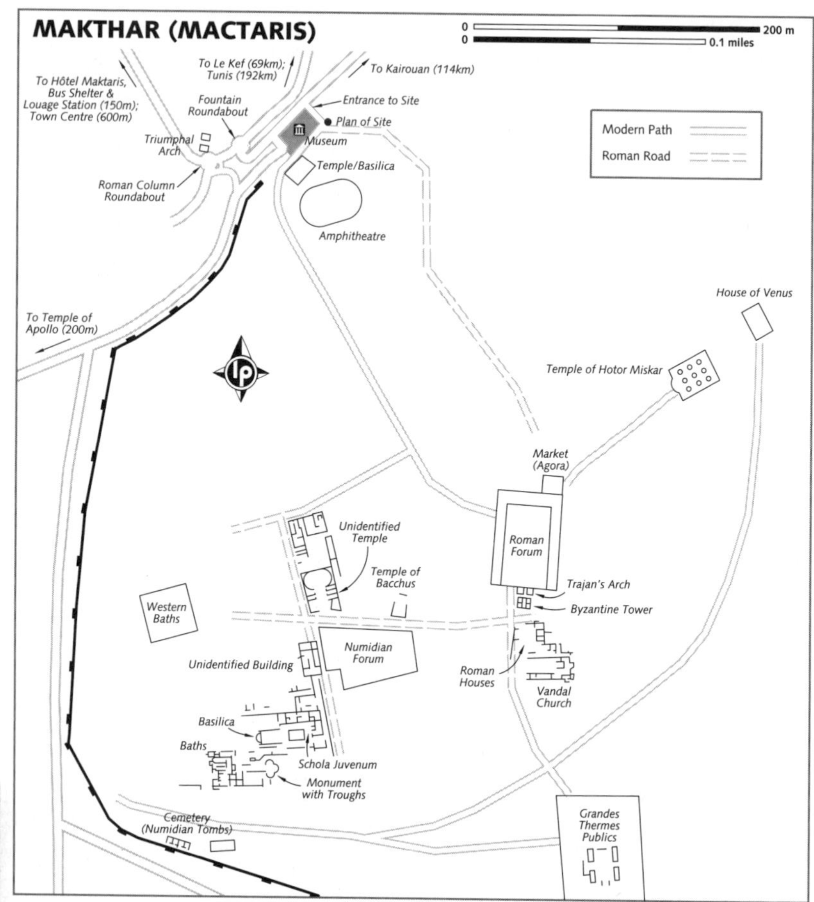

is about 400m northeast of the hotel in the area between the two minarets.

If you're visiting in the winter come suitably dressed – at an altitude of more than 1000m, the winds that blow off the surrounding hills can be bitterly cold.

Ancient Mactaris

The entrance to **Mactaris** (admission TD3, plus camera TD1; 8am-7pm Apr–mid-Sep, 8.30am-5.30pm mid-Sep–Mar) is through the **museum**, which houses a mosaic portraying a veritable menagerie, including peacocks, some interesting Roman and Christian gravestones decorated with Latin inscriptions and *haut-relief* figures, coins and Christian-era terracotta lamps.

Immediately south of the museum are the remains of the town's small **amphitheatre**, built in the 2nd century AD.

The main path runs south from the amphitheatre towards **Trajan's Arch** (AD 116), which has an ornate pediment and is dedicated, naturally, to the emperor Trajan; on the south side, part of a Latin inscription is still readable. The arch overlooks the stone-paved **Roman forum**, built at the same time. The four columns at the northeastern corner of the forum mark the location of the town's **market**. The foundations south of the arch belong to a 6th century Byzantine tower.

A path leads northeast from the forum to the scanty remains of the **Temple of Hotor Miskar**, dedicated to the Carthaginian god of the same name. Nearby are the remains of a Roman villa known as the **House of Venus**, named after the mosaic of Venus found there that's now in the museum.

The group of columns south of Trajan's Arch belong to a small **Vandal church** (5th century AD) with two rows of columns running down the middle. The baptismal font, hidden behind the rounded apse at the eastern end, still has traces of the original mosaics.

The jumble of arches and columns standing at the southwestern corner of the site was once home to the town's **schola juvenum**, a youth club where local boys learned how to be good Romans. Converted into a church in the 3rd century AD, it's a pleasant, shady spot. The area just south of the schola was the town's **cemetery** and is dotted with **Numidian tombs**.

The southern part of the site is dominated by the massive walls of the **Grandes Thermes Publics** (Great Southeastern Baths). Built in the 2nd century AD, they were converted into a fortress by the Byzantines in the 6th century but are nonetheless among the best preserved Roman baths in Tunisia. The star feature is the extraordinary deep blue, jade green, dark red and orange mosaic floor of the central hall, with its three imposing arches.

The ruins of the **Temple of Apollo** are about 200m southwest of town (they're signposted from the museum). Built on the site of an earlier Carthaginian temple dedicated to Baal Hammon, this was the town's principal temple in Roman times. Adjoining the site are the crumbling remains of the Roman aqueduct that once supplied water to the town.

Sleeping & Eating

Hôtel Maktaris (☎ 22 204 995; s, d or tr with sink TD12) Makthar's only hotel is the dilapidated, five-room hotel, situated 400m from the archaeological site above the only bar in town. This juxtaposition is fortuitous because you'll need to drink a fair bit before even considering lying down on one of the beds, whose slats can be felt through the flimsy mattresses. The general air of dereliction also pervades the boot-camp-grade toilets.

Makthar doesn't have any proper restaurants but you'll find a few cafés and small eateries in the town centre.

Getting There & Away

Makthar is on the bus line linking Le Kef (TD3, 1¼ hours, four daily; last bus at 3pm or 3.30pm) with Kairouan (TD4.6, 1¾ hours) and can be visited on a day trip from Le Kef; the stop is in front of the Hôtel Maktaris. SNTRI buses to Tunis (TD7.7, three hours) leave from the town centre.

Destinations served by louage include Tunis, Kairouan, Le Kef (until the early afternoon) and Sousse (TD8.5, until about 4pm). Stops are next to the Hôtel Maktaris.

HAIDRA (AMMÆDARA) حيدرة

The remote border village of Haidra is the site of ancient Ammædara, one of the oldest Roman towns in Africa. It's a wonderfully evocative site, spread along the northern bank of Oued Haidra, and the atmosphere is especially magical as the sun slowly sets behind the mountains of Algeria to the west, bathing the site in a rich orange glow.

The modern town is little more than a sleepy customs post on the road to the Algerian town of Tébessa, 41km to the southwest. Along both sides of the main street, a colonnaded arcade shades shops, several groceries and two tiny eateries from the fierce North African sun.

The nearest midrange accommodation is in Kasserine, 69km to the southeast, or Le Kef, 78km to the north. Basic hotels can be found in Tajerouine (see p177) and in Thala, 54km north of Kasserine, where you could try the Hôtel Bouthelja, a nondescript building with light-blue bars on all the windows. From the police station, it's 100m down the main drag and across the street.

History

Ammædara is a Berber name, although the only evidence of pre-Roman occupation is the foundations of a Carthaginian temple to the god Baal Hammon overlooking Oued Haidra to the southeast of the site.

The first Roman settlement here was a base established by the troops of the Augustine Third Legion at the beginning of the 1st century AD during their campaign to suppress a rebellion by the Numidian chief Tacfinares. Only a cemetery near the Arch of Septimius Severus survives from this period. After Tacfinares was defeated, Ammædara was repopulated with retired soldiers and became a prosperous trading town.

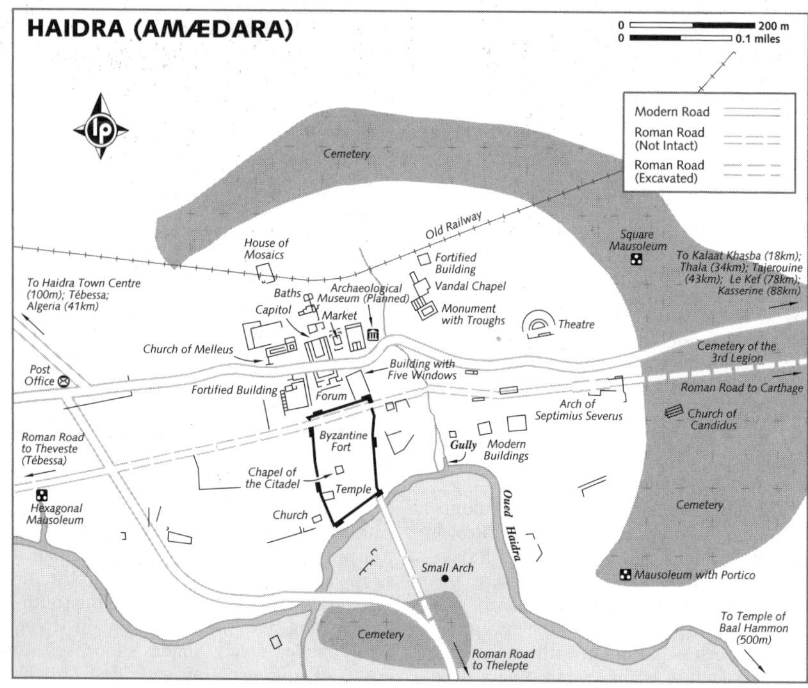

Ancient Ammædara

The road from Kalaat Khasba passes through the middle of the site, which is not enclosed and can be visited at any time. Admission is free but the amiable custodian appreciates a tip. There are plans to turn the former French customs house (1886), on the main road, into an **archaeological museum** featuring mosaics, inscribed gravestones and stone sarcophagi; it *may* open in 2007 or 2008.

The site, strewn with stone blocks, is dominated by the walls of an enormous **Byzantine fort**, built in AD 550. It straddles the old Roman road and extends down to the banks of Oued Haidra. The ruins of an earlier Roman temple are incorporated into the southwestern corner.

The principal Roman monument is the extremely well preserved **Arch of Septimius Severus**, which stands on the eastern edge of the site. It was built in AD 195 and remains in good condition because it was protected for centuries by a surrounding Byzantine wall. About 300m south of here, the **mausoleum**, with its portico, stands silhouetted on a small rise overlooking the *oued* (river).

The modern road passes over the old forum. A single giant column marks the site of the great temple that once stood at the **capitol**; right nearby are the remains of the old **baths** and the **market**.

Although the site is dotted with the ruins of numerous small churches, the only one that warrants serious inspection is the partially reconstructed **Church of Melleus**, just west of the forum, which has a rounded apse and two rows of columns separating the nave from the aisles. Originally built in the 4th century, it was later expanded by the Byzantines.

Getting There & Away

Getting to Haidra by public transport is a bit of a challenge but eminently doable, though don't count on finding any buses or louages out of town after mid-afternoon. From Kasserine or Le Kef, it's possible to visit both Haidra and Jugurtha's Table on a day trip if you catch your first bus or louage very early in the morning.

(Continued on page 177)

CRAIG PERSHOUSE

Illuminated clock tower (p77), Place du 7 Novembre, Ville Nouvelle, Tunis

ARIADNE VAN ZANDBERGEN

Zaytouna (Great) Mosque (p71) through traditionally tiled terrace window, Tunis

L'Acropolium (p93), Carthage, Tunis

CHRISTOPHER WOOD

BETHUNE CARM

Statues and mosaics (p47), Bardo Museum, Tunis

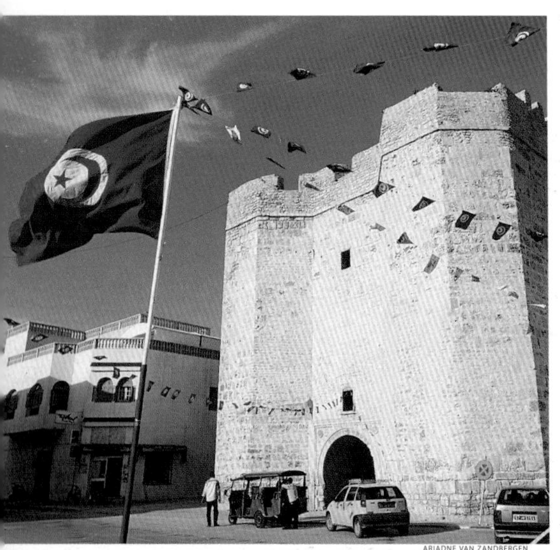

ARIADNE VAN ZANDBERGEN

Entrance to old medina (p103), Hammamet, Cap Bon

Statue of Venus from Carthage, Bardo Museum (p50), Tunis

ARIADNE VAN ZANDBERGEN

View across city buildings to Tabarka Island and its Genoese fort (p137)

BETHUNE CARMICHAEL

CHRISTOPHER WOOD

The sunken House of the Hunt (p146), Bulla Regia

Fishing boats in the old port (p125), Bizerte

DAMIEN SIMONIS

ARIADNE VAN ZANDBERGEN

Remains of Roman temple (p182), Sbeitla

Street leading to Zaouia of Sidi Abdallah Boumakhlouf (p162), Le Kef

JANE SWEENEY

Roman theatre (p156), Dougga

JANE SW

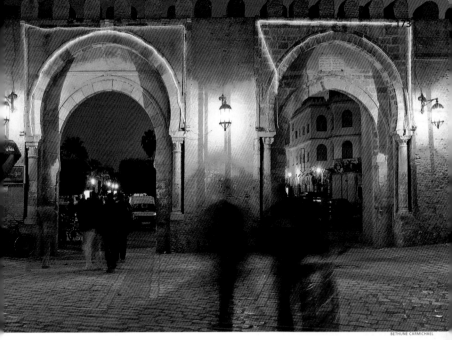

BETHUNE CARMICHAEL

Gateway to the medina (p202), Kairouan

Market stall selling brassware (p296)

VERONICA GARBUTT

CHRISTOPHER WOOD

Detail of mosaic (p47)

ANTHON

Ancient Berber hill-top village (p235), Ksour district

Jebel Dahar near Toujane (p230), south of Matmata

BETHUNE CARMICHAEL

ARIADNE VAN ZANDBERGEN

Berber woman, troglodyte (underground) home (p228), Matmata

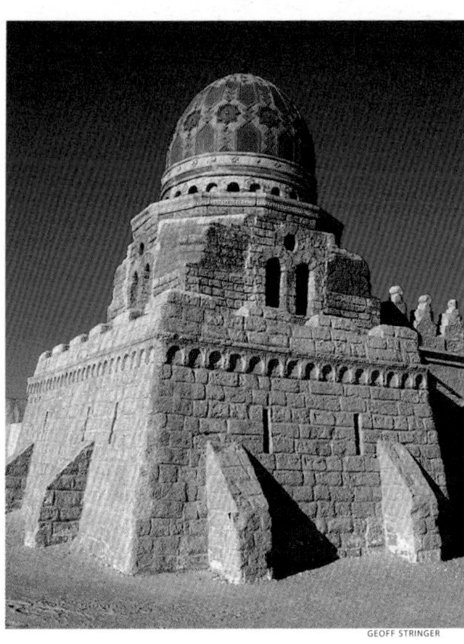

GEOFF STRINGER

Islamic military architecture (p53) near the Great Dune, Douz

CRAIG PERSHOUSE

Tuareg man at Sahara Festival, Douz (p243)

Stunt horsemen at Sahara Festival (p245), Douz

CRAIG PERSHOUSE

ARIADNE VAN ZANDE

Horse-riding acrobatics at traditional Berber (p234) wedding, Jerba

Talmudic scholar, El-Ghriba Synagogue (p277), Erriadh

ANTHONY HAM

Mosque (p53), Jerba

ARIADNE VAN ZANDE

(Continued from page 168)

Haidra is linked by louage with Kalaat Khasba (TD1, 15 minutes), 18km to the northeast, which is served by all Le Kef–Kasserine buses and by two daily trains from Tunis (TD10, five hours; departures in both directions are at around 6am and in the early afternoon).

An SRTK bus links Haidra with Kasserine (TD3.6, 2¼ hours, twice daily via Thala) – departures from Kasserine are at 6.45am and 9.30am; the last bus back leaves Haidra at 3.30pm.

Getting from Haidra to Jugurtha's Table involves taking three louages: one to Kalaat Khasba (TD1) – get off at the big roundabout on the Le Kef–Kasserine road; then one to Tajerouine (TD1.2), a distance of about 25km; and finally a third louage to Kalaat es-Senan (TD1.4), a further 27km.

JUGURTHA'S TABLE مايدرة يوغرطة

This spectacular flat-topped mountain (1271m), or mesa, rises almost vertically from the surrounding plains 98km northwest of Kasserine. Its sheer, impregnable walls make it a superb natural fortress and, indeed, the mountain bears the name of the ruthless Numidian king Jugurtha (p27), who used it as a base during his seven-year campaign against the Romans (112–105 BC).

Known as the Plateau de Jugurtha on some road signs, Jugurtha's Table can be seen from the Le Kef–Kasserine highway, between Tajerouine and Kalaat Khasba, on the far western horizon.

The only access to the summit is via a twisting set of steps hewn into the escarpment; the small gate at the base was added by the Byzantines. The reward for those who climb to the top is a spectacular view over the surrounding countryside; the hills you can see off to the west are across the border in Algeria. The small shrine honours a local *marabout* (holy man).

The gateway to Jugurtha's Table is the sleepy, low-rise town of **Kalaat es-Senan**, whose less-than-thriving local economy gets a lift from some smuggling from nearby Algeria. The walking route up the mesa (two hours return) starts 3km southeast of Kalaat es-Senan in the hamlet of **Ain Senan**, on the western side of the mountain. Take sufficient water because there's none to be found along the way.

Tourists are supposed to register at the friendly Garde Nationale (National Guard) office – *not* the same thing as the Police – on the main street of Kalaat es-Senan before they set out.

Two French-language websites with details on the area are www.jugurtha.com and www.kalaat.com.

Sleeping

It is permitted to camp atop Jugurtha's Table, making it possible to wake up to a spectacular sunrise. Make sure you bring *plenty* of water.

Otherwise, extremely basic accommodation is on offer at the eight-room **Hôtel Jugurtha** (☎ 78 296 356; s/d TD3/6), 200m south of the Garde Nationale office. The sign is in Arabic only. Reception is in the grocery and sheets are available on request. This place doubles as the only bar in town.

Another option is to stay in Tajerouine, 35km south of Le Kef, at the Hôtel de la République, on the main street a few hundred metres from the louage and taxi station.

Getting There & Around

Good sealed roads connect Kalaat es-Senan with Kalaat Khasba, 28km to the southeast, and Tajerouine, 27km to the northeast, both on the Le Kef–Kasserine road.

Buses to/from Le Kef stop in front of the Garde Nationale.

Red louages go to Tunis, while blue louages link Kalaat es-Senan with Le Kef and with Tajerouine, a stop on the bus line linking Le Kef (TD2, 45 minutes) with Kasserine (TD4, 1½ hours; last bus to Kasserine at about 4.45pm). For details on getting to Kalaat Khasba (linked to Tunis by two trains a day) and Haidra by louage, see p168.

A taxi from Kalaat es-Senan to Ain Senan costs TD0.5 per person (TD2 for the whole shebang).

KASSERINE القصرين

pop 38,000

Kasserine, famous for a WWII battle that raged just west of here (see p178), would be a strong contender in any poll to determine the dullest town in Tunisia. However, it does make an excellent base for exploring the remote western reaches of the country – including Sbeitla, Haidra, Jugurtha's Table and Chambi National Park (see opposite) – either by car or by public transport. If you come in winter bring warm clothing.

Kasserine's main industry is the production of high-quality paper from esparto grass (see boxed text, p180) – you'll see a mountain of the stuff, piled up waiting to be processed, at the steam- and smoke-belching factory a bit west of the centre of town.

Online information on Kasserine is available (in French) at www.kasserine.com.

Orientation & Information

Kasserine stretches for over 5km along east–west-oriented ave Habib Bourguiba, from the Cillium ruins, in the west, to the bus and louage station, in the east. The main square, place de l'Indépendance – also known as place de l'Ancienne Gare (Old Train Station Square) – is situated on ave Habib Bourguiba about 4km east of Cillium and 1.5km west of the bus station.

The four banks at place de l'Indépendance – Banque du Sud, Banque de l'Habitat, BNA and STB – all change money and have ATMs.

Post office (place de l'Indépendance)

Publinet (internet per hr TD1.5; 8am-2am) One short block north of place de l'Indépendance, next to the police station.

Publinet (ave Habib Bourguiba; internet per hr TD1.5; 8am-2am) Conveniently situated about 300m west of place de l'Indépendance in the Complexe Commercial, behind the pizzeria on the 1st floor overlooking the inner courtyard.

Sights

The minor Roman site of **Cillium** (admission free) was, like modern-day Kasserine, an important regional centre. The ruins are scattered over a wide area but are centred on a low hill overlooking the broad bed of Oued Dhrib, on the southwestern edge of town about 4km west of place de l'Indépendance.

The main features are a well-preserved **triumphal arch** and a large **theatre** carved into the hillside. Both date from the 3rd century, when Cillium was at the height of its prosperity. The **capitol** and **forum** are also identifiable, as are the main **baths**. The site is signposted to the east of the road to Gafsa, about 250m south of Hôtel Cillium.

Cillium's most famous monument, on ave Habib Bourguiba 3km west of the centre, is the **Mausoleum of the Flavii**. This triple-tiered monument to Flavius Secundus and his family, standing by the roadside, looks stunning at night when spotlights sometimes highlight the 110 lines of poetry inscribed on the bottom tier.

Every Tuesday a huge **open-air market** is held in the field across the street from the bus station.

Sleeping

Hôtel de la Paix (Nazal as-Salaam; ☎ 77 471 465; ave Habib Bourguiba; s/d with breakfast TD10/14) This friendly place, 50m east of place de l'Indépendance, is a bit noisy but clean. For a warm shower ask the guy at reception to turn on the gas heater.

Hôtel Amaïdra (☎ 77 470 750; fax 77 477 397; 232 ave 7 Novembre; s/d TD25/50;) With its exuberant

THE BATTLE OF KASSERINE PASS

In February 1943, the hills northwest of Kasserine, towards the Algerian town of Tébessa, were the site of WWII's first major confrontation between American and German ground forces.

In the Battle of Kasserine Pass, German Afrika Korps units – commanded, in part, by Field Marshal Erwin Rommel – tried to block the advance of the US Army's II Corps, which was moving eastward from Algeria into Nazi-occupied Tunisia. The inexperienced American forces suffered heavy casualties and were pushed back some 80km but American commanders quickly learned from their mistakes and implemented wide-ranging structural and strategic reforms. In the meantime, British forces advanced westward from Libya, setting the stage for the fall of Tunis – and the end of Axis power in North Africa – three months later.

The opening scene of the Academy Award–winning film *Patton* (1970) takes place immediately after the Battle of Kasserine Pass. More recently, a variety of computer games based on the battle have appeared.

To find original maps and sketches of the battle published by the US Army's Center of Military History, go to www.army.mil and search for 'Kasserine maps'.

CHAMBI NATIONAL PARK

About 15km west of Kasserine – that is, about halfway to the Algerian border – is Tunisia's highest mountain, **Jebel Chambi** (1544m), which is often snow-capped between December and March. The extreme weather doesn't seem to bother the Phoenician juniper, Aleppo pines or Holm oaks that flourish above 1000m, or the park's rich wildlife, which includes plentiful wild boars, endangered mountain gazelles (Cuvier's gazelles), striped hyenas, foxes, Barbary partridges and the recently reintroduced Barbary sheep. Hares and other small rodents have to keep a sharp eye out for peregrine falcons, Egyptian vultures, Bonelli's eagles and Eurasian sparrowhawks.

A biosphere reserve since 1977, the **Parc National du Djebel Chambi** (as the park is known in French) has seen a regeneration of plant life since it received protected status.

A rough track, suitable for 4WD vehicles, takes you up the mountain to 1300m. From there a trail leads to the summit (two hours), where you'll find a metal crescent erected by Tunisian boy scouts shortly after independence.

but awkward neo-Andalusian façade, this 30-room, two-star establishment – named after the ruins at Haidra – has 30 spacious but tastelessly furnished rooms with all-tile bathrooms. Opened in 2001, the building already feels several decades old. It's situated about six long blocks due west of place de l'Indépendance (ave 7 Novembre is four blocks north of ave Habib Bourguiba).

Hôtel Cillium (☎/fax 77 474 682; s/d TD30/40; ❄) Situated 4km west of place de l'Indépendance near the Cillium ruins (just off the road to Le Kef), this completely round hotel – which for some reason lacks a sign – has spacious, trapezium-shaped rooms arrayed around a central atrium. Virtually unchanged (though kept in pristine condition) since it was built in 1963, it's a classic of its architectural genre. It's easy to imagine jet-set French tourists in period bathing suits lounging around the long-disused pool, meticulously tiled in blue, and sliding down the now crumbling wooden slide.

Eating

Along the east side of place de l'Indépendance there are several **basic restaurants** with chickens roasting out front. The **pâtisserie** in the southeast corner of place de l'Indépendance sells – for breakfast – semolina porridge with halvah and crushed pistachios (TD1).

Pizzeria al-Amir al-Saghir (☎98 276 927, 20 236 999; ave Habib Bourguiba; pizzas TD2.8-5; 🕑 6am-midnight) Hugely popular with local young people who can afford it, this modern, international-style establishment, outfitted with red banquettes and a Starbucks-like café area, is named after Le Petit Prince, AKA the Little Prince. Food options include hamburgers (TD1.5 to TD2), crepes (TD0.8 to TD1.8) and *paninis* (TD1.5 to TD1.8). It's situated 300m west of place de l'Indépendance in the Complexe Commercial building.

The outdoor food market is a few hundred metres east of place de l'Indépendance, just off the main road.

Getting There & Away

The bus and louage stations are on the eastern outskirts of town (towards Sbeitla) about 1.5km from place de l'Indépendance.

SNTRI buses to Tunis (TD12.9, five hours, seven daily) pass by El-Fahs, near Thuburbo Majus.

The Société Régionale de Transport de Kasserine (SRTK) has services to Gabès (TD10.2, twice daily), Gafsa (TD4.5, five daily), Haidra (TD3.6, 2¼ hours, twice daily at 6.45am and 9.30am; last bus back at 3.30pm), Kairouan (TD6.6, three daily), Le Kef (TD5.6, two hours, five daily), Sbeitla, Sfax (TD8.2, four daily), Sousse (TD8.8, twice daily) and Thala (TD2.3, 1¼ hours, four daily).

Red louages go to Gafsa (TD5.8), Le Kef (TD6.6), Kairouan (TD6.5), Sfax, Sousse (TD10) and Tunis (TD13.5, four hours). To get to Gabès you'll probably have to change at Gafsa. Blue louages go to Sbeitla (TD1.7) and Thala; the latter is linked by louage with Haidra and, via Tajerouine, with Kalaat es-Senan (Jugurtha's Table).

Passenger trains link Kalaat Khasba, 65km north of Kasserine, with Tunis (TD10, five hours; departures in both directions are at around 6am and in the early afternoon).

ESPARTO GRASS

Never heard of it? That's hardly surprising – this tenacious, grey-green grass, one of the few plants that thrives in the harsh conditions of the Tunisian interior, hardly calls attention to itself. Wiry and narrow-bladed, *Stipa tenacissima* – as it's known, quite accurately, in Latin – grows to a height of about 1m in dense clumps topped by graceful, feathered seed heads. It's a popular water-saving garden plant in some parts of the world.

In ancient times, esparto was gathered and woven into a variety of household items, including mats, baskets and sandals. It was even strong and flexible enough to make ropes, animal harnesses and saddlebags.

These days, skilled artisans still make esparto into decorative baskets but commercially the tough, stiff leaves are exploited primarily for the production of high-quality book paper. Large areas of the countryside around Kasserine and Sbeitla are devoted to its cultivation, and you'll often see rows of women working their way across fields of esparto armed with small sickles.

In the past, raw esparto fibre was exported to places like Edinburgh for processing into paper. These days, though, the cut grass – 43,000 tonnes of which were produced in Tunisia in 2004 – is bailed and trucked to a huge paper factory in Kasserine.

A local bus from the bus and louage station into Kasserine costs TD0.3.

SBEITLA (SUFETULA) سبيطلة

pop 7500

Out in the middle of nowhere on the plains 107km southwest of Kairouan and 38km east of Kasserine, Sbeitla is home to the evocative ancient town of Sufetula, famous for its remarkably preserved Roman temples.

The drab modern town has very little going for it except for one really first-rate budget hotel.

History

Roman Sufetula, established at the beginning of the 1st century AD on the site of a Numidian settlement, seems to have followed an evolutionary path similar to that of other Roman towns in the region, such as Ammædara (Haidra) and Mactaris (Makthar).

The surrounding countryside proved ideal for olive growing (it still is) and Sufetula quickly waxed wealthy, building its finest temples in the 2nd century, when the town – like all of Roman Tunisia – was at the height of its prosperity. Fortuitously, its olive groves ensured that Sufetula continued to prosper long after other Roman towns slipped into decline, helping it to become an important Christian centre in the 4th century.

The Byzantines made Sufetula their regional capital, transforming it into a military stronghold from where they could tackle the area's rebellious local tribes. It was here in AD 647 that Prefect Gregory declared himself independent of Constantinople. However, his moment of glory lasted only a few months before he was killed by the Arabs, who simultaneously destroyed much of Sufetula. The Arab victory is celebrated with the **Festival of the Seven Abdullahs**, held in the last week of July.

Orientation & Information

The Sufetula ruins are about 1km north (towards Kasserine) from the modern town, whose French street grid is almost as regular as Sufetula's Roman one. The main street is northwest–southeast-oriented ave de la Libération.

The entrance to the archaeological site is across the road from the museum and the new Complexe Touristique, which houses the **tourist office desk** (☎ 77 466 506; approximately 8am-noon & 3-6pm, no midday closure in summer), a café and Publinet centre for internet access.

Sufetula

The **ruins** (☎ 77 465 813; admission TD2.1, plus camera TD1; 7am-7pm Apr–mid-Sep, 8am-5.30pm mid-Sep–Mar) are especially spectacular early in the morning, when the temples glow orange.

The **museum** (Tue-Sun), across the road from the site, has some fine mosaics and a statue of Bacchus reclining on a panther, discovered at the theatre.

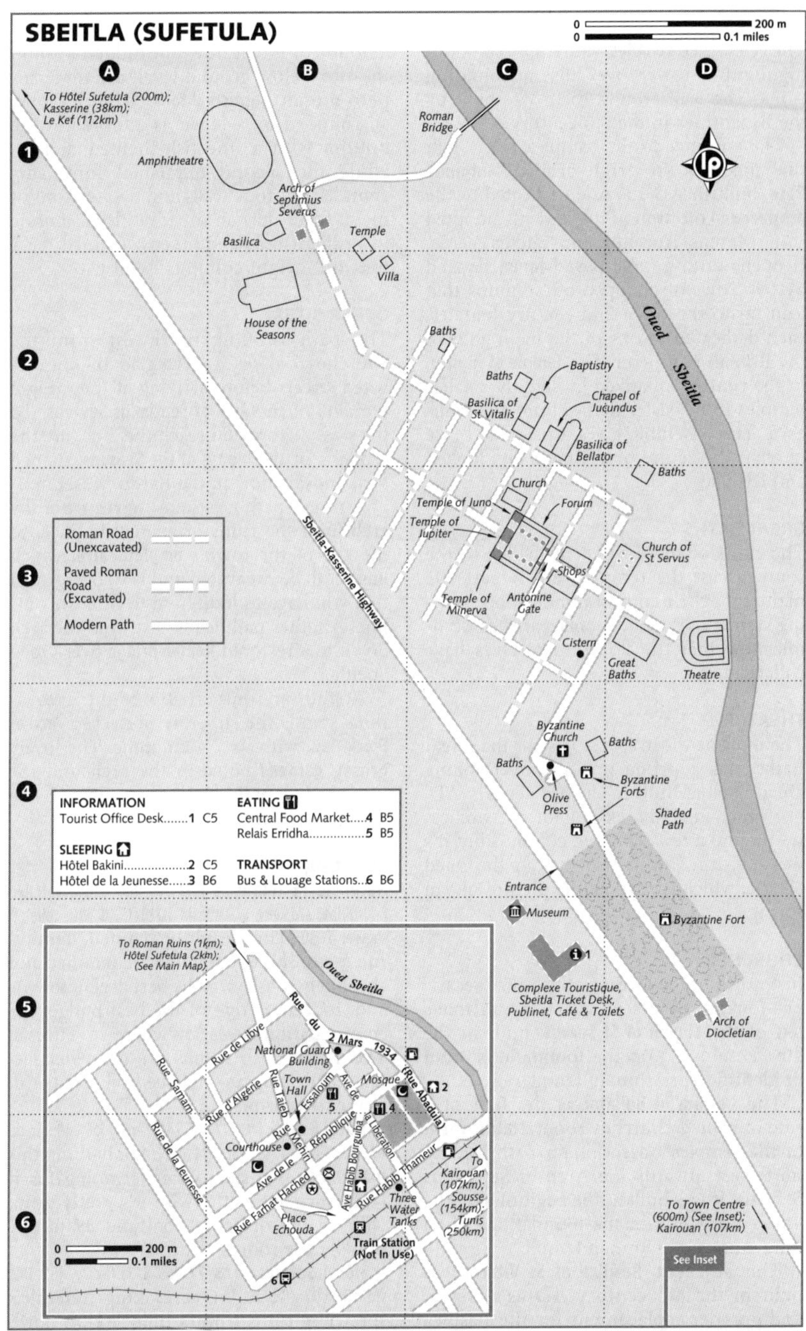
SBEITLA (SUFETULA)
0 200 m
0 0.1 miles
To Hôtel Sufetula (200m); Kasserine (38km); Le Kef (112km)
Amphitheatre
Roman Bridge
Arch of Septimius Severus
Basilica
Temple
Villa
House of the Seasons
Oued Sbeitla
Baths
Baptistry
Basilica of St Vitalis
Chapel of Jucundus
Basilica of Bellator
Baths
Church
Temple of Juno
Forum
Temple of Jupiter
Church of St Servus
Shops
Temple of Minerva
Antonine Gate
Sbeitla-Kasserine Highway
Cistern
Great Baths
Theatre
Roman Road (Unexcavated)
Paved Roman Road (Excavated)
Modern Path
Byzantine Church
Baths
Baths
Byzantine Forts
Olive Press
Shaded Path
INFORMATION
Tourist Office Desk.......1 C5
SLEEPING
Hôtel Bakini..................2 C5
Hôtel de la Jeunesse.....3 B6
EATING
Central Food Market....4 B5
Relais Erridha................5 B5
TRANSPORT
Bus & Louage Stations..6 B6
Entrance
Museum
Byzantine Fort
Complexe Touristique, Sbeitla Ticket Desk, Publinet, Café & Toilets
Arch of Diocletian
To Roman Ruins (1km); Hôtel Sufetula (2km); (See Main Map)
Oued Sbeitla
Rue du 2 Mars 1934 (Rue Abadula)
Rue de Libye
National Guard Building
Rue Samam
Rue d'Algérie
Rue Taieb
Town Hall
Rue Essaloum
Ave de la Libération
Mosque
Rue de la Jeunesse
Rue Mehiri
Courthouse
Ave de la République
Ave Habib Bourguiba
Rue Habib Thameur
Rue Farhat Hached
Place Echouda
Three Water Tanks
Train Station (Not In Use)
To Kairouan (107km); Sousse (154km); Tunis (250km)
To Town Centre (600m) (See Inset); Kairouan (107km)
See Inset

TEMPLES

The celebrated **temples** – Sufetula's standout highlight – tower over the surrounding ruins. The wall around them was built by the Byzantines in the 6th century AD.

The entrance to the complex is through the magnificent triple-arched **Antonine Gate**, built in AD 139 and dedicated to the emperor Antoninus Pius and his adopted sons Marcus Aurelius and Lucius Verus. It opens onto a large paved **forum** flanked by two rows of chopped-off columns that lead up to the three 2nd-century temples, each dedicated to one of the main gods of the Roman pantheon. The **Temple of Jupiter**, in the centre, is flanked by slightly smaller temples to his sister deities Juno and Minerva. The ensemble gives a palpable sense of what the centre of a Roman city looked and felt like.

GREAT BATHS

The ruins of these extensive baths, to the southeast of the temples, are remarkable mainly for their complex under-floor heating system in the hot rooms, easily discernible now that the floors themselves have collapsed.

THEATRE

The ancient theatre, just east of the Great Baths, has a prime position overlooking Oued Sbeitla. Built in the 3rd century AD, not much remains except for the orchestra pit and a few scattered columns but it's worth visiting for the views along the Oued Sbeitla, which is particularly picturesque in spring.

CHURCHES

Just north of the Great Baths, four precarious-looking pillars of stone are all that's left of the **Church of St Servus**, built in the 4th century AD on the foundations of an unidentified pre-Roman temple.

The **Basilica of Bellator** is the first of a row of ruined churches about 100m north of the temples on the main path leading northwest towards the Arch of Septimius Severus. It was built at the beginning of the 4th century AD on the foundations of an unidentified pre-Roman temple.

The adjacent **Basilica of St Vitalis** was built in the 6th century AD as a bigger and grander replacement for the Basilica of Bellator. The basilica itself doesn't amount to much now but hidden around the site, below ground level, are three superb mosaic **baptismal fonts**. The first one, surrounded by a fence, is adorned at the bottom with a fine fish-themed mosaic, while the second baptismal font, surrounded by stone walls and two sections of metal fence, has an intricate floral mosaic in brilliant reds and greens. A third, near four full-height columns, is all white.

OTHER SITES

The path running northwest from the churches crosses a neat grid of unexcavated streets before arriving at the meagre remains of the **Arch of Septimius Severus**. To the west, before you reach the arch, are the remains of the **House of the Seasons**, named for a mosaic now in the Bardo Museum.

A rough path continues north from the arch, past the ruins of a small basilica, to the site of the town's **amphitheatre**, which has yet to be excavated and is so overgrown that you have to look hard to find the outline. Another path leads east from the arch down to a restored **Roman bridge** over Oued Sbeitla.

At the far southern tip of the excavations stands the superbly preserved **Arch of Diocletian**, with its 7½ columns. The lovely grassy **gardens** between the arch and the tree-shaded pathway just inside the site entrance are perfect for a picnic

Sleeping

Hôtel de la Jeunesse (☎ 77 466 528; ave Habib Bourguiba; s/d with washbasin TD10/18, d with toilet & shower TD30) This brightly painted, family-run establishment, lovingly maintained and absolutely spotless, is the best deal in town – and, indeed, is one of the best budget accommodation deals anywhere in Tunisia. The 12 smallish rooms are off a delightful, North African–style central courtyard, home to a tortoise.

Hôtel Bakini (☎ 77 465 244; fax 77 465 048; rue du 2 Mars 1934; s/d TD35/50; ❄) The only thing this ostensibly two-star place has going for it is the air-con – otherwise it's pretty grim, with an out-of-order pool and 39 utterly uninspiring rooms.

Hôtel Sufetula (☎ 77 465 311; fax 77 465 582; s/d TD64/92; ❄ 🏊) Overlooking Sufetula's sprawling ruins from a hillock 2km north of the town centre (towards Kasserine), this extremely comfortable, pleasingly modern, three-star hotel has spotless rooms with balconies.

Eating

Fruits and vegies are sold at the **central food market** (cnr ave de la Libération & rue de la République). There are several cafés along ave de la Libération.

Relais Erridha (☎ 77 467 500; rue Essaloum; mains TD3-6; 7am-midnight) Opened in 2006, this sparkling, spotless restaurant has cheerful blue-and-white tiling – in fact, it has cheerful blue-and-white everything. It serves meat and fish mains, sandwiches and several kinds of cake.

Getting There & Away

Buses and louages leave from a lot on the southern edge of town, off rue Habib Thameur. Bus destinations include Le Kef (TD7, four daily), Kairouan (TD6, 1½ hours, two daily), Kasserine (25 minutes, frequent) and Tunis (TD12, four hours, four daily). Frequent louages go to Kairouan (TD6), Kasserine (TD1.7, 25 minutes), Sousse (TD9) and Tunis (TD12).

The Central Coast & Kairouan

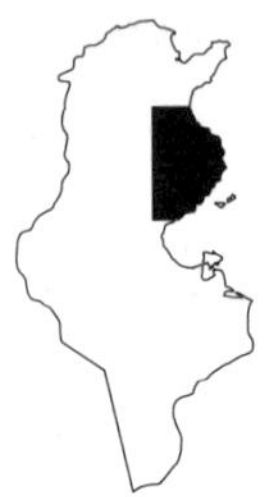

Considered by many to be the heartland of Tunisia and home to one of Islam's most important mosques, several of the country's largest beach resorts and its most impressive Roman monument, this region is hardly lacking in superlatives. Its diversity, from fortified ancient medinas to exclusive modern beach resorts, from religious conservatism to western hedonism, from bastions of the tourist-industrial-complex to quiet, timeless villages, is belied by the short commute it takes to get from one to the other. This is the Tunisia of postcards and brochures, where architecture and landscapes unchanged for centuries meet facilities designed for the busloads of foreign visitors that fuel much of the economy.

The fortified medinas of the central coast, which once protected these cities that became wealthy from the trade of the Mediterranean and the Sahara, house Tunisians going about their everyday lives in what, to the average foreigner's eye, looks like an elaborate and exotic Hollywood set. Each is distinctive: Sfax's is the least touched by tourism, Mahdia's looks like a Greek fishing village and is by far the most inviting, Sousse's is a shopping Mecca and Monastir's the birthplace and final resting place for the country's independence leader, Habib Bourguiba.

It is also Tunisia's Islamic heartland, with Kairouan ranking only behind Mecca, Medina and Jerusalem as one of the holiest cities of Islam. The well preserved colosseum of El-Jem rivals that of Rome's in terms of sheer size but may be an even more spectacular, and certainly more incongruous, sight. During the summer months the beach resorts along the Mediterranean become the holiday playground for what seems to be all of Europe.

HIGHLIGHTS

- Become part of the vast parade taking a sunset stroll along the promenade of Sousse's **Boujaffar Beach** (p191)
- Be rendered speechless standing in the middle of North Africa's most impressive Roman monument, El-Jem's awesome **colosseum** (p208)
- Breathe in the sea air while wandering the shady cobblestone streets of the charming medina at **Mahdia** (p211)
- Listen for the call to prayer in the holy Islamic city of **Kairouan** (p199)
- Indulge in the cosmopolitan luxury at the beach resort of **Port el-Kantaoui** (p195)
- Explore the bustling alleyways of the best medina in the country, to see how residents of these ancient cities live and work, in **Sfax** (p215)

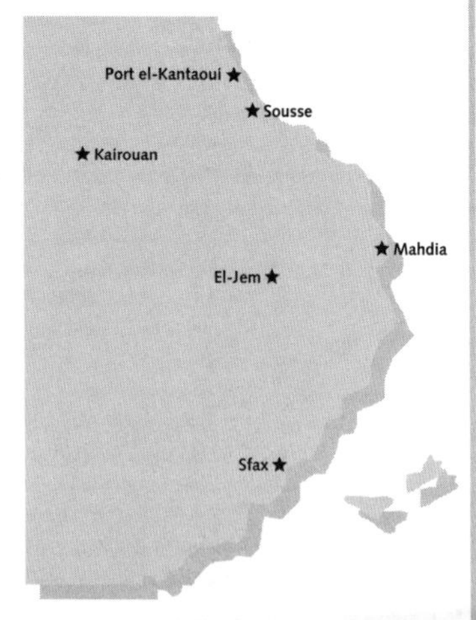

History

The Sahel, the large coastal bulge between the Gulf of Hammamet and the Gulf of Gabès, has always been a battleground for other people's wars. Sousse, the home base of Hannibal in the Carthaginian battles against the Romans, again found itself on the losing side when Pompey made it his headquarters in his doomed civil war against Julius Caesar (based at Monastir). It was finally destroyed by the first wave of Islamic armies that swept across North Africa in the 7th century. These Islamic armies founded the holy city of Kairouan and ushered in the reign of Islamic dynasties, the most productive of which were the Aghlabids (who left a splendid architectural legacy in all of the coastal towns) and the Cairo-based Fatimids (whose mark can still be seen in Mahdia).

For some reason, the indigenous Berbers took umbrage at their traditional land being taken over by foreigners. Whether confronted with the Roman Empire from the north or the Islamic dynasties from the east, they fought them all, mounting rebellion after rebellion, one of which destroyed Kairouan. During another, they held out against vastly superior numbers in the colosseum of El-Jem.

In modern Tunisian history, Monastir is revered as the birthplace of the nation's founder, Habib Bourguiba.

Climate

Tunisia's central coast gets very hot in summer but you're never too far from a sea breeze. The further you go inland, the hotter it gets – Kairouan and El-Jem bake in summer, but can be quite cold in winter.

Getting There & Away

All the towns covered in this chapter are well-connected to the rest of the country by bus, louage (shared taxi) and (apart from Kairouan) train, which is easily the most comfortable and convenient mode of travel. Many buses heading north or south originate elsewhere and are often full by the time they arrive here.

Getting Around

Again, louage or train are the easiest ways to get around. There are no direct connections between Kairouan and either El-Jem or Mahdia, while visiting El-Jem at sunset requires some planning (see the boxed text, p208).

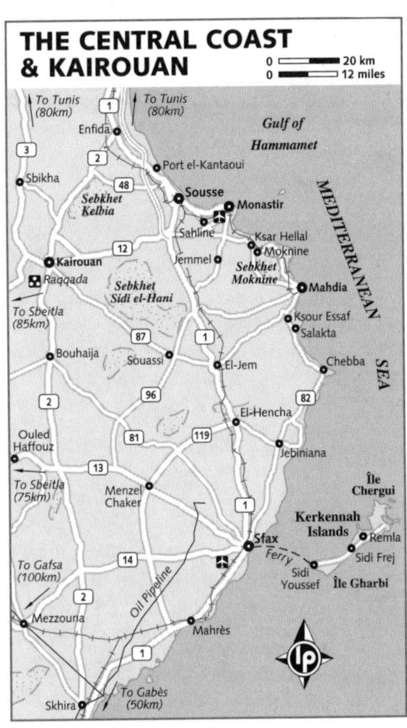

SOUSSE سوسة

pop 173,000

This raucous city – by Tunisian standards – doesn't make a great first impression. The city centre mix of modern high-rise buildings and derelict port do nothing to explain Sousse's popularity. However, once you're settled in and you've grabbed your beach towel, the seductive simplicity of the warm water, the soft sand and the ready availability of all manner of quick bites becomes apparent. Throw in a vibrant medina with several historical and religious sites and an enormous selection of hotels and it's easy to understand why Sousse is one of the country's most highly touted holiday destinations.

In the summer it feels like Europeans outnumber Tunisians. The dress code, especially for Tunisian women, is more liberal here than other parts of the country. During the day, the beach is packed with Tunisians and foreigners alike, but it's from

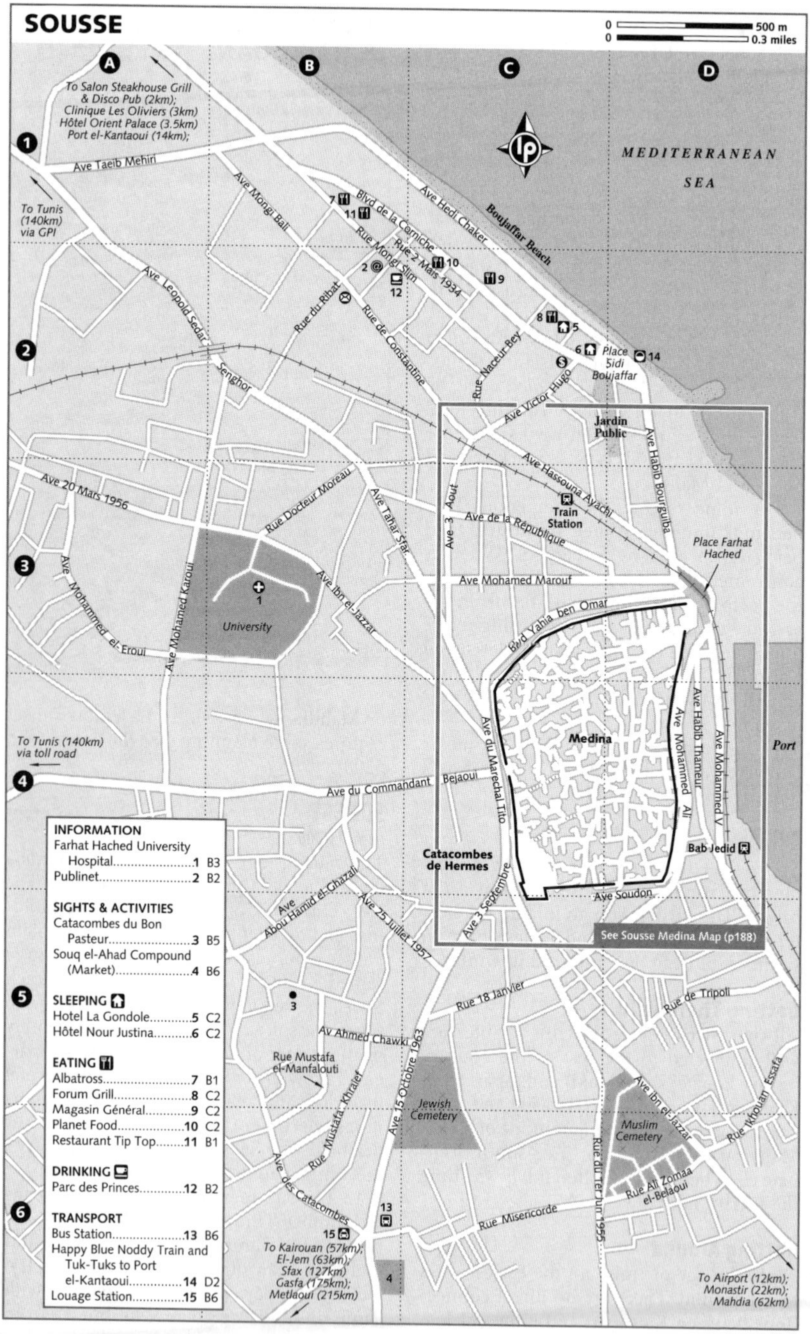

SOUSSE

INFORMATION
Farhat Hached University Hospital......1 B3
Publinet......2 B2

SIGHTS & ACTIVITIES
Catacombes du Bon Pasteur......3 B5
Souq el-Ahad Compound (Market)......4 B6

SLEEPING
Hotel La Gondole......5 C2
Hôtel Nour Justina......6 C2

EATING
Albatross......7 B1
Forum Grill......8 C2
Magasin Général......9 C2
Planet Food......10 C2
Restaurant Tip Top......11 B1

DRINKING
Parc des Princes......12 B2

TRANSPORT
Bus Station......13 B6
Happy Blue Noddy Train and Tuk-Tuks to Port el-Kantaoui......14 D2
Louage Station......15 B6

early evening till late when Boujaffar Beach really comes alive and young people and families take part in a nightly ritual, essentially the equivalent of teenagers cruising up and down the strip.

The Ville Nouvelle streets are lined with hotels and restaurants. Inevitably shops in the medina cater more to tourists than to residents.

History

Founded in the 9th century BC as the Phoenician outpost of Hadrumète, Sousse fell under the sway of Carthage from the middle of the 6th century BC. The famous Carthaginian general Hannibal used the town as his base against the Romans in the final stages of the Second Punic War in 202 BC.

The town allied itself with Rome during the Third (and final) Punic War (see History, p24), but Hadrumètum, as it became known, later chose the wrong side when it became Pompey's base during the Roman civil war, and suffered badly after his forces were defeated by Julius Caesar at the Battle of Thapsus in AD 46. Sousse's formidable defences proved of little use when it was levelled, wall and all, by Okba ibn Nafaa al-Fihri, falling to the Arabs in the late 7th century. Rebuilt as the Arab town of Soussa, it became the main port of the 9th-century Aghlabid dynasty based in Kairouan.

By the time the French arrived in 1881, it had declined to a modest settlement of just 8000 people.

Orientation

Life in Sousse revolves around two very different landscapes. The first is the medina, with its maze-like cobblestone streets containing many sights of historical and religious interest and a fair number of hotels. The second is Boujaffar Beach, running from just north of the port all of the way to Port el-Kantaoui and beyond. The pedestrian promenade that runs alongside ave Hedi Chaker and parallel to the beach is stop and go for much of the time during the summer months. Blvd de la Corniche is behind ave Hedi Chaker and is where many of the hotels, restaurants, banks and shops are found. Ave Habib Bourguiba connects the two different parts of Sousse to place Farhat Hached in the south and place Sidi Boujaffar in the north.

Information

INTERNET ACCESS

Publinet rue Remada (Map p188; 2nd fl, rue Remada; per hr TD2; 🕑 8am-midnight); Mongi Slim (Map p186; per hr TD2; 🕑 9.30am-midnight); ave Mohamed Maarouf (Map p188; per hr TD2; 🕑 8am-10pm Mon-Sat, noon-10pm Sun) The latter, near the post office is the largest and has the fastest connections.

MEDICAL SERVICES

Clinique Les Oliviers (☎ 73 242 711) North of town; it is more used to dealing with insurance forms.

Farhat Hached University Hospital (Map p186; ☎ 73 221 411; ave Ibn el-Jazzar) The city's main hospital, northwest of the medina.

MONEY

Almost all of Tunisia's banks have branches here; many are located along ave Habib Bourguiba and blvd de la Corniche and almost all have ATMs.

POST & TELEPHONE

There are quite a few Taxiphone offices around the city centre and along rue de la Corniche.

Main post office (Map p188; ave Mohamed Maarouf) Just up from place Farhat Hached.

TOURIST INFORMATION

Tourist office (Map p188; ☎ 73 25 157; fax 73 224 262; 1 ave Habib Bourguiba; 🕑 7am-7pm Mon-Sat & 9am-noon Sun summer, 8.30am-1pm & 3-5.45pm Mon-Thu & 8.30am-1.30pm Fri & Sat winter) An unusually efficient branch, on the north side of place Farhat Hached. Has useful maps and a notice board with timetables for buses and trains and opening hours of local attractions. Staff speak a variety of languages, including English.

Sights & Activities

MEDINA

An attraction as stimulating as the beach is relaxing, Sousse's medina, outside the one in Tunis, probably has the most interesting combination of religious and historical monuments and lively commercial activity. Where one ends and the other begins is sometimes hard to discern.

The walls of Sousse's fine old medina stretch 2.25km at a height of 8m and are fortified with a series of solid square turrets. They were built by the Aghlabids in AD 859 on the foundations of the city's original Byzantine walls. Within the walls are 24 mosques (12 for men and 12 for women)

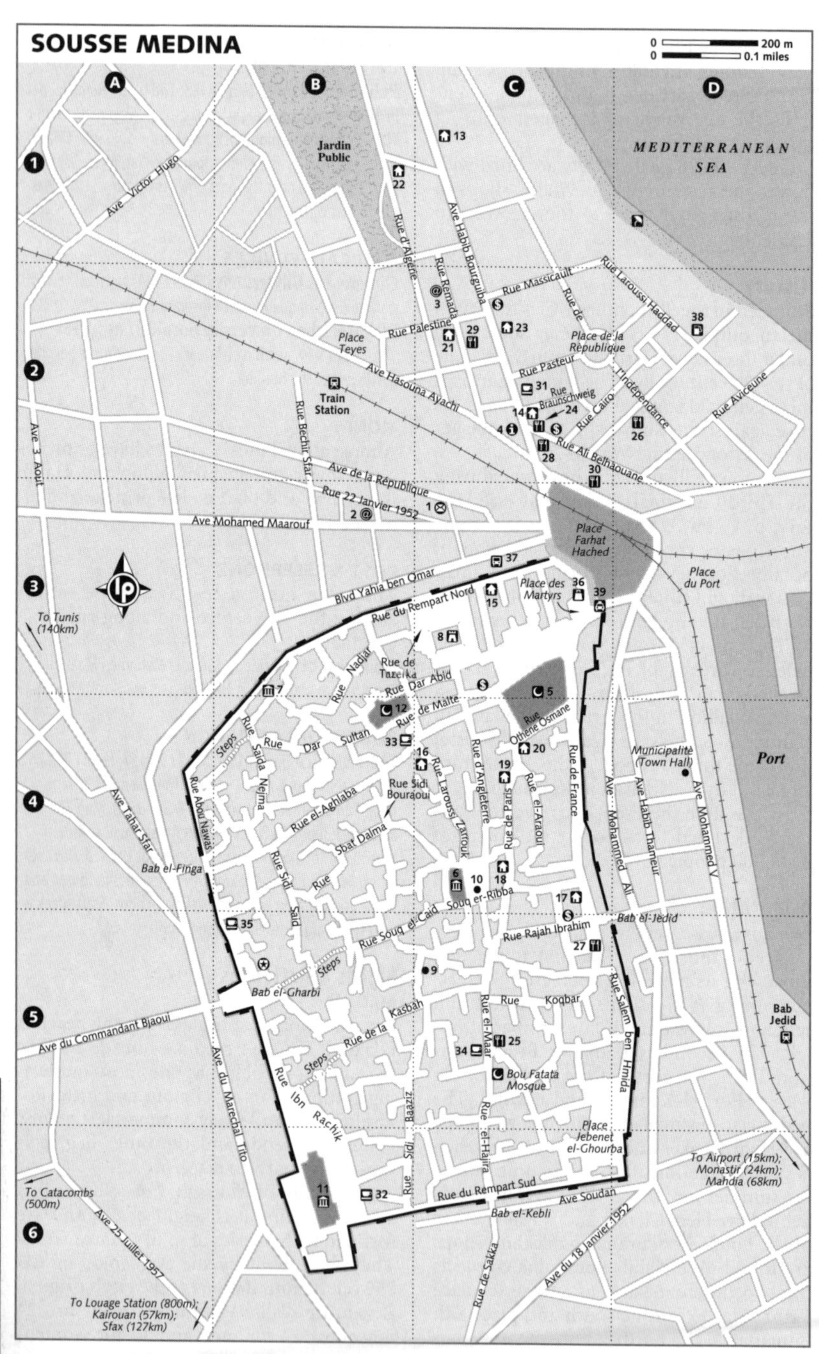
SOUSSE MEDINA
0 200 m
0 0.1 miles
MEDITERRANEAN SEA
Jardin Public
Ave Victor Hugo
Rue d'Algérie
Rue Remada
Ave Habib Bourguiba
Rue Massicault
Rue Laroussi Haddad
Rue de
Place de la République
Rue Palestine
Place Teyes
Ave Hasouna Ayachi
Train Station
Rue Pasteur
Rue Braunschweig
Rue Cairo
l'Indépendance
Rue Aviceune
Rue Ali Belhaouane
Rue Bechir Sfar
Ave 3 Août
Ave de la République
Rue 22 Janvier 1952
Ave Mohamed Maarouf
Place Farhat Hached
Place du Port
Blvd Yahia ben Omar
Rue du Rempart Nord
Place des Martyrs
To Tunis (140km)
Rue Nadjar
Rue de Tazerka
Rue Dar Abid
Rue de Malte
Rue Othene Osmane
Rue Dar Sultan
Rue Saida Nejma
Steps
Rue Abou Nawas
Rue Laroussi Zarrouk
Rue d'Angleterre
Rue de Paris
Rue el-Araoui
Rue de France
Municipalité (Town Hall)
Port
Ave Mohammed Ali
Ave Habib Thameur
Ave Mohammed V
Ave Tahar Sfar
Rue Sidi Bouraoui
Rue el-Aghlaba
Sbat Dalma
Bab el-Finga
Rue Sidi Saïd
Soug er-Ribba
Rue Souq el-Caid
Bab el-Jedid
Rue Rajah Ibrahim
Bab el-Gharbi
Rue Koqbar
Rue Salem ben Hmida
Ave du Commandant Bjaoui
Rue de la Kasbah
Rue el-Maar
Bab Jedid
Bou Fatata Mosque
Rue Ibn Rachik
Ave du Marechal Tito
Rue Sidi Baaziz
Rue el-Hajira
Place Jebenet el-Ghourba
To Airport (15km); Monastir (24km); Mahdia (68km)
To Catacombs (500m)
Rue du Rempart Sud
Ave Soudan
Bab el-Kebli
Ave 25 Juillet 1957
Ave du 18 Janvier 1952
Rue de Sakka
To Louage Station (800m); Kairouan (57km); Sfax (127km)

INFORMATION	
Main Post Office	1 C3
Publinet	2 B3
Publinet	3 C2
Tourist Office	4 C2
SIGHTS & ACTIVITIES	
Great Mosque	5 C3
Kalat el-Koubba	6 C4
Museum Dar Essid	7 B3
Ribat	8 C3
Sofra Cistern	9 C5
Souq er-Ribba	10 C4
Sousse Archaeological Museum & Kasbah	11 B6
Zaouia Zakkak	12 B4
SLEEPING	
Hotel Abou Nawas Boujafaar	13 C1
Hôtel Claridge	14 C2
Hôtel de Paris	15 C3
Hôtel el-Aghlaba	16 C4
Hôtel Emira	17 C4
Hôtel Ezzouhour	18 C4
Hôtel Gabès	19 C4
Hôtel Medina	20 C4
Hôtel Residence Monia	21 C2
Hôtel Sousse Azur	22 B1
Hôtel Sousse Palace	23 C2
EATING	
Caracas	24 C2
Dodo Restaurant	25 C5
Magasin Général	26 D2
Market	27 C5
Monoprix Supermarket	28 C2
Restaurant Du Peuple	(see 15)
Restaurant Marmite	29 C2
Restaurants	30 C2
DRINKING	
Café Theatre Municipal	31 C2
Café des Nomades	32 B6
Café Sidi Bouraoui	33 B4
Café Yasmine	34 C5
Restaurant-Café Seles	35 B5
SHOPPING	
Soula Shopping Centre	36 C3
TRANSPORT	
Buses to Mahdia, Monastir & Port el-Kantaoui	37 C3
Local Buses	(see 37)
Petrol Station	38 D2
Taxi Rank	39 C3
Tunisair	(see 31)

and a wealth of historical landmarks well worth seeking out.

The main entrance to the medina is at the northeastern corner at place des Martyrs. The area was created when Allied bombs blew away this section of the wall in 1943. Of the other gates, the most historically interesting is **Bab el-Finga** (*bab* means gate and *finga* means blade in Arabic); the French set up their guillotine outside the gate.

GREAT MOSQUE

The **Great Mosque** (Map p188; admission TD1.1; 8am-2.30pm Sat-Thur, 8am-12.30pm Fri summer, 8am-2.30pm daily winter) is a typically austere Aghlabid affair. It was built, according to a Kufic (early Arabic) inscription in the courtyard, in AD 851 by a freed slave called Mudam, on the instructions of the Aghlabid ruler Abul Abbas. Mudam adapted an earlier kasbah (fort), which explains the mosque's turrets and crenellated wall, as well as its unusual location; the great mosque is usually sited in the centre of a medina. The mosque is also unusual in that it has no minaret; its proximity to the *ribat* (fortified Islamic monastery) meant that the latter's tower could be used to call the faithful to prayer. The structure underwent 17th-century modifications and 20th-century restoration.

Non-Muslims aren't allowed beyond the courtyard but from there you can see the grand barrel-vaulted prayer hall.

RIBAT

The **ribat** (Map p188; admission TD2.1, plus camera TD1; 8am-6pm summer, 8am-7pm winter) is northwest of the mosque and is the oldest monument in the medina, built in the final years of the 8th century AD.

The entrance is through a narrow arched doorway flanked by weathered columns salvaged from the ruins of Roman Hadrumètum. The small **antechamber** was the last line of the building's defences – from high above the columns, projectiles and boiling liquids were rained down on intruders. A vaulted passage opens out into a courtyard surrounded by porticos. The *ribat,* designed principally as a fort, was garrisoned by devout Islamic warriors who would divide their time between fighting and silent study of the Quran in the tiny, cell-like rooms built into the walls. The **prayer hall** on the first floor has an elegant vaulted ceiling and reflects this dual purpose with a simple *mihrab* (the prayer niche in the mosque wall that indicates the direction of Mecca, this is one of the oldest in North Africa) and fortified windows that were used by archers.

Scramble up the narrow 76-step spiral staircase of the *nador* (watch tower), which was added by the Aghlabids in AD 821, for unparalleled views over the medina up the hill to the kasbah and down into the courtyard of the Great Mosque.

ZAOUIA ZAKKAK

The splendid octagonal stone minaret belongs to the 17th-century **Zaouia Zakkak** (Map p188; cnr rue Dar Abid & rue de Tazerka), the medina's leading example of Ottoman architecture. Non-Muslims can do no more than admire from the street the minaret's wonderful blue-green stone and tile work, with its echoes of Andalusia.

SOFRA CISTERN

This great underground cistern (Map p188), once the medina's principle water supply, was created in the 11th century by enclosing a large Byzantine church. It's an eerie place with the columns of the church rising from the black waters. The entrance is on the northeastern side, but the battered old metal door is often locked.

SOUQ ER-RIBBA

This souq (market) is the closest Sousse comes to a medieval bazaar. The roof is unmistakably modern, yet the sales-pitch beneath it is age-old. Far from the tranquillity of the southern medina, Souq er-Ribba (Map p188) forms the commercial heart of the medina. The place is a riot of colour, packed with haggling merchants, browsing tourists and barrow boys trying to squeeze through with their improbably overloaded carts. This is not the world's most evocative bazaar but worth exploring nonetheless.

KALAT EL-KOUBBA

The **Koubba** (a small domed tomb; Map p188; ☎ 73 229 574; rue Laroussi Zarrouk; admission TD2.1, plus camera/video TD1/3; 🕒 10am-1pm & 3-6pm summer, 10am-1pm & 4.30-7.30pm Sat-Thu winter) was an ancient *funduq* (*caravanserai* or inn) and the rooms surrounding the courtyard are now given over to mannequin displays of day-to-day life under the Ottomans. It's thought to have been built in the late 11th century AD. The most striking feature is the cupola with its remarkable zigzag ribbing; the fluted interior is also impressive.

SOUSSE ARCHAEOLOGICAL MUSEUM & KASBAH

Sousse's excellent archaeological **museum** (Map p188; ☎ 73 219 011; ave du Maréchal Tito; admission TD2.1, plus camera TD1; 🕒 9am-noon & 2-6pm Tue-Sun summer, 8am-noon & 3-7pm Tue-Sun winter) occupies the southern section of the kasbah.

One of the best collections of mosaics in the country is housed in the rooms around the kasbah's two main courtyards. The highlight is the room on the northern side of the entrance courtyard with exceptional exhibits, including the *Triumph of Bacchus*, which depicts the Roman god of wine riding in a chariot at the head of a parade of satyrs, as well as many superb fishing scenes. Other rooms contain a collection of funerary objects from a Punic grave beneath the museum and a resident artist demonstrating the patient and painstaking artistry of mosaic-making.

Standing at the high point of the medina, the kasbah was built onto the city walls in the 11th century. It incorporates the imposing square **Khalef tower**, built by the Aghlabids in AD 859 at the same time as the city walls, which superseded the *ribat* as the city's watchtower. It's now a lighthouse.

Note that there is no entrance from inside the medina walls.

MUSEUM DAR ESSID

This small, private **museum** (Map p188; ☎ 73 220 529; 65 rue du Remparts Nord; admission TD2, plus camera TD1; 🕒 10am-1pm & 3-6pm summer, 10am-7pm winter) is also not to be missed. In a quiet part of the medina, it occupies a beautiful old home, furnished in the style of a well-to-do 19th-century Sousse official and his family. The dimensions of the elaborately decorated, arched door are the first indication of the owner's status. It opens into a small anteroom for meeting strangers, and then into a tiled courtyard surrounded by the family rooms. A plaque in the courtyard reveals that the house was built in AD 928, making it one of the oldest in the medina. There's an extravagance reflected in the Andalusian tiled façades and items ranging from European antique furniture to traditional perfume bottles, from decorative plaster work to a 700-year-old wedding contract, and marble from Carrara in Italy. Check out the Roman lamp with the graphic depiction of a copulating couple; it's by the master bed to remind the husband to demonstrate his control and stamina until the lamp went out.

The upstairs area, reached by a heavily restored staircase, is the old servant's quarters and there's a pleasant café with splendid panoramic views. It's a good place to catch the breeze.

CATACOMBS

The **catacombs** (Map p186; ave des Catacombes; admission TD1.1; 9am-noon & 2-6pm Tue-Sun summer, 8am-noon & 3-7pm winter) include an estimated 5.5km of tunnels containing the graves of more than 15,000 local Christians, mostly from the 4th and 5th centuries AD. The only section open to the public is about 100m of the Catacombes du Bon Pasteur, named after an engraving of the *bon pasteur* (good shepherd) found inside. Most of the graves have been bricked in; a few have glass fronts, revealing skeletal remains.

BOUJAFFAR BEACH

Sousse's **Boujaffar Beach** (Map p186), with its multikilometre stretch of high-rise hotels, cafés and restaurants, is the city's landmark. Named somewhat incongruously after a local Muslim holy man, the soft, sandy strip is a playground where families picnic, children frolic, foreigners sunbathe and the warm, calm waters of the Mediterranean is everyone's bathtub. Only a few small parts of the strip are claimed by beachfront hotels with chaise longues and parasols. Though these are usually not roped off, they are 'protected' by staff that generally looks kindly on foreigners while tending to treat rudely any Tunisians who wander through. Access to these areas is generally open to nonhotel guests for a small sum, however it's unlikely anyone will ask you for proof of residency. You'll find all sorts of water-sports equipment for hire along the beach. Don't leave valuables lying around unattended since petty theft is not unheard of.

In summer, the beachfront is packed with people sitting in the cooler evening air or strolling along the waterfront – a wonderful way to pass an evening.

MARKETS

Sousse's weekly market is held on Sunday in the **Souq el-Ahad compound** (Map p186) just south of the bus and louage stations. You'll find everything from handicrafts to livestock to souvenirs for the busloads of tourists.

There's another **market** (Hamman Sousse) *sans* tacky stuffed camels 5km northwest of the city centre on Friday evenings and Saturday mornings.

Sleeping

MEDINA

Hôtel Gabès (Map p188; ☎ 73 226 977; 12 rue de Paris; mattress on roof TD5, s/d TD9/15) If sleeping under the stars surrounded by an ancient medina sounds appealing, then the Gabès is for you. Otherwise the basic and ordinary rooms with shared facilities aren't much.

Hôtel el-Aghlaba (Map p188; ☎ 73 211 024; rue Laroussi Zairouk; s/d/tr TD8/12/15) This medina cheapie should really only be considered as a last resort since the bare-bones rooms are reminiscent of prison cells and the bathroom facilities are shared.

Hôtel de Paris (Map p188; ☎ 73 220 564; fax 73 219 038; 15 rue du Rempart Nord; s/d TD14/22) The Paris has small and sparse rooms with shared facilities, which is a shame since the sunny terrace has excellent views of the medina. There's a good restaurant attached on the ground floor.

Hôtel Ezzouhour (Map p188; ☎ 73 228 729; 48 rue de Paris; d TD15) Duck into the entrance and up the stairway to the reception area of the Ezzouhour and you'll think you've entered the living room of a private villa. Walk up the stairs to the basic rooms and you'll think you've entered a 'short-time' hotel. Some of the rooms have showers but bathrooms are all shared.

Hôtel Emira (Map p188; ☎ 73 226 325; 52 rue de France; s/d TD22/30) Easily the best of the medina hotels, the quality of the rooms at the Emira rivals those of top-end places in terms of sheer appeal. Brightly painted and done up with gleaming blue tiles, even rooms have balconies, though views of nothing. Fans are available and breakfast is included.

Hôtel Medina (Map p188; ☎ 73 221 722; fax 73 221 794; 15 rue Othene Osmane; s/d TD30/45;) On a shady corner opposite the Great Mosque, this hotel would be an excellent choice though on our visit the scowling manager made it less so. This is unfortunate since the motel-style rooms are large, bright and comfortable and even have fair-sized balconies. Fan rooms are cheaper.

CITY CENTRE & ZONE TOURISTIQUE

The beachfront north of Sousse has been entirely taken over by massive hotel complexes, virtual city-states unto themselves.

Most are booked out in summer, and don't quite know what to do with walk-in guests. Cheap deals can be found in winter. Prices include breakfast and almost all offer half-board and full-board rates. All of the following hotels are located in the city centre.

Hôtel Residence Monia (Map p188; ☎/fax 73 210 469; rue Remada; s/d TD28/50;) On a small side street only a block from ave Habib Bourguiba, the Monia is likely the best option in this price range though you won't exactly feel you're on a beach holiday staying here. The rooms are clean and modern, if a little dark, but the friendly and personable staff makes up for any shortcomings. Breakfast is served in a pleasant little nook on the ground floor.

Hôtel Claridge (Map p188; ☎ 73 224 759; fax 73 227 277; 10 ave Habib Bourguiba; s/d TD30/45;) It's hard to know what to make of the Claridge, occupying one of the busiest intersections in the city only a block or two from both the medina and the beach. The large rooms have ornate high ceilings but fraying furniture, faux marble floors, little balconies with alleyway views and exposed showers in the rooms but shared toilets in the hallways.

Hotel Sousse Azur (Map p188; ☎ 73 227 760; fax 73 228 145; 5 rue Amilcar; s/d with TV TD43/64;) This hotel is good value in the winter when its rates drop substantially, otherwise the room rates are a bit high for a hotel several blocks from the beach. The rooms are a little stuffy and the high-school-cafeteria–style tile floors not the best choice, though it is professionally run and some of the rooms have balconies. The rooftop terraces have good views.

Hôtel Nour Justina (Map p186; ☎ 73 227 189; fax 73 225 993; 4 ave Hedi Chaker; s/d TD50/85;) Popular with Eastern European package tourists, the Nour Justina doesn't make a good first impression. The front-desk staff makes you feel like you're being hustled and the street-side pool seems like an afterthought. However, the large and nicely decorated rooms are worth the hassles. Ones with balconies and amazing sea views cost the same as others.

Hotel La Gondole (Map p186; ☎ 73 214 500; lagondole@planet.tn; ave Hedi Chaker; r TD70/100;) A professionally run high-rise, La Gondole feels more like a business hotel than a beach resort with modern, comfortable and well kept rooms. There's no pool and no sea views.

Hôtel Abou Nawas Boujaffar (Map p188; ☎ 73 226 030; www.abounawas.com; ave Habib Bourguiba; s/d TD100/146;) A *zone touristique*–style hotel in the centre of the city, the Abou Nawas, as the name indicates, is also directly on the beach. It's an enormous complex with a few restaurants and bars and a health centre.

Hotel Sousse Palace (Map p188; ☎ 73 219 220; www.soussepalace.com; ave Habib Bourguiba; s/d TD111/160;) Typical of four-star hotels in Tunisia, room décor receives little attention here compared to the time it must have taken to find the perfect red-leather swivel bar chairs to match the dull red carpet. The Sousse Palace does have more facilities than a cruise ship, and like a low-end Club Med, staff patrol the pool and private beach areas, usually for young foreign women, looking for participants for impromptu aerobics classes and volleyball games. Low season discounts (singles/doubles TD36/52) are a steal.

Hôtel Orient Palace (☎ 73 241 888; fax 73 243 345; s/d TD155/200;) The further north you go from the city centre, the bigger and generally more upmarket the hotels become, culminating in this five-star hotel, 4km north of town.

Eating

Most of the beachfront area restaurants cater to tourists and have English menus with inflated prices. It's almost impossible to stay away from all of these, and while the food is usually nothing special, they are pleasant enough. The further inland you go from the beach, the more likely you are to find a place that's strictly for locals.

RESTAURANTS

You'll find half a dozen restaurants with outdoor seating bunched together on the northern side of place Farhat Hached, all advertising very similar menus at similar prices (mains TD6). There are two good cheap basic eateries (meals TD4) on either side of Hôtel Residence Monia on rue Remada. There are several *gelaterias* along ave Habib Bourguiba, perfect but temporary antidotes for the summer heat.

Caracas (Map p188; rue Ali Belhaouane; mains TD4;) One of the better places to eat in the city centre, frequented by young and hip

Tunisians, Caracas is built to resemble some version of the Latin American city. Well, there are faux stone walls and colonial archways but it's a modern restaurant with TVs tuned to Arab language music videos. The eclectic menu has everything from pizza to deli sandwiches and Tunisian and western standards. The enormous chicken omelette (TD4) is a meal unto itself.

Forum Grill (Map p186; ☎ 73 228 399; ave Hedi Chaker; mains TD4.5-9) This is a beachfront tourist restaurant that is nevertheless not a bad option since the service is friendly and it has a large, eclectic menu.

Planet Food (Map p186; Blvd de la Corniche; mains TD5) For homesick Americans, this Planet Hollywood imitator should do the trick. From the movie posters to the headshots of famous actors to the TVs playing movies and videos, Planet Food is all American. However, it's Tunisians who mostly come here, young people on dates and families enjoying the enormous menu at cheaper prices than the tourist traps. Pizzas (TD5), hamburgers (TD1.9), fish, chicken, salads etc are served. Paella for two (TD18) is delicious. Until the kinks are worked out don't be surprised if the service is desultory.

Dodo Restaurant (Map p188; rue el-Maar; mains TD5) This, the most modern of the medina restaurants, is a bit of a surprise. Surrounded by the clutter of commerce, the Dodo is a little bit of a refuge though it is expensive by medina standards. Pizzas and Tunisian meat dishes are on the menu.

Restaurant Du Peuple (Map p188; rue de Rempart Nord; mains TD5) The owner of this little medina restaurant has the tourist trade cornered and rightly so. Hearty meat and couscous dishes are served off an assembly line, and tea and watermelon come free with dessert. It's a bright and pleasant spot just inside the medina walls next to the Hôtel de Paris.

Restaurant Tip Top (Map p186; ☎ 73 226 158; 73 Blvd de la Corniche; mains TD8) Tip Top is your standard tourist restaurant though it seems to be more popular than others, possibly because its street-side touting waiters are more vocal. The seafood is good though expensive (TD15).

Albatross (Map p186; ☎ 73 228 430; Blvd de la Corniche; mains TD10) Just past Tip Top is the Albatross, another of the tourist-class restaurants that spend a great deal of attention on translating the menu and dressing the waiters in uniforms, and give at least a few nods in the direction of elegance, but that serve up unspectacular Tunisian and continental fare. Pizzas are good (TD5).

Restaurant Marmite (Map p188; ☎ 73 226 728; 8 rue Remada; mains TD12) Across from the Hôtel Residence Monia, this posh, at least as far as cost goes, restaurant serves up seafood and other Tunisian fare for around TD20 per person, plus wine. A *marmite*, by the way, in Tunisia is a large urn-shaped cooking pot.

Saloon Steakhouse Grill & Disco Pub (mains TD16) If you've ever wanted to eat on what appears to be the movie set for an American western in Tunisia, then this surreal restaurant around 2km from the Ville Nouvelle should not be missed. Hearty steaks are the deserved speciality though you have to pay extra for the custom sauces.

SELF-CATERING

The **Magasin Général** (Map p188; blvd Abdelhamid el-Kahdi) is the best supermarket with a good selection of Tunisian wine. There's another

JASMINE – IT'S A BOY THING

Sitting in any restaurant in Sousse can involve saying no to a seemingly endless stream of men selling jasmine. Any look around will tell you that the main buyers aren't tourists but other Tunisian men.

According to some locals, there's a strict delineation of how to wear your jasmine. If you wear it behind your left ear, you have a girlfriend and want to advertise that happy fact to the world. Wear it in the right ear and chances are that you don't have a girlfriend but would very much like one. Some men buy the jasmine as a gift for women. If they accept the gift, many women will wear it on their shirt or collar, although solely for decorative purposes, not to signify anything.

Of course not all Tunisians agree that the humble jasmine carries such weighty significance. The most common reason given to us by Tunisian men was the simple and unarguable 'because it smells nice'.

branch at rue de la Corniche. There is also a **Monoprix supermarket** (Map p188; cnr ave Habib Bourguiba & rue Ali Belhaouane).

The main produce markets are in the medina, just inside the Bab el-Jedid.

Drinking

Coffeehouses or restaurants with outdoor street-side seating are chock-a-block along ave Habib Bourguiba. Most restaurants here serve alcohol, and the only habitable nightclubs are in the big hotels far out in the Zone Touristique.

Café Theatre Municipal (Map p188; ave Habib Bourguiba) This is one especially good café. Squeezed into the street corner next to the theatre, which at the time of research was undergoing renovations, it boasts one of the prime people watching spots in the city.

Parc des Princes (Map p186; rue Mongi Slim) This is a strictly Tunisian affair for soccer fanatics; TVs play important matches of the day.

There is a bunch of good coffeehouses in the medina including **Café Sidi Bouraoui** (Map p188; rue el-Aghlaba) and **Café Yasmine** (rue el-Maar). **Restaurant-Café Seles** (Map p188; rue Abou Nawas) is a cosy little spot with cushion benches, perfect for a drink or food. And **Café des Nomades** (Map p188; rue Ibn Rachik) is another small inviting spot like the Seles in the very southwestern corner of the medina below the kasbah.

Shopping

The Sousse medina is one of the most convenient places to shop in all of Tunisia. Besides an enormous array of traditional shops, and souvenir shops that operate on the barter system, there are many price-fixed centres scattered around the medina and along blvd de la Corniche in the Ville Nouvelle.

Soula Shopping Centre (Map p188; place des Martyrs; 8.30am-10pm) Placed at the entrance to the medina, this mega four-storey complex is probably the largest price-fixed centre in the country. Most credit cards are accepted.

Getting There & Away

AIR

Sousse is served by Monastir's airport 15km to the southeast, but only by international flights. There's a **Tunisair** office (Map p188; ☎ 73 227 955; 5 ave Habib Bourguiba).

BUS

Buses leave from the **bus stop** (Map p188; blvd Yahia ben Omar), just outside the medina, heading for Monastir (bus 52, TD0.85, 40 minutes, every 30 minutes), Mahdia (TD2.5, 1½ hours, every 45 minutes) and Port el-Kantaoui (bus 12 and 18, TD0.5, 20 minutes, every 30 minutes).

Buses to all other destinations depart from the new **bus station** (Map p186; Souq el-Ahad), 800m southwest of the medina.

Destination	Fare	Duration	Frequency (per day)
Douz	TD16.9	6½hr	2
El-Jem	TD3.2	1¼hr	8
Gabès	TD11.8	4¼hr	8
Hammamet	TD5	1½hr	2
Jerba	TD17	7hr	2
Kairouan	TD4.5	1½hr	2
Kebili	TD16.6	6hr	2
Nabeul	TD5.5	2hr	3
Sfax	TD7	2½hr	8
Tozeur	TD15.7	5¾hr	1
Tunis	TD7.4	2½hr	8

There are also local buses to Kairouan from the new bus station (TD3) every 30 minutes from 6am to 7pm.

SRTG Nabeul operates three services a day to Hammamet (TD3.8, 1½ hours) and Nabeul (TD4.4, two hours). These depart from the bus stop located just outside the medina.

LOUAGE

The **louage station** (Map p186; rue 1 Juin 1955) is about a kilometre south of the medina in a large warehouse-like space. Major destinations include El-Jem (TD3.3), Hammamet (TD4.8), Kairouan (TD4), Mahdia (TD3.4), Monastir (TD1.7), Sfax (TD6.3) and Tunis (TD7). Tickets can be purchased from the modern ticket office inside.

TRAIN & MÉTRO

The mainline station is conveniently central. There are 10 trains a day north to Tunis (TD8.6, 2¼ hours) and six to Nabeul (2nd/1st class TD3.4/4.5). There's only one convenient departure time (8.01am) for Sfax (1¾ hours) and Gabès (3¾ hours). The only train to Gafsa (5¾ hours) and Metlaoui (6¼ hours) departs at 11.23pm.

The métro, essentially decommissioned train cars, connects Sousse to the airport, Monastir (TD1, 40 minutes), Mahdia (TD3, 1¾ hours) and hotels in between. Trains depart from the Bab el-Jedid station near the southeastern corner of the medina every 45 minutes or so from 6am to 9pm.

Getting Around

TO/FROM THE AIRPORT

The airport is 15km south of town, TD8 by taxi from the town centre. You can also get there by métro (TD1, 20 minutes). From Sousse there are 20 métro departures between 6am and 9pm, whereas services from the airport start around 5am.

BUS

The local bus network operates from the **bus stop** (Blvd Yahia ben Omar) just north of the medina. Useful services include buses 8, 21 and 22, which all travel past the bus and louage stations at Souq el-Ahad (280 mills).

TAXI

There are lots of taxis, particularly in the main tourist areas; you'll struggle to run up a fare of more than TD3 around the city. There's a **taxi rank** (Map p188; place des Martyrs) at the entrance to the medina.

TRAIN & TUK-TUK

The easiest way to get from Sousse to Port el-Kantaoui is to take one of the 'Happy Noddy Trains' that run up and down the main road of the tourist strip. They go from the northern end of ave Habib Bourguiba to Port el-Kantaoui, 14km to the north. Trains are colour-coded (with a round-trip ticket you must return on the same 'colour' train) and leave every 15 minutes from 9am to 11pm in summer and to 6pm in winter. The fare is TD3.5/2.5 one way per adult/child and TD5/4 return. From the same point, five-wheel motorcycle 'tuk-tuks' (one way/return TD2/3) do the same journey quicker and cheaper although you may need to wait as they won't depart with less than five passengers.

AROUND SOUSSE

Port el-Kantaoui عناء القنطاوي

You may experience a feeling of dislocation walking around the Andalusian-style marina complex at Port el-Kantaoui. After all, it's a familiar yet strange combination of the southern California mall, the Italian *piazza* and the Tunisian *zone touristique*. To say it's inauthentic and artificial is beside the point. It's meant to be and that's what Tunisians and others like about it. Grafted onto the coast 14km north of Sousse and advertised as 'the pleasure port of the Mediterranean', it's an expansive and classy custom-built village of hotels, restaurants and souvenir shops clustered around a large yachting harbour. Many visitors spend their entire holiday here without leaving. For those staying in Sousse, it's a convenient side trip. The beach north of the marina is nicer than Boujaffar Beach in Sousse and inevitably less crowded as most sunbathers here are guests of one of the luxury hotels. In addition, there are mock **pirate ships**, **glass-bottom boats**, **charter fishing trips**, **diving schools** (from TD20 per dive, around TD300 for a course), floating restaurants, banks, international newspapers, an **aromatic garden and zoo** (admission TD2.5), two quality 18-hole **golf courses** (around TD100 incl club hire), nightclubs and **amusement parks (admission TD7 to TD12)** for children and the young-at-heart. If the waters of the Mediterranean are too calm for you, it's only a short walk to the **Acqua Palace** (☎ 73 348 855; www.acquapalace.com; rue des Palmiers; adult/child TD12.5/7.5; 9.30am-6pm May-Oct), a nearby water park with slides and wave pools. Look for signs by the Happy Noddy Train stop across the road from the entrance to the marina complex.

The price for all this is high and hotels here cater to high-end package tour groups. Rates can be prohibitive (and, in summer, rooms unavailable) for the independent traveller though it's still worth a visit if you're in the area. The food spans the full range of European and local cuisine and the atmosphere is thoroughly multinational. Depending on your perspective, you'll feel like you've stumbled onto a movie set or found the last word in luxury.

SLEEPING & EATING

Hotels stretch for miles north of the marina area and the further you go the better, or at least less crowded, the beach tends to be. Most places are of higher quality than their counterparts in Sousse.

Hannibal Palace (☎ 73 348 577; fax 73 348 321; s/d TD141/196;) This is the closest five-star place to the marina (around 200m), one of the original Port el-Kantaoui hotels.

There are plenty of other options.

Hadstrubal (☎ 73 348 944; fax 73 348 969; s/d TD112/160;) Just south of Hannibal Palace, with a beachfront that tends to be quieter than the hotels on the northern side of the marina.

Les Maisons de la Mer (☎ 73 348 799; fax 73 348 961; 2/4/6 persons TD90/130/160;) For self-catering apartments.

Marhaba Palace (☎ 73 347 071; fax 73 347 077; s/d TD112/160;)

Meliá El Mouradi Palm Marina (☎ 73 246 900; info.palmmarina@elmouradi.com) A five-star north of the golf course.

Sol Club El Kantaoui (☎ 73 348 450; info.clubkantaoui@elmouradi.com) A four-star resort.

All of the hotels have their own restaurants, most have more than one, plus a bar and sometimes a disco. The marina complex itself is filled with restaurants and cafés; most are indistinguishable from one another and offer the same level of service and food. Some seem to justify their higher prices simply if they have tablecloths and fancier signs.

The choice of where to eat is more a question of price and ambience; wander around until one takes your fancy. Not everything is pricey, in fact there are several marina restaurants that serve sandwiches and mains for less than TD5. At the higher-end places expect to pay more than TD20 per person plus drinks. **Les Emirs** (☎ 73 240 865; marina) and **Misk Ellil** (☎ 73 348 952) come recommended.

GETTING THERE & AWAY

There are ample transport options to/from Sousse – see p195 for details.

From Port el-Kantaoui, all buses, tuk-tuks and 'noddy trains' leave from the station around 150m west of the marina.

MONASTIR المنستير

pop 71,500

Possessing neither the cosmopolitanism of Sousse and Port el-Kantaoui, its neighbours to the north, nor the picturesque charm of Mahdia to the south, Monastir is a little like the disadvantaged stepchild of the central coast resorts. It does have an imposing well preserved *ribat*, the Mausoleum of Habib Bourguiba and a horseshoe-shaped municipal beach. The inevitable Zone Touristique is even less integrated into Monastir proper than in other coastal towns, however this also means Monastir retains its character and pace more so than other beach towns.

History

Monastir was founded as the Phoenician trading settlement of Rous, living then (as now) in the shadow of its larger and more illustrious neighbour, Hadrumète (Sousse).

It briefly took the limelight in AD 46 when Julius Caesar based himself here before defeating Sousse-based Pompey at the Battle of Thapsus, the decisive moment of the Roman civil war. It subsequently became the Roman town of Ruspina.

Two millennia later, Habib Bourguiba was born here and lived on the outskirts of town until his death in April 2000.

Information

INTERNET ACCESS

Publinet Pubinet La Gare (train station entrance; 8am-8pm; per hr TD2); ave Farhat Hached (8am-midnight; per hr TD2)

MONEY

There are branches of all the major banks on and around place du 3 Septembre 1934, including the **Banque du Tunisie** (place du 3 Septembre 1934), which has an ATM, as does the **STB** (place du Gouvernorate).

POST & TELEPHONE

There are Taxiphone offices all around the town centre.

Main post office (ave Habib Bourguiba) Just south of the medina.

TOURIST INFORMATION

ONTT tourist office (☎ 73 461 960; rue de l'Indépendance; 8am-1pm & 3-5.45pm Mon-Thu, 8.30am-1.30pm Fri & Sat) Opposite the Bourguiba Mosque.

Sights & Activities

MEDINA

Monastir's medina was largely demolished after independence in an ill-considered rush to modernise the town in keeping with its status as the birthplace of the president. Thankfully the *ribat* (see opposite) survived, as did the **Great Mosque**. Built in the 9th century, it's a severe Aghlabid creation, apart from the graceful horseshoe arches at

the northern end. The Roman columns supporting these arches and those of the prayer hall (closed to non-Muslims) were salvaged from the ruins of ancient Ruspina.

The **walls** in the western part of the medina remain largely intact and are dotted with some interesting old gates. The finest is **Bab el-Gharbi**, at the centre of the western wall. It was built by the Hafsids in the 15th century. **Bab Tunis**, in the northwestern corner, was built in 1780 while the main southern gate, **Bab Briqcha**, was built by the Ottomans at the end of the 17th century.

The **Costume Museum** (rue de l'Indépendance; admission TD1.1; 9am-1pm & 3-7pm Tue-Sat summer, 9am-4pm winter) is around the corner from the tourist office and worth a quick look.

RIBAT

Monastir's star attraction is its immaculately preserved **ribat complex** (admission TD2.1, plus camera TD1; 8am-7pm summer, 8.30am-5.30pm winter), regarded as the country's finest example of Islamic military architecture. Its seemingly chaotic design with labyrinthine passageways and staircases is a legacy of the *ribat*'s many periods of construction and renovation. The consequence is an evocative structure devoid of any uniformity.

The original *ribat*, known as the Ribat de Harthama, was built in AD 796. Its original scope would have occupied only the central courtyard and museum area. The oldest remaining sections (though heavily restored) include the *nador* and the area around its base, all of which date from the 8th to 10th centuries.

The walls as they currently appear were begun by the Aghlabids at the end of the 9th century and completed in the 11th century. They contained built-in accommodation for defenders and the small courtyard behind the museum is known as the women's *ribat*, with its own prayer room and accommodation. The walls have been remodelled many times since, notably in the 17th century when the octagonal corner towers were added.

There are excellent views of the town and the coastline from the ramparts and the top of the *nador*; those suffering from vertigo should tread carefully.

The *ribat*'s prayer room houses a **Museum of Islamic Art** (Tue-Sun). Apart from early Arab coins and pottery, the collection includes an interesting map of Monastir's medina before independence and early photos of the town.

And if it all looks familiar, that's because the complex is a great favourite of film directors in search of accessible Islamic architecture. Many scenes from *Monty Python's Life of Brian* were filmed here, including hundreds of Tunisian extras laughing at Biggus Dickus. Franco Zeffirelli also came here to shoot scenes for his *Life of Christ*, and Monastir again became Jerusalem in *Jesus of Nazareth*.

BEACHES

Backed not by palm trees, lush vegetation or mountains, the beach at Monastir nonetheless has a dramatic setting. After all, you emerge from the water confronted by the centuries-old *ribat*. During the summer months locals flock to the beach leaving little room to spread a towel. There's a smaller, quieter beach immediately southeast of El-Kebira Island.

The beaches west of town are dominated by the resort hotels of the Zone Touristique.

MAUSOLEUM OF HABIB BOURGUIBA

The **Mausoleum of Habib Bourguiba** (admission free; 2-4.30pm Mon-Thu, 9am-4.30pm Fri & Sat, to 6pm summer) and his family is a must-see. Reached via a long, paved walkway, the gold-and-green cupolas are superb as are the marble courtyard, green-tiled arches and elegant eastern door. The mausoleum houses tombs of the family and a small display of items that belonged to the great man. If it's open, climb the small staircase on the southern side of the building to a 1st floor interior balcony from where you can appreciate the full extravagance of the mausoleum's interior.

Opening times can be erratic and shorts aren't permitted. If the main gate is closed, walk around the fence to the small gate on the northern side.

Sleeping

The *zone touristique* hotels are strung out along the beaches west of town all the way from Monastir to Skanes, 8km away. Like other resort hotels, Monastir's are self-contained complexes and provide little motivation for guests to leave.

Hôtel Monastir Beach (73 464 766; monastirbeach@yahoo.com; s/d with fan TD27/40, with air-con TD32/45;) Bringing new meaning to the expression 'beachfront property,' this hotel is strung out in a shallow niche below the corniche. Every room has large French doors that open out onto the frenzied crowds only a few feet away. Age and the salt air have taken their toll on the furnishings but the rooms are large and provide an interesting alternative for beach-minded travellers priced out of the Zone Touristique.

Hôtel Yasmine (73 501 546; route de la Falaise; s/d TD40/60) This family-run pension 2km north of town has charming and simple rooms; some have private shower and toilet while others share the latter. Sea-view rooms have balconies.

Hôtel Club Esplanade (73 461 146; hotel.lac@planet.tn; route de la Corniche; s/d TD45/70;) This is a three-storey complex whose brochure was made in another century; fortunately the rooms aren't as dated, though they're in need of attention. It is centrally located and sea-view rooms have balconies.

Marina Cap Monastir (73 462 305; marina@planet.tn; Marina complex; d TD106, 4-/6-/8-bed apartments TD115/133/172;) The reception for this low-slung complex is all of the way in the back, past the yacht-filled harbour and all of the restaurants. The simple and modern rooms are good for groups or families though it's far from the luxury of Port el-Kantaoui.

Regency (73 460 033; Marina complex; s/d TD150/225; P) This luxury resort is so exclusive that it's doubtful they even take walk-in guests. Everyone seems to have booked through a French travel agency. If you can find your way here, you'll be satisfied with modern and posh luxury and all the facilities you'd expect. It has a Club Med feel and is good for families. There's a small private beach in front of the resort.

Eating

Several of Monastir's best restaurants are clustered together out at the marina. They're all good and it's a matter of ambience and budget; most are not cheap.

Roi du Couscous (mains TD3.5) On the beach side of place du Gouvernorate, this locally popular restaurant, if not quite the king of couscous, is at least Monastir royalty.

Al Hambra (☎ 73 465 358; rue Sidi el-Mezri; mains TD5) The nicest place to eat in Monastir proper, Al Hambra is highly recommended. From the outdoor patio seating to the stylish indoor dining room, it has a European feel to it. The service is excellent and the menu includes large pasta dishes, pizza, salads, steaks and especially seafood.

Dar Chakra (off rue de l'Indépendance; mains TD5) Inside a quiet courtyard across from the tourism office and housed in an old mansion, Dar Chakra is an atmospheric place to eat. There are also tables set outside on the patio. The calamari and grilled fish are specialities.

Café La Medina (place du 3 Septembre 1934) This popular place on an interesting intersection in the middle of the medina is good for a drink, snack or full meal. The *briqs* (crispy pastries with a variety of different fillings; TD1.6) are a bargain and there's a choice of salads, pizzas and meat dishes.

Self-caterers can head to the Monoprix supermarket, next to the post office in the front of the marina complex, or the even nicer one outside one of the gates to the medina on ave Habib Bourguiba.

Getting There & Away

AIR

Monastir's airport handles a lot of international traffic, but no domestic flights. It's the primary gateway for charter flights handling tourists booked at resorts in *zone touristiques* up and down the coast.

There's a **Tunisair** (☎ 73 468 189; route de la Corniche) office in the Habib Complex.

BUS

The bus station is at the western edge of the medina. There are services to Sousse (TD1.3, 30 minutes) every 30 minutes and to Mahdia (TD1.8, one hour) hourly.

CAR

Avis (☎ 73 521 031), **Europcar** (☎ 73 520 799) and **Hertz** (☎ 73 521 300) are all based at Monastir's airport.

LOUAGE

Louages to Sousse (TD1.2), Kairouan (TD4.4) and Tunis (TD7.5) leave from next to the bus station. Louages to Mahdia leave from their own station on the southeastern side of town.

TRAIN

There are 16 trains a day (less often in winter) to Sousse (TD1, 30 minutes) and eight to Mahdia (TD1.7, one hour).

There's also one train a day to Tunis (2nd/1st class TD8.5/11, three hours).

Getting Around

TO/FROM THE AIRPORT

Monastir's **airport** (☎ 73 460 300) is at Skanes, 9km west of town on the road to Sousse. The trip costs about TD4.5 by taxi from the town centre. You can also get to the airport on any of the trains between Monastir and Sousse; L'Aeroport station is 200m from the airport terminal.

KAIROUAN القيروان

pop 118,000

Considered the fourth holiest site in Islam because of the presence of the Great Mosque, the oldest in North Africa, Kairouan feels far removed from the relative hedonism of the beach resorts to the east. Unlike many of the cities and towns in the region that cultivate tourism as an industry, Kairouan seems able to absorb the busloads of day-trippers and retain its conservative, low-key relationship to outsiders. Besides the religious significance, the medina is an interesting and beautiful place to wander, especially in the late afternoon when the sun creates shadows, highlighting the charming and ornate doors, and the blue-and-green window shutters and balconies. Kairouan has always been a place of travellers, whether here for trade or the purposes

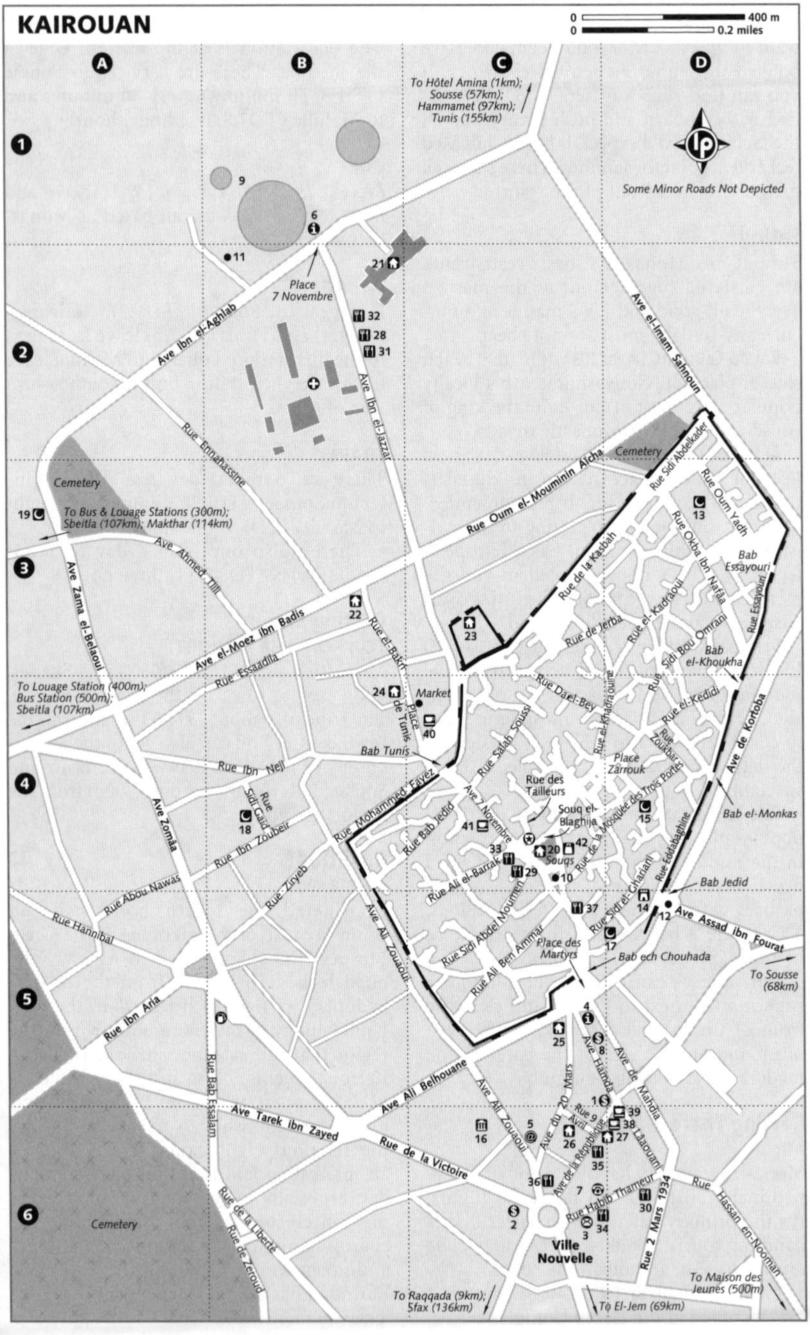

KAIROUAN

0 400 m
0 0.2 miles

A B C D

1 2 3 4 5 6

To Hôtel Amina (1km); Sousse (57km); Hammamet (97km); Tunis (155km)

Some Minor Roads Not Depicted

Place 7 Novembre

Ave Ibn el-Aghlab

Ave Ibn el-Jazzar

Ave el-Imam Sahnoun

Rue Ennahassine

Cemetery

To Bus & Louage Stations (300m); Sbeitla (107km); Makthar (114km)

Ave Ahmed Tlili

Ave Zama el-Belaoui

Rue Oum el-Mouminin Aïcha

Rue Sidi Abdelkader

Rue Oum Yadh

Rue Okba ibn Nafâa

Bab Essayouri

Rue Essayouri

Rue de la Kasbah

Rue el-Kadraoui

Rue de Jerba

Rue Sidi Bou Omrani

Bab el-Khoukha

Ave el-Moez ibn Badis

Rue el-Bakri

Rue Essaadila

To Louage Station (400m); Bus Station (500m); Sbeitla (107km)

Market

Place de Tunis

Rue Dar el-Bey

Rue el-Khadraouine

Rue el-Kedidi

Rue Zoukbar

Ave de Kortoba

Bab Tunis

Rue Salah Soussi

Place Zarrouk

Rue Ibn Nejl

Rue Sidi Gaid

Ave Zomâa

Rue Mohammed Fayez

Ave 7 Novembre

Rue des Tailleurs

Souq el-Blaghija

Rue de la Mosquée des Trois Portes

Bab el-Monkas

Rue Bab Jedid

Souqs

Rue Ibn Zoubeir

Rue Eddabaghine

Rue Ali el-Barrak

Rue Sidi Abdel Moumen

Rue Sidi el-Ghariani

Bab Jedid

Rue Abou Nawas

Rue Ziryeb

Ave Assad ibn Fourat

Rue Hannibal

Ave Ali Zouaoui

Rue Ali Ben Ammar

Place des Martyrs

Bab ech Chouhada

To Sousse (68km)

Rue Ibn Aria

Ave Hamda

Ave de Mahdia

Rue Bab Essalam

Ave Ali Belhouane

Ave du 20 Mars

Rue 9 Avril

Ave Tarek ibn Zayed

Rue de la Victoire

Ave de la République

Rue Lâaouani

Rue Hassan en-Nooman

Rue Habib Thameur

Rue 2 Mars 1934

Rue de la Liberté

Rue de Zeroud

Cemetery

Ville Nouvelle

To Raqqada (9km); Sfax (136km)

To El-Jem (69km)

To Maison des Jeunes (500m)

1 2 3 4 5 6 7 8 9 10 11 12 13 14 15 16 17 18 19 20 21 22 23 24 25 26 27 28 29 30 31 32 33 34 35 36 37 38 39 40 41 42

INFORMATION
Banque du Tunisie....................1 C5
BIAT....................2 C6
Main Post Office....................3 C6
ONTT....................4 C5
Publinet....................5 C6
Publinet....................(see 22)
Syndicat d'Initiative....................6 B1
Taxiphone Office....................7 C6
UIB....................8 C5

SIGHTS & ACTIVITIES
Aghlabid Basins....................9 B1
Bir Barouta....................10 C4
Entrance to Aghlabid Basins....................11 B2
Giant Anchors....................12 D5
Great Mosque....................13 D3
Maison du Gouverneur....................14 D5
Mosque of the Three Doors....................15 D4
ONAT Museum....................16 C6
Zaouia of Sidi Abid el-Ghariani....................17 D5
Zaouia of Sidi Amor Abbada....................18 B4
Zaouia of Sidi Sahab....................19 A3

SLEEPING
Hôtel Barouta....................20 C4
Hôtel Continental....................21 B2
Hôtel el-Menema....................22 B3
Hôtel la Kasbah....................23 C3
Hôtel Les Aghlabites....................24 B4
Hôtel Sabra....................25 C5
Hôtel Splendid....................26 C6
Tunisia Hôtel....................27 C6

EATING
Gelateria Italiana....................28 B2
Outdoor Patisserie Stalls....................29 C4
Patisserie Rabaoui Kairouan....................30 D6
Patisserie Royal Opera....................31 B2
Picolomondo....................32 B2
Restaurant de la Jeunesse....................33 C4
Restaurant Karawan....................34 C6
Restaurant Sabra....................35 C6
Roi Roi du Couscous....................36 C6
Segni....................37 C5

DRINKING
Bars....................(see 36)
Café Amar....................38 D6
Café Belhadj....................39 D6
Café Les Soirées de L'Orient....................40 C4
Turkish Coffeehouse....................41 C4

SHOPPING
Centre des Traditions et des Métiers d'Art de Kairouan....................42 C4

of pilgrimage, a city accustomed to strange people from far-off lands. There's something fundamentally Tunisian about the place – Islamic to its core and with deep roots in tradition, but adapted to the commercial necessities of the modern world.

History

It was in Kairouan that Islam gained its first foothold in the Maghreb. The original Arab settlement lasted only a few years before it was destroyed by a Berber rebellion. It was re-established in AD 694 by Hassan ibn Nooman and has been Islamic ever since.

The city's golden age began when it became the capital of the Aghlabid dynasty in AD 797. Although they preferred to rule from their palace at Raqqada, 9km south of Kairouan, it was the Aghlabids who endowed the city with its most important historic buildings, most notably the Great Mosque.

Kairouan fell to the Fatimids in AD 909, and declined after the capital was moved to Mahdia. Its fortunes hit rock bottom when it was sacked in 1057 during the Hilalian invasions (p185). It never regained its position of political pre-eminence but it retained its significance as a seat of Islamic scholarship and a holy city of Islam.

Orientation

Life in Kairouan revolves around the medina at the centre of town and the Ville Nouvelle to the south. The two meet at the large open space (place des Martyrs) outside the medina's main southern gate, the Bab ech Chouhada. The medina's principal street, ave 7 Novembre, runs northwest from here to the main northern gate, Bab Tunis.

Information

INTERNET ACCESS

Publinet Hôtel el-Menema (per hr TD1.5; 8am-10pm); ave Ali Zouaoui (per hr TD2; 8am-midnight)

MONEY

There are branches of all the major banks on the streets south of place des Martyrs.

THE FOUNDING OF KAIROUAN

The origins of many cities in North Africa (eg Ghadames in neighbouring Libya) centre on the chance discovery of wells. As a modern traveller on the barren plains of the Maghreb, you'll appreciate why such sites were chosen for cities. But Kairouan was different.

Kairouan was founded in AD 670 by the Arab general Okba ibn Nafaa al-Fihri and takes its name from the Arabic word *qayrawan*, meaning 'military camp'. According to legend, the site for the city was chosen after Okba's horse stumbled on a golden goblet that lay buried in the sands. The goblet turned out to be one that had mysteriously disappeared from Mecca some years previously. When it was picked up, water sprang from the ground – supplied, it was concluded, by the same source that supplied the holy well of Zem-Zem in Mecca. Legend has it that the well survives at Bir Barouta, in the heart of the medina (p203).

Banque du Tunisie (cnr aves de la République & Hamda Lâaouani) ATM.
BIAT (rue de la Victoire) ATM.
UIB (ave Hamda Lâaouani) Near place des Martyrs; ATM.

POST & TELEPHONE

Taxiphone offices are everywhere. The main post office is southwest of Bab ech Chouhada.

TOURIST INFORMATION

ONTT tourist office (☎ 77 231 897; Place des Martyrs; 8am-4pm) South of the medina. Transport schedules and not much else are available here.
Syndicat d'Initiative (cnr aves Ibn el-Jazzar & Ibn el-Aghlab; 8am-6pm summer, 8.30am-5.30pm winter) On the northern edge of town in front of the Aghlabid Basins. Some of the staff here speak English and can arrange tours with officially licensed guides. This is the place to purchase the all-in-one ticket for the sites around Kairouan.

Sights

MEDINA

Less commercial than other medinas in the country, Kairouan's feels even more like it ebbs and flows to a different rhythm from modern Tunisia. Most of it is given over to quiet residential streets whose rather derelict façades are set off by grand and ornate doors, and windows, arches and shutters in bright blues and greens, more reminiscent of the Caribbean than of North Africa. It's possible to wander much of the medina without being confronted by a single souvenir-buying opportunity as virtually all of the commerce is restricted to the main north–south thoroughfare of ave 7 Novembre. Here you'll find several carpet shops selling high quality products and all the usual trinkets for sale to tourists.

The first walls of the medina were built towards the end of the 8th century, but those you'll see today date mainly from the 18th century. Of the numerous gates, the oldest is **Bab el-Khoukha**, which features a horseshoe arch supported by columns. It was built in 1706.

ENTRY TICKETS & GUIDES

Most of the sites in Kairouan can be visited on a single ticket, which can be purchased at the Great Mosque, the *syndicat d'initiative* (tourist office) or the Zaouia of Sidi Sahab. The tickets (TD6) are valid for the Great Mosque, the Aghlabid Basins, the Zaouia of Sidi Sahab, the Zaouia of Sidi Amor Abbada, Bir Barouta, the Zaouia of Sidi Abid el-Ghariani and the Raqqada Islamic Art Museum (see p207). The ticket is valid only for one day and one entry per site. The camera permit (TD1) is valid at all of the sites mentioned.

If you want a guide to show you around, you can arrange one through the *syndicat d'initiative*. These guys carry accreditation, with photos, and they know their stuff. They charge TD15 for a tour of all the major sites. They all speak Arabic and French; some also speak English and/or German. Some of the accredited guides double as low-key lookouts for carpet shops.

GREAT MOSQUE

The **Great Mosque** (8am-2pm Sat-Thu, to noon Fri), in the northeast corner of the medina, is North Africa's holiest Islamic site. It's also known as Sidi Okba Mosque, after the founder of Kairouan who built the first mosque here in AD 670. The original version was completely destroyed, and most of what stands today was built by the Aghlabids in the 9th century. Entry is with the multiple-site ticket (see left).

The exterior, with its buttressed walls, has a typically unadorned Aghlabid design. Impressions change once you step into the huge marble-paved courtyard, surrounded by an arched colonnade. The courtyard was designed for water catchment, and the paving slopes towards an intricately decorated central drainage hole that delivers the collected rainwater into the 9th-century cisterns below. The decorations were designed to filter dust from the water. The marble rims of the two wells both have deep rope-grooves worn by centuries of hauling water up from the depths.

The northwestern end of the courtyard is dominated by a square three-tiered minaret. The lowest level was built in AD 728. At its base, note the two Roman slabs (one upside down) bearing Latin inscriptions.

The prayer hall is at the southern end of the courtyard. The enormous, studded wooden doors here date from 1829; the carved panels above them are particularly fine. Non-Muslims are not allowed inside, but the doors are left open to allow a glimpse of the interior. The 414 pillars that support the horseshoe arches and roof were, like those of the colonnade, originally Roman or Byzantine, salvaged from Carthage and Hadrumètum (Sousse), and no two are the same. At the far end of the hall, it's just possible to make out the precious 9th-century tiles behind the *mihrab* between two red marble columns. The tiles were imported from Baghdad along with the wood for the richly adorned *minbar* (pulpit) next to them.

Visitors must be appropriately dressed; robes are available at the entrance. Entry is via the main gate on rue Okba ibn Nafaa. The other eight gates are closed to non-Muslims.

For an overview of the Great Mosque, take in the view from the roof of a neighbouring carpet shop on rue Okba ibn Nafaa. The owners will cheekily claim that the view is included in the price of the entry ticket; so too is a period spent inspecting carpets.

ZAOUIA OF SIDI ABID EL-GHARIANI

Just inside the Bab ech Chouhada, the restored **Zaouia of Sidi Abid el-Ghariani** (rue Sidi el-Ghariani) dates from the 14th century and contains some fine woodcarving and stuccowork. The *zaouia* (complex surrounding the tomb of a saint) also houses the tomb of the Hafsid sultan Moulay Hassan who ruled from 1525 to 1543. There are no official opening hours, but you're most likely to find it open in the morning. Entry is with the multiple-site ticket (see opposite).

MAISON DU GOUVERNEUR

This 18th-century residence of the former beys or pashas of Kairouan called the **Maison du Gouverneur** (admission free; 8am-5pm), signposted as 'Tapis-Sabra', is an exquisitely restored medina house and an extravagant counterpoint to the austerity of the Aghlabids. The interior is a sumptuous combination of cedar and teak, marble latticework, plaster moulding and elegant tiled arches adorning the entrance hall, harem and reception hall where the governor received official guests and held meetings. The house doubles, of course, as a carpet shop; after watching a woman demonstrate the painstaking art of carpet making (women make the carpets, men sell them), you'll be expected to view the carpets. If you only experience the carpet ritual once in Kairouan, make it here.

BIR BAROUTA

The Bir Barouta, north of ave Ali Belhouane, was built by the Ottoman ruler Mohammed Bey in 1676 to surround the well that features in the city's foundation legend. Its waters are supposedly linked to the well of Zem-Zem in Mecca. The scene itself is a little staged for the uninitiated with a blinkered camel turning the wheel to draw water from the well for people to taste. That said, this is an important religious moment for most visitors, many of whom genuinely believe that the well is connected to Mecca. Entry is with the multiple-site ticket (see opposite).

MOSQUE OF THE THREE DOORS

250m northeast of the Bir Barouta, the **Mosque of the Three Doors** (rue de la Mosquée des Trois Portes), was founded in AD 866 by Mohammed bin Kairoun el-Maafri, a holy man from the Spanish city of Cordoba. The interior is closed to non-Muslims, but the main feature is the elaborate façade, with its strong Andalusian influences. The mosque's three arched doorways are topped by intricate friezes of Kufic script (two of which name the mosque's founder) interspersed with floral reliefs and crowned with a carved cornice. It's well worth a detour.

AGHLABID BASINS

These **cisterns** (ave Ibn el-Aghlab; 7.30am-6.30pm summer, 8.30am-6pm winter), built by the Aghlabids in the 9th century are more impressive because of their engineering sophistication than as sights in themselves. Water was delivered by aqueduct from the hills 36km west of Kairouan into the smaller settling basin and then into the enormous main holding basin, which was 5m deep and 128m in diameter. In the centre of the main pool was a pavilion where the rulers could come to relax on summer evenings. Most visitors do nothing more than peek at the cisterns from the rooftop of the *syndicat d'initiative* office nearby, but you can enter with the multiple-site ticket (see opposite).

ZAOUIA OF SIDI SAHAB

This extensive **zaouia** (ave Zama el Belaoui; 7.30am-6.30pm), about 1.5km northwest of the medina, houses the tomb of Abu Zama el-Belaoui, a *sahab* (companion) of the Prophet Mohammed. He was known as the barber because he always carried three hairs from the Prophet's beard with him, and the *zaouia* is sometimes referred to as the Mosque of the Barber. While the original mausoleum dates back to the 7th century AD, most of what stands today was added at the end of the 17th century. The additions include a *funduq* to house pilgrims, a *medersa* (Quranic school) and a mosque.

Entry to the zaouia is with the multiple-site ticket (see p202). The entrance is along an unusually decorative marble passageway that leads to a stunning white central courtyard. Sidi Sahab's mausoleum is in the northwestern corner, topped by a cupola added in 1629. Non-Muslims are not permitted to enter. The small room on the opposite side of the courtyard contains the tomb of the architect of the Great Mosque.

ZAOUIA OF SIDI AMOR ABBADA

This **zaouia** (off rue Sidi Gaid; 7.30am-6.30pm), identifiable by its seven white cupolas, was built in 1860 around the tomb of Sidi Amor Abbada, a local blacksmith with a gift for prophecy. He specialised in the production of oversized things, like a set of giant anchors (now standing north of place des Martyrs) that were supposed to secure Kairouan to the earth. Entry is with the multiple-site ticket (see p202).

ONAT MUSEUM

The **ONAT Museum** (ave Ali Zouaoui; admission free; 7.30am-1.30pm summer, 8.30am-1pm & 3-5.45pm Mon-Sat, 8am-1pm Fri & Sat winter) houses a collection of rugs. It could be missed, although these are the people who accredit all carpets sold in Kairouan; if you plan to buy one, look here at the various styles.

Sleeping

The only place to stay in the medina is the **Hôtel Barouta** (off ave 7 Novembre), but it can't be recommended.

BUDGET

Maison des Jeunes (☎ 77 230 309; ave de Fes; dm TD5) There's little reason for the budget minded to stay here since the perfectly located Hôtel Sabra is only a few dinars more. The city's uninspiring youth hostel is about 1km southeast of the medina.

Hôtel Les Aghlabites (☎ 77 230 880; off place de Tunis; s/d TD8/16) Other than the atmosphere of staying in a converted *funduq*, this hotel, north of the medina, isn't an especially good choice though it's reasonably popular with Tunisians. Ask for a room off the central courtyard. Most of the rooms have shared bathrooms.

Hôtel Sabra (☎ 77 230 263; Place des Martyrs; per person TD10) Other than the Hôtel la Kasbah, this hostel-like dump has the best location in Kairouan opposite the Bab ech Chouhada, and the views from the rooftop (where you may be able to sleep in summer) are breathtaking. It's mostly big teen tours that stay here since all they need is a mattress and space to toss a backpack. Bathrooms are shared and the thin walls don't do much to dampen the street noise or that from your neighbours.

Hôtel el-Menema (☎ 77 225 003; fax 77 226 182; rue Moez Ibn Badis; r with/without bathroom TD20/10) For those who love cyberspace, el-Menema is attached to one of the Publinets in town; however it's less convenient to the medina than the hotels in the Ville Nouvelle. The only good thing that can be said about the old, decaying rooms is that they're large. Breakfast is included.

MIDRANGE

Tunisia Hôtel (☎ 77 231 775; fax 77 231 597; ave de la République; s/d TD20/40; ❄) There's not much to recommend this old, rather rundown hotel over the nearby Hôtel Splendid, which is only a few dinars more. The rooms are small and dark but they are clean and the front desk is friendly.

Hôtel Splendid (☎ 77 230 041; fax 77 230 829; rue 9 Avril; s/d TD28/41; ❄) Only a short walk from the main entrance to the medina and boasting newly painted and refurbished rooms, the Splendid is...well a splendid choice. There are high ceilings and modern bathrooms and a restaurant on the ground floor.

Hôtel Continental (☎ 77 232 006; fax 77 229 900; ave Ibn el-Aghlab; s/d TD33/46; ❄) It's a shame the lobby here feels a little like an airport terminal and the empty pool (plans are to fill it in the near future) is surrounded by minigolf-like felt since the spacious rooms are comfortable if a little strangely furnished. It's across the street from the Aghlabid Basins.

Hôtel Amina (☎ 77 225 555; hotel.amina@topnet.tn; ave Ibn el-Aghlab; s/d TD52/77; ❄) This large whitewashed complex is inconveniently located several kilometres north of town. If you have your own vehicle it may be worth the commute since the nice rooms are better than most in this price range and have balconies overlooking the baking concrete of the pool area.

TOP END

Hôtel la Kasbah (☎ 77 237 301; kasbah.kairouan@goldenyasmin.com; ave Ibn el-Jazzar; s/d TD103/160;) This is no artificial Disney-like Alladin hotel. Occupying the old kasbah in the northern section of the medina, this is the real thing, albeit generously reimagined and re-appointed. The rooms are quite possibly some of the nicest in the country, tastefully done up in fine textiles and linens and subdued tones. Rare for a tourist-class hotel of this calibre, the facilities are refined and elegant without the usual slapdash nods to the *Arabian Nights*. The pool in the central courtyard is heated.

Eating

PATISSERIES

Kairouan is famous for a date-filled semolina cake soaked in honey called *makhroud*, which can be found everywhere. Expect to pay 150 mills a piece.

Segni (ave 7 Novembre) This is the best place to sample *makhroud* and other local Tunisian specialities. Signed only in Arabic in the middle of the medina, Segni's interior is a wonderful example of a traditional medina shop.

Other places to try include the outdoor stalls just off the main thoroughfare near the arch, or the brightly lit and modern **Patisserie Rabaoui Kairouan** (rue Soukina bint el-Hassan).

RESTAURANTS

There is a cluster of restaurants in the streets south of the medina and several places serving good rotisserie chicken can be found around ave El Moez Ibn Badiss and ave Ibn el-Jazzar.

Gelateria Italiana (ave ibn el-Jazzar; gelato TD1.3-2.4) Next door to Picolomondo, this place has a good selection of gelati.

Picolomondo (ave ibn el-Jazzar; pizzas from TD2.5;) A short walk from the Aghlabid Basins, Picolomondo is a modern restaurant with pizza and other Tunisian fare.

Patisserie Royal Opera (ave ibn el-Jazzar; pizzas TD3.5) Next door to Gelateria Italiana is this pastry shop/takeout restaurant, or you can eat in at one of the standup tables.

Roi Roi du Couscous (ave Ali Zouaoui; mains around TD4) A raucous place by Tunisian standards, this restaurant-bar is filled with men, smoke and beer, even in the middle of the day. It's not exactly the cleanest place in town but big servings of couscous are served.

Restaurant de la Jeunesse (ave 7 Novembre; mains TD5) This is the place to get couscous in the heart of the medina. The restaurant is tourist-friendly though it's worth double checking your bill.

Restaurant Sabra (ave de la République; set meals TD7) Next to the Tunisia Hôtel, the Sabra serves good filling meals though don't order off the set menu, which is more expensive than simply ordering the same à la carte. Chicken or couscous by itself is TD3.

Restaurant Karawan (rue Soukina bint el-Hassan; set meals TD8) A clean, friendly family-run place, the Karawan serves the usual couscous and meat dishes, though the *tajines* (a Tunisian omelette) and *briqs* appetizers are particularly good.

SELF-CATERING

Lots of fruit is grown around Kairouan; you'll find whatever's in season at the stalls around place de Tunis, just north of the medina.

Drinking

There are plenty of outdoor places to enjoy a coffee, soft drink, mint tea or a *sheesha* (water pipe). Most popular in the evenings are the tables around place des Martyrs in front of the Hôtel Sabra. South of here near the intersection of ave Hamda Laaouani and ave de la République are two good coffeehouses: Café Belhadj and Café Amar.

Just north of the medina in front of Bab Tunis is the Café Les Soirées de L'Orient.

Easily the best place to soak up the atmosphere in the medina is the **Turkish Coffeehouse** (ave 7 Novembre).

If you're looking for bars with an all-male ambience, head to the main roundabout south of the medina on ave Ali Zouaoui, next to the Roi Roi du Couscous restaurant. For a beer in posh surrounds try the bar at the **Hôtel la Kasbah** (ave Ibn el-Jazzar).

JUST LOOK, NO BUY

Viewing vast numbers of carpets and *kilims* (woven rugs decorated with Berber motifs) is as much a part of the Kairouan experience as visiting the Great Mosque. However averse you might be to the idea, you're likely at some stage to find yourself in a carpet shop. Resistance is futile. The secret is to accept the hospitality, enjoy the ceremony and not feel in the least obliged to buy – easier said than done.

The process starts with a passing glance as you walk through one of the medina's lanes. You're invited inside and offered sweet tea or Turkish coffee while you sit around and discuss the fact that the salesman (they're all men and all very charming) has a brother or uncle living in your country and indeed, what providence, sold a carpet, a very beautiful carpet, from his private collection, to one of your countrymen just last week.

While you wait for your drinks, why not look, looking is free, just for the pleasure of your eyes. Choices are unfurled by a boy, while another brings tea and coffee that is too hot to drink quickly. You ask a price and are told in a conspiratorial whisper that, because you have not come as part of a group, you will be offered a 30% discount. You're an honoured guest in Tunisia and hospitality demands such things.

The ones you don't like are rolled up and stacked against a wall. The designs are explained and more young men arrive to hold the carpets at viewing level. They might even try to burn the carpet with a cigarette lighter to show its durability. Suddenly the room is filled with young men at your service. Carpets are expertly rolled into tiny bundles to show how easily they will fit in your bag for carrying home.

This is the point at which you might decide that carpet-buying is not for you. You say that you want to think about it. The salesman, possibly now casting furtive glances in the direction of the shop owner, is suddenly serious, knowing full well that the vast majority of tourists never return despite promises to do so, knowing even better that most visitors to Kairouan will be leaving on the next bus out of town. Prices drop. They might even do so dramatically. Looks of sadness will be exchanged that such beautiful carpets must be let go for such a price. As you walk out the door – you might be left to find your own way out as hospitality suddenly evaporates – you might well hear dark mutterings and grim curses directed towards you. More likely, you'll look over your shoulder and see the salesman deflated on a chair, like a child who has lost his toy.

If you do decide to stay, bargain and buy, most of what the salesmen say about their carpets is true (apart from the price) – they are a wonderful keepsake to remember your journey. Your carpet is wrapped before you can reconsider. You hand over your credit card. The salesman looks aggrieved one last time. Cash is not possible, madam? Credit cards involve too much paperwork, sir. You might be able to get a few dinars more off the price for breach of contract, offset by requests for tips for the boys.

You leave with your carpet under your arm and walk past all the other carpet dealers who'll tell you that you paid too much. You can't help but smile at the whole performance. Rest assured, the man who sold you the carpet is smiling too.

Shopping

Kairouan is the carpet capital of the country. If you're in the market for a carpet, this is a good place to do your shopping.

There are two basic types of carpet: knotted and woven. The traditional (pre-Islamic) carpet industry was based on the weaving of *mergoums* and *kilims*. *Mergoums* feature very bright, geometric designs, with bold use of reds, purples, blues and other vivid colours. *Kilims* use traditional Berber motifs on a woven background. Both are reasonably cheap to buy. The Berber *guetiffa* is another type of knotted carpet: thick-pile and normally cream coloured, with Berber motifs.

The most well-known of the knotted carpets are the classical (Persian-style) Kairouan carpets. This style of carpet-making was first introduced to Tunisia by the Turks. Legend has it that the first knotted carpet to be made in Tunisia was by the daughter of the Turkish governor of Kairouan.

Knotted carpets are priced according to the number of knots per square metre. On the back of each carpet is a small certificate containing the dimensions and type of carpet. Official prices are:

Dimensions	Knots per sq m	Price per sq m
10x10	10,000	TD110-160
12x12	14,000	TD160-210
20x20	40,000	TD220-300
30x30	90,000	TD300-380
40x40	160,000	TD380-450
50x50	250,000	TD1400-1700
kilims	(usually silk)	TD170-220

To see carpets being made without the hard sell, the Centre des Traditions et des Métiers d'Art de Kairouan, just north of Bir Barouta on a side street leading to the souqs, was set up by ONAT to promote local Tunisian handicrafts. The rooms upstairs are specifically set up to demonstrate traditional techniques for weaving, embroidery and carpet making. The artisans are usually more than happy to show you how it's done.

Another option you might consider is to attend the carpet auctions where Berber women sell their traditional carpets to shop-owners. You may even be able to bid if you speak Arabic. It all takes place in the Souq el-Blaghija, with most of the action between 11am and 1pm on a Saturday. Needless to say, the carpet dealers will make you feel as unwelcome as possible, just in case you realise the extent of their profit margins.

Getting There & Around

The bus and louage stations are next to each other about 300m west of the Zaouia of Sidi Sahab. A taxi from the centre of town to place des Martyrs costs about TD1 on the meter but many taxi drivers ask three times that.

Note that for El-Jem, you'll have to go via Sousse.

BUS

Most of the services are operated by the national line, SNTRI, which has its own booking office in the terminal, together with an information board displaying destinations and departure times.

Destination	Fare	Duration	Frequency (per day)
Douz	TD18.7	7hr	1
Gabès	TD9.4	4¼hr	5
Gafsa	TD9.8	3hr	6
Jerba	TD15.1	5hr	2
Kélibia	TD7.2	3hr	1
Medenine	TD12.3	5¼hr	1
Nabeul	TD5	2¼hr	3
Nefta	TD13.8	7½hr	2
Sfax	TD5.8	3hr	3
Sousse	TD2.4	2½hr	16
Tozeur	TD13.7	4½hr	3
Tunis	TD7.8	3hr	hourly

Other destinations are served by regional companies with separate booking offices at the terminal. They include buses every 30 minutes (6.30am to 7.30pm) to Sousse (TD3, 1½ hours), three buses a day to Sfax (TD5.5, two hours) and two to Makthar (TD4.5, 1¾ hours).

LOUAGE

There are frequent departures to Sousse (TD3.5), Sfax (TD6.7) and Tunis (TD7.4), and occasional services to Makthar (TD4.8), Sbeitla (TD5.7) and Hammamet (TD4.5).

AROUND KAIROUAN

Raqqada Islamic Art Museum (9.30am-4.30pm Tue-Sun) occupies a former presidential palace at Raqqada, 9km south of Kairouan; take any transport heading to Sfax. Exhibits on display here include a model of the Great Mosque of Kairouan, a faithfully reproduced plaster copy of the *mihrab* and lots of calligraphy. There are ambitious plans for expansion, until which time it's probably not worth the effort. Entry is with the multiple-site ticket (see p202).

EL-JEM الجم

pop 18,300

The ancient colosseum of El-Jem is a dramatic and impressive sight, both because of its awesome size and solidity in relation to the modern buildings surrounding it, and because, like all ruins, it's a sober reminder of the inevitable fleetingness of achievement. Built on a low plateau halfway between Sousse and Sfax, the colosseum is all the evidence you need to begin to grasp the scope of Roman civilization in Africa.

History

E-Jem's colosseum was once the crowning glory of ancient Thysdrus, a thriving market town that grew up at the junction of the Sahel's lucrative trade routes during the 1st century AD and that derived its wealth from the olive oil produced in the area. Thysdrus, a town of sumptuous villas, reached the peak of its prosperity in the 2nd and 3rd centuries AD.

In the 17th century, the troops of Mohammed Bey blasted a hole in the western wall to flush out local tribesmen and the breach was widened during another rebellion in 1850.

Orientation & Information

Ave Habib Bourguiba runs from the colosseum to the train station on the southern edge of town. The post office and bank are just west of here on ave Fahdel ben Achour (the road to Sfax). The main thoroughfare into town from Sousse is ave Heidi Chaker, which turns into ave Taieb Mehiri just past the train station and continues northeast out of town on the way to Mahdia.

Sights

COLOSSEUM

This World Heritage–listed **colosseum** (admission TD6, plus camera TD1; 7am-7pm summer, 8am-5.30pm winter) was the third largest in the Roman world; it was 138m long by 114m wide, with three tiers of seating 30m high. Its seating capacity has been estimated at 30,000 – considerably more than the population of the town itself.

The colosseum is believed to have been built between AD 230 and 238, and is generally attributed to the African proconsul Gordian, a local landowner and patron. Stone for construction had to be hauled all the way from the quarries at Sullectum (modern Salakta), 30km away on the coast, and water was brought 15km by underground aqueduct from the hills northwest of town.

In AD 238, Gordian was declared emperor of Rome here during an ill-fated rebellion against the Emperor Maximus. Gordian reportedly committed suicide in the amphitheatre when it became obvious that the rebellion was doomed.

The colosseum later doubled as a last line of defence. The Berber princess Al-Kahina was besieged here by Arab forces at the end of the 7th century. According to legend, the colosseum was linked by tunnel to the coastal town of Salakta, enabling Al-Kahina to torment her besiegers by waving fresh fish from the top of the walls (see the boxed text, p233).

When you enter the colosseum for the first time, you'll be struck by the indulgent grandeur of the Roman vision. The south side of the amphitheatre is the most intact, allowing a sense of how the seats swept down from the upper tiers to the marble-walled arena, beneath which ran arched corridors. To see how the colosseum must once have appeared, check out the artist's impression displayed just inside the entrance gate.

You can still climb up to the upper seating levels and gaze down on the arena. It's also possible to explore the two long underground passageways that were used to hold animals, gladiators and other unfortunates in their last moments before they were thrust into the arena to provide entertainment for the masses. It was here that many spent their last lonely minutes, listening to 30,000 people baying for their blood.

For a relatively uninterrupted view back towards the colosseum, take any of the streets behind the colosseum, heading north.

Admission is free for holders of an international student ID card.

SEEING THE COLOSSEUM AT SUNSET

The best time to see the colosseum is at sunset when the sun bathes the amphitheatre's interior in golden light. But for independent travellers this is more difficult than it should be.

One option is to charter a private taxi. As you'll need to pay for the driver to return home anyway, it can be a good idea to take a taxi from Mahdia (around TD35 return) or Sousse or Sfax (both around TD45).

The other option is to visit from Sfax and return on the 8.57pm train. If you're quick (and the train is late), you might also catch the 7.13pm train to Sousse. Check current departure times at the stations in Sousse and Sfax before setting out.

Either that or get up (very) early and catch a louage from Mahdia or Sousse (they start filling from 6am) and content yourself with the almost-as-impressive sunrise.

MUSEUM

This **museum** (8am-7pm summer, 8am-5.30pm winter), 1km south of the amphitheatre on the road to Sfax, houses a small but exceptionally beautiful collection of mosaics. Highlights include a splendid array of scenes from the colosseum, a dramatic depiction of Dionysius astride a tiger and the delightful if quixotic Genius of the Year. The turnoff to the museum is at the intersection occupied by the Restaurant Le Bonheur. Admission is included in the colosseum ticket.

OTHER SITES

The colosseum was not the first amphitheatre to be built at Thysdrus. Opposite the museum and across the railway line to the east are the ruins of an earlier **amphitheatre**, dug into a low hill. There's also a second area of **Roman villas** to the north of the colosseum, though these will probably only be of interest to passionate amateur archaeologists. Look for signs posted off ave Farhat Hached, the road to Sousse or off ave Hedi Chaker, the road to Kairouan.

Festivals & Events

From mid-July until mid-August, the colosseum is transformed into a splendid floodlit venue for the **El-Jem International Symphonic Music Festival** (73 631 621; www.festivaleljem.com). You can buy tickets (TD10.5 to TD27) and find a programme at the tourist office in Sousse (p187). The tourist office in Tunis organises an evening bus to and from the colosseum (see p70 for contact details).

Sleeping & Eating

Hôtel Julius (s/d TD24/38) The only place to stay in El-Jem proper is next to the train station at this hotel, though there's not much to recommend it other than the fact that it's easy to find. There's an especially surly vibe and the downstairs bar isn't the most inviting. Rooms are window cooled and have thin carpeting and mismatched furniture.

Elyeses Chez Faruch (73 631 253; pizzas TD4) This is a nice, clean pizzeria.

Restaurant Le Bonheur (73 632 384; mains TD6;) A short walk from the train station, this is the best and most tourist-oriented restaurant in town. The English menu offers a small selection of traditional dishes like spicy couscous with chicken (TD4).

Restaurant Le Bonheur 2 This place, owned by the nephew of the original Le Bonheur, is behind the colosseum and has a similar menu.

There are several cafés serving snacks and grilled meat in front of the colosseum entrance.

Getting There & Away

The louage station is 500m west of the train station along ave Hedi Chaker. The most frequent departures are to Mahdia (TD1.9), but there are also semi-regular departures for Tunis (TD8.8), Sousse (TD3.3) and Sfax (TD3.3). For Kairouan, you'll need to change at Sousse. The last louage has usually left the station by 7.15pm and often well before.

Buses leave from outside the train station. A lot of SNTRI buses pass through town, but they're often full. There are buses to Tunis (TD9.5, three hours, four daily), Sousse (TD3.1, 1¼ hours), Sfax (TD3, 1¼ hours) and Mahdia (TD2, one hour).

There are trains north to Sousse (TD4.4 in 1st class, one hour) and Tunis (TD11, three hours), and south to Sfax (TD4.2, one hour), but only a couple in each direction are at decent times and of any use to colosseum visitors.

MAHDIA المهدية

pop 46,000

Occupying a narrow peninsula jutting out into the Mediterranean, Mahdia is blessed with a spectacular setting and a wonderful old-world charm. More than any other of the central coast towns, the heart of Mahdia is refreshingly free of the heavy architectural imprint of modern tourism and is the most inviting place to slow down and settle into your own daily routine. A walk anywhere along Ave 7 Novembre or Rue du Borj, both of which hug the narrow peninsula, offers wonderful views of the shimmering Mediterranean. The large and very developed Zone Touristique stretches along the coast to the north of town.

History

Mahdia was founded as a port in AD 916 by the first Fatimid caliph, Obeid Allah, known as El-Mahdi, who used Mahdia's narrow rugged peninsula as a coastal base from which to plan his attack on his ultimate

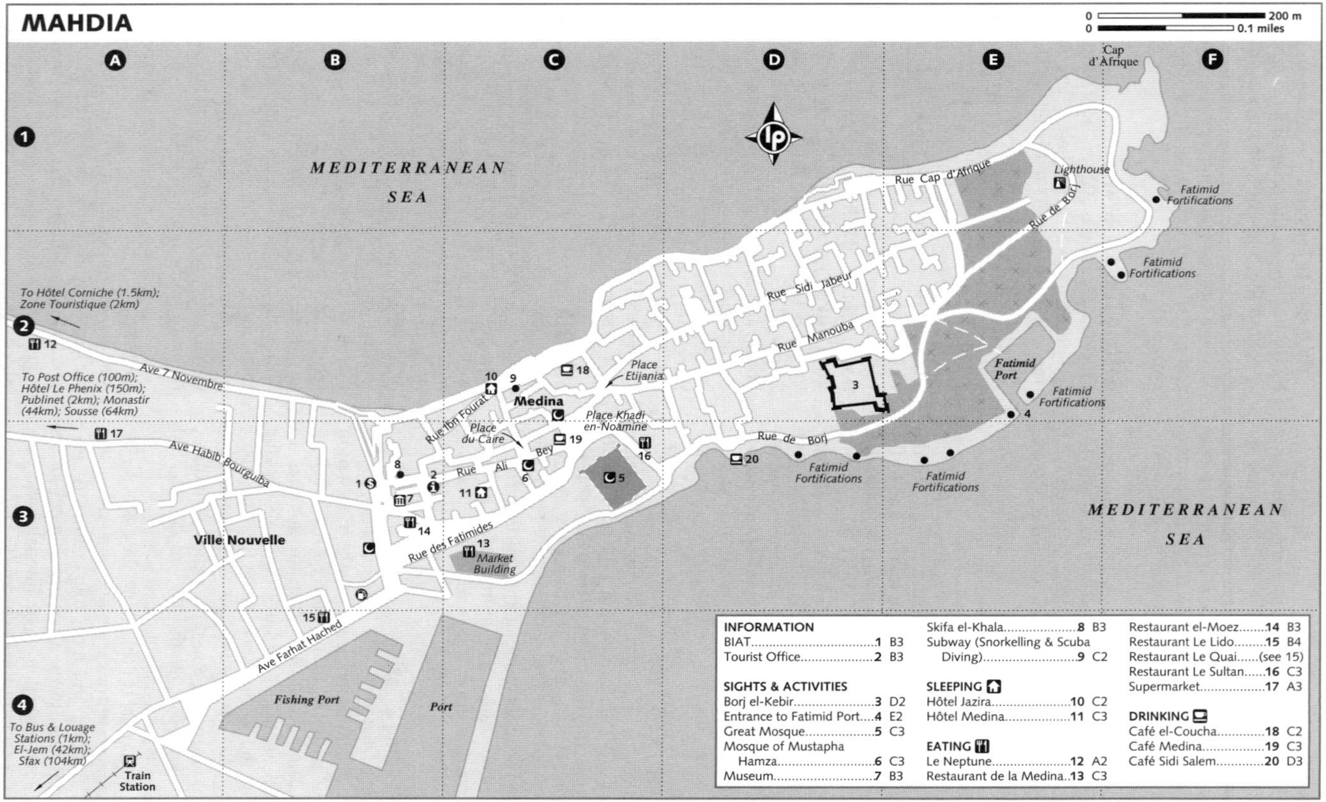

MAHDIA

0 200 m
0 0.1 miles

A B C D E F
1 2 3 4

MEDITERRANEAN SEA
Cap d'Afrique
Lighthouse
Fatimid Fortifications
Fatimid Port
Rue Cap d'Afrique
Rue de Borj
Rue Sidi Jabeur
Rue Manouba
Place Etijania
Place Khadi en-Noamine
Place du Caire
Rue Ibn Fourat
Rue Ali Bey
Medina
Rue des Fatimides
Market Building
Ville Nouvelle
Ave 7 Novembre
Ave Habib Bourguiba
Ave Farhat Hached
Fishing Port
Port
Train Station
To Hôtel Corniche (1.5km); Zone Touristique (2km)
To Post Office (100m); Hôtel Le Phenix (150m); Publinet (2km); Monastir (44km); Sousse (64km)
To Bus & Louage Stations (1km); El-Jem (42km); Sfax (104km)

INFORMATION
BIAT.......1 B3
Tourist Office.......2 B3

SIGHTS & ACTIVITIES
Borj el-Kebir.......3 D2
Entrance to Fatimid Port.......4 E2
Great Mosque.......5 C3
Mosque of Mustapha Hamza.......6 C3
Museum.......7 B3
Skifa el-Khala.......8 B3
Subway (Snorkelling & Scuba Diving).......9 C2

SLEEPING
Hôtel Jazira.......10 C2
Hôtel Medina.......11 C3

EATING
Le Neptune.......12 A2
Restaurant de la Medina.......13 C3
Restaurant el-Moez.......14 B3
Restaurant Le Lido.......15 B4
Restaurant Le Quai.......(see 15)
Restaurant Le Sultan.......16 C3
Supermarket.......17 A3

DRINKING
Café el-Coucha.......18 C2
Café Medina.......19 C3
Café Sidi Salem.......20 D3

goal, Cairo, and as an easily defensible refuge for his minority Shiite followers.

The original Fatimid city was protected by a massive wall, up to 10m thick, which cut across the peninsula at its narrowest point, where the Skifa el-Kahla now stands. A smaller wall encircled the remainder of the peninsula. The area within these walls was a royal compound, reserved for the Mahdi and his entourage while his subjects lived outside the walls.

When the Fatimids abandoned Mahdia in AD 947, the inhabitants of Zawila moved inside the walls. The present medina was well established by the time the famous historian Ibn Khaldun visited in the 14th century and reported that Mahdia had become the wealthiest city on the Barbary Coast.

The medina remains a residential area, but the majority of the town's 30,000 inhabitants have reversed the trend of their ancestors and now live in the modern suburbs that spread west from Skifa el-Kahla.

Information

Friday is market day in Mahdia.

BIAT This bank with ATM is right outside the Skifa el-Kahla.

Post office (ave Habib Bourguiba) About 650m west of the medina.

Publinet (ave Habib Bourguiba; TD1.5 per hr; 8am-midnight;) West of the centre on the way to the Zone Touristique.

Tourist office (73 681 098; 8am-1pm & 3-5.45pm Mon-Thu, 8.30am-1.30pm Fri & Sat) There's a small office just inside the medina, through the Skifa el-Kahla. There was a reasonable range of brochures when we visited but even the exact location of the bus station was a mystery.

Sights & Activities

MEDINA

There's less commerce and more peaceful residential streets in Mahdia's medina than others in Tunisia, especially the closer you get to the lighthouse at Cap d'Afrique where the peninsula narrows and the sea is only steps away. The narrow, cobblestone streets are definitely photogenic.

SKIFA EL-KAHLA

The Skifa el-Kahla, a massive fortified gate and one of Tunisia's finest, is all that survives of the original Fatimid city. Entry is through a narrow, vaulted passageway, almost 50m long, that was once protected by a series of gates – one of them a suitably oversized iron portcullis. On market day, the interior is lined with impromptu stalls; it's just possible to imagine you're entering an ancient town little changed in centuries. For the view from the top of the gate, you'll need to enter the museum adjacent to the Skifa.

MUSEUM

The **museum** (admission TD3; 9am-1pm & 4-7pm Tue-Sat Apr–mid-Sep, 9am-4pm Tue-Sat mid-Sep–Mar), just south of the Skifa el-Kahla, is small but excellent. The ground floor has three superb, expansive mosaics and nicely displayed marble statues dating from 3rd-century El-Jem. There are also oil lamps that once illuminated the corridors of the colosseum at El-Jem.

Upstairs are cedar panels adorned with Kufic script from the Great Mosque at Kairouan, as well as local costumes and coins from more recent Tunisian history.

Before leaving, don't forget to climb to the top of the Skifa el-Kahla for the best views over the medina.

PLACE DU CAIRE

The compact place du Caire is Mahdia at its best. The outdoor cafés under the generous shade of trees and vines are the perfect place to relax and contemplate the ornate arched doorway and octagonal minaret on the southern side of the square. They belong to the **Mosque of Mustapha Hamza**, built in 1772 when the square was the centre of the town's wealthy Turkish quarter. There are also some wonderful old Mahdia houses to admire.

GREAT MOSQUE

The Great Mosque stands on the southern side of place Khadi en-Noamine. What you see today is a modern replica of the original Fatimid mosque, built by Obeid Allah in AD 921, which was destroyed when retreating Spanish troops blew up the city walls in 1554. Non-Muslims are allowed into the courtyard outside prayer times.

BORJ EL-KEBIR

The **Borj el-Kebir** (admission TD1.1; 9am-1pm & 4-7pm Sat-Thu summer, 9am-4pm Sat-Thu winter) is a large fortress standing on the highest point of the peninsula, rising above the medina with a brooding and unadorned severity. It was built in the 16th century on the ruins of an earlier Fatimid structure. There's not much to see inside, but the views from the ramparts are well worth the entry fee. It's also aesthetically pleasing, as much for its simplicity as the clear evidence of its original purpose.

FATIMID FORTIFICATIONS

Fragments of the original **Fatimid walls** dot the shoreline from near the Great Mosque all the way to Cap D'Afrique, and provide just enough hints to imagine a walled town protected from sea-borne invasion. The **Fatimid port** remains in evidence here, as do the crumbling pillars which once flanked the entrance and dominated the harbour's defences. If you're having difficulty imagining what it must have been like, the Borj el-Kebir contains an artist's representation of Mahdia in Fatimid times.

BEACHES

Mahdia's main beach is northwest of town and is fronted by the big hotels of the Zone Touristique; you can use the beach even if you're not staying at one of the hotels. Local kids make do with swimming off the rocks that run along rue Cap d'Afrique and families head to the beach that starts in town almost parallel to the Skifa.

The waters here are as clear and blue as anywhere in the Mediterranean. To take a closer look, head to **Subway** (☎ 73 696 492; subway@topnet.tn; rue Cap D'Afrique), which can arrange snorkelling (TD15 per hour) or diving (TD44 per dive). It caters to beginners (to whom it offer a 'baptism in the sea') and experienced divers (TD55 for a night dive).

Sleeping

BUDGET

Hôtel Medina (☎ 73 694 664; fax 73 691 422; rue el-Kaem; s/d with shared bathroom TD10/20) A quiet oasis in the heart of the medina, this hotel is housed in a large converted home with a number of rooms surrounding a pleasant central courtyard. The simple rooms are kept spotless.

Hôtel Jazira (☎ 73 681 629; fax 73 680 274; 36 rue Ibn Fourat; s/d with shared bathroom TD14/24) The entrance to the Jazira, on a small alleyway just around the corner from the road that skirts the seafront, is hard to find. However, it is well worth the search if you get one of the cosy rooms with sea views, otherwise the Hôtel Medina is probably a better choice. There's a rooftop 'patio' with excellent views.

Hôtel Corniche (☎ 73 694 201, fax 73 692 196; route de la Corniche; s/d TD16/32) Almost 2km northwest of the medina and just before the restaurant Neptune, the friendly Corniche is a budget beach hotel, which means you'll probably want to spend most of your time at the beach and not in the basic and plain rooms.

TOP END

With one exception, Mahdia's more expensive hotels are spread along the beaches in the Zone Touristique, which starts about 2.5km northwest of the medina. They're quite removed from the town and are designed to provide all that you need without leaving – beach, swimming pools, restaurants and high levels of comfort. As elsewhere in Tunisia, they're packed in summer and dead in winter.

Hôtel Le Phenix (☎ 73 690 101; ave Habib Bourguiba, s/d TD70/120;) Within in walking distance of the beach and the medina this four-star boutique hotel is the only upmarket choice in Mahdia proper and even a step above the *zone touristique* hotels in terms of service and room quality. With a stylish café, restaurant and lobby area and rooftop pool, Le Phenix would be equally at home in New York City's Soho as it is here.

Eating

RESTAURANTS

Minimalls with cafés and restaurants, not to mention shops, line the road out in the Zone Touristique. The restaurant in the Hôtel Le Phenix is the best in the city centre.

Le Neptune (☎ 73 681 927; ave 7 Novembre; mains TD8, set menu TD15) Grilled seafood and seafood couscous are the in-house specialities at this restaurant just west of the medina on the corniche. The 2nd floor terrace has views of the medina jutting out into the Mediterranean.

Restaurant el-Moez (mains TD5) Between the Skifa el-Kahla and the markets, el-Moez is a no-frills place with large servings of daily specials and fresh-caught grilled fish and calamari.

Restaurant de la Medina (mains TD5) At the rear of the market building by the port and next to the fish market, this restaurant features fish and more fish.

Restaurant Le Sultan (pizzas TD3.5;) Another place to try is this air-con place just east of the Great Mosque.

Facing the port along ave Farhat Hached are **Restaurant Le Lido** (8am-midnight) and **Restaurant Le Quai** (Chez Farhat), which offer pleasant outdoor dining and alcohol, although the quality is nothing special; expect to pay TD14 per person plus drinks.

SELF-CATERING

The produce section of the market building is the best bet for self-caterers. The only **supermarket** (ave Habib Bourguiba) is about 400m west of the Skifa el-Kahla.

Drinking

There are few more pleasant spots on the coast for a morning or afternoon drink than in the shady place du Caire. The cafés there serve a limited range of pastries for breakfast. **Café Medina** (place Khadi en-Noamine) is equally lovely, while on the north side of the medina, head for the large and less atmospheric Café el-Coucha, which serves breakfast and croissants. The opening hours here are hard to predict.

Café Sidi Salem is a magical place overlooking the Mediterranean on the south side of the medina. Several levels of tables jut out into the water as if you were in the Greek Islands, and kids and families frolic in the water below. It's wonderful any time of the day for a drink or bite to eat and should not be missed.

Getting There & Away

BUS

The bus station is next to the louage station, about 1km southwest of the train station. Most people prefer louages or the train.

There are regular departures to Sousse (TD3.1, 1½ hours) and El-Jem (TD2.4, one hour).

LOUAGE

The louage station, also 1km southwest of the train station, has noticeboards listing fares. Regular departures include Sousse (TD2.9, 1½ hours), El-Jem (TD1.9, one hour), Monastir (TD2, 1¼ hours), Sfax (TD4.8, two hours) and Tunis (TD8.8, four hours). For Kairouan, change at Sousse.

TRAIN

The **train station** (ave Farhat Hached) is just west of the port. There are 16 trains a day to Monastir (TD2.5, one hour) and Sousse (TD3.3, 1¾ hours).

There's also a daily service to Tunis (1st/2nd class TD11.4/8.5, four hours).

Getting Around

A taxi from the louage station to the medina should cost no more than TD2.

SFAX صفاقس

pop 281,000

Other Tunisians describe the residents of Sfax, the second largest city in the country as hard working, dull and thrifty. No doubt there's some truth to the stereotype, however a visit here is an opportunity to experience contemporary Tunisian life unmediated by the demands of tourism. An afternoon stroll through the medina, which outside of the one in Tunis is probably the most fascinating to explore, provides a look at how the modern and the ancient, the mercantile and the spiritual coexist in apparent harmony.

History

The coast around Sfax has been settled since Phoenician times, but none of the towns amounted to very much until Sfax was established by the Arabs at the beginning of the 8th century AD. The city's massive stone ramparts were built by the Aghlabids in the middle of the 9th century AD. They proved effective enough for the city to hold out against the Hilalian invasions in the 11th century (see p185), and Sfax emerged as the major city in the south of Tunisia. In the 14th century, it controlled a stretch of coastline reaching as far as Tripoli in Libya and it remained largely independent of the central government in Tunis until the beginning of the 17th century.

The French built the Ville Nouvelle in the 19th century and developed the port to handle the export of phosphate from the mines at Gafsa.

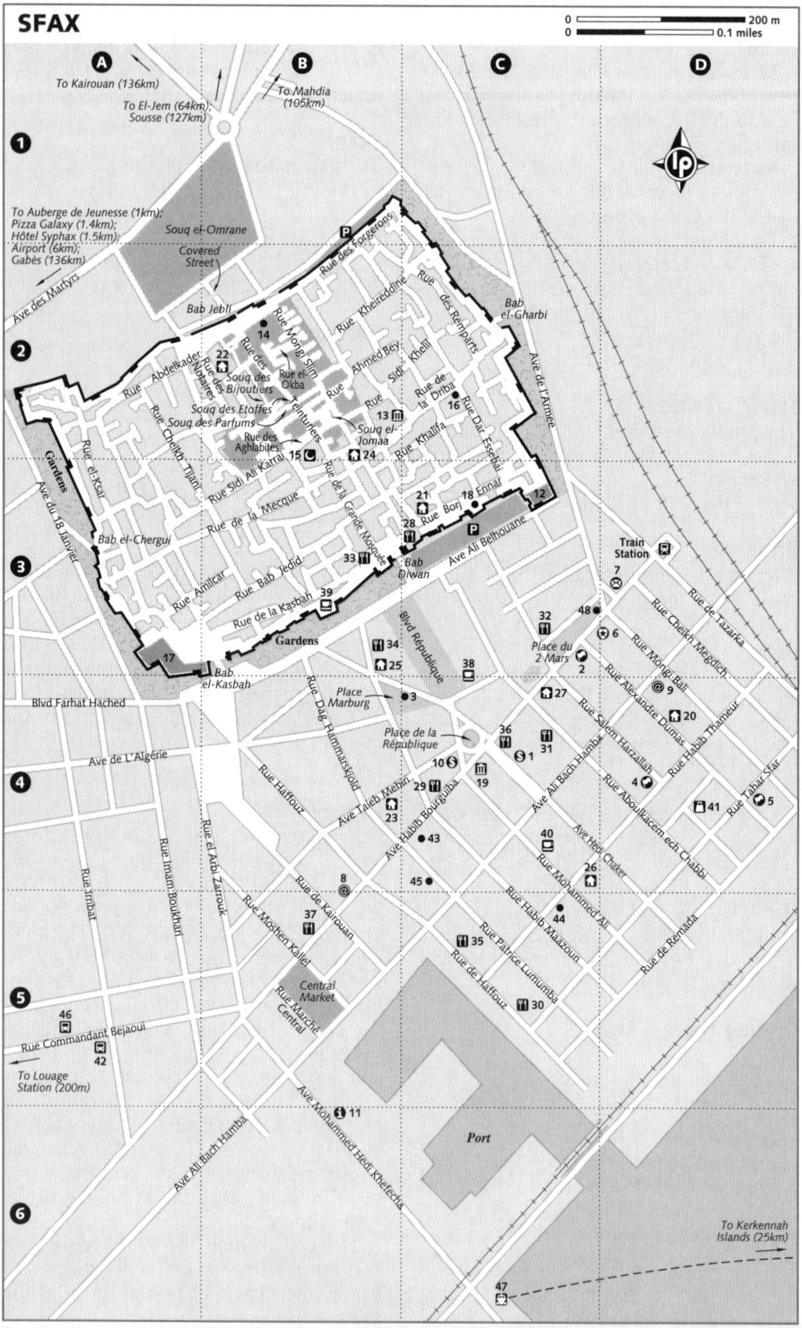

SFAX

0 200 m
0 0.1 miles

To Kairouan (136km)
To El-Jem (64km); Sousse (127km)
To Mahdia (105km)
To Auberge de Jeunesse (1km); Pizza Galaxy (1.4km); Hôtel Syphax (1.5km); Airport (6km); Gabès (136km)
Ave des Martyrs
Souq el-Omrane
Covered Street
Bab Jebli
Rue des Forgerons
Rue Kheireddine
Rue des Remparts
Bab el-Gharbi
Ave de l'Armée
Rue Mongi Slim
Rue des Notaires
Rue Abdelkader
Rue des Notaires
Souq des Bijoutiers
Rue el-Okba
Rue Ahmed Bey
Rue Sidi Khelil
Rue de la Driba
Souq des Etoffes
Souq des Parfums
Teinturiers
Souq el-Jomaa
Rue Dar Essebai
Rue des Aghlabites
Rue Khalifa
Rue el-Ksar
Rue Cheikh Tijani
Rue Sidi Ali Karray
Rue de la Grande Mosquée
Rue Borj Ennar
Gardens
Ave du 18 Janvier
Rue de la Mecque
Bab el-Chergui
Ave Ali Belhouane
Bab Diwan
Train Station
Rue Amilcar
Rue Bab Jedid
Rue de la Kasbah
Gardens
Blvd République
Bab el-Kasbah
Place du 2 Mars
Rue de Tazarka
Rue Cheikh Megdich
Rue Mongi Bali
Rue Alexandre Dumas
Rue Salem Harzallah
Rue Habib Thameur
Blvd Farhat Hached
Rue Dag Hammarskjold
Place Marburg
Place de la République
Ave de L'Algérie
Rue Haffouz
Ave Taieb Mehiri
Ave Habib Bourguiba
Ave Ali Bach Hamba
Rue Aboulkacem ech Chabbi
Rue Tahar Sfar
Ave Hedi Chaker
Rue el Arbi Zarrouk
Rue Imam Boukhari
Rue Irribat
Rue Mohammed Ali
Rue de Kairouan
Rue Habib Maazoun
Rue Moshen Kallel
Rue Patrice Lumumba
Rue de Remada
Rue de Haffouz
Central Market
Rue Marché Central
Rue Commandant Bejaoui
To Louage Station (200m)
Ave Mohammed Hedi Khefecha
Ave Ali Bach Hamba
Port
To Kerkennah Islands (25km)

A B C D
1 2 3 4 5 6

INFORMATION
BIAT....................1 C4
French Consulate....................2 C3
International Newspapers....................3 C4
Italian Consulate....................4 D4
Libyan Consulate....................5 D4
Police Station....................6 D3
Post Office....................7 D3
Publinet....................8 B4
Publinet....................9 D4
STB....................10 C4
Tourist Office....................11 B6

SIGHTS & ACTIVITIES
Association de Sauvegarde de la Medina....................(see 12)
Borj Ennar....................12 C3
Dar Jellouli Museum....................13 B2
Funduq des Forgerons....................14 B2
Great Mosque....................15 B2
Hammam Sultan....................16 C2
Kasbah....................17 A3
Mausoleum of Sidi Amar Kammoun....................18 C3
Town Hall & Archaeological Museum....................19 C4

SLEEPING
Hôtel Alexander....................20 D4
Hôtel Besbes....................21 C3
Hôtel de la Paix....................(see 20)
Hôtel el-Mokhtar....................(see 21)
Hôtel Ennacer....................22 B2
Hôtel La Colisée....................23 B4
Hôtel Medina....................24 B2
Hôtel Thyna....................25 B3
Les Oliviers....................26 C4
Mercure Accor Hôtel....................27 C4

EATING
Cheap Restaurants....................28 C3
La Perla....................29 C4
Le Petit Navire....................30 C5
Monoprix Supermarket....................31 C4
Restaurant au Bec Fin....................32 C3
Restaurant Budaya....................33 B3
Restaurant Le Corail....................34 B3
Restaurant Speciality Lebanese..35 C5
Sandro Pizzeria....................36 C4
Twings....................37 B5

DRINKING
Black In White Café....................38 C3
Café Maure Diwan....................39 B3
Club My House....................40 C4

SHOPPING
ONAT....................41 D4

TRANSPORT
Bus Station....................42 A5
Hertz....................43 C4
Location 2000....................44 C5
Mattei....................45 C4
SNTRI Bus Station....................46 A5
Soretrak Ferries to Kerkennah Islands....................47 C6
Tuninter....................48 C3

Orientation

Modern Sfax is spread out over a large area though the centre is fairly compact. The train station and rail line marks the eastern edge of town and the port defines the southern border. Ave Habib Bourguiba, a primary thoroughfare, runs east to west through the central part of the Ville Nouvelle. Blvd République is a wide pedestrian boulevard that connects Bourguiba to the Bab Diwan entrance to the medina. North of the medina is an even newer section of the city that's going through a mini construction boom similar to those in Arabian Gulf States. Gleaming white towers are rising at a surprising pace.

Information

INTERNET ACCESS

Publinet ave Habib Bourguiba (2nd fl, ave Habib Bourguiba; per hr TD2; 8am-midnight); Ali Bach Hamba (7 ave Ali Bach Hamba; per hr TD2; 8am-10pm Mon-Sat, 9am-8pm Sun)

MEDIA

International newspapers are sold at the kiosk on the northern side of place Marburg.

MONEY

All the Tunisian banks here have branches either on ave Habib Bourguiba or ave Hedi Chaker.

BIAT (ave Hedi Chaker) ATM.

STB (place de la République) ATM.

POST

Post office (ave Habib Bourguiba) Occupies an entire block just west of the train station.

TOURIST INFORMATION

Tourist office (☎ 74 211 040; ave Mohammed Hedi Khefecha; 9am-1pm & 3-5.30pm Mon-Thu, 9am-1.30pm Fri & Sat) Out by the port. Bus, train and ferry timetables are available.

Sights & Activities

MEDINA

Apart from the imposing walls, the medina lacks the monumental grandeur of Sousse or Kairouan, but its considerable charm lies in the fact that it is remarkably untouched by tourism.

The main thoroughfares are narrow and crowded with stalls and local shoppers, while away to the northeast and southwest wind quiet, twisting lanes where you can admire the flourishes of iron balconies and window frames, ornate doors and the sound of artisans from an upstairs window.

If you need a bath, the **Hammam Sultan** (rue de la Driba; admission TD1.5; women noon-4pm, men 4pm-midnight) is near the Dar Jellouli Museum in the heart of the medina. It's a good earthy place for a scrub.

Any exploration of the medina is bound to start at the medina's main southern gate, the triple-arched **Bab Diwan**. This gate was added in 1306, and stands in the middle of the most impressive section of the ramparts.

THE LIFE OF THE MEDINA

Despite their chaotic appearance, medinas were laid out according to strict Islamic principles, thought to have originated in 8th-century Baghdad. Their layout is carefully adapted to the rigours of the climate. The deep, narrow streets keep the sun's rays from the centre during the day, and draw in the cool evening air during the night. Earth, stone and wood were used to absorb water, which then evaporates and cools the surrounding air.

Medinas also served a military purpose, surrounding the city with fortified, crenellated walls and towers (Sfax's are among the best preserved in Tunisia), elaborate *babs* or *skifas* (gates) designed to impress as much as to regulate entry to the city, and fortresses occupied by Islamic warriors.

Inside the walls, the heart of any medina was the city's main mosque, normally known as the Jami el-Kebir or Great Mosque. This should be located at the exact centre of the medina, as is the case in Sfax and Tunis. Radiating out from the Great Mosque were the souqs – still today the heartbeat of any medina. Closest to the mosque were purveyors of the 'noble trades': vendors of candles, incense and other objects used in the rites of worship. Next to them were the booksellers, venerated in Muslim cultures, and the vendors of leather goods. These were followed by the clothing and textile stalls, long the domain of the richest and most powerful merchants.

The hierarchy then descended through furnishings, domestic goods and utensils. Finally, on the city perimeter and away from the piety of the mosque, the caravans used to assemble and here were found the ironmongers, blacksmiths and the other craftsmen and vendors serving the caravan trade.

The *funduqs* or *caravanserais* (ancient hotels) were important features of any medina. Here, traders, nomads, pilgrims and scholars stayed while in town, usually on their route elsewhere (eg Kairouan or Mecca). Traditionally, an unadorned façade provided a doorway wide enough to allow camels or heavily laden beasts to enter. The central courtyard was open to the sky and surrounded by a number of stalls, bays or niches. The ground floor housed shops, warehouses, teahouses and stabling for the animals; the upper floor accommodated the travellers. The Funduq des Forgerons (opposite) in Sfax is an evocative example.

Apart from these buildings around which the public life of the city revolved, most of the medina was the domain of residential quarters. The Tunisian town house, known as the *dar* or interior-courtyard house, has remained largely unaltered for 3000 years. The principal feature is a central courtyard, around which are grouped suites of rooms in a symmetrical pattern. In the wealthier houses, service areas were often tacked on to one side. The courtyard was designed to keep the house light and cool as well as provide a space for communal family life. Rooms could be used interchangeably for eating, relaxing and sleeping. The hottest part of the day is spent in the cool of the courtyard, and at night, the roof terrace can be used as a sleeping area. The Dar Jellouli Museum (opposite) in Sfax is a fine example of just such a house.

The street façade is usually just a plain wall, and the only opening is the entrance door. Any other openings are small, grilled and above the line of vision of passers-by, reflecting the strict demarcation of public and private life in Islamic society.

To the north is the ornate eastern wall of the **Great Mosque** (closed to non-Muslims), founded by the Aghlabids in the middle of the 9th century AD. The eastern wall is the only section that's visible, as the other sides are hidden by souqs. The elaborate sandstone **minaret**, a smaller replica of the three-tiered square minaret at Kairouan, was added by the Fatimids in AD 988. It's best viewed from rue des Aghlabites, to the north of the mosque; take the stairs next to the entrance of the teahouse for the best view.

Further north you can discover the wonderful world of the **covered souqs**. The main souq heading north is the celebrated **Souq des Etoffes**, which was used as the setting for the Cairo markets in the film *The English Patient*.

Souq des Etoffes emerges on rue des Teinturiers, where the dyers once carried on their business. If you keep going until you hit rue Abdelkader, which runs inside the medina's northern wall, you'll get to the delightful **Bab Jebli**, one of the original Aghlabid gates.

Nearby, the **Funduq des Forgerons** no longer functions as a *funduq*, but still serves as a base for the city's *forgerons* (blacksmiths). It's like walking back a century in time, into a world of blackened faces, smoking fires, red-hot metal and constant hammering. Climb up to the 1st floor for views down into the courtyard. This is the most recognisable of the sites used for *The English Patient*.

The **Dar Jellouli Museum** (admission TD1.1, plus camera TD1; 9.30am-4.30pm Tue-Sun) is in a classic courtyard house, built by the wealthy Jellouli merchant family in the 17th century, and is filled with beautiful carved-wood panels, rich tile decoration and ornate stuccowork. The displays include traditional costumes and jewellery, but the building is the star attraction.

The **Borj Ennar** is a small fort added in the 17th century to protect the southeastern corner of the medina, and is now the headquarters of the Association de Sauvegarde de la Medina, the group responsible for preserving the medina. It has a good map of the medina showing all 69 mosques and all sites of historical interest.

West along rue Borj Ennar, the minaret on the left after 50m belongs to the **Mausoleum of Sidi Amar Kammoun**, built at the start of the 14th century. To the west is the **kasbah**. Built by the Aghlabids, it began life as a watchtower but was steadily expanded into a kasbah over the centuries.

VILLE NOUVELLE

South of the medina is the Ville Nouvelle, a fairly compact and walkable area where the majority of the restaurants, shops and hotels are located. It's a mix of sophisticated clothing boutiques, apartment buildings and government buildings that close fairly early in the evening.

The focal point is the **place de la République**, fronted by a number of superb French-era buildings at the junction of ave Hedi Chaker and ave Habib Bourguiba. The grand building on the southern side of the square is the **town hall**. As well as housing the city's bureaucrats, it's also the home of the **archaeological museum** (admission TD1.1, plus camera TD1; 8.30am-3pm summer, 8.30am-1pm & 3-6pm winter), housing some impressive finds from nearby Roman sites.

Other architectural highlights in the area include the fine **French consulate** (13 ave Habib Bourguiba) and the **police station** (11 ave Habib Bourguiba) – no photos are permitted at either place, though.

Sleeping

MEDINA

The cheapest places are found in the medina. All budget places listed here have shared bathrooms unless stated.

Hôtel Medina (74 220 354; 53 rue Mongi Slim; d TD8) If you can find it, the Medina is only acceptable during the cooler months as there is no air-con nor fans and the small bare rooms get hot.

Hôtel Ennacer (74 211 037; 100 rue des Notaires; r TD20;) By far the best of the medina budget hotels, the Ennacer is near Bab Jebli on the northern edge. Air-con is available in a few rooms for TD5 more, though most stay cool from natural breezes and all are kept immaculate. What makes it special, however, are the views from the rooftop – it's conceivable management will let you sleep on the roof in summer.

On a sliding scale downwards to the grim but very cheap end of the scale, there are some basic places just inside Bab Diwan. The least bleak among them include **Hôtel Besbes** (rue Borj Ennar) and **Hôtel el-Mokhtar** (rue Borj Ennar).

VILLE NOUVELLE

Budget

Auberge de Jeunesse (74 243 207; www.ibn-sina.org.tn; rte de l'Aéroport; dm TD6) A kilometre or so northwest of the medina is the spick and span Sfax youth hostel. Toilets are shared and there are separate showers for men and women.

Hôtel de la Paix (74 296 437; fax 74 298 463; 17 rue Alexandre Dumas; s/d TD12/18) The bottom of the barrel as far as accommodation in the Ville Nouvelle goes, La Paix is well located and cheap. And what else could you expect at this price? Top-floor rooms with shared bathroom are even cheaper.

Hôtel Alexander (74 221 613; 21 rue Alexandre Dumas; s/d TD15/25) What once could be called character, now is nothing more than old age at this four-storey hotel next to La Paix. The vestiges of what it was once can be seen in the high ceilings and balconies. Rooms with shared facilities are a few dinars cheaper.

Midrange

Hôtel Thyna (74 225 317; fax 74 225 773; 37 rue Habib Maazoun; s/d with breakfast & TV TD30/46;) Only a block or so from the southern entrance to the medina, the Thyna is both ideally located and excellent value. The attractively done lobby suggests a high-end boutique hotel but the rooms, while perfectly comfortable and kept immaculate, are more Ikea. There's a charming little café on the 3rd floor and you can store your bags there if you want to lighten your load when heading to the Kerkennah Islands.

Hôtel La Colisée (☎ 74 227 800; fax 74 299 350; 32 ave Taieb Mehiri; s/d TD31/40;) Formerly the top of the line as far as midrange accommodation in the city centre goes, this high-rise hotel has fallen far. Rooms here are large, especially the bathrooms, some of which have large bathtubs, but from the lobby to the hallways everything is dark.

Top End

Hôtel Syphax (☎ 74 243 333; fax 74 245 226; ave des Martyrs; s/d with breakfast TD75/90;) Formerly part of the Novotel chain, this hotel 2km west of the medina on the way to the airport is a rapidly fading, low-slung complex that does little to justify its out-of-the-way location. Staff are friendly and there is an outdoor pool, however there's little attention to detail or upkeep in the rooms or of the facilities.

Mercure Accor Hôtel (☎ 74 225 700; sfax@abounawas.com.tn; 15 ave Habib Bourguiba; s/d TD105/135;) Previously the Abou Nawas Sfax, the Mercure Accor is conveniently located only a few blocks from the train station right in the middle of town. However, its service is far from courteous and the rooms themselves are simply not worth the high price, though they do have balconies. There is a rooftop pool and several restaurants, though they may only open for groups and the food is unremarkable.

Les Oliviers (☎ 74 201 999; www.goldenyasmin.com; 25 ave Hedi Chaker; s/d TD130/170;) It's a bit of a surprising sight, this beautiful looking faux palace hotel, one of the classiest in the country, sitting across from a neglected patch of grass and surrounded by pot-holed and derelict looking buildings. The lobby and the rooms of Les Oliviers are as impressive as the façade, all mahogany and fine finishing and there's a sunny atrium that houses a pleasant café. Downstairs is a dark and atmospheric pub, the walls lined with posters of Hollywood and Arab film stars and musicians. There's a business centre, though internet access is unreliable.

Eating

RESTAURANTS

There's a cluster of cheap restaurants on the right just inside the medina's Bab Diwan. Most are signed only in Arabic and are very popular, with locals chowing down on rotisserie chicken and couscous.

Sandro Pizzeria (sandwiches TD2) This place directly across the street from the place de la République is open later than most and serves excellent *gyros* – pick your filling – bursting at the seams. Pizza (TD3.5) is also available and you can eat in or take away.

Twings (ave Habib Bourguiba; mains TD3;) This is a US-style fast food joint with a wide selection of menu items from chicken wings and hamburgers to pitta sandwiches.

Restaurant Budaya (rue de la Kasbah; mains TD3;) This is another cheap medina eatery serving up rotisserie chicken, though the Budaya is slightly more modern and comfortable than the others and has air-con.

Restaurant Speciality Lebanese (rue de Haffouz; mains TD3;) Across from the port, this place serves up an excellent variety of pizzas in a comfortable 2nd-floor dining area.

Restaurant au Bec Fin (place du 2 Mars; mains TD4) Centrally located and popular with regular locals, this restaurant has a large, plain dining room and Tunisian fare to match.

Pizza Galaxy (ave des Martyrs; mains TD7;) Convenient only if you're staying at the Hôtel Syphax outside of town, Pizza Galaxy is a big, modern restaurant with a massive menu serving pizza, pasta and meat dishes.

La Perla (ave Habib Bourguiba; mains TD7) Conveniently located close to several of the hotels, La Perla is somewhat elegant in that there are tablecloths and silverware. Besides pasta, fish and meat dishes, alcohol is served.

Le Petit Navire (☎ 74 212 890; rue de Hafouz; mains TD7, set menu TD15) One of Sfax' more elegant restaurants, the high ceilinged, 2nd floor dining room at Petit Navire overlooks the harbour area. As you might expect, fish is the speciality here.

Restaurant Le Corail (☎ 74 227 301; 39 rue Habib Maazoun; mains TD13) Next to the Hôtel Thyna this place doesn't serve food of remarkably better quality than any of the less expensive options but you're paying for the waiters' uniforms and the slightly upscale décor.

SELF-CATERING

Monoprix supermarket (rue Aboulkacem ech Chabbi; 8.30am-9pm) This is a nice and modern supermarket in the centre of town.

Drinking

Café Maure Diwan (off rue de la Kasbah; 6am-midnight) This is a great atmospheric place to kick back and smoke a *sheesha* or kill a few hours with a coffee or the house speciality *thé au pignons et menthe* (mint tea with pine nuts; TD1). Cut into the medina wall between Bab Diwan and Bab el-Kasbah, Maure Diwan is a refuge from the heat, sun and claustrophobia of the medina streets.

Club My House (rue Mohammed Ali) From the outside, Club My House looks like it's part of a set for the film *Pirates of the Caribbean*. Inside, it's a two-storey modern hangout for the young and hip of Sfax. A huge flat-screen TV plays Arabic-language music videos, while friends and dates share milk-shakes (TD2), ice cream, floats, coffee etc on comfy lounge chairs. Food is also served, such as crepes (TD2), *paninis* (TD2) and hamburgers (TD1.5).

Black In White Café (blvd République) This is a typical outdoor café patronized by regulars, young and old alike, along the pedestrian plaza near ave Habib Bourguiba.

Shopping

The shops in the **Souq des Etoffes** stock a range of Berber rugs, blankets and other handicrafts from the villages of the Gafsa region. Although the selection is somewhat more limited compared with Tunis, Sousse and Kairouan, shop owners here are less likely to adopt hard-sell techniques and more likely to start off with a price somewhere in the ballpark of what items reasonably cost.

ONAT (rue Salem Harzallah; 8am-1pm & 5-8pm Mon-Sat) This is a good crafts shop on the southern part of rue Salem Harzallah.

Getting There & Away

AIR

Tuninter (☎ 74 228 028; 4 ave de l'Armée) has two flights a week between Tunis and Sfax (one way/return TD58/113, 45 minutes).

BOAT

Soretrak (☎ 74 498 216, ave Mohammed Hedi Khefecha) ferries for the Kerkennah Islands leave from the southwestern corner of the port. There are 11 crossings a day in summer, four in winter. Timetables are displayed at the port and at the tourist office. The trip costs 800 mills for passengers and TD4 for a car. The crossing takes about 1¼ hours in good weather and there can be long queues to take a vehicle across in summer. In summer, the last boat back from the islands leaves around 8.45pm. Grab a seat in the shade or else you'll be baking in the sun the entire trip. Food and snacks are sold on board.

BUS

All buses leave from the **bus station** (rue Commandant Bejaoui) southwest of the medina. SNTRI is on the north side of the road, while the depot for the local company Soretras is to the south.

SNTRI also operates a daily international bus service to Tripoli, in Libya (TD17.8, seven hours); ask at the SNTRI office for the latest departure times.

Destination	Fare (per day)	Duration	Frequency
Douz	TD15	5 hrs	2
El-Jem	TD3	1¼ hrs	10
Gabès	TD6.3	2 hrs	10
Houmt Souq (Jerba)	TD14.5	5 hrs	3
Medenine	TD9.2	3 hrs	2
Sousse	TD6.1	2 hrs	10
Tataouine	TD11.7	4 hrs	2
Tunis	TD13.5	5 hrs	8

Soretras operates a busy intercity schedule, including hourly services to Mahdia (TD2.7) and three daily buses to Kairouan (TD5.5).

CAR

The main international rental-car companies with a presence in Tunisia are represented here, as is a slew of small local companies.

Avis (☎ 74 224 605; rue Tahar Sfar)
Europcar (☎ 74 226 680; 40 rue Tahar Sfar)
Hertz (☎ 74 228 626; 47 ave Habib Bourguiba)
Location 2000 (☎ 74 221 763; ave Habib Thameur)
Mattei (Ada; ☎ 74 296 404; 18 rue Patrice Lumumba)

LOUAGE

The **louage station** (cnr rues Commandant Bejaoui & de Maurianie) is a compound 200m west of the bus stations. There are departures to Gabès

(TD5.9), Sousse (TD5.9) and Tunis (TD10.9). Other destinations include El-Jem (TD3.2), Mahdia (TD4.8) and Jerba (TD11.2).

There are also louages to Tripoli (TD30). These vehicles are yellow and white, and often have Libyan markings.

TRAIN

There are three trains a day south to Gabès (three hours) and one late-night train to Gafsa (3½ hours) and Metlaoui (4¼ hours). Heading north, there are five trains daily to El-Jem (one hour), four to Sousse (two hours) and six to Tunis (3½ hours).

Destination	2nd class	1st class	Confort
El-Jem	TD3.1	TD4.1	TD4.4
Gabès	TD5.3	TD7.2	TD7.9
Gafsa	TD7	TD9.4	TD10.1
Sousse	TD4.9	TD6.5	TD6.9
Tunis	TD10.2	TD13.5	TD12.6

Getting Around

TO/FROM THE AIRPORT

The **airport** (☎ 74 241 740) is 6km from town on the Gafsa road at Thyna – TD3.5 by taxi.

KERKENNAH ISLANDS جزر القرقنة

pop 16,000

To Tunisians born and raised here, this cluster of nine low-lying islands, 25km east of Sfax, evokes warm memories of peaceful evening strolls with family along the shore. To visitors, the flat, desolate landscape, once valued as a place of exile, is less liable to provoke nostalgia though it is a chance for a beach holiday away from the mass tourism found elsewhere along the coast.

Tourism here means residents of Sfax gathering up the kids and heading out on the ferry for a Sunday picnic. So far, the islanders have resisted any large-scale development and prefer the timeless rhythms dictated by nature. Fishermen still use traditional traps made from palm fronds. Lines of fronds are stuck in the sea bed in a 'V' shape, and the fish are then driven into this large funnel to a small trap at the end.

Orientation

The two main islands, Île Gharbi and Île Chergui, are connected by a small causeway dating back to Roman times.

Most of the population lives on Chergui. The only place of any consequence is the small town of Remla, the administrative and service 'capital' of the islands.

Information

There's a branch of the UIBC bank in Remla with an ATM, on the road leading down to the sea next to the Hôtel el-Jazira, or change money at one of the hotels. Remla also has a hospital, post office and police station.

Sights & Activities

BORJ EL-HISSAR

Borj el-Hissar is an old fort on the coast, about 3km north of the hotels at Sidi Frej. It's

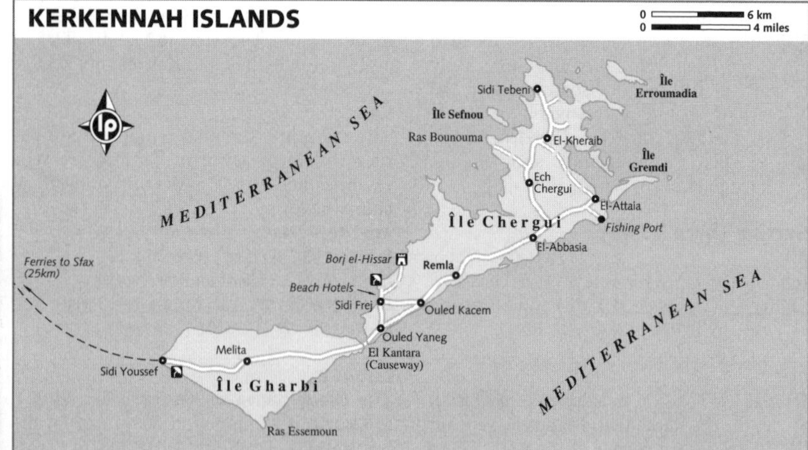

well worth the 40-minute walk; it's clearly signposted from near the Hôtel Le Grand. The small fort itself was built by the Spanish in the 16th century, but Roman ruins surround the fort. You get the feeling that you are stumbling across something previously undiscovered, with mosaics covered by sand and ruins disappearing into the sea.

BEACHES

The sea is very shallow – good for kids and adults who don't like to get their hair wet. You can walk out 100m before even your knees get wet. The best beach is at **Ras Bounouma**, northeast of Sidi Frej, but there's no public transport.

Sleeping & Eating

REMLA

Youth Hostel (☎ 74 481 148; per person TD5) Situated across the road from the beach, this place has clean and well-maintained facilities. Reservations in summer are recommended and camping is an option if you have your own equipment.

Hôtel el-Jazira (☎ 74 481 058; s/d TD14/22) The one and only hotel in Remla, opposite the bus station on the main street, has plain but clean rooms, a restaurant and the only bar in town. Breakfast is included.

The Restaurant La Sirène has a shady terrace overlooking the sea and does meals for around TD15, plus wine. The Dauphin, next to El-Jazira does basic Tunisian dishes.

SIDI FREJ

Appart Hôtel Aziz (☎ 74 259 933; s/d TD25/42; 🏊) Just up and across the road from the Club Residence, this hotel has no beachfront property and it won't exactly feel like an island holiday staying here. It can feel lonely here with no other guests for company. The rooms are big and come with stand-up fans.

Kerkennah Islands Club Residence (☎ 74 489 999; s/d TD35/50; ❄ 🏊) This large complex feels like an empty warehouse with large spaces given over to functions that seem to only rarely happen – there's even a small amphitheatre on the grounds. Accommodation is in simple whitewashed rondavels on a grassy lawn set back from the pool area. There's isn't much of a beach to speak of though you can conceivably enter the water from here. An extra TD5 gets you air-con.

Hôtel Cercina (☎ 74 489 953; hotel.cercina@planet.tn; s/d TD40/60) The first hotel you come to in Sidi Frej, the Cercina won't win any architectural awards for it's Soviet-style concrete block aesthetic, but it's comfortable enough if you get a room with a sea view. Rooms in a newer annexe are more modern though most don't front the sea.

Grand Hotel (☎ 74 489 861; www.grand-hotel-kerkennah.com.tn; s/d TD60/90; ❄ 🏊) The inappropriately named Grand caters to both package-tour groups from Britain and Tunisians looking for a version of *zone touristique* hotels found elsewhere. It all feels a little down on its luck with a sad-sack looking lobby area and aging rooms. What it does have is the only good beach around, with water excellent for wading, and a nice pool area.

All of the hotels have restaurants and the food is generally unspectacular except for the local speciality, a thick, spicy octopus soup called *tchich*, and freshly caught fish. There's a pleasant restaurant and café on the main road just before the turnoff for the Hotel Cercina.

Getting There & Away

See p219 for details of ferries between Sfax and Sidi Youssef.

Getting Around

BICYCLE

The flat terrain is ideal for cycling although shady spots are few and far between. Most of the hotels rent out bicycles (TD2 per hour, TD10 per day).

BUS

There's a small network of buses connecting the villages of the islands and at least two or three meet each ferry; all go to Remla. One (with a 'hotel' sign in the window) goes via Sidi Frej (TD1). There are buses from Remla and the Sidi Frej junction to Sidi Youssef departing about an hour before the ferry. Times are posted in the bus station window in Remla.

The Remla bus station is opposite the Hôtel el-Jazira.

TAXI

Dozens of shared taxis also meet each ferry as it docks. These are much more convenient and quicker than the buses and only slightly more expensive (TD1.5).

Gabès, Matmata & the Ksour

Covering a good chunk of territory from the Gulf of Gabès to the Libyan border, this fairly remote region of southern Tunisia is a forbidding landscape of inhospitable desert, though not the sandy sort that inspires poetry and romantic fantasies. Recognisable to anyone who has travelled in the western part of the United States or *Star Wars* fans, the land here ranges from scrub brush flats to low mountain escarpments, all of which looks like the ends of the earth.

The area receives few visitors, most on lightning-quick Land Rover 'safaris' of the underground troglodyte dwellings of Matmata and one or two of the ruined hilltop Berber villages around Tataouine. It's easy to find yourself staring at the empty fortress-like homes imagining what life would be like, so isolated not only by distance from other settlements but by the mere physical challenge of visiting the neighbours. Each of the villages has at least one *ksar* (the plural is *ksour*), the wonderfully idiosyncratic fortified strongholds that are the region's trademark. Gabès, the terminus of the rail line, is the de facto transport centre and while its *palmeraie* (palm grove) is an attractive place in which to get lost, the city's industrial character holds few visitors in its thrall.

HIGHLIGHTS

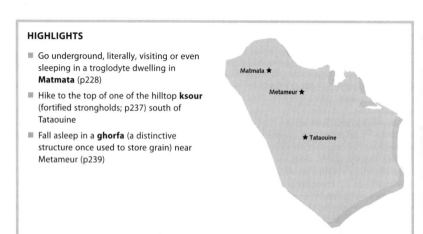

- Go underground, literally, visiting or even sleeping in a troglodyte dwelling in **Matmata** (p228)
- Hike to the top of one of the hilltop **ksour** (fortified strongholds; p237) south of Tataouine
- Fall asleep in a **ghorfa** (a distinctive structure once used to store grain) near Metameur (p239)

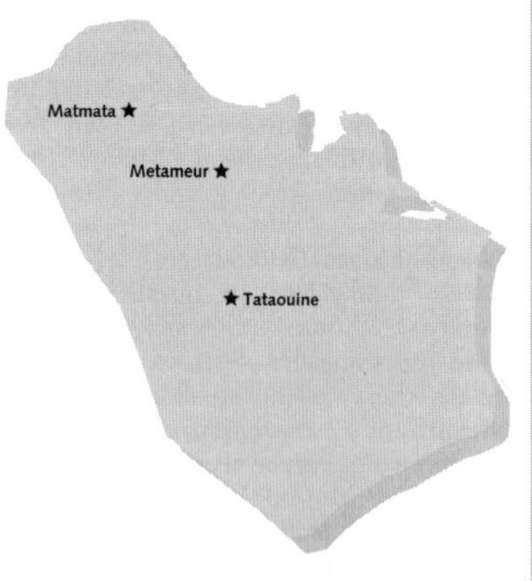

History

The Ksour district, centred on the hills of the Jebel Dahar has long been a stronghold of Berber culture – ever since the seminomadic Berber tribes who inhabited the Jeffara were driven into the hills by the Hilalian invasions of the 11th century. The villages around here are among the last places where the local Berber language, Chelha, can be heard. With the deaths of elderly speakers, the language too is dying out.

Getting There & Away

Other than flying to Jerba and then crossing the Roman causeway or ferry to the mainland, the quickest way to the region is to arrive in Gabès via the train. There are no commercial flights from Tunis or elsewhere in the country.

Getting Around

Most people zip around the region in a 4WD as part of a group tour. A rental vehicle allows you the luxury of choosing your itinerary. Public transport connects the towns in the region though it's sometimes difficult to do more than two legs of a trip in one day.

GABÈS قابس

pop 116,300

For a seaside city at a major transport crossroads, Gabès does little to take advantage of its location, at least as far as tourism

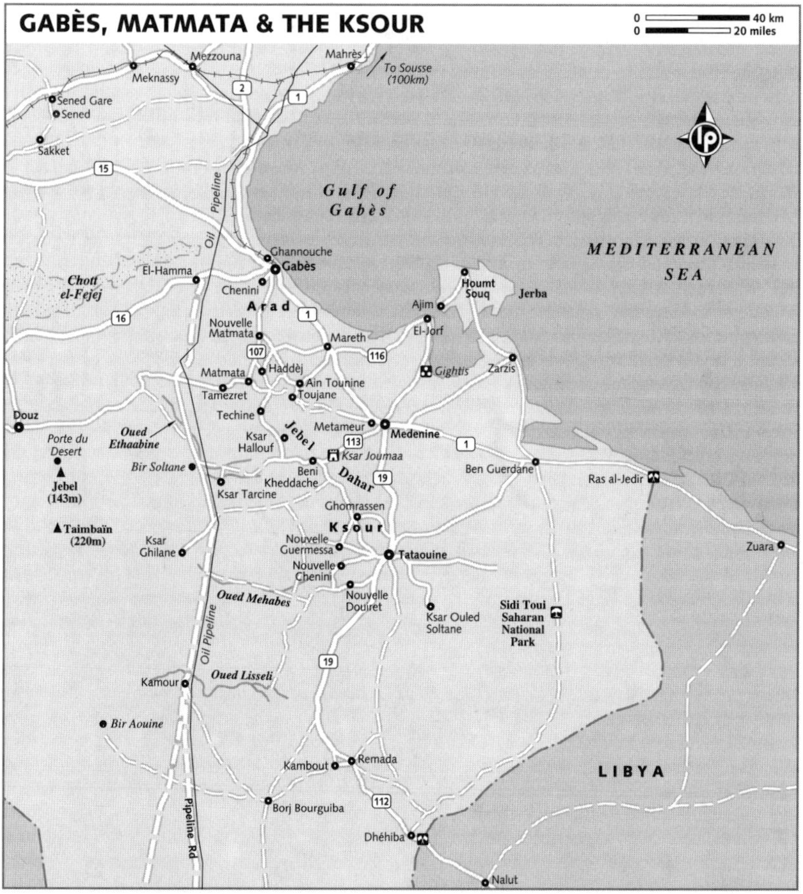

GABÈS, MATMATA & THE KSOUR

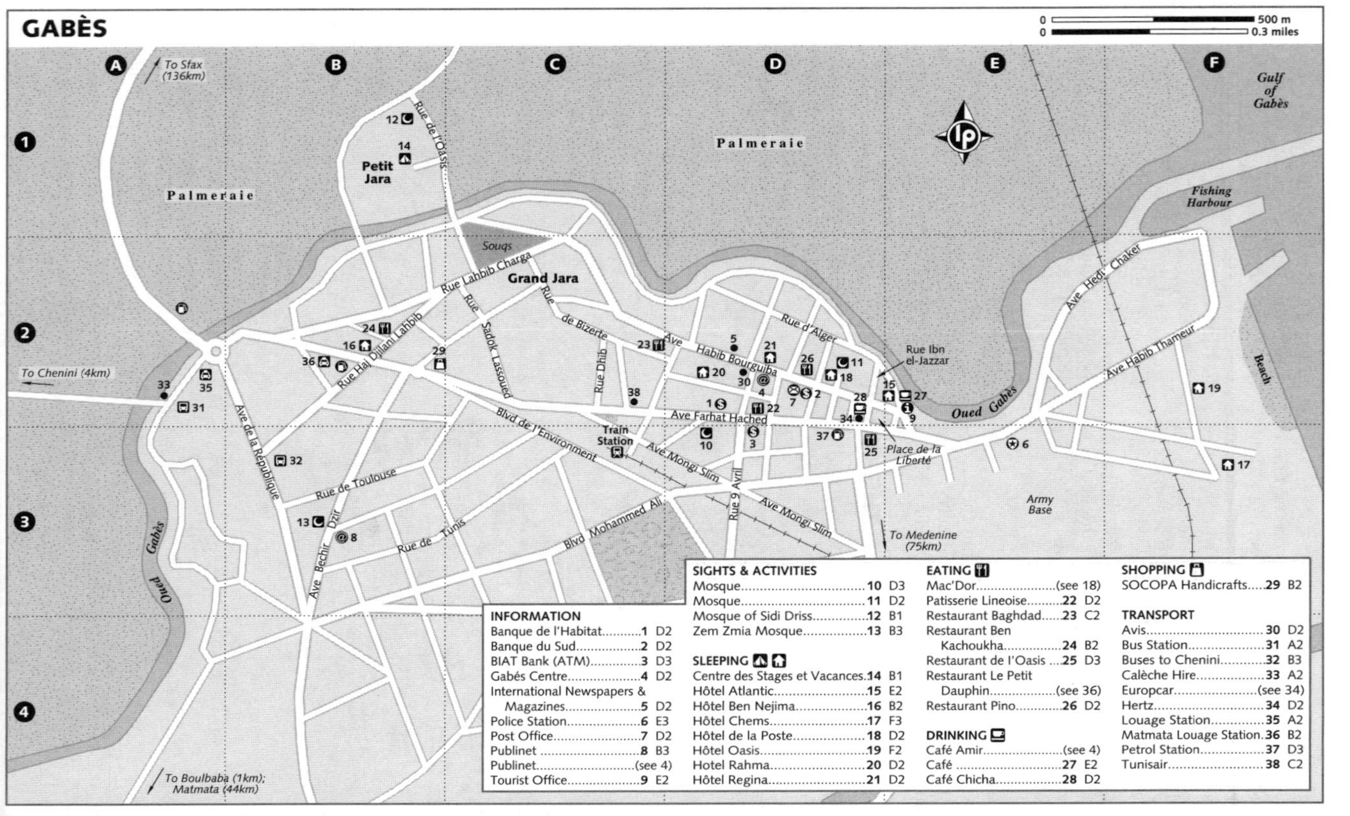
GABÈS
0 500 m
0 0.3 miles
To Sfax (136km)
Gulf of Gabès
Palmeraie
Palmeraie
Petit Jara
Grand Jara
Souqs
Fishing Harbour
Beach
Army Base
Train Station
Oued Gabès
Oued Gabès
To Chenini (4km)
To Boulbaba (1km); Matmata (44km)
To Medenine (75km)
Rue de l'Oasis
Rue Lahbib Charga
Rue Sadok Lassoued
Rue de Bizerte
Rue Hai Djilani Lahbib
Ave de la République
Rue de Toulouse
Ave Bechir Dziri
Rue de Tunis
Blvd Mohammed Ali
Blvd de l'Environment
Ave Mongi Slim
Rue 9 Avril
Rue Dhib
Ave Habib Bourguiba
Ave Farhat Hached
Rue d'Alger
Rue Ibn el-Jazzar
Place de la Liberté
Ave Hedi Chaker
Ave Habib Thameur
INFORMATION
Banque de l'Habitat 1 D2
Banque du Sud 2 D2
BIAT Bank (ATM) 3 D3
Gabès Centre 4 D2
International Newspapers & Magazines 5 D2
Police Station 6 E3
Post Office 7 D2
Publinet 8 B3
Publinet (see 4)
Tourist Office 9 E2
SIGHTS & ACTIVITIES
Mosque 10 D3
Mosque 11 D2
Mosque of Sidi Driss 12 B1
Zem Zmia Mosque 13 B3
SLEEPING
Centre des Stages et Vacances 14 B1
Hôtel Atlantic 15 E2
Hôtel Ben Nejima 16 B2
Hôtel Chems 17 F3
Hôtel de la Poste 18 D2
Hôtel Oasis 19 F2
Hotel Rahma 20 D2
Hôtel Regina 21 D2
EATING
Mac'Dor (see 18)
Patisserie Lineoise 22 D2
Restaurant Baghdad 23 C2
Restaurant Ben Kachoukha 24 B2
Restaurant de l'Oasis 25 D3
Restaurant Le Petit Dauphin (see 36)
Restaurant Pino 26 D2
DRINKING
Café Amir (see 4)
Café 27 E2
Café Chicha 28 D2
SHOPPING
SOCOPA Handicrafts 29 B2
TRANSPORT
Avis 30 D2
Bus Station 31 A2
Buses to Chenini 32 B3
Calèche Hire 33 A2
Europcar (see 34)
Hertz 34 D2
Louage Station 35 A2
Matmata Louage Station 36 B2
Petrol Station 37 D3
Tunisair 38 C2

goes. The infrastructure of the busy port and industrial sector blocks much of the seafront and pollutes the air, so that the city focus is directed instead inland towards the impressive *palmeraie*. Most people who have travelled this far, 137km southwest of Sfax, are on their way to or from Matmata, the Ksour or Jerba. The city is home to a recently established university that specialises in information technology and engineering. The main campus is in the southern part of the city on the road to Matmata.

History

Gabès has been inhabited since prehistoric times though little of note happened here until the town grew rich in the 14th century as the main Tunisian destination for the great camel caravans that brought gold and slaves from across the Sahara. The French invasion of the Sahara in the 19th century killed off the caravans and Gabès slipped back into obscurity. It boomed again after the discovery of oil in the gulf in the mid-20th century.

Orientation

Although Gabès is a coastal city, its orientation is towards the *palmeraie* that surrounds the modern town to the north and west. The town centre is about 2km inland, skirted by the Oued Gabès to the north. Most of the services required by travellers are on or near the two main east–west thoroughfares – ave Farhat Hached and ave Habib Bourguiba. The Gabès Centre, a hulking shell of concrete with a few shops, is at the heart of the town. There's a small, unspectacular beach next to the fishing harbour.

Information

INTERNET ACCESS

Publinet (2nd fl, Gabès Centre, ave Habib Bourguiba; per hr TD2; 🕑 8am-10pm)
Publinet (ave Bechir Dzir; per hr TD2; 🕑 8am-midnight)

MEDIA

There's a shop that sells international newspapers and magazines on ave Habib Bourguiba.

MONEY

There's a cluster of banks on ave Habib Bourguiba around the Gabès Centre.

Banque de l'Habitat (ave Farhat Hached) ATM.
Banque du Sud (ave Habib Bourguiba) ATM.
BIAT (ave Farhat Hached) ATM.

POST & TELEPHONE

You can use any of the Taxiphone offices around town.

Post office (ave Habib Bourguiba) Centrally located; telephones.

TOURIST INFORMATION

Tourist office (☎ 75 274 248; cnr aves Farhat Hached & Habib Bourguiba; 🕑 8.30am-1pm & 3-5.45pm Mon-Thu, 8am-1pm Fri & Sat) Doesn't see many tourists but more helpful than most. There's a complete list of bus departures, hotel prices and an old Lonely Planet map of the town posted on the door.

Sights & Activities

PALMERAIE

The *palmeraie* stretches inland along the Oued Gabès. It begins on the coast at **Ghannouche** and ends more than 4km west of Gabès at the oasis village of **Chenini** (not to be confused with Chenini near Tataouine – see p236). This western section is the most interesting (and least polluted) part.

Walking is the best way to explore. You can follow the shortcut used by the *calèches* (horse-drawn carriages), crossing the *oued* (dry riverbed) by the bridge behind the bus station and turning left onto the Chenini road. The road then twists and turns through the *palmeraie* to El-Aouadid, where a left turn leads down to Chenini. It's a pleasant walk of about one hour. The *palmeraie* looks its best during the pomegranate season in November and December, when the trees are weighed down with huge ruby-red fruit.

Chenini itself has not much more to offer other than loads of souvenir stalls. A path (negotiable by bicycle) heads off around the back of a partially reconstructed Roman dam and winds through the *palmeraie* to an open-air café tucked away in the palms. It's about a 20-minute walk and you can continue along the *oued* to the end of the valley. Climb up the small escarpment for a view of the surrounding area.

To get back to Gabès from Chenini, bus 7 runs between the village and rue Haj Djilani Lahbib, or pay around TD3 for a taxi. Horse-drawn carriages (TD15), which can hold up to four people, are a popular alternative to walking; find them behind the bus station.

JARA

The Jara is the old district that straddles the *oued* on the northern edge of town. The **Petit Jara**, amid the palm trees north of the *oued*, is the oldest part of town. The **Mosque of Sidi Driss**, at the far end of rue de l'Oasis, dates back to the 11th century. The old market, where the slaves once were sold, is in **Grand Jara**, south of the *oued*. These days you're as likely to find cheap tourist souvenirs as gold, and silversmiths and henna.

Sleeping

BUDGET

Centre des Stages et Vacances (☎ 75 270 271; dm TD5, camping for 2 TD7) In a shady location in the *palmeraie* of Petit Jara, this government-run youth hostel provides typical bare-bones accommodation with, on average, seven to nine beds a room. There's a large canteen that will serve up grub for groups.

Hôtel de la Poste (ave Habib Bourguiba; s/d TD8/15) This hotel doesn't have much going for it besides its central location and cheap price tag but for many that's enough. It's been around since the '20s and it shows in the chipped paint and less-than-comfortable beds. Bathrooms are shared.

Hôtel Ben Nejima (☎ 75 271 591; cnr ave Farhat Hached & rue Haj Djilani Lahbib; s/d TD10/16) Even if the lobby décor is chintzy and artificial, the friendly Ben Nejima should be applauded for the effort. For better of worse, none of this was carried over to the fairly spartan rooms, however, it's hard to beat for the price and convenience to the *palmeraie* and local transport. Bathrooms are shared.

Hôtel Regina (☎ 75 272 095; fax 75 221 710; ave Habib Bourguiba; s/d with private bathroom TD13/20) It has a good location opposite the Gabès Centre and popular street-side cafés but the Regina is a little dreary. Basic rooms with large bathrooms surround a big and bare concrete courtyard that could be put to better use.

Hôtel Atlantic (☎ 75 220 034; fax 75 221 358; ave Habib Bourguiba; s/d TD15/28; ❄) Dramatically framed by two towering palm trees that reach to the 5th floor rooftop, the Atlantic's ornate colonial façade is best seen at night when, like an aging movie star its flaws are harder to see. The rooms themselves are not in terrible condition though the size and quality vary but be warned that there's some kind of DJ booth/bar on the ground floor that blasts music loud enough to hear in Libya.

> **HENNA**
>
> Gabès is well known for its high-quality henna, which is made by grinding the dried leaves of the henna tree (*Laussonia inermis*), a small evergreen native to the region. Gabès' henna produces a deep red-brown dye. Berber women use it to decorate their hands and feet, as well as to colour and condition their hair. You'll see henna powder for sale in the souqs, piled up in colourful green pyramids. Henna costs about TD1.5 for 100g.
>
> If you want a henna tattoo, ask any of the stall holders around the souq on rue Lahbib Charga or in the *palmeraie* village of Chenini. Prices vary as wildly as the designs.

MIDRANGE & TOP END

Hotel Rahma (☎ 75 275 385; fax 75 275 710; rue Boulbaba Mrabet; s/d TD30/45; ❄) Easily the best choice in Gabès, the Rahma has small, modern, well-kept rooms with cable TV. The only downside is not much natural light makes it into the rooms. There's a ground floor restaurant and café and it's only a short walk from the train station.

Hôtel Chems (☎ 75 270 547; www.hotelchems.com.tn; off ave Habib Thameur; s/d TD55/80; ❄ 💻 🏊) The Chems is a better choice than the next door Oasis though it too suffers from grandiose ambitions, maybe best exemplified in its very own small bowling alley. Most of the rooms are well kept and have balconies with sea views and the pool is a pleasant spot to relax.

Hôtel Oasis (☎ 75 270 381; www.sdts.tourism.tn; off ave Habib Thameur; s/d TD64/104; ❄ 🏊) Don't judge this hotel by its stars – four are too many and the rates are high for rooms that are far from posh. The fitness centre looks like it hasn't been used since the days of Charles Atlas but there is a thermal swimming pool and bar, and it fronts the beach. The restaurant is merely adequate.

Eating

Patisserie Lineoise (ave Farhat Hached; ❄) The Lineoise is a friendly and modern bakery with good coffee and ice cream to boot.

As You Like Chapati (ave Habib Bourguiba; sandwiches TD2) The name says it all at this fast-food-style joint.

Mac'Dor (ave Habib Bourguiba; sandwiches TD2) Like its American namesake, Mac'Dor is usually hopping, though the menu here is mostly hearty *shwarmas* (sliced meat in pitta-type bread) and pizzas.

Restaurant Le Petit Dauphin (ave Farhat Hached; mains around TD3.5) For those heading out of town, this is conveniently located as part of the louage (shared taxi) station complex, but it's also worth a visit for the friendly ambience and big helpings of couscous. Open for breakfast, closed Sunday night.

Restaurant Ben Kachoukha (☎ 75 220 387; rue Haj Djilani Lahbib; mains TD4) An unassuming and no nonsense place, Ben Kachoukha serves a regular clientele but will welcome strangers. It serves standard Tunisian fare and freshly caught fish.

Restaurant Baghdad (ave Habib Bourguiba; mains TD4) This modest place in the quiet part of town is accustomed to foreign travellers. There are tablecloths, an English menu and healthy sized servings.

Restaurant Pino (ave Habib Bourguiba; set menus TD5;) One of the best places to refuel, Pino is a pleasant and modern restaurant, serving up large portions of the standard meat dishes plus salads and pizzas. The 2nd floor dining room is quiet.

Restaurant de l'Oasis (☎ 75 273 087; ave Farhat Hached; mains TD8; closed Sun) As close to a culinary institution as you can come in Gabès, the Oasis adds a touch of class to the usual fare, with both Tunisian and continental dishes served up in elegant if not baroque dining rooms. It's one of the few places in town where credit cards are accepted.

Drinking

Maybe the most popular night-time spot for men, women and children is the café behind the tourism office. There's a small park with a duck pond and trees for shade.

Café Chicha (cnr aves Habib Bourguiba & Farhat Hached) In the gravel spot in the place de la Liberté, the aptly named Chicha is a little more refined than the average plastic chair joint.

Café Amir (Gabès Centre) Most of the tables here are set up in the interior courtyard of the Gabès Centre though there's a fan cooled indoor area as well.

Shopping

Gabès is a major centre for straw goods – baskets, hats, fans and mats. There's plenty to choose from in the souqs off rue Lahbib Charga in the Grand Jara district.

Getting There & Away

BUS

At least three companies operate out of the bus station at the western end of town. Daily departures include: Tozeur (TD9.7, 9am, 1pm), Jerba (TD6, seven daily), Sfax (TD7.3, six daily), Sousse (TD12.2, four daily), Tunis (TD17, six daily), Tataouine (TD6, 10am, 4.15pm), Douz (TD8, noon, 3.45pm, 6pm), Matmata (TD1.7, six daily) and Gafsa (TD8, six daily).

CAR

Because of its location Gabès is a good place to begin and end a trip further south if you intend to rent a car. Avis, Europcar and Hertz all have offices in town.

LOUAGE

The louage station adjoins the bus station, with departures for Kebili (TD6.2), Jerba (TD6, includes cost of ferry), Medenine (TD4), Sfax (TD7), Sousse (TD12), Tunis (TD18.3), Douz (TD7.7), Tozeur (TD10) and Tataouine (TD6.5). Most departures are in the morning; things quieten down considerably as the afternoon wears on.

For Matmata, louages leave from a separate lot along ave Farhat Hached. Services go to Nouvelle Matmata (TD1.4) where you'll have to change to old Matmata (a further 750 mills).

TRAIN

The **train station** (☎ 75 270 944) is just off ave Mongi Slim, a five-minute walk from ave Habib Bourguiba. There are four trains daily to Tunis (2nd/1st class TD14.9/20.1, six hours, 5am, 11.15am, 4.10pm, 12.05am).

MATMATA مطماطة

pop 1000

From above, the underground troglodyte dwellings Matmata is famous for looking like bomb craters, providing an interesting and unique inverse skyline. Home to around 500 people, the ingenious dwellings only come into focus up close and are a testament to our urge to domesticate anywhere. Some of these are hard to find, blocked by conventional, modern buildings that are now in the majority. Surrounded by a barren, eroded landscape of fissures and craters, the Berbers of Matmata found a way to rig up air conditioning naturally. More recently, Matmata, 45km southwest of Gabès gained a measure of cinematic fame as the setting for the home planet of Luke Skywalker of *Star Wars*. Residents and tourism officials have eagerly embraced this fact, and it's sometimes hard to tell whether the busloads of visitors, most on overnight excursions from Jerba, are more excited by the *Star Wars* memorabilia or the unusual architecture.

There are licensed guides who charge TD10 for a guided tour of the village or TD15 for tours of both Matmata and Tamezret (you'll have to provide the transport to Tamezret). You can reach the guides through the *syndicat d'initiative* (tourist office) or ask at your hotel.

Orientation & Information

The road from Gabès descends into Matmata from the north and continues through town to the east as the back road to Medenine. In the centre of town, ave de l'Environnement branches off to the west towards Tamezret and Douz. All of the town's attractions are on or just off these two main thoroughfares and all of the hotels are just off the southern side of the road.

The closest bank is the Banque Nationale Agricole in Matmata Nouvelle, 15km away. Midrange and top end hotels might be able to help with exchanging cash. The post office is in the centre of town, opposite the turn-off to Douz. The small **syndicat d'initiative** (☎ 75 230 114; ⌚ 8am-noon & 3-5.30pm Mon-Thu, 8am-noon Fri & Sat) is just downhill from the bus station, at the turn-off to the Hôtel Kousseila. The staff aren't trained to provide any real help.

Troglodyte Homes

Matmata's underground homes are easily accessible to travellers though many people are satisfied after visiting several of the budget hotels. Just about all group tours stop at the **Hôtel Sidi Driss**, which outdoes the others in terms of sheer tackiness, as if nailing a *Star Wars* beach towel to the wall proves its screen credentials. Spread over five pit courtyards, all connected by underground tunnels, the hotel courtyard did stand in for the young Skywalker's childhood home and the hotel was used again in *The Phantom Menace, Attack of the Clones* and *Episode IV – A New Hope*. Of the other hotels, **Hôtel Marhala** has some of the best-looking grottoes and tunnels.

Another option for viewing the pit dwellings is the small **Musée Berber** (⌚ daily), run by local women who have displays of carpet-making and traditional keys – because doors are secured by long, wooden bolts that disappear into the wall, these keys are up to a foot long, and open the door by releasing the bolt through a keyhole in the wall. The long, sloping entrance tunnel is one of the best in town. It's all quite rustic and unadorned, wherein lies its charm. Opening hours are unpredictable but mornings are the best times. A donation of TD2 is expected.

You'll probably be accosted by children offering to take you around to visit private homes. You may even be flagged down while driving and stop, thinking someone is in danger only to be offered a tour for an inflated price. If you do decide to take one of the kids up on their offer, agree to a price in advance. The people of Matmata get little enough privacy so visiting by invitation is infinitely more respectful than seeking them out on your own.

There are also a couple of homes set up for tourists on the last 3km into town from Gabès.

Sleeping

Matmata has an excellent choice of accommodation for all budgets. Some places, however, are often completely booked out by large tour groups passing through for the night. The town's three budget hotels are traditional troglodyte dwellings.

BUDGET

Hôtel Marhala (☎ 75 240 015; fax 75 240 109; s/d with breakfast TD13.5/18, half board TD15/22) The best of the below ground hotels, the Marhala is run by the Touring Club de Tunisie, though it has anything but a tourist group vibe. There are plenty of compact and cosy doubles with comfortable mattresses and electricity and the share bathrooms are immaculate. Meals are served in a dining room cave.

Hôtel Les Berbères (☎ 75 240 024; fax 75 240 097; off ave de l'Environnement; s/d with breakfast TD14/25) This is the last of the troglodyte options before heading out of town on the road to Douz. Long labyrinthine passages lead to simple bedroom grottoes.

Hôtel Sidi Driss (☎ 75 240 005; fax 75 240 005; s/d with breakfast TD16/32) Stop by if you're interested in standing where Luke Skywalker dined in *Star Wars*, otherwise it's best to avoid the Sidi Driss, easily the worst of the troglodyte hotels. Accommodation is an afterthought here and beds seem to have been tossed into the underground rooms willy-nilly. Don't be surprised if your wake-up call is a group of camera toting tourists.

MIDRANGE & TOP END

All of the hotels in this category are above ground and prices include breakfast.

Hôtel Kousseila (☎ 75 303 355; fax 75 240 265; s/d TD32/64;) Housed in a large rambling complex without any effort to blend in to the desert surrounds, this modern hotel in the middle of town is popular with large groups. Be sure to ask for one of the doubles with the vaulted ceiling since these are quite large and comfortable compared with some of the more basic rooms on offer. There's a restaurant and bar and good views from a series of rooftops.

Hôtel Matmata (☎ 75 240 066; matmatahotel@yahoo.fr; s/d TD35/70;) A cross between Berber architecture and a *zone touristique* hotel, the Matmata combines the strengths of both. It has modern rooms, some with vaulted domed ceilings, rose petals scattered on the beds, tile floors and colourful carpets, but it's designed to resemble a traditional *ksar* from the outside. There's a pool, restaurant and bar. Highly recommended.

Hôtel Ksar Amazigh (☎ 75 240 088; fax 75 240 173; s/d TD35/60;) Looking like a run-down Berber village, this hotel 1.5km out of town on the way to Tamezret, has equally run-down rooms, though the pool and views do provide compensation. It has a restaurant and bar but it's bound to feel lonely if there isn't a big group in residence.

Hôtel Diar el-Berber (☎ 75 240 074; www.diarelbarbar.com; route de Tamazret; s/d TD70/120, half board TD80/120;) Like the Matmata, this hotel 1.8km west of town has the façade of a traditional *ksar* but the Diar el-Berber ratchets things up a few notches in terms of luxury. The courtyards, surrounded by several floors of modern barrel-vaulted rooms, look surreal and the views over the desert from the poolside terrace are breathtaking. Buffet meals are served in the restaurant and there's a relatively posh bar with a big-screen TV.

Eating

The two restaurants in town, the **Chez Abdoul** (mains TD4) and the **Restaurant Ben Khalifa** (mains TD4), both across from the bus and louage stations, serve standard fare and all of the hotels, including the troglodyte ones have restaurants. It helps to order in advance and if there's a big group in residence there's often no choice but to order the more expensive set meal. The Hôtel Diar el-Berber has the nicest restaurant in terms of décor and service and you can sit outside for excellent sunset views.

If you're staying the night, you're better off taking a room with half board.

Getting There & Away

The bus and louage stations are in the centre of town. Louages run throughout the day to Nouvelle Matmata (750 mills), from where louages go to Gabès (TD1.4). This is the only way to get to Douz or Tataouine without your own transport.

There are nine buses a day to Gabès (TD1.7), as well as an afternoon bus to Tamezret (900 mills, 1.30pm) that returns to Matmata an hour later, although check with the driver before setting out. There are also two to Techine (900 mills), one to Jerba that leaves at 10am and one evening SNTRI bus to Tunis (TD18.6, eight hours).

AROUND MATMATA

Haddèj حدّاج

The village of Haddèj, 3km northeast of Matmata, provides a chance to see **pit dwellings** without feeling like you're following in well-trodden footsteps. Though hardly developed compared with Matmata, the purpose of your visit is no secret to locals and you'll probably be surrounded by enterprising and persistent children hoping to act as guides. It's best to take one of them up on the offer – a tip of course is expected – since you'll likely feel uncomfortable bounding into homes on your own, many of which were abandoned after the severe floods of 1969. The most interesting attraction is an underground olive press, where big millstones are turned by a camel in an impossibly small space. There's also a press operated by weights and levers. It was in Haddèj that the crucifixion scene in *Monty Python's Life of Brian* was filmed.

GETTING THERE & AWAY

The road to Haddèj is signposted to the east 4km north of Matmata on the road to Gabès. There's no public transport from old Matmata, but there are occasional buses and *camionnettes* (small pick-ups used as taxis) to and from Nouvelle Matmata. Otherwise, catch a bus as far as Tijma and walk the remaining 3km to Haddèj.

If the weather is favourable, there's an excellent walk back to Matmata along the mule track that cuts directly through the hills. It takes about 1½ hours at a steady pace. Ask the locals in Haddèj to point it out to you, as it's not obvious where it starts. Once you are on it, it's well trodden and easy to follow. There's little shade to protect you from the scorching sun.

Tamezret تمزرات

If you're driving between Matmata and Douz you'll pass through this quiet village overlooking the Nefzaoua plains. Though only 13km west of Matmata, Tamezret sees few tourists stop for anything more than a photo op and maybe a drink at the roadside café. The houses here are built above ground, using the abundant local rock. The old quarter, above the bus stop, is a maze of alleyways that winds around the hillside. There are two afternoon buses from Matmata.

An excellent sealed road continues from Tamezret to Douz, 97km further west; the turn-off for the route south to Ksar Ghilane is signposted along here. There are several cafés along this desolate route, though they are really nothing more than a shack with coffee and some cold drinks available. This is one of those routes where drivers take sympathy on anyone unfortunate or unlucky enough to be caught out here walking – it's a mystery where they're coming from – and are expected to pick up hitchhikers.

East of Matmata

The dramatic scenery east of Matmata on the back road to Medenine justifies a journey out here. It's a good sealed road as far as the turn-off to **Techine**, 12km to the southeast of Matmata. Techine is a smaller version of Matmata, minus the tour buses; you'll find plenty of volunteers for the job of leading the way to the pit homes, which are unusual for their built-in furniture. There are two afternoon buses from Matmata to Techine (900 mills).

You'll need your own transport if you want to continue further east. The road runs through some wild hill country, much of it covered by esparto grass, which the locals gather and use for making all sorts of things, from mats to mule harnesses (see the boxed text, p180). It finally emerges at **Toujane**, 23km southeast of Matmata. This extraordinary place of stone houses spread around a hillside and beneath the ruins of an old kasbah, is cut by a gorge that leads down to the coastal plain. It's very photogenic, particularly in the early morning light. Several informal tourist facilities have sprung up recently, indicating a possible future transformation. Signs in English announce carpets for sale, little shacks offer coffee or tea and the **Auberge Shambhala** (r TD 12) has a few rooms in a troglodyte dwelling or more conventional ones up the hill. A few other enterprising villagers have more informal accommodation on offer but bathroom facilities may be either entirely lacking or in the least wanting.

A 4WD is necessary to continue on the back road from Toujane to Medenine, 38km to the southeast, but there's a good sealed road northeast from Toujane to the town of **Mareth**, on the main road from Gabès to Medenine, which has a **WWII Museum**.

An alternative is to turn northwest at **Ain Tounine**, 4km north of Toujane, and head back to Matmata Nouvelle, passing the charming stone village of **Ben Zeiten** on the way.

TATAOUINE تطاوين

pop 64,000

There's no photogenic medina to explore and little to recommend this town; however, it's an excellent and logical place to base yourself if you're venturing further south to see the ruined hilltop *ksour*. Despite Tataouine's popularity on the southern tourist trail, few solo travellers make it here, so you're bound to get more attention than elsewhere.

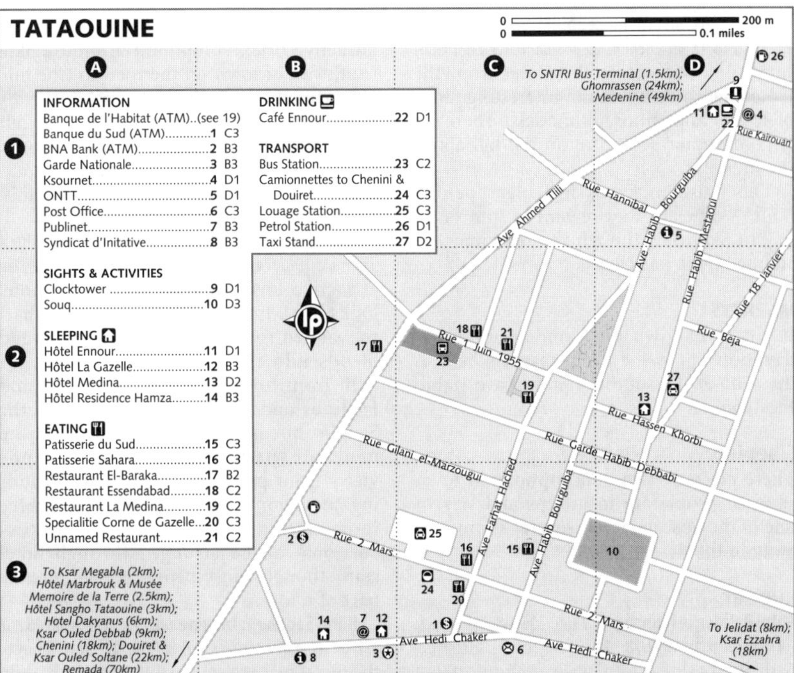

Almost everything of importance for the traveller is found within the town centre, between the east–west ave Hedi Chaker and the small clocktower in the north.

Information

INTERNET ACCESS

Ksournet (rue Habib Mestaoui; per hr TD2; 9am-midnight;) Opposite the clocktower; modern and good connections.

Publinet (ave Hedi Chaker; per hr TD1.5; 9am-midnight) Next to the Hôtel La Gazelle; generally slow connections.

MONEY

Most major banks have offices in town and all change money.

Banque de l'Habitat (ave Farhat Hached) ATM.

Banque du Sud (ave Farhat Hached) ATM.

BNA (ave 2 Mars) ATM.

POST & TELEPHONE

There are plenty of Taxiphone offices around the town centre.

Post office (ave Hedi Chaker) Opposite the southern end of ave Habib Bourguiba.

TOURIST INFORMATION

ONTT tourist office (☎ 75 850 686; ave Habib Bourguiba; 7.30am-1pm & 3-6pm summer, 8am-12.30pm daily & 3-5.30pm Sat-Thu winter) At the northern end of town.

Syndicat d'initiative (☎ 75 850 850; ave Hedi Chaker; 8.30am-1pm & 3-5.45pm Mon-Thu, 8.30am-1pm Fri & Sat) Small but helpful.

Sights & Activities

KSAR MEGABLA

This small *ksar*, about 2km from the town centre, is a good place to start your exploration of the *ksour*, although much of the façade originally built in 1409 is no longer intact. It does, however, retain glimpses of its original character that can be lacking in some of the more heavily restored *ksour*. The villagers still keep their livestock in the cells and the courtyard can be uneven underfoot. Ksar Megabla is signposted to the right off the Remada road; it takes about one hour to walk up there from the main road.

MUSÉE MEMOIRE DE LA TERRE

It's no surprise that dinosaurs once called the barren and parched land around here home. This small **museum** (Memory of the Earth Museum; route de Chenini; admission TD1.5), 2.5km south of town across the street from the Hôtel Mabrouk, houses an interesting range of fossils and dinosaur models. There's a large dinosaur sculpture on the hill above the museum.

The museum keeps irregular opening hours – officially they're 9am to 7pm Tuesday to Saturday, though the few times we stopped by it was closed.

MARKETS

If you're in town on Monday or Thursday, don't miss the lively markets held in the souq at the southern end of ave Habib Mestaoui.

Sleeping

There are only two good options in town as most people are in groups and stay in one of the upscale hotels several kilometres away in the desert.

BUDGET

Hôtel Residence Hamza (☎ 75 863 506; ave Hedi Chaker; s/d with breakfast TD17/28;) For those satisfied with the basics – four walls, a comfortable bed and light – the Hamza is actually a better deal than the nearby La Gazelle. Admittedly, the entrance is none too promising but reception is on the 2nd floor and the family that runs the place is very welcoming. Every four rooms share a bathroom.

None of the other budget options can really be recommended though **Hôtel Ennour** (☎ 75 860 131; ave Ahmed Tili; s/d TD3/6) and **Hôtel Medina** (☎ 75 860 999; rue Habib Mestaoui; s/d TD9/15) are clean enough to be occupied. All facilities are shared.

MIDRANGE & TOP END

Hôtel La Gazelle (☎ 75 860 009; fax 75 862 860; ave Hedi Chaker; s/d TD33/49;) Resting on its laurels as the only midrange option in town, La Gazelle isn't especially good value though the large and simple, characterless rooms are comfortable enough. It has some cavernous public spaces including a bar and a restaurant that's kept so dark it's hard to read the menu. Large groups tend to pull in here for the night and vacate early the next morning.

Hôtel Mabrouk (☎ 75 853 853; hotelmabrouk@messagerie.net; route de Chenini; s/d TD45/80;) A less costly alternative to the Sangho is this attractive brick compound around 2.5km southwest of town on the road to Chenini. Unfortunately, it's not the most friendly place, especially if you show up on your own, but the stone and marble rooms, charming vaulted hallways and large outdoor garden more than make up for this. Plans call for a pool in the near future.

Hôtel Dakyanus (☎ 75 832 199; www.dakyanushotel.com; s/d TD62/74;) From the front, the attractive low slung façade of this hotel looks like a traditional *ghorfa* (a long, barrel-vaulted room built to store grain) and blends into the desert environment. It's 6km from town, has modern rooms and facilities and is not quite as nice as the Sangho but is a good choice for a more moderate price. There are panoramic views from parts of the property including 2nd-floor room balconies. It has three restaurants, a pool and a tennis court. Excursions can be arranged through hotel staff, though most people arrive already part of a tour.

Hôtel Sangho Tataouine (☎ 75 860 124; fax 75 862 177; off route de Chenini; s/d TD86/120;) This is the nicest place to stay in Tataouine, not only for the facilities but also for the large and relatively posh low slung bungalows. There's a pool (nonguests TD10), tennis courts (netfree when we stopped by), bar (rum TD2.3) and a good restaurant. The Sangho is around 3km southwest of town; to find it make the left just before the Mabrouk.

Eating

RESTAURANTS

Few restaurants in Tataouine are geared to tourists; most are coffeehouses-cum-cafés or holes in the wall that aren't especially inviting.

Hôtel La Gazelle (starters from TD2.5, mains TD6; lunch & dinner) For a true sit down experience, your best bet is to head here or better yet, to one of the top end hotels outside of town. Expect to pay around TD12 or more for a meal and if there's a big group in residence you'll probably be limited to whatever set menu they're having.

Restaurant Essendabad (closed Sun) Across from the bus station, Essendabad has a range of daily specials though it's filled as much with people waiting for their transport as it is with diners.

THE BERBERS

The Berbers, the indigenous people of North Africa, got their name (the Greek *barbarikos* means 'foreign') from the Arabs who arrived at the end of the 7th century and sought to distinguish the Berbers from those who had adopted Roman/Byzantine culture. The ancient Egyptians knew them as the Libou (nomads); the Greeks called them Libyans, as did the Phoenicians; and the Romans called them Africans.

Ethnically, the Berbers are a cultural melting pot – the result of successive waves of immigration from the Near East, sub-Saharan Africa and southern Europe. By the time the Phoenicians arrived in the 10th century BC, these diverse peoples had adopted a uniform language and culture.

Berber territory was divided up into tribal confederations. Northern Tunisia was the territory of the Numidians, founders of the cities of Bulla Regia, Sicca (El-Kef) and Thugga (Dougga). Other tribes had settled in the major oases of the south, while others lived a seminomadic pastoral existence.

Although conquered many times through history, the Berbers proved hard to repress. Military resistance to Roman rule continued until AD 24, and later resurfaced in the 4th century. They were probably at the peak of their political and military power when the Arabs arrived. The Berbers' greatest success against these latest invaders was the capture of Kairouan, which became the base for a short-lived Berber kingdom until 689.

The next wave of rebellion was led by Al-Kahina, a legendary figure in Berber lore. The widow of a tribal chief from the Aures Mountains in Algeria, she defeated Hassan bin Nooman at Tebessa in 695 and pushed back the Arab armies as far as Gabès, before fighting her last stand in the colosseum of El-Jem (p208). More trouble was to follow in the form of Berber-led Kharijite rebellions that flared intermittently over the following 250 years, but effective resistance to Arab rule ended with the Hilalian invasions in the 11th century.

Tunisia's Berbers have become all but totally assimilated with the Arab population. Berber customs, however, continue to survive – particularly in rural areas. Many women still wear the traditional *bakhnoug* (shawl) and *assaba* (headband) and tattoo their faces with ancient tribal symbols; men still favour the *burnous,* a hooded woollen cape.

Restaurant La Medina (ave Farhat Hached) and **Restaurant el-Baraka** (ave Ahmed Tili) have similar menus of cheap Tunisian standards for around TD2 a dish.

For bargain, good-sized *briqs* (pastries; 400 mills) with a hint of onion, it's hard to beat the small unnamed restaurant just along from the bus station on rue 1 Juin 1955; look for the orange-and-yellow awning outside.

PATISSERIES

All of Tataouine's many pâtisseries sell the local speciality, *corne de gazelle* (350 mills) – a pastry case, shaped like a gazelle's horn, filled with chopped nuts and soaked in honey. Good places to try are the hole-in-the-wall **Patisserie Sahara** (ave Farhat Hached), **Specialitie Corne de Gazelle Restaurant** (ave Farhat Hached) or **Patisserie du Sud** (ave Habib Bourguiba).

Drinking

Not surprisingly, the coffeehouse is the centre of social activity in Tataouine for men.

Café Ennour (ave Habib Bourguiba) This place is at the intersection just south of the clocktower and spills out onto the street in the afternoon.

Café de l'Union (ave Hedi Chaker) Next to Hôtel la Gazelle, this café is a standard no frills coffeehouse, but enough groups of tourists stop here so female foreigners should feel perfectly comfortable.

Hôtel La Gazelle has the only bar in town and it's this monopoly that may explain why little effort has been made at decoration. Cold beers cost TD2.

Getting There & Away

BUS

The bus station occupies the large compound at the western end of rue 1 Juin 1955. There are four daily buses to Medenine (TD2.4, one hour), one to Houmt Souq (Jerba; TD6.4, 2½ hours) and six to Ghomrassen (TD1.3, 30 minutes); the last bus back from Ghomrassen leaves at 4.30pm. There's a daily bus southeast to

Beni Barka, Maztouria and Ksar Ouled Soltane (TD1, 45 minutes), leaving town at 6am, and returning at 6pm.

SNTRI runs three daily air-con buses to Tunis (TD23, eight hours) that travel via Gabès (TD6.4, two hours), Sfax (TD11.5, four hours) and Sousse (TD16.5, 6½ hours). Buses leave from the SNTRI terminal 1.5km north of town on the road to Medenine.

CAMIONNETTE

Camionnettes leave from opposite the louage station on rue 2 Mars with fairly regular departures for Chenini (TD1), Douiret (TD1.3) and Maztouria (TD1); some continue to Ksar Ouled Soltane (TD1.4). The earlier you set off the better as the system slows down around noon and is virtually nonexistent after 3pm.

LOUAGE

Louages leave from the northern side of rue 2 Mars. There are regular departures for Medenine (TD2.2) and Remada (TD3.8), and occasional services to Jerba (TD6.5), Ghomrassen (TD1.2) and Tunis (TD22.5). For Matmata, change at Gabès.

AROUND TATAOUINE

The land immediately west of Tataouine doesn't look hospitable for human beings ,which is perhaps why George Lucas chose to name Luke Skywalker's desert home planet after the city itself. Despite the conditions,

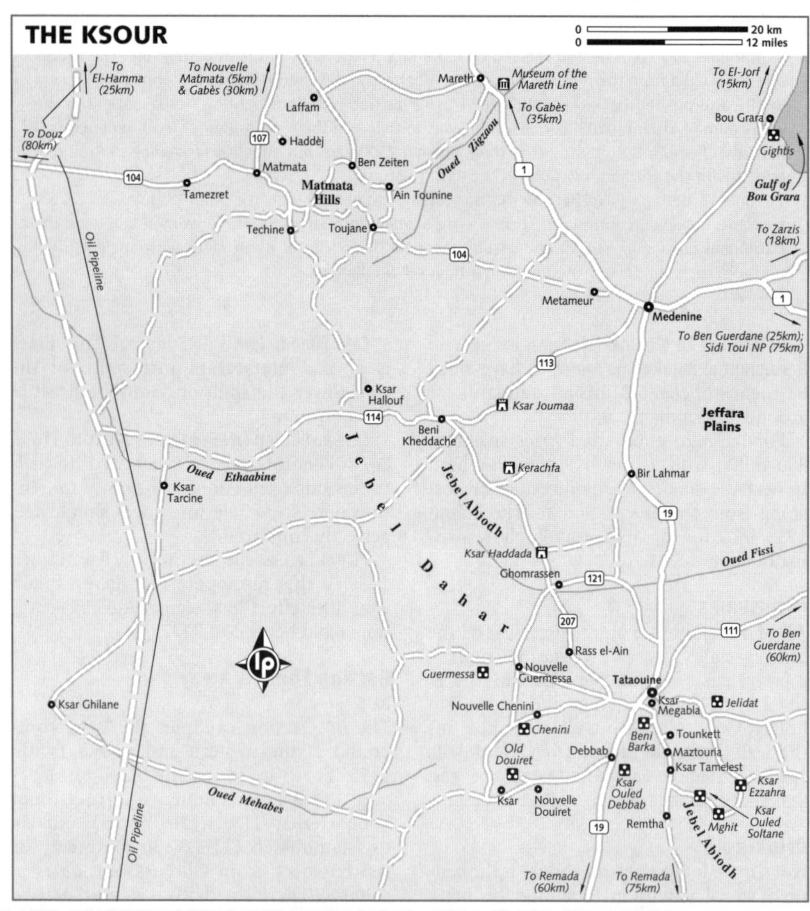

the area is home to centuries-old Berber and Arab villages clinging to hilltops with a few *ksour* dotted among them. South of Tataouine, in the low hills of the Jebel Abiodh, is somewhat different – more Arab than Berber and home to some of Tunisia's best *ksour*.

GETTING AROUND

Easily the best way to get around the area is to have your own vehicle. Chartering a taxi is the next best option. Rates quoted by taxi drivers vary wildly, but count on TD60/30 for a day/half day. This gives you more freedom to stop where and for how long you want. A good half day could take in Ksar Haddada, Guermessa, Chenini and Douiret, or a loop through the *ksour* south of Tataouine.

Using public transport is extremely inefficient and you'll be limited to one or two sites a day. *Camionnettes*, buses and other vehicles are thin on the ground.

Berber Villages & Ksar Haddada

GHOMRASSEN غمراسّن

Once the stronghold of the powerful Ouergherma federation, which ruled from here until it moved to Medenine in the 17th century, Ghomrassen now has a modern town that is continuing to expand with a bank, shops, a Publinet and a couple of restaurants – but no hotels. It's 24km northwest of Tataouine and is the main town of the Jebel Demmer.

The old part of town, to the south on the way to Guermessa, is a fine place to wander. It is spread along a gorge carved out by a broad *oued*, and protected by the ramshackle walls of the old **kalaa** (Berber hill fort) on both sides. It does have a couple of *ksour* in the vicinity, notably the **Ksar Rosfa**, which affords fine views over the surrounds, and **Ksar Bani Ghedir**, north of town, which is a typical one-storey plains *ksar*. You'll need to ask directions for both in town.

The best day for getting transport to Ghomrassen is Friday, when the market draws traders from all over the region. Otherwise, there are six buses a day to Tataouine (TD1, 30 minutes), and five to Medenine (TD2, one hour), as well as services to Guermessa (500 mills, 15 minutes) and Ksar Haddada.

HILLTOP VILLAGES

Southern Tunisia's oldest surviving settlements are the spectacular hilltop villages built to take advantage of the region's dramatic rocky outcrops. The outcrops are formed by alternate layers of soft and hard rock, which have weathered into a series of natural terraces.

They are dotted with natural caves, which became a place of refuge for Berber tribes who were forced to flee the plains by the Hilalian invasions of the 11th century. The caves were extended into houses by tunnelling rooms into the soft rock, and further expanded by the addition of walled courtyards at the front. The highest point of the villages was occupied by a *ksar*, where the food supplies and valuables of the village were stored, while the village itself stretched out along the terraces below.

The best examples of Berber hilltop villages are those of Chenini, Guermessa and Douiret.

KSAR HADDADA قصر حادادة

Ksar Haddada, 5km north of Ghomrassen, draws a steady stream of visitors who marvel at the maze of small alleyways and courtyards. A restored section of the *ksar* was once occupied by the fabulous Hôtel Ksar Haddada, which became a place of pilgrimage for *Star Wars* fans following its appearance in *Star Wars IV – A New Hope*. The orange door jams were part of the set. The hotel has closed and the place is falling apart. Despite this, it's a special place. The old palm doors are superb and it's a wonderful site for exploring and reliving all those *Star Wars* memories.

There are occasional buses from Ghomrassen, but it's quicker to stand by the road and flag down whatever comes your way (for information on the risks associated with hitching see p311).

GUERMESSA قرماسة

Like most of the villages in the area now, there are two Guermessas – there's the nondescript modern town in the plains below and the fairly impressive ruined Berber village strung out along the hilltop above. The abandoned stone village makes exemplary use of the region's fortresslike hills and spreads across two peaks, linked by a narrow causeway. The larger peak is topped by a ruined *kalaa*. Less intact than some of the other villages, old Guermessa gives an impression of the village slowly merging back into the mountain, an effect that the photogenic white mosque below merely highlights. Guermessa remains relatively undiscovered by large numbers of visitors.

You need a 4WD to drive up to the site, which can be reached via the road to Ksar Ghilane and Douz, signposted to the east 1km north of the modern village. The turn-off to the site is 3km along this road, and loops back to Guermessa. This approach provides a great view. If you're walking, take plenty of water.

You might find the occasional bus to Nouvelle Guermessa from Ghomrassen, but the best option is to charter a taxi from Tataouine (see p235) and combine your visit with one to Chenini and Douiret.

The most direct road from Guermessa to Chenini is 4WD only.

THE SEVEN SLEEPERS

The area around Tataouine lends itself to legend and fairy tale, whether in dramatic hilltop villages or improbable *ksour* architecture that has drawn the directors of Hollywood.

One local fable is not out of place in such company. Beyond the white mosque of Chenini, a 20-minute walk leads to a mosque and a series of strange 5m-long grave mounds known locally as the graves of the Seven Sleepers. According to local legend, seven Christians (and a dog) went into hiding in a nearby cave to escape persecution by the Romans. They slept for 400 years and awoke to find a world of Islam, long devoid of Romans. While they had slept, their bodies had continued to grow until they were 4m tall. They awoke only to die almost immediately, which must have been quite disappointing. To compensate, the story goes that, before dying, the men converted to Islam, assuring them of their place in paradise.

CHENINI شنني

Part of the 4WD 'safari' circuit, Chenini, the best known of the hill villages can get crowded by mid-morning. The approach to this village, only 18km west of Tataouine, is a scenic rollercoaster of small hills and turns but the village only comes into focus after rounding the mountain bend and looking up.

The picturesque ruins of the original *kalaa*, dating from the 12th century AD, stand at the junction of two ridges. The settlement tumbles down and out from this point, built into the rock along a series of small terraces that leads around the steep hillside. The houses consist of a cave room, which has a fenced front courtyard containing one or two more rooms. Highlights include doors made from palm trunk, and the interiors of some cave rooms still containing the faded remnants of decorative paintwork and carvings on the roof. Some of the doorways here are so small they require a contortionist's flexibility to enter. The *ksar* is still used to store grain and the village even retains a few occupants (unlike the other villages), although most of Chenini's inhabitants have moved to the modern settlement of Nouvelle Chenini.

A path leads up from the road to a beautiful white mosque situated on a saddle between the two ridges.

To get the most out of your visit, it can be worth allowing one of the village children to show you around, as some of the features can be hard to find. There's a very nice and modern **restaurant** (⏰ 7am-3pm) and café at the base of the village where you'll park. It has an à la carte menu though if there's a big group in town the set menu may be your only option.

Camionnettes from Tataouine stop at Nouvelle Chenini; sometimes it's possible to persuade the driver to continue the last 2km to the ruins. A charter taxi from Tataouine starts at about TD20 return.

There's a good sealed road south to Douiret, following the course of an *oued* through the hills to Nouvelle Douiret. The road directly north from Chenini to Guermessa is best tackled by 4WD; there's another sealed road that's more roundabout though only slightly longer.

DOUIRET دويرات

Most of old Douiret is abandoned, both by residents and tourists, so a visit here is a chance to wander around an ancient and crumbling *ksar* at your leisure. Perched high on the spur of a hill 22km southwest of Tataouine, and above a dazzling whitewashed mosque, white *marabout* (holy man or saint) and other tombs dot the plains below. As at Chenini, the houses are built into the rock along terraces that follow the contour lines around the hill. The main terrace leads south for 1km to more houses, some of which are still occupied. Look out for some of the ornate carved doorways and Berber designs painted on the walls. Stairs lead up the hill next to the mosque and the higher you climb, the better the views.

The road to Douiret is signposted from Debbab, 9km south of Tataouine on the road to Remada. Unless you've chartered a taxi, transport to Douiret is few and far between. Early morning is the best time to catch a *camionnette* from Tataouine, but they normally go only as far as Nouvelle Douiret, 1.5km before old Douiret. You may be able to persuade the driver to take you the rest of the way, but you'll certainly have to walk back afterwards to find a ride to Tataouine.

Ksour القصور

KSAR OULED DEBBAB قصر أولاد دباب

This huge *ksar* sits on a low hill just east of the modern village of Debbab, 9km south of Tataouine on the Remada road. It was occupied until several years ago and most of the buildings are still in good condition. There's a sealed road leading up to the entrance gate from Debbab; the walk takes about 20 minutes.

KSAR OULED SOLTANE قصر أولاد صلطان

Ksar Ouled Soltane, 22km southeast of Tataouine, has the best set of *ghorfas* (long barrel-vaulted rooms built to store grain) in the south, rising a dizzying four storeys around two courtyards. The *ghorfas* have been renovated to give a sense of how they must once have appeared. It's a terrific place that shouldn't be missed. The lower courtyard is used as a stage for performances during the **Festival of the Ksour** in late November.

The views of the sunset from here are wonderful, but don't get here too late or the courtyards will be quite dark. There's a small, friendly café in one of the *ghorfas*.

THE KSAR

The structure that typifies Berber architecture is the *ksar* (plural *ksour*), the traditional fortified granary built by the region's tribes. Its design reflects the main priority of its builders – to preserve and protect the precious grain crops produced in good seasons. *Ksour* were usually built on natural defensive positions, and occupy some spectacular ridge and hilltop locations.

A single *ksar* consists of many *ghorfas* (long, narrow, barrel-vaulted rooms built of stone and gypsum and finished with a mud render). The *ghorfas* themselves were like caves, with a single tiny door opening onto the courtyard. The very low humidity of this arid region, combined with the cool conditions inside the *ksar*, meant that grain could be kept for years in the *ghorfas* without deteriorating. The storage areas were sealed with doors made of palm trunks and warded off insects, thieves and inclement weather alike. Sometimes a caretaker, often a local religious figure, regulated how much could be taken by the owners during times of scarcity. Its purpose was, therefore, akin to a modern bank and prevented the crop-holders from squandering their resources through a system of enforced saving and stockpiling.

Entry to the courtyard was by a single fortified gate or *skifa*. The *ghorfas* were stacked three or four storeys high and access to the upper levels was by a narrow staircase. Where no such staircase existed, precarious stone steps were built into the walls. The tree branches protruding from the top of the upper *ghorfas* were part of a pulley system, allowing the *ghorfas* to be filled and emptied without having to carry the grain up the difficult stairs.

Although the practice varied from town to town, in general each *ghorfa* belonged to a particular family or group of families. Grains like barley and wheat were usually kept in the rooms above the ground with olive oil stored in underground chambers.

The oldest examples of *ksour* are to be found occupying the highest peaks of the ancient hilltop villages west of Tataouine, but these are in poor condition. Most of the best examples are more recent constructions dating from the 15th and 16th centuries, built by Arab settlers who had adopted Berber traditions.

The only bus to Ksar Ouled Soltane (TD1, 40 minutes) leaves Tataouine at 6am; *camionnettes* are a better bet. There are occasional services to Ksar Ouled Soltane, but plenty to Maztouria. There's quite a lot of traffic along this road, so hitching shouldn't be a problem (for information on the risks associated with hitching see p311).

OTHER KSOUR

On the way between Tataouine and Ksar Ouled Soltane, it's worth looking in at the **Ksar Beni Barka** and **Ksar Tamelest**, which are more modest than Ksar Ouled Soltane, but nonetheless interesting examples of small village *ksour*.

If you have your own transport, you can continue on beyond Ksar Ouled Soltane, southeast to **Mghit**, which also has its own little *ksar*.

The road turns northeast to **Ksar Ezzahra**, which almost rivals Ouled Soltane as the best *ksar* in the region. It is almost uniformly four storeys with two courtyards, many staircases and multilayered tiers. Because it's further from Tataouine, you'll have the place to yourself. The small section of dirt road between Mghit and Ksar Ezzahra is easily traversed by conventional vehicle.

The road continues beyond Ksar Ezzahra to Tataouine. En route back to town, don't miss the expansive ruined complex of *ghorfas* at **Ksar Jelidet**.

Remada & South

There's little reason to visit Remada, unless of course you're travelling to or from Libya, which in theory should be possible now that the relationship between the two countries has normalised. There's direct transport from Tataouine to Tripoli so there's no need to spend a night in Remada; if you are stuck there's little choice but to throw yourself on the hospitality of a local family. See p306 for information on border formalities.

MEDENINE مدنين

pop 61,700

This uninspiring modern town 76km southeast of Gabès is a convenient place to break up a trip further south, though really only for petrol or lunch since there's little quality accommodation in town. There is a well preserved *ksar*, which sees busloads of tourists stop by for a quick visit.

Orientation & Information

The main street is ave Habib Bourguiba, which runs north–south through the centre of town. The other main thoroughfare, where you'll find the *ksar* and your probable route into the city if coming from Jerba, is ave 7 de Novembre. The streets in the market area and to the north of Place 7 Novembre are confusing to navigate.

The **post office** (place des Martyrs) is south of the town centre, although most other things of importance – banks (with ATMs), hotels and restaurants – are north of the *oued*.

Ksar Medenine

Medenine's only attraction is its well preserved *ksar*, though the fact that almost every square inch of every *ghorfa* surrounding the courtyard is covered with souvenirs, ceramics and carpets on sale for visiting tourists, detracts from the atmosphere. It was built by the Ouergherma Federation in the 17th century following the decision to leave the mountain stronghold of Ghomrassen and assert authority over the plains.

It's on ave 7 Novembre; the ruins of two other *ksour* are to the north, in varying stages of disrepair, though they're not always open.

Sleeping

There's little reason to spend the night in Medenine since there is much better accommodation elsewhere, whether at Matmata, Tataouine or one of the *ksar* hotels in the area. The one tourist-class hotel in town, the Étape Sangho was closed for the foreseeable future.

Hôtel Essaada (☎ 75 640 300; ave Habib Bourguiba; s/d TD7/10) Everything here could use a paint job but at least the rooms open up onto a relatively quiet courtyard set back from the street. Toilets are shared but some of the rooms have private showers.

Hôtel el-Hana (☎ 75 640 690; ave Habib Bourguiba; s/d with shared bathroom TD10/20) Another option with bare-bones rooms that could use some attention, at least this hotel has a restaurant on the ground floor where you can hang out.

Hôtel Le Sahara (☎ 75 640 007; ave 2 Mai; s/d TD20/30; ❄) It's a backhanded compliment to say this is the best hotel in Medenine since the competition is hardly fierce. The rooms are slightly nicer than you'd expect from the building itself and while some have air-con units they're not always functioning. Check before checking in.

Eating

There is a bunch of cheap restaurants on and around ave Habib Bourguiba and ave 7 Novembre.

Montazah Al-Meria (ave 7 Novembre; mains TD4) Just north of the *ksar*, this is probably the most pleasant place for a meal. There's a huge garden out the back where you can chow down on pizza and hearty pitta sandwiches.

The other places are all fairly similar: indoor/outdoor seating with standard fare like couscous and *merguez* (spicy sausages), all for around TD3.

Restaurant Chrigui (ave Habib Bourguiba) is in the same building as Hôtel el-Hana and the **Restaurant Carthage** (rue 18 Janvier) is a no frills place to wait while your louage fills up. **Café de Paris** (ave Habib Bourguiba) is a basic coffeehouse where you can get soup and pastries and maybe a meat dish or two. **Café el-Ksours** is a tiny little place at the entrance to the Ksar Medenine.

Self-caterers can stock up on supplies at the **Grand Magasin supermarket** (ave Habib Bourguiba).

Getting There & Away

BUS

All services leave from the bus station 1.5km north of town on the Gabès road.

SNTRI has seven buses daily to Tunis. The buses via Kairouan are quicker and cheaper (TD18.8, seven hours) than those via Sfax, El-Jem and Sousse. Getting a seat in summer can be difficult because only one service originates in Medenine.

There are frequent local buses to Jerba; services via the ferries at El-Jorf are faster and cheaper (TD3.7, 1½ hours) than those via Zarzis and the causeway (TD4.8, 2½ hours). Four buses daily head to Tataouine (TD2.4, one hour) and Gabès (TD4, 1¼ hours).

Local services include two daily buses to Metameur (500 mills, 15 minutes) and Beni Kheddache (TD1.6, 45 minutes).

LOUAGE

Louages to the north and Tataouine (TD2.2) leave from next to the bus station. Gabès (TD3.6) is the main destination. Louages to Jerba (TD4.5) leave from the centre of town on the small street linking rue 18 Janvier and ave Mansour el-Houch.

Louages for Beni Kheddache (TD1.5) leave from ave Masbah el-Jarbou.

AROUND MEDENINE

Metameur متامر

The small village of Metameur, 4km west of Medenine, has **Le Café Metameur** (☎ 75 640 294), which is set in the renovated *ghorfas* of a 17th-century *ksar*. It's a favourite of tour groups and a nice detour if you're exploring the area. The café is clearly visible from the Gabès–Medenine road, 1km to the east, on a low hill above the modern village. The **Hôtel les Ghorfas** (☎ 75 560 533; fax 75 656 458; per person TD15) offers rustic accommodation in one of the restored *ghorfas*. A taxi from Medenine costs about TD3 or there are two daily buses.

Ksar Joumaa قصر جومة

Joumaa, 30km southwest of Medenine, is as good a *ksar* as you could hope to find, and one of the few that's easily accessible by public transport.

The *ksar* is strung out along a narrow spur to the east of the modern village of Joumaa, the first place you come to after climbing the escarpment on the road to Beni Kheddache. The best approach is via a rough track signposted to the left about 1km before Joumaa on the road from Medenine. It's easy to spend an hour or so exploring the many *ghorfas*. Look out for unusual motifs on some of the ceilings. An archway leads to an inner courtyard and the ruins of the old *kalaa*.

Buses and louages running between Medenine and Beni Kheddache pass through Joumaa.

Beni Kheddache بني خداش

Beni Kheddache, 36km southwest of Medenine, is the main town of the northern Jebel Demmer. The remnants of the town's old *ksar* are signposted on the way into the village, but there are better *ksour* in other towns, most notably Tataouine. There are two buses a day to Medenine (TD1.6, 45 minutes) and more frequent louages (TD1.5).

The road southwest to Ksar Ghilane is best left to 4WDs, but there are good roads northwest to Ksar Hallouf and south to Ksar Haddada and Ghomrassen.

Ksar Hallouf قصر حلوف

Ksar Hallouf, 14km northwest of Beni Kheddache, provides a great opportunity to retreat from the stresses of everyday modern life and experience the stresses of the Berber life, well heat and isolation for a day or so. But whether you decide to simply hang out and take it easy or meditate in a cave like St Anthony, an overnight stay at the **Relais Touristique de Ksar Hallouf** (☎ 75 837 148; fax 75 837 320; bed TD5, full board TD15), a 13th-century *ksar* overlooking a picturesque valley, is a highlight of any Tunisian visit. Accommodation is in a small restored section of *ghorfas* and even though it's rudimentary, it's clean and kept fairly cool by natural air conditioning. Ablutions are available in cold showers and toilets are of the squatting variety.

The road to Ksar Hallouf is clearly signposted from the centre of Beni Kheddache. There are a couple of unsignposted forks in the road along the way; take the right fork both times. The first 10km is a good sealed road, which finishes at an army base; the final 4km of dirt road presents no problems for conventional vehicles. A taxi from Beni Kheddache costs TD5.

Gightis قطيس

The Roman port of **Gightis** (admission TD1.1, plus camera TD1; 🕒 8am-noon & 3-7pm Sat-Thu Apr-Sep, 8.30am-5.30pm Oct-Mar), 20km south of El-Jorf on the back road from Medenine, is one of Tunisia's least-visited ancient sites.

Established by the Phoenicians, Gightis became a busy port during Roman times, exporting gold, ivory and slaves delivered by trans-Saharan caravans. Most of the buildings date from the 2nd century AD and are spread around the ancient capitol and forum. The site lay buried until the early 20th century and is largely undeveloped. It's a good spot for a stroll, with clumps of palms and acacia trees dotting the coast above the gleaming waters of the Gulf of Bou Grara.

Don't worry if the site appears closed – the guardian lives opposite and will emerge.

GETTING THERE & AWAY

Buses and louages between Houmt Souq and Medenine can drop you at the site, which is just south of the tiny modern village of Bou Grara. You'll have to pay the full fare for Houmt Souq to Medenine if you catch a louage. Getting away is more difficult; you may have a long wait for a bus, and louages are likely to be full. The local practice is to flag down whatever comes by.

The Sahara الصحراء

There's something undeniably moving about standing on top of a shifting sand dune and surveying the emptiness – what seems to be the end of the earth can be so beautiful. The novelty of finding sand so far from the ocean can spark anxious nightmares about global warming and yet for certain temperaments there's the temptation to simply walk off into the distance to see how far you can go before feeling like you're truly on an alien planet. *Lawrence of Arabia* fantasies aside, don't underestimate the inviting soft dunes of the Grand Erg Oriental, one of the Sahara's most expansive sand seas. It's an inhospitable place for all but the experienced and travel here should be done with the utmost precaution. It's a remarkable and breathtaking setting, as long as you travel with a guide or in a group, and could be the highlight of your trip.

The *erg* (sand sea) begins 50km south of Douz and extends 500km southwest into neighbouring Algeria. All along the Sahara's northern perimeter are oasis towns huddled amid vast *palmeraies* (palm groves), fed by underground water and producing the finest dates in Tunisia. Conveniently, Douz is the best of these oases from which to launch your desert expeditions.

The Sahara and its northern hinterland is the home of the Berbers. With the decline of the Roman Empire, tribes began to move in from the south at the end of the 4th century AD, bringing with them the first camels to be seen in Tunisia. The Berbers and their camels are still there and many continue to live a seminomadic existence in the south around Douz.

HIGHLIGHTS

- Take the camel by the hump on a **trek** (p248) through the otherworldly dunes of the Grand Erg Oriental for a Saharan experience
- Soak your tired bones in the **hot springs** (p251) at the oasis of Ksar Ghilane

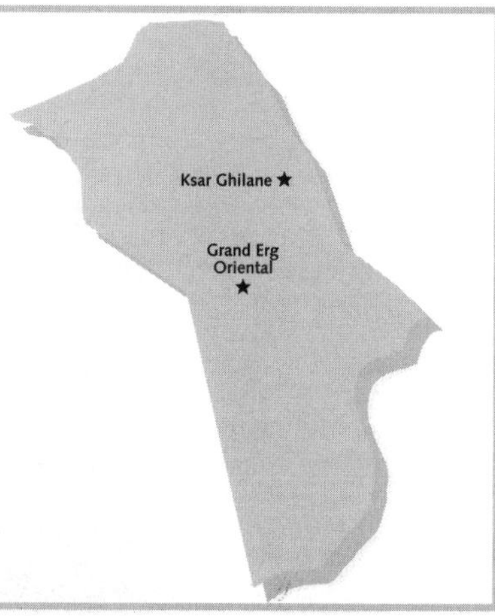

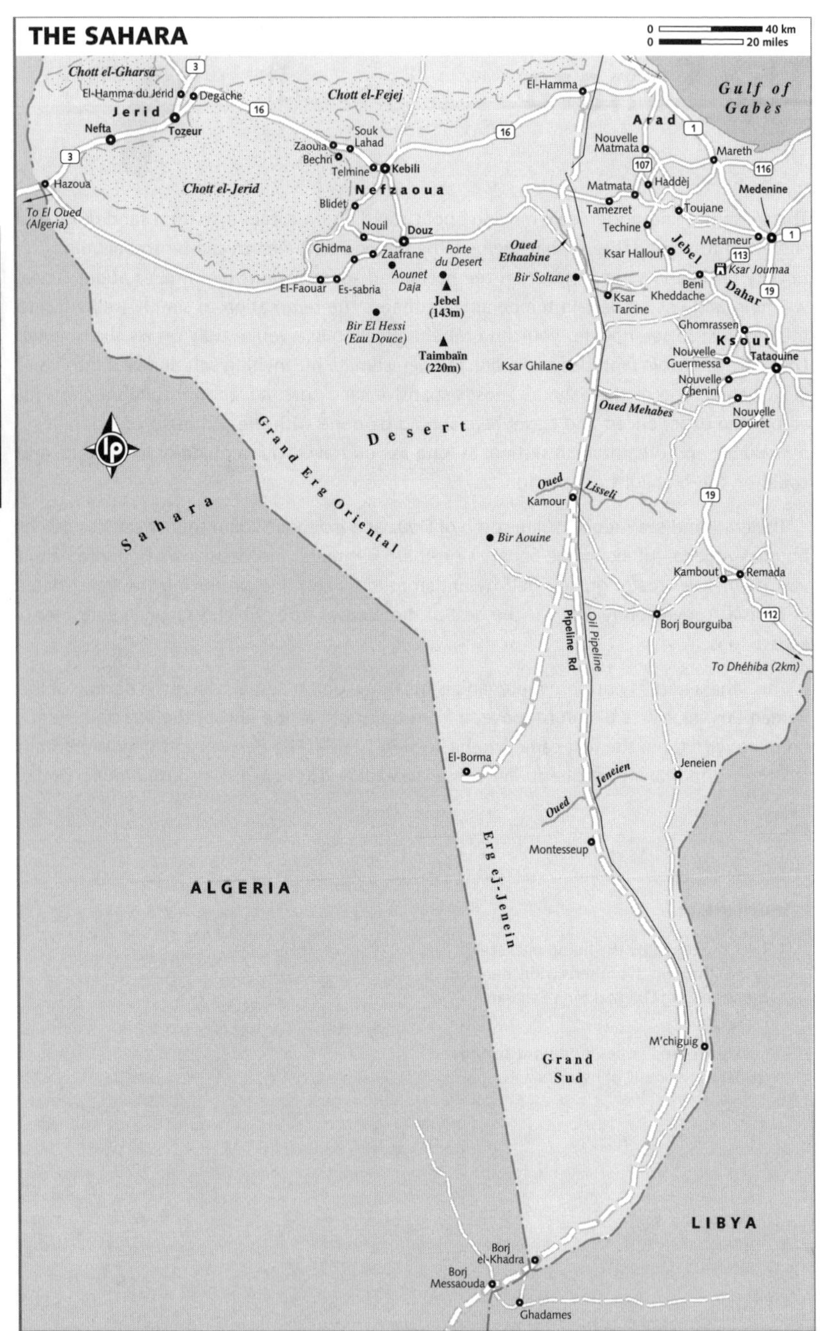
THE SAHARA
0 40 km
0 20 miles
Chott el-Gharsa
El-Hamma du Jerid
Degache
Jerid
Tozeur
Nefta
Hazoua
To El Oued (Algeria)
Chott el-Fejej
Chott el-Jerid
Souk Lahad
Zaouia
Bechri
Telmine
Kebili
Nefzaoua
Blidet
Nouil
Douz
Ghidma
Zaafrane
El-Faouar
Es-sabria
Aounet Daja
Porte du Desert
Jebel (143m)
Bir El Hessi (Eau Douce)
Taimbaïn (220m)
El-Hamma
Gulf of Gabès
Arad
Nouvelle Matmata
Mareth
Haddèj
Matmata
Tamezret
Toujane
Medenine
Techine
Metameur
Oued Ethaabine
Ksar Hallouf
Jebel Dahar
Ksar Joumaa
Bir Soltane
Beni Kheddache
Ksar Tarcine
Ghomrassen
Ksour
Nouvelle Guermessa
Tataouine
Nouvelle Chenini
Nouvelle Douiret
Ksar Ghilane
Oued Mehabes
Desert
Grand Erg Oriental
Sahara
Oued Lisseli
Kamour
Bir Aouine
Kambout
Remada
Borj Bourguiba
To Dhéhiba (2km)
Pipeline Rd
Oil Pipeline
El-Borma
Jeneien
Oued Jeneien
Montesseup
Erg ej-Jenein
ALGERIA
M'chiguig
Grand Sud
LIBYA
Borj el-Khadra
Borj Messaouda
Ghadames
3
16
1
107
116
113
19
112

History

Southern Tunisia was the southernmost point of Roman Africa, with towns such as Tozeur forming part of the Limes Tripolitanus – a defensive line that guarded the southwestern boundaries of Roman Africa. The Berbers were largely left to themselves, which is why strongholds of Berber culture and architecture have survived.

Although administered nominally by the occupying powers of the north, the region was largely the domain of Berber confederations, most notably the Nefzaoua (around Kebili) and Ouergherma (around Tataouine). The orientation of the south has also always been different, facing as much towards the arriving and departing trade caravans from across the desert as to the coast.

Climate

Spring and autumn are the best times to visit, although tour operators claim that the season lasts from late September to early May. Summer is the worst time as far as your comfort is concerned and camel treks are restricted to overnight excursions. Besides the high temperatures, it's also the season of the sirocco, a hot, southerly wind that can blow for days on end, filling the air (and lungs) with fine, desert sand.

Getting There & Away

The major southern towns are well connected to the rest of Tunisia by bus and louage. Trains connect Gabès to Tunis and coastal cities to the north.

Getting Around

Most tourists are ferried around the south as part of a 4WD tour arranged in advance. If you are an independent traveller, having your own vehicle makes getting around immeasurably easier and more convenient. Many of the places worth visiting in the south don't necessarily call for an allday or overnight stop and some are infrequently served by public transport. The major towns and even most of the villages are connected by well-maintained sealed roads.

If car rental isn't an option, you'll have to rely on a mix of louage, bus, *camionnette* (pick-up truck used as a taxi), hitching and (for Ksar Ghilane, the area around Tataouine, and the mountain oases around Tozeur) organised 4WD tour; see the Douz (p248), Tozeur (p260) and Gabès (p227) sections for details. There are no direct public transport connections between the towns of Douz, Matmata and Tataouine; you'll need to backtrack to Gabès to connect.

DOUZ دوز

pop 28,000

Strictly modern and functional, the town of Douz acts like a curtain to the wonders just to the south. Driving through the compact narrow streets of the centre, you'll wonder what all the hype is about. Why journey to this remote outpost that appears abandoned during the intense midday summer heat? But as the sun sets and the streets cool, Douz comes alive, the cafés around the central souq fill up and as you pass through the intervening *palmeraie,* the sight of the Grand Erg Oriental reveals its magical self, a seeming mirage until you set foot on its sandy shore.

People here are naturally open and friendly, accustomed to the fact that the local economy is largely dependent on groups of foreigners turning giddy at the prospect of riding a camel. In addition to the Zone Touristique hotels, whose inflated prices are mostly justified by their desert-side locations, there are several hotels in the town centre that cater to independent travellers. Every Thursday, the souq is home to a colourful weekly market; it's worth arranging to be here just to see it. For good reason Douz is the most popular gateway to the Sahara.

Orientation

There are basically two parts to Douz. There's the compact and walkable town centre with restaurants, budget and midrange accommodation and banks laid out in a rough grid around the souq. And there's the Zone Touristique, which is found 3km southwest of the centre down ave des Martyrs and through the *palmeraie*. This is also the way to the desert and the start of the great dune.

Information

INTERNET ACCESS

Publinet (Map p244; cnr rue 20 Mars & rue el-Hounine; per hr TD2; 8am-10pm) Good connections.

MONEY

The post office has an exchange counter as do most hotels in the Zone Touristique.

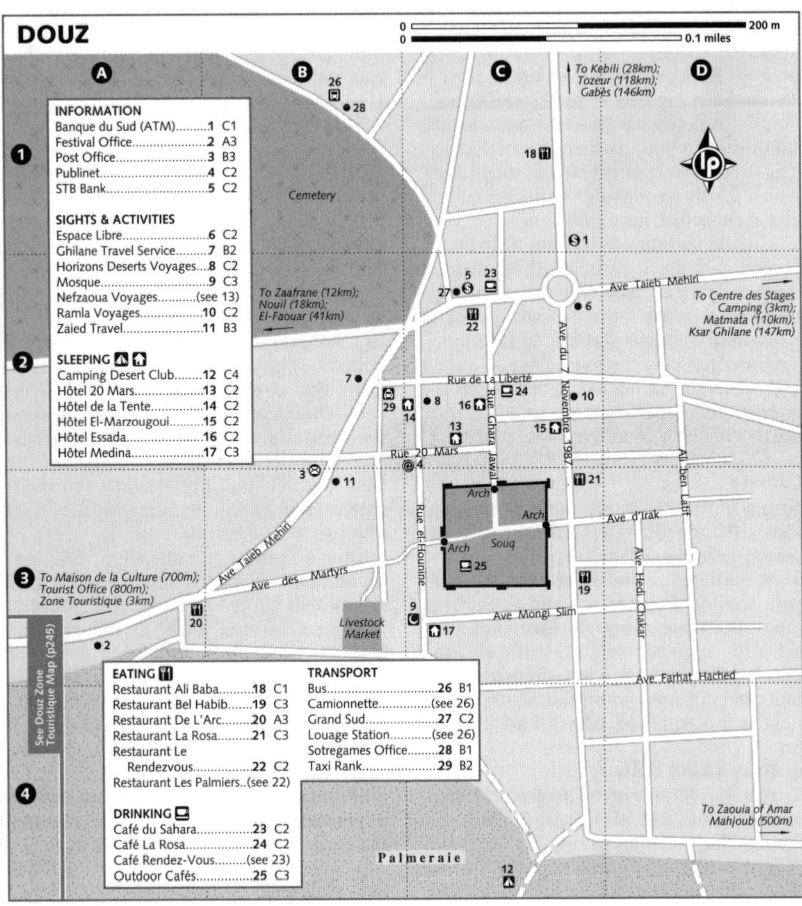

Banque du Sud (Map p244; route de Kebili) ATM.
STB bank (Map p244; ave Taieb Mehiri) ATM.

POST

Post office (Map p244; ave Taieb Mehiri) Just west of the town centre.

TOURIST INFORMATION

ONTT tourist office (Map p245; ☎ 75 470 351; place des Martyrs; 🕑 8am-1pm & 3-5.45pm Sun-Thu, 8.30am-1.30pm Fri & Sat) Helpful in giving recommended prices for camel expeditions.

Sights & Activities

MUSÉE DU SAHARA

A visit to the small folk **museum** (Map p245; place des Martyrs; admission TD1.1; 🕑 7-11am & 4-7pm Tue-Sun Jun-Aug, 9am-4.30pm Tue-Sat Sep-May) provides some perspective and context on the desert lifestyle. It has a good collection of regional costumes, a mock nomad tent and an interesting section explaining the tattoos worn by local women. There is also information on camel husbandry and a section on desert plants. It's definitely worth a visit although text is in Arabic and French.

PALMERAIE

Not that you're counting, but the *palmeraie* here is the largest of all the Tunisian desert oases, with almost half a million palm trees. A wonderfully productive place, it turns out a remarkable assortment of fruit and vegetables – as well as prized *deglat ennour* (finger of light) dates.

The best way to explore it is to walk out along one of the two roads leading south through the *palmeraie* from the western end of ave des Martyrs. The roads link up at the Zone Touristique.

DESERT ACTIVITIES

Douz is the most convenient place to get a taste for the Sahara, though it's really only a taste. The Sahara desert proper starts 50km south of the Zone Touristique. Unless you're planning a longer excursion into the desert (see p248), the action centres around the **great dune**. It can't compare with the sand seas of the Grand Erg Oriental, but is a gentle introduction for those with limited time.

Pegase (Café de Dunes; ☎ 75 470 793; fax 75 470 835) is a one-stop shop that seems to have a monopoly on most of the tourist business around the great dune. You could probably arrange things on your own with any of the tour companies (see below), your hotel or one of the freelance guides who will likely introduce themselves to you around town or near the great dune. Most people arrive as part of a large group and everything is prearranged. Part of the fun of a camel trip into the dunes (if alone you should be able to negotiate a ride for around TD10 per hour) is being outfitted in a long Berber style tunic. A lap around a desert track on a **go-cart** is TD10 but for a much more exciting ride in the dunes it's a whopping TD60 for 30 minutes. To view the dunes from on high, though not too high, a 10-minute **flight** in a light plane is TD60.

Tours

Most people show up in Douz already part of a tour though it's also quite easy to arrange a trip into the desert through one of the companies with offices in town; the more people, the better the individual rates. Here's some officially recognised agencies:

Espace Libre (Map p244; ☎ 75 470 620; www.libre-espace-voyages.com; cnr ave Taieb Mehiri & ave du 7 Novembre)

Ghilane Travel Services (Map p244; ☎ 75 470 692; gts@planet.tn; 38 ave Taieb Mehiri)

Horizons Deserts Voyages (Map p244; ☎ 75 471 688; www.horizons-deserts.com; 9 rue el-Hounine)

Nefzaoua Voyages (Map p244; ☎ 75 472 920; age.nefzaoua@planet.tn; Hotel 20 Mars, rue 20 Mars)

Ramla Voyages (Map p244; ☎ 75 472 805; www.ramlavoyages.com.tn; rue 7 Novembre)

Zaied Travel (Map p244; ☎ 75 455 118; www.zaiedtravel.com; ave Taieb Mehiri)

Festivals & Events

Consider yourself lucky if you happen to be in Douz for the **Sahara Festival**, which is

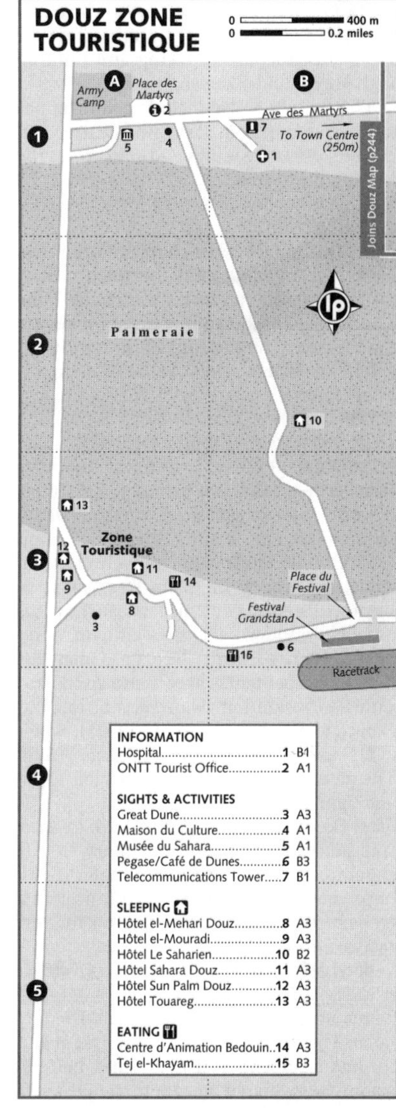

normally held at the beginning of November – although the dates can be hard to track down. It's one of the few genuine festivals in the country, and draws large numbers of domestic visitors as well as foreign tourists.

Most of the action takes place around place du Festival out near the Great Dune, where a large concrete grandstand has been erected to handle the big crowds who come to watch the displays of traditional desert sports, such as camel racing and hunting with greyhound-like Saluki dogs.

The festivities also include colourful parades and music in the town centre, and evening poetry readings and concerts at the Maison du Culture.

Sleeping

All of the budget and a couple of midrange places are in or around the town centre; the more upmarket hotels are in the Zone Touristique, 3.5km southwest of town, facing the desert on the edge of the enormous *palmeraie*. There's great value to be found in all categories, especially during the low season.

TOWN CENTRE

Camping Desert Club (Map p244; ☎/fax 75 470 575; off ave du 7 Novembre; motorbike/car/campervan TD2/3/4, per person TD5) This is one of the better camp sites in the country, not only because of its setting among the palm trees south of the town centre, but also because it has excellent modern facilities. If you don't have a tent, you can sleep on a mattress inside a Berber tent. There is also an Italian-Tunisian restaurant. Showers are free, but expect to pay for electricity (TD1), water (TD2) and use of a washing machine (TD5). The gates are closed to cars between 11pm and 7am.

Hôtel Essada (Map p244; ☎75 472 955; rue Ghara Jawal; per person TD5) The rudimentary Essada should only be a last resort though if you have your own equipment you can pitch a tent or conceivably a mattress on the terrace for only TD3.

Hôtel de la Tente (Map p244; ☎/fax 75 470 468; rue el-Hounine; s/d with toilet & shower TD10/20) A much better budget option is this small, friendly hotel. The rooms are basic but well kept and the management is friendly and helpful. Rooms with shared bathroom are cheaper.

Hôtel el-Marzougoui (Map p244; ☎/fax 75 475 480; ave du 7 Novembre; s/d TD10/20) For this price, the fantastic views of town from the rooftop patio are a bargain though the small rooms with arched ceilings are about in line with the costs. Most of the rooms have private showers though bathrooms are shared, and plans call for some air-con rooms in the near future.

Hôtel 20 Mars (Map p244; ☎75 470 269; hotel20mars@planet.tn; rue 20 Mars; s/d with shower TD11/16, with shower & toilet TD15/20; ❄) A small centrally located hotel, 20 Mars feels more like a guesthouse because of its friendly, helpful staff and the interior courtyard, ideal for hanging out during the midday heat. But the place really shines because of the immaculate rooms – with their high ceilings and colourful tiles, they are more comfortable and better quality than most top end places around the region. Rates include breakfast and there are several air-con rooms for TD10 more. The Nefzaoua Voyages tour company is run out of here.

Hôtel Medina (Map p244; ☎75 470 010; rue el-Hounine; per person without/with bathroom & air-con TD20/30; ❄) Another excellent choice is the Medina whose flowering courtyard is even more appealing though the clean, modern rooms are more basic than those at the Hôtel 20 Mars.

ZONE TOURISTIQUE

All of the hotels in the Zone Touristique are typical of the complexes found throughout the country: all have bars, multiple restaurants and *hammams* (public bathhouses). Prices include breakfast and most people book half board. Reservations are recommended in the summer.

Hôtel Le Saharien (Map p245; ☎75 471 337; fax 75 470 470; hotoasis@gnet.tn; s/d with breakfast TD55/80; ❄ 🏊) An enormous step down in quality from the other hotels out this way, Le Saharien does at least boast shady surroundings in the heart of the *palmeraie* on the road to place du Festival. Everything, including the lobby and small pool area is ragged and there seems little attempt at upkeep.

Hôtel Mehari Douz (Map p245; ☎75 471 088; www.goldenyasmin.com; s/d TD75/110; ❄ 🏊) Once you pass through the entrance of the imposing fortress façade, the Mehari Douz opens up onto a wonderfully light and bright large inner courtyard with two pools, one filled with thermal therapeutic water. One of the original Zone Touristique hotels, it's still the classiest and the closest to the great dune. The small rooms are nothing spectacular but there is an intimate feel here absent from the others.

Hôtel el-Mouradi (Map p245; ☎ 75 470 303; info.douz@elmouradi.com; s/d TD80/144;) More luxurious than its neighbour the Sun Palm, el-Mouradi boasts an enormous glitzy domed lobby and an aesthetic that's best described as faux palace. There's a large outdoor pool traversed by a bridge and an indoor pool, just in case the sun is too intense. A gym, *hammam* (public bathhouse) and several restaurants are part of the complex.

Hôtel Sun Palm Douz (Map p245; ☎ 75 470 123; www.goldenyasmin.com; s/d TD90/140;) Part of the Golden Yasmin hotel chain, the Sun Palm looks like an imposing fort from the outside but a standard tourist class hotel inside. Rooms are disappointingly no frills, in stark contrast to the obvious attempt at lavishness evident in the lobby and restaurant. The pool area is nice and the *hammam* (TD5) a good post-desert treat.

The two other Zone Touristique hotels, **Hôtel Touareg** (Map p245; ☎ 75 470 057; www.hotel-touareg.com;) and **Hôtel Sahara Douz** (Map p245; ☎ 75 470 864; saharadouz@planet.tn;) are unremarkable and offer singles/doubles for around TD70/100.

Eating

The majority of visitors are virtually sequestered to their hotel dining rooms, in part because most of the meals are already prepaid. All of the Zone Touristique hotels have at least one restaurant and while the furnishings and waiters' uniforms are usually high end, the food is usually voluminous if not especially spectacular. Expect to pay around TD15 for a buffet.

Restaurant Ali Baba (Map p244; route de Kebili; mains TD3.5) It's a little derelict looking and the backyard garden is cramped, still this traveller-friendly place about 100m north of the roundabout, is a pleasant spot for a quiet evening.

Restaurant Bel Habib (Map p244; ave du 7 Novembre 1987; mains TD4.5;) On the ground floor of the cheapie hotel of the same name, the Bel Habib is comfortable and tourist friendly. The menu is no surprise: couscous, meat and chicken dishes.

Tej el-Khayem (Map p245; ☎ 75 472 446; Zone Touristique; mains TD10;) Whether you eat indoors, in a Berber style tent or out on the sand, Tej el-Khayem serves up some of the best meals in Douz. The à la carte menu includes all the standards but if you order in advance and/or are part of a large group you can experiment with camel (TD12) or try the *coucha agneau* – a local speciality of meat cooked underground in *gargoulette* (pottery). Wine and beer are served and dancing and performances can be arranged in advance.

Centre d'Animation Bedouin (Map p245; ☎ 75 470 639; Zone Touristique) This place, just past the Hotel Sahara Douz near Tej el-Khayem also offers the chance to eat in a Berber tent, though one done up for tourists, and puts on 'traditional dance' shows, though it's generally only used for large groups who book in advance.

There are several other restaurants in town that are fairly indistinguishable from one another. All serve up couscous and meat dishes for around TD4.

Restaurant De l'Arc (Map p244; ave des Martyrs)

Restaurant La Rosa (Map p244; ave du 7 Novembre 1987)

Restaurant Le Rendezvous (Map p244; ☎ 75 470 802; ave Taieb Mehiri) Slightly nicer than the next door Les Palmiers.

Restaurant Les Palmiers (Map p244; ave Taieb Mehiri)

Drinking

The open-air cafés stay busy till late in the night, especially during the summer months when the plastic tables in and around the souq area buzz with conversation. Café les Arcades (Map p244) is in the southwest corner of the souq.

Café Rendez-Vous (Map p244) and Café du Sahara (Map p244), almost side-by-side on ave Taieb Mehiri, are also very popular. **Café La Rosa** (Map p244; Rue Ghara Jawal) has a quiet courtyard at the back.

Of course you can sip a tea, coffee or beer for that matter at most of the hotels out in the Zone Touristique, but it's also fun to hang out at the Café de Dunes (Map p245), part of the Pegase outdoor activity centre, and watch the bustle when groups arrive and the calm after the storm.

Beer and alcohol are served at the restaurants and bars of the Zone Touristique hotels.

Shopping

Not surprisingly, sand roses are commonly sold in the shops around town. Tourist versions of Saharan sandals (comfortable slip-on shoes made from camel skin) decorated with palm motifs etc are also widely available. All around the souq and surrounding streets, you'll find Berber rugs, sand roses, Touareg jewellery and a range of other pots and pieces.

Getting There & Away

BUS

SNTRI has two air-con services a day to Tunis. The 6am one is direct (TD24, eight hours) and the 10am one goes via Gabès (TD16, two hours) and Sfax (TD11, four hours). There are also two non air-con trips a day: one at 6am via Tozeur and another at 9pm via Gabès. There's also a 6am bus to Sfax via Gabès.

DESERT EXPEDITIONS

Camels are the Toyota Corollas of the desert: neither stylish nor luxurious, strictly functional vehicles to get you from one dune to the next. But to the average visitor who doesn't live in desert climes, there's something inherently romantic and exotic about these clumsy looking animals. The one humped Arabian camel or dromedary could be the illegitimate offspring of a crazy night between a giraffe, a horse and the Hunchback of Notre Dame, but this animal with a bad case of scoliosis is a cash cow for the tourist industry in Douz.

About as difficult as finding a taxi in New York City's Times Square, everyone from restaurant waiters to bank clerks has a friend with a camel ready to take you into the desert at a moment's notice. If you come in summer, only overnight excursions are possible since even this beast that can go a week without water can't take the heat.

The possibilities start with one-hour rides, available in the morning and late afternoon at the Pegase Centre in the Zone Touristique. You shouldn't have to pay more than TD10 for an hour-long circuit that gives you a taste of the serene and magical beauty of the desert; the large majority of people show up as part of a busload of other tourists who have prepaid for their camel experience. Camel riding newbies should definitely try out one of these short jaunts before signing on to something longer since the slow back and forth rocking motion doesn't exactly feel like an easychair.

Overnight treks are equally easy to organise; longer treks generally require 24-hours notice. It's possible to even arrange trips of two to three weeks during the winter months. The biggest challenge is choosing between the range of treks on offer. The tourist office advises travellers to stay clear of the town's many unlicenced guides, pointing out that they are uninsured and unaccountable if problems arise. Some of the 10 registered tour companies are listed under Tours (p245).

In practice, many independent travellers end up using unlicenced guides operating through one of the hotels in town. Most charge TD35 for overnight treks or TD80 for two days and one night. You could try bargaining, but you run the risk of operators taking short cuts with food and water.

These treks leave Douz in the afternoon, and involve about four hours riding before pitching camp at sunset. Guides prepare an evening meal of damper bread, cooked in the ashes of a camp fire, and stew, before bedding down beneath the stars (blankets provided on request). An early breakfast of damper and jam is followed by the return ride, arriving in Douz mid-morning. Sometimes a visit to a village or Berber encampment is included.

The main complaint about these treks is that the desert immediately south of Douz isn't very interesting. The real desert, the Grand Erg Oriental, is a long way further south.

Longer expeditions can range as far as Ksar Ghilane (seven to 10 days). If you don't have that much time, most companies arrange overnight 4WD trips to Ksar Ghilane, leaving Douz around 4pm and arriving back mid-morning the following day. Count on around TD200 to TD250 per 4WD per day with one of the licenced operators.

You'll need to be properly equipped to go trekking. Essential items include a sensible hat that you can secure to your head, sunscreen and sunglasses. Long trousers are a good idea to prevent your legs getting chafed. Cameras and watches should be kept wrapped in a plastic bag to protect them from the very fine Saharan sand that gets into everything.

Regional company Sotregames has daily buses to Kebili (TD1.5, 30 minutes), Tozeur (TD7, two hours) and Gabès (TD5.7, three hours). Some of these have air-con. There are also three daily buses to Zaafrane (500 mills, 20 minutes, 7am, 2.30pm, 9pm), Sabria (TD1.5) and El-Faouar.

CAR & MOTORCYCLE

The road between Douz and Matmata, 110km to the east, is good. There are several small cafés – forlorn looking wooden shacks – along the way, but no petrol stations. The pipeline road to Ksar Ghilane intersects the Douz–Matmata road 66km east of Douz.

LOUAGE & CAMIONNETTE

There are regular departures to Kebili (TD1.8) and Gabès (TD7.5), but none to Tozeur or Matmata – change at Kebili or Gabès respectively. There are regular *camionnettes* to Zaafrane (600 mills) and the other oases south of Douz. There's also one a day to Tunis (TD23) though this is only for transport masochists.

Getting Around

BICYCLE

Bicycles can be rented from **Grand Sud** (Map p244; ☎ 75 590 177; ave Taieb Mehiri; per hr TD2.5, per day TD15).

TAXI

The best place to find taxis is on rue de la Liberté, near the corner with ave Taieb Mehiri. A trip from the centre of town to the Zone Touristique should cost around TD2.

AROUND DOUZ

A sealed road runs southwest from Douz through Zaafrane, Ghidma, Es-sabria and El-Faouar, a string of small oasis towns, which are bases for the region's semi-nomadic tribes who prefer life in the desert to the concrete-block settlements provided by the government. West beyond El-Faouar to Hazoua on the Algerian border is a desolate landscape, with the Chott el-Jerid on one side and the beginnings of the Grand Erg Oriental on the other. Be sure you have petrol and water if you come this way.

Zaafrane زعفران

The small, fly bitten town of Zaafrane, nothing more than a string of low slung pockmarked concrete buildings, is redeemed by its location. It sits about 12km southwest of Douz on the edge of the desert like a port on the Mediterranean. Members of the Adhara tribe, who call the area home, have turned their desert skills into a commercial enterprise by ferrying tourists into the dunes. It's a less developed and busier departure point than Douz; most people turn up here as part of a large group so small crowds are usually part of the experience.

If you stay at **Hôtel Zaafrane** (☎ 75 450 020; fax 75 450 033; s/d with breakfast TD35/50; ❄ 🅟) you'll have a front row view of the fleet of camels parked across the road. Fortunately as the only hotel, restaurant and bar in town, the Zaafrane's simple and modern aesthetic is good value and you'll feel less anonymous here than at the *zone touristique* hotels in Douz.

Operating out of the hotel is **La Mer des Sables** (☎ 75 450 032; www.lamerdessables.com), Zaafrane's only indigenous tour company. The director, Ben Mna Ahmed, can arrange all manner of camel and 4WD trips in the south.

There are around three buses a day from Douz, as well as frequent *camionnettes* (600 mills). The flow of traffic dries up around 4pm and there's never anything much on Friday afternoons.

Beyond Zaafrane

The road continues from Zaafrane to **El-Faouar**, 41km southwest of Douz. This is the region's second-largest oasis, after Douz, with a population approaching 6000. It's also the source of the bulk of the 'sand roses' that are sold at souvenir stalls throughout the country. The best day to visit El-Faouar is Friday, when the market comes to town.

Hôtel Faouar (☎ 75 460 531; fax 75 460 576; s/d with half board TD50/80; ❄ 🅟) is a three-star place signposted to the left on the road into town from Zaafrane. It's a reasonably comfortable hotel with spacious but rustic rooms; you can also sleep in a Berber tent for TD30. As well as the standard swimming pool, it offers the chance to try the X game activity of dune skiing (TD10). The sand may look deceptively soft but it hurts if you fall.

There's a back road that loops north from Zaafrane to Kebili via the oasis villages of **Nouil** and **Blidet**. The turn-off is just west of

Zaafrane on the road to El-Faouar. Nouil is nothing much, but Blidet has a great setting on the edge of the Chott el-Jerid. Blidet can be reached by bus and *camionnette* from Kebili.

Campement Touristique Saharien (☎ 75 455 118; fax 75 455 014; per person half board TD12) outside of Nouil offers mattresses in nomad-style tents and bungalows or you can pitch your own tent. Meals can be provided.

Kebili قبلي

pop 19,000

It's a stretch to label any town on the edge of such a stark and forbidding landscape as ordinary, but Kebili, the main town and administrative centre of the Nefzaoua region, seems to fit the bill. Normally only a pit stop before or after crossing the Chott el-Jerid on the way between Douz and Tozeur, those who stay longer will be afforded the chance to experience what is essentially an oasis lifestyle, beating to rhythms both modern and timeless, undisturbed by passing visitors.

The abandoned town of **Ancienne Kebili** crumbles away in obscurity in the *palmeraie* to the south of the modern town. To get there, head south towards Douz on ave Bourguiba for about 10 minutes until you reach the **hot springs** on the left. The springs feed a *hammam* and pool complex. The houses may be collapsing, but the gardens are neatly tended. The **mosque** is still in use, and an ancient **koubba** (shrine) has been given a coat of blue paint.

Opposite the springs is a signposted track that winds through the *palmeraie* to the old town. In the modern centre, facilities include a post office, several banks and a well-stocked supermarket a few blocks west of ave Habib Bourguiba near the main bus and louage stations.

SLEEPING & EATING

Hôtel Kitam (☎ 75 491 338; fax 75 491 076; route de Gabès; s/d TD32/41; ❄) This is an acceptable, modern two-star hotel on the road into town.

Hôtel Les Dunes (☎ 75 785 364; fax 75 795 106; s/d TD64/94; ❄ 🏊) Another alternative before crossing the *chott* (salt lake or marsh) is Hôtel Les Dunes, near the village of Bechri 22km west of Kebili. The turn-off for the hotel is clearly signposted. Its most distinctive feature is a rather uninteresting tower that offers fantastic panoramic views when open. The Moorish inspired complex comes with a large pool area, forlorn disco and spacious rooms that were closed for improvements when we stopped by.

Hôtel de l'Oasis Dar Kebili (☎ 75 491 113; www.darhotels.com; s/d TD104/136; ❄ 🏊) This hotel is a rather overstuffed but comfortable option outside of the town centre. The staff's eagerness is either a sign of professionalism or that they're lonely for conversation. If entering Kebili on the Blvd de l'Environnement from Douz, take a right just before the hospital.

Hôtel Fort des Autruches (☎ 75 490 933; fax 75 491 111) Prices are similar at this nearby option. It was being renovated at the time of writing, but should reopen soon.

Restaurant Kheireddine (ave Bourguiba; mains TD2) This is one of the best places to soak up local atmosphere. It's near the louage stations. There are two entrances on parallel streets and in between a small outdoor courtyard. One side is a dining room with tablecloths and the other is a bustling café with outdoor tables and chairs.

Restaurant Bei Chabeen (ave Bourguiba; mains TD2.5) Look for the green-and-white awning diagonally opposite Kheireddine this place, for another popular indoor/outdoor café and restaurant.

There are a few other cheap eateries around the louage station.

GETTING THERE & AWAY

The bus station is no more than an office on the main street, near the junction with the Gabès–Tozeur road. There are frequent buses to Douz (TD1.3, 30 minutes) as well as regular departures for Tozeur and Gabès. The SNTRI office is 100m away on the opposite side of the dusty square.

Louages to Gabès (TD5.5) and Tozeur (TD4.6) leave from the street running between place de l'Indépendance and ave Habib Bourguiba, although those to Douz (TD1.5) leave from one block further south.

SOUTH INTO THE SAHARA

The country immediately south of Douz is flat and fairly featureless – low dunes interspersed with small *chotts*. The first point of interest is the evocative abandoned village of **Aounet Dajah**, about 15km

THUMBING IT IN THE DESERT

Hitchhiking in southern Tunisia isn't a matter of a philosophical or existential stand or youthful experiment but a matter of necessity. And picking up hitchers is an extension of the age old virtue of showing hospitality to strangers in need – like letting camels drink from your well since yours will be thirsty one day too. In a region where public transport is few and far between it's not entirely unusual to come upon Tunisians walking by the side of the road in the middle of nowhere, without a single home or settlement in sight. If there's space in your car it's entirely expected that you pull over and pick up the weary pedestrians. There's none of the taboo or risk of danger associated with hitchhiking in many parts of the Western world; that's not to say it's unreasonable to be cautious but that the practice has a different context here. Besides, more often than not your passengers will be police or National Guard officers looking for a lift to or from their remote post. And if you're driving solo, not only is it an opportunity for meeting Tunisians, but you'll likely feel more comfortable and less lonely with a companion. There's something about all that emptiness that makes every strange sound from your beat up Fiat sound like a sign of its impending breakdown.

southwest of Douz, which has all but disappeared beneath a large dune. A small domed marabout tomb at the crest is the only building that remains intact; elsewhere all that remains are the tops of old walls poking from the sand.

Officially, the desert begins at **La Porte du Desert**, about 20km south of Douz. This gleaming white crenellated arch is visible from miles around.

Tour companies refer to this area as *jebel* (small mountain), which is the low hill nearby. It is the starting point for trips to **Taimbaïn** (pronounced Tembayine), 5km further south. Taimbaïn itself is a large, crescent-shaped outcrop of rock that offers magnificent views from its summit (220m). The main attraction is the journey through some magnificent dune country, crossing three great walls of gleaming white sand that the wind has thrown up like defensive ramparts around Taimbaïn.

KSAR GHILANE قصر غلان

The sand dunes of the Grand Erg Oriental offer some of the country's most awe-inspiring landscapes. They have provided the backdrop for many films including *The English Patient* and it's easy to see how such a photogenic and surreal looking topography is perfect for the fantasy of cinema. The remote oasis of Ksar Ghilane, 138km southeast of Douz, has developed into the most visited outpost in the far south; as a consequence the pristine quality of the oasis has been impacted by the tourism industry that sustains it. But no matter how many others you share the vistas with, the human presence feels like but a pinprick in the vast ocean of the desert.

The amazing *ksar* (fortified stronghold) here is the ancient Roman fort of Tisavar, once a desert outpost on the Limes Tripolitanus defensive line. It was modified and renamed by the local Berber tribespeople in the 16th century. The *ksar* now lies abandoned on a low hill about 2km west of a magical little oasis where hot springs feed a small swimming hole shaded by graceful tamarisk trees. There are impressive dunes between the oasis and Tisavar, particularly once you get among them, and of course they're especially wonderful at sunset and sunrise.

There are cafés around the swimming hole, but no shops or other facilities.

Accessible by overnight 4WD excursion from Tozeur or Douz, Ksar Ghilane is where you'll understand the power of the Sahara's lure.

Camel Rides

Locals charge around TD15 for the 1½-hour return journey from the oasis to the fort. Evening is the best time, when the setting sun produces some stunning plays of light and shadow across the dunes.

Sleeping & Eating

Camping is tolerated around the fringe of the oasis, but most visitors use one of the three camp sites. All offer beds in large nomad-style tents as well as providing areas for pitching tents. All also have

THE GREAT DESERT

The Sahara Desert stretches from the Atlantic to the Red Sea, covering, at last count, more than 9.065 million sq km, passing across 15 degrees of latitude in the process. This vast space is home to just over two million people and encompasses large parts of Mauritania, Morocco, Algeria, Libya, Tunisia, Mali, Niger, Chad, Egypt, Sudan and a small slice of Burkina Faso.

The Sahara is home to haunting mountain ranges, particularly in southern Algeria, Libya, northern Niger and Chad where the Sahara reaches its high point at Emi Koussi, 3415m above sea level. Most of the Sahara is a high plateau while the Qattara Depression of northwestern Egypt is its lowest point, 133m below sea level.

Contrary to popular myth, as little as one-ninth of the Sahara's surface is covered with sand. Some of the unimaginably beautiful sand seas nonetheless cover areas larger than many European countries and the Grand Erg Oriental, which straddles Algeria and southern Tunisia, is one of the largest and one of the most stunning.

In ancient times, the Sahara was the domain of camel caravans numbering up to 30,000 beasts and carrying salt (that once traded ounce for ounce with gold), gold and slaves from the heart of Africa to the northern coast and beyond. Tunisian oasis towns such as Gabès, Tozeur and Gafsa grew rich on the trade.

The Sahara is a place of myth and legend. You can get a taste of the silent gravitas of its many moods and the beauty of its diverse landscapes, but the Sahara rewards those who linger. As Antoine de Saint-Exupéry observed: 'If at first it is merely emptiness and silence, that is because it does not open itself to transient lovers'.

Above all, the Sahara is home to its once-nomadic people, primarily Berbers, Touareg and Tubu who alone understand the Sahara's lure. Nigerien Touareg Mano Dayak wrote that the desert could not be described, but could only be lived.

restaurants. There is one luxury four-star hotel.

Camping Ghilane (☎ 75 460 100; per person half board TD23) This camping ground is ideally located next to the hot springs on the northern edge of the oasis. A three-course evening meal costs an extra TD10.

Campement el Bibène (☎ 75 470 178; per person TD23) This place is located between the oasis and the barracks. It's also possible to camp *sauvage* in the dunes behind the hot springs; inform the National Guard here of your plans.

Camping Paradise (☎ 75 900 507; half board TD25) This place is run by Douz-based Mrazig Voyages and offers sleeping in either Bedouin tents or in more permanent military style tents in the middle of the *palmeraie*.

Hôtel Pansea (☎ 75 900 506; www.pansea.com/ksar.html; s/d TD100/163; ❄ 🏊) This is an extraordinary and fabulous place. Situated on the edge of Grand Erg Oriental, the internationally renowned Pansea has air-con linen tents with private bathrooms, a swimming pool, restaurant and a decided touch of class. This is one of the best places in the country for a splurge.

Getting There & Away

There's no public transport to Ksar Ghilane and previously this remote spot was only accessible by 4WD along the rough pipeline road that runs south from El-Hamma, on the Gabès–Kebili road, all the way to Borj el-Khadra. By late 2006 this road should be sealed all the way south to Ksar Ghilane from the turn-off. However, a 4WD vehicle is still your best bet in case parts of the road are covered with sand drifts.

If you have a 4WD, there are several other possibilities, including the roads from Beni Kheddache, Guermessa and Douiret (see The Ksour, p235).

AROUND KSAR GHILANE

There are a couple of interesting diversions off the pipeline road between Ksar Ghilane and the Douz–Matmata road.

Most popular is **Bir Soltane**, where a small stone dome surrounds an ancient well. Centuries of use has cut deep rope grooves into the well-head. The only other building here is the nearby National Guard post, which uses a windmill to draw its water. Bir Soltane is about 2km west of the pipeline road, reached by signposted tracks both north and south of the **Café Bir Soltane**, 32km south of the Douz–Matmata road.

Hardly anyone heads out to **Ksar Tarcine**, about 12km southeast of Bir Soltane. This remote outpost began life as part of the Roman Limes Tripolitanus – when it was called Centenarium Tibubuci. As occurred with Ksar Ghilane, it was later modified by local Berber tribes and is now in ruins. It stands on a rise overlooking the broad bed of the Oued Ethaabine, which stretches away towards the Jebel Dahar range, silhouetted to the east. There's a well on the bank of the *oued* (river bed), as well as some cisterns.

Access is from the road to Beni Kheddache, which is signposted to the east off the pipeline road 500m south of the Café Bir Soltane. Keep going along here for 8km until you reach a small settlement with a well and a few struggling saplings. The turn-off to Ksar Tarcine is signposted to the south just beyond the settlement.

GRAND SUD الجنوب الكبير

The desert south and west of Ksar Ghilane is remote Saharan country that brings many rewards for those who venture deep into this largely uninhabited area. Tunisia's southernmost settlement is **Borj el-Khadra**, 292km south of Kamour. The pipeline road to reach it curves around the edge of the Grand Erg Oriental, across barren steppe country dotted with great outcrops of weathered rock and crisscrossed by the boulder-strewn beds of *oueds* that might flow only once in a hundred years. There's very little along the way save the odd military post. Borj el-Khadra itself comprises no more than a small military garrison and airfield. Sadly, it's impossible to continue to the legendary Libyan oasis of Ghadames, just across the border.

Dunes – seriously large ones – are the main reason tourists come to this part of the world. Some of the best examples are found between **Bir Aouine** and **El-Borma**, and this trek is popular with the tour operators in Douz.

This is border country and much of the area lies within a military zone so you need a permit to continue beyond **Kamour**, on the pipeline road 110km south of the Douz–Matmata road, and **Kambout**, about 10km east of Remada. Unless you're travelling as part of a group, you will need to apply in person to the governorate in Tataouine; ask about the current situation at the **syndicat d'initiative** (☎ 75 850 850) in Tataouine. The permit can take up to two days to process and it's essential you have a 4WD vehicle.

If you're heading for the Grand Sud, the best access is from Remada, 70km south of Tataouine.

THE SAHARA

DESERT HOTTIES

It's hard to believe anything can live in the Sahara as everything seems stacked against life – the heat, the lack of shade, the lack of food. One species of ant, the *Cataglyphis fortis* or Sahara ant found in Tunisia, however, has developed ingenious survival techniques, ones scientists hope to be able to fully understand one day in order to find adaptations for human purposes. These ants can be active with internal temperatures over 50°C and in ambient heat over 70°C. And while these ants don't wear big floppy hats or apply loads of Hawaiian Tropic sunscreen, they have their own methods of keeping cool. For one thing, they're fast, for ants, which means they can be back in their hole quicker and their relative speed also means things like sweating and their own internal cooling mechanisms work harder. They also have long legs that act like stilts and keep most of their body off the hot desert surface.

But equally fascinating to scientists is their ability to navigate, to find their way home after foraging for their meals of other dead insects that have generally succumbed to the heat. After all, there are few landmarks in the Sahara, especially for these creatures whose perspective is decidedly low to the ground. Initially, it was thought that they used the sun and light patterns like we may use the stars – a solar version of MapQuest. But only recently researchers have postulated that these ants also possess some ability to count or to at least keep track of the number of steps they have taken. Although this internal pedometer is not yet fully understood, experiments strongly suggest it helps explain how these ants are the homing pigeons of the desert.

Tozeur & the Jerid

One of the more pleasant towns in the south is Tozeur and because of its location and facilities, it's the logical base from which to explore this diverse region. Only a short drive from the sophisticated comforts of Tozeur's Zone Touristique, its attractive, brick old town and its enormous *palmeraie* (palm grove) are several oases towns – Tamerza, Chebika and Midès. This area along the Algerian border is carved with small canyons and offers swimming and hiking opportunities.

The Jerid itself, which all of these towns occupy, is the narrow strip of land between the region's two major salt lakes, the Chott el-Jerid and the Chott el-Gharsa. It has long been one of the most important agricultural districts in Tunisia and the oases around here are famous for their high-quality dates. The harvest is in October, which is a good time to visit the area.

While cartographers tend to label the Chott el-Jerid as a lake, for most of the year this bone-dry depression looks more like the moon. It's easy to lose your focus driving along the causeway that bisects the Chott, to try to catch a glimpse of the gypsum crystals that form in small pools alongside the road or to stare off into the hazy distance; later you may swear you saw odd things in the heat, like a desert wookie, the species heretofore known only to *Star Wars* fans. There are several cafés along the way, though we use that term loosely since these are nothing more than wooden shacks with optimistic signs inviting weary travellers in for a drink.

HIGHLIGHTS

- Catch some shade wandering through the manicured forests of Tozeur's **palmeraie** (p256)
- Don your hiking boots and navigate your way between Midès and Tamerza along the **gorge** (p262)
- Drive – don't walk or take a camel – across the mesmerizing flat expanse of **Chott el-Jerid** (p261) where just looking out the window will make you feel dehydrated

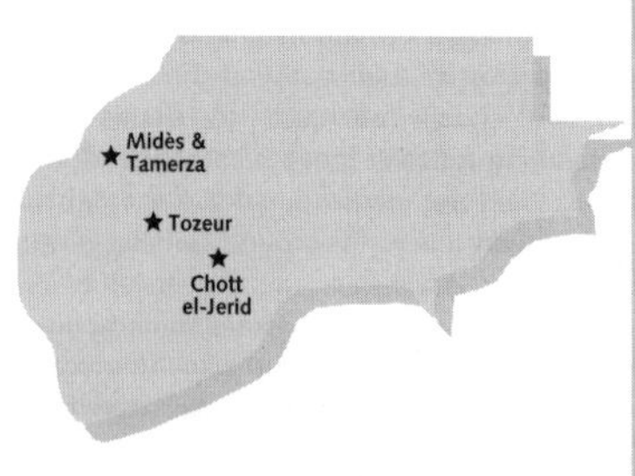

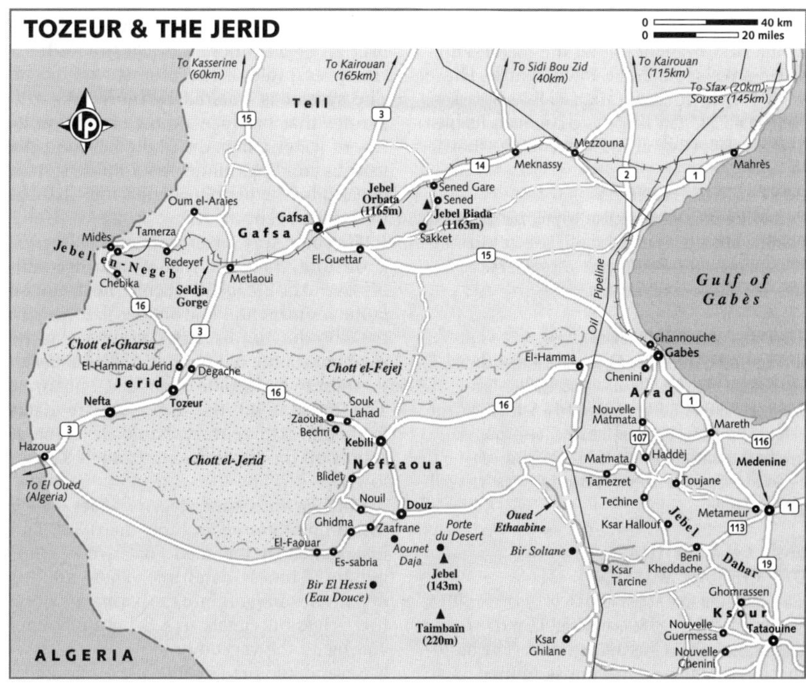

TOZEUR توزر

pop 35,500

For travellers in the south, Tozeur, boasting the widest range of hotels and restaurants, makes an excellent base for longer forays into the surrounding area. Bounded on one side by an enormous forest of palm trees and then the desolate Chott el-Jerid, the town itself feels simultaneously far-flung and welcoming. It's easy to spend a few days here occupied by the labyrinthine Ouled el-Hadef with its distinctive traditional brickwork and a few interesting and unique museums located in the town itself.

History

The oasis at Tozeur has been inhabited since Capsian times (from 8000 BC; see p24). It developed into the small Roman town of Thuzuros, which lay within the *palmeraie* around the area now occupied by the district of Bled el-Hader. Tozeur's prosperity peaked during the age of the great trans-Saharan camel caravans, between the 14th and 19th centuries.

Orientation

Tozeur is easy to navigate. Most of the accommodation and many of the restaurants are on ave Abdulkacem Chebbi, which runs along the edge of the *palmeraie* on the southern side of town and continues into the Zone Touristique. Ave Farhat Hached skirts the northern edge of town and is your likely route into the city if coming from Kebili or Gafsa; it has several banks, cafés and restaurants. Ave Habib Bourguiba links the two primary roads and is lined with stalls and shops selling souvenirs and other goods.

Information

INTERNET ACCESS

Publinet (11 ave de 7 Novembre; per hr TD2; 24hr) Good connections.

LAUNDRY

Pressing (ave Abdulkacem Chebbi) Next door to the Au Couer du Désert office.

MEDIA

Kiosk (ave Habib Bourguiba) There's a kiosk with English-language and other international newspapers.

MONEY

You'll find branches of all the major Tunisian banks around the town centre. Those with ATMs include **STB** (ave Habib Bourguiba), **Banque du Sud** (ave Habib Bourguiba), **Arab Tunisien Bank** (ave Farhat Hached) and **BNA** (ave Farhat Hached).

POST & TELEPHONE

Post office (off place Ibn Chabbat) By the market.

Publitel office (ave Farhat Hached) There are telephone offices all over town, including this (allegedly) 24-hour office opposite place Bab el-Hawa.

TOURIST INFORMATION

ONTT office (☎ 76 454 503; ave Abdulkacem Chebbi; 🕒 7.30am-1.30pm & 5-8pm Jul-Aug, 8.30am-1pm & 3.30-6pm Sun-Thu, 8.30am-1.30pm Fri & Sat Sep-Jun) Between the town centre and the Zone Touristique.

Syndicat d'initiative (☎ 76 462 034; place Bab el-Hawa) Can provide times for bus and air departures and not much else.

Sights & Activities

DAR CHARAÏT MUSEUM

The **museum** (ave Abdulkacem Chebbi; admission TD3.4, plus camera TD1.7; 🕒 8am-midnight) is part of the impressive Dar Charaït complex. The building in which the museum is housed is an extravagant reproduction of an old palace and contains collections of pottery, jewellery, costumes and other antiques, as well as an art gallery. Scattered throughout the rooms off the splendid main courtyard is a series of replicas of scenes from Tunisian life, past and present. They include the bedroom of the last bey (provincial governor in the Ottoman Empire), a palace scene, a typical kitchen, a *hammam* (public bathhouse), wedding scenes and a Bedouin tent. The museum attendants, dressed as servants of the bey, set the tone for the museum.

The complex also includes attractions aimed at children. **Dar Zaman – 3000 years of Tunisian History** features scenes from the nation's long history using some good models. **La Medina – 1001 Nights** is a theme park full of cartoon characters. Both are open the same hours as the museum and each charges TD5 admission.

The whole complex is tastefully lit at night, which is a good time to visit.

PALMERAIE

Tozeur's *palmeraie* is the second largest in the country with at least 200,000 palm trees (locals claim twice that number) spread over an area of more than 10 sq km. It's a classic example of tiered oasis agriculture. The system is watered by more than 200 springs that produce almost 60 million litres of water a day, distributed around the various holdings under a complex system devised by the mathematician Ibn Chabbat in the 13th century AD.

The best way to explore the *palmeraie* is on foot. Take the road that runs south off ave Abdulkacem Chebbi next to the Hôtel Continental and follow the signs to the Zoo du Paradis. After about 500m the road passes the old quarter of **Bled el-Hader**, thought to be the site of ancient Thuzuros. The mosque in the main square dates from the 11th century, while the minaret stands on the square base of an old Roman tower.

Further on is the village of **Abbes**, where the tomb of *marabout* (holy man) Sidi Bou Lifa stands in the shade of an enormous jubube (Chinese date) tree. There are lots of paths leading off into the *palmeraie* along the irrigation canals. It's delightfully cool among all the vegetation.

Several kilometres southeast of the statue of Ibn Chabbat is the incongruous and trippy **Chak Wak Park** (admission TD15; 🕒 8am-11pm Mon-Fri, 9am-11pm Sat & Sun), an enormous testament to the vision of one passionate and wealthy man. The former mayor of Tozeur and the driving force behind the Dar Charaït museum has created what amounts to a three-dimensional liberal education on evolution, history and religion. Surrounded by high walls reminiscent of the *King Kong* films, inside is a circuit that takes you from dinosaur-sized replicas of dinosaurs to a replica of Noah's Ark with models of animals lining up two by two while a sound system pipes in rain effects. Even the biblical parting of the Red Sea is represented here with walls of papier-mâché ocean. Other exhibits are truly worthwhile including an excellent history of Hannibal and the Carthaginian wars in English, Italian, Spanish, French, Arabic and German and a building given over to the symbols and icons of the world's major religions.

If you want to see more of the oasis, you can hire bicycles from a number of places around town (see p261). Thus equipped, you can complete a loop through the *palmeraie* that emerges further west on ave

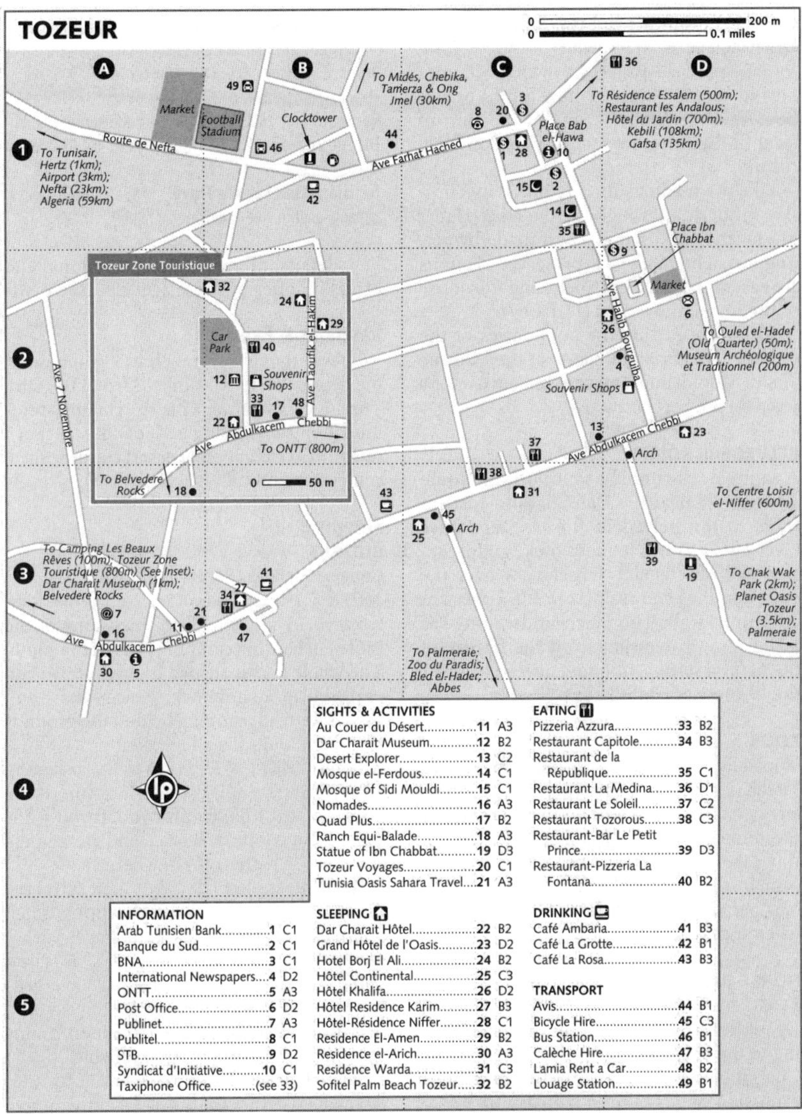

Abdulkacem Chebbi near the Grand Hôtel de l'Oasis.

OULED EL-HADEF

The town's delightful **old quarter** was built in the 14th century AD to house the el-Hadef clan, which had grown rich on the proceeds of the caravan trade. The area is a maze of narrow, covered alleys and small squares. It's famous for its amazing traditional brickwork, which uses protruding bricks to create intricate geometric patterns in relief. The style is found only here and in nearby Nefta.

The easiest entrance to the Ouled el-Hadef is from ave de Kairouan. Follow the signs pointing to the small **Museum Archéologique et Traditionnel** (admission TD1.1; 8am-noon & 3-6.30pm Tue-Sun), which occupies the old *koubba* (small domed tomb) of Sidi Bou Aissa. It houses a small collection of local finds, costumes and displays on local culture.

Like the medinas further north in Tunisia, wandering through the Ouled el-Hadef is a journey of discovery best made by getting lost. The most well-preserved sections are east of the museum, including the house of the former governor (Dar Bey).

Although outside the boundaries of the old town, the brick minarets of the Mosque of Sidi Mouldi and **Mosque el-Ferdous** (ave Habib Bourguiba) are very attractive.

BELVEDERE ROCKS

A sandy track running south off the Route Touristique near the Dar Charaït Museum leads to the Belvedere Rocks. Steps have been cut into the highest rock, giving access to a spectacular sunset view over the oasis and the *chott* (salt lake). It's a pleasant 20-minute walk. Too much landscaping has taken away somewhat from the beauty of the natural setting, but not entirely; look for the likeness of Abdulkacem Chebbi.

ZOOS

Ironically, or cynically, named, the **Zoo du Paradis** (admission TD2; 8am-7pm), on the southern side of the *palmeraie,* is anything but for the animals housed, if it can be called that, in tiny cages. The star is a Coca-Cola–drinking camel… The closing time isn't set in stone and paradise usually closes its pearly gates when it gets dark.

HORSE-RIDING

Ranch Equi-Balade (☎ 76 452 613; fax 76 462 857; off ave Abdulkacem Chebbi), based on the road leading to the Belvedere Rocks just past the Dar Charait Hôtel, charges TD15 for a one-hour excursion or TD45 for a half-day trip.

OFF-ROADING

Quad Plus (☎ 76 452 502; ave Abdulkacem Chebbi) rents all-terrain vehicles for fun out in the desert.

Tours

There are dozens of travel agencies around town. Recommended agencies:

Au Coeur du Désert (☎ 76 453 570; aucoeur.dudesert@gnet.tn; ave Abdulkacem Chebbi)
Desert Explorer (☎ 76 460 950; fax 76 460 900; ave Abdulkacem Chebbi)
Nomades (☎ 76 453 423; 196 ave Abdulkacem Chebbi)
Tozeur Voyages (☎ 76 452 203; fax 76 452 038; 58 ave Farhat Hached)
Tunisian Oasis Sahara Travel (☎ 76 460 466; oasis.sahara@gnet.tn; ave Abdulkacem Chebbi)

For details of available excursions and prices on offer by these agencies, see p261.

Festivals & Events

Whoever thought so much was going on in the desert? Every November (3rd to the 6th), Tozeur comes alive with storytelling, traditional music, dancing and, of course, camel racing in a celebration of desert culture called, somewhat ironically, the **Oasis Festival**.

Sleeping

BUDGET

Camping Les Beaux Réves (☎ 76 453 331; beauxreves.koi29.com; ave Abdulkacem Chebbi; per person tents/bungalows TD5/8, showers TD1.5) This is one of the more enchanting camping sites in the south. The whole area is shaded by trees – you can even set up a hammock to sleep on – and there's a stream running behind the grounds that backs onto the *palmeraie*.

Hôtel Khalifa (☎ 76 454 858; ave Habib Bourguiba; s/d TD8/16) If it's a noisy central location you're after then the Khalifa is for you. If you're interested in comfort, service and cleanliness then you're better off elsewhere.

Residence Essalem (☎ 76 462 881; ave de l'Environnement; s/d TD9/18) This small charming hotel, 150m east of the intersection of aves Farhat Hached and Habib Bourguiba, is good value. Clean and simple rooms have ceiling fans and the owners are friendly and accustomed to travellers. Cheaper rooms with shared bathroom are available.

Hôtel-Résidence Niffer (☎ 76 460 610; fax 76 461 900; place Bab el-Hawa; s/d TD13/20) Occupying one of the busiest intersections in Tozeur, this small pension has spacious but ordinary rooms. Breakfast is included.

Hôtel Residence Karim (☎ 76 454 574; 150 ave Abdulkacem Chebbi; s/d TD15/26;) Travellers give this place high marks and we can see why – the Karim has bright and cheerful tiled rooms, shady courtyards and a rooftop terrace. Rooms minus air-con are TD4 less.

TOZEUR & THE JERID

Residence Warda (☎ 76 452 597; fax 76 452 744; 29 ave Abdulkacem Chebbi; s/d TD18.5/28.5;) A friendly and centrally located hotel accustomed to independent foreign travellers, the Warda has basic, clean rooms surrounding a small shady courtyard. Rooms with fan are a few dinars less.

MIDRANGE

Tozeur easily has the best choice of midrange accommodation in the south and for that matter much of the country.

Residence el-Amen (☎ 76 463 522; amentozeur@yahoo.fr; 10 ave Taoufik el-Hakim; s/d TD 20/34;) Part of the poor man's *zone touristique*, the friendly el-Amen, on a side street off ave Abdulkacem Chebbi, has tiny, cute rooms painted in bright pinks and blues. For real quiet and privacy take one of the rooftop rooms with direct access to the patio and its excellent views.

Residence el-Arich (☎ 76 462 644; www.elarichtozeur.8m.com; 93 ave Abdulkacem Chebbi; s/d TD21/36;) With midrange prices and top-end quality rooms, the el-Arich is possibly the best value in Tozeur. Some of the upper floor rooms are more like suites with separate sitting rooms and foyers that lead to the bathroom and bedroom. The vistas from the rooftop lounge area are superb and there's a large outdoor garden out back.

Hôtel du Jardin (☎ 76 454 196; medmoncef@voila.fr; ave de l'Environnement; s/d TD31/41;) You'll feel much further than only 1km from the town centre staying at this place set amid a grassy lawn and lush garden on the road from Kebili. The rooms are colourful and mostly well kept and there's an attractive restaurant attached.

Hotel Borj El Ali (☎ 76 462 650; ave Taoufik el-Hakim; s/d TD30/50;) This new hotel across the street from the el-Amen is no doubt the realisation of a personal vision. The end result is a sort of Holiday Inn meets *Arabian Nights* – garish and functional furnishings collide to create an interesting effect. There are several nooks with beautifully tiled benches and other ornate touches throughout.

TOP END

Tozeur's Zone Touristique is on steroids compared with other towns in the south. The massive, gated complexes line the road west of town, perched on a hill overlooking the Chott el-Jerid.

Hôtel Continental (☎ 76 461 526; fax 76 461 411; 79 ave Abdulkacem Chebbi; s/d TD43/70;) In a large and somewhat bland building, the Continental is nothing more than a bottom-of-the-line *zone touristique* wannabe that knows its guests are there for only a night.

Grand Hôtel de l'Oasis (☎ 76 452 300; Place des Marytrs; s/d TD76/112;) Occupying prime real estate at the intersection of aves Bourguiba and Abdulkacem Chebbi, the Grand has the amenities of a *zone touristique* hotel with a central location. The Grand eschews the gaudy trappings of the other hotels for more modern and functional décor. There's a large outdoor pool and restaurant.

Sofitel Palm Beach Tozeur (☎ 76 453 111; www.accorhotels.com; route Zone Touristique; s/d TD180/240;) The five-star Palm Beach is not nearly as unique or elegant as the Dar Charait, but it has all the facilities and luxuries you'd expect.

Dar Charait Hôtel (☎ 76 454 888; www.darcherait.com.tn; route Zone Touristique; s/d TD195/270;) The five-star Dar Charait is one of the few places where the opulent interior fulfils the promise of its palatial façade. It's worth the splurge if you have the extra dinars since you'll be treated like royalty and everything from the fabulously designed suites to the luxurious lobby lounge and restaurants is refined and tasteful. It's adjacent to the museum in the Zone Touristique.

Eating

Compared with the dining scene in the rest of the southern part of the country, Tozeur's restaurants qualify as *haute cuisine*.

Restaurant La Medina (ave Farhat Hached; mains from TD2.8) A no-nonsense eatery 100m northeast of place Bab el-Hawa, the Medina is clean and friendly and the service prompt. Try the *ragout d'haricot* (bean stew; TD2.8).

Restaurant Capitole (☎ 76 462 631; 152 ave Abdulkacem Chebbi; mains from TD3) This small place is popular with Tunisian families but the service is slow and it's worth pre-ordering; the *metabgha* (Berber pizza; TD3) is available by pre-order only. Camel steak is also on the menu.

Restaurant Tozorous (ave Habib Bourguiba; mains TD3.5;) This highly recommended restaurant serves up pizza (TD3), meat and chicken dishes (TD6) in a brick-walled dining room complete with a working fountain in the centre.

Restaurant Le Soleil (☎ 76 454 220; 58 ave Abdulkacem Chebbi; mains from TD4) There's an extensive menu with a couple of vegetarian dishes. The service is attentive and it's a good place to try camel steak (TD6) because you generally don't have to pre-order it as in other restaurants. It also does pizzas (TD5 to TD7) and sandwiches (TD1.5 to TD2).

Restaurant de la République (☎ 76 452 354; 108 ave Habib Bourguiba; mains from TD4) Tucked away in an arcade next to the Mosque el-Ferdous, this is another good place with a pleasant eating area and decent food.

Restaurant-Bar Le Petit Prince (☎ 76 452 518; off ave Abdulkacem Chebbi; mains TD5-17) Dining under the palms, sipping a fine wine while listening to music is a special experience. This restaurant is tucked in behind a wall a short walk past the arch and serves quality French and Tunisian cuisine.

Restaurant Les Andalous (Hôtel du Jardin; mains TD7) Overlooking the garden of Hôtel du Jardin, this restaurant has high-end trappings and a better-than-average menu and, at least as important, wine and other alcohol is served.

Pizzeria Azzura (route Zone Touristique; pizzas from TD4) and **Restaurant-Pizzeria La Fontana** (pizzas TD2.5-8, pasta from TD3), a few doors north at the start of the Zone Touristique, serve pies of comparable quality.

Planet Oasis Tozeur (☎ 76 460 310; www.planet-oasis.com; meals TD35) Gorge on a buffet while watching a sound and light show at this place, deep in the middle of the *palmeraie*. These are only staged for large groups.

Handy for a snack and very much a part of the Tozeur experience are the dates available in the market. The best dates are harvested in October, but you'll usually find something on offer throughout summer. For reasonable quality, expect to pay TD3.5 per kilogram, although the best method is to taste before you buy.

Drinking

Outdoor *sheesha* (water pipe) places and coffeehouses are everywhere. Beer and other alcohol is available at all of the Zone Touristique hotels.

Café La Grotte (ave Farhat Hached; ❄) A step up from the streetside cafés, La Grotte, *à la* its name, is fitted out to look like the inside of a cave, albeit a cool, air-conditioned one. It tends to draw a younger crowd of men.

Café La Rosa (ave Abdulkacem Chebbi) This busy café spills over onto the street and can get rowdy in the evenings, but it's pleasant enough if you don't mind the choir of all-male voices.

Café Ambaria (ave Abdulkacem Chebbi) A cut above the rest in terms of décor and service, although again it's mostly all men. *Sheesha* cost TD1.5 and there's a real live coffee machine if you're craving an espresso or cappuccino.

Centre Loisir el-Niffer (🕑 9.30am-midnight) Set in the *palmeraie*, this is a great place for a *sheesha* (TD1 to TD2) under the palm trees, or a coffee or cool drink. There's a swimming pool (TD3) and a few courting couples and families sitting at the tables spread throughout the garden. To get here, take the road past the Restaurant-Bar Le Petit Prince and follow the signs (about 700m).

Getting There & Away

AIR

Tuninter runs five flights a week to Tunis (TD66/128 one way/return). The airport handles a growing number of international flights, mainly charters from Europe. The **Tunisair** (☎ 76 460 038) office, which sells Tuninter tickets, is out towards the airport along the Nefta road.

BUS

There are five air-con SNTRI buses a day to Tunis (TD20.75, seven hours), travelling via Gafsa (TD5, 1½ hours) and Kairouan (TD13.7, 4½ hours). SNTRI also has a service to Sousse (TD14.6, 5¾ hours) in the morning.

Regional services include six buses a day to Gafsa (TD4), five to Nefta (TD1.1) and two to Tamerza (TD3). There are also daily buses to Douz (TD6.3, three hours) and Gabès (TD11, 4½ hours).

CAR

There are half a dozen car-rental outlets in town. You'll find better deals at local agencies like **Lamia Rent a Car** (☎ 76 462 433), opposite La Palmeraie Hotel in the Zone Touristique.

International agencies include **Avis** (☎ 76 454 356; 96 ave Farhat Hached) and **Hertz** (☎ 76 460 214; route de Nefta), out towards the airport.

CHOTT EL-JERID

The Chott el-Jerid is an immense salt lake covering an area of almost 5000 sq km, the bulk of which is south of the Kebili–Tozeur road and part of a system of salt lakes that stretches deep into Algeria from the Gulf of Gabès. It is a scene of desolation – dry for the greater part of the year, when the flat, flat surface stretching to the horizon becomes blistered and shimmers in the heat. It was here that Luke Skywalker contemplated the two moons in the first *Star Wars* movie. The Kebili–Tozeur road crosses the northern reaches of the *chott* on a 2m-high causeway – it's a trip not to be missed. At times, the wind-driven salt piles up into great drifts by the roadside, creating the impression that you're driving through a snowfield. Just one litre of water can yield as much as 1kg of salt. Mirages are common, and if you've picked a sunny day to cross you may see some deceptive optical effects.

LOUAGE

The louage (shared taxi) station has regular departures to Nefta (TD1.7), Gafsa (TD5.1) and Kebili (TD5.3). There are also occasional louages to Tamerza (TD4.6) and Gabès (TD10).

TRAIN

An overnight train departs Tunis at 8.50pm, arriving in Tozeur the next morning at 5.15; trains turn west after Sfax and pass through Graiba, Meknassy, Sned, Gafsa and Metlaoui before the end of the line in Tozeur.

Getting Around

TO/FROM THE AIRPORT

Tozeur's taxis don't have meters – the fare depends on your bargaining skills and how wealthy you look. Most charge around TD5 for the 4km trip, although some ask as much as TD10 late at night.

BICYCLE

Bicycles can be rented from lots of places, including along ave Abdulkacem Chebbi and from the Taxiphone office opposite the Dar Charaït complex at the Zone Touristique. Rates range from TD2 to TD5 per hour. Motor-scooters cost around TD10 per hour.

CALÈCHE

Calèches (horse-drawn carriages) can be hired from opposite the Hôtel Residence Karim for TD10 per hour.

AROUND TOZEUR

There are plenty of worthwhile excursions that can be made from Tozeur; see the table opposite. Almost all the hotels in Tozeur, as well as the tour agencies (see p258) can organise such trips. They include food and some water, though always bring your own as well.

Destination	Duration	Cost (per person)
Tamerza (p262), Chebika (p262) & Midès (p262)	4 hrs	TD45
Nefta (p263) & Ong Jemal (p263)	3-4 hrs	TD45
Kebili (p250), Douz (p243) & La Porte du Désert	½ day	TD60
Lezard Rouge (p268)	½ day	TD40
Ksar Ghilane (p251), Douz & Matmata (p227)	2 days	TD120
Ksar Ghilane, Douz, Tataouine (p230) & Matmata	3 days	TD150

The half-day excursions are best done in the afternoon, as in the morning most 4WD vehicles are booked out by the tour buses that roll into town. Also, if you're on your own, you may need to wait a day or two for enough other travellers to arrive to make the trip viable for the operators. And one final thing: no matter when you go, each site will be inundated with convoys of 4WD vehicles. It just comes with the territory in this part of the world.

Mountain Oases

The allure, in part, of these beautiful, ancient Berber villages is the result of a natural disaster. After this region, near the Algerian border in the rugged Jebel en-Nebeg ranges, was hit by 22 days of torrential rain in 1969, the villages of Chebika, Tamerza and Midès were abandoned for hastily built run-of-the-mill settlements. The remaining ruined houses still cling evocatively to the cliff faces. The three villages were once part of the Limes Tripolitanus defensive line developed by the Romans to keep out marauding Saharan tribes.

CHEBIKA شبيكة

After passing through bleak and barren land and several camel-crossing signs, you reach this village, 59km north of Tozeur on the southern edge of the mountain range overlooking the Chott el-Gharsa. The *palmeraie* is visible for miles – a great slash of green set against the barren mountains. Up the hill, past the nondescript settlement of new Chebika and behind the *palmeraie,* next to a small spring-fed stream, is **old Chebika**. The best way to explore is to climb up through the deserted village to the narrow cleft in the rock from where there are great views over the oasis. On the other side of the rock, steps lead down into a pretty little **canyon** fed by a spring and with a tiny waterfall. The path follows the gorge back up to the town.

There's a cluster of souvenir shops and drink-and-snack stalls at the foot of old Chebika.

TAMERZA تمغزة

The road from Chebika twists and turns up a steep mountainside before finally dropping down into the small valley where Tamerza, the largest of the villages, is located.

The shell of the **old walled town** is about 1km east of new Tamerza (a characterless modern sprawl). Strung out along a ridge on the southern bank of the Oued Horchane, this is one of the most photogenic old villages in Tunisia, set against the backdrop of the rugged mountain range and with the *palmeraie* to the west.

Tamerza's water comes from a spring that rises in the hills south of old Tamerza. The spring supplies water to the old town and then to an extensive *palmeraie,* which locals claim produces the finest dates in Tunisia.

If you're on a half-day trip, most of your time will be spent at one of the town's small **waterfalls** (bring your swimmers) and there's considerable novelty value to be swimming in such a barren landscape. Local children jump with reckless abandon into the 10m-high falls south of town. On the main road is the **syndicat d'initiative** (☎ 76 485 288; 🕑 8am-1pm & 3-6pm), which can arrange guides for the hike along the gorge to Midès. A ballpark price is TD15 for the 2½-hour trip. If you're in town for the day, it should not be missed.

The **Hôtel Les Cascades** (☎ 76 485 322; s/d TD20/25) is beautifully placed at the edge of the *palmeraie,* near one of the smaller falls and the entrance to one of the gorges, but the palm-frond bungalows are dirty and falling apart and surely not worth the price.

The four-star **Hôtel Tamerza Palace** (☎ 76 485 322; www.tamerza-palace.com; route de Midès; s/d TD165/265, junior ste TD350; 3-course set menu TD15; ❄ 🏊) is also wonderfully situated overlooking the oasis and old village. The pool is especially nice but the rooms themselves are fairly ordinary. You can picnic in the palms and the hotel arranges all manner of 4WD excursions, from half-day to overnight, and guided hikes as well.

Tamerza has several restaurants, most of which cater to tour groups and serve set menus with couscous as the main dish. The tiny **Restaurant Chedli** (dishes TD7.5) and the **Restaurant Gelain** (dishes TD6.5) are both on the right side of the road leading down to the Hôtel Les Cascades.

Tamerza is the only one of the three oasis villages with public transport. There are two SNTRI buses a day from Tunis (TD22, seven hours), three buses a day from Gafsa (TD4.8, 2½ hours) and two from Tozeur (TD4.6, 1½ hours).

MIDÈS ميداس

A good road connects this small oasis village to Tamerza only 6km away, however a more adventurous route between the two is the 4.5km hike that passes through some stunning scenery including some tight passages in one of the gorges (see above for more information). Only 1km from the Algerian border (the National Guard has a customs post on the road to the border), Midès is perched high above a dramatic gorge that was previously employed as the town's southern fortification. The gorge has been used as a setting for many movies, including *The English Patient*. If you have time it's worth walking down into the canyon; if not the views from above are stunning.

The two places at Midès calling themselves camping grounds were closed indefinitely at the time of research. Food and drinks are available at the cluster of souvenir stalls at the top of the canyon.

Ong Jemal عنق الجمال

Ong Jemal (Neck of the Camel) is a popular place for watching the sunset out over the sand dunes. Visiting this remote spot, around 30km north of Nefta, is only possible as part of an organised tour from Tozeur.

The name derives from an unusual rock formation, shaped, not surprisingly, like the neck and head of a camel, overlooking the barren plains. Not far away is a line of sand dunes where *The English Patient* crew indulged in lots of billowing, sand-blown romantic stuff. Drivers of 4WDs love this spot for exhilarating descents of the dunes and it's a stunning place to watch the sunset.

Just over a hill to the west is **Mos Espa**, a very well preserved *Star Wars* set. This was Darth Maul's lookout in *The Phantom Menace,* and the location for his and Qui-Gon's tussle, as well as lots of pod-race scenes. It's remarkably intact and one of the best *Star Wars* sites in the country. Film crews spent 4½ months here (including building the now-decaying road) for 12 minutes of footage.

NEFTA نفطة

pop 22,000

Technically, it qualifies as an oasis. However, Nefta, an elongated and smaller version of Tozeur, 23km to the east, is too dusty and spread out to justify the images that word conjures up. There are fine examples of distinctive ornamental brickwork in the old town, which seems abandoned in the middle of the day. The greenery of the sunken *palmeraie,* unlike any other in the country, is best appreciated from the road above as a counterpoint to the barren Chott el-Jerid, which spreads out to the horizon beyond.

Nefta is also the home of Sufism in Tunisia, and there are a couple of important religious sites here.

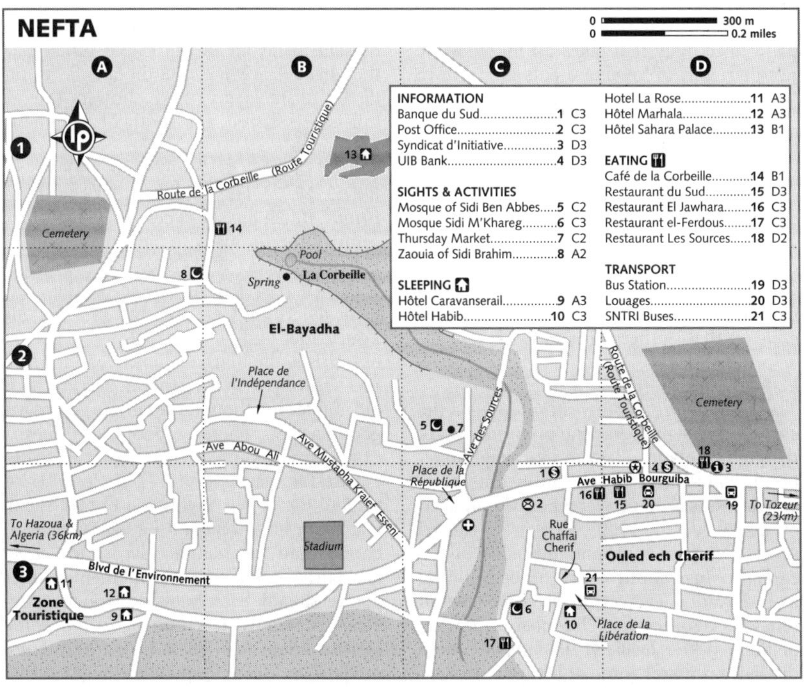

Orientation & Information

Nefta's main street, ave Habib Bourguiba, is also the main Tozeur–Algeria road. The route de la Corbeille does a loop around the *corbeille* (palm-filled gully) off ave Habib Bourguiba. The bulk of the *palmeraie* borders the southern edge of the town and the Chott el-Jerid to the south. Ave Habib Bourguiba turns into Blvd de l'Environnement west of the gorge and Place de la République; the small and unimpressive Zone Touristique is a little further west along here.

The small **syndicat d'initiative** (☎ 76 430 236) is on the right as you come into town from Tozeur, just before the ring-road junction and almost across from the Mobil station. Its primary function is to sell guide services (TD15 for a two-hour tour of Nefta, full day TD40 plus vehicle, four-hour camel rides TD24).

There's also a **post office** (ave Habib Bourguiba) and a branch of the **Banque du Sud** (ave Habib Bourguiba) and **UIB bank** (ave Habib Bourguiba).

Sights & Activities

LA CORBEILLE

La Corbeille (literally 'Basket'), the deep palm-filled gully that takes up much of the northern part of town and cuts the town in two, is the highlight of Nefta. It measures almost 1km across at its widest point and is about 40m deep. The best views are from the northwestern side. Take in the setting over a coffee at the Café de la Corbeille, which has a terrace overlooking the *corbeille*.

Below the cafés is a large spring-fed concrete **pool**, a popular swimming spot with local kids. The *corbeille* contracts to a narrow gorge that leads to the main *palmeraie* on the southern side of town.

EL-BAYADHA

The cafés at the northwestern edge of the *corbeille* are a good starting point for a walk through the old El-Bayadha neighbourhood, which lies to the southwest. Many of the houses here were badly damaged by heavy rain in 1990, which also caused several landslides around the edge of the *corbeille*. Just about every other building in El-Bayadha seems to have some level of religious significance. The most important of them is the **Zaouia of Sidi Brahim**, where the Sufi saint and some of his followers are buried. The *zaouia* (complex surrounding the tomb of a saint) is 100m south of the cafés. There's an open space opposite the **Mosque of Sidi Ben Abbes**, off ave des Sources at the eastern edge of El-Bayadha, where Nefta's **Thursday market** is staged.

OULED ECH CHERIF

The best preserved of Nefta's old districts is the Ouled ech Cherif. To get there, follow the signs to the Hôtel Habib on the main road leading south next to the bus station. The layout is very similar to the Ouled el-Hadef in Tozeur, with winding, vaulted alleyways and some stunning examples of traditional brick designs. Check out the street that runs west off place de la Libération to the *palmeraie*, emerging next to the quarter's principal mosque, the **Mosque of Sidi M'Khareg**.

Sleeping

None of the accommodation in Nefta measures up to Tozeur and there's little reason to spend the night here. There's a small cluster of big hotels in the Zone Touristique on the southwestern side of town.

Hôtel Habib (☎ 76 430 497; place de la Libération; r per person with breakfast TD7.5) Nothing much can be said in favour of the Habib other than the cheap price tag. Rooms are fairly little and dismal; most have showers though toilets are shared. It's south of ave Habib Bourguiba.

Hotel La Rose (☎ 76 430 696; fax 76 430 385; s/d TD40/60; ⛶ ⛶) This cookie-cutter *zone touristique* hotel boasts excellent views from some of the rooms with balconies.

Hôtel Marhala (☎ 76 430 027; hotelmarhala@voila.fr; s/d TD43/62; ⛶ ⛶) Directly across the street from the Hôtel Caravanserail in the Zone Touristique and catering to itinerant groups of tourists, the Marhala looks abandoned if you show up solo. In general, everything is old and fading though the simple rooms are good enough. There's a pool but it doesn't exactly invite sunbathing.

Hôtel Caravanserail (☎ 76 430 355; fax 76 430 344; s/d TD100/130; ⛶ ⛶) Saying the Caravanserail is a more luxurious and better maintained choice than the Marhala across the street is a fairly backhanded compliment. Unless you've already been booked through a prearranged tour, there's little to justify shelling out the dinars here. The rooms are large and modern and there's a pool and nightclub.

Hôtel Sahara Palace (☎ 76 432 005; www.saharapalace.com.tn; s/d TD135/200;) The best hotel in town, the Sahara Palace commands panoramic views directly over the *corbeille* from both the rooms and a terrace, a wonderful place for a sunset drink. Rooms here are clean and large and better looking than the more forlorn lobby area.

Eating

The dining scene in Nefta is about what you'd expect in the desert.

Restaurant Les Sources (ave Habib Bourguiba; mains TD4;) This is the only place worth noting. It's a small, modern restaurant geared to tourists, which isn't such a bad thing, though the English menu could use some variety. As it is, there are around five options of basic meat and chicken dishes.

There are a few basic eateries including **Restaurant El Jawhara** (ave Habib Bourguiba; mains TD3) and the next door **Restaurant du Sud** (ave Habib Bourguiba; mains TD2.5) on ave Habib Bourguiba and near the bus station, and around place de la Libération, plus hotel restaurants.

Although it looked closed at the time of our most recent visit, Restaurant el-Ferdous is a bar-restaurant in the *palmeraie,* crowded in the evenings.

Getting There & Away

BUS

SNTRI has two daily buses to Tunis (TD20, seven hours) from the station on place de la Libération.

Regional services operate from the bus station on the southern side of ave Habib Bourguiba. There are five buses to Tozeur (TD1.7, 30 minutes) and six a day to Gafsa (TD5.8, three hours).

LOUAGE

Louages leave from outside the restaurants on ave Habib Bourguiba. You won't have to wait long for a ride to Tozeur (TD1.7).

GAFSA قفصة

pop 84,700

The approach from the west is rather striking; the modern city of Gafsa lies below in a valley backed by a low range of mountains that glow orange in the sunset. However, from ground level the utilitarian buildings on the outskirts and the congested centre will disappoint all but the least demanding traveller. Tour groups do breeze through, mostly though because it's on the way to Tozeur. Gafsa is historically significant as the site of Capsa (see p24), which was captured and destroyed by the Roman consul Marius in 107 BC as part of the campaign against the Numidian king Jugurtha. It went on to become an important Roman town.

Information

All the major banks have branches around Jardin du 7 Novembre in the centre of town. Most have ATMs. There are plenty of Taxiphone offices around the town centre.

L'Univers de l'Internet (ave Abdulkacem Chebbi; per hr TD2; 8.30am-11pm;) Strangely enough, this is one of the largest and most modern internet centres in the country. Fast connections.

Post office (ave Habib Bourguiba) This is 150m north of the kasbah.

Tourist office (☎ 76 221 664; 8am-1pm & 3-5.45pm Mon-Thu, 8.30am-1.30pm Fri & Sat) There's a small office in the small square by the Roman Pools.

Sights

The twin **Roman Pools** (Piscines Romaine; ave Habib Bourguiba; admission free) are Gafsa's main attraction and it's a pleasant spot although you've seen all there is to see after a few minutes. Apart from the entertainment provided by local children diving, and you're welcome to join them, note the Latin inscriptions just above water level in the eastern pool. The pools are located at the southern end of ave Habib Bourguiba.

Beside the entrance to the pools is a small **museum** (admission TD1.1; 7.30am-12.30pm & 3-7pm Tue-Sun Apr–mid-Sep, 9am-4.30pm mid-Sep–Mar), which houses, among other things, a couple of large mosaics from ancient Capsa.

Sleeping

The cheap hotels clustered around the bus station area are probably best avoided. In general, Gafsa has plenty of accommodation though none of it is particularly good.

BUDGET

Hôtel de la République (☎ 76 221 807; rue Ali Belhaouane; s/d TD5.5/7) Not exactly a quiet spot, sandwiched between the street and bus station, this cheapie does have fairly spacious rooms, though they're a little worse-for-wear and only a few have private showers with intermittent hot water.

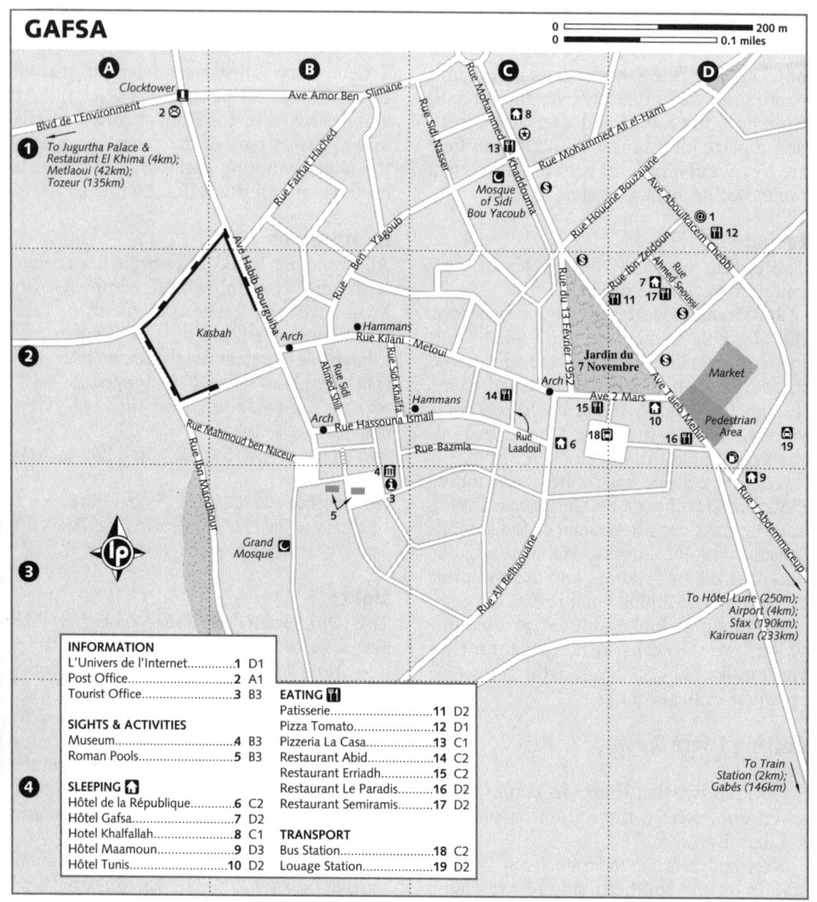

Hôtel Tunis (☎ 76 221 660; ave 2 Mars; s/d TD6/8) A small step up from the République, rooms here are smaller though in better shape. Look at several rooms before choosing one since some have small balconies while others don't even have windows to the outside. Use of the common shower is an extra TD1.5.

Hotel Khalfallah (ave Taieb Mehri; s/d TD10/20) The best of the cheapies, the friendly Khalfallah is OK so long as you don't need air-con and you're not a light sleeper. Some of the rooms get lots of street noise, though you could always take refuge in one of the bunker-sized bathtubs. A few rooms have balconies that open on to an alleyway.

MIDRANGE & TOP END

Hôtel Lune (☎ 76 220 218; fax 76 220 980; rue Jamel Abdennaceur; s/d TD24/36) A poor entry in the midrange category, the Lune has no air-con. Sure the rooms are spacious but so is the Kremlin; the incongruous ripped leather couches are an interesting touch. The hotel is located about 300m south of the town centre.

Hôtel Gafsa (☎ 76 224 000; fax 76 224 747; rue Ahmed Snoussi; s/d TD25/40; ❄) There's little to recommend this high-rise hotel except the friendly staff. If the elevator doesn't work, rest up for a long climb.

Hôtel Maamoun (☎ 76 224 441; fax 76 226 440; rue Jamel Abdennaceur; s/d TD40/80; ❄) The empty rooftop pool says it all. While it's possible the Maamoun was once a tourist-class hotel, it's now a sad, aging relic that still hosts large groups, mostly young tourists, only because of lacklustre competition. The rooms themselves are OK though the air-con is old and the bathrooms in need of repair. It's well located just south of the main market square. Play hardball for a reduced rate and it won't seem like such a bad deal.

Jugurtha Palace (☎ 76 211 200; Sidi Ahmed Zarroug; s/d TD63/100;) The best and most expensive place to stay in Gafsa, the Jugurtha covers a lot of property 4km west of town. Typical of this genre of hotel in Tunisia, the Jugurtha's royal ambitions translate into cheesy, grandiose furnishings in the rooms, though they're perfectly comfortable. It's kitsch galore in the lobby, lounge, bar and restaurant, and it can be hard to find your way around, what with all the mirrors and the dim lighting. There's a pool out back.

Eating

There are lots of small restaurants around the bus station, especially clustered on Rue Laadoul and on rue Mohammed Khadouma north of Jardin du 7 Novembre.

Restaurant Abid (rue Laadoul; mains TD3.5) This is a sparkling clean place in less than salubrious surroundings serving Tunisian fare. It's especially popular at lunch.

Pizza Tomato (rue Abdulkacem Chebbi; pizzas TD4) Next door to L'Univers de l'Internet, this is a small, modern place done up in Italian/Tunisian décor. A lot of pride goes into the authenticity of the large pizzas but they can taste kind of off. Meat toppings are scarce in the summer.

Pizzeria La Casa (rue Mohammed Khaddouma) This is a less ambitious place with no pretensions to authenticity.

Of the other cheapies, **Restaurant Erriadh** (ave 2 Mars) next to the bus station is good, while chicken is the (only) order of the day at **Restaurant Le Paradis** (ave Taieb Mehri). A couple of pâtisseries are dotted around the centre.

Restaurant El Khima (mains TD12) If you want to eat in over-the-top kitsch surroundings, try this place in the Jugurtha Palace west of town.

It's a bit of a dive but if you want to drink wine with your meal, try the **Restaurant Semiramis** (rue Ahmed Snoussi; mains TD4), below the Hôtel Gafsa, or the restaurant at the **Hôtel Maamoun** (mains TD9), though service and food might be hard to muster if there's no large group chowing down on a fixed-price meal and it's equally hard to get the attention of a waiter if they are.

Getting There & Away

AIR

Tuninter flies to Tunis twice a week (TD99/122 one way/return). The airport is 4km east of town; taxis cost TD3.

BUS

The bus station in the centre of town has ticket windows for booking.

SNTRI runs at least five buses a day to Tunis (TD16, 5½ hours), most of which go via Kairouan (TD9.3, three hours).

The local company, Sotregafsa, drives an amazing collection of wrecks eight times a day to Tozeur (TD4.3, two hours) and Nefta (TD4.9, 2½ hours); it also has services to Gabès (TD6, 2½ hours, three daily), Kasserine (TD4.6, 1¾ hours, two daily) and Sfax (TD8.2, 3½ hours, three daily). There are also nine buses to Metlaoui (TD2, 45 minutes); three of these continue via Redeyef to Tamerza (TD4.1, 2½ hours).

LOUAGE

There are regular louage departures from just north of Taieb Mehiri, on the way south out of town, for Metlaoui (TD2.4) and Tozeur (TD4.9). Other possibilities include Tunis (TD16.3), Sfax (TD8.5), Sousse (TD13) and Gabès (TD7.1). There are occasional direct services to Kasserine (TD5.5), otherwise change at Feriana.

TRAIN

The station is 3km south of town and about TD2.5 by taxi. The only departures are a night train to Tunis (2nd/1st class TD18.6/13.9) and a morning service to Metlaoui at 5am.

AROUND GAFSA

Metlaoui & the Seldja Gorge متلوي و سالجة

When a town's *raison d'être* is phosphate mining, odds are it holds little appeal for the non-phosphate miner. Unfortunately that truism holds true for Metlaoui, a drab, utilitarian town 42km southwest of Gafsa.

It is the starting point for rides through the Seldja Gorge on the **Lezard Rouge** (Red Lizard) train.

Built in 1910, the Lezard Rouge was once used by the bey of Tunis for journeys between Tunis and his summer palace at Hammam Lif. It was given a complete refit by the national railway company SNCFT in 1995, and put back to work transporting tourists, if not in style at least in a modicum of comfort. Unfortunately the chairs and couches look like they were the same ones used in the time of the bey. The scenery, several gorges featuring weird and wonderful rock formations following the path carved out by the Oued Seldja, is dramatic enough to warrant the trip.

The two-hour return journey leaves Metlaoui at 10.30am on Monday, Friday and Sunday and at 10am on Tuesday and Thursday from 1 May to 30 September. However, you should definitely contact the **Bureau de Lezard Rouge** (☎ 76 241 469, fax 76 241 604; Metlaoui) or the tourist office in Tozeur (p256) to check that the train is running; reservations are highly recommended. The return fare is TD20. Tour companies in Tozeur (p258) offer the trip on the Lezard Rouge as a half-day tour for TD40, which is good value and probably the best option.

The only acceptable lodging option in Metlaoui is the **Hôtel Seldja** (☎ 76 241 570; fax 76 241 486; s/d TD30/40;), on the way out of town towards Gafsa. It's not exactly an uplifting place but rooms have air-con and satellite TV and there's a bar and restaurant.

All transport between Gafsa and Tozeur passes through Metlaoui and there are regular louages to Gafsa and Tozeur.

East of Gafsa

There are half a dozen traditional Berber villages east of Gafsa, spread along the mountain range that runs south of the Gafsa–Sfax road. Most of them are very difficult to get to unless you have a 4WD. The most accessible is **Sened**, 10km south of modern Sened Gare and spread along the banks of a river in the hills below Jebel Biada (1163m). The houses are built of stone and are still in reasonable condition. People have lived around here for thousands of years – the escarpment behind the village is dotted with caves.

Jerba

For such a small island, Jerba contains the ingredients of most people's idea of the ideal holiday vacation: soft sandy beaches, warm Mediterranean waters, a warren of shops selling every imaginable handicraft, a maze of cobblestone streets and a history of ethnic and religious diversity more pronounced than the rest of the country. To the classically inclined, the name Jerba conjures up images of Homer's Land of the Lotus Eaters, an island so seductive that it's impossible to leave. But many visitors voluntarily sequester themselves at the McHotels along beautiful Sidi Mahres beach, and while the appeal of a luxury beach resort speaks for itself, the rest of Jerba shouldn't be missed.

The heart of the island is Houmt Souq, its largest town and one of Tunisia's most unique. So polished and charming it's like eye candy for those living in concrete jungles. It's chock-a-block with outdoor cafés, has enough carpets, souvenirs and crafts to satisfy the most demanding shopaholic and has a handful of ancient *funduqs* (inns), the town's architectural trademark, set around a central courtyard and converted into hotels.

Inland amongst crumbling homesteads you'll find one of the last remaining Jewish communities in North Africa, with their synagogue at Erriadh, as well as an equally unusual population of Ibadis (an offshoot of the Kharijite sect found only in Jerba). Jerba's postcard-perfect beaches are as good as advertised, but it's the interior with its distinctive above- and below-ground mosques and the small villages shaded by palm trees that lingers in your memory after you have left.

HIGHLIGHTS

- Shop till you drop in **Houmt Souq** (p274)
- Soak up the sun at **Sidi Mahres beach** (p280)
- Visit the ancient Jewish community at the **El-Ghriba synagogue** (p277) in Erriadh

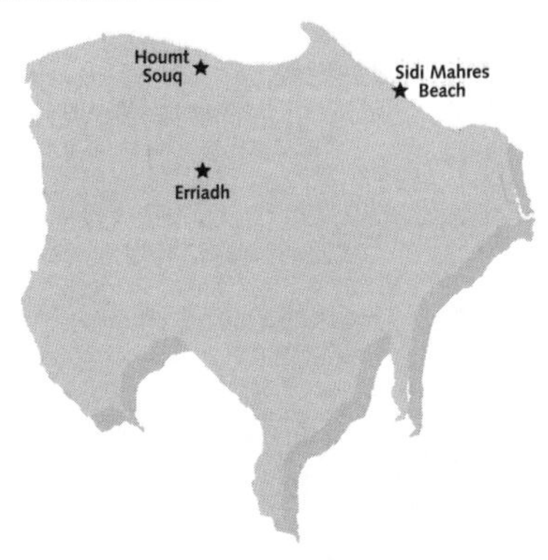

History

When Phoenicians arrived on the scene about 2700 years ago, Berber tribes were already well established on Jerba. Among them was the Gerbitani of Gerba (near modern Houmt Souq). The Phoenicians established settlements at Gightis on the mainland and Meninx (modern El-Kantara) on Jerba. The island was one of the first places to fall to the Arabs on their march into Tunisia, but it later became a stronghold and refuge of the Kharijites in the wake of the Kharijite rebellion and subsequent Fatimid backlash that erupted across North Africa in AD 740. They belonged to the Ibadite sect of Kharijism (see the boxed text, p280) and were largely responsible for the over 200 mosques on the island.

Jerba later became a home base for some of the Mediterranean's most renowned pirates, including the Barbarossa brothers and later their offsider Dragut – who became Dargouth Pasha, ruler of Tripoli. Dragut's renown was enhanced by a famous escape from the Spanish in 1551 when his fleet was trapped in the Gulf of Bou Grara; he escaped at night by hauling the ships across a breach in the causeway. Returning in 1560, he massacred Spanish forces the next year, leaving the Tower of Skulls near Houmt Souq.

Climate

For sun worshippers Jerba is a great place to visit year-round since even in the middle of winter temperatures rarely drop below 15°C. However, as in the rest of Tunisia, summers are hot though a regular sea breeze cools things down along the coast.

Getting There & Away

AIR

Jerba's airport, near Mellita village in the northwest, handles a busy schedule of international flights with a constant flow of charter flights from Europe (see p304). **Tuninter** (☎ 75 650 320; ave Habib Bourguiba) has an office in Houmt Souq and four flights a day to Tunis (TD84 one way, one hour) in summer.

BUS

The bus station is a block west of ave Habib Bourguiba at the southern edge of Houmt

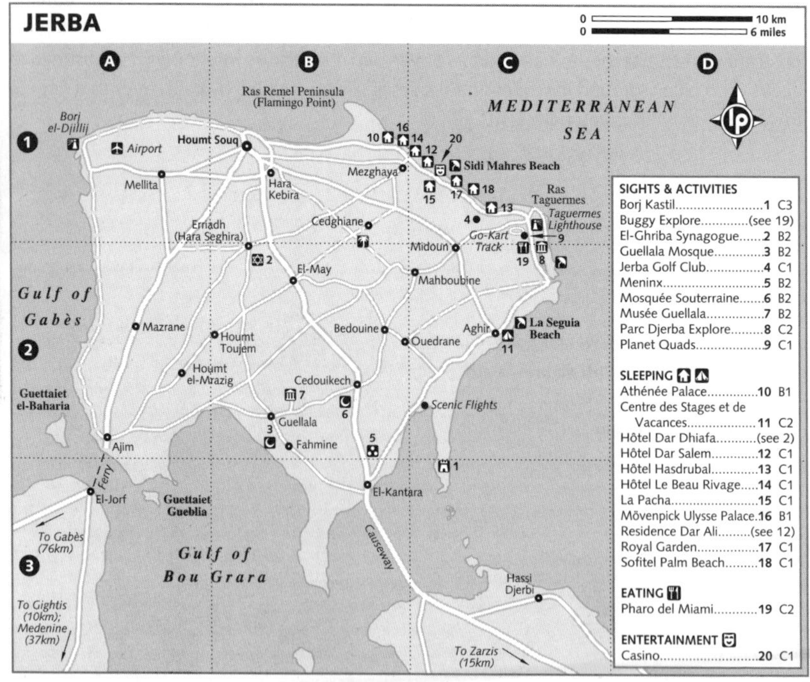

Souq. Scheduled departures are listed on a board above the ticket windows.

SNTRI runs at least three air-con services a day to Tunis (TD21). Two of these travel via Kairouan (TD15, six hours) and take eight hours; the other service goes via Sfax (TD12, five hours) and Sousse (TD16.5, seven hours) and takes nine hours. All SNTRI services stop at Gabès (TD6.1, 2½ hours).

The regional company, Sotregames, has five buses a day to Medenine. Make sure you catch one of the services that travel via the Ajim–El-Jorf ferry. These services cost TD3.7 and take 1½ hours; services via Zarzis take an hour longer and cost TD4.8. Two of these buses continue to Tataouine (TD6, 2½ hours). The afternoon service travels via Zarzis, stretching the journey time to 3½ hours and the fare is TD6.9.

There are three buses a day to Gabès (TD6.1, three hours). One service continues to Matmata (TD6.5, three hours).

CAR

An efficient car ferry service operates 24 hours a day between the Jerban port of Ajim and El-Jorf on the mainland, leaving every 20 minutes from 6.30am to 9.30pm; hourly from 9.30pm to 11.30pm; twice-hourly from 11.30pm to 4.30am; and hourly again from 4.30am to 6.30am. The trip takes 15 minutes and the fare is 800 mills for a car. Passengers travel free.

The other alternative is to take the old Roman causeway that links El-Kantara and the mainland. This only makes sense if you are heading south to Zarzis or if you're approaching Jerba from the south.

LOUAGE

Louages (shared taxis) leave from the parking lot at the southern entrance to Houmt Souq. There are frequent departures for Gabès (TD6) and Medenine (TD5.2), and services to Tataouine (TD7). Occasional louages leave for Tunis, Sfax and Sousse.

Getting Around

TO/FROM THE AIRPORT

The airport is 8km west of Houmt Souq, past the village of Mellita. There are three buses (570 mills) a day from the central bus station, which doesn't make it a very convenient option. Taxis are hassle free and cost only around TD3.5 from Houmt Souq, or TD8.5 from the Zone Touristique.

BICYCLE & MOPED

Renting a bicycle or motor scooter is an enjoyable and relatively inexpensive way to get around the island. Keep in mind that you're unlikely to be covered by your insurance policy when riding a moped so keep an eagle eye out for young children, wayward cyclists and attacking dogs. On the plus side, the roads on Jerba are very flat. **Raïs Rentals** (☎ 75 650 303; ave Abdelhamid el-Kadhi), north of the Mosque of the Strangers in Houmt Souq, has a good selection of bikes and motor scooters. Bicycles/50cc-scooters cost from TD10 to TD45 per day.

BUS

For those with more time than dinars, the cheapest way to get around the island is with the reasonably extensive local bus network, which operates from Houmt Souq to Guellala (TD1, 30 minutes, nine daily) via Erriadh (Hara Seghira; 600 mills), Cedouikech (800 mills, seven daily), the Zone Touristique (TD1, 13 daily), and Midoun (900 mills, 30 minutes, 12 daily) among other villages. There's a timetable and a colour-coded route map of the services above the ticket windows in Houmt Souq's bus station. You can also purchase tickets on the bus.

CAR RENTAL

If you're after flexibility and freedom and plan to explore sights on the mainland, then renting a car is an efficient option though not inexpensive. All the companies have offices in Houmt Souq and out at the airport. The offices in town include **Avis** (☎ 75 650 151; blvd de l'Environnement), **Budget** (☎ 75 635 444; ave Abdelhamid el-Kadhi), **Europcar** (☎ 75 650 357; ave Abdelhamid el-Kadhi) and **Hertz** (☎ 75 650 196; ave Habib Bourguiba). It's possible to return the car at an office in another city on the mainland for a surcharge. There is a cluster of local companies at the northern end of ave Abdelhamid el-Kadhi; these tend to be less expensive than the international companies though the quality of the vehicles is more suspect.

TAXI

Renting a taxi can be a good way to see the island. Rates start at TD10 per hour, but

THE LAND OF THE LOTUS-EATERS

According to legend, Jerba is the Land of the Lotus-Eaters, where Ulysses paused in the course of the *Odyssey* and had a lot of trouble persuading his crew to get back on board. Today's islanders are said to be descendants of these people.

In a passage that more than a few visitors to Jerba can relate to, Homer described how, after landing in 'the country of the Lotus-Eaters' and being given flowering food by the natives, the companions of Ulysses did not want to leave and couldn't even remember the way home.

These days there's scarcely a lotus to be found anywhere on the island, although many visitors to Jerba wish that they could forget the way home. Even louage drivers, not normally the most poetic of men, seem to have eaten of the lotus. When we boarded our louage to Jerba, the driver told us: 'You are going to the island of dreams'.

you may be able to bargain for less. Taxi drivers know the island inside out, but do have a tendency to take you to where they think you should go rather than where you want; be firm. There are two taxi ranks in Houmt Souq – on ave Habib Bourguiba in the centre of town and place Sidi Brahim. Some of the big hotels in the Zone Touristique have their own taxi ranks. It's about TD7 from Houmt Souq to Sidi Mahres.

HOUMT SOUQ حومة السّوق

pop 70,000

Imagine a Greek fishing village crossed with a Middle Eastern souq with a little Italian piazza thrown in and you have some idea of the beguiling charm of the island's capital. While its name in Arabic is ordinary and strictly descriptive – it literally means 'marketplace', which is all it was until the 20th century – the compact mix of uniformly whitewashed architecture (see the boxed text, p274), slow island pace and labyrinthine alleyways means Houmt Souq is one of Tunisia's gems. The ideal time to appreciate the town's charm is in the evening when the day trippers have gone, the shops have closed up, the temperature has cooled and you can wander the streets in dreamy silence.

Orientation

Ave Habib Bourguiba runs north through the town centre from the bus and louage stations and finishes near the port, while ave Abdelhamid el-Kadhi skirts the eastern edge of town. The souqs and most of the town's hotels and restaurants are found within the large V formed by these streets.

Information

BOOKSHOPS

The bookshop just north of the post office on ave Habib Bourguiba stocks international newspapers, magazines, a small collection of novels in French and an even smaller number of airport paperbacks in English.

INTERNET ACCESS

Cyber Planet (8am-10pm; per hr TD1.5) Northwest of place Sidi Brahim; fast connections.

Djerba Cyber Espace (9am-midnight; per hr TD2) Stairs to the 2nd-floor entrance are inside the courtyard for Restaurant el-Foundouk.

MEDICAL SERVICES

Clinique Dar ech-Chifa (75 650 441; fax 75 652 215; off ave Abdelhamid el-Kadhi) Private clinic northeast of town.

Hospital (75 650 018) Large regional facility about 500m southeast of the town centre on the road to Midoun.

MONEY

All the major banks have branches around the town centre and most have ATMs. There's always one bank rostered to be open on Saturday and Sunday; the *syndicat d'initiative* (tourist office) can tell you which one.

POST & TELEPHONE

There are dozens of Taxiphone offices around the town centre, including one on ave Habib Bourguiba and another on ave Abdelhamid el-Kadhi.

Main post office (ave Habib Bourguiba)

TOURIST INFORMATION

ONTT (75 650 016; blvd de l'Environnement; 8.30am-1pm & 3-5.45pm Mon-Thu, 8.30am-1.30pm Fri & Sat) Out on the beach road, about a 15-minute walk from the centre.

Syndicat d'initiative (75 650 915; ave Habib Bourguiba; 8am-2pm summer, to 3pm Mon-Sat winter) A little building set back from the street, behind the two large maps of the island opposite place Mongi Bali. Friendly staff.

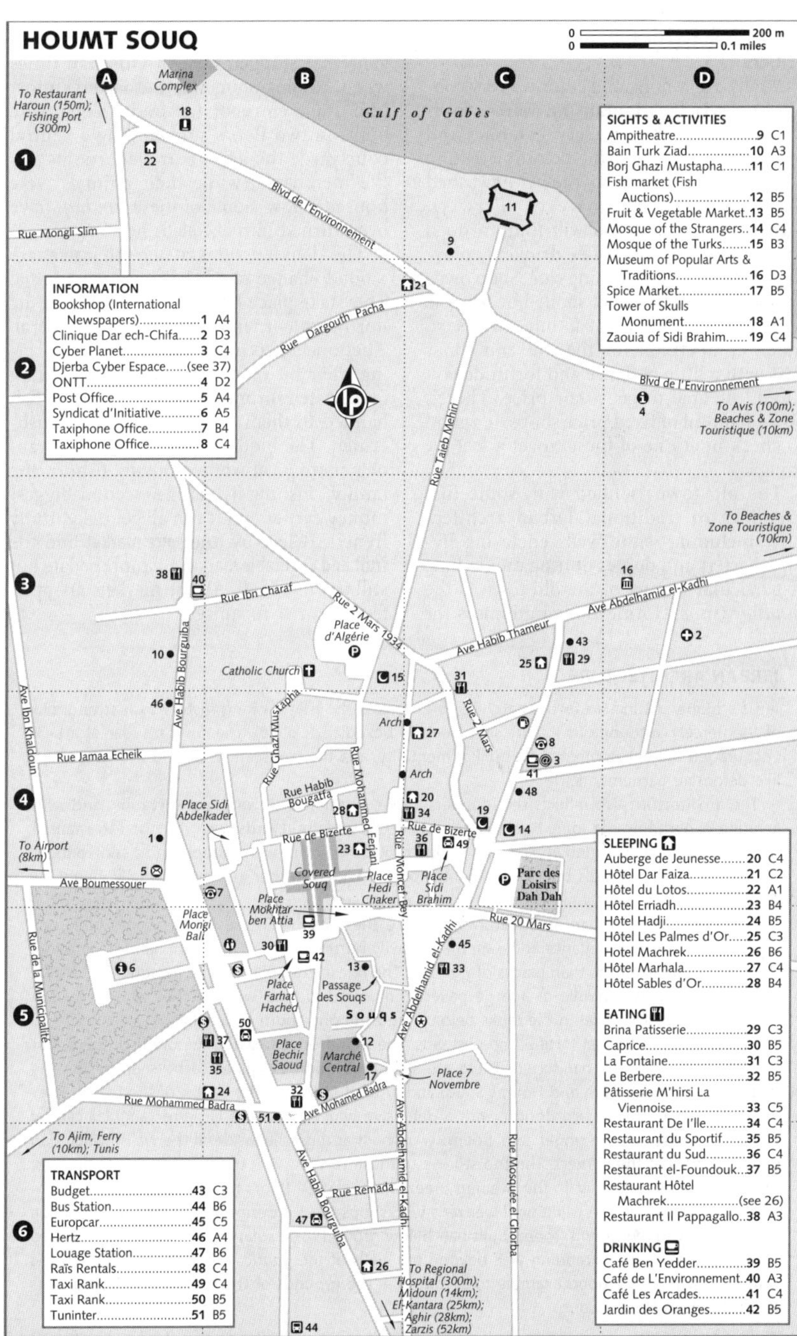
HOUMT SOUQ
0 200 m
0 0.1 miles
A
B
C
D
1
2
3
4
5
6
Marina Complex
Gulf of Gabès
To Restaurant Haroun (150m); Fishing Port (300m)
Blvd de l'Environnement
Rue Mongli Slim
Rue Dargouth Pacha
Rue Taieb Mehiri
To Avis (100m); Beaches & Zone Touristique (10km)
To Beaches & Zone Touristique (10km)
Ave Abdelhamid el-Kadhi
Ave Habib Thameur
Rue Ibn Charaf
Rue 2 Mars 1934
Place d'Algérie
Catholic Church
Ave Habib Bourguiba
Ave Ibn Khaldoun
Rue Jamaa Echeik
Rue Ghazi Mustapha
Rue Mohammed Ferjani
Rue Habib Bougatfa
Rue 2 Mars
Arch
Arch
Place Sidi Abdelkader
Rue de Bizerte
Rue de Bizerte
To Airport (8km)
Ave Boumessouer
Covered Souq
Place Hedi Chaker
Place Sidi Brahim
Rue Moncef Bey
Parc des Loisirs Dah Dah
Place Mokhtar ben Attia
Place Mongi Bali
Rue 20 Mars
Rue de la Municipalité
Place Farhat Hached
Passage des Souqs
Souqs
Ave Abdelhamid el-Kadhi
Place Bechir Saoud
Marché Central
Place 7 Novembre
Rue Mohammed Badra
Ave Mohamed Badra
To Ajim, Ferry (10km); Tunis
Ave Habib Bourguiba
Rue Remada
Rue Mosquée el Ghorba
To Regional Hospital (300m); Midoun (14km); El-Kantara (25km); Aghir (28km); Zarzis (52km)
INFORMATION
Bookshop (International Newspapers) 1 A4
Clinique Dar ech-Chifa 2 D3
Cyber Planet 3 C4
Djerba Cyber Espace (see 37)
ONTT 4 D2
Post Office 5 A4
Syndicat d'Initiative 6 A5
Taxiphone Office 7 B4
Taxiphone Office 8 C4
SIGHTS & ACTIVITIES
Ampitheatre 9 C1
Bain Turk Ziad 10 A3
Borj Ghazi Mustapha 11 C1
Fish market (Fish Auctions) 12 B5
Fruit & Vegetable Market 13 B5
Mosque of the Strangers 14 C4
Mosque of the Turks 15 B3
Museum of Popular Arts & Traditions 16 D3
Spice Market 17 B5
Tower of Skulls Monument 18 A1
Zaouia of Sidi Brahim 19 C4
SLEEPING
Auberge de Jeunesse 20 C4
Hôtel Dar Faiza 21 C2
Hôtel du Lotos 22 A1
Hôtel Erriadh 23 B4
Hôtel Hadji 24 B5
Hôtel Les Palmes d'Or 25 C3
Hotel Machrek 26 B6
Hôtel Marhala 27 C4
Hôtel Sables d'Or 28 B4
EATING
Brina Patisserie 29 C3
Caprice 30 B5
La Fontaine 31 C3
Le Berbere 32 B5
Pâtisserie M'hirsi La Viennoise 33 C5
Restaurant De l'Ile 34 C4
Restaurant du Sportif 35 B5
Restaurant du Sud 36 C4
Restaurant el-Foundouk 37 B5
Restaurant Hôtel Machrek (see 26)
Restaurant Il Pappagallo 38 A3
DRINKING
Café Ben Yedder 39 B5
Café de L'Environnement 40 A3
Café Les Arcades 41 C4
Jardin des Oranges 42 B5
TRANSPORT
Budget 43 C3
Bus Station 44 B6
Europcar 45 C5
Hertz 46 A4
Louage Station 47 B6
Raïs Rentals 48 C4
Taxi Rank 49 C4
Taxi Rank 50 B5
Tuninter 51 B5

JERBA

Sights & Activities

SOUQS

Virtually every nook and cranny, every cobblestone displays tantalising wares, from striking carpets to jewellery, ceramics and miniature bird cages, the colours creating a beautiful contrast to the whitewashed buildings lining the maze of alleyways. Turn a corner and you will find an open square peopled with coffee drinkers enjoying the shade in a charming café. Shop owners have been somewhat spoiled by tourists who don't bargain hard, but there's so much competition for the souvenir dinar that with a little patience and fortitude you should be able to get a fair price. There's also a handful of fixed price shops; it's good to check in at one of these to get a feel for things.

The old town is filled with some fine examples of traditional Jerban architecture, including white walls enclosing living quarters and domes dotting the skyline. A particular feature of the old town is the *funduqs* (inns), former lodging houses for the travelling merchants of the camel caravans that stopped here in Ottoman times when Houmt Souq was the island's most important entrepôt for trade. They were built on two floors surrounding a central courtyard; the top floor had rooms for the merchants, while their animals were housed below. Some of these *funduqs* have been turned into excellent hotels.

The daily auctions at the **fish market** are a good change of pace from tourist Jerba. They take place late in the morning in the northeast corner of the Marché Central. Auctioneers command attention performing their bit of mercantile theatre: sitting on elevated thrones they tout strings of fish handed to them by their helpers and fishermen. The bidders range from restaurant owners to local women buying fish for the family. Fishing is Jerba's second-biggest money earner and it can all get delightfully frenetic. Close by, the **spice market** and the **fruit and vegetable market** are more sedate but still worth a look. All the markets are open from sunrise to sunset.

JERBAN ARCHITECTURE

Jerba's highly distinctive fortress architecture reflects the island's long history as a stronghold of the fiercely autonomous Ibadite sect (see the boxed text, p280). The constant fear of attack encouraged the development of a bunker mentality, and the landscape is dotted with what look like defensive battlements.

The architecture also reflects the islanders' preoccupation with water conservation, and with keeping cool during the long, hot summers. Rooftops and courtyards were designed to channel rainwater into underground *impluviums* (tanks), providing both a water supply and a cool foundation. Thick rendered walls built of mud and stone provided further insulation. Finally, buildings were painted a brilliant white to deflect the summer sun.

Nothing typifies Jerban architecture quite like the mosque. These squat, square buildings positively bristle with defiance and with their heavily buttressed walls and minimalist decoration, they look more like forts than places of worship. The finest examples are the mosque at El-May – which stands in the middle of a large paved compound, dotted with hatches where you can check out the water level in the tanks below – and the one south of Guellala.

Menzels are traditional fortified homesteads. The island once boasted hundreds of them, but most have now been abandoned. There are still some good examples to be seen beside the main road between Ajim and Houmt Souq, and around El-May in the centre of the island. They were all built to a standard design, with a defensive wall enclosing a large rectangular central compound entered by a single gate. Rooms were built around the inside of the walls. which had square towers at the corners. The top storeys of these towers were used as summer bedrooms, with window grates to let in the evening breezes and slatted floors for extra ventilation.

Known as *harout*, the traditional weaver's workshops have a design that is simplicity itself: a long, barrel-vaulted *ghorfa* (room) built half below ground for insulation. They are characterised by a triangular front, extending well beyond the walls of the *ghorfa*, and buttressing along the outer walls. There's a good example to be found in the grounds of the Museum of Popular Arts & Traditions in Houmt Souq.

ISLAMIC MONUMENTS

There are some interesting Islamic monuments around town. On the edge of the souq is the imposing **Zaouia of Sidi Ibrahim** (rue 2 Mars 1934), which contains the tomb of the 17th-century saint. On the other side of the road is the multi-domed **Mosque of the Strangers** (ave Abdelhamid el-Kadhi). The 18th-century **Mosque of the Turks** is north of the souq on place d'Algérie. Built in the same fortress style as the island's traditional mosques, the only clue to its Turkish origins is the distinctive Ottoman minaret. All of these monuments are closed to non-Muslims but can be admired from the courtyard outside.

MUSEUM OF POPULAR ARTS & TRADITIONS

Though the displays aren't especially exciting, a visit to this little **museum** (☎ 75 650 540; ave Abdelhamid el-Kadhi; admission TD2.1, plus camera TD1; 🕑 8am-noon & 3-7pm Sat-Thu summer, 9.30am-4.30pm Sat-Thu winter) does provide some context and perspective on the culture of the island, one you're unlikely to get at the beaches of Sidi Mahres. It houses a good collection of local costumes as well as pottery and jewellery though exhibits are only labelled in Arabic and French. The room housing the latter still has the original terracotta domed tile ceiling as well as superbly intricate latticework design around the base. Indeed, the building itself is as interesting as the exhibits, with courtyards, arches and underground workshops. The museum occupies the Zaouia of Sidi Zitouni under the eucalyptus trees about 200m from the town centre; look for the ticket office in the small traditional weaver's hut near the entrance.

BORJ GHAZI MUSTAPHA

The town's old **fort** (Borj el-Kebir; admission TD3, plus camera TD1; 🕑 8am-7pm Sat-Thu summer, 9.30am-4.30pm Sat-Thu winter) is on the coast 600m north of the Mosque of the Turks. It was built by the Aragonese in the 13th century on the rubble of a 9th-century Aghlabid *ribat* (fortified monastery). It was extended early in the 16th century.

The fort was the scene of a massacre in 1560 when a Turkish fleet under Dragut (see p270) captured the fort and put the Spanish garrison of around 6000 men to the sword. The skulls of the victims were stacked up on the shoreline 500m west of the fort as a grim reminder to others not to mess with Dragut. This macabre **Tower of Skulls** stood for almost 300 years until it was dismantled in 1848. A simple monument now stands in its place, although a drawing in the room next to the fort's entrance shows how it must have appeared.

The fort's interior has dozens of rooms and a mosque crammed into a small space. The ramparts are accessible and offer good views along the coast. Look for the mounds of cannonballs, both stone and rusting iron, that have been found in the course of restoration.

There's a large recently constructed **amphitheatre**, the planned setting for performances and a sound and light show, next to the fort.

On Mondays and Thursdays, Rue Taieb Mehiri, the road that leads directly back to town from the fort, is the place to find the **Libyan market**. Traders from Tunisia's neighbour to the south once set up shop here though these days it's T-shirts, jeans and other everyday Western goods. It's only open for two days of the week; ask at your accommodation for details.

THE OCTOPUS CATCHERS

On this island that has been transformed by tourism, not everything has changed. The most distinctive features of Houmt Souq's fishing harbour are the great piles of terracotta pots shaped like Roman amphorae. Each bears its own mark signifying the local octopus fisherman who uses it in a traditional technique known as *gargoulette* that has changed little from Phoenician times. The 45cm to 50cm pots are tied together and cast out on long lines; they sink to the bottom and are left there for the octopus to discover. The slow-learning octopus mistakes the pot for its favourite underwater rocky nook or cranny, and obligingly crawls into the pot, only to be caught when the pots are hauled to the surface.

FISHING PORT & MARINA

Houmt Souq's busy little fishing port is at the northern end of ave Habib Bourguiba, about a 25-minute walk from town. Early mornings are the busiest and most interesting times to visit. Also out in the same direction is a brand new multimillion-dollar marina complex of apartments, shops, cafés and restaurants. At the time of research only about half the space was occupied.

Festivals & Events

Created and engineered for the delight of tourists, the **Ulysses Festival** is held in July to August and includes events like a Miss Ulysses beauty contest. Any of the tourist offices (see p272) can provide details.

Sleeping

There's a good array of sleeping options in Houmt Souq though none are top-end or resort quality. Prices here include breakfast unless stated. For camping on the island, head to Aghir (p281), 28km southeast of Houmt Souq.

For those who find the Zone Touristique too sterile or expensive and want a little more quiet than what's available in Houmt Souq proper, there are two hotels facing the beach on blvd de l'Environnement just to the west of the fort.

BUDGET

Auberge de Jeunesse (☎ 75 650 619; rue Moncef Bey; dm TD6) The old *funduq* this youth hostel occupies is picturesque enough for the casual tourist to stop to snap a photo; however, the rooms with two to four beds are rudimentary. Reservations are definitely recommended during the high season. Bathrooms are shared.

Hôtel Sables d'Or (☎ 75 650 423; rue Mohammed Ferjani; s/d TD13/25) This charming and attractive old home is decorated with antiques and the small but stylish rooms are immaculate. There are private showers but toilets are shared.

Hôtel Marhala (☎ 75 650 146; fax 75 653 317; rue Moncef Bey; s/d TD18/28) An atmospheric place to stay in Houmt Souq, the Marhala (owned by the Touring Club de Tunisie) has barrel-vaulted rooms surrounding a central courtyard. You may feel like a medieval monk in some of the more unadorned ones.

Hôtel Erriadh (☎ 75 650 756; mounirherbegue@gnet.tn; rue Mohammed Ferjani; s/d TD19/30; ❄) Besides being a comfortable and charmingly decorated place, the Erriadh is architecturally delightful, housed in one of the old *funduqs*. Some of the rooms have ceiling fans.

MIDRANGE

Hôtel Hadji (☎ 75 650 630; hotel.hadjires@gnet.tn; 44 rue Mohammed Badra; s/d TD22/32; ❄) Just around the corner from a supermarket, the Hadji won't win any interior design awards but the rooms are functional and the bathrooms are kept clean. There's a small café on the ground floor.

Hôtel Les Palmes d'Or (☎ 75 653 369; fax 75 653 368; 84 ave Abdelhamid el-Kadhi; s/d TD32/50; ❄) Less modern and comfortable than the Machrek, this friendly hotel on the northeastern edge of town, nevertheless is popular with groups and has large, clean rooms.

Hôtel du Lotos (☎ 75 650 026; blvd de l'Environnement; s/d TD25/50; ❄) This hotel situated opposite the Tower of Skulls monument near the marina complex is an attractive and airy whitewashed complex. Most of the rooms get good sunlight but the wooden furnishings are basic. There's a pleasant outdoor patio area with a restaurant and bar.

Hotel Machrek (☎ 75 653 155; hôtel.elmachrek@planet.tn; ave Habib Bourguiba; s/d TD28/56; ❄) Easily the best value option in Houmt Souq, the Machrek has comfortable and modern rooms, at least as nice as many of the *zone touristique* hotels. There's a sunny central courtyard, good restaurant and professional front desk staff.

Hôtel Dar Faiza (☎ 75 650 083; www.darfaiza darsalem.com; blvd de l'Environnement; s/d TD39/74; ❄ 🏊) Almost directly across the street from the amphitheatre, the friendly Dar Faiza feels like the private villa of a once prosperous family whose fortunes have changed. There's no denying the appeal of the small pool but the rooms are older and more basic than you'd expect from the outside; however, it's still a good choice.

Eating

The streets and alleyways of central Houmt Souq are a veritable moving feast with a café or restaurant seemingly every few feet.

Le Berbere (ave Habib Bourguiba; sandwiches TD2) Chow down on custom filled pitta sandwiches and fries at this fast food–style stand-up restaurant.

Caprice (place Farhat Hached; mains TD3) Claiming a particularly prime piece of real estate on the edge of one of the busiest squares, Caprice is a modern restaurant with indoor and outdoor seating. Food is Italian crossed with fast food: pizza (TD2.8), hamburgers, spaghetti and meat dishes.

Restaurant du Sportif (ave Habib Bourguiba; mains TD3) Frequented by locals rather than tourists, du Sportif is a friendly no-nonsense eatery serving good portions of basic couscous, meat and chicken dishes for bargain prices.

La Fontaine (☎ 75 254 205; rue 2 Mars; mains TD4) Choose from a variety of distinctive dining areas at this fairyland like restaurant, from the wooden Swiss tea house to the Moroccan-style patio. There seems to be more than one menu and it's hard to work out the theme but you can choose from pizza (TD3.7), crepes (TD1.5) and sandwiches (TD1.5) as well as drinks and ice cream. A set menu is offered from 4pm on.

Restaurant el-Foundouk (☎ 75 653 238; off ave Habib Bourguiba; mains from TD4.5, set menu TD7-15) Set back from the road in a courtyard, el-Foundouk feels a little lonely, even more so because service can seem half-hearted and despite the French, German, English and Arabic menus, they seem unprepared for diners. One way around this is to order the special fish couscous for four (TD28) 24 hours in advance.

Restaurant Il Pappagallo (☎ 75 416 216; ave Habib Bourguiba; mains TD6) Big hearty portions of pasta are served here with an unusual amount of elegance and attention to detail. If this lovely Italian restaurant isn't crowded it's only because there's no pedestrian traffic on this road leading out of town. Even the dishes and silverware, to say nothing of the service, is a step above the rest. Pizzas (TD6.5), salads and meat dishes are also on the menu.

Restaurant du Sud (☎ 75 650 479; mains TD6) Between place Hedi Chaker and place Sidi Brahim, du Sud is fairly cookie cutter as tourist souq restaurants go, but the large helpings of seafood are fresh and comparatively inexpensive.

Restaurant de l'Ile (rue de Bizerte; mains TD7) A more sophisticated version of the souq restaurants catering specifically to tourists, this place has classy trappings and tasty seafood specials for moderate prices, including overflowing plates of fresh clams. The *briq au fruits de mer* is almost big enough for a meal in and of itself. Wine is available.

Restaurant Haroun (☎ 75 650 488; mains TD15) Posh and lovely, this restaurant on the edge of the new marina complex is the most upmarket place in Houmt Souq. Whether you eat in the docked pirate-like ship or the main dining room with high ceilings and stonework, it's worth the price. *Haute cuisine* fish and meat dishes are served.

Patisserie M'hirsi La Viennoise (ave Abdelhamid el-Kadhi) and **Brina Patisserie** (ave Abdelhamid el-Kadhi) have a good array of cakes and pastries.

Of the hotel restaurants, one of the best is the streetside one at the **Hotel Machrek** (ave Habib Bourguiba; mains TD5).

Drinking

Café Ben Yedder (place Mokhtar ben Attia) Popular with locals and tourists alike, Ben Yedder is a prime people watching spot with an above average collection of pastries and snacks.

Jardin des Oranges (place Farhat Hached) Tables here are scattered over the entire square, on the lawn, under the pavilion and inside, and while it's hard to determine who in fact your waiter is, there's no hurry. Most of the territory is marked by small baskets of oranges. Beware: the juice is pricey (TD3.5).

Café de l'Environnement (ave Habib Bourguiba) Just down the road from the Restaurant Il Pappagallo on the northern edge of town, this café, nothing more than plastic tables set up in a garden, is a good place to stop for a breather on a walk to or from the marina complex.

Café Les Arcades (ave Abdelhamid el-Kadhi) More distinctive than the average coffeehouse because of the marble tables, Les Arcades feels slightly Parisian even if it's strictly filled with local regulars.

ERRIADH (HARA SEGHIRA) الرّياض

The village of Erriadh or Hara Seghira (Small Ghetto), 7km south of Houmt Souq, is notable only because of its ancient synagogue and the presence of one of the island's finer hotels.

El-Ghriba Synagogue

The most important synagogue on Jerba and the oldest in North Africa is **El-Ghriba** (The Miracle; admission TD1; 🕑 7.30am-6pm Sun-Fri), signposted 1km south of the town. It's a major place of pilgrimage during *Lag Ba'Omer*, usually occuring in May, when Jews come to pay tribute to the grand master of the Talmud, Shimon Bar Yashai, who died more than 400 years ago. As part of the festivities, local Jews and pilgrims carry the community's holy books through the town.

The site dates back to 586 BC, although the present building was built early in the 20th century. The original synagogue is thought to have been founded here after a holy stone fell from heaven at the site and a mysterious woman appeared to direct the construction of the synagogue. It is also believed that when the last Jew leaves Jerba, the keys to the synagogue will return to heaven.

The interior is an attractive combination of blue tilework and sombre wooden furniture. The inner sanctuary, with its elevated pulpit, is said to contain one of the oldest Torahs (Jewish holy book) in the world. Numerous silver plaques from pilgrims adorn the eastern wall.

Because of the 2002 attack on the synagogue, security at the site is now as tight as you'll see in Tunisia with airport style detectors (independent travellers may be asked for their passport).

Sleeping & Eating

Hôtel Dar Dhiafa (☎ 75 671 166; www.hoteldardhiafa.com; d TD180, ste TD220-260;) This is an elegantly opulent hotel with 10 rooms, four suites, all wonderfully and uniquely decorated with fine artwork and local handicrafts, wrought iron beds under a cupola and elaborate doorways to each private residence. The Dar Dhiafa is the anti-*zone touristique* hotel, so discreet, subtle and tasteful in its lavishness that you feel like royalty or a celebrity in a private hideaway. Facilities include an excellent restaurant, two swimming pools, a *hammam* (public bathhouse) and a Moorish café. The hotel is well signposted in town.

Getting There & Away

Buses from Houmt Souq to Guellala go past the synagogue (600 mills).

GUELLALA قلالة

If you arrive in the middle of the day at this village on the south coast of the island, it will seem almost like a ghost town since shopkeepers shutter their doors and seek refuge from the heat. When a big tourist bus rolls down the street the pottery workshops and galleries come alive with activity. Though the selection is similar to what you'll find in Houmt Souq, odds are you'll get the real goods rather than an imitation and a better chance of striking a good deal. However, other than shopping and the museum, Guellala is not an especially exceptional place to visit.

THE JEWS OF JERBA

The Jewish community dates its arrival in Jerba either from 586 BC, following Nebuchadnezzar's conquest of Jerusalem, or from the Roman sacking of the same city in AD 71; either way this makes it one of the oldest Jewish communities in the world outside Israel. Some historians, however, argue that many Jerban Jews are descended from Berbers who converted to Judaism. Over the centuries the community also received several influxes of Jews fleeing from persecution in Spain, Italy and Palestine.

In the 19th century, Jews in Jerba were required to wear distinctive clothes: black pantaloons, black skull cap and sleeveless blue shirts. Discrimination ended with the arrival of the French in 1881. The community was known for being staunchly traditional, like its neighbours the Kharijite Muslims, and it rejected financial and educational aid from the rest of the Jewish world. Communities of Jerban Jews settled all over southern Tunisia, usually working as blacksmiths famed for their jewellery, but returned to the island for the summer and for religious festivals.

Most Jerban Jews emigrated to Israel after the 1956 and 1967 Arab-Israeli wars; after centuries of relative peace, the clash between Arab and Israeli nationalism made their position untenable across North Africa. The community also suffered during WWII, when the Germans extorted 50kg of gold as a communal fine.

The Jewish community on Jerba now numbers only a few hundred. The community's survival on Jerba was called into question in April 2002 when a truck bomb exploded at El-Ghriba synagogue, killing 19 people in an event locals call 'Le Catastrophe'. Muslim and Jewish locals are quick to point out that the two communities have lived in harmony alongside one another for generations, pointing the finger at external elements for the bombing.

JERBA AND TOURISM

The at-times-difficult relationship between tourism and traditional Tunisian society is best evident than on Jerba, particularly in Houmt Souq and the Zone Touristique. Environmentally, ground water has become less potable and agriculture less tenable as supplies are exhausted by thirsty resorts and other tourist infrastructure on the island. For many of the older inhabitants of Jerba, the tourism inundation has also been profoundly alienating, with liberal displays of flesh putting the best beaches out of bounds for Tunisian families, and prices pushed ever higher to catch the tourist euro.

The most visible example of the impact of tourism upon traditional life can be found at the fishing harbour north of Houmt Souq, where local fishermen have been following millennia-old techniques passed down from father to son. Behind the little harbour is a new luxury marina complex modelled on those at Monastir and Port el-Kantaoui, intended as the domain of wealthy yachters, while the fishermen are shunted further along the coast.

Traditional ways survive in the Berber-speaking Ibadite villages of the south, like Guellala and Cedouikech, but they're fading as young people are drawn away to jobs in the tourist business.

Tourism has also brought good things to Jerba, including a renewed interest in preserving the architectural heritage of the island, the revival of the manufacturing of traditional handicrafts and the providing of much-needed jobs; government statistics suggest that every hotel bed in Tunisia supports 1.1 direct local jobs.

Your impact is likely to be diminished if you avoid the temptation to fly through the souq, make a couple of rapid-fire purchases and eat at a restaurant visited only by tourists, only to hasten back to your hotel. Take the time to talk to locals – whether it's the youngster who serves you breakfast, the vendor who sells you the stuffed camel or the old men sitting in the cafés frequented only by locals. Chances are that they'll appreciate someone taking the time to stop and listen to a different story of Jerba.

Sights & Activities

CAVE D'ALI BERBERE

Be sure to check out the Cave d'Ali Berbere, on the southeastern edge of town. Ali is an endearing man who, in French, will tell you that the cave, supported by a series of stone arches, dates back to Roman times. He'll demonstrate pottery-making as it used to be done, climb into a massive amphora to show how Ali Baba and his 40 thieves were able to hide and take you to an ancient underground olive press. There's no entrance fee but a tip is both appreciated and deserved.

GUELLALA MOSQUE

The 15th-century waterfront mosque 1.5km south of town is a fine example of Jerban Islamic architecture, and a favourite spot to watch the sunset.

MUSÉE GUELLALA

This large whitewashed complex of buildings sits in a commanding position at the top of a hill nearly 2km east of town on the road to Cedouikech. The **museum** (Museum of Guellala, Musée du Patrimonie; ☎ 75 761 114; admission TD5, plus camera TD3; 🕑 7am-11pm summer, 8am-6pm winter) is really a collection of life-size dioramas using mannequins past their prime to illustrate Jerban customs and folklore. The rather kitschy reproductions of 'scenes from Jerban life' range from weddings (the depilation scene graphically captures the pain of hair removal!) and the solemn rite of circumcision to Sufi dancers and olive pressing. Music is piped through the rooms, and there are labels in four languages. There are also displays of wedding costumes from around Tunisia. Even if the dummies leave you unimpressed, there are fine views over Guellala and down to the Gulf of Bou Grara.

Getting There & Away

There are seven buses a day between Guellala and Houmt Souq (800 mills, 30 minutes). If you take a taxi, be sure to arrange the return trip in advance; transport here is extremely sparse.

GUELLALA TO THE ZONE TOURISTIQUE

The most interesting road northeast of Guellala runs through the quiet town of **Cedouikech**, notable for its subterranean mosque, the **mosquée souterraine** or Louta Mosque, with only the white domes visible above ground. It was an Ibadite mosque and dates from the 12th century. Continuing northeast takes you to **Mahboubine**, where the Turkish or El-Kaatib Mosque is worth stopping for. The road from here to Midoun is a good place to see examples of traditional *menzels* (Jerban dwellings) along the roadside.

Midoun, the island's second-largest town, is a smaller, less charming version of Houmt Souq. It does have a busy Friday market; however, it's crowded with tourists on the prowl for souvenirs most days of the week during the summer because of its proximity to the hotels on Sidi Mahres beach. Pretty much everything you can find in Houmt Souq is also available here though the experience is less atmospheric. The town also stages a traditional **Jerban wedding ceremony** in the open-air theatre for the benefit of tourists every Tuesday at 4pm (TD2). An excellent place to catch your breath before again entering into high stakes negotiations for that ceramic dish you were eyeing is Le Palais Royal Café Patisserie, a sophisticated Parisian style place with indoor and outdoor seating. Les Delices de Jerba has great pastries, gelati and sandwiches. Restaurant de l'Orient and Restaurant Constantine serve reasonably priced Tunisian fare. There are several banks with ATMs.

Another worthwhile detour is to the oasis of **Cedghiane**. It's in the most fertile part of the island, with an ample supply of sweet artesian water, which has allowed the development of traditional, tiered desert oasis agriculture. Tall palms provide shade for citrus and pomegranate trees, which in turn protect vegetable crops. The huge *menzels* of the area are evidence that this was once an important settlement, but most are in ruins.

ZONE TOURISTIQUE

Like other *zone touristiques* throughout Tunisia, Jerba's (which occupies most of the island's eastern cost) is filled with artificially enhanced resorts, the equivalent of an athlete on steroids. There's nothing modest about these all-inclusive behemoths – whether it's the Las Vegas meets the Kasbah design schemes or the cavernous chandelier-filled atriums, it's a little bit of a disorienting experience to stay here.

In some ways it would be unfortunate if **Sidi Mahres**, a long sweep of golden sand, was all one saw of the country, though for some it's a perfectly wonderful vacation full of sun, sand and banana boating for the kids. It begins east of the low-lying Ras Remel Peninsula, which protrudes from the middle of the north coast 10km east of Houmt Souq. The peninsula is known as **Flamingo Point** because of the large number of flamingos that gathers there in winter. Sidi Mahres beach then continues east all the way to **Ras Taguermes**, the cape at Jerba's eastern tip. A

THE IBADIS

Jerba is home to one of the last remaining communities of Ibadis, an offshoot of the Kharijites. The word 'Kharijite' means 'those who go out to fight jihad (holy war)'. The Kharijites separated from other Islamic doctrines in the years after Islam was born when they accepted the legitimacy of the first two caliphs but held all others to be in error. Indeed, some argue that the Kharijites were responsible for the death of Ali (the fourth caliph, whose followers founded the Shiite Islamic sect).

When Islam spread across North Africa in the 7th century AD, the rebellious Berber tribes accepted the new religion, but typically were drawn to sects, such as the Kharijites, which rejected the prevailing hierarchies.

The Ibadis believe that the imam or head of the Muslim community should be the most worthy candidate, regardless of their origin or family background. The imam, chosen by the community, can also be removed if he fails to adhere to the Islamic principles of his office. The Ibadis even believe that it is not necessary for there to be an imam at all times. Again this suited the Berbers who would sometimes appoint an imam to mediate between the disparate tribes during times of conflict only to dispense with his services when he was deemed no longer necessary.

Under the Ottomans, the Ibadis, who lived under a council of learned elders, were tolerated and left to their own devices, but their unorthodox beliefs have always made them vulnerable to attack from zealots, hence their retreat to a few well-defended refuges like Jerba.

long sand spit extends south from the cape, enclosing a large lagoon.

South of here on the east coast is **La Seguia**. The hotels are spaced further apart here and the beaches are less crowded.

Most of the beaches are the private domain of the hotels, but there are some small public beaches (ask for *la plage populaire;* the only ones left for locals) just south of the Mövenpick Ulysse Palace resort.

The road running along the coast behind the hotels has a range of restaurants, souvenir shops and bicycle/scooter-hire places.

Sights & Activities

Most people indulge in the activity of lethargy and a trip from the bar to the pool can be considered an aerobic workout. For the more energetic, all the hotels offer every imaginable **water sport** from windsurfing to catamarans, jet skiing and parasailing. For those hoping to change their financial future through the hard work of gambling, Jerba has its very own **casino** (☎ 75 757 537; ⏰ 24hr); it only accepts foreign currency.

A fairly sterile attempt to beef up the island's cultural offerings is the new **Parc Djerba Explore** (☎ 75 745 277; djerbaexplore.commercial@planet.tn; adult/child TD12/6), a combination museum, heritage zone and crocodile park out next to the Taguermes Lighthouse. The crocs are mesmerising, the museum houses a good collection of Islamic ceramics, textiles and manuscripts but the small heritage zone is nothing more than an empty house surrounded by sand. The large, modern whitewashed complex includes souvenir shops and a few restaurants and cafés.

Across the road from the Parc is **Buggy Explore** (☎ 75 745 162; per 1½ hrs TD45), where you can rent go-cart-like 4WDs to take for a spin on the sandy track down the road. Also near the lighthouse is **Planet Quads** (☎ 75 836 911) offering vehicles of lesser quality.

The **Jerba Golf Club** (☎ 75 745 055; www.djerbagolf.com; 9/18 holes TD40/70, club hire TD15) is out at the eastern edge of the Zone Touristique; reservations are required.

Sleeping & Eating

There seem to be as many hotels lining the Jerban coast on the route Touristique as there are grains of sand on the beach. The gaudy architecture and rather impersonal service are redeemed by the natural assets – soft sand and warm water – that lie just beyond the back doors of these gargantuan pleasure palaces. Walk-up travellers are about as common as snow in the Sahara and you'll probably be given strange looks if you just show up looking for a room. Even if the roads and towns are deserted the hotel pools and lobbies tend to be packed. Most are totally booked out in the summer and really only worthwhile if you book as part of a package. Most are city-states unto themselves with several swimming pools, private beaches, massage centres, tennis courts, nightclubs, bars, restaurants, coffee shops, boutiques and a programme of daily activities to keep guests entertained.

Centre des Stages et de Vacances (☎ 75 750 266; dm without breakfast TD5, tent TD2.5) This is the island's centre for campers or for that matter budget travellers after a beachfront vacation. There are no bells and whistles but the four-bed dorm rooms are comfortable enough. Expect to have to walk to one of the nearby hotels for your meals if there isn't a large group in residence. It's located by the beach at Aghir at the junction of the Midoun road 28km southeast of Houmt Souq. To get there from Houmt Souq, catch the bus (TD1, 40 minutes) to Club Med via Midoun.

Pharo del Miami (mains TD4) This pleasant restaurant is directly across the street from the Parc Djerba Explore; tasty crepes, sandwiches and pizzas are served.

At the time of writing there were several five-star resorts including the **Athénée Palace** (☎ 75 757 600), the **Sofitel Palm Beach** (☎ 75 757 777), the **Mövenpick Ulysee Palace** (☎ 75 758 777), the **Hôtel Hasdrubal** (☎ 75 657 657) and the **Royal Garden** (☎ 75 658 777). Plans for even more are in the works. Summer rates for these run around TD170/218 for a single/double. Dozens of other three- and four-star hotels line the road along Sidi Mahres and while the facilities tend to be similar, the level of service and attention can be hit or miss. A few that have been recommended are the **Djerba Holiday Beach** (☎ 75 758 177, 75 758 192), **Al Jazira** (☎ 75 758 860; bravoclub@planet.tn) and **Abou Nawas** (☎ 75 657 022; fax 75 657 700).

There are several hotels at the western edge of the Zone Touristique that are more welcoming to individual travellers, in part because they tend not to be as heavily booked as the three-star and up places directly on the beach. Most are close to the beach but not right on it, and are more intimate, pension-style accommodation. Expect to pay around TD70/100 for a single/double. The **Hôtel Dar Salem** (☎ 75 757 667; www.darfaizadarsalem.com;), which has a large pool, is certainly one of the nicest. Others to try are the **Hôtel Le Beau Rivage** (☎ 75 758 230), **Residence Dar Ali** (☎ 75 758 045; fax 75 758 045) and **La Pacha** (☎ 75 731 827; hedi.sassi@tunet.tn).

SOUTHEASTERN COAST

Most visitors never make it to this part of the island and for good reason, unless you're interested in some solitude and fairly uninspiring scenery. The **Borj Kastil** is a reconstructed Roman fort visible on a narrow peninsula southwest of La Seguia. It's only accessible if you're on a bike.

Near the town of **El-Kantara** are the meagre ruins of Roman **Meninx**, an ancient trading post. Many of the ruins are visible from the road, especially west and north of El-Kantara. The old Roman causeway links Jerba to the mainland.

Directory

CONTENTS

Accommodation	283
Activities	285
Business Hours	287
Children	287
Climate Charts	288
Courses	288
Customs	288
Dangers & Annoyances	289
Discount Cards	290
Embassies & Consulates	290
Festivals & Events	291
Food & Drink	292
Gay & Lesbian Travellers	292
Holidays	292
Insurance	293
Internet Access	293
Legal Matters	293
Maps	294
Men Travellers	294
Money	294
Photography	295
Post	296
Shopping	296
Solo Travellers	298
Telephone & Fax	298
Time	299
Toilets	299
Tourist Information	299
Travellers with Disabilities	300
Visas	300
Women Travellers	300

ACCOMMODATION

As a well-established tourist destination, Tunisia has accommodation ranging from rock-bottom basic to five-star glitz. Recently it has acquired a number of smaller, chic, boutique hotels – welcome additions to the market. Throughout this book, accommodation is divided into three price categories: budget, midrange and top end. Some hotels add an air-con supplement to their prices in summer – this is usually around TD5 to TD10. To make things simpler, we have included this supplement in the prices listed where appropriate.

Although it can vary from town to town, budget accommodation includes camping, hostels and cheap hotels – where a bed will usually range from TD3 per person to TD30 for a double. In the cheapest places, your few dinars won't get you much more than a dorm bed or a cell with a shared bathroom. At the upper end of the scale you'll probably get somewhere quite pleasant with a private bathroom of some description. Lone women travellers will feel

PRACTICALITIES

Newspapers & Magazines

Daily newspapers include the French-language *La Presse* (www.lapresse.tn, in French only) and *Le Temps* (www.letemps.com.tn), and Arabic *Assabah* (www.tunisie.com/Assabah, in French only) and *Al-Houria*. In English, *Tunisia News* is available weekly, plus (two-day-old) major European and US papers, and (week-old) *Time* and *Newsweek*.

Radio

Tune in to local French-language Radio Tunis (98FM; www.radiotunis.com) or BBC World Service on short wave (15.070MHz and 12.095MHz).

TV

The French-language TV station (www.tunisiatv.com) includes 30 minutes of news at 8pm daily; satellite TV (CNN etc) screens in top-end hotels.

Video Systems

Like Europe and Australia, Tunisia uses PAL, which is incompatible with the North American and Japanese NTSC system.

Electricity

Almost universal and reliable, electricity is 220V; wall plugs have two round pins (as in Europe).

Weights & Measures

Tunisia uses the metric system (weight in kilograms, distance in metres); conversion charts are on the inside back cover of this book.

uncomfortable in the lowest-end cheapies, though exceptions are specified throughout the book; youth hostels are usually a good bet. Classified hotels are those that have been inspected by the government and awarded from one to five stars. Non-classified hotels haven't been inspected (these are indicated by the initials NC – *nonclassifié* – on accommodation lists handed out by tourist offices). They can still be very good though – they tend to be the most budget places and many are listed in this book. At classified hotels prices usually include breakfast, while at non-classified hotels you normally have to fend for yourself.

Midrange accommodation can start at TD30 per double, rising to TD100. In this price range, you'll usually have a private bathroom, more space and higher standards of cleanliness than some budget places, and – on occasion – charm, views and a pool.

For top-end rates (from TD100 for a double), you can expect luxurious rooms with satellite TV, fluffy towels, direct-dial telephone and a bathtub. Most places in this price bracket also have a pool, spas and a *hammam* (bathhouse).

Camping

There are few camp sites in Tunisia and facilities tend to be basic. Most charge between TD3 and TD7 per person, and some in the south rent on-site Bedouin tents if you don't have a tent. Showers are either free or around TD1.5, while those with cars and campervans pay a few extra dinars for water and electricity. The best camp sites are those in Tozeur (p258), Ksar Ghilane (p251), Douz (p246) and near Kélibia (p116).

Camp sites apart, it should be possible to camp anywhere as long as you obtain permission from the landowner. You can also ask locals where good camping spots are. Sleeping on the beach is the accepted thing at Raf Raf and Ghar el-Melh in the north. The same does not apply, however, to the resort beaches around the Cap Bon, Jerba and Sousse.

BOOK ACCOMMODATION ONLINE

For more accommodation reviews and recommendations by Lonely Planet authors, check out the online booking service at www.lonelyplanet.com. You'll find the true, insider lowdown on the best places to stay. Reviews are thorough and independent. Best of all, you can book online.

Hostels

Hostels fall into two categories: *auberges de jeunesse,* affiliated to Hostelling International (HI); and government-run *maisons des jeunes.*

The *auberges de jeunesse* are thoroughly recommended. Most have prime locations, such as a converted palace in the Tunis medina (p80) and an old *funduq* (*caravanserai;* inn) in Houmt Souq on Jerba (p276). Others are at Remel Plage (p128) outside Bizerte and at the beach in Nabeul (p112).

You must be a member of Hostelling International to stay at an *auberge de jeunesse.* The hostels generally charge about TD6 to TD8 per night, with breakfast available for TD1 and other meals for TD3 each. Many impose a three-night limit during high season.

Maisons des jeunes, on the other hand, often have all the charm of a barracks, though there are exceptions, such as Hammamet's central beachside option (p106). Almost every town has one, but they can be far-flung and hard to reach without private transport. However, they're sometimes the only budget accommodation option. They all charge around TD5 for a dorm bed.

There are a few places where the *maison des jeunes* concept has evolved into a *centre des stages et vacances,* combining hostel and camp site. These are on the beach at Aghir on Jerba (p281), and in the oasis at Gabès (p226). Camping charges are usually TD3 per person. Power and hot showers are available for a few dinars extra.

Hotels

Tunisian hotels fall into two main categories: classified hotels, which have been awarded between one and five stars by the government; and nonclassified hotels, which haven't. The latter are indicated by the initials NC *(nonclassifié)* on tourist office accommodation lists.

Most budget places recommended in this book are nonclassified and some are excellent. The cheapest are in the town medinas. They're basic, often with no showers, and you pay for a bed in a shared room. These

APARTMENT RENTAL

For longer-term lettings, particularly in and around Tunis, and at resorts such as Hammamet and Sousse, try the following websites.

- http://properties.tunisia.com
- www.homelidays.com
- www.oasisimmobilier.com (in French only)
- www.meteotunisie.com/annonce (in French only)
- www.oleaimmobilier.com (in French only; for Hammamet rentals)

hotels are totally unsuitable for women travellers. However, there are plenty of nonclassified places that are more appealing.

One- and two-star hotels tend to be small, and often built in colonial times. They're generally clean, if rundown, and are popular with local business travellers and tourists who want a decent double room with private bathroom and hot water. A three-star rating usually indicates a hotel built to cater for tour groups. Four- and five-star hotels have the facilities you would expect, but people often find that four- and five-star places here, though often splendid, fall short of international standards.

Hotel prices are normally listed according to three seasons – *haute* (high), *moyenne* (middle) and *basse* (low). High season usually corresponds with the European summer (from 1 July to 15 September) and Christmas holidays. It's the same in the south, despite the incredibly hot temperatures. Low season is from 1 November to 15 March (excluding the Christmas holidays), and the rest is middle season. Generally low-season prices for top-end places can be remarkable: between 30% and 60% less than high-season rates. Differences are less marked at midrange places and only a few dinars cheaper at budget hotels. Prices listed in this book are high-season rates.

At classified hotels, room rates usually include breakfast; at nonclassified hotels and at top-end places, breakfast is often quoted separately, so make sure you ask. At budget and midrange level, you'll soon tire of the typical hotel breakfast, which consists of coffee, French bread, butter and jam, and occasionally a croissant. Hotels catering for package groups normally offer a buffet breakfast. At top-end places you'll usually be brought a sumptuous feast that includes pastries, eggs, fruit, yoghurt and so on.

Resorts

Tunisia's coastline is awash with resort-style hotels, generally clustered together in what's known as a Zone Touristique. These are not aimed at the independent traveller, for whom the prices quoted are the full five- or four-star rates – still cheaper than European prices but expensive for Tunisia. Most people who stay at resorts do so as part of an airfare-and-accommodation package where prices are great value. Most resort hotels will have bars, restaurants, at least one swimming pool, a travel desk and shops, as well as a *hammam,* games room, private beach, gym and activities club. The most popular resorts are at Hammamet (p106), Sousse (p191), Port el-Kantaoui (p195), Monastir (p198) and Jerba (p280).

ACTIVITIES

Although the lure of the beach is hard to fight, Tunisia has a surprising range of activities besides lounging on the sand and plunging in the sea. Most popular are camel trekking, 4WD Saharan excursions and water sports. Trekking in the north is another great option – all the better because this is little-explored territory.

Beaches & Swimming

Roman remains, the Saharan desert and *Star Wars* sets may be temptations, but beaches remain Tunisia's main tourist draw. Beaches ring Cap Bon, including the remarkably clear waters at Mansourah Plage (Kélibia) and beyond, with another great option at El-Haouaria. Hammamet has grown up around its glorious curve of golden sand, which begins in the shadow of a picturesque old kasbah (fort) and stretches for miles along the coast. More good beaches lie all along the central coast. The best beach in the south is Sidi Mahres on Jerba.

There are also some fine spots in the north. Sidi Ali el-Mekki, between Tunis and Bizerte, is particularly lovely and much loved by Tunisian holidaymakers. Cap Serrat, at the centre of the rugged north coast, shelters a glorious small sandy bay that's all but deserted for most of the year.

If you can't afford to stay at top-end *zone touristique* hotels, rest assured that it's easy to use their pools if you look like you belong there.

Bird-Watching

Tunisia is a great place for bird-watchers. You can spot rarities, such as Audouin's gull and local species such as Levaillant's woodpecker and Moussier's redstart.

Spring and autumn are the best times to see a wide range of migratory birds resting on their way elsewhere. In winter, the Unesco-listed Ichkeul National Park wetlands (see p132) are home to migratory waterfowl from all over Europe, including the rare greylag goose. Winter is also the time for flamingos that visit the northeast coast of Jerba and the beautiful 15km-long Korba Lagoon on Cap Bon.

At El-Haouaria on Cap Bon, May and June are when to spot Europe-bound migratory species.

For more information about birds in Tunisia, see p55. **Nature Trek** (☎ 01962-733051; www.naturetrek.co.uk) offers specially tailored bird-watching tours.

Camel Trekking

The Saharan town of Douz is the main camel-trekking centre (see the Desert Expeditions boxed text, p248). You can organise anything from a one-hour ride (TD4) to an eight-day, oasis-hopping trek to Ksar Ghilane and back (from TD40 per day).

Diving & Water Sports

The best place to go diving or snorkelling is Tabarka on the north coast (see p137), which has three good diving centres. Other places to try include Mahdia (p212), Bizerte (p127), Hammamet (p105) and Port el-Kantaoui (p195). At each place, there are agencies that organise trips, rent equipment and run courses for beginners.

Prices for snorkelling start from TD15 per hour, while diving costs about TD35 per dive.

The big tourist resorts (Hammamet, Sousse, Monastir and Jerba) are where to go for water sports, with plenty of places offering everything from windsurfing to waterskiing and paddleboats to parasailing.

Dune Skiing, Go-Karting & Microlight Flights

The thrill of sand-dune skiing is only possible in the tiny oasis village of El-Faouar, 30km southwest of Douz, at Hôtel Faouar (see p249).

Go-karting-type rides are also available in Douz (see p245), and you can take a short microlight flight over the desert from here too.

4WD Trips

The most popular way of exploring the desert, particularly for those with little time, is by 4WD. Although the coastal resort hotels can set things up, independent travellers may prefer to organise their own tour. Costs work out roughly at TD50 per person (vehicles take up to seven people), if you're in a group, per day. The most popular expedition is from Douz to Ksar Ghilane. For more information, see the Desert Expeditions boxed text (p248).

Golf

Tunisia is a popular place to play golf, particularly in winter when the fairways of northern Europe are covered in snow, and there are some excellent facilities.

Hammamet is the best served, with two beautifully manicured courses; see p105. There are also good layouts at Jerba (p281), Port el-Kantaoui (p195), Tabarka (p137) and Carthage (p95). Green fees cost about TD85 for 18 holes. Usually a handicap of around 36 or over is required.

Hammams

The Tunisian *hammam* (public bathhouse) experience is just about vigorous enough to qualify as an activity and should be tried at least once. Every town has one – some of the best and most historic are in Tunis.

The standard service (TD1 to TD2) includes a rubdown with a *kassa* – a coarse mitten that is used to remove the grime and dead skin after your stint in the steam room. It's usually possible to have a massage as well. It's a good idea to bring along a towel and shorts for moving around the *hammam*, as nudity is a no-no. The idea is to wear a pair of underpants while washing, so bring a second dry pair. And be warned: a rubdown with the *kassa* and the massage are not for the faint-hearted; it can be quite vigorous.

For a description of the *hammam* experience see the boxed text Steam & Sociability, p71.

Hiking/Mountain Biking

Walking in the hills is a newly developing pursuit in Tunisia. The Kroumirie Mountains forests around Ain Draham have enormous potential as a trekking destination; the region is stunningly beautiful and conditions are perfect for walking in spring and autumn. The potential is limited by the lack of detailed maps required to venture off the beaten track independently. **Siroko Travel** (☎ 71 965 267; www.sirokotravel.com) offers trekking holidays in both the north and Saharan south. Royal Rihana Hôtel (p141), in Ain Draham, also runs trekking and mountain-biking trips with overnight stays in Berber tents.

Horse-Riding

Sitting astride a horse is an excellent way to see the landscape. Horse-riding is available in Tabarka (p137), Hammamet (p106) and Tozeur (p258).

Quad-Biking

You can have off-road desert fun in Tozeur (see p258).

Sailing

Berthing in Tunisia is remarkably cheap compared with the northern Mediterranean, and there are lots of conveniently placed marinas along the coast. The largest are at Monastir, Port el-Kantaoui, Sidi Bou Saïd, Tabarka and Zarzis. You can hire a yacht at Sidi Bou Saïd (see p96). For information on Tunisian sailing, go to www.noonsite.com/Countries/Tunisia.

Thalassotherapy

Many upmarket hotels are equipped with spas specialising in thalassotherapy – from the Greek for sea treatment – a range of therapies using seawater to relax, revive and relieve pain, including seaweed wraps and water-jet treatments. In Tunisia you can indulge in these for a fraction of the cost of the same in Europe. The best include Hasdrubal Thalassa (p107) in Hammamet, La Residence (p99) in Gammarth (Tunis) and Villa Didon (p96) in Carthage. You can also indulge in water treatments in Korbous in Cap Bon (p121) and El Moradi at Hammam Bourguiba (p142).

BUSINESS HOURS

See the inside front cover for a summary of countrywide opening hours for shops, post offices, banks, offices and restaurants. Note that during July and August, many businesses open earlier and close around noon. Hours also change dramatically during Ramadan (October/November), when most museums close at around 3pm, and businesses open for the morning only, with some re-opening for an evening session. In tourist areas, one bank is rostered to open on Saturday morning. Souvenir shops tend to stay open as long as there are tourists around.

CHILDREN

Tunisians adore children. Everyone finds Tunisians friendly, but the welcome's even warmer for those travelling with kids. The extended family is the centre of Tunisian life. Expect to be stopped in the street, to have your child kissed, admired and doted upon, and to have an extra special effort made to make sure you're comfortable. On beaches popular with locals you are bound to acquire new friends.

Practicalities

Although the benefits of travelling with children almost always outweigh the hassles, there are a few practical matters to bear in mind.

Airlines usually allow children up to two years old to fly for 10% of the adult fare or free. For children from two to 12, the fare on international flights is usually 50% of the regular fare or 67% of a discounted fare.

Breastfeeding is a private affair in Tunisia; doing it in public will attract lots of stares.

Safety seats in hire cars are more likely to be available from international companies, though it's always worth asking, while highchairs in restaurants are only occasionally available. Hotels often charge a daily rate for cot rental, anything from TD5 to TD30 per night.

Baby products (baby food, nappies etc) are widely available although they can be expensive. Baby wipes cost from TD8 to

TD11 for a pack of 72, and pots of prepared baby food cost around TD3. Disposable nappies are cheaper than in Europe, the most popular brand being Peaudouce at around TD9 for a pack of about 25, but these are plastic-sealed so they're a bit less breathable than brands such as Pampers.

Many recognised brands are available in Tunisia, but expect to find them only in larger cities.

Sun lotion for babies and children is widely available but can be expensive, so bring a good supply.

For more comprehensive advice on travelling with children, get Lonely Planet's *Travel with Children* by Cathy Lanigan.

Sights & Activities

With beaches galore, swimming pools, camel rides, the Saharan desert and *Star Wars* sets, there's a lot to keep children happy here. That said, there are few organised forms of entertainment, though most of the resort hotels have some form of dedicated playgroup or playground (and many have child-care services). Impromptu football games spring up on just about any open patch of ground most evenings; everyone's welcome.

For activities in Tunis, see Tunis for Children, p79, and for the best across the country, see Kids Stuff in the Top 10s boxed text (p15).

CLIMATE CHARTS

Northern Tunisia has a typical Mediterranean climate, with hot, dry summers (June to September) and wet winters (November to March) – which are quite mild by northern European standards. However, be warned that it can feel chilly in winter, and few places have adequate heating. The mountains of the northwest occasionally get snow.

The further south you go, the hotter and drier it gets. Annual rainfall ranges from 1000mm in the north down to 150mm in the south, although some Saharan areas go for years without rain. Desert nights can get very cold.

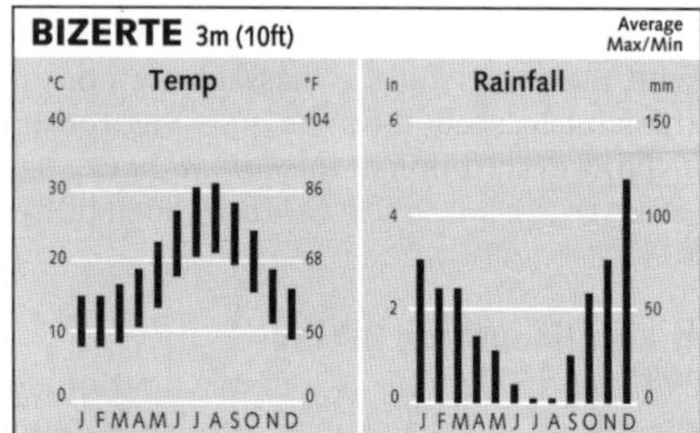

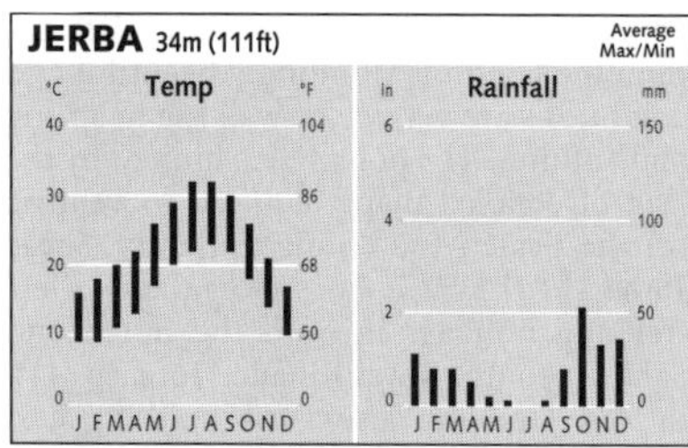

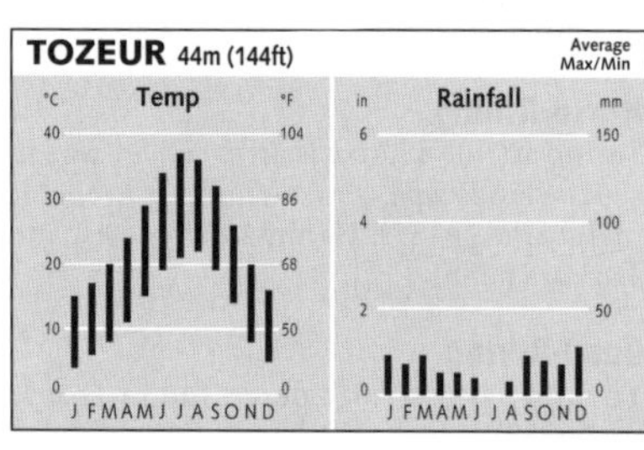

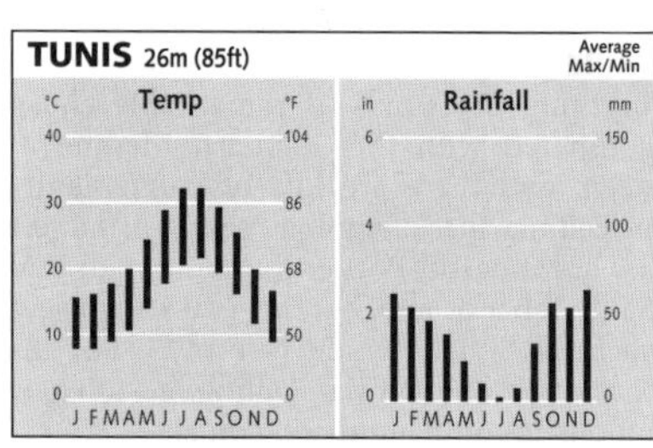

COURSES

The Institut Bourguiba des Langues Vivantes in Tunis runs courses in classical and Tunisian Arabic, while Langue Arabe pour Étrangers and Université Libre de Tunis (ULT) offer lessons in Modern Standard Arabic (see p79). Courses in Arabic are available in Bizerte (p128).

CUSTOMS

Baggage searches at Tunisia's airports are rare, but those arriving or leaving with their car by boat often find that every bag is opened and searched – a process that can take hours and includes completing forms listing valuable items. Apart from prohibited goods (such as illicit drugs and excessive amounts of alcohol), officials are also keen to ensure that you don't intend to sell goods from Europe while in Tunisia – hence the list, which must be presented on departure from the country.

The duty-free allowance is 400 cigarettes, 2L of wine, 1L of spirits and 250ml of perfume.

DANGERS & ANNOYANCES

Tunisia is a generally safe place to travel and attacks on Westerners are extremely rare. One exception was in April 2002, when a suicide bomber blew himself and 19 others up at Erriadh's El-Ghriba Synagogue on the island of Jerba. The Tunisian government has spent decades cracking down on Islamic fundamentalism and such acts, claimed by Al-Qaeda, are extremely rare, but always do your research before going to Tunisia to get an idea of the risks as assessed by Western intelligence services.

Americans and other English-speaking visitors are likely to hear frequent comments expressing opposition to American foreign policy. In most cases, these are made in a friendly way, with the speaker emphasising that they differentiate between the US government and the American people. In extremely rare cases (we've heard one report), outrage at US foreign policy can become personal and result in heated argument.

> **GOVERNMENT TRAVEL WARNINGS**
>
> Before setting out, it's always wise to check on the prevailing safety and health situation. Most governments have travel advisory services detailing potential pitfalls and areas to avoid. Some of these include the following.
>
> - **Australian Department of Foreign Affairs & Trade** (☎ 1300 139 281; www.smartraveller.gov.au/zw-cgi/view/Advice/Tunisia)
> - **Canadian Department of Foreign Affairs & International Trade** (☎ 800-267 6788; www.voyage.gc.ca)
> - **UK Foreign and Commonwealth Office** (☎ 0845-850 2829; www.fco.gov.uk/travel)
> - **US Department of State** (☎ 202-501 4444; www.travel.state.gov/travel)

Mosquitoes

In some of the southern oasis towns (such as Tataouine, Tozeur and, to a lesser extent, Douz), sleeping with your window open is a good way to wake up the next morning covered in mosquito bites.

Rubbish

Rubbish, particularly plastic bottles and bags, scattered over the countryside is a distressing problem in Tunisia. Some small towns have no rubbish-collection system in place and rely on tips in public spaces – not a pretty sight. Don't add to the problem.

Sexual Harassment

Both female and male travellers have reported varying degrees of sexual harassment. For men, this seems to take place mostly in *hammams,* whereas women will soon realise that unwanted attention is a frequent occurrence whatever your location; see Women Travellers p300.

Smoking

Tunisians make the Chinese look like doctors of the National Cancer Institute. There are few public non-smoking areas – restaurants will often be very smoky – and the prevalence of smoke can be extremely aggravating for those who are bothered by second-hand smoke.

Stone-Throwing Children

Some readers have reported children throwing stones, particularly in some of the *ksour* (fortified strongholds) around Tataouine, the *palmeraie* (palm groves) around Gabès, and near the entrance of the medina in Sfax. Don't throw back.

Taxi Cons

Some cab drivers fiddle with their meters to increase the fare. This is mostly likely when you take a taxi from Tunis-Carthage airport, at large resorts, or when taking a taxi around tourist sights. For more information see the Tunis chapter, p70.

Theft

Tunisia has low levels of street crime. Still, it pays to take precautions, particularly in busy areas like the medinas of Tunis and Sousse. There have also been a few reports of beach thefts, so don't leave your belongings unattended. Crimes such as mugging are very rare. One reported scam, which might be a problem in resorts, is where you are asked to exchange currency for a euro or a pound, but if you produce your wallet, the person will grab the contents and run away.

The best place to keep your valuables (passport, travellers cheques, credit cards etc) is in a moneybelt or pouch around the neck under your clothes where, hopefully, you will be aware of an alien hand before it's too late. Put your valuables in a plastic bag first, otherwise they'll get soaked in sweat as you wander around in the heat of the day.

Touts

Touts are not a major hassle in Tunisia, but you sometimes might get someone warmly professing recognition and claiming to be a waiter at your hotel, then leading you to a local shop.

In Kairouan, people sometimes attach themselves to tourists as guides and are so persistent that people end up following them and giving them a few dinars, only to find they need another guide (who magically appears) to get them back from where they have been guided.

Unethical salespeople

At Tunisia's archaeological sites, you may well meet shifty men offering ancient coins for sale to tourists. Buying looted ancient artefacts is unethical and illegal, and if this does not deter you, bear in mind that they may well be fakes.

DISCOUNT CARDS

Hostel Cards

You need to be a member of **Hostelling International** (HI; www.hihostels.com) if you want to stay at any of Tunisia's four affiliated *auberge de jeunesse* hostels; see under Accommodation, p284, for their locations. You can join on the spot at the hostel in Tunis (p80).

Student & Youth Cards

There are no advertised discounts for students, although it never hurts to ask. An international student card can get you in free to various monuments, including the Colosseum at El-Jem and Great Mosque at Kairouan. Note that most museums are free for under-18s. Most internet cafés offer small student discounts.

EMBASSIES & CONSULATES

It's important to realise what your own embassy can and can't do. Generally speaking, it won't help much in emergencies if the trouble you're in is remotely your own fault. Embassies will not be sympathetic if you end up in jail after committing a crime locally, even if such actions are legal in your own country. In genuine emergencies you might get some assistance, but only if other channels have been exhausted (the embassy would expect you to have insurance). If you have all your money and documents stolen, it might assist with getting a new passport.

Tunisian Embassies & Consulates

Following is a list of Tunisian embassies and consulates abroad.

Australia (☎ 02-9327 1258; GPO Box 801, Double Bay, Sydney, NSW 2028)

Belgium (☎ 2-771 7395; 278 ave De Tervueren, Brussels 1150)

Canada (☎ 613-237 0330; 515 O'Connor St, Ottawa, Ontario K1S 3P8)

Egypt (☎ 2-735 8962; 26 El-Gizera St, Zamalek, Cairo)

France (www.amb-tunisie.fr, in French only) Paris (☎ 01 45 55 95 98; 25 rue Barbet de Jouy, 75007); Lyon (☎ 04 78 93 42 87; 14 ave du Maréchal Foch, 69453); Marseilles (☎ 04 91 50 28 68; 8 blvd d'Athènes, 13001); Nice (☎ 04 93 96 81 81; 18 ave des Fleurs, 06000); Toulouse (☎ 05 61 63 61 61; 19 allée Jean Jaurès, 31000)

Germany Berlin (☎ 30-364 10 70; Lindenallee 16, 14050); Munich (☎ 089-55 46 35; Herzog-Heinrich-Straße 1, 80336)

Italy Rome (☎ 06-860 30 60; Via Asmara 5, 00199); Palermo (☎ 091-32 12 31; 24 Piazza Ignazio Florio, 90139)

Japan (☎ 3-3511 6622; 3-6-6 Kudan-Minami, Chiyoda-ku, Tokyo 102-0074)

Libya (☎ 21-607181; Ave Jehara, Sharia Bin Ashur, Tripoli 3160)

Morocco (☎ 37-730 636; 6 Rue de Fès & 1 rue d'Ifrane, Rabat 1000)

Netherlands (☎ 70-351 22 51; Gentestraat 98, the Hague 2587 HX)

South Africa (☎ 12-342 6283; 850 Church St, Arcadia, Pretoria 0007)

UK (☎ 020-7584 8117; 29 Princes Gate, London SW7 1QG)

USA (☎ 202-862 1850; 1515 Massachusetts Ave NW, Washington DC 20005)

Embassies & Consulates in Tunisia

There is a bevy of foreign embassies and consulates concentrated in the capital, Tunis, including the following.

Algeria (Map p69; ☎ 71 783 166; fax 71 788 804; 18 rue du Niger, 1002 Tunis)
Australia The Australian embassy in Egypt and the Canadian embassy in Tunis handle consular affairs in Tunisia for the Australian government.
Austria (☎ 71 751 091; fax 71 767 824; 6 rue Ibn Hamdis, 1004 El-Menzah)
Belgium (☎ 71 781 655; fax 71 792 797; 47 rue du 1 Juin, 1002 Tunis)
Canada (Map p69; ☎ 71 104 000; fax 71 792 371; 3 rue du Sénégal, 1002 Tunis)
Denmark Consulate (Map p69; ☎ 71 792 600; fax 71 790 797; 5 rue de Mauritanie, 1002 Tunis)
Egypt (☎ 71 792 233; fax 71 794 389; rue 8007, Montplaisir 1073, 1002 Tunis)
France (Map pp72-3; ☎ 71 105 111; fax 71 105 100; 1 place de l'Indépendance, ave Habib Bourguiba, 1000 Tunis) Consulate (Map pp72-3; ☎ 71 105 050; 1 rue de Hollande, 1000 Tunis)
Germany (☎ 71 786 455; fax 71 788 242; 1 rue el-Hamra, 1002 Tunis)
Italy (Map pp72-3; ☎ 71 321 811; ambitalia.tunis@email.ati.tn; 37 rue J Abdennasser, 1000 Tunis)
Japan (☎ 71 791 251; eog.tunis@planet.tn; 10 rue Apollo 11, 1002 Tunis)
Libya (☎ 71 781 913; fax 71 795 338; 48 rue du 1 Juin, 1002 Tunis)
Morocco (☎ 71 782 775; fax 71 787 103; 39 rue du 1 Juin, 1002 Tunis)
Netherlands (☎ 71 797 724; tun@minbusa.nl; 6-8 rue de Meycen, 1002 Tunis)
South Africa (☎ 71 801 918; sa@emb-safrica.intl; 7 rue Achtart, 1002 Tunis)
Spain (☎ 71 782 217; fax 71 786 267; 22 rue Dr Ernest Conseil, 1002 Tunis)
UK (☎ 71 108 700; www.britishembassy.gov.uk; rue du Lac Windermere, 1053 Berges de Lac)
USA (☎ 71 107 000; http://tunis.usembassy.gov; route de la Marsa, Zone Nord-Est, 2045 Berges de Lac)

FESTIVALS & EVENTS

Colourful local festivals celebrate everything from fishing to falconry, and in addition Tunisia has some major international cultural festivals as well. July and August are prime festival months, with classical music and drama at some of the country's best-known ancient sites. A useful site listing upcoming events is www.tunizik.com (in French only). You will find a full listing of festivals, complete with dates, on the ONTT's website: www.tourismtunisia.com/culture/festlist.html.

For those keen to see as many festivals as possible, see the Following the Festivals itinerary, p21.

MARCH

Octopus Festival (Kerkennah) People dress up in octopus costumes to celebrate the many-legged.

JUNE

Falconry Festival (El-Haouaria) Displays of falconry, sailing competitions, street stalls and concerts.

JULY

El-Jem International Symphonic Music Festival (www.festivaleljem.com) Uses the town's magnificent floodlit colosseum to great effect.
Festival of Malouf (Testour) Tunisia's musical emblem, *malouf* resonates in rural Testour.
Tabarka International Jazz Festival (www.tabarkajazz.com, in French only) Staged in early July, is one of Tunisia's best-loved events.

JULY/AUGUST

Carthage International Festival (www.festival-carthage.com.tn) Features events at Carthage's Roman Theatre and French-built cathedral, as well as Dougga's Roman theatre.
Hammamet International Festival (Hammamet) Attracts an impressive cast of international musicians and theatre groups to its coastal amphitheatre.

AUGUST

International Short Film Festival (Kélibia) Showcases up-and-coming Tunisian movie-makers.
World & Latin Music Festivals (www.tabarkajazz.com, in French only) In Tabarka.

AUGUST/SEPTEMBER

Raï Music Festival (www.tabarkajazz.com, in French only) In Tabarka.

OCTOBER

Carthage International Film Festival Biennial event, screened even-numbered years in Tunisia (other years this prestigious festival is held in Ouagadougou, Burkina Faso); two weeks of international film, with an Arabian and African emphasis.

OCTOBER/NOVEMBER

Medina Festival During Ramadan expect memorable concerts of traditional music in the Tunis medina.

NOVEMBER

Festival of the Ksour (Tataouine) Performances of Berber dance at nearby Ksar Ouled Soltane.

Sahara Festival Held in Douz, in early November, expect camel racing and displays of traditional desert skills, as well as music, parades and poetry reading.

Oasis Festival Held in Tozeur; mid-November.

FOOD & DRINK

For a comprehensive insight into Tunisian food written by an expert, see the Food & Drink chapter, p58.

Throughout this book, restaurant information includes whether the restaurant opens for breakfast, lunch and/or dinner, and the main-course price range. For more information about meal times, see the inside front cover.

Alcohol is generally only available at more expensive restaurants. Some supermarkets sell alcohol, but usually only in larger towns and resorts. Most towns will have a bar or two serving alcohol, but these are the preserves of men only.

Vegetarians may have difficulty finding purely vegetarian dishes, as the idea of not eating meat or fish is anathema to many Tunisians. Salads often come with tuna sprinkled on the top. You'll usually end up having to pick the meat or fish out of many dishes, which can make eating difficult for strict vegetarians.

GAY & LESBIAN TRAVELLERS

While the Tunisian lifestyle is generally liberal by Islamic standards, Tunisian society has yet to come to terms with overt homosexuality, which remains illegal under Tunisian law – in theory you can go to jail and/or be fined. However, although it's not openly admitted or shown, male homosexuality remains relatively common (men are occasionally propositioned in *hammams*) and there is a long tradition of gay male travellers visiting Tunisia. These days Tunisians seem relatively easygoing on the subject and, certainly in touristy places, they are finding it less bizarre to see gay couples. Some harassment has been reported, in the form of unpleasant stares and laughter, but this appears fairly unusual.

In some of the more touristy areas, local 'beach gigolos' looking to pick up foreign men are common, and some foreign men travel here specifically to seek out such action.

Lesbianism, on the other hand, is completely taboo and lesbian travellers will not find any kind of scene going on.

Regardless of your sexual orientation, discretion is the key.

HOLIDAYS

Some of Tunisia's secular public holidays, such as Women's Day and Evacuation Day, pass without notice. On others (particularly Islamic holidays), everything closes and comes to a halt (although transport still runs). On some long weekends, such as the Eid al-Fitr (celebrating the end of Ramadan), public transport is strained to the limit as everyone tries to get home for the festival.

As the Gregorian (Western) and Islamic calendars are of different lengths, the Islamic holidays fall 11 days earlier every Western calendar year.

Ramadan is the main holiday to watch out for, because for the whole month opening hours are disrupted (as well as the patience of many officials). Most places work a half-day, but then some places are open much later at night. It's an extraordinary time to be in Tunisia. The days are subdued but after dark the streets come alive and shops are often open till midnight, with impromptu concerts in cafés.

Islamic Holidays

Hejira Year	Ras as-Sana	Moulid an-Nabi	Ramadan Begins	Eid al-Fitr	Eid al-Adha
1428	20.01.07	29.03.07	13.09.07	11.10.07	19.12.07
1429	10.01.08	20.03.08	02.09.08	02.10.08	09.12.08
1430	29.12.08	09.03.09	22.08.09	21.09.09	28.11.09
1431	18.12.09	26.02.10	12.08.10	10.09.10	17.11.10

Other Public Holidays

New Year's Day 1 January

Independence Day 20 March

Youth Day 21 March

Martyrs' Day 9 April

Labour Day 1 May

Republic Day 25 July

Public Holiday 3 August (celebrates the birthday of Habib Bourguiba)

Women's Day 13 August

Evacuation Day 15 October

Anniversary of Ben Ali's Accession 7 November

INSURANCE

Travel Insurance

A travel insurance policy to cover theft, loss, damage, cancellations and medical problems is essential if you want to avoid potential nightmare bills.

If you have a medical insurance policy at home, you may be covered for travel abroad – ask your provider. Likewise home contents insurance policies sometimes cover items lost abroad.

Check the small print: some travel insurance policies specifically exclude dangerous activities, which can include scuba diving, motorcycling, even trekking. Also ensure that the policy covers ambulances or an emergency flight home.

With most policies, you have to pay on the spot and claim later, so make sure you obtain the appropriate documentation and retain it for when you claim.

For more information on health issues, see the Health chapter (p314), while for details on car insurance see p310.

INTERNET ACCESS

Public access to the internet in Tunisia is handled by Publinet, which has at least one internet café in every medium-sized town in the country; addresses are listed throughout this book. Connections are usually slow, some are reasonable, none are super-fast. The normal cost is TD1.5 to TD2 per hour.

WHERE'S THE @ SIGN?

Your first encounter with a Tunisian computer keyboard is likely to be frustrating, especially for touch-typists. Most letters are where you always thought they were, but the few that are not make typing a tricky business. You'll soon get used to the changes, but here are some helpful tips.

- If you're trying to insert the '@' symbol for an email address, use the 'Alt Gr' key plus the number '0'
- Numbers require the 'shift' key
- dash ('-') can be accomplished with '6' (without using the 'shift' key)
- The apostrophe also doesn't require the 'shift' key; simply press '4'
- A full stop needs the 'shift' key plus ';'

Previously Hotmail accounts were not accessible in Tunisia, but this was no longer a problem at the time of research. However, just for insurance, if your normal account is Hotmail, it may be worth setting up an alternative web-based email (eg Google Mail; www.gmail.com) before you go. Web pages considered subversive or corrupting (politics and porn) are blocked.

If you wish to have access to your home email account, you'll need to carry three important pieces of information with you: your incoming (POP or IMAP) mail server name, your account name and your password. With this information, you should be able to access your internet mail account from any Net-connected machine in the world.

If you're travelling with a portable computer, internet access from your hotel room is possible only in top-end hotels. Most international ISPs with global roaming facilities do not have agreements with Tunisian service providers. You may also need to buy a reputable 'global' modem before you leave home, or to buy a local PC-card modem; contact **Planet Tunisie** (www.planet.tn, in French only), Tunisia's service provider. However, unless you plan to be in the country for an extended period of time, it's not worth the hassle. Wi-fi is available in a few top-end hotels in Tunis only.

If you intend to use your computer in your hotel room, always check that there are power sockets as even a few midrange hotels don't have any.

See Internet Resources, p16, for useful websites relating to Tunisia.

LEGAL MATTERS

Tunisian police are everywhere, and if you behave oddly you are likely to attract their attention. They are prolific, keeping a keen eye on the population's behaviour and regularly checking locals' paperwork. However, as a tourist, it's unlikely that you'll encounter any difficulties. Incidents of visitors being approached by police or asked for identification are rare. At Erriadh's El-Ghriba Synagogue in Jerba, scene of the April 2002 bombing, independent travellers may be asked to show identification and be asked a few questions. And if travelling close to the Algerian border, you might also be stopped.

> I visited Jugurtha's Table, and I was stopped by military police every few kilometres. Usually it was just a friendly talk where they asked if everything was OK, but in one case we had to show our passports.
>
> *Ada Valencic, Slovenia*

Drug laws are very strict, and possession of even the smallest amount of cannabis resin is punishable by one year in jail and/or a hefty fine.

In Tunisia, the legal age for voting, driving, drinking and having sex is 20; in the last case, the dictates of traditional family mores render the legal position somewhat irrelevant.

MAPS

If you plan on driving in Tunisia, it's a good idea to buy a map before you go, though they are also available locally at bookshops in larger towns. The Michelin *Tunisia 744* (956; 1:800,000) is probably the best, although Freytag & Berndt's *Tunisia* (1:750,000) is also comprehensive.

The best locally produced maps come from the Tunisian **Office de la Topographie et de la Cartographie** (OTC; www.otc.nat.tn). It produces the *Carte Touristique et Routiére* (1:750,000), which is the most up-to-date road map around. The OTC also produces a series of street maps of major cities, including Tunis, Sfax and Sousse (all 1:10,000); Kairouan (1:8000); and Hammamet and Nabeul (1:5000). At the time of research, you could buy these at the OTC office in Tunis (see p67 for details) and the various regional offices listed on its website, as well as from some bookshops.

The government-run Office National du Tourisme Tunisien (ONTT) supplies a reasonable (and free) 1:1,000,000 road map, but it's more of general use than a helpful navigational tool. Most local ONTT offices also hand out free town maps. They range from the useful to the barely comprehensible.

MEN TRAVELLERS

Men travelling in Tunisia will encounter few pitfalls; it's certainly easier than travelling as a woman (see Women Travellers, p300).

In most Arab countries the only people you'll get to speak with are men, but Tunisian women have greater freedoms and often enjoy talking to foreigners, whether male or female. Although men should never be the one to initiate contact with a Tunisian woman, proximity in shops and particularly on transport will sometimes lead to women starting a conversation.

Low-level sexual harassment from other men in *hammams* occurs occasionally.

MONEY

The unit of currency is the Tunisian dinar (TD), which is divided into 1000 millimes (mills). There are five, 10, 20, 50, 100 and 500 mills coins and one- and five-dinar coins. Dinar notes come in denominations of five, 10, 20 and 30. Changing the larger notes is not usually a problem, apart from in the occasional small shop.

The TD is a soft currency, which means that exchange rates are fixed artificially by the Tunisian government (thus rates are the same everywhere). It cannot be traded on currency markets and it is also illegal to import or export it, so you will be unable to equip yourself with any of the local currency before you arrive. It is not necessary to declare your foreign currency on arrival.

Within the country, the euro, UK pound and US dollars are readily exchangeable, while the Canadian dollar and Japanese yen should be fine in most banks. Australian and New Zealand dollars and South African rand are not accepted.

Tunisian banks will usually want to see your passport when you change money, especially for travellers cheques, and may want to see your receipt for the cheques. Post offices change cash only.

When leaving the country, you can re-exchange up to 30% of the amount you changed into dinars, up to a limit of TD100. You may need to produce bank receipts to prove you changed the money in the first place.

Note that the Tunis-Carthage airport duty free does not accept dinars so don't count on using up any surplus there.

You should be able to change money after leaving the country – ie on arrival at any large international airport – but the rate will be terrible.

ATMs

ATMs are found in almost all medium-sized towns, and certainly in all the tourist areas. If you've got MasterCard or Visa, there are plenty of places to withdraw money. Many of them will allow you to access international savings accounts; look for the Cirrus or Visa Electron logo. However, it pays to plan ahead and have enough to tide you over in case an ATM is out of order – they often are and some only operate during office hours.

Cash

Nothing beats cash for convenience – or for risk. If you lose it, it's gone for good and few travel insurers will come to your rescue. Those who do will normally limit the amount to about US$300. Don't carry too much cash on you at any one time, and set aside a small amount of cash, say US$50, as an emergency stash.

Credit Cards

Credit cards (mostly MasterCard and Visa) are accepted in a few places in major towns and tourist areas. They can be used to pay for upmarket meals, top-end accommodation, car hire, some souvenir shopping and very occasionally at petrol stations. However, compared with other countries, credit coverage is not widespread. Outside major centres you won't be able to use them much, and less in the south than in the north.

Credit cards can also be used as cash cards to withdraw dinars from the ATMs of affiliated Tunisian banks in the same way as at home. The issuing bank sets daily withdrawal limits. Cash advances are given in local currency only. Both MasterCard and Visa say they can replace a lost card in Tunisia within 24 hours, and will supply you with a phone number in your home country that you can call, reverse charges, in an emergency; ask your bank for details.

The main charge cards are American Express (Amex) and Diners Club, which are accepted in a few places in tourist areas, but unheard of elsewhere.

Tipping

Tipping is not a requirement but underpaid waiters often appreciate small change; cafés and local restaurants provide a saucer for customers to throw in their small change. Waiters in tourist restaurants are accustomed to tips: 10% is plenty. Taxi drivers do not usually expect tips, but will appreciate them.

Travellers Cheques

The main reason for carrying your funds as travellers cheques rather than cash is the protection they offer against theft. They are, however, losing popularity as more and more travellers opt to withdraw their money from ATMs as they travel.

Amex, Visa and Thomas Cook cheques are widely accepted and have efficient replacement policies. Maintaining a record of the cheque numbers and when you use them is vital when it comes to replacing lost cheques. Keep this record separate from the cheques themselves. US dollars and euros are the best currencies. It's wise to have the customer purchase record with you, in case the bank wants to see it. STB Bank is your best bet for cashing cheques in smaller towns.

PHOTOGRAPHY

Name-brand film, such as Kodak and Fuji, is widely available and reasonably priced. Expect to pay about TD4.5 for 24-exposure 100 ISO film, and TD5.5 for 36 exposures. Slide film is increasingly available in more touristy areas (expect to pay around TD10 for a 36-exposure 100 ISO roll) but always check the expiry date. Never buy film that has been sitting in a shop window in the sun. Digital equipment, such as memory cards, is rarely available. You can sometimes download pictures onto CDs in Net cafés, usually those in larger towns.

You should always ask permission before taking photographs of people. While Tunisians expect every tourist to carry a camera, most don't like to have the lens turned on them. This applies particularly to Tunisian women and to people in rural areas.

It's forbidden to take photographs of airfields, military installations, police stations and government buildings. Soldiers, police and security around official haunts don't appreciate being snapped.

For detailed technical advice, get hold of Lonely Planet's *Travel Photography: A Guide to Taking Better Pictures,* written by internationally renowned travel photographer, Richard I'Anson. It's full colour throughout and designed to take on the road.

POST

Post offices are known as PTTs. See the inside front cover for opening times.

Air-mail letters cost 600 mills to Europe and 700 mills to Australia and the Americas; postcards are 100 mills cheaper. You can buy stamps at post offices, major hotels and some general stores and newsstands.

Receiving Mail

Mail can be received poste restante at any Tunisian post office. It should be addressed clearly, with your family name in capitals. Address mail to: (Your Name), Poste Restante, PTT Central, City Name, Postcode, Tunisia. Ask the clerks to check under your given name if you think mail is missing. There's a collection fee of TD0.5 per letter.

Sending Mail

The Tunisian postal service is slow but reliable. Letters to/from Europe generally take about a week to arrive; for further afield expect about two weeks. If you want to ensure that your mail arrives quickly, the Rapide Poste service guarantees to deliver anywhere in Europe within two working days (TD25 for up to 1kg), or within four working days to the Americas, Asia and Oceania (TD35). The service is available from all post offices. Posting your letter from a big city post office will ensure it arrives more quickly.

Parcels that weigh less than 2kg can be sent by ordinary mail. Larger parcels should be taken, unwrapped for inspection, to the special parcel counter.

SHOPPING

Bargaining

Handicrafts and medina souvenirs are about the only items you'll have to bargain for in Tunisia. To be good at bargaining, you need to enjoy the banter. Once you get the hang of it, it can be a lot of fun, and kinder on your wallet – often you can get things for less than a third of the price quoted. Knowing a few words of Arabic really helps smooth the way. If you don't like bargaining, you can buy your souvenirs from the Socopa stores (see Where to Shop, opposite for details).

What to Buy

CHECHIAS

Chechias are the small, red felt hats sported by older Tunisian men. The Grande Souq de Chechias in Tunis (p76) is the obvious place to look, and you'll doubtless also get an interesting demonstration of how they were made – they start off life as a loosely knitted, saggy white bag. Quality varies, but an average price is around TD6.

COPPER & BRASS

You'll see people engraving beaten copper and brass items in the medina shops. Beaten plates make good souvenirs and can be anything from saucer to coffee-table size, though you might find the latter rather weighs down your luggage.

ESPARTO GOODS & BASKETWARE

Rectangular, woven esparto baskets are practical and cheap. Some are pure tack, with pictures of camels and desert scenes, but there are plenty of other simpler, less cheesy designs. Most esparto items come from Gabès and Jerba in the south. See the Esparto Grass boxed text (p180) for more details.

You can also buy the attractive large baskets that local people use for going to the market – a large one costs around TD4. Straw hats – as seen on Tunisian farm workers everywhere – and fans are other popular, practical pieces to snap up.

JEWELLERY

Arabic jewellery (particularly from gold) is often extremely ornate and glitzy, but there is also plenty more tourist-friendly silver folk jewellery on sale here. A traditional Arabic motif is the Hand of Fatima (daughter of the Prophet) or *khomsa,* used in everything from small earrings to large neck pendants, and usually made of silver. In pre-Islamic times this same design represented Baal, the protector of the Carthaginians. It's thought to ward off the evil eye (of envy), an enduring superstition.

Other traditional pieces of jewellery include the *hedeyed,* which are wide engraved or filigree bracelets made of gold or silver, and *kholkal,* which are similar but worn around the ankle. In Carthaginian times *kholkal* were commonly worn to signify chastity; today they're still a symbol of fidelity and are often part of a bride's dowry. You'll also see *khlal* brooches. Made from silver, and usually a triangular or crescent shape with a pin, these are used to fasten clothes.

The quality of pure silver and gold jewellery can be established by the official stamps used to grade all work, and the quality of unstamped items is immediately suspect. The stamps in use are: the horse's head (the Carthaginian symbol for money and used to mark all 18-carat gold jewellery); the scorpion (all nine-carat gold jewellery); grape clusters (silver graded at 900 mills per gram); and the Negro head (poorer-quality silver graded at 800 mills per gram).

LEATHER

There's a huge variety of leather goods on sale, but check the quality, as often stitching can be on the shoddy side.

Kairouan is the country's leading producer of leather goods, supplying the nation's souvenir shops with belts, wallets, purses and handbags embossed with camels and palm trees.

Other articles for sale include traditional pieces such as camel and donkey saddles, water skins and cartridge pouches.

In Douz, and elsewhere in the south, you can slip on comfortable camel-leather sandals.

OILS & PERFUME

Cap Bon is famous for the production of essential oils, especially orange blossom and geranium. Most of the output goes to the international perfume market, but some is kept and used to make the scented oils that are sold in tourist shops everywhere. Prices start at TD1.5 for 5mL.

POTTERY & CERAMICS

Ceramics is big business in Tunisia, and the main centres of production are Nabeul (p109) in Cap Bon, and the town of Guellala (p278) on Jerba. Styles range from simple terracotta to bright Andalusian-style vases and tiling.

The Berber villages around the small northern town of Sejnane (p134) are famous for a primitive style of pottery, producing unusual moulded bowls and naive figures decorated in ochre and black. It's found in the Tunis medina at Hanout Arab (see p85), and stalls around Sidi Mahres (p75).

RUGS & CARPETS

There are some really beautiful rugs and carpets for sale, though they are not especially cheap. The main carpet-selling centres are Tunis, Kairouan, Tozeur and Jerba.

Look for traditional *alloucha* (thick-pile Berber rugs) in Ain Draham, where they are produced by a small women's cooperative called Les Tapis de Kroumirie (see the boxed text, p141). They are also sold in Tunis at Mains des Femmes (p85).

All types are sold at the government-run Socopa emporiums (see Where to Shop, below) found in the major tourist centres. They have been inspected by the Organisation National de l'Artisanat (ONAT) and classified according to type and number of knots. They come with an affixed label giving this information.

SAND ROSES

Sand roses are the speciality of southern Tunisia, although they're sold all over the country. They are formed of gypsum, which has dissolved from the sand and then crystallised into spectacular patterns that resemble flower petals.

They range from about 5cm in diameter up to the size of a large watermelon. They do make good cheap souvenirs, but carting around a great chunk isn't much fun.

SHEESHAS

The ubiquitous water pipes are everywhere in souqs and tourist shops, just ready to clutter up a corner of your sitting room. They range in price from around TD4 for a small, cheap one up to TD70 for a good-quality, full-size version.

Where to Shop

These Tunisian crafts are available from souvenir shops all over the country. The problem is finding the right price. The tourist shops in the big medinas are the worst place to start, especially if you have no idea what you should be paying. First prices are sometimes 10 times higher than the real price.

Best is to head first to one of the government-run Société de Commercialisation des Produits de l'Artisanats (Socopa) emporiums found in all the major tourist centres. Expert bargainers may be able to find cheaper prices elsewhere, but not the guarantee of quality that Socopa provides. Sales staff in these shops are paid to assist shoppers, not to apply hard-sell techniques. Even if you don't buy, it's an excellent idea to visit a Socopa shop to mug up on prices before heading into the fray.

If you do opt to shop in the medina, be careful – many a TD100 carpet has been sold for TD500 on the strength of a practised patter and complimentary cup of mint tea.

There are a few cooperatives and organisations around that help rural artisans and sell quality goods at fixed prices. These include Les Tapis de Kroumirie (p141), Mains des Femmes (p85) and Cooperative des Tisserands El Faouz (p114).

Tunis has crafts from all over the country (as well as junk from Egypt, India and China) in its markets, while Houmt Souq and Midoun on Jerba are also fantastic places to buy Tunisian odds and sods.

MARKETS

Town and village life often revolves around the weekly markets. Market day is the liveliest day to be in a town, as it'll be packed with traders and shoppers from all around the region.

A few markets have become tourist traps, such as that in Nabeul, but this also means they have more souvenirs geared for tourists than at the usual weekly market. At a regular market, you may find some quality handicrafts, but it's mostly cheap clothes and mundane household goods that heap the stalls. See Market Days, below, for the dates of the main town market days.

SOLO TRAVELLERS

Tunisia is a friendly, manageable country to travel around, and doing so on your own should present few problems, although it's much easier for men than for women (see Women Travellers, p300).

If you are counting the dinars, it's more expensive to travel alone. In hostel dorms the price is per bed, but in hotels single rooms are usually over half the price of a double, so it's cheaper if you hook up with other solo travellers and share a room. Another cost consideration will arise if you want to rent a taxi for the day in places like Tataouine and Jerba, or a 4WD in Tozeur or Douz to explore surrounding sites inaccessible by public transport. Sharing a taxi reduces costs considerably (the price quoted by taxi drivers is for the car, regardless of the number of people), while 4WD tours or expeditions will be expensive for a single person. If you want to share the cost of a trip, you'll need to gather a group together, which can involve a few days of waiting around, particularly during the low season; always ask at a number of agencies to increase your chances.

Unless you're on one of the private hotel beaches, travelling alone means having noone to watch your belongings on the beach while you go for a swim – petty theft can be a problem on some of the busier public beaches, so leave any valuables locked up in your hotel.

Solo travellers will encounter some curiosity as it's quite rare for Tunisians to travel without a friend. This is especially the case for women.

On the plus side, you are more likely to meet local people and be outgoing if you're on your own and don't have a readily available companion to talk to. As Tunisia is a friendly place, you're unlikely to be lonely for long.

TELEPHONE & FAX

The telephone system is fairly modern and straightforward. Few people have a phone at home, so there are lots of public telephones, known as Taxiphones. They accept

MARKET DAYS

Day	Location
Monday	Ain Draham, El-Jem, Houmt Souq, Kairouan, Kélibia, Matmata and Tataouine
Tuesday	Ghardimao, Kasserine and Kebili
Wednesday	Gafsa, Jendouba and Sbeitla
Thursday	Douz, Hammamet, Le Kef, Nefta, Remla (Kerkennah), Sejnane and Teboursouk
Friday	El-Haouaria, Mahdia, Nabeul, Sfax, Tabarka, Tamerza and Zaghouan
Saturday	Ben Guerdane, El-Fahs, Gabès and Monastir
Sunday	Hammam Lif and Le Kef

100-mills, 500-mills, one-dinar and five-dinar coins. Look out for Publitel offices, which are prevalent across the country and contain rows of telephone booths. Some are open 24 hours.

In 2001, local telephone codes were incorporated into telephone numbers, so there are no longer any local telephone codes – you have to dial the entire 8-digit number when calling locally. Landline numbers start with '7', while mobile numbers usually start with '98' or '21'.

Fax

Almost every classified hotel has a fax machine, but it costs less to use the public facilities at telephone offices and some post offices in major towns. Telegrams can be sent from any post office.

International & Local Calls

All public telephones can be used for international direct dialling. Taxiphone offices usually keep a copy of **Yellow Pages** (Pages Jaunes; www.pagesjaunes.com.tn), published in both Arabic and French, and have information on international area codes.

Rates for local and international calls are 10% cheaper between 8pm and 6am.

Mobile Phones

Mobile phones of most European carriers function in Tunisia, although it's a bit more hit-and-miss with North American and Australian mobile companies. Contact your phone company before setting out to check that it has reciprocal arrangements and that you don't have to activate a global roaming facility. Coverage is almost universal throughout the country, save for more remote desert locations such as Ksar Ghilane.

A cheaper option than using your home mobile company is to set up a Tunisian number while you are here. You can buy a SIM card for TD5 from either Tunisie Telecom or Tunisiana – both of which have branches in most medium-sized towns. You'll need your passport, a photocopy of your passport details, and a completed form. You can buy phone credit at most small grocery shops advertising top-up cards. A recharge card of TD5 is valid for five months, TD10 or TD25 are valid for six months. Check that your phone operates with a different SIM card before you leave home.

TIME

Standard time is one hour ahead of Greenwich Meantime/Coordinated Universal Time (GMT/CUT); it's two hours ahead from April to October. That means that when it's noon in Tunisia, the time elsewhere is:

Cairo – 1pm
London – 1pm
Paris – noon
New York – 6am
Sydney – 8pm

TOILETS

Public toilets are almost unheard of, except in places like airports and major bus and train stations. If you're caught short, your best bet is to go to a café: you'll be expected to buy something, unless it's really busy and they don't notice.

TOURIST INFORMATION

The government-run **Office National du Tourisme Tunisien** (ONTT; ☎ 80 100 333; www.tourismtunisia.com) handles tourist information. The standard of service from tourist offices inside Tunisia varies from efficient to barely awake. Most can supply no more than glossy brochures in half-a-dozen languages and a map. Some can supply an accommodation list and one or two have transport details. Some have no qualms about giving you incorrect information, so it's always wise to check things out yourself.

Many towns also have municipal tourist offices, called *syndicats d'initiative,* which usually open only in the high season.

For tourist office details, see the Information section of the relevant town throughout this book.

The ONTT's foreign representatives tend to be better equipped, and more enthusiastic, than their domestic counterparts. Have a look at www.tourismtunisia.com/adresses/international.html for a full listing of overseas addresses, which includes the following.

Belgium (☎ 2-511 11 42; tourismetunisien@skynet.be; Galerie Ravenstein 60, Brussels 1000)
Canada (☎ 514-397 1182; tunisinfo@qc.aira.com; 1253 McGill College, Quebec, Montreal H3 B2 Y5)
France Paris (☎ 01 47 42 72 67; ontt@wanadoo.fr; 32, Ave de l'Opéra, 75002); Lyon (☎ 03 78 52 35 86; 12, rue de Séze, 69006)

Germany Berlin (☎ 30-885 0457; Kurfuerstendamm 171, 10707); Düsseldorf (☎ 211-880 0644; Flingerstrasse 66 23, 40213); Frankfurt (☎ 29-706 40; Goethplatz, 60313); Munich (☎ 29-16 36 85; Burgerstrasse 12, 80331)
Italy Rome (☎ 06-42 01 01 49; Via Calabria 25, 00187); Milan (☎ 02-86 45 30 44; Via Baracchini 10, 20123)
Spain (☎ 01 548 14 35; tunezturismo@mad.servicom.es; Plaza de Espana 18, Torre de Madrid, Madrid 28008)
UK (☎ 020-7224 5598; tntolondon@aol.com; 77a Wigmore St, London W1H 9LJ)
USA (☎ 202-466 2546; tourism@tunisiaguide.com; 1515 Massachussets Ave, Washington DC 20005)

TRAVELLERS WITH DISABILITIES

If mobility is a problem, the hard fact is that most Tunisian hotels, museums and tourist sites are not wheelchair-friendly, though some upper-range places do have rooms adapted for disabled travellers.

Take heart in the knowledge that disabled people do come to Tunisia and that the absence of infrastructure is compensated for by the friendliness and willingness to help of most Tunisians. However, the trip will need careful planning, so get as much information as you can before you go. The British-based **Royal Association for Disability & Rehabilitation** (Radar; ☎ 020-7250 3222; www.radar.org.uk; 12 City Forum, 250 City Rd, London EC1V 8AF) has links to and can recommend organisations facilitating travel abroad. It publishes a guide to nonlocal transport *There & Back*, with information on air travel (see the website for details). Also British-based, **Canbedone Ltd** (☎ 020-8907 2400; www.canbedone.co.uk; 11 Woodcock Hill, Harrow HA3 0XP) and **Katalan** (☎ 01494 580816; www.katalantravels.com) can arrange tailor-made holidays.

VISAS

Visas are not a problem for most visitors. Nationals of most Western European countries can stay up to three months without a visa – you just collect a stamp in your passport at the point of entry. Americans can stay for up to four months.

Australians and South Africans can get a three-month visa at the airport for UK£20. There's a separate counter for visas, so don't join the queue for an entry stamp until you've been to the visa desk. At most entry points, you'll need to leave your passport at the visa counter and talk your way through immigration and customs (without your passport) to reach a bank to change money, then go all the way back through to pay the visa fee and collect your passport. It's usually easy enough but can take a while.

Other nationalities need to apply before arrival; the visa costs around UK£20, takes 14 to 21 days in person or via post, and the length of stay is up to the embassy. Israeli passport holders can visit Tunisia (subject to visa approval, like everyone else).

Visa Extensions

Avoid having to extend your visa if you can. Applications can be made only at the **Interior Ministry** (Map pp72-3; Ave Habib Bourguiba) in Tunis. They cost TD1.5 to TD10 (payable only in *timbres fiscales* – revenue stamps available from post offices) and take up to 10 days to issue. You'll need two photos, and may need bank receipts and a *facture* (receipt) from your hotel, for starters. An easier, though costlier, way to extend your stay is to leave the country and return.

Visas for Onward Travel

The Algerian and Libyan embassies in Tunis do not issue visas. If you want to visit either country from Tunisia, you should apply to the Algerian or Libyan representatives in your home country. Australians and New Zealanders can apply in London. Don't leave it until the last minute – it can be a lengthy process. For both countries you usually need an invitation to visit the country, obtained from a citizen or through a travel agency.

WOMEN TRAVELLERS

What to Expect

Even if Tunisian men have female friends or girlfriends, restrictions on unmarried men and women mixing, on people having relationships before marriage, and the expectation that women should be virgins when they marry mean that pre-marital sex is a minefield. The expense of getting married also means that, for many, male-female sexual relationships are delayed further.

Despite the freedom enjoyed by Tunisian women, it's undeniable that foreign women are almost always much freer. They also exist outside the social structure, and hence, from the point of view of Tunisian men, are a separate species, tantalisingly related to the free-and-easy types that appear on satellite TV or in foreign films.

The country's beach resorts are the territory of Casanovas, who spend their summers attempting to charm their way into the bedrooms of female (and male) tourists. Plenty of foreign women do have holiday romances with local men and the mythology arising from these encounters fuels expectations.

These factors mean that sexual harassment is par for the course and the tidal waves of testosterone that women encounter in some places can be intimidating and unpleasant. However, unpalatable though it is, harassment is usually low key, taking the form of being stared at or subjected to slimy chat-up strategies. Don't be surprised to receive proposals of marriage, swooning statements about your incredible beauty, and declarations of undying love (or considerably less noble suggestions). Physical harassment is rare, but does happen occasionally.

Among those women who wrote to us was the following perspective.

> We quickly learnt to be on our guards. Although Tunisians are a very friendly bunch and most will bend over backwards to please you, at times the stares, calls and propositions were overwhelming and discouraging. However, that said, we never felt in danger and learnt that a firm 'no' or simply walking away was all that was needed. We were disappointed not to be able to communicate more with the local women (at times, we weren't even sure if they existed) and we wish that we had a better overall understanding of women in an Islamic culture… Our two weeks in Tunisia have been fantastic. The amazing things we've seen, tasted, heard and experienced definitely outweigh any negatives. A country not to be missed.
>
> *Ruth Gould & Monique Menard, Australia*

Strategies

You can try a few strategies to reduce your hassle quota.

If you're travelling alone or without a male companion, Tunisian men usually will be befriending you with one intention in mind. The simple and obvious rule is to be careful. If you get a bad vibe, then get away immediately. Don't be afraid of completely ignoring people or asking them to stop bothering you. Most men will immediately leave you alone. If someone does touch you, shout.

The best policy is to ignore sexist remarks and sound effects, and sunglasses can form a good way of avoiding eye contact (many men try out the staring-you-into-submission technique). It can be advisable to sit next to other women on buses and louages, sit in the back seat of taxis, and avoid staying in cheap medina hotels. Books are useful props on trains, at restaurants and cafés and so on, as you can immerse yourself and ignore any unwanted attention.

Dressing modestly – cover your shoulders, upper arms and legs, and a headscarf can be useful to indicate modesty – makes a difference and you'll gain more respect by doing so, especially in rural areas. That said, dressing conservatively doesn't necessarily mean that you won't be hassled. What local women are wearing is also a reasonable guide to prevailing attitudes wherever you are. It's also a good idea to take some extra items to wear on the beach if venturing outside the main resorts – most local women wear a pair of knee-length shorts (and maybe a T-shirt) over their bathing costume to go in the sea, and you might feel more comfortable doing the same.

Transport

CONTENTS

Getting There & Away	**302**
Entering the Country	302
Air	302
Land	306
Sea	306
Getting Around	**307**
Air	307
Bicycle	308
Boat	308
Bus	308
Camionnette	309
Car & Motorcycle	309
Hitching	311
Local Transport	311
Tours	312
Train	313

GETTING THERE & AWAY

ENTERING THE COUNTRY

Most people face few bureaucratic obstacles when entering the country. Arriving by air is the easiest method, with immigration and customs completed with a minimum of fuss. It takes longer for those who have to apply for a visa on arrival (see p300 for details), but is still relatively easy. Note that a few nationalities have to get a visa prior to arrival. On board your flight to Tunisia, you should be given an arrivals card (keep the departures section until you leave the country as immigration will require it), which asks for all of the usual passport details.

Those arriving by sea with a car can expect a tedious three or four hours taking care of bureaucratic matters on arrival, though police are helpful and tourists receive prior attention. Bags and vehicles are often searched thoroughly on arrival or departure. In addition, if the boat is running late, it can mean that you enter the country in the wee hours; you should be able to find a few petrol stations and shops open late, but to be on the safe side come prepared with a full tank.

Land borders with Algeria and Libya are not really an option, as most are closed to foreigners, with the exception of Ras al-Jedir in Libya; expect long queues of vehicles.

Flights, tours and rail tickets can be booked online at www.lonelyplanet.com/travel_services.

THINGS CHANGE...

The information in this chapter is particularly vulnerable to change. Check directly with the airline or a travel agent to make sure you understand how a fare (and ticket you may buy) works and be aware of the security requirements for international travel. Shop carefully. The details given in this chapter should be regarded as pointers and are not a substitute for your own careful, up-to-date research.

Passport

It's not usually a problem to enter the country if you have an Israeli stamp or evidence that you have visited Israel in your passport, and Israeli passport holders are allowed into the country subject to visa approval (like all other nationalities requiring a visa). For more details on visa requirements see p300.

AIR

Airports & Airlines

There are six airports handling international traffic in Tunisia. The Tunisian Civil Aviation and Airports Authority (OACA) website (www.oaca.nat.tn) contains general information on each airport.

7 Novembre-Tabarka (TBJ; ☎ 78 680 005)
Jerba-Zarzis (DJE; ☎ 75 650 233)
Monastir-Habib Bourguiba (MIR; ☎ 73 520 000)
Sfax-Thyna (SFA; ☎ 74 279 007)
Tozeur-Nefta (TOE; ☎ 76 453 525)
Tunis-Carthage (TUN; ☎ 71 755 000)

AIRLINES FLYING TO/FROM TUNISIA

The national carrier is **Tunisair** (airline code TU; Map pp72-3; ☎ 71 330 100; www.tunisair.com.tn,

CLIMATE CHANGE & TRAVEL

Climate change is a serious threat to the ecosystems that humans rely upon, and air travel is the fastest-growing contributor to the problem. Lonely Planet regards travel, overall, as a global benefit, but believes we all have a responsibility to limit our personal impact on global warming.

FLYING & CLIMATE CHANGE

Pretty much every form of motorised travel generates CO_2 (the main cause of human-induced climate change) but planes are far and away the worst offenders, not just because of the sheer distances they allow us to travel, but because they release greenhouse gases high into the atmosphere. The statistics are frightening: two people taking a return flight between Europe and the US will contribute as much to climate change as an average household's gas and electricity consumption over a whole year.

CARBON OFFSET SCHEMES

Climatecare.org and other websites use 'carbon calculators' that allow travellers to offset the level of greenhouse gases they are responsible for with financial contributions to sustainable travel schemes that reduce global warming – including projects in India, Honduras, Kazakhstan and Uganda.

Lonely Planet, together with Rough Guides and other concerned partners in the travel industry, support the carbon offset scheme run by climatecare.org. Lonely Planet offsets all of its staff and author travel.

For more information check out our website: www.lonelyplanet.com.

in French only; 48 ave Habib Bourguiba, Tunis; 8am-6.15pm Mon-Sat, 7am-12.45pm & 4-6.45pm Mon-Sat Jul–mid-Aug, 7am-6.45pm Mon-Sat, 8am-12.45pm Sun Sep–Aug). It has offices throughout the country and an excellent safety record.

Other airlines flying to and from Tunisia include the following.

Air Berlin (airline code AB; www.airberlin.com)
Air Europa (airline code UX; ☎ 71 285 144; www.air-europa.com; ave du Japon, 1073 Montplaisir, Tunis)
Air France (airline code AF; Map pp72-3; ☎ 71-105 324; www.airfrance.com; 1 rue d'Athènes, Tunis)
Air Malta (airline code KM; ☎ 71 235 822; www.airmalta.com; Tunis-Carthage Airport)
Alitalia (airline code AZ; ☎ 71 767 722; www.alitalia.com; Tunis-Carthage Airport)
British Airways (airline code BA; ☎ 71 963 120; www.british-airways.com; rue du Lac Michigan, 1053 Berges du Lac, Tunis)
EgyptAir (airline code MS; Map pp72-3; ☎ 71 341 182; www.egyptair.com.eg/docs/home.asp; 49 ave Habib Bourguiba, Tunis)
GB Airways (airline code GT; www.gbairways.com)
Interflug (airline code IF; www.interflug.de, in German only)
Karthago Airlines (airline code KAJ; ☎ 71 940 540; www.karthagoairlines.com, in French only; 8 bis, rue Mustapha Sfar, 1002 Tunis Le Belvédère)
Lufthansa Airlines (airline code LH; ☎ 71 751 096; www.lufthansa.com; Tunis-Carthage Airport)
Nouvelair (airline code BJ; ☎ 73 520 600; www.nouvelair.com, in French & German only; Monastir-Habib Bourguiba Airport)
Royal Air Maroc (airline code AT; ☎ 71 847 051; www.royalairmaroc.com; 6 ave Kheireddine Pacha, 1073 Montplaisir, Tunis)
Royal Jordanian (airline code RJ; ☎ 71 754 000; www.rj.com; Tunis-Carthage Airport)
Turkish Airlines (airline code TK; ☎ 71 787 033; www.thy.com; Complex el-Mechtel, ave Ouled Hafouz, Tunis)

Tickets

If you're looking for bargain airfares, go to a travel agency rather than directly to the airline, which generally only sells fares at the official listed price. The exception is the expanding number of 'no-frills' carriers operating in the USA and Europe, which sell direct to travellers (many of them sell tickets over the internet).

Some reliable online flight-booking sites include the following.

- www.cheapflights.co.uk
- www.deckchair.com
- www.ebookers.com
- www.expedia.co.uk
- www.lastminute.com
- www.opodo.com
- www.travelocity.co.uk

However, online super-fast fare generators are no substitute for a travel agency that knows all about special deals and can offer advice on other aspects of your trip.

Tickets to Tunisia are also invariably cheaper if you buy some sort of flight-and-accommodation package through a travel agency. Departure tax is included in the price of your ticket. High season usually corresponds with the European summer (from 1 July to 15 September) and Christmas holidays. It's the same in the south, despite the incredibly hot temperatures. Low season is from 1 November to 15 March (excluding the Christmas holidays), and the rest is middle season.

From Africa & the Middle East

EgyptAir and Tunisair both operate between Cairo and Tunis (from TD600), while Royal Air Maroc and Tunisair share the route between Tunis and Casablanca (from around TD560). Tunisair also flies to Tripoli (Libya). Tunisair and Royal Jordanian Airlines connect Tunis with Amman, which has good connections throughout the Middle East, and Tunisair flies to Jeddah.

Recommended agencies in the region include the following:

Al-Rais Travels (www.alrais.com; Dubai)
Egypt Panorama Tours (www.eptours.com; Cairo)
Orion-Tour (www.oriontour.com; Istanbul)

Tunisia is not well connected with sub-Saharan Africa and you'll usually need to change in Cairo or Casablanca. Tunisair flies to Nouakchott (Mauritania), Bamako (Mali) and Dakar (Senegal), via Nouakchott.

From Australia & New Zealand

There are no direct flights between Australia or New Zealand and Tunisia. The easiest option is first to travel to Europe or Egypt, then fly to Tunis as a side trip. Qantas, Singapore and British Airways fly to Cairo, while Singapore, British and Malaysian fly to Rome. Alitalia, Air France and Tunisair fly Cairo to Tunis and Alitalia and Tunisair fly Rome to Tunis.

In Australia, **STA Travel** (☎ 134 782; www.statravel.com.au) and **Flight Centre** (☎ 133 133; www.flightcentre.com.au) are both good places to check on ticket prices. Both agencies have offices throughout Australia; call or visit the websites for office locations. For online bookings, try www.travel.com.au.

In New Zealand, both **Flight Centre** (☎ 0800 243 544; www.flightcentre.co.nz) and **STA Travel** (☎ 0800 474 400; www.statravel.co.nz) have nationwide branches. The site www.travel.co.nz is recommended for online bookings.

From Canada

There are no direct flights between Canada and Tunisia. You can either use one of the major European airlines and take a connecting flight to Tunis, or fly to Europe or Egypt as cheaply as possible and then shop around.

Travel Cuts (☎ 1-866 246 9762; www.travelcuts.com) is Canada's national student travel agency. For online bookings try www.expedia.ca and www.travelocity.ca. For tailored packages try **Adventures Abroad** (☎ 1-800 665 3998; www.adventures-abroad.com) or **Goway.com** (☎ 416-322 1034; www.goway.com).

From Continental Europe

Just about any European travel agency that's worth its salt can drum up a cheap airfare-and-accommodation package to Tunisia. Expect to pay at least €300 for a simple return flight in the high season. Charter flights are cheaper; you may get tickets for as little as €250 in the high season for a return flight plus an extra €100 to €150 for seven nights' accommodation, although the deals vary widely.

FRANCE

Unsurprisingly, France has excellent connections with Tunisia. Air France and Tunisair between them have regular flights to Tunis, Sfax and Tozeur from Paris, Lyon, Marseille, Nice and Bordeaux.

Recommended agencies include the following:

Anyway (☎ 0892 302 301; http://voyages.anyway.com)
Lastminute (☎ 0899 785 000; www.lastminute.fr)
Nouvelles Frontières (☎ 0825 000 747; www.nouvelles-frontieres.fr)
OTU Voyages (☎ 0155 823 232; www.otu.fr) This agency specialises in student and youth travel.
Voyageurs du Monde (☎ 0173 008 188; www.vdm.com)

GERMANY

Lufthansa have direct flights from Frankfurt (with connections onto Berlin) for €300.

Recommended agencies include:
Expedia (☎ 018 050 071 46; www.expedia.de)
Just Travel (☎ 089 747 3330; www.justtravel.de)
Lastminute (☎ 018 052 843 66; www.lastminute.de)
STA Travel (☎ 069 743 032 92; www.statravel.de) For travellers under the age of 26.

ITALY

Alitalia and Tunisair offer some good direct flights, costing around €200 to €300 return in the high season. In Italy try **CTS Viaggi** (☎ 06 462 0431; www.cts.it), specialising in student and youth travel.

THE NETHERLANDS

Alitalia and Lufthansa have return flights from Amsterdam for around €300. A useful online agency serving the Netherlands is **Airfair** (☎ 090 077 177 17; www.airfair.nl).

SPAIN

Air Europa flies Madrid to Tunis direct.

Recommended agencies include **Barcelo Viajes** (☎ 902 200 400; www.barceloviajes.com) and **Viajes Zeppelin** (☎ 915 425 154; www.v-zeppelin.es).

From the UK

GB Airways (a subsidiary of British Airways) and Tunisair operate scheduled flights from London to Tunis. Alitalia also flies from London, with a change at Milan. Expect to pay from around £240 for a high-season fare, although these fares can sell for as low as £140.

Charter flights offer a much wider choice of departure points, and most tickets are for a two-week stay. Try the **Charter Flight Centre** (☎ 0845 045 0153; www.charterflights.co.uk).

Discount air travel is big business in London. Advertisements for travel agencies appear in the travel pages of the weekend broadsheet newspapers, in *Time Out*, the *Evening Standard* and *TNT*.

Recommended travel agencies include:
Ebookers.com (☎ 0800 082 3000; www.ebookers.com)
Flight Centre (☎ 0870 499 0040; www.flightcentre.co.uk)
North-South Travel (☎ 01245 608 291; www.northsouthtravel.co.uk) Donates part of its profit to projects in the developing world.
Quest Travel (☎ 0871 423 0135; www.questtravel.com)
STA Travel (☎ 0870 163 0026; www.statravel.co.uk) For travellers under the age of 26.
Trailfinders (☎ 0845 058 5858; www.trailfinders.com)
Travel Bag (☎ 0800 082 5000; www.travelbag.co.uk)

Agencies offering packages to Tunisia include:
Adventures Abroad (☎ 0114 247 3400; www.adventures-abroad.com)
Cadogan Holidays (☎ 0800 082 1006; www.cadoganholidays.com)
Dragoman Overland (☎ 01728 861133; www.dragoman.com)
Explore Worldwide (☎ 0870 333 4001; www.exploreworldwide.com)
Imaginative Traveller (☎ 0800 316 2717; www.imaginative-traveller.com)
Panorama Holidays (☎ 0870 759 5595; www.panoramaholidays.co.uk)
Thomson Holidays (☎ 0870 165 0079; www.thomson-holidays.com)
Tunisia First (☎ 01276 600100; www.tunisiafirst.co.uk)
Wigmore Holidays (☎ 020-7836 4999; www.aspectsoftunisia.co.uk)

From the USA

New York has both the cheapest airfares and the largest choice of airlines. The cheapest option is to buy a discount ticket to Europe and then to shop around (London is the ideal place to head, but there's not much point in doing this unless you want to spend a few days hanging around).

Discount travel agents in the USA are known as consolidators. San Francisco is the ticket consolidator capital of America, although some good deals can be found in Los Angeles, New York and other big cities.

The following agencies are recommended for online bookings:

- www.cheaptickets.com
- www.expedia.com
- www.lowestfare.com
- www.orbitz.com
- www.statravel.com (travellers under 26)
- www.travelocity.com

Package operators include the following.
Adventures Abroad (☎ 1-800 665 3998; www.adventures-abroad.com)
Adventure Center (☎ 1-800 228 8747; www.adventurecenter.com)
Far Horizons (☎ 1-800 552 4575; www.farhorizons.com)
Goway.com (☎ 800 387 8850; www.goway.com)
Promo Tunisia (☎ 1-888 701 3202; www.promotunisia.com)
TunisUSA (☎ 610 995 2788; www.tunisusa.com)

LAND

Border Crossings

The only land border crossing open to foreigners is between Tunisia and Libya at Ras al-Jedir; see From Libya below. All other crossings from Tunisia to Libya or Algeria were closed to foreigners at the time of publication.

Car & Motorcycle

Those driving their own cars and motorcycles will need their vehicle's registration papers, liability insurance and a drivers licence (preferably an international drivers' permit in addition to their domestic licence, although usually the latter is sufficient). There's no need for a *carnet de passage en douane* (effectively a passport for the vehicle and acts as a temporary waiver of import duty). Contact your local automobile association for up-to-date details about the documentation required. See p309 for information about driving in Tunisia.

From Algeria

Algeria has been effectively out of bounds to travellers since the start of the civil war in early 1993. The conflict has forced the cancellation of all bus and train services between the two countries.

Louages (shared taxis) are the only form of public transport still operating between the two countries. They operate from place Sidi Bou Mendil in the Tunis medina to Annaba and Constantine.

From Libya

The only crossing point open to foreigners is at Ras al-Jedir, 33km east of Ben Guerdane. For a tourist, the main obstacle is obtaining a visa, which is difficult; the best approach is to take a tour to Libya with an agency that will arrange a visa for you.

There are daily buses to Tripoli from the southern bus station in Tunis. The trip costs TD29.6 and takes up to 16 hours. You should reserve three days ahead. There are also services from Sfax (TD17.8).

Louages are faster and more convenient than buses. There are regular (though not daily) services to Tripoli via Ras al-Jedir from many Tunisian towns, including Tunis, Sfax, Gabès, Medenine, Houmt Souq and Ben Guerdane. The louages that work these routes are yellow with a white stripe.

SEA

Crossing by ferry from Italy or France is a popular option, with ferries operating year-round. Ferries are heavily booked in summer, so book well in advance. If you're arriving with your vehicle, see Entering the Country p302. Child fares usually cost 50% of adult fares.

Shipping agents and ferry companies that operate on these routes include:

Compagnie Tunisienne de Navigation (CTN; www.ctn.com.tn) Tunis (Map pp72-3; ☎ 71 322 802; fax 71 354 855; 122 rue de Yougoslavie); Marseille (☎ 04 91 56 30 10; fax 04 91 56 35 86; 61 blvd des Dames)

Linee Lauro (☎ 081-497 2222; www.lauro.it, in Italian only)

SNCM (Map pp72-3; ☎ 71 338 222; www.sncm.fr; 47 ave Farhat Hached, Tunis)

Tirrenia Navigazione (☎ 39 081 017 1998, 892 123 from within Italy; www.tirrenia.it)

Viamare Travel (www.viamare.com) London (☎ 0870 410 6040; 1230 High Rd, Whetsone N20 0LH); Tunis (☎ 71 737 3 07; Biglietteria Medmar, Agenzia Marittima Unima, Stazione Marittima di La Goulette)

From Italy

Throughout the year, ferries run between Tunis and the Italian ports of Genoa, Naples, Citavecchia, Palermo (Sicily), Salerno and Livorno. **Viamare Travel** (www.viamare.com) has a full listing of services and fares.

GENOA–TUNIS

The route between Tunis and the northern Italian port of Genoa is operated by CTN and Grandi Navi Veloci (Viamare). The frequency of services ranges from four a month in winter to one every couple of days in July and August. The trip for an adult/child costs around €116/58 and takes between 22 and 24 hours. For small vehicles it costs about €426 one way.

CITAVECCHIA–TUNIS

From Citavecchia in northern Italy, ships take around 24 hours, operated by Grandi Navi Veloci (Viamare). Fares for an adult cost €116, while a small vehicle costs €182.

PALERMO–TUNIS

Grandi Navi Veloci (Viamare) operates ferries to/from Palermo, which take about 10 hours. Passenger fares for an adult start at €62, while a car costs €123.

NAPLES–TUNIS

Medmar (Viamare) runs around one ferry per week from June to September (there is no service at other times of the year) to/from Naples (about 24 hours). Tickets for an adult cost from €90; a car costs €125.

SALERNO–TUNIS

Grimali Ferries (Viamare) operates ferries between Salerno and Tunis (24 hours); a passenger fare costs €99, while a car costs €129.

LIVORNO–TUNIS

Medmar (Viamare) runs ferries to/from Livorno (24 hours). Passengers cost €88, and cars €176.

From France

CTN and the French company SNCM operate ferries year-round between Marseilles and Tunis. Between them there are at least two ferries a week, even in the middle of winter. There are sailings almost every day between late June and the middle of November. The trip for an adult/child costs around €126/63 and takes around 21 hours. For small vehicles it costs about €578.

GETTING AROUND

Tunisia has a well-developed, efficient transport network that includes buses, louages, trains and ferries. Just about anywhere that's anywhere has daily connections with Tunis.

AIR

Tunisia's domestic air network is fairly limited.

Domestic flights are operated by Tunisair subsidiary Tuninter (www.tuninter.com.tn, in French only), which did have an

TOP 10 TIPS FOR GETTING AROUND TUNISIA

Travelling around Tunisia is generally hassle-free, but there are some things you can do to avoid getting stranded or getting cramp, and to show the locals that you're as savvy as they are.

- A 1st-class train ticket on a popular summer route doesn't mean you have a reserved seat; 1st-class carriages have quotas for standing passengers, so get there early and fight for your (or any) seat.
- Always check whether the bus you're waiting for originates elsewhere; if so, chances are it will be full when it arrives.
- In the old louages (shared taxis, usually Peugeot station wagons), avoid the back seats unless you're under 5ft tall.
- In the new louages (eight-seater 'people-mover' vans), avoid the middle front seat where the combination of dashboard, radio and gearstick can play havoc with knees.
- In the new louages, don't choose a back seat until you've seen how much luggage will be piled in behind you; suitcases can considerably diminish head space.
- Don't expect louages to run after 7pm.
- If the sun is sinking low, always consider paying for the last empty louage seat(s) (or sharing the cost with other passengers) to get it going; it's better than not leaving at all or arriving late at night.
- If you want to see the El-Jem colosseum at sunset, see the boxed text on p208.
- A louage linking Town A with Town B will leave only when completely full of passengers going all the way to Town B. As a result, if you want to get off en route you may have to pay the fare all the way to Town B. And if you're waiting for transport on a remote bit of highway between Town A and Town B, almost all the louages passing by will be full. It's in such circumstances that you'll be glad you checked the schedule for buses, which can always squeeze in one more passenger.
- Watch out for rogue cyclists, maverick moped drivers and wildly unobservant pedestrians when driving.

excellent safety record up until August 2005, when one of its planes crashed near the Sicilian coast, with 16 fatalities.

There are direct flights between Tunis and Jerba (TD85, up to four daily in summer), Tozeur (TD65), Sfax (TD58), Gafsa (TD99) and Tabarka (TD26).

BICYCLE

Tunisia is developing a good reputation as a cycling destination. The road network is extensive and well maintained, and most of the country's roads are flat, although it's too hot in summer and can get very cold in winter in the north. The rest of the year conditions are ideal. It's also possible to put a bike on the train if you want to skip a long stretch or get yourself back to Tunis quickly (it may be necessary to send the bike the day before or afterwards by freight train; check in advance). All louages are equipped with roof racks and can also carry bikes.

The downside of riding a bike in Tunisia is that you share the road with motorists. Most Tunisian drivers aren't accustomed to driving alongside cyclists (some barely manage to avoid larger vehicles). Bicycle lanes are nonexistent and most roads are two-lane stretches of tarmac with no hard shoulder. Traffic on the coastal routes and roads into and out of Tunis can be very heavy, though elsewhere roads are generally quite empty. Your experience will be entirely different – more pleasant and less dangerous – if you keep off major roads; they're not only busier but also more boring.

Though most people you pass on the way will be wreathed in smiles, rock-throwing kids can be an annoyance – this seems to be most prevalent in the north.

If you want a decent touring bike, you should bring your own; check with the airline before buying your ticket to see if your bicycle can be carried as checked baggage. For safety, you should also pack high-visibility clothing, good lights and so on. While it is not compulsory to wear a helmet in Tunisia, we recommend that you bring your own.

Before you leave home, go over your bike with a fine-toothed comb and fill your repair kit with every imaginable spare, as you won't necessarily be able to buy spares for your machine if it breaks down in the middle of nowhere.

Hire

There are a few places that rent bicycles and it can be a great way to explore a town, especially if it's very spread out. This is particularly the case with the massive *palmeraies* (palm groves) in the south. Most charge TD2.5 to TD4 per hour, but you can usually negotiate cheaper day or half-day rates. Note that this does not include helmet or lock. Never take the first bike offered to you – check through the bikes to find the best one, and make sure that the brakes work.

BOAT

There are two regular scheduled ferry services in Tunisia. The first connects Sfax with the Kerkennah Islands (p219), about 25km off the coast. In summer, there are up to 11 crossings daily, dropping to four in winter.

The second service runs from El-Jorf on the mainland to Ajim on the island of Jerba (p271) throughout the day and night.

BUS

The national and regional bus companies normally operate from a communal bus station (ask for the *gare routière*), although there are exceptions (eg Tabarka and Tataouine).

Buses are preferable to louages if you're on a longer journey as they are more comfortable.

National Buses

The national bus company, the Société Nationale du Transport Rural et Interurbain (referred to as SNTRI and pronounced 'sintry'), operates daily air-conditioned buses from Tunis to just about every town in the country. Frequency ranges from one daily bus (small towns) to half-hourly (to major cities like Sousse and Sfax). The buses run pretty much to schedule, and they're fast, comfortable and inexpensive.

In summer, many of the long-distance departures are at night to avoid the heat of the day, which means you don't get to see any of the country you're travelling through. Booking ahead is usually recommended.

Regional Buses

Besides the national company, there are regional bus companies that run buses around their area and to nearby cities in neighbouring regions.

These buses are reliable enough, but most have seen better days, are slow and never air-conditioned. Coverage of routes is good; in some cases, they're the only form of transport to smaller towns. The only way to be sure of bus schedules is to go to the bus station and ask. Some larger towns are served by two or three regional companies.

Costs

Buses cost around the same as louages. Sample long-distance fares from Tunis include Jerba (TD21.2), Sfax (TD12.5) and Tozeur (TD20.8).

Reservations

Almost every bus station has a SNTRI booking office for reservations. Regional companies maintain similar windows but they often open only an hour or so before departure, so advance reservations can be difficult.

CAMIONNETTE

Camionnettes (pick-ups used as taxis) go where buses and louages fear to tread. There aren't many and they make few pretensions to comfort, but they're indispensable if you want to get to some of the out-of-the-way places in the south (especially around Tataouine). Try to establish what the locals are paying before you pay, and remember that they don't operate much beyond mid-afternoon.

CAR & MOTORCYCLE

Automobile Associations

The **Touring Club de Tunisie** (☎ 71 323 114; fax 71 324 834; 15 rue d'Allemagne, Tunis 1000) has reciprocal arrangements with many European automobile clubs, including the UK's Automobile Association. If your car conks out, it can direct you to an affiliated breakdown service.

Bring Your Own Vehicle

For an explanation of the documents required if you're bringing your own car, see p306.

Driving Licence

Your own country's driving licence is sufficient for driving (or hiring a car) in Tunisia, but international driving permits are also acceptable, and recommended if you come from a country outside Western Europe.

Fuel & Spare Parts

Fuel is very inexpensive by European standards and prices are the same everywhere: 740 mills per litre for diesel and two-stroke mix, and TD1.1 per litre for super (high octane), regular (low octane) and unleaded fuel.

Spare parts are generally available in Tunisia for most well-known European cars (especially French ones), but that really only applies in larger towns; get your car comprehensively serviced before leaving your home country.

ROAD DISTANCES (KM)

	Bizerte	Gabès	Gafsa	Houmt Souq	Kairouan	Nabeul	Sfax	Sousse	Tabarka	Tataouine	Tozeur	Tunis
Bizerte	---											
Gabès	375	---										
Gafsa	409	149	---									
Houmt Souq	547	106	255	---								
Kairouan	220	215	209	321	---							
Nabeul	130	357	323	463	114	---						
Sfax	332	137	197	243	136	220	---					
Sousse	208	264	277	132	68	96	127	---				
Tabarka	147	496	347	602	277	239	441	317	---			
Tataouine	563	122	271	118	337	479	259	259	672	---		
Tozeur	502	242	93	348	302	416	290	370	440	364	---	
Tunis	66	375	343	481	154	64	266	142	175	497	436	---

If you're bringing your own motorcycle, make sure you carry some basic spare parts. These are virtually impossible to find within the country.

Hire

CAR

Hire cars are the best way to see more of the country at your own pace, but they're relatively expensive to rent. Some international agencies include:

Avis (www.avis.com)
Hertz (www.hertz.com)
Europcar (www.europcar.com)

Details of local agents for these are given in the individual chapters.

International agencies typically charge from about TD30 per day plus 250 mills per kilometre, or TD54 per day for unlimited kilometres and a minimum of seven days for the smallest cars (eg Fiat Uno). On top of these rates you'll usually have to pay 18% tax, insurance of at least TD8 per day, contract fees and so on. Medium-sized, air-con cars (Renault Clio or VW Polo) are listed as costing about TD65 per day plus 325 mills per kilometre.

Both international and local companies are usually willing to offer cheaper rates than those listed. In winter, it may be possible to find someone willing to hire a Renault Clio with air-con (all-inclusive with unlimited kilometres) for less than TD350 per week, and for TD450 per week in summer. Tunis, Sfax and Houmt Souq (on Jerba) are the best places to look for bargains. You'll get a much better deal if you hire on arrival rather than booking a car from abroad. Agencies often try to charge a surcharge for dropping off at a different location to where you pick up, but you may be able to avoid this by informing the agency that you want to drop off at a different point towards the end of your trip rather than when you hire the car.

Child seats are usually available, at a cost of around TD5 to TD10 per day extra.

A deposit of roughly the equivalent of the rental is usually required (unless you're paying by credit card). Rental companies require that drivers be aged over 21 and hold a driving licence that has been valid for at least a year.

When you hire the car, make sure that an accident-report form has been included with the car's papers; in the event of an accident, both parties involved must complete the form. If the form is not completed, you may be liable for the costs, even if you have paid for insurance.

MOTORCYCLE

A few places rent scooters or mopeds for which no licence or insurance is required, although for a machine of more than 50cc you need to be over 21 years old and held a valid motorcycle licence for more than one year.

Insurance

If you hire a car, you usually pay an extra charge for insurance – check this part of the agreement carefully to understand what protection you have. If you're travelling with your own vehicle and have insurance with a

WITH A SMILE AND A WAVE

All along Tunisia's roads you'll come across policemen keeping watch over the nation's safety. While that may be reassuring, not all Tunisians see it that way. Anyone who has spent any time in a louage will know the ritual well.

As the driver approaches the intersection or police checkpoint, or an area where his local knowledge tells him that there may be one, he slows the car almost to walking speed, puts on his seat belt and asks front-seat passengers to do the same. At a snail's pace, he draws near, pretending not to look at the police, yet unable to take his eyes off them. When he catches their eye and receives the shrug indicating permission to pass, the driver smiles innocently and waves genially in the direction of the men in uniform, all the while muttering dark curses about scorpions under his breath.

As a driver in Tunisia, you'd be well advised to follow the same procedure (except that you should wear your seatbelt at all times), although before you curse the police, remember that your status as a foreigner almost always guarantees you unimpeded passage.

European company, ask your insurer about the possibility of an extension to your home-insurance cover. If you take out travel insurance, this may also cover vehicle damage or accidents – again, check the small print.

Road Conditions

Tunisia has a good road network. All but the most minor roads are tar sealed, though smaller roads can be bumpy. Potholes are more common in the south. Many of the roads that are marked as unsealed on maps have now been sealed, particularly in the south where the army has heavily involved itself in the road-building effort. Of the unsealed roads in the south, most are graded regularly and can usually be negotiated easily with a 2WD vehicle (see the regional chapters for more details). Of course, negotiating unsealed roads wherever you are in the country depends on the weather conditions.

There is only one *péage* (road toll) in Tunisia – the new A1 expressway between Tunis and Msaken, south of Sousse. The trip costs TD1.2 by car. There are plans to extend the system north to Bizerte and south to Sfax and Gabès.

Police officers rarely stop foreigners, but it's best to ensure you have your passport, licence and car registration papers handy at all times.

Road Hazards

If you're used to driving in Italy or France, you'll have no trouble adapting to Tunisian roads. Those coming from the highways of Britain, Germany or the US may find it trickier to assimilate to road etiquette here. However, Tunisian drivers are generally well behaved, and drive fairly predictably, if sometimes badly. Overtaking manoeuvres are often launched with little regard for what's coming the other way, and frequently on bends or when approaching a hill. Yet the worst hazards are moped riders, who weave suicidally in and out of traffic, and pedestrians, who think they have an inalienable right to walk on the road regardless of traffic conditions. In country towns, watch out for animals and small children making unexpected forays onto the road.

Road Rules

The road rules in Tunisia are much the same as in continental Europe. You drive on the right and overtake on the left. Speed limits are 50km/h in built-up areas and 90km/h on the open road. The only exception is on the toll road from Tunis to Sousse, where the speed limit is 110km/h.

The regulation that causes the most problems for tourists is the one giving priority to traffic coming from the right in built-up areas. This also extends to roundabouts, where you are obliged to give way to traffic approaching from the right even if you are already at the roundabout.

The special intersections for turning left off major roads are another curiosity of Tunisian driving. Instead of using a turning lane in the centre of the road, the Tunisian system involves a special lane leading off to the right, which loops back and crosses the main road at right angles. It can be very confusing if you're driving along looking for a sign pointing to the left – and then find a sign telling you to turn right.

Seat belts are not compulsory in cities or towns, but are obligatory for front-seat passengers on the open road. That said, it's highly recommended to wear seat belts at all times.

It's almost unheard of for a tourist to be booked – unless the infringement causes an accident, when the police are obliged to act.

HITCHING

Many local people hitch as a matter of course, and picking them up can be a good way of having local contact. However, before sticking your own thumb out, remember that hitching is not an entirely safe method of transport and comes with an element of risk. Women should never attempt to hitch without a male companion.

LOCAL TRANSPORT

Most towns are small enough to get around on foot. The problem comes in summer, when it's too hot to walk far during the day.

Taxis are the best alternative. They can be found in all but the smallest towns and are cheap by European standards. The day rate (tariff A or tariff 1) applies from 5am to 8pm; flag fall is 340 mills, and fares work out at about 500 mills per kilometre. At night the flag fall is 510 mills and fares are 50% higher. Most taxis are only allowed to take three passengers, though some will take more without a murmur, while others will negotiate a fixed price for taking more passengers. Police usually turn a blind eye.

Major towns like Sousse, Sfax and Tunis have local bus networks. Tunis also has a modern tram network and a suburban train line (TGM) connecting the city centre with the northern suburbs.

Some towns, including Gabès, Houmt Souq, Nabeul and Tozeur, have *calèches* (horse-drawn carriages) for hire. All charge TD10 per hour.

Louage

Louages (long-distance shared taxis – usually white with a red, blue or yellow stripe) are the workhorses of the Tunisian road and by far the simplest and fastest means of public transport, as well as a good way to meet local people. Fares cost around the same as buses (working out around TD3 per 100km). Louages leave when full rather than to any timetable, but you'll rarely have to wait more than 45 minutes. However, don't leave your run too late – most louages stop running after 7pm, sometimes earlier.

In most towns, the louage station is close to, or combined with, the bus station, enabling you to choose between the services. At the louage stations, drivers stand by their vehicles and call out their destinations. A foreigner is sure to be asked their destination and given assistance. Occasionally you have to buy your ticket from a booth beforehand, but usually you pay the driver on board. If it's the latter, ask the fare before you get in. If you think you're being ripped off, ask to see the list of tariffs (set by the government) that all drivers are required to carry.

Most of the old Peugeot or Renault station wagons (with an extra bench seat in the back and licensed to carry five passengers) are being replaced by more comfortable people-carrier vans, which are licensed to carry eight passengers. Fares are quoted *par place* (per person). There are no discounts for children. There is a small charge for luggage. At least in Kasserine, taxi regulations provide for an extra fee of TD0.4 for each bag over 10kg.

Although some louages are licensed to operate nationwide, most can operate only within their local government area on a specific route. The town name on the roof of each louage indicates where it's licensed, which is not necessarily where it's going.

TOURS

For information about package tours from abroad, see Air p302.

Most sites in Tunisia can be reached by public transport, but there are two types of organised tour that will be of use to travellers.

The first is a Sahara desert tour. Indeed, unless you have your own vehicle, a tour is the only way to see the desert. Options range from overnight camel treks to week-long 4WD expeditions. Douz (p245) is the main base for launching desert tours, although good operators also work from Tozeur (p258). Many resort hotels from the coast (especially Jerba) can also make the arrangements for a desert exploration. Be aware that tours leaving from resorts such as Hammamet, Nabeul and Sousse will entail a lot of time on the road as it's quite a journey to get to the south. For more information on what sort of trip is possible, see Desert Expeditions, p248.

The second type of tour is a day trip. This usually involves a hotel or agency rounding up enough people to make the trip viable. This is a popular way of visiting Matmata, the oasis villages near Tozeur or the sights in and around Tunis. To get the most out of a tour, check that it's not covering too much in one day – those taking in Carthage, the Bardo and the Medina in Tunis, for example, will feel rather rushed.

Chartering a taxi privately is a popular do-it-yourself alternative for exploring Jerba or the Berber villages and *ksour* (fortified strongholds) around Tataouine – it's best to bargain for a fixed price before you set out.

ECOTOURS

Guides with a good understanding of ecology are hard to find in Tunisia, and ecotours are rarely on the agenda.

One company worth seeking out is **Becasse** (☎ 71 960 314, 97-462 460; www.becasse-ecologie.com; apt 10 1002, 38 bis, rue de Cologne, Tunis), which specialises in small-group nature and bird-watching tours to areas of outstanding natural interest. It is affiliated with Hammamet-based agency **Visit Tunisia** (☎ 72 280 860; www.visit-tunisia.com).

TRAIN

Trains are run by the **Société Nationale des Chemins de Fer Tunisiens** (SNCFT; ☎ 71 345 511; www.sncft.com.tn). The rail network is extensive (though not comprehensive) and train travel is comfortable (unless you are standing), but trains are slow, and can run late. For shorter journeys you're usually better off taking a bus or a louage.

The main train line runs north–south between Tunis and Gabès via Sousse and Sfax, and there are frequent services along this route. One train per day branches off at Mahres, south of Sfax, to Gafsa and Metlaoui. There are also lines to Bizerte, via Mateur; Ghardimao, via Jendouba; and Kalaat Khasba (halfway between Le Kef and Kasserine).

Cap Bon is serviced by a branch line from Bir Bou Regba to Nabeul, while the Metro du Sahel network operates south from Sousse to Monastir and Mahdia. Both these lines are linked to the main north–south line. Other rail lines shown on maps are for freight only.

The *Lezard Rouge* (Red Lizard) is a restored train that belonged to the former bey, who used it to go on pleasure trips into the mountains. It runs between Metlaoui and Redeyef five days per week, offering great views of the Seldja Gorge. For more details, see p267.

Classes

Passenger trains offer three classes: 2nd, 1st and *confort*. Second class costs about the same as a bus, and is normally packed with people, parcels and livestock – a circus that can be fun to experience for a short journey. Unless you get on at the start and have sharp elbows, you're unlikely to find a seat.

First class has reclining, upholstered seats, and a better chance of actually sitting in one. *Confort* doesn't offer much more apart from a smaller, slightly more exclusive compartment. Most mainline trains have a restaurant car, which sends out a regular supply of sandwiches, soft drinks and coffee.

Costs

Sample fares from Tunis to:

Destination	1st class	2nd class	confort
Sousse	TD6.5	TD8.6	TD9.2
Sfax	TD10.5	TD14.1	TD15
Gafsa	TD14.35	TD19.25	TD20.45
Monastir	TD37.85	TD10.35	TD11

Reservations

Trains can get crowded in summer, especially going south. To get a seat, it's a good idea to make a reservation the day before, which can be done at train stations in any medium-sized town around the country.

Health

Dr Caroline Evans

CONTENTS

Before You Go	**314**
Insurance	314
Recommended Vaccinations	314
Medical Checklist	315
Internet Resources	315
Further Reading	315
In Transit	**315**
Deep Vein Thrombosis (DVT)	315
Jet Lag & Motion Sickness	315
In Tunisia	**316**
Availability & Cost of Healthcare	316
Infectious Diseases	316
Environmental Hazards	317
Travelling with Children	318
Women's Health	318

Prevention is the key to staying healthy while travelling in Tunisia. A little planning before departure, particularly for pre-existing illnesses, will save you trouble later: see your dentist before a long trip to sort out any loose fillings; carry spare contact lenses and glasses and take your optical prescription with you. Infectious diseases can and do occur in Tunisia, but they are extremely rare. Medical facilities can be excellent in large cities, but in remote areas they may be more basic.

BEFORE YOU GO

It's tempting to leave it all to the last minute – don't! Many vaccines don't ensure immunity for two weeks, so visit a doctor four to eight weeks before departure. Ask your doctor for an International Certificate of Vaccination (otherwise known as the yellow booklet), which will list all the vaccinations you've received. This is mandatory for countries that require proof of yellow fever vaccination upon entry, but it's a good idea to carry it wherever you travel.

Travellers can register with the **International Association for Medical Advice to Travellers** (IAMAT; www.iamat.org). Its website can help travellers to find a doctor with recognised training.

Bring medications in their original, clearly labelled containers. A signed and dated letter from your physician describing your medical conditions and medications, including generic names, is also a good idea. If carrying syringes or needles, be sure to have a physician's letter documenting their medical necessity.

INSURANCE

Find out in advance if your insurance will make payments directly to providers or reimburse you later for overseas health expenditures (in many countries doctors expect payment in cash); it's also worth ensuring that your travel insurance will cover repatriation home, or to better medical facilities elsewhere. Your insurance may be able to locate the nearest source of medical help, or you can ask at your hotel. In an emergency contact your embassy or consulate. Your travel insurance will not usually cover you for any dental work other than emergency treatment. Not all insurance covers emergency aeromedical evacuation home or to a hospital in a major city, which may be the only way to get medical attention for a serious emergency.

RECOMMENDED VACCINATIONS

The World Health Organization recommends that all travellers regardless of the region they are travelling in should be covered for diphtheria, tetanus, measles, mumps, rubella and polio, as well as hepatitis B. While making preparations to travel, take the opportunity to ensure that all of

TRAVEL HEALTH WEBSITES

It's usually a good idea to consult your government's travel health website before departure, if one is available.

Australia (www.dfat.gov.au/travel)
Canada (www.travelhealth.gc.ca)
UK (www.dh.gov.uk) Click on the links for 'Policy and Guidance' and then 'EHIC and Health advice for travellers'.
US (www.cdc.gov/travel)

your routine vaccination cover is complete. The consequences of these diseases can be severe and there is a small risk of contracting them in Tunisia.

MEDICAL CHECKLIST

Following is a list of items you should consider packing in your medical kit.

- Antibiotics if travelling off the beaten track
- Antidiarrhoeal drugs (eg loperamide)
- Acetaminophen (Tylenol) or aspirin
- Anti-inflammatory drugs (eg ibuprofen)
- Antihistamines (for hay fever and allergic reactions)
- Antibacterial ointment (eg Bactroban) for cuts and abrasions
- Steroid cream or cortisone (allergic rashes)
- Bandages, gauze, gauze rolls
- Adhesive or paper tape
- Scissors, safety pins, tweezers
- Thermometer
- Pocket knife
- DEET-containing insect repellent for the skin
- Permethrin-containing insect spray for clothing, tents and bed nets
- Sun block
- Oral rehydration salts
- Iodine tablets (for water purification)
- Syringes and sterile needles if travelling to remote areas

INTERNET RESOURCES

There is a wealth of travel-health advice on the internet. For further information, the **Lonely Planet** (www.lonelyplanet.com) website is a good place to start. The World Health Organization publishes a superb book, *International Travel and Health,* which is revised annually and is available online at no cost at www.who.int/ith. Another website of general interest is **MD Travel Health** (www.mdtravelhealth.com), which provides complete travel health recommendations for every country, updated daily, also at no cost. The **Centers for Disease Control and Prevention** (www.cdc.gov) website is a very useful source of travellers' health information.

FURTHER READING

Lonely Planet's *Healthy Travel* is packed with useful information including pretrip planning, emergency first aid, immunisation and disease information and what to do if you get sick on the road. Other recommended references include *Traveller's Health* by Dr Richard Dawood (Oxford University Press), *International Travel Health Guide* by Stuart R Rose, MD (Travel Medicine Inc) and *The Travellers' Good Health Guide* by Ted Lankester (Sheldon Press), an especially useful health guide for volunteers and long-term expatriates working in the Middle East.

IN TRANSIT

DEEP VEIN THROMBOSIS (DVT)

Deep vein thrombosis occurs when blood clots form in the legs during plane flights, chiefly because of prolonged immobility. The longer the flight, the greater the risk. Though most blood clots are reabsorbed, some may break off and travel through the blood vessels to the lungs, where they may cause life-threatening complications.

The chief symptom of deep vein thrombosis is swelling or pain of the foot, ankle, or calf, usually but not always on just one side. When a blood clot travels to the lungs, it may cause chest pain and difficulty breathing. Travellers with any of these symptoms should immediately seek medical attention.

To prevent the development of deep vein thrombosis on long flights you should walk about the cabin, perform isometric compressions of the leg muscles (ie contract the leg muscles while sitting), drink plenty of fluids, and avoid alcohol and tobacco.

JET LAG & MOTION SICKNESS

Jet lag is common when crossing more than five time zones; it results in insomnia, fatigue, malaise or nausea. To avoid jet lag try drinking plenty of (nonalcoholic) fluids and eating light meals. Upon arrival, seek exposure to natural sunlight and readjust your schedule (for meals, sleep etc) as soon as possible.

Antihistamines such as dimenhydrinate (Dramamine) and meclizine (Antivert, Bonine) are usually the first choice for treating motion sickness. Their main side effect is drowsiness. A herbal alternative is ginger, which works like a charm for some people.

IN TUNISIA

AVAILABILITY & COST OF HEALTHCARE

The healthcare system in Tunisia varies. Medical care can be excellent in larger towns (eg Tunis, Sousse, Sfax and Houmt Souq, where many of the doctors completed their studies in Europe). Reciprocal arrangements with countries rarely exist and you should be prepared to pay for all medical and dental treatment. Charges are less expensive than European countries but medical insurance is always advisable.

Medical care is not always readily available outside major cities. Medicine, and even sterile dressings or intravenous fluids, may need to be bought from a local pharmacy. Nursing care may be limited or rudimentary as this is something families and friends are expected to provide. The travel assistance provided by your insurance may be able to locate the nearest source of medical help, otherwise ask at your hotel. In an emergency contact your embassy or consulate.

Standards of dental care are variable and there is an increased risk of hepatitis B and HIV transmission via poorly sterilised equipment. Keep in mind that your travel insurance will not usually cover you for anything other than emergency dental treatment.

For minor illnesses such as diarrhoea, pharmacists can provide valuable advice and sell over-the-counter medication. They can also advise when more specialised help is needed and recommend good local clinics.

INFECTIOUS DISEASES

Diphtheria

Diphtheria is spread through close respiratory contact, causing a high temperature and severe sore throat. Sometimes a membrane forms across the throat requiring a tracheostomy to prevent suffocation. Vaccination is recommended for those likely to be in close contact with the local population in infected areas. The vaccine is given as an injection alone, or with tetanus, and lasts 10 years.

Hepatitis A

Hepatitis A is spread through contaminated food (particularly shellfish) and water. It causes jaundice, and although rarely fatal, it can cause prolonged lethargy and delayed recovery. Symptoms include dark urine, a yellow colour to the whites of the eyes, fever and abdominal pain. Hepatitis A vaccine (Avaxim, VAQTA, Havrix) is given as an injection: a single dose gives protection for up to a year while a booster 12 months later will provide a subsequent 10 years of protection. Hepatitis A and typhoid vaccines can also be given as a single dose vaccine (hepatyrix or viatim).

Hepatitis B

Infected blood, contaminated needles and sexual intercourse can all transmit hepatitis B. It can cause jaundice, and affects the liver, occasionally causing liver failure. All travellers should make this a routine vaccination. (Many countries now give a hepatitis B vaccination as part of routine childhood vaccination.) The vaccine is given singly, or with the hepatitis A vaccine (hepatyrix). A course will give protection for at least five years. It can be given over four weeks, or six months.

HIV

HIV is spread via infected blood and blood products, sexual intercourse with an infected partner and from an infected mother to her newborn child. It can be spread through 'blood to blood' contact such as contaminated instruments during medical, dental, acupuncture and body piercing procedures, and sharing used intravenous needles.

Poliomyelitis

This disease is generally spread through contaminated food and water. It is one of the vaccines given in childhood and should be boosted every 10 years, either orally (a drop on the tongue) or as an injection. Polio may be carried asymptomatically, although it can cause a transient fever and, in rare cases, potentially permanent muscle weakness or paralysis.

Rabies

Spread through bites or licks on broken skin from an infected animal, rabies is fatal. Animal handlers should be vaccinated, as should those travelling to remote areas where a reliable source of post-bite vaccine is not available within 24 hours. Three injections are needed over a month. If you have not been vaccinated you will need a course of five injections starting within 24 hours or as soon as possible after the injury. Vaccination does not give you immunity, it merely buys you more time to seek appropriate medical help.

Travellers' Diarrhoea

To prevent diarrhoea, avoid tap water unless it has been boiled, filtered or chemically disinfected (iodine tablets); only eat fresh fruits or vegetables if cooked or if you have peeled them yourself and be wary of dairy products that might contain unpasteurised milk. Buffet meals are risky, as food should be piping hot; food freshly cooked in front of you in a busy restaurant is more likely to be safe.

If you develop diarrhoea, drink plenty of fluids, preferably an oral rehydration solution with lots of salt and sugar. A few loose stools don't require treatment, but if you start having more than four or five stools a day you should start taking an antibiotic (usually a quinolone drug) and an antidiarrhoeal agent (such as loperamide). If diarrhoea is bloody or persists for more than 72 hours or is accompanied by fever, shaking chills or severe abdominal pain, seek medical attention.

Tuberculosis

Tuberculosis (TB) is spread through close respiratory contact and occasionally through infected milk or milk products. BCG vaccine is recommended for those likely to be mixing closely with the local population. It is more important for those visiting family or planning on a long stay, and those employed as teachers and healthcare workers. TB can be asymptomatic, although symptoms can include cough, weight loss or fever months or even years after exposure. An x-ray is the best way to confirm if you have TB. BCG gives a moderate degree of protection against TB. It causes a small permanent scar at the site of injection, and is usually only given in specialised chest clinics. As it's a live vaccine it should not be given to pregnant women or immunocompromised individuals. The BCG vaccine is not available in all countries.

Typhoid

This is spread through food or water that has been contaminated by infected human faeces. The first symptom is usually fever or a pink rash on the abdomen. Septicaemia (blood poisoning) may also occur. Typhoid vaccine (typhim Vi, typherix) will give protection for three years. In some countries, the oral vaccine Vivotif is also available.

ENVIRONMENTAL HAZARDS

Heat Illness

Heat exhaustion occurs following heavy sweating and excessive fluid loss with inadequate replacement of fluids and salt. This is particularly common in hot climates when taking unaccustomed exercise before full acclimatisation. Symptoms include headache, dizziness and tiredness. Dehydration is already happening by the time you feel thirsty – aim to drink sufficient water such that you produce pale, diluted urine. The treatment of heat exhaustion consists of fluid replacement with water and/or fruit juice, and cooling by cold water and fans. The treatment of the salt loss component consists of salty fluids as in soup or Bovril, and adding a little more table salt to foods than usual.

Heat stroke is much more serious. This occurs when the body's heat-regulating mechanism breaks down. An excessive rise in body temperature leads to sweating ceasing, irrational and hyperactive behaviour and eventually loss of consciousness and death. Rapid cooling by spraying the body with water and fanning is an ideal treatment. Emergency fluid and electrolyte replacement by intravenous drip is usually also required.

Prickly heat is a heat rash that occurs when sweat-gland pores get clogged, resulting in a red rash and sometimes small water blisters. It can feel quite itchy or prickly. Wearing loose cotton clothing will help prevent or reduce the rash, as will having frequent cool baths or showers. Calamine lotion may soothe it, or you can try antihistamines to relieve the itching. If it persists, see a pharmacist or doctor.

Insect Bites & Stings

Mosquitoes may not carry malaria but can cause irritation and infected bites. Using DEET-based insect repellents will prevent bites. Mosquitoes also spread dengue fever.

Bees and wasps only cause real problems to those with a severe allergy (anaphylaxis). If you have a severe allergy to bee or wasp stings you should carry an adrenaline injection or similar.

Sand flies are found around the Mediterranean beaches. They usually only cause a nasty itchy bite but can carry a rare skin disorder called cutaneous leishmaniasis. Bites may be prevented by using DEET-based repellents.

Scorpions are frequently found in arid or dry climates. They can give a painful bite which is rarely life threatening.

Bed bugs are often found in hostels and cheap hotels. They lead to very itchy lumpy bites. Spraying the mattress with an appropriate insect killer will do a good job of getting rid of them.

Scabies are also frequently found in cheap accommodation. These tiny mites live in the skin, particularly between the fingers. They cause an intensely itchy rash. Scabies is easily treated with lotion from a pharmacy; people who you come into contact with also need treating to avoid the spread of scabies between asymptomatic carriers.

Snake Bites

Avoid being bitten – do not walk barefoot or stick your hand into holes or cracks. Half of those bitten by venomous snakes are not actually injected with poison (envenomed). If bitten by a snake, do not panic. Immobilise the limb with a splint (eg a stick) and apply a bandage over the site, firm pressure, similar to a bandage over a sprain. Do not apply a tourniquet, or cut or suck the bite. Get the victim to medical help as soon as possible so that antivenin can be given if necessary.

Water

Tap water is safe to drink throughout Tunisia, with the notable exception of Jerba where salt water has seeped into underground water sources; stick to bottled water, boil water for 10 minutes or use water purification tablets or a filter. Do not drink water from rivers or lakes, as this may contain bacteria or viruses that can cause diarrhoea or vomiting.

TRAVELLING WITH CHILDREN

All travellers with children should know how to treat minor ailments and when to seek medical treatment. Make sure the children are up to date with routine vaccinations, and discuss possible travel vaccines well before departure as some vaccines are not suitable for children aged under one year.

In hot, humid climates any wound or break in the skin may lead to infection. The area should be cleaned and then kept dry and clean. Remember to avoid contaminated food and water. If your child is vomiting or experiencing diarrhoea, lost fluid and salts must be replaced. It may be helpful to take rehydration powders for reconstituting with boiled water. Ask your doctor about this.

Bear in mind that children are more susceptible to heat than adults, and should drink plenty of fluids in hot weather. They are more prone to prickly heat (see p317); discuss any treatment with a doctor before you apply it.

Children should be encouraged to avoid dogs or other mammals because of the risk of rabies and other diseases. Any bite, scratch or lick from a warm-blooded, furry animal should immediately be thoroughly cleaned. If there is any possibility that the animal is infected with rabies, immediate medical assistance should be sought.

WOMEN'S HEALTH

Emotional stress, exhaustion and travelling through different time zones can all contribute to an upset in the menstrual pattern. If using oral contraceptives, remember some antibiotics, diarrhoea and vomiting can stop the pill from working and lead to the risk of pregnancy, so remember to take condoms with you just in case (they're readily available over the counter in pharmacies in Tunisia). Condoms should be kept in a cool dry place or they may crack and perish.

Emergency contraception is effective if taken within 24 hours after unprotected sex. See the **International Planned Parent Federation** (www.ippf.org) website for details on the availability of contraception in Tunisia. Tampons are usually only found in supermarkets, and can be hard to find outside medium towns.

Travelling during pregnancy is usually possible but there are important things to consider. Have a medical check-up before embarking on your trip. The most risky times for travel are during the first 12 weeks of pregnancy, when miscarriage is most likely, and after 30 weeks, when complications such as high blood pressure and premature delivery can occur. Most airlines will not accept a traveller after 28 to 32 weeks of pregnancy, and long-haul flights in the later stages can be very uncomfortable. Antenatal facilities should be relied on only in larger cities. Taking written records of the pregnancy including details of your blood group is likely to be helpful if you need medical attention while away. Ensure your insurance policy covers pregnancy delivery and postnatal care, but remember insurance policies are only as good as the facilities available.

Language

CONTENTS

Arabic	**319**
Transliteration	319
Pronunciation	321
Accommodation	321
Conversation & Essentials	322
Directions	322
Emergencies	323
Health	323
Language Difficulties	323
Numbers	323
Paperwork	324
Question Words	324
Shopping & Services	324
Time & Dates	324
Transport	324
Travel with Children	325
French	**326**
Pronunciation	326
Accommodation	326
Conversation & Essentials	327
Directions	327
Emergencies	327
Health	327
Language Difficulties	328
Numbers	328
Paperwork	328
Question Words	328
Shopping & Services	328
Time & Dates	329
Transport	329
Travel with Children	330

ARABIC

Arabic is the official language of Tunisia. However, the Arabic spoken on the streets differs greatly from the standard Arabic written in newspapers and spoken on the radio (which is known as Modern Standard Arabic or MSA). MSA is the written and spoken lingua franca that is common to all Arabic-speaking countries.

Tunisian Arabic is from the group of Arabic dialects known as the Western dialects, which also includes Moroccan Arabic and Algerian Arabic. It is fun, but difficult to learn. It's basically a dialect of the standard language, but so different in many respects as to be virtually another language. As with most dialects, it's the everyday language that differs the most from that of Tunisia's other Arabic-speaking neighbours. More specialised or educated language tends to be pretty much the same across the Arab world, although pronunciation may vary considerably. An Arab from, say, Jordan or Iraq will have no problem having a chat about politics or literature with a Tunisian, but might have more trouble making themselves understood in a Tunisian grocery shop.

There is no official written form of the Tunisian Arabic dialect, although there is no practical reason for this – The Tunisian writer 'Abd al-'Aziz Laraoui wrote his famous collections of short stories exclusively in Tunisian Arabic. However, the use of Tunisian Arabic in literary fields is generally not readily accepted. A 1997 translation into Tunisian Arabic of Antoine de Saint-Exupéry's *Le Petit Prince* was greeted with much criticism by those who felt it was a threat to the national written language of the country – Modern Standard Arabic. For some reason though, foreigners who specifically want to learn Tunisian Arabic instead of MSA are told that it can't be written in script, and are then presented with one system or other of transliteration – none of them totally satisfactory. If you're getting a headache now, you'll have some idea of why few non-Arabs and non-Muslims embark on the study of the language.

Nevertheless, if you take the time to learn even a handful of words and phrases, you'll discover and experience much more while travelling through the country.

TRANSLITERATION

Converting what for most outsiders is just a bunch of squiggles into meaningful words (ie those written using the Roman alphabet) is a tricky business – in fact, no really satisfactory system of transliteration has been established, and probably never will be. For

THE STANDARD ARABIC ALPHABET

Final	Medial	Initial	Alone	Transliteration	Pronunciation
ـا			ا	**ā/aa**	as in 'father'/as the long 'a' sound in 'air'
ـب	ـبـ	بـ	ب	**b**	as in 'bet'
ـت	ـتـ	تـ	ت	**t**	as in 'ten'
ـث	ـثـ	ثـ	ث	**th**	as in 'thin'
ـج	ـجـ	جـ	ج	**j**	as in 'jet'
ـح	ـحـ	حـ	ح	**H**	a strongly whispered 'h', like a sigh of relief
ـخ	ـخـ	خـ	خ	**kh**	as the 'ch' in Scottish *loch*
ـد			د	**d**	as in 'dim'
ـذ			ذ	**dh**	as the 'th' in 'this'; also as **d** or **z**
ـر			ر	**r**	a rolled 'r', as in the Spanish word *caro*
ـز			ز	**z**	as in 'zip'
ـس	ـسـ	سـ	س	**s**	as in 'so', never as in 'wisdom'
ـش	ـشـ	شـ	ش	**sh**	as in 'ship'
ـص	ـصـ	صـ	ص		emphatic 's' (see below)
ـض	ـضـ	ضـ	ض		emphatic 'd' (see below)
ـط	ـطـ	طـ	ط		emphatic 't' (see below)
ـظ	ـظـ	ظـ	ظ		emphatic 'dh' (see below)
ـع	ـعـ	عـ	ع	**’**	the Arabic letter *'ayn*; pronounce as a glottal stop – like the closing of the throat before saying 'Oh-oh!' (see Other Sounds on p321)
ـغ	ـغـ	غـ	غ	**gh**	a guttural sound like Parisian 'r'
ـف	ـفـ	فـ	ف	**f**	as in 'far'
ـق	ـقـ	قـ	ق	**q**	a strongly guttural 'k' sound; also often pronounced as a glottal stop
ـك	ـكـ	كـ	ك	**k**	as in 'king'
ـل	ـلـ	لـ	ل	**l**	as in 'lamb'
ـم	ـمـ	مـ	م	**m**	as in 'me'
ـن	ـنـ	نـ	ن	**n**	as in 'name'
ـه	ـهـ	هـ	ه	**h**	as in 'ham'
ـو			و	**w**	as in 'wet'; or
				oo	long, as in 'food'; or
				ow	as in 'how'
ـي	ـيـ	يـ	ي	**y**	as in 'yes'; or
				ee	as in 'beer', only softer; or
				ai/ay	as in 'aisle'/as the 'ay' in 'day'

Vowels Not all Arabic vowel sounds are represented in the alphabet. For more information on the vowel sounds used in this language guide, see Pronunciation on p321.

Emphatic Consonants To simplify the transliteration system used in this book, the emphatic consonants have not been differentiated from their non-emphatic counterparts.

this book, an attempt has been made to standardise some spellings of place names and the like.

There is only one article in Arabic: al (the). It's also sometimes written as 'il' or 'el', occasionally contracted to 'l' and sometimes modifies to reflect the first consonant of the following noun, eg in Saladin's name, Salah ad-Din (righteousness of the faith), the 'al' has been modified to 'ad' before the 'd' of 'Din'. The article el is used only in a few instances in this book, such as well-known places (El-Jem, Borj el-Khadra) or where locals have used it in restaurant and hotel names.

The whole business of transliteration is fraught with pitfalls, and the reality is that it simply isn't possible to devise a truly 'correct' system. The locals themselves can only guess at how to make the conversion – and the result is often amusing. The fact that French and English have had a big influence in Tunisia has also led to many interesting ideas on transliteration. Don't be taken aback if you start noticing half a dozen different spellings for the same thing.

For some reason, the letters **q** and **k** have caused enormous problems, and have been interchanged willy-nilly in transliteration. For a long time, Iraq (which in Arabic is spelled with what can only be described in English using its nearest-sounding equivalent: 'q') was written, even by scholars, as 'Irak'. Other examples of an Arabic **q** receiving such treatment are *souq* (market), often written 'souk', and *qasr* (castle), sometimes written 'kasr'. It's a bit like spelling English 'as she is spoke' – imagine the results if Australians, Americans, Scots and Londoners were all given free rein to write English the way they pronounce it!

PRONUNCIATION

Pronunciation of Arabic can be somewhat tongue-tying for those unfamiliar with the intonation and combination of sounds. The following guide should help, but it isn't complete because the myriad rules governing pronunciation and vowel use are too extensive to be covered here.

Vowels

a as in 'had' (sometimes very short)
aa like the long 'a' sound in 'air'
ā as the 'a' in 'father'
e as in 'bet' (sometimes very short)
ee as in 'beer', only softer
i as in 'hit'
o as in 'hot'
oo as in 'food'
u as in 'put'

Diphthongs

ow as in 'how'
ai as in 'aisle'
ay as in 'day'

Consonants

Pronunciation of Arabic consonants is covered in the alphabet table on p320. Note that when double consonants occur in transliterations, each consonant is pronounced. For example, *il-Hammaam*, (bathhouse), is pronounced 'il-ham-maam'.

Other Sounds

Arabic has two sounds that are very tricky for non-Arabs to produce, the 'ayn and the glottal stop. The letter 'ayn represents a sound with no English equivalent that comes even close – it is similar to the glottal stop (which is not actually represented in the alphabet) but the muscles at the back of the throat are gagged more forcefully and air is allowed to escape, creating a sound that has been described as reminiscent of someone being strangled! In many transliteration systems 'ayn is represented by an opening quotation mark, and the glottal stop by a closing quotation mark. To make the transliterations in this language guide (and throughout the rest of the book) easier to use, we have not distinguished between the glottal stop and the 'ayn, using the closing quotation mark to represent both sounds. You'll find that Arab speakers will still understand you.

ACCOMMODATION

I'm looking for a ... *ana infarkis 'ala ...*
hotel *ooteel*
youth hostel *dār ash-shabaab*

Where can I find a cheap hotel?
birabbi ween famma ooteel rakhees?
What is the address?
shneeya l-adreesa?
Could you write the address, please?
mumkin tiktibshee l-adreesa
Do you have rooms available?
'andkumshee beet faarigha?

I'd like (a) ... *inHebb*
I'd like to book (a) ... *birabbi inHebb naHjiz ...*
  bed *farsh*
  single room *beet li waaHid*
  double room *beet doobal*
  room with two beds *beet ma' zooz afraash*
  room with a bathroom *beet ma' beet banoo*
  room with air-con/fan *beet ma' akleemateesur/marwaha*

in the name of ... *bi 'ism ...*
date *taareekh*
from (date) **to** (date) *min yoom (...) li yoom (...)*
credit card ... *kart kredee ...*
  number *noomroo*
  expiry date *taareekh al-'intihaa*
How much is it ...? *qaddaash ...?*
  per night *bi qaddaash il-leela*
  per person *lil waaHid*

Do you have any cheaper rooms?
'andkumshee byoot arkhas?
May I see it?
mumkin inshoofoo?
Where is the bathroom?
ween il-beet banoo?
I'm/We're leaving today.
(ana nimshi/aHna nimsheeoo) l-yoom.

CONVERSATION & ESSENTIALS

Hello. *'aslaama*
  (response) *'aslaama*
Hello/Welcome. *marHaba beek* (to one person)
  marHaba beekum (to a group)
  (response) *'ayshik*
Good morning. *sbāH al-kheer*
  (response) *sbāH al-kheer*
Good evening. *masa' l-kheer*
  (response) *masa' l-kheer*
Good night. *tisbaH 'ala kheer*
  (response) *tisbaH 'ala kheer*
Goodbye. *bi s-slaama*
Yes. *ayy* (or *na'am* – more formal)
No. *la*

Please.
birabbi (used when asking for something in a shop)
tfaddel/tfaddloo (to man/group; used when offering something or inviting someone)
itfaddel//itfaddloo (to man/group; similar, or can mean 'Please, go ahead and do something)

Thank you. *barkallaoo feek/'ayshik*
  (response) *min gheer muziyya*

Excuse me. *saamaHnee* (to one person)
  saamHoonee (to group)
That's fine/You're welcome. *min gheer muziyya*
Sorry. (ie forgive me) *mitaasif/a* (m/f)
What's your name? *shnuwwa ismek inti?*
My name is ... *ismee ...*
Pleased to meet you. *nitsharrafoo* (pol)
How are you? *shnuwwa Hawaalek?* (to one person)
  shnuwwa Hawaalkum? (to a group)
I'm fine. *la baas ilHamdu lillah*
Where are you from? *mineen inti?*
I'm from ... *ana min ...*
I like/don't like ... *ana inHebb/manHebbish*
Just a minute. *daqeeqa waaHida*

DIRECTIONS

Where is ...? *ween ...?*
Go straight ahead. *tool*
Turn left. *door al-lisaar*
Turn right. *door al- limeen*
at the (next) corner *fi l-kwan (illi jayy)*
at the traffic lights *fi dhow laHmar*
behind *wara*
in front of *quddaam*
far (from) *ba'eed ('ala)*
near (to) *qreeb (min)*
opposite *mqābil*
here *hoonee/hnaa*
there *ghādee*
this address *haadhee l-adreesa*
north *shamaal*
south *janoob*
east *sharq*
west *gharb*

beach *il-bHar*
bridge *il-qantra*
castle *il-qala'*
my hotel *il-ooteel mtaa'ee*
island *jazeera*
main square *is-saaHa l-kabeera*
mosque *il-jaami'*
museum *il-matHaf*
old city *il-madeena*
palace *il-qasr*
ruins *il-athār*
sea *il-baHr*
square *il-saaHa*
street *ish-shaara'*
village *al-qarya*

EMERGENCIES – ARABIC

Help!	*'awnoonee!*
There's been an accident.	*famma Hādith!*
I'm lost.	*ana dhāyi'/dhāy'a*
Go away!	*khalleenee rāyidh/a!*
Call a doctor!	*jeeboolee it-tabeeb!*
Call the police!	*jeeboolee il-bolees!*
I've been robbed.	*sarqoolee Hwayji*
Where are the toilets?	*ween it-twalet?*

HEALTH

I'm ill. *ana mreedh/a* (m/f)
My friend is ill. *sāHbi/sāHibti mreedh/a* (m/f)
It hurts here. *yuwja'ni hnaa*

I'm ... *ana mreedh/a bi ...* (m/f)
asthmatic *l-fadda*
diabetic *s- sukkar*
epileptic *l-epilepsee*

I'm allergic ... *'andee Hasasiyya ...*
to antibiotics *min antbiotique*
to aspirin *min asbireen*
to bees *min naHl*
to nuts *min looz*
to peanuts *kakwiyya*
to penicillin *min penisileen*

antiseptic *dwaa l-aHmar*
aspirin *asbireen*
condoms *preservateef* (*rifel*, brand name)
contraceptive *wasaa'il mana' il Haml*

I have ... *'andee ...*
diarrhoea *kirshee tijree*
fever *skhāna*
headache *wjee'it ir-rās*

hospital *sbeetār*
medicine *dwaa*
pharmacy *saydaliyya*
pregnant *Hebla*
prescription *warqit at-tabeeb*
sanitary napkins *alwees* (brand name)
stomachache *wjee'it il-maada*
sunblock cream *kreema did ish-shams*
tampons *tampax*

LANGUAGE DIFFICULTIES

Do you speak English?
titkallim ingleeziyya?
Does anyone here speak English?
famma skhoon yitkallim bi l-ingleeziyya?
How do you say ... in Tunisian Arabic?
kifaash taqool ... bi t-toonsee?
What does ... mean?
aash ta'nee ...
I understand.
nifhim
I don't understand.
ma nifhimsh
Please write it down.
mumkin tiktibhaalee
Can you show me (on the map)?
mumkin twarreenee (fi l- khareeta)?

NUMBERS

Arabic numerals are simple to learn and, unlike the written language, run from left to right. Pay attention to the order of the words in numbers from 21 to 99. When followed by a noun, the pronunciation of *miyya* changes to *meet* for the numbers 100 and 300–900, and the noun is always used in its singular form.

0	*sifr*	٠
1	*waaHid*	١
2	*zooz/ithneen*	٢
3	*thlaatha*	٣
4	*arb'a*	٤
5	*khamsa*	٥
6	*sitta*	٦
7	*sab'a*	٧
8	*thmaanya*	٨
9	*tis'a*	٩
10	*'ashra*	١٠
11	*Hadaash*	١١
12	*ithnāsh*	١٢
13	*thlattāsh*	١٣
14	*arba'tāsh*	١٤
15	*khamastāsh*	١٥
16	*sittāsh*	١٦
17	*saba'tāsh*	١٧
18	*thamantāsh*	١٨
19	*tisa'tāsh*	١٩
20	*'ashreen*	٢٠
21	*waaHid oo 'ashreen*	٢١
22	*ithneen oo 'ashreen*	٢٢
30	*thalatheen*	٣٠
40	*arba'een*	٤٠
50	*khamseen*	٥٠
60	*sitteen*	٦٠
70	*sab'een*	٧٠
80	*thamaneen*	٨٠

90	*tis'een*	٩٠
100	*miyya* (*meet* before a noun)	١٠٠
200	*meeteen*	٢٠٠
1000	*alf*	١٠٠٠
2000	*alfeen*	٢٠٠٠

How many? *qaddaash min?*

PAPERWORK

name *ism*
nationality *jinsiyya*
date/place of birth *tareekh/maHal il-milād*
sex (gender) *jins*
passport *paspoor*
visa *veeza*

QUESTION WORDS

Who? *shkoon?*
What? *shnuwwa/aash?*
When? *waqtaash?*
Where? *ween?*
How? *keefaash?*
Which? *aama?*

SHOPPING & SERVICES

I'd like to buy ... *inHebb nishree ...*
How much is it? *qaddaash haadha?*
I don't like it. *ma y'ajibneesh*
May I look at it? *mumkin inshoofu?*
I'm just looking. *qa'ad inshoof bark*
It's cheap. *hiyya rakheesa*
It's too expensive. *ghaalee shwayya*
No more than ... *mush akthār min ...*
I'll take it. *nishreeha*

Can you give me ...? *tnajjemshee t'amelee ...?*
a discount *takhfeedh*
a good price *soom behee*

Do you accept ...? *taakhudh ...?*
credit cards *kart kredee*
traveller cheques *sheekaat siyaHiyya*

more *akthir*
less *aqall*
smaller *asghar*
bigger *akbar*

I'm looking for ... *ana infarkis 'ala*
a bank *banka*
the bazaar/market *is-sooq*
the city centre *wist il-blaad*
the (...) embassy *as-sifāra (...)*
the post office *il-boosta*
the telephone centre *it-taxiphone*
the tourist office *maktab is-siyaaHa*

I want to change ... *inHebb nijbid ...*
money *fuloos*
travellers cheques *sheekaat siyaHiyya*

Where is an internet café? *wayn famma intanet kafay?*

TIME & DATES

What time is it? *qaddaash il-waqt?*
It's (8 o'clock). *tawwa (ith-thmaanya)*
in the morning *fi s-sbaaH*
in the afternoon *fi l-'asheeya*
in the evening *fi l-leel*
today *il-yoom*
tomorrow *ghudwa*
yesterday *ilbaaraH*
day *yoom*
month *sh-har*
week *jim'a*
year *'ām*
early *bikree*
late *makhkhir*
daily *kull yoom*

Monday *inhar il-ihtneen*
Tuesday *inhar ith-thlaatha*
Wednesday *inhar il-arba'*
Thursday *inhar il-khamees*
Friday *inhar ij-juma'*
Saturday *inhar is-sibt*
Sunday *inhar il-aHadd*

January *janfee*
February *feevree*
March *māris*
April *avreel*
May *may*
June *jwān*
July *jweelya*
August *oot*
September *sibtamber*
October *uktoober*
November *nuvamber*
December *disamber*

TRANSPORT

Public Transport

When does the ... leave/arrive? *Waqtaash timshee/tuwsil ...?*
boat *il-flooka*
bus *il-kār*

ferry	*il-ferry*
plane	*it-tayyāra*
train	*it-treenoo*

I'd like a ... ticket.	*inHebb tiskira ...*
one-way	*maashee akahow*
return	*maashi oo jayy*
1st-class	*daarija oola*
2nd-class	*daarija thaanya*

I want to go to ...
inHebb nimshee
The train has been delayed.
it-treenoo wakher
The train has been cancelled.
naHāoow it-treenoo
Which bus goes to ...?
enayhee il-kār timshee li- ...?
Does this bus go to ...?
il-kār haadhee timshee li ...?
Please tell me when we arrive in ...
birabbi qullee waqtillee nuwsiloo fi ...
What is the fare to ...?
qaddaash it-tiskira li ...?
Stop here, please.
birabbi waqif hoonee
Wait!
istanna!

the first	*il-awwil/oola* (m/f)
the last	*il-aakhir*
the next	*illi jayy*
airport	*il-matār*
bus station	*mHattat il-kār*
bus stop	*mHatta*
city	*il-madeena*
platform number	*noomroo il-qay*
station	*il-maHatta*
ticket office	*il-geeshay*
timetable	*jadwal awqāt*
train station	*maHattat il-treenoo*

Private Transport

I'd like to hire a/an ...	*inHebb nikree ...*
car	*karhaba*
4WD	*too terran*
motorbike	*mutoor*
bicycle	*bisklaat*
camel	*jmal*
donkey	*bheem*
guide	*geed*
horse	*Hsān*

Is this the road to ...?
it-treeq haadha iyhizz li ...?

(How long) Can I park here?
mumkin inwaqqif karhabti hoonee (Hatta waqtaash)?
Where do I pay?
ween inkhallis?
I need a mechanic.
Haajti bi mekanisyan
The car/motorbike has broken down (at ...)
il-karhaba tāHit on pan 'and ...
The car/motorbike won't start.
il-karhaba ma tHebbish tikhdim
I have a flat tyre.
'andee 'ajla mafshoosha
I've run out of petrol.
wfaalee l-essans
I've had an accident.
'amelt hādith
Where's a service station?
ween il-kiyosk?
Please fill it up.
birabbi 'abbeelee
I'd like (30) litres.
inHebb thalaatheen eetra

diesel	*diyaysel*
leaded petrol	*essans normaal* (regular)
	essans sooper (super)
unleaded petrol	*essans son plom*

TRAVEL WITH CHILDREN

Is there a/an ...?
famma ...?
I need a/an ....
Haajti bi...
car baby seat
kursi mtaa' baybiyaat li l-karhaba
child-minding service
kresh
children's menu
menyu mtaa' li s-sghār
(disposable) nappies/diapers
koosh
infant milk formula
Haleeb baybiyaat
(English-speaking) babysitter
babysitter (illi titkallim bi l-ingleeziyya)
highchair
kursi baybiyaat
potty
kasreeya
stroller
karoosa

Are children allowed?
tiqbloo is-sghār?

FRENCH

Almost everybody in Tunisia speaks French, so if the thought of getting your mind around Arabic is too much, it'd be a good investment to learn a little French instead.

In French, an important distinction is made between *tu* and *vous*, which both mean 'you'. The informal *tu* is only used when addressing people you know well, or children. When addressing an adult who is not a personal friend, *vous* should be used unless the person invites you to use *tu*.

PRONUNCIATION

The pronunciation guides included with each French phrase should help in getting your message across. Here are a few of the trickier letters used in written French:

- **j** — as the 's' in 'leisure', eg *jour* (day)
- **c** — before **e** and **i**, as the 's' in 'sit'; before **a**, **o** and **u** it's pronounced as English 'k'. When undescored with a 'cedilla' (ç) it's pronounced as the 's' in 'sit'.
- **r** — pronounced from the back of the throat while constricting the muscles to restrict the flow of air
- **n, m** — where a syllable ends in a single **n** or **m**, these letters are not pronounced, but the vowel is given a nasal pronunciation

ACCOMMODATION

I'm looking for a ...	*Je cherche ...*	zher shersh ...
campground	*un camping*	un kom·peeng
guesthouse	*une pension (de famille)*	ewn pon·syon (der fa·mee·ler)
hotel	*un hôtel*	un o·tel
youth hostel	*une auberge de jeunesse*	ewn o·berzh der zher·nes

Where is a cheap hotel?
Où est-ce qu'on peut trouver un hôtel pas cher?
oo es·kon per troo·vay un o·tel pa shair

What is the address?
Quelle est l'adresse?
kel e la·dres

Could you write it down, please?
Est-ce que vous pourriez l'écrire, s'il vous plaît?
e·sker voo poo·ryay lay·kreer seel voo play

Do you have any rooms available?
Est-ce que vous avez des chambres libres?
e·sker voo·za·vay day shom·brer lee·brer

MAKING A RESERVATION

(for phone or written requests)

To ...	*A l'attention de ...*
From ...	*De la part de ...*
Date	*Date*
I'd like to book ...	*Je voudrais réserver ...* (see the list under 'Accommodation' for bed and room options)
in the name of ...	*au nom de ...*
from ... (date) **to ...**	*du ... au ...*
credit card	*carte de crédit*
number	*numéro*
expiry date	*date d'expiration*
Please confirm availability and price.	*Veuillez confirmer la disponibilité et le prix.*

I'd like (a) ...	*Je voudrais ...*	zher voo·dray ...
single room	*une chambre à un lit*	ewn shom·brer a un lee
double-bed room	*une chambre avec un grand lit*	ewn shom·brer a·vek un gron lee
twin room with two beds	*une chambre avec des lits jumeaux*	ewn shom·brer a·vek day lee zhew·mo
room with a bathroom	*une chambre avec une salle de bains*	ewn shom·brer a·vek ewn sal der bun
to share a dorm	*coucher dans un dortoir*	koo·sher don zun dor·twa

How much is it ...?	*Quel est le prix ...?*	kel e ler pree ...
per night	*par nuit*	par nwee
per person	*par personne*	par per·son

May I see it?
Est-ce que je peux voir la chambre? — es·ker zher per vwa la shom·brer

Where is the bathroom?
Où est la salle de bains? — oo e la sal der bun

Where is the toilet?
Où sont les toilettes? — oo·son lay twa·let

I'm leaving today.
Je pars aujourd'hui. — zher par o·zhoor·dwee

We're leaving today.
Nous partons aujourd'hui. — noo par·ton o·zhoor·dwee

LANGUAGE

CONVERSATION & ESSENTIALS

Hello.	*Bonjour.*	bon·zhoor
Goodbye.	*Au revoir.*	o·rer·vwa
Yes.	*Oui.*	wee
No.	*Non.*	no
Please.	*S'il vous plaît.*	seel voo play
Thank you.	*Merci.*	mair·see
You're welcome.	*Je vous en prie.*	zher voo·zon pree
	De rien. (inf)	der ree·en
Excuse me.	*Excuse-moi.*	ek·skew·zay·mwa
Sorry. (forgive me)	*Pardon.*	par·don

What's your name?
Comment vous appelez-vous? (pol) — ko·mon voo·za·pay·lay voo
Comment tu t'appelles? (inf) — ko·mon tew ta·pel
My name is ...
Je m'appelle ... — zher ma·pel ...
Where are you from?
De quel pays êtes-vous? — der kel pay·ee et·voo
De quel pays es-tu? (inf) — der kel pay·ee e·tew

I'm from ...
Je viens de ... — zher vyen der ...
I like ...
J'aime ... — zhem ...
I don't like ...
Je n'aime pas ... — zher nem pa ...
Just a minute.
Une minute. — ewn mee·newt

DIRECTIONS

Where is ...?
Où est ...? — oo e ...
Go straight ahead.
Continuez tout droit. — kon·teen·way too drwa
Turn left.
Tournez à gauche. — toor·nay a gosh
Turn right.
Tournez à droite. — toor·nay a drwa
at the corner
au coin — o kwun
at the traffic lights
aux feux — o fer

behind	*derrière*	dair·ryair
in front of	*devant*	der·von
far (from)	*loin (de)*	lwun (der)
near (to)	*près (de)*	pray (der)
opposite	*en face de*	on fas der

beach	*la plage*	la plazh
castle	*le château*	ler sha·to
island	*l'île*	leel
main square	*la place centrale*	la plas son·tral
mosque	*la mosquée*	la mos·kay
museum	*le musée*	ler mew·zay
old city	*la vieille ville*	la vyay veel
ruins	*les ruines*	lay rween
sea	*la mer*	la mair
street	*la rue*	la roo
village	*le village*	ler vee·lazh

EMERGENCIES

Help!
Au secours! — o skoor
There's been an accident!
Il y a eu un accident! — eel ya ew un ak·see·don
I'm lost.
Je me suis égaré/e. (m/f) — zhe me swee·zay·ga·ray
Leave me alone!
Fichez-moi la paix! — fee·shay·mwa la pay

Call ...!	*Appelez ...!*	a·play ...
a doctor	*un médecin*	un mayd·sun
the police	*la police*	la po·lees

HEALTH

I'm ill.	*Je suis malade.*	zher swee ma·lad
It hurts here.	*J'ai une douleur ici.*	zhay ewn doo·ler ee·see

I'm ...	*Je suis ...*	zher swee ...
asthmatic	*asthmatique*	(z)as·ma·teek
diabetic	*diabétique*	dee·a·bay·teek
epileptic	*épileptique*	(z)ay·pee·lep·teek

I'm allergic to ...	*Je suis allergique ...*	zher swee za·lair·zheek ...
antibiotics	*aux antibiotiques*	o zon·tee·byo·teek
aspirin	*à l'aspirine*	a las·pee·reen
bees	*aux abeilles*	o za·bay·yer
nuts	*aux noix*	o nwa
peanuts	*aux cacahuètes*	o ka·ka·wet
penicillin	*à la pénicilline*	a la pay·nee·see·leen

antiseptic	*l'antiseptique*	lon·tee·sep·teek
aspirin	*l'aspirine*	las·pee·reen
condoms	*des préservatifs*	day pray·zair·va·teef
contraceptive	*le contraceptif*	ler kon·tra·sep·teef
diarrhoea	*la diarrhée*	la dya·ray
medicine	*le médicament*	ler may·dee·ka·mon
nausea	*la nausée*	la no·zay
sunblock cream	*la crème solaire*	la krem so·lair
tampons	*des tampons hygiéniques*	day tom·pon ee·zhen·eek

LANGUAGE DIFFICULTIES

Do you speak English?
Parlez-vous anglais? par·lay·voo ong·lay
Does anyone here speak English?
Y a-t-il quelqu'un qui parle anglais? ya·teel kel·kung kee par long·glay
How do you say ... in French?
Comment est-ce qu'on dit ... en français? ko·mon es·kon dee ... on fron·say
What does ... mean?
Que veut dire ...? ker ver deer ...
I understand.
Je comprends. zher kom·pron
I don't understand.
Je ne comprends pas. zher ner kom·pron pa
Could you write it down, please?
Est-ce que vous pouvez l'écrire? es·ker voo poo·vay lay·kreer
Can you show me (on the map)?
Pouvez-vous m'indiquer (sur la carte)? poo·vay·voo mun·dee·kay (sewr la kart)

NUMBERS

0	*zero*	zay·ro
1	*un*	un
2	*deux*	der
3	*trois*	trwa
4	*quatre*	ka·trer
5	*cinq*	sungk
6	*six*	sees
7	*sept*	set
8	*huit*	weet
9	*neuf*	nerf
10	*dix*	dees
11	*onze*	onz
12	*douze*	dooz
13	*treize*	trez
14	*quatorze*	ka·torz
15	*quinze*	kunz
16	*seize*	sez
17	*dix-sept*	dee·set
18	*dix-huit*	dee·zweet
19	*dix-neuf*	deez·nerf
20	*vingt*	vung
21	*vingt et un*	vung tay un
22	*vingt-deux*	vung·der
30	*trente*	tront
40	*quarante*	ka·ront
50	*cinquante*	sung·kont
60	*soixante*	swa·sont
70	*soixante-dix*	swa·son·dees
80	*quatre-vingts*	ka·trer·vung
90	*quatre-vingt-dix*	ka·trer·vung·dees
100	*cent*	son
1000	*mille*	meel
How many?	*Combien?*	kom·byun

PAPERWORK

name	*nom*	nom
nationality	*nationalité*	na·syo·na·lee·tay
date/place of birth	*date/place de naissance*	dat/plas der nay·sons
sex/gender	*sexe*	seks
passport	*passeport*	pas·por
visa	*visa*	vee·za

QUESTION WORDS

Who?	*Qui?*	kee
What?	*Quoi?*	kwa
What is it?	*Qu'est-ce que c'est?*	kes·ker say
When?	*Quand?*	kon
Where?	*Où?*	oo
Which?	*Quel/Quelle?*	kel
Why?	*Pourquoi?*	poor·kwa
How?	*Comment?*	ko·mon

SHOPPING & SERVICES

I'd like to buy ...
Je voudrais acheter ... zher voo·dray ash·tay ...
How much is it?
C'est combien? say kom·byun
I don't like it.
Cela ne me plaît pas. ser·la ner mer play pa
May I look at it?
Est-ce que je peux le voir? es·ker zher per ler vwar
I'm just looking.
Je regarde. zher rer·gard
It's cheap.
Ce n'est pas cher. ser nay pa shair
It's too expensive.
C'est trop cher. say tro shair
I'll take it.
Je le prends. zher ler pron

Can I pay by ...?	*Est-ce que je peux payer avec ...?*	es·ker zher per pay·yay a·vek ...
credit card	*ma carte de crédit*	ma kart der kray·dee
travellers cheques	*des chèques de voyage*	day shek der vwa·yazh

more	*plus*	plew
less	*moins*	mwa
smaller	*plus petit*	plew per·tee
bigger	*plus grand*	plew gron

Where can I can find ...?	*Où est-ce qu'on peut trouver ...?*	oo es·kon per troo·vay ...

I'm looking for ...	*Je cherche ...*	zhe shersh ...
a bank	*une banque*	ewn bonk
the bazaar	*le bazar*	ler ba·zar
the ... embassy	*l'ambassade de ...*	lam·ba·sahd der ...
the hospital	*l'hôpital*	lo·pee·tal
the market	*le marché*	ler mar·shay
the police	*la police*	la po·lees
the post office	*le bureau de poste*	ler bew·ro der post
a public phone	*une cabine téléphonique*	ewn ka·been tay·lay·fo·neek
a public toilet	*les toilettes*	lay twa·let

TIME & DATES

What time is it?	*Quelle heure est-il?*	kel er e til
It's (8) o'clock.	*Il est (huit) heures.*	il e (weet) er
It's half past ...	*Il est (...) heures et demie.*	il e (...) er e day·mee
in the morning	*du matin*	dew ma·tun
in the afternoon	*de l'après-midi*	der la·pray·mee·dee
in the evening	*du soir*	dew swar
today	*aujourd'hui*	o·zhoor·dwee
tomorrow	*demain*	der·mun
yesterday	*hier*	yair
day	*jour*	zhoor
month	*mois*	mwa
week	*semaine*	se·men
year	*année*	a·nay
early	*tôt*	to
late	*en retard*	on rer·tar
daily	*quotidien* (m)	*ko·tee·dyun*
	quotidienne (f)	*ko·tee·dyen*

Monday	*lundi*	lun·dee
Tuesday	*mardi*	mar·dee
Wednesday	*mercredi*	mair·krer·dee
Thursday	*jeudi*	zher·dee
Friday	*vendredi*	von·drer·dee
Saturday	*samedi*	sam·dee
Sunday	*dimanche*	dee·monsh

January	*janvier*	zhon·vyay
February	*février*	fayv·ryay
March	*mars*	mars
April	*avril*	a·vreel
May	*mai*	may
June	*juin*	zhwun
July	*juillet*	zhwee·yay
August	*août*	oot
September	*septembre*	sep·tom·brer
October	*octobre*	ok·to·brer
November	*novembre*	no·vom·brer
December	*décembre*	day·som·brer

TRANSPORT

Public Transport

What time does ... leave/arrive?	*À quelle heure part/arrive ...?*	a kel er par/a·reev ...
boat	*le bateau*	ler ba·to
bus	*le bus*	ler bews
plane	*l'avion*	la·vyon
train	*le train*	ler trun

I'd like a ... ticket.	*Je voudrais un billet ...*	zher voo·dray un bee·yay ...
one-way	*simple*	sum·pler
return	*aller et retour*	a·lay ay rer·toor
1st class	*de première classe*	der prem·yair klas
2nd class	*de deuxième classe*	der der·zyem klas

I want to go to ...
Je voudrais aller à ... zher voo·dray a·lay a ...

The train has been delayed.
Le train est en retard. ler trun et on rer·tar

The train has been cancelled.
Le train a été annulé. ler trun a ay·tay a·new·lay

the first	*le premier* (m)	ler prer·myay
	la première (f)	la prer·myair
the last	*le dernier* (m)	ler dair·nyay
	la dernière (f)	la dair·nyair
platform number	*le numéro de quai*	ler new·may·ro der kay
ticket office	*le guichet*	ler gee·shay
timetable	*l'horaire*	lo·rair
train station	*la gare*	la gar

Private Transport

I'd like to hire a/an...	*Je voudrais louer ...*	zher voo·dray loo·way ...
car	*une voiture*	ewn vwa·tewr
4WD	*un quatre-quatre*	un kat·kat
motorbike	*une moto*	ewn mo·to
bicycle	*un vélo*	un vay·lo

Is this the road to ...?
C'est la route pour ...? say la root poor ...

Where's a service station?
Où est-ce qu'il y a une station-service? oo es·keel ya ewn sta·syon·ser·vees

Please fill it up.
Le plein, s'il vous plaît. ler plun seel voo play

I'd like ... litres.
Je voudrais ... litres. zher voo·dray ... lee·trer

petrol/gas	*essence*	ay·sons
diesel	*diesel*	dyay·zel

(How long) Can I park here?
(Combien de temps) Est-ce que je peux stationner ici? (kom·byun der tom) es·ker zher per sta·syo·nay ee·see?

Where do I pay?
Où est-ce que je paie? oo es·ker zher pay?

I need a mechanic.
J'ai besoin d'un mécanicien. zhay ber·zwun dun may·ka·nee·syun

The car/motorbike has broken down (at ...)
La voiture moto est tombée en panne (à ...) la vwa·tewr/mo·to ay tom·bay on pan (a ...)

The car/motorbike won't start.
La voiture/moto ne veut pas démarrer. la vwa·tewr/mo·to ner ver pa day·ma·ray

I have a flat tyre.
Mon pneu est à plat. mom pner ay ta pla

I've run out of petrol.
Je suis en panne d'essence. zher swee zon pan day·sons

I had an accident.
J'ai eu un accident. zhay ew un ak·see·don

TRAVEL WITH CHILDREN

Is there a/an ...?
Y a-t-il ...? ya teel ...

I need a/an ...
J'ai besoin ... zhay ber·zwun ...

car baby seat
d'un siège-enfant dun syezh·on·fon

child-minding service
d'une garderie dewn gar·dree

children's menu
d'un menu pour enfants dun mer·new poor on·fon

disposable nappies/diapers
de couches-culottes der koosh·kew·lot

infant milk formula
de lait maternisé de lay ma·ter·nee·zay

(English-speaking) babysitter
d'une baby-sitter (qui parle anglais) dewn ba·bee·see·ter (kee parl ong·glay)

highchair
d'une chaise haute dewn shay zot

potty
d'un pot de bébé dun po der bay·bay

stroller
d'une poussette dewn poo·set

Are children allowed?
Les enfants sont permis? lay zon·fon son pair·mee

LANGUAGE

Glossary

This glossary includes terms and abbreviations you may come across during your travels in Tunisia. Where appropriate, the capital letter in brackets indicates whether the terms are French (F) or Arabic (A).

Abbasids – Baghdad-based ruling dynasty (AD 749–1258) of the Arab/Islamic Empire
Africa Proconsularis – Roman province of Africa
Aghlabids – Arab dynasty based in Kairouan who ruled Tunisia (AD 800–909)
ain (A) – water source or spring
Allah (A) – Muslim name for God
alloucha (A) – thick-pile, woven, woollen Berber rug
Almohads – Berber rulers of Spain and North Africa (1130–1269)
Almoravids – dynasty of Berbers from the Sahara; reigned from 1061 to 1106 in Morocco and the Maghreb, and later in Andalusia, after 1086.
ASM – Association de Sauvegarde de la Medina; group charged with preserving the medinas of a number of Tunisian towns
assaba (A) – headband worn by Berber women
auberge de jeunesse (F) – youth hostel affiliated to Hostelling International

bab (A) – city gate
bakhnoug (A) – traditional shawl worn by Berber women
Barbary Coast – European term for the Mediterranean coast of North Africa in the 16th to 19th centuries
basilica – Roman building used for public administration; early Christian church
Berbers – indigenous (non-Arab) people of North Africa
bey – provincial governor in the Ottoman Empire; rulers of Tunisia from the 17th century until independence in 1957
bezness – local slang for beach-gigolo 'business'
borj (A) – fort (literally 'tower')
boukha (A) – local spirit made from figs
brochette (F) – kebab
burnous (A) – hooded winter cape worn by men

calèche (F) – horse-drawn carriage
caliph – Islamic ruler, originally referred to the successors of the Prophet Mohammed
camionnette (F) – small pick-up used as a taxi
capitol – main temple of a Roman town, usually situated in the forum
caravanserai – see *funduq*
casse-croûte (F) – Tunisian fast food; a sandwich made from half a French loaf stuffed with a variety of fillings
centre des stages et des vacances (F) – holiday camps
chechia (A) – red felt hat
chorba (A) – soup, also spelt *shorba*
chott (A) – salt lake or marsh
confort (F) – class above 1st class on passenger trains
corniche (F) – coastal road
corsairs – pirates, especially those who operated on the North African coast from the 16th to the 19th century
couscous – semolina granules, the staple food of Tunisia

dar (A) – town house or palace
deglat ennour (A) – type of date (literally 'finger of light')
destour (A) – literally 'constitution' but also the name for Habib Bourguiba's political party before independence
dey – the Ottoman army's equivalent of a sergeant; rulers of Tunisia in the 16th century
diwan – assembly (in the Ottoman Empire)

eid (A) – feast
Eid al-Adha (A) – feast of Sacrifice marking the pilgrimage to Mecca; sometimes called Eid al-Kebir
Eid al-Fitr (A) – feast of the Breaking of the Fast, celebrated at the end of Ramadan
emir (A) – military commander or governor
erg (A) – sand sea; desert

Fatimids – Muslim dynasty (AD 909–1171) who defeated the Aghlabids and ruled Tunisia from Mahdia from AD 909 to 969
forum – open space at the centre of Roman towns
fouta (A) – cotton bath towel provided in a *hammam*
funduq (A) – former lodging houses or inns for the travelling merchants of the camel caravans, also known as *caravanserai;* Arab word for hotel

gare routière (F) – bus station
gargotte (F) – cheap restaurant that serves basic food
gargoulette (F) – pottery amphora used in traditional octopus catching technique on Jerba
ghar (A) – cave
ghorfa (A) – literally, room; especially a long, barrel-vaulted room built to store grain
guetiffa – a thick-pile, knotted Berber carpet

Hafsids – rulers of *Ifriqiyya* from the 13th to the 16th century
haj (A) – the pilgrimage to the holy sites in and around Mecca, the pinnacle of a devout Muslim's life
hammam (A) – public bathhouse

harissa (A) – spicy chilli paste
harout (A) – traditional Jerban weaver's workshop
hedeyed (A) – finely engraved, wide bracelets made of gold or silver
hejab (A) – woman's veil or headscarf
Hejira (A) – Mohammed's flight from Mecca in AD 622; also the name of the Muslim calendar
Hilalian tribes – tribes of Upper Egypt who invaded the Maghreb in the 11th century, causing great destruction
Hizb al-Nahda – Renaissance Party, the main Islamic opposition party
Husseinites – dynasty of beys who ruled Tunisia from 1705 to 1957

Ibadites – an offshoot of the Kharijite sect found only on Jerba, in the villages of the M'Zab Valley in Algeria and in Oman
ibn (A) – son of
Ifriqiyya – Arab province of North Africa, including Tunisia and parts of Libya
iftar (A) – (also spelt *ftur*) the breaking of the day's fast during Ramadan
imam (A) – religious teacher

jebel (A) – hill or mountain
jihad (A) – holy war

kalaa (A) – Berber hill fort
kasbah (A) – fort or citadel
kassa (A) – a coarse mitten used in the steam room of a *hammam*
Kharijites – puritanical Islamic sect, which broke away from the mainstream Sunnis in AD 657 and inspired Berber rebellions from the 8th to the 10th century
kholkal (A) – gold or silver anklets
khomsa – Hand-of-Fatima motif
khutba (A) – weekly sermon in the mosque
kilim (A) – woven rug decorated with typical Berber motifs
koubba (A) – small domed tomb
ksar (A) – (plural *ksour*) a fortified Berber stronghold consisting of many *ghorfas*
ksibah (A) – small fort
ksour (A)– (singular *ksar*) fortified Berber stronghold consisting of many *ghorfas*
kuttab (A) – Quranic primary school

Limes Tripolitanus – the defensive line developed by the Romans in southern Tunisia
louage (F) – shared long-distance taxi

Maghreb – term used to describe northwest Africa, including Morocco, Algeria and Tunisia
maison des jeunes (F) – government-run youth hostel
malouf (A) – musical form that originated in Andalusia and adopted as traditional Tunisian music
marabout (A) – Muslim holy man or saint
masjid (A) – small local mosque
medersa (A) – Quranic school
medina (A) – city; the old quarter of Tunisian towns and cities
menzel (A) – fortified family dwelling found on Jerba
mergoum (A) – woven carpet with geometric designs
mihrab (A) – vaulted niche in a mosque, which indicates the direction of Mecca
minaret(A) – tower (literally 'lighthouse') of a mosque from which the *muezzin* calls the faithful to prayer
minbar (A) – the pulpit in a mosque
mouloud (A) – Maghreb term for the Moulid an-Nabi, the feast celebrating the birth of the Prophet Mohammed
moussem (A) – pilgrimage to a shrine or to a tomb of a *marabout*
muezzin (A) – mosque official who calls the faithful to prayer
Muradites – line of Tunisian *beys*, ruling from the 17th to 18th century

nador (A) – watchtower
Numidians – tribe from present-day Algeria, who once controlled Northern Tunisia; founders of the cities of Bulla Regia, Sicca (El-Kef) and Thugga (Dougga)

ONAT – the Office National de l'Artisanat Tunisien; government-run fixed-price craft shops
ONTT – Office National du Tourisme Tunisien; government-run national tourist office
Ottoman Empire – former Turkish Empire, of which Tunisia was part; based in Constantinople from the late 13th century to the end of WWI
oud – lute
oued (A) – river; also dry riverbed
Ouergherma (A) – 17th-century Berber confederation that ruled from Medenine

palmeraie (F) – palm grove; the area around an oasis where date palms, vegetables and fruit are grown
pasha – provincial governor or high official in the Ottoman Empire
pâtisserie (F) – cake and pastry shop
pension (F) – guesthouse
Phoenicians – a great seafaring nation, based in modern Lebanon, which dominated trade in the Mediterranean in the 1st millennium BC; founders of Carthage
PSD – Parti Socialiste Destourien (called the Neo-Destour Party before 1964); the first nationalist party in Tunisia
Punic – the Phoenician culture that evolved in North Africa
Punic Wars – three wars waged between Rome and Carthage in the 3rd and 2nd centuries BC, resulting in the destruction of Carthage by the Romans in 146 BC

qibla (A) – the direction of Mecca in a mosque, indicated by the *mihrab*
Quran (A) – the holy book of Islam

Ramadan – ninth month of the Muslim year, a time of fasting
razzegoui (A) – a large white grape that ripens to a pink blush
RCD – Rassemblement Constitutionel Democratique; President Ben Ali's ruling party
ribat (A) – fortified Islamic monastery
rôtisserie (F) – basic restaurant serving roast chicken

Sahel – eastern part of central Tunisia occupying the large, fertile coastal bulge between the Gulf of Hammamet and the Gulf of Gabès
sand rose – crystallised gypsum found in desert and sold as souvenirs
Sharia'a (A) – Quranic law
sheesha (A) – water pipe used to smoke tobacco; also spelt *chicha*
Shiite – one of two main Islamic sects (see also Sunni); its followers believe that the true *imams* are descended from Ali
sidi (A) – saint
skifa (A) – gate
SNCFT – Société Nationale des Chemins de Fer Tunisiens; the national railway company
SNTRI – Société Nationale du Transport Interurbain; the national bus company
souq (A) – market
stele – gravestone
Sufi – follower of Islamic mystical orders that emphasise dancing, chanting and trances to attain unity with God
Sunni – the main Islamic sect (see also Shiite) derived from followers of the Umayyad caliphate
syndicat d'initiative (F) – municipal tourist office

Taxiphone – public telephone
Tell – the high plains of the Tunisian Dorsale, in central Tunisia
thibarine – a local spirit from the village of Thibar near Dougga
tophet – sacrificial site
tourbet (A) – mausoleum

Umayyad – first great dynasty of Arab Muslim rulers (AD 661–750), based in Damascus

zaouia (A) – a complex surrounding the tomb of a saint
zone touristique (F) – tourist strip

Behind the Scenes

THIS BOOK

The first two editions of Tunisia were written by David Willett, the third-edition authors were Anthony Ham and Abigail Hole and this fourth edition was written by Abigail Hole, Michael Grosberg and Daniel Robinson. Dr Caroline Evans wrote the Health chapter and Rafik Tlatli wrote the Food & Drink chapter with Abigail Hole. This guidebook was commissioned in Lonely Planet's Melbourne office, and produced by the following:

Commissioning Editors Jessa Boanas-Dewes, Stefanie di Trocchio
Coordinating Editor Jeanette Wall
Coordinating Cartographer Sally Gerdan
Coordinating Layout Designer Cara Smith
Managing Editor Suzannah Shwer
Managing Cartographer Adrian Persoglia
Assisting Editors Michelle Bennett, Monique Choy, Simone Egger, Alexandra Payne, Helen Yeates
Assisting Cartographer Joshua Geoghegan
Cover Designer Mary Nelson-Parker
Colour Designer Steven Cann
Project Managers Eoin Dunlevy, Craig Kilburn
Language Content Coordinator Quentin Frayne
Language Consultant Kathryn Stapley

Thanks to Shahara Ahmed, Yvonne Bischofberger, Carolyn Boicos, David Burnett, Sin Choo, Sally Darmody, Mark Germanchis, Rebecca Lalor, Raphael Richards, Averil Robertson, Fiona Siseman, Nick Stebbing, Marg Toohey, Celia Wood

THANKS

ABIGAIL HOLE

Biggest cheers to my on-the-road research team: Luca and Gabriel (and especially to Luca for making this possible). Many thanks also to Mum and Ant for their help in Tunisia, to Rafik Tlatli and to my co-authors Michael and Daniel. Thanks to Vittorio Romiti for help with recommendations, as well as the many readers who sent in contributions. Mille grazie a Anna, Marcello, Mum e Ant per il loro lavoro di babysitting, and to all those at Lonely Planet who worked so hard on the guide, especially Stefanie, Jessa, Marg and Jeanette.

MICHAEL GROSBERG

Thanks go out to Mahor, the National Guard officer in need of a ride in the desert, who shared his thoughts and insight into Tunisian culture and politics; to Najwa Meki for her reflections on the media, education and women's issues; to all the Tunisians who without fail were warm and hospitable to a sweaty and hot stranger; to my fellow authors Abigail Hole and Daniel Robinson; to Rebecca Tessler for keeping me sane while I stayed up nights writing with only her affection, support and coffee in my belly; and finally to my niece the Sashmeister who somehow managed to learn how to walk while I was gone.

DANIEL ROBINSON

Countless Tunisians from all walks of life went out of their way to assist me in my travels, most of

THE LONELY PLANET STORY

The story begins with a classic travel adventure: Tony and Maureen Wheeler's 1972 journey across Europe and Asia to Australia. There was no useful information about the overland trail then, so Tony and Maureen published the first Lonely Planet guidebook to meet a growing need.

From a kitchen table, Lonely Planet has grown to become the largest independent travel publisher in the world, with offices in Melbourne (Australia), Oakland (USA) and London (UK). Today Lonely Planet guidebooks cover the globe. There is an ever-growing list of books and information in a variety of media. Some things haven't changed. The main aim is still to make it possible for adventurous travellers to get out there – to explore and better understand the world.

At Lonely Planet we believe travellers can make a positive contribution to the countries they visit – if they respect their host communities and spend their money wisely. Every year 5% of company profit is donated to charities around the world.

them completely unaware that I was researching a guidebook. Especially useful was the practical advice on transport options proffered enthusiastically by louage and bus drivers and by Tunisian railways staff.

People who shared their intimate knowledge of Tunisia's rich heritage include Rachid Bouallegue, technical director of the ASM in Le Kef; Hedi Selini of Utica; and Kamel Aloui of the Chemtou museum. I wish Asma and Douha of Béja success in their exams. It was a real pleasure louaging it through the remotest Kroumirie Mountains with Brendan Markey of Oz and Leeds. Lara Gibson and Lewis Kinnair of the UK displayed admirable forbearance as I covered the northern coast. During the write-up stage, Yossi Buki and his staff – Eugen, Lev, Roman and Slava – as well as Orit Ram and Nava Engel provided ever-constructive diversions. I am also indebted to Meital Lior and Shiri Rosen for their online encouragement as the manuscript inched towards completion.

Finally, I'd like to express my special thanks to Réka Kocsis of Sopron, Hungary for meticulously keeping tabs on my Tunisian peregrinations.

OUR READERS

Many thanks to the travellers who used the last edition and wrote to us with helpful hints, useful advice and interesting anecdotes:

A J Adams, Stephen Arthur **B** Margaret Bahr, D L & D C Baker, Liz & Mike Bissett, Susan Boxall, Samuel Brind, Antonella Broglia, Linda Brown, Leslie Burnett **C** Fiona Cleland, Nick Comfort, Jimmy Cornell, Angela Costanzo, Kylie Crawley, Helen & David Crewe **D** Richard Davies **E** Paul Engels **F** Gail Falk, Debbie Flint **G** Manish Gandhi, Damaris Garzon-Marques, Maximilan Gauger, Marina Greco, Liesl Groenewald, Linda Gunnewegh **H** Hotan Haghiran, Lesley Hall, Heikki Happonen, Kate Hawkins, Sarah Hedley, Beth Hollowell, Valerie M Hume **J** Jussi Jaaskelainen, Nicola James, Anja Jelavic, Tom Jestico, Simon Jeynes **K** Anna Kadlecková, Martin Kent, M Krasik **L** Duncan Lamberton, Domonkos Lendvai, Andrea Lewis, Peter Lilley, Christian Lyng **M** Aryn Machell, Dave Manderscheid, Sara Marcelli, Roberto Marcos, Donald & Emily Martini, Cedric McCallum, Gregory McElwain, Larry Meilack, Graham Mitchell, Peter Murakami **N** Serhat Narsap, Jakhan Nguyen, Willemijn Noom **O** Daniel O'Kelly, Peter & Therese O'Neill, Sylvia Osche **P** Francesco Paterno, Gustavo & Stina Pena, Cissi Persson, Ruth Pojer **R** Tony Rees, Luis Rodríguez **S** Enrico Salvotti, Chris Score, Adrain Scott, Dave Shackson, Karen Shaw, Christopher Sorensen, Jennifer Spreen, Christian Steen, Isla Stephenson **T** Gustavo Tommasini, Bruno Trematore **V** Ada Valencic, Ton van de Vis, Isabelle Velleman, Saffier Verkaik, Serena Viviani **W** Ian Wadley, Andrea Wallis, Duncan Watson, L Wong

SEND US YOUR FEEDBACK

We love to hear from travellers – your comments keep us on our toes and help make our books better. Our well-travelled team reads every word on what you loved or loathed about this book. Although we cannot reply individually to postal submissions, we always guarantee that your feedback goes straight to the appropriate authors, in time for the next edition. Each person who sends us information is thanked in the next edition – and the most useful submissions are rewarded with a free book.

To send us your updates – and find out about Lonely Planet events, newsletters and travel news – visit our award-winning website: **www.lonelyplanet.com/contact**.

Note: we may edit, reproduce and incorporate your comments in Lonely Planet products such as guidebooks, websites and digital products, so let us know if you don't want your comments reproduced or your name acknowledged. For a copy of our privacy policy visit www.lonelyplanet.com/privacy.

Index

4WD trips 286

A

Abbes 256
accommodation 283-5, *see also individual locations*
activities 285-7, *see also* camel trekking, cycling, diving, dune skiing, go-karting, golf, hiking, horse-riding, microlight flights, quad biking, sailing, water sports
Aeneid, The 25, 49, 90, 91
Aghlabid basins 203
Aghlabids 29, 53, 185, 201, 203
Ain Draham 139-42
air travel
  airfares 303-4
  to/from Tunisia 302-5
  within Tunisia 307
alcohol 61
Aleppo pine 55, 179
Almohads 30
Ammædara 167-8, 177, **168**
animals 54-6, *see also* birds, camels, cats, crocodiles, elephants, flamingos
Antonine Baths 94
apartments 285
archaeological sites
  Ammædara 167-8, **168**
  Bulla Regia 145-7, **145**, 171
  Carthage 93
  Chemtou 147-9
  Cillium 178
  Dougga 156-9, **157**, 5, 172
  Gightis 240
  Kerkouane 117-19, **117**
  Mactaris 165-7, **166**
  Meninx 282
  Neapolis 111
  Pupput 104
  Sufetula 180-2, **181**, 172
  Thuburbo Majus 153-5, **154**
  Uthina 151
  Utica 130-1
architecture 48-53
  Berber 52, 228, 235, 237, 8, 174
  Islamic 52-3, 175, 176
  Jerban 274
  Punic 49
  Roman 49
arts 44-53, *see also* calligraphy, carpets, dance, literature, mosaics, painting
ATMs 295
auberge de jeunesse 284, 290

B

Barbossa, Khair ed-Din 30, 135, 270
Bardo Museum 47, 50, 66, **51**, 170
bargaining 296
bars 63
bathrooms 299
El-Bayadha 26
beaches 102, 285-6
  Barrage Port Princes 121
  Bizerte 127
  Boujaffar Beach 191
  Cap Serrat 134
  Hammamet 105
  Hamman Jebli 115
  Korba Lagoon 114
  El-Mansourah 115
  Oued Kassab 115
  Raf Raf 131-2
  Ras el-Drek 120
  Sidi Ali el-Mekki 132
  Sidi Mahres 132, 280
Béja 143
Belvedere Rocks 258
ben Ali, Hussein 30, 75, 160
ben Ali, Zine el-Abidine 33
Beni Kheddache 239-40
Beni Khiar 114
Beni Metir 142-3
Berber people 26, 27, 29, 49, 52, 162, 233
Berber villages 235-7, 174
Bey, Ahmed 132
bicycle travel, *see* cycling
bin Nooman, Hassan 67, 234
Bir Barouta 203
Bir Soltane 252
bird-watching 286
birds 114, 131, 286
Bizerte 123-30, **126**, 171
boat travel 306-8
books 43, 48, 54, *see also* literature
  food 58, 60, 61, 62, 64, 65
  health 315
  history 24, 28, 29, 31, 32, 40, 43
  Islam 40
  travel 14, 16, 288
border crossings 306
Borj Enna 217
Borj Ghazi Mustapha 275
Borj el-Hissar 220
Borj Kastil 282
Borj el-Kebir 211
Borj el-Khadra 253
Bou Hedma National Park 55, 56
Boujaffa Beach 191
Boukornine National Park 56
Bourguiba, Habib 24, 28, 31-2, 33, 43, 196, 198
briq 59, 64
Bulla Regia 49, 145-7, **145**, 171
bus travel 308-9
business hours 287
Byrsa Hill 93
Byzantines 28, 47, 125, 156, 181

C

Caesar, Julius 27, 185, 196
cafés 63
calligraphy 46
camel trekking 243, 248, 286, 312, 8
camels 54, 162, 248
camionnette travel 309
camping 284
Cap Bon 100-21, **101**
Cap Serrat 134-5
Capsian people 24, 255
car travel 306, 309-12
carbon offset scheme 303
carpets 48, 141, 206-7, 297, 8
Carthage 24-6, 66, 90-6
  attractions 91-5
  history 90-1
  travel to/from 96
Carthage International Festival 291
Carthage International Film Festival 291
cash 295
casino 281

catacombs 191
cathedrals, *see* churches
cats 55
Cave d'Ali Berbere 279
Cedghiane 280
Cedouikech 279
cell phones 299
cemeteries 94, 143, 144
ceramics 48, 111, 134, 297
Chak Wak Park 256
Chambi National Park 179
Chebika 262
Chemtou 147-9
Chenini 236
children, travel with 287-8, 318, 325
  food 64
  itineraries 15
  Tunis 79-80
Chott el-Jerid 261, 7
churches
  Cathedral of St Vincent de Paul 77
  Church of St Peter 163
  Damous el-Karita Basilica 94
  La Basilique 137
Cillium 178
cinema 44-5, 84
climate 288
climate change 303
Colosseum (El-Jem) 208, 5
consulates 290-1
cork 148
corsairs, *see* pirates
costs 14, 283-4
courses 79, 128, 288
couscous 60
credit cards 295
crocodiles 281
culture 36-43
customs regulations 288-9
cycling 140, 308, *see also* mountain biking

D

Dah Dah Happy Land Park 79
dance 46
Dar Ben Abdallah Museum 76
Dar Chaabane 114
Dar Ennejma Ezzahra 96-7
Dar Jellouli Museum 217
Dar Othman 76
date palms 60

000 Map pages
000 Photograph pages

deep vein thrombosis (DVT) 315
dehydration 317
Destour (Constitution) Party 31
diarrhoea 317
Dido 91
digital photography 295
dinosaurs 232, 256
diphtheria 316
disabled travellers 300
diving 286
  Bizerte 127
  Hammamet 105
  Mahdia 212
  Port el-Kantaoui 195
  Tabarka 137
Dougga 156-9, **157**, 5, 172
Dougga Festival 156
Douiret 236-7
Douz 243-9, **244**, **245**
Dragut 135, 270, 275
Drake, Sir Francis 132
drinks 61
driving licence 309
dune skiing 286

E

economy 34
ecotourism 140, 312-3
Eid al-Adha 42, 62, 292
Eid al-Fitr 41, 62, 292
electricity 283
elephants 26, 54
Elissa, *see* Dido
email services 293
embassies 290-1
emergencies, *see inside front cover*
English Patient, The 216, 251, 262
environmental issues 56-7, 133, 148
erosion 56
Erriadh 277-8
esparto grass 180, 296
etiquette 36, 64
exchange rates, *see inside front cover*

F

El-Faouar 249
Fatimids 29, 67, 201, 211
fax services 299
El-Feija National Park 56, 149
ferry travel 307, 308
festivals 291-2
  Cap Bon International Festival 106
  Carthage International Festival 95-6
  Carthage International Film Festival 291
  Dougga Festival 156
  Falconry Festival 120
  Festival of Malouf 291
  Festival of the Ksour 46, 237, 292
  itineraries 21
  Jazz Festival 138
  El-Jem International Symphonic Music Festival 209
  Latinos Festival 138
  Oasis Festival 258
  Raï Festival 138
  Sahara Festival 245-6, 175
  Tabarka International Jazz Festival 138
  World Music Festival 138
film festivals 291
films 25, 34, 44-5
  English Patient, The 216, 251, 262
  Monty Python's Life of Brian 14, 17, 198, 230
  Star Wars 22, 52, 228, 229, 235, 261, 263
Flamingo Point 280
flamingos 114, 131, 286
food 58-65, 292
  books 58, 60, 61, 62, 64, 65
  customs 64
  eating places 63
  internet resources 58, 62
  vegetarianism 64
football 38-43, 84
French Protectorate 30-1

G

Gabès 223-7, **223**, **224**
Gafsa 265-7, **266**
galleries 47-8
Gammarth 99
gay travellers 292
Genoese Fort 137, 171
geography 54-7
Ghar el-Melh 132
Ghardimao 149
Ghomrassen 235
Al-Ghriba Synagogue 162
El-Ghriba Synagogue 277, 176
Gightis 240
go-karting 286
golf 281, 286
government 23
Grand Erg Oriental 252
Grand Sud 253
Great Mosque (Béja) 143

Great Mosque (Bizerte) 125
Great Mosque (Kairouan) 202-3
Great Mosque (Le Kef) 162
Great Mosque (Mahdia) 211
Great Mosque (Sfax) 216
Great Mosque (Sousse) 189
Guellala 278-9
Guermessas 235-6

H
Haddèj 229-30
Hadrian 94, 130, 153, 155
Haidra 167-8, 177, **168**
Hammam Bourguiba 142
Hammam Lif 99
Hammam Mellegue 164-5
Hammamet 101-9, **103**, **105**, 170
Hammamet International Festival 291
hammams 71, 286
Hamuda Pasha Mosque 75
Hand of Fatima 162, 296
handicrafts 141, 296
Hannibal Barca 26, 187
El-Haouaria 119-20
Hara Seghira 277-8
harissa 58
health 314-18
heat illness 317
henna 226
hepatitis 316
hiking 140, 287
history 24-35
  books 24, 27, 28, 31, 32, 40, 43
  Byzantine 28
  French Protectorate 30-1
  independence 31-2
  Islam 28
  Ottomans 30
  Phoenicans 24
  Roman rule 26-7
  Vandal 28
hitchhiking 251, 311
HIV 316
holidays 292
Homer 272
horse-riding 140, 258, 287
hostels 284
hot springs 133, 164, 250
  Hammam Bourguiba 142
  Hammam Mellegue 164-5
  Korbous 121
  Ksar Ghilane251
Hôtel Sidi Driss 228, 229
hotels 284-5
Houmt Souq 272-7, **273**

I
Ibadis 280
ibn al-Aglab, Ibrahim 29
Ichkeul National Park 56, 132-3, 286
Île Chergui 220
Île Gharbi 220
immigration regulations 302
independence 31-2
insurance
  car 310-11
  health 293, 314
  travel 293
International Short Film Festival 291
internet access 293
internet resources 16, 45
  arts 40, 46
  environmental issues 56, 57
  food 58, 62
  health 315, 318
  religion 39, 41, 58
  travel 303-6, 310
Islam 39-43
  customs 41-3
  history of 39-43
  in Tunisia 42-3
Islamic holidays 41, 292
Islamic Museum 50
itineraries 11, 17-22

J
jasmine 193
Jebel Abiod 119
Jebel Biri 140
Jebel Chambi 54, 179
Jebel Dahar 223
El-Jem 207-9
El-Jem International Symphonic Music Festival 291
Jendouba 143-5
Jerba 269-82, **270**
Jericho rose 56
jewellery 296-7
Judaism 39, 278
Jugurtha 151, 177
Jugurtha's Table 177, 6
Justinian 28

K
Al-Kahina 208, 233
Kairouan 199-207, **200**, 173
  accommodation 204-5
  attractions 202
  travel to/from 207
  travel within 207
Kasbah Mosque 74
kasbahs 53
  Bizerte 125
  Hammamet 104
  Le Kef 162
  Sousse 190
Kasserine 177-80
Kebili 250-1
Kélibia 114-17
Kerkennah Islands 220-1, **220**
Kerkouane 49, 117-19, **117**
Kharijites 280
Klee, Paul 47
Korba Lagoon 114
Korbous 121, 6
Kroumirie Mountains 54-5
Ksar Beni Barka 238
Ksar Beni Ghedir 235
Ksar Ezzahra 238
Ksar Ghilane 251-2
Ksar Haddada 235
Ksar Hallouf 240
Ksar Jelidet 238
Ksar Joumaa 239
Ksar Medenine 238
Ksar Megabla 232
Ksar Ouled Debbab 237
Ksar Ouled Soltane 237-8, 5
Ksar Rosfa 235
Ksar Tamelest 238
Ksar Tarcine 253
Ksour district 237, **234**

L
La Basilique 137
La Corbeille 264
La Goulette 89-90, **89**
La Marsa 98-9
La Porte du Desert 251
La Seguia 281
Lake Ichkeul 131
language 319-30
  Arabic 319-25
  French 326-30
  emergencies 323
Le Kef 160-4, **161**
legal matters 293-4
Les Aiguilles 137
lesbian travellers 292
Levaillant's woodpecker 286
Lezard Rouge 268
Limes Tripolitanus 251, 253, 262
literature 31, 43, 44, 49, *see also* books
louage travel 312-13
Louta Mosque 279

INDEX

M
Macke, Auguste 47
Mactaris, *see* Makthar
magazines 283
Mahdia 209-13, **210**
maisons des jeunes 284
Makthar 165-7, **166**
malouf 45
maps 294
Mareth 230
markets 111, 178, 298, *see also* souqs
Massinissa 25, 26, 27, 156, 165
Matmata 227-9, **223**
Mausoleum of Habib Bourguiba 198-9
Medenine 238-9
medersas 53, 75
medical services 316, *see also* health
Medina Festival 291
Meninx 282
meshoui 63
metalwork 296
Metameur 239
Metlaoui 267-8
metric conversions, *see inside front cover*
Mghit 238
microlight flights 286
Midès 262
Midoun 280
mobile phones 299
Monastir 196-9, **197**, 6
money 290, 294-5, *see also inside front cover*
Monty Python's Life of Brian 14, 17, 198, 230
mosaics 47, 173
mosques
  Great Mosque (Béja) 143
  Great Mosque (Bizerte) 125
  Great Mosque (Kairouan) 202-3
  Great Mosque (Le Kef) 162
  Great Mosque (Mahdia) 211
  Great Mosque (Sfax) 216
  Great Mosque (Sousse) 189
  Guellala Mosque 279
  Louta Mosque 279
  Hamuda Pasha Mosque 75
  Kasbah Mosque 74
  Mosque of Sidi Mahres 75
  Mosque of the Dyers 75
  Mosque of the Strangers 275
  Mosque of the Three Doors 203
  Mosque of the Turks 275
  Mosque of Youssef Dey 75
  Sahib El-Tabía Mosque 75
  Zaytouna (Great) Mosque 71-4, 169
motorcycle travel 306, 309-12
mountain biking 287
Mouvement des Démocratique Socialist (MDS) 34
museums
  Bardo Museum 47, 50, 66, **51**, 170
  Chemtou Museum 147
  Dar Ben Abdallah Museum 76
  Dar Charaït Museum 256
  Dar Jellouli Museum 217
  Gafsa Museum 265
  El-Jem Museum 209
  Kerkouane Museum 119
  Mactaris Museum 166
  Mahdia Museum 211
  Monastir Costume Museum 195
  Musée Berber 228
  Musée de Carthage 93
  Musée des Arts et Traditions Populaires 162
  Musée du Sahara 244
  Musée Memoire de la Terre 232
  Museum Dar Essid 190
  Museum of Islamic Art 198
  Museum of Popular Arts & Traditions 275
  Nabeul Museum 111
  Oceanographic Museum (Bizerte) 127
  Oceanographic Museum (Carthage) 95
  ONAT Museum 204
  Raqqada Islamic Art Museum 207
  Sbeitla Museum 180
  Sousse Archaeological Museum 190
  Utica Museum 130
  World War II Museum 230
music 45-6
  festivals 138, 209, 291

N
Nabeul 109-14, **110**, **112**
national parks 56-7
  Chambi National Park 179
  El-Feija National Park 56, 149
  Ichkeul National Park 132
natural air conditioning 240
Neapolis 111
Needles, the 137
Nefta 263-5, **263**
Néo-Destour Party 31-2
newspapers 39, 283
Nouil 249-50
Numidians, the 26, 27, 123, 151, 233

O
Oasis Festival 292
Oceanographic Museum (Carthage) 95
Octopus Festival 291
oils 75-6, 297
ONAT Museum 204
Ong Jemal 263
Othman Dey 30, 76
Oudhna 151
Ouled el-Cherif 264
Ouled el-Hadif 257-8

P
painting 47
palmeraies 225, 244, 256
passports 302
perfume 297
Phoenicians 24, 90, 118, 119, 233, 270
photography 295
pirates 30, 31, 76, 101, 115, 123, 270
planning 17-22, 290, 292, 295, 314
plants 55-7
poliomyelitis 316
politics 23
pollution 56
Pompey 130, 185
population 36, 38-43
Port el-Kantaoui 195-6
postal services 296
pottery, *see* ceramics
Punic Ports 95
Punic Wars 25, 130, 187
Pupput 104-5

Q
quad biking 287

R
rabies 316
radio 39, 283
Raf Raf 131-2
Raï Music Festival 291
Ramadan 34, 41-2, 292
Raqqada Islamic Art Museum 207
Ras as-Sana 41, 62
Ras el-Ain 163
Ras el-Drek 120
religion 39-43

000 Map pages
000 Photograph pages

Remada 238
resorts 285
restaurants 63
ribats
Monastir 197
Sousse 189-90
road rules 311-2
Roman caves 119-20
Roman rule 26-7
rugs, *see* carpets

S

safety 289-90, 311, 314
Sahara Desert 241-53, **242**, 7
Sahara Festival 245-6, 292, 175
sailing 287
Sanctuary of Tophet 95
sand roses 297
Sbeitla 180-3, **181**, 172
Sebastian, George 104
Sejnane 134
Seldja Gorge 267-8
Sfax 213-20, **214**
sheeshas 297
shopping 111, 141, 296-8
Sidi Ali el-Mekki 132
Sidi Bou Lifa 256
Sidi Bou Saïd 66, 96-8, **97**
Sidi Frej 221
Sidi Mahres 132, 280
Sidi Mechrig 135
Sidi Toui Saharan National Park 56
Skifa el-Kahla 211
Socopa shops 297
Sofra Cistern 190
Soliman 120-1
solo travellers 298
souqs 75-6, 190, 216, 274
Sousse 185-95, **186, 188**
travel to/from 194-5
travel within 195
souvenirs 296
Spanish Fort 125
spas 142
Star Wars 22, 52, 228, 229, 235, 261, 263
Sufetula 180-3, **181**
Sufism 42, 263
synagogues
Al-Ghriba Synagogue (Le Kef) 162
El-Ghriba Synagogue (Erriadh) 277

T

Tabarka 135-9, **136**
Tabarka International Jazz Festival 291
Tamerza 262
Tamezret 230
Tataouine 230-4, **231**
taxi travel 311
Teboursouk 159-60
Techine 230
telephone services 298-9
television 38, 283
temples 158, 167, 180, 154
terrorism 289
thalassotherapy 77, 287
theft 289-90
Thuburbo Majus 153-5, **154**
time 299
tipping 295
toilets 299
Toujane 230
Tourbet el-Bey 76
tourism, effects of 34, 279
tourist information 299-300
tours 312
Tozeur 255-61, **255**, **257**
train travel 313
transport 302-13
travellers cheques 295
trekking 140, 287
troglodyte homes 54, 228, 8, 174
tuberculosis 317
Tunis 66-99, **68**, **69**, **72-3**, **78**, **88**
accommodation 80-1
attractions 71-6
drinking 82, 84
entertainment 84
food 81-3
history 67
internet access 68
shopping 85
tourist offices 70
tours 80
travel to/from 86-7
travel within 87-9
walking tour 77-9
typhoid 317

U

Ulysses 50, 272
underground villas 145-7
Uthina 151
Utica 130-1

V

vacations 292
vaccinations 314
Vandals, the 28, 91, 94
vegetarian travellers 64
video systems 283
Virgil 50, 90, 91
visas 300, *see also* passports

W

water 56
water sports 286
weather 288
websites, *see* internet resources
weddings 37
weights & measures 283, *see also inside front cover*
wildlife, *see* animals
wine 61
women in Tunisia 43
women travellers 30-1, 318
World Heritage sites
Dougga 156-9
El-Jem colosseum 208
Ichkeul National Park 132
Tunis Medina 71
World War II 31, 178

Y

Yasmine Hammamet 102

Z

Zaafrane 249
Zaghouan National Park 155
Zaouia of Sidi Abdallah Boumakhlouf 162, 172
Zaouia of Sidi Abid el-Ghariani 203
Zaouia of Sidi Amor Abbada 204
Zaouia of Sidi Brahim 264
Zaouia of Sidi Mahres 75
Zaouia of Sidi Mokhtar 125
Zaouia of Sidi Sahab 203-4
Zaouia of Sidi Ibraham 275
Zaouia Zakkak 190
Zaytouna (Great) Mosque 71-4, 169

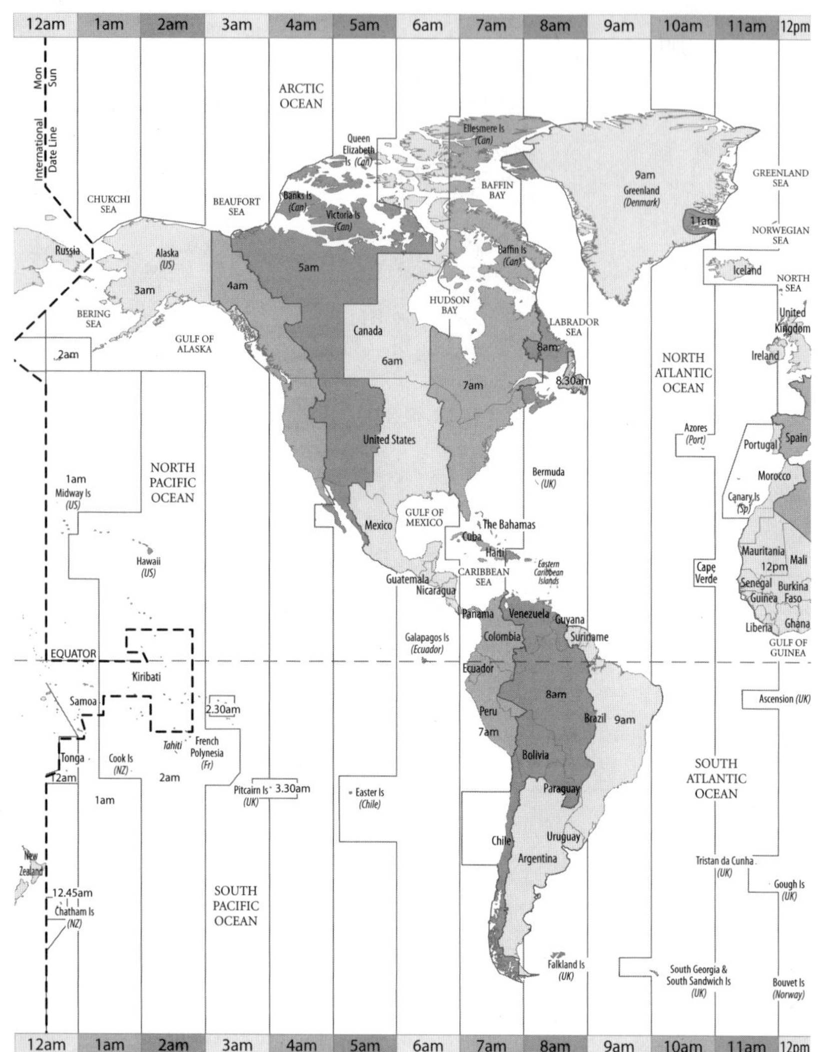
12am
1am
2am
3am
4am
5am
6am
7am
8am
9am
10am
11am
12pm
Mon
Sun
International Date Line
ARCTIC OCEAN
Queen Elizabeth Is (Can)
Ellesmere Is (Can)
CHUKCHI SEA
BEAUFORT SEA
Banks Is (Can)
Victoria Is (Can)
BAFFIN BAY
9am
Greenland (Denmark)
11am
GREENLAND SEA
NORWEGIAN SEA
Russia
Alaska (US)
3am
4am
5am
Baffin Is (Can)
Iceland
NORTH SEA
BERING SEA
HUDSON BAY
Canada
LABRADOR SEA
United Kingdom
GULF OF ALASKA
2am
6am
8am
Ireland
8.30am
7am
NORTH ATLANTIC OCEAN
United States
Azores (Port)
Portugal
Spain
1am
Midway Is (US)
NORTH PACIFIC OCEAN
Bermuda (UK)
Morocco
Canary Is (Sp)
GULF OF MEXICO
Mexico
The Bahamas
Cuba
Haiti
Hawaii (US)
Eastern Caribbean Islands
CARIBBEAN SEA
Guatemala
Nicaragua
Cape Verde
Mauritania
Mali
12pm
Senegal
Guinea
Burkina Faso
Liberia
Ghana
Panama
Venezuela
Guyana
Suriname
Colombia
Galapagos Is (Ecuador)
GULF OF GUINEA
EQUATOR
Ecuador
Kiribati
Samoa
2.30am
8am
Ascension (UK)
Peru
7am
Brazil
9am
Tahiti
French Polynesia (Fr)
Bolivia
Tonga
Cook Is (NZ)
2am
12am
1am
Pitcairn Is (UK)
3.30am
Easter Is (Chile)
Paraguay
SOUTH ATLANTIC OCEAN
Chile
Uruguay
Argentina
New Zealand
Tristan da Cunha (UK)
Gough Is (UK)
12.45am
Chatham Is (NZ)
SOUTH PACIFIC OCEAN
Falkland Is (UK)
South Georgia & South Sandwich Is (UK)
Bouvet Is (Norway)